D1644151

# Contents

# PART ONE
# The Nature of Public Policy

CHAPTER 1

# What Is Public Policy?

GOVERNMENT IN THE UNITED STATES has grown from a small, simple "night watchman state" providing defense, police protection, tax collection, and some education into an immense network of organizations and institutions affecting the daily lives of all citizens in countless ways. The United States is not a welfare state in the sense that most European states are, but there is now an extensive array of social and health programs that serve an increasing proportion of the population. The size and complexity of modern government make it necessary to understand what public policies are, how those policies are made and changed, and how to evaluate the effectiveness and morality of policies.

Government in the United States is large. Today, its revenues account for one dollar in three of total national production. Despite the widespread political rhetoric, this money is rarely wasted; most of it returns to citizens through a variety of cash benefit programs or in the form of public services. Likewise, one working person in six is employed by government—mostly in local governments. But the range of activities of modern government in the United States is not confined to such simple measures as spending money or hiring workers. Governments also influence the economy and society through many less obvious instruments such as regulation, insurance, and loan guarantees.

Government in the United States today also is complex and is becoming more complex every day. The institutions of government are becoming more complicated and numerous. More than 89,500 separate governments now exist in the United States, many of which provide a single service and undergo little or no public oversight through elections.[1] Much public business is now conducted through public corporations and quasi-autonomous public bodies. There are also a number of increasingly complex relationships between the public and private sectors, as the private and not-for-profit sectors are becoming heavily involved in delivering public services.[2] The subject matter of government policy is more complex and technical than it was even a few years ago. Governments must make decisions about the risks of nuclear energy, the reliability of technologically sophisticated weapons systems, and the management of a huge and remarkably convoluted economic system. Attempting to influence socioeconomic problems—poverty, homelessness, deficiencies in education—may be even more difficult than addressing problems arising in the physical and scientific worlds, given the absence of a proven method of solving social problems.[3] Even when the subject matter of policy is less complex, increasing requirements for participation and accountability make managing a public program a difficult undertaking, often more difficult than managing in the private sector.

This book is intended to help the reader understand the fundamental processes and content of public policy that underlie the size and complexity of American government. It is meant to increase knowledge about how public policies are made, what the policies of the United States are in certain areas, and what standards should be applied in evaluating those policies. I begin with a discussion of the policy process in the United States—concentrating on the federal level—and the impact of the structures and procedures of that government on the content of policies. I then discuss the means that those in government and citizens alike can use to evaluate the effects of public policies and the methods that will enable them to decide what they want, and can expect, to receive from government.

## Defining Public Policy

Samuel Johnson once commented that patriotism is the last refuge of fools and scoundrels. To some degree, public policy has become just such a refuge for some academic disciplines. As public policy studies are now popular, everything government does is labeled *policy*. I adopt a somewhat more restrictive definition of *public policy*.

Stated most simply, *public policy* is the sum of government activities, whether pursued directly or through agents, as those activities have an influence on the lives of citizens. Operating within that definition, we can distinguish three separate levels of policy, defined by the degree to which they make real differences in the lives of citizens. At the first level, we have policy *choices*—decisions made by politicians, civil servants, or others granted authority that are directed toward using public power to affect the lives of citizens. Congress members, presidents, governors, administrators, and pressure groups, among others, make such policy choices. What emerges from all those choices is a policy that can be put into action. At the second level, we can speak of policy *outputs*—policy choices being put into action. Here, the government is actually doing things: spending money, hiring people, or promulgating regulations that are designed to affect the economy and society. Outputs may be virtually synonymous with the term *program* as it is commonly used in government circles.[4]

Finally, at the third level, we have policy *impacts*—the effects that policy choices and policy outputs have on citizens, such as making them wealthier or healthier or the air they breathe less polluted. These impacts may be influenced in part by other factors in the society—economic productivity, education, and the like—but they also reflect to some degree the success or failure of public policy choices and outputs. These policy impacts also may reflect the interaction of a number of different programs. Successful alleviation of poverty, for example, may depend upon a number of social programs, education, economic programs, and the tax system. If any of these does not perform well, it may be impossible for government, and the society that it represents, to reach its desired goals.

Several aspects of public policy require some explanation. First, although we are focusing on the central government in Washington, we must always remember that the United States is a federal system in which a large number of subnational governments also make decisions. Even when they attempt to cooperate, the levels of government often experience conflicts over policy. For example, attempts by the George W. Bush administration to enforce national standards for education through the No Child Left Behind program encountered opposition from the states and eventually also from Congress, each with its own ideas about what those standards should be and how they should be enforced. Even within the federal government, the actions of one agency may conflict with those of another. The U.S. Department of Agriculture, for example, still subsidizes the growing of tobacco, while the U.S. Office of the Surgeon General encourages citizens not to smoke.

Second, not all government policies are implemented by government employees. Many are actually implemented by private organizations or by individual citizens, and the involvement of the private sector in implementation continues to increase.[5] We must understand this if we are to avoid an excessively narrow definition of public policy as concerning only those programs directly administered by a public agency. A number of agricultural, social, and health policies involve the use of private agencies operating with the sanction of, and in the name of, government. Even the cabin attendant on an airplane making an announcement to buckle seat belts and not to smoke is implementing a public policy. As government has begun to use an increasing number of alternative mechanisms, such as contracts, for implementation, private sector providers are becoming increasingly important in delivering public policy.

Even if a government implements a program directly, it may not act through its own employees. The federal government in particular depends on state and local governments to implement a large number of its programs, including major social programs such as Medicaid, the "workfare" reforms to the welfare system, and a good portion of environmental policy. The degree of control that the federal government can exercise in those instances may be as small as, or even smaller than, when programs are delivered through private sector agents, who often depend on government for contracts and loans and therefore may be very compliant with demands from Washington.

Third, and most important, we are concentrating on the effects of government choices on the lives of individuals within the society. The word *policy* is commonly used in a number of ways. In one usage, it denotes a stated intent of government, as expressed in a piece of legislation or a presidential speech. Unfortunately, any numbers of steps are required to turn a piece of legislation into an operating program, and all too frequently, significant changes in the intended effects of the program result from difficulties in translating ideas and intentions into actions. In this analysis, we will place greater emphasis on the effects of policies than on the intentions of the individuals who formulated them. We must also have some degree of concern for the legislative process, which produces the good intentions that may or may not come to fruition.

Our definition recognizes the complexity and the interorganizational nature of public policy. Few policy choices are decided and executed by a single organization or even a single level of government. Instead, policies, in terms of their effects on the public, emerge from a large number of programs, legislative intentions, and organizational interactions that affect the daily lives of citizens. For example, environmental issues now are handled not only by the Environmental Protection Agency but also by the Department of the Interior, the Department of Agriculture, the Department of Health and Human Services, and even the Department of Defense.[6] This conception of policy also points to the frequent failure of governments to coordinate programs, with the consequence that programs cancel one another out or produce a costly duplication of effort.[7] The question about government that Harold Lasswell posed many years ago, "Who gets what?" is still central for understanding public policy.

## The Instruments of Public Policy

Governments have a number of instruments through which they can influence society and the economy and produce changes in the lives of citizens. For example, government can choose to provide education by directly supplying that service, by providing vouchers that parents can use to pay for their children's education, or by subsidizing privately managed charter schools (see chapter 13). The choice of which instrument to employ for any particular situation may depend on the probable effectiveness of the instrument, its political palatability, the experiences of the policy designers, and national or organizational tradition. Furthermore, some policy instruments may be effective in some circumstances but not in others. Unfortunately, governments do not yet have sufficient knowledge about the effects of their "tools," or the relationship of particular tools to particular policy outcomes, to be able to make effective matches.[8] It appears that most choices are now made out of habit and familiarity, not out of certain knowledge of effectiveness.

### Law

Law is a unique resource of government. It is not available to private actors, who have access to the other instruments of policy discussed here.[9] Governments have the right to make authoritative decrees and to back up those decrees with the legitimate power of the state. In most instances, simply issuing a law is sufficient to produce compliance, but monitoring and enforcement are still crucial to the effectiveness of the instrument. Citizens may obey speeding laws most of the time, but the prospect of a police officer with a radar set makes compliance more probable. Citizens daily obey many laws without thinking about them, but police, tax collectors, and agencies monitoring environmental damage, occupational safety, and product safety (to name only a few) are also busy attempting to ensure compliance through their enforcement activities.

We should make several other points about the use of law as an instrument of public policy. First, laws are used as the means of producing the most important outputs of government: rights. Such laws are usually of a fundamental or constitutional nature and are central in defining the position of citizens in society. In the United States, the fundamental rights of citizens are defined in the Constitution and its amendments, but rights also have been extended in a variety of other legislation. This extension has been most significant for the rights of nonwhites and women, as reflected in the passage of the Voting Rights Act of 1965, the Equal Employment Opportunity Act of 1972, and the Civil Rights Act of 1991. The Americans with Disabilities Act (1990) extended a variety of rights to people with various forms of disability, with the courts tending to expand the applicability of that law to groups, such as AIDS sufferers,[10] for whom it was perhaps not intended by the framers of the legislation. Law is now being used by some groups to attempt to extend rights to homosexuals, and other groups also use law to attempt to limit those rights (see chapter 16).

Second, the United States uses laws to regulate economic and social conditions to a greater extent than most countries do. The United States is frequently cited as having a small public sector in comparison with other industrialized countries because of lower levels of taxing and spending. If, however, the effects of regulations are included, government in the United States approaches being as pervasive as it is in Europe.[11] The costs of government's interventions in the United States tend to appear in the price of products, however, as much as in citizens' tax bills.[12] This indirect effect of intervention tends to be less visible to the average citizen than a tax and therefore is more palatable in a society that tends to be skeptical about government.

Third, law can be used to create burdens as well as benefits. This is certainly true for tax laws and is also true, for example, of legislation that mandates the recycling of metal, glass, and plastic. Often, a law that creates benefits for one group of citizens is perceived by others to be creating a burden; environmental laws satisfy conservationists but often impose costs on businesses. Any action of government requires some legal peg on which to hang, but the ability of a simple piece of paper to create both rights and obligations is one of the essential features of American public policy.

### Services

Governments also provide a number of services directly to citizens, ranging from defense to education to recreation. In numbers of people employed, education is by far the largest directly provided public service, employing more than nine million people. The Department of Defense employs just under another three million people, military and civilian. Government tends to provide services when there is a need to ensure that the service is provided in a certain way (education) or where the authority of the state (policing) is involved. Furthermore, services tend to be delivered directly to parts of the population that are less capable of making autonomous decisions on their own, such as children and the mentally impaired.

The direct provision of public services raises several questions, especially as continuing pressures exist for government to control expenditures and to "privatize."[13] An obvious question is whether the direct provision of services is the most efficient means of ensuring that a service is delivered to citizens. Could that service be contracted out instead? A number of public services have been contracted out to private corporations, including traditional government services, such as firefighting, tax collection, and operating prisons.[14] Contracting out removes the problem of personnel management from government, a problem magnified by the tenure rights and pension costs of public employees under merit systems. Also, government tends to build a capacity to meet maximum demand for services such as fire protection and emergency medical care, resulting in underutilization of expensive personnel and equipment. This tendency to create too much capacity can be corrected in part by contracting out.

Another interesting development in the direct provision of services is the use of quasi-governmental organizations to provide services.[15] There are some services that government does not want to undertake entirely but that require public involvement for financial or other reasons. The best example is Amtrak, a means of providing public subsidies for passenger train service in the face of declining rail service in the United States. Government may also choose quasi-governmental organizations for programs that require a great deal of coordination with private sector providers of the same service, or when the service is in essence a marketable one. At an even greater degree of separation, governments also use not-for-profit organizations to provide public services. The George W. Bush administration pressed for wider use of such organizations, especially faith-based organizations. President Barack Obama continued the emphasis, working to mobilize not-for-profit organizations early in his administration.

### Money

Governments also provide citizens, organizations, and other governments with money. Approximately 65 percent of all money collected in taxes by the federal government is returned to the economy as transfer payments to citizens. Transfers to citizens range from Social Security and unemployment benefits to payments to farmers to support commodity prices. Interest on the public debt is also a form of transfer payment, one that now absorbs nearly 8 percent of total federal spending. Another 10 percent of tax receipts is transferred to other levels of government to support their activities.

The use of money transfers to attempt to promote certain behaviors is in many ways an inefficient means for reaching policy goals. The money paid out in Social Security benefits, for example, is intended to provide the basics of life for the recipients, but nothing prevents those recipients from using it to buy food for their pets rather than for themselves. The claims about how "welfare" payments are used and abused are legion, if often inaccurate. Thus, although the direct provision of services is costly and requires hiring personnel and erecting buildings, many transfer programs, though less expensive, are much less certain of reaching the individuals and achieving the goals for which they were intended.

Money dispersed to other levels of government can be restricted or unrestricted. Of the over $500 billion given to state and local governments in 2010, most were distributed as categorical grants, with an increasing proportion being given as block grants. Categorical grants channel resources more directly to the problems identified by the federal government as needing attention, but they also tend to centralize decision making about public policy in Washington.[16] Categorical grants also tend to encourage state and local spending through matching requirements and to create clienteles that governments may not be able to eliminate after the federal support has been exhausted. Although this pattern of funding was largely associated with social and economic programs, the Clinton administration's program for funding the hiring of additional police created expectations among citizens that local governments will have to fulfill in the future, and Homeland Security funding has created the same effect after the Bush administration.

The federal government has less control over the impact of block grants than over the effects of categorical grants.[17] Block grants allow greater latitude for state and local governments to determine their own priorities, but most still have some strings attached. Also, giving block grants to the states tends to concentrate power in state governments rather than allowing local (especially city) governments to bargain with Washington directly. Given that state governments are, on average, more conservative than local governments—especially large city governments that need federal grant money the most—block grants have been a useful tool for Republican administrations to control public spending.[18]

### Taxes

The government giveth and the government taketh away. But the way in which it chooses to take away may be important in changing the distribution of burdens and benefits in society. In the United States, we are familiar with tax "loopholes," or, more properly, *tax expenditures*.[19] The latter term is derived from the theory that granting tax relief for an activity is the same as subsidizing that activity directly through an expenditure program.[20] For example, in 2010, the federal government did not collect roughly $79 billion in income tax payments because of mortgage interest deductions and another $16 billion because state and local property taxes were deductible. This is in many ways exactly the same as government subsidizing private housing in the same amounts, a sum far greater than the amount spent on public housing by all levels of government. The use of the tax system as a policy instrument as well as for revenue collection is perhaps even less certain in its effects than transfer payments, for the system is essentially providing incentives rather than mandating activities. Citizens have a strong incentive to buy a house, but there is no program to build houses directly. These instruments are, however, very cheap to administer, given that citizens make all the decisions and then file their own tax returns.

Taxes may also be used more directly to implement policy decisions. For example, there are proposals to substitute taxes on pollution for direct prohibitions and regulation of emissions. The logic is that such an action would establish a "market" in pollution; those firms willing to pay the price of polluting would be able to pollute, while those less willing (or, more important, less able) because of inefficient production means would have to alter their modes of production or go out of business. The use of market mechanisms is assumed to direct resources toward their most productive use, whereas regulations at times may inhibit production and economic growth. Critics argue that what is being created is a "market in death," when the only real solution to the problem is the prohibition or severe restriction of pollution.

Tax incentives are a subset of all incentives available to government to encourage or discourage activities. The argument for their use, as was well expressed by Charles Schultze, is that private interests (e.g., avarice) can be used for public purposes.[21] If a system of incentives can be structured effectively, then demands on the public sector can be satisfied in a more efficient and inexpensive manner than through direct regulation. Clearly, this form of policy instrument is applicable to a rather narrow range of policies, mostly those now handled through command and control regulation, but even in that limited range, the savings in costs of government and in the costs imposed on society may be significant. The use of such incentives, as opposed to command and control regulation, also conforms to traditional American ideas about limited government and the supremacy of individual choice.[22]

### Other Economic Instruments

Government has a number of other economic weapons at its disposal.[23] Governments supply credit for activities such as a farmer's purchase of land and supplies.[24] When it does not directly lend money, the government may guarantee loans, thus making credit available (e.g., for student loans or Federal Housing Administration [FHA] mortgages) where it might otherwise be denied. Governments can also insure certain activities and property. For example, federal flood insurance made possible the development of some lands along the coasts of the United States, thereby creating both wealth and environmental degradation. Almost all money in banks and thrift institutions is now protected by one of several insurance corporations within the federal government. Thus, in the economic downturn of 2008 and 2009, individual bank accounts were protected.

Although these instruments may be important to their beneficiaries and may influence the spending of large sums of money, they do not appear as large expenditures in most government accounting schemes. Thus, as with regulations and their costs, the true size of government in the United States may be understated if one looks simply at expenditure and employment figures. In addition, the ability of these programs to operate "off budget" makes them not only less visible to voters but also more difficult for political leaders and citizens to control. Only when there are major problems, as in the bursting of the housing bubble and the credit crisis in 2008, do government insurance, guarantee schemes, and federal "bailouts" make the news.

### Suasion

When all other instruments of policy fail, governments can use moral suasion to attempt to influence society. Government as a whole or particular political officials are often in a good position to use such suasion because they can speak in the name of the public interest and make those who oppose them appear unpatriotic and selfish. As Theodore Roosevelt said, the presidency is a "bully pulpit." Suasion, however, is often the velvet glove disguising the mailed fist, for governments have formal and informal means of ensuring that their wishes are fulfilled. So when John F. Kennedy "jawboned" steel industry officials to roll back a price increase, the patriotism of the steel officials was equaled by their fear of lost government contracts and Internal Revenue Service investigations of their corporate and personal accounts.

Suasion is an effective instrument as long as the people regard the government as a legitimate expression of their interests. There is evidence that the faith and trust of American citizens in government has been declining (see Table 1.1) in response to the excesses of Vietnam, Watergate, budget deficits, the inadequate response to Hurricane Katrina, and so forth. Congress members in particular are regarded very poorly by the public. As governments lose some of their legitimacy, their ability to use suasion naturally declines, pushing them toward more direct tools of intervention; that could lead to increases in government employment and taxation and perhaps to an accelerated downward spiral of

TABLE 1.1    Public Perception of Honesty and Ethics in Various Professions (percentages of "Very high" and "High" responses combined)

| | 1976 | 1981 | 1985 | 1990 | 1992 | 1995 | 2005 | 2008 | 2011 |
|---|---|---|---|---|---|---|---|---|---|
| Pharmacists | n.a. | 59 | 65 | 62 | 66 | 66 | 67 | 70 | 73 |
| Clergy | n.a. | 63 | 67 | 57 | 54 | 56 | 54 | 56 | 52 |
| Medical doctors | 56 | 51 | 50 | 52 | 52 | 54 | 65 | 64 | 70 |
| College teachers | 49 | 45 | 53 | 51 | 50 | 52 | n.a. | n.a. | n.a. |
| Engineers | 49 | 48 | 53 | 50 | 48 | 53 | n.a. | n.a. | n.a. |
| Police | n.a. | 44 | 47 | 49 | 42 | 41 | 61 | 56 | 54 |
| Journalists | 33 | 32 | 31 | 30 | 27 | 23 | 28 | 25 | 26 |
| Bankers | n.a. | 39 | 38 | 32 | 27 | 27 | 41 | 23 | 25 |
| Lawyers | 25 | 25 | 27 | 22 | 18 | 16 | 18 | 18 | 19 |
| Business executives | 20 | 19 | 23 | 25 | 18 | 16 | 16 | 12 | 18 |
| Local officeholders | n.a. | 14 | 18 | 21 | 15 | 21 | n.a. | 20 | n.a. |
| Real estate agents | n.a. | 14 | 15 | 16 | 14 | 15 | 20 | 17 | 20 |
| Labor union leaders | 12 | 14 | 13 | 15 | 14 | 14 | 16 | 16 | 18 |
| U.S. senators | 19 | 20 | 23 | 24 | 13 | 12 | 16 | n.a. | n.a. |
| State officeholders | n.a. | 12 | 15 | 17 | 11 | 15 | n.a. | 12 | n.a. |
| Members of Congress | 14 | 15 | 20 | 20 | 11 | 10 | 14 | 12 | 7 |
| Car salesmen | n.a. | 6 | 5 | 6 | 5 | 5 | 8 | 7 | 7 |

Sources: *Gallup Poll Monthly*, November 1995, 31; Gallup Poll, January 18, 2005; Gallup Poll, November 7, 2008; Gallup Poll, June 23, 2011.

Note: n.a. = not available.

government authority. In 2012, the public views Congress members as only slightly more favorably than car salesmen, who anchored the bottom of the scale. On the other hand, police had achieved a major increase in respect, in part because of their heroism after 9/11. One exception to the trend of declining trust in government may be in times of war, as President George H. W. Bush showed during the Persian Gulf crisis. The second President Bush also used suasion and manipulated powerful national symbols in the "war on terror," although his ability to do so declined as his term ended.

### The Effects of Tools

Governments have a number of instruments with which they attempt to influence the economy and society by distributing what burdens and benefits they have at their disposal. The most fundamental benefits governments have to confer are rights. These are largely legal and participatory, but with the growth of large entitlement programs that distribute cash benefits to citizens, rights may now be said to include those programs as well.

Governments also distribute goods and services. They do so directly by giving money to people who fall into certain categories (e.g., the unemployed) or by directly providing public services, such as education. They also do so less directly by structuring incentives for individuals to behave in certain ways and to make one economic decision rather than another. Governments also distribute goods and services through private organizations and through other governments, in attempts to reach their policy goals. A huge amount of money flows through the public sector, where it is shuffled around and given to different people.[25] The net effect is not as great as might be expected from the number of large expenditure and revenue programs in operation in the United States, but that effect is to make the distribution of income and wealth somewhat more equal than would be the case through the market alone.[26]

Finally, governments distribute burdens as well as benefits. They do this through taxation and through programs such as conscription for military service.[27] Like expenditures, taxes are distributed broadly across the population, with state and local taxes tending to be collected from an especially broad spectrum. Even the poorest citizens have to pay sales taxes on many things they purchase, and they must pay Social Security taxes as soon as they begin to work. In other words, everyone in society benefits from the activities of government, but everyone also pays for them.

## The Environment of Public Policy

Several characteristics of the political and socioeconomic environment in the United States influence the nature of policies adopted and the effects of those policies on citizens. Policy is not constructed in a vacuum; it is the result of the interaction of all the background factors with the desires and decisions of those who make policies. Neither individual decision makers nor the nature of "the system" appear capable alone of explaining policy outcomes. Instead, policy emerges from the interaction of a large number of forces, many of which are beyond the control of decision makers.

### Conservatism

American politics is relatively conservative in policy terms. The social and economic services usually associated with the mixed-economy welfare state are generally less developed in the United States than in Europe, and to some extent they have declined since the 1990s. In general, that is the result of the continuing American belief in limited government. As Anthony King has said, "The State plays a more limited role in America than elsewhere because Americans, more than other people, want it to play a limited role."[28] The Republican domination of electoral politics for much of the past three decades emphasizes the underlying conservatism of Americans. The election of Barack Obama, however, also shows that there are limits to that conservatism and that the American public has some underlying commitment to social values. That said, the rise of the Tea Party movement and the appeal of some libertarian candidates in the Republican primaries of 2012 indicate how intense the conservative ideology is for some elements within the population.

Several points should be brought out that counter the description of American government as a welfare state laggard. First, the government of the United States regulates and controls the economy in ways not common in Europe, and in some areas such as consumer product safety, it appears to be ahead of many European governments. If the effects of regulation are tabulated along with more direct public interventions into the economy, the U.S. government appears more similar to those of other industrialized countries. We also tend to forget about the activities of state and local governments, which frequently provide gas, electricity, water, and even banking services to their citizens.

It is easy to underestimate the extent of the changes in public expenditures and the public role in the economy that followed World War II. Let us take 1948 as the starting point. Even in that relatively peaceful year, defense expenditures were 29 percent of total public expenditures and 36 percent of federal expenditures. At the height of the Cold War, in 1957, defense expenditures were 62 percent of federal expenditures and 37 percent of total public expenditures. In contrast, in 2006, defense expenditures were 7 percent of total expenditures and 15 percent of federal expenditures. Spending on social services—including education, health, social welfare, and housing—increased from 7 percent of total spending in 1948 to over 64 percent in 2003. Even for the federal government, social spending now accounts for more than 50 percent of total expenditures. American government and its policies may be conservative, but they are less so than commonly believed, and less so in the early twenty-first century than in the 1950s.

It is also easy to overestimate the conservatism of the American public because Americans are often very ambivalent about government.[29] Lloyd A. Free and Hadley Cantril described Americans as "ideological conservatives" and "operational liberals"[30] because they tend to respond negatively to the idea of a large and active government but positively to individual public programs (e.g., Social Security, police protection, and education). For example, a majority of voters leaving the polls in California after voting in favor of Proposition 13, to cut taxes severely in that state, were in favor of reducing public expenditures for only one program—social welfare. For most programs the researchers mentioned, larger percentages of respondents wanted to increase expenditures than wanted to reduce them.[31] Likewise, citizens express great skepticism about government in polls, but in the 2008 elections, the voters approved most propositions on state and local ballots to raise revenues for specific purposes, as well as voting for a liberal president and Congress. Even in the tide of conservative victories in the 2010 election, a number of ballot initiatives proposing new taxing and spending were successful.

The huge federal deficit is to some degree a function of this set of mismatched ideas about government; politicians can win votes both by advocating reducing taxes and by advocating spending for almost any program. For example, surveys show that the majority of Americans believe that they pay too many taxes and that the federal government wastes almost half of all the tax money it collects.[32] On the other hand, there are generally majorities in favor of a variety of social programs, especially those for the more "deserving poor"—the elderly, unemployed workers whose companies have closed, divorced and widowed mothers, and the like. Furthermore, although Americans dislike the idea of socialized medicine, they also dislike the inequality in health in the United States (see chapter 11).

## Participation

Another attitudinal characteristic that influences public policy in the United States is the citizen's desire to participate directly in government. A natural part of democratic politics, public participation has a long history in the United States. The cry "No taxation without representation" was essentially a demand to participate. More recently, populist demands for participation and the right of "the little man" to shape policy have been powerful political forces. In a large and decentralized political system that deals with complex issues, however, effective participation may be difficult to achieve. Although the 2008 elections saw an increase in voter turnout, especially among young people and minorities, the low rate of participation in most elections appears to indicate that citizens do not consider the voting process a particularly effective means of influencing government. Furthermore, many experts believe that citizens are not sufficiently informed to make decisions about such complex technical issues as nuclear power. Still, citizens argue that they should and must have a role in those decisions.

Government has increasingly fostered participation. The laws authorizing "community action" in 1964 were the first to mandate "maximum feasible participation" of the affected communities in urban renewal decisions. Similar language was written into a number of other social and urban programs. The regulatory process also imposes requirements for notification and participation that, in addition to their positive effects, have slowed the process considerably. Government also has been allowing more direct participation in agency rulemaking, with affected interests allowed to negotiate among themselves the rules that will govern a policy area.

The desire for effective participation has to some degree colored popular impressions of government. Citizens tend to demand local control of policy and to fear the "federal bulldozer." Although objective evidence may be to the contrary, citizens tend to regard the federal government as less benevolent and less efficient than local governments. The desire to participate and to exercise local control then produces a tendency toward decentralized decision making and a consequent absence of national integration. In many policy areas, such decentralization is benign or actually beneficial. In others, it may produce inequities and inefficiencies. But ideological and cultural desires for local control may override practical arguments.

Ideas about participation in the United States also have at times had a strong strand of populism, meaning the belief that large institutions—whether in government, business, or even labor—are inimical to the interests of the people. The antigovernment, antitax rhetoric that President George W. Bush used so effectively is one example of that populist style in American politics. That style of populism can be contrasted with a rather different approach by President Obama, who appealed to the American people with an all-inclusive message of unification that defies partisanship. The populist ideas have reasserted themselves in 2010 and after in both the Tea Party and the Occupy movements. The institutions of government have begun to respond to demands for effective participation, and *empowerment* has become one of the more commonly used words in government circles.[33] Balancing popular demands for greater direct democracy with the requirements of governing an immense landmass with over 300 million citizens will continue to be a challenge for American democracy.

*Elections determine who controls Congress and the presidency, and therefore set the parameters for policy choices in American government. A volunteer for Rep. Marcy Kaptur, D-OH, hands out campaign literature on January 29, 2012.*

### Pragmatism

The reference to ideological desires seemingly contradicts another cultural characteristic of American policymaking, pragmatism—the belief that one should do whatever works rather than follow a basic ideological or philosophical system. For most of our collective history, American political parties have tended to be centrist and nonideological; perhaps the surest way to lose an election in the United States has been to discuss philosophies of government. Ronald Reagan questioned that characteristic of American politics to some degree, interjecting an ideology of government that was partly continued by George H. W. Bush. Bill Clinton's self-description as a "new Democrat" represented a return to greater pragmatism. George W. Bush claimed to be a "compassionate conservative" in his first election campaign, but his style, and especially that of members of Congress, transformed American politics into something of a battle of ideologies.

The years following the election of Barack Obama as President have, however, been marked by partisan and ideological debate. A long history of compromise was transformed into one of opposition and gridlock. The clearest manifestations of this were in battles over the debt ceiling and over the administration's policies to combat the recession. While Congress, the president, and other political elites continue to wrangle and make partisan pronouncements, the American public has expressed its dismay and disgust with the inability of the political system to make effective decisions to address the problems of the nation.[34]

One standard definition of what will work in government is "that which is already working," and so policies tend to change slowly and incrementally.[35] The fundamentally centrist pattern of U.S. political parties has tended to produce agreement on most basic policies, and each successive president tends to jiggle and poke policy but not attempt significant change. A crisis such as the Great Depression or a natural political leader such as Reagan may introduce some radical changes, but stability and gradual evolution are the most acceptable patterns of policymaking. Indeed, American government is different after Reagan but not as different as he had hoped or intended.[36] Nor was George W. Bush able to change very much of the system, and even during the Great Recession, Barack Obama was generally incapable of bringing about the type of grand change that he proposed during his campaign. The battle over reform of Social Security typifies this persistence of policies (see chapter 12). There has been concern about the financial soundness of this crucial program for years, but no agreement has coalesced on the direction or degree of change. The pragmatism of the policy process in the United States was clearly manifested in the defeat in 2005 of attempts at radical change in the Social Security program.[37]

As mentioned above, the pragmatism of American politics has been declining. Several issues over which there appears to be little room for compromise have split the American public. The obvious example is the abortion issue, which intruded into the debate over national health care reform during the Clinton administration, with some members of Congress refusing to support any bill that paid for abortions and others opposing any bill that did not.[38] Other issues with a moral, religious, or ethnic basis also have taken more prominent places in the political debate, leaving fewer possibilities for compromise or pragmatic resolution of disputes. The religious right has become especially important in the internal politics of the Republican Party, as groups such as the Christian Coalition and the Family Research Council have taken over at local and even state levels and attempted to shape the party's national policies.[39]

The seeming decline in pragmatism in American politics is not just a function of religion. The political parties themselves have become more ideological.[40] Congressional politics has become more sharply divided along party lines, and compromise has become much more difficult to achieve. Even when the country was facing potential financial disaster, President Obama's stimulus plan received no Republican votes in the House of Representatives and only three in the Senate.[41] The votes on subsequent economic issues such as raising the debt ceiling were partisan based. Citizens say that they do not like the wrangling among parties, but the parties seem more committed to their own views of politics than in the past.

## Wealth

Another feature of the environment of American public policy is the country's great wealth. Although it is no longer the richest country in the world in per capita terms, the United States is the largest single economy in the world by a large margin. This wealth permits the U.S. government great latitude for action so that even the massive deficits experienced in the 1980s and 1990s (and now recurring in the twenty-first century) have not required government to alter its folkways. The federal government can continue funding a huge variety of programs and policy initiatives, even while trying to control the size of the budget (see chapter 7).

That great wealth is threatened by two factors, however. First, the U.S. economy is increasingly dependent on the rest of the world. That is apparent in financial and monetary policy, as the United States has become the world's largest debtor, but it is true especially in dependence on raw materials from abroad. We are familiar with the nation's dependence on foreign oil, but the economy is also heavily dependent on other countries for a range of commodities necessary to maintain its high standard of living. The American economy historically has been relatively self-sufficient, but increasing globalization in recent decades has emphasized its relationship to the world economy.[42]

Wealth in the United States is also threatened by the relatively slow rate of capital investment and savings. The savings rate for the average American family was 2.7 percent in 2011, indicating that relatively little capital is available for investment. The average American worker is still very productive but has lost some ground to workers in other countries. Also, many U.S. factories are outmoded, so competition on the world market is difficult. These factors, combined with relatively high wages, mean that many manufacturing jobs have gone overseas and more are likely to do so. The U.S. government has had to borrow abroad to fund its deficits, and the country has chronic balance of payments problems because exports trail imports. Such international trade problems are not often direct domestic concerns of American politicians, although the Democrats have attempted to make them more of a concern in recent presidential campaigns.

In addition to the changing distribution of wealth in the United States relative to the remainder of the world, the internal distribution of wealth has been changing and changing rapidly. Although there was substantial economic growth in the first decade of the twenty-first century, most of economic growth went to the most affluent segments of society, while the real earnings of most citizens were stagnant or even declining. The economic (and political) strength of the United States has been built on a large middle class, a group that is now under threat. They are in part under threat because of the international trade issues and falling wages used as a means of competing with overseas manufacturers.

## Diversity

The diversity of the American society and economy provides a great deal of richness and strength to the country, as well as real policy problems. One of the most obvious diversities is the uneven distribution of income and wealth. Even with the significant social expenditures mentioned earlier, approximately forty-six million people (1 in 6) in the United States live below the poverty line (see chapter 12). The persistence of poverty in the midst of plenty remains perhaps the most fundamental policy problem for the United States, if for no other reason than that it affects so many other policy areas, including health care, housing, education, crime, and race relations. Moreover, there is growing concentration of income and wealth in the very affluent stratum at the top of society that may undermine confidence in the economic and social justice of the political system.

Diversity of racial and linguistic backgrounds is another significant factor affecting policy in the United States. The underlying problems of social inequality and racism persist despite many attempts to correct them. The "two Americas" had never been so visible as they were in New Orleans after Hurricane Katrina.[43] The concentration of minority group members in urban areas, the continuing influx of immigrants, and the unyielding economic distress of some cities combine to exacerbate the underlying problems. Again, this diversity affects a variety of policy areas, especially education. Race in particular pervades policymaking and politics in the United States, and that fundamental fact conditions our understanding of education, poverty, and human rights.[44] These issues of diversity have now become more apparent politically in the debate over immigration policy.

The social and economic characteristics of the country taken as a whole are also diverse. The United States is both urban and rural, both industrial and agricultural, both young and old. It is a highly educated society with several million illiterates; it is a rich country with millions of people living in poverty. In at least one state, California, there already is no majority ethnic group, and in a few generations that may be true for the country as a whole. American policymakers cannot concentrate on a single economic class or social group but must provide something for everyone if the interests of the society as a whole are to be served. But serving that whole range of social interests forces government to spend for other purposes the resources that could be applied to rectifying the worst inequalities of income and opportunity.

## World Leadership

The United States is an economic, political, and military world leader. Since the collapse of the Soviet Union, it is the only remaining superpower. If America sneezes, the world still catches cold because the sheer size of the American economy is so important in influencing world economic conditions, as the 2008 financial crisis demonstrated. Despite the upheaval in global political alignments, the world still expects military and diplomatic leadership for the West to come from the United States. For example, the heavy involvement of the American military in Iraq and Afghanistan may have made world response to humanitarian crises in Darfur and other parts of Africa less feasible.

The U.S. position as world leader imposes burdens on American policymakers. Although the Cold War had ended, the role of peacekeeper required a good deal of U.S. military might even before the war on terror escalated military spending. Burdens also arise from the need to provide diplomatic and political leadership. The U.S. dollar, despite some battering and significant competition, is still a major reserve currency in the world economy, and that status imposes additional economic demands on the country. The role of world leader is an exhilarating one, but it is also one filled with considerable responsibility and economic cost. Indeed, the globalization of the economic system is making many Americans rethink the desirability of major international involvement. American acceptance of such a role may also be waning as the costs (human and material) of involvement in Iraq and Afghanistan and a greater sense of insecurity at home have turned more attention inward rather than outward to the world.

The policies that emerge from all these influences are filtered through a large and extremely complex political system. The characteristics of that government and the effects of those institutional characteristics on policies are the subject of the next chapter. Policy choices must be made, and thousands are made each day in government; the sum of those choices, rather than any one, decides who gets what as a result of public policies. In the United States, more than in most countries, there are a number of independent decision makers whose choices must be factored into the final determination of policy.

## Summary

American public policy is the result of complex interactions among a number of complex institutions. It also involves a wide range of ideas and values about what the goals of policy should be and what are the best means of reaching them. In addition to the interactions that occur within the public sector are the interactions with an equally complex society and economy. Indeed, society is playing an increasingly important role in policymaking and implementation, with reforms in the public sector placing increasing emphasis on the capacity of the private sector to implement, if not make, public policy.

Making policy requires reaching some form of social and political consensus among all these forces. There does not have to be full agreement on all the values and all the points of policy, but enough common ground must be found to pass and implement legislation. Building those coalitions can extend beyond reaching ideological agreement to include bargaining and horse trading, which assign a central role to individual policy entrepreneurs and brokers. There is so much potential for blockage and delay in the American political system that some driving force may be needed to make it function.

CHAPTER 2

# The Structure of Policymaking in American Government

THE STRUCTURES THROUGH WHICH public policy is formulated, legitimated, and implemented in the United States are extremely complex. It could be argued that American government has a number of structures but no real organization, for the fundamental characteristic of the structures is the absence of effective coordination and control. The absence of central control is largely intentional. The framers of the Constitution were concerned about the potential for tyranny of a powerful central executive; they also feared the control of the central government over the constituent states. The system of government the framers designed divides power among the three branches of the central government and further between the central government and state and local governments. As the system of government has evolved, it has become divided even further, as individual policy domains have been able to gain substantial autonomy from central coordination. To understand American policymaking, therefore, we must understand the extent of the fragmentation that exists in this political system and the (relatively few) mechanisms devised to control that fragmentation and enhance coordination.

The fragmentation of American government presents some advantages. First, having a number of decision makers involved in every decision should reduce errors, as all must agree before a proposal can become law or be implemented as an operating program; there will be full deliberation. The existence of multiple decision makers should also permit greater innovation both in the federal government and in state and local governments. And as the framers intended, diffused policymaking power reduces the capacity of central government to run roughshod over the rights of citizens or the interests of socioeconomic groups. For citizens, the numerous points of access to policymaking permit losers at one level of government, or in one institution, to become winners at another point in the process.

Americans also pay a price for this lack of policy coherence and coordination. It is sometimes difficult to accomplish *anything,* and elected politicians with policy ideas find themselves thwarted by the large number of decision points in the policymaking system. The policymaking situation in the United States in the 1980s and 1990s was described as *gridlock,* in which the different institutions blocked one another from developing and enforcing policies.[1] The crisis provoked by the attacks of September 11, 2001, eliminated that gridlock for a short period, but it soon returned, even in some aspects of national security. For example, the USA PATRIOT Act could not be renewed in late 2005 because of sharp partisan differences over domestic wiretapping. That partisan gridlock became even more of a barrier to policymaking after the 2010 election, with a Republican-controlled House of Representatives facing a Democratic Senate and president.

The division of government into many separate policy fiefdoms also means that programs may cancel one another out. For example, progressive (if decreasingly so) federal taxes and regressive state and local taxes combine to produce a tax system in which most people pay about the same proportion of their income as tax. The surgeon general's antismoking policies and the Department of Agriculture's tobacco subsidies attempt to please both pro- and antitobacco interests. The apparent inability or unwillingness of policymakers to choose among options means that policies will be incoherent, and the process continues seemingly without any closure. It also means that because potential conflicts are resolved by offering every interest in society some support from the public sector, taxes and expenditures are higher than they might otherwise be.

I have already mentioned the divisions that exist in American government. I now look at the more important dimensions of that division and the ways in which they act and interact to effect policy decisions and real policy outcomes for citizens. *Divided government* and *gridlock* have become standard descriptions of American government, and their impact, as well as that of federalism, must be considered in analyzing the way in which policy emerges from the political system. But we should be careful to understand the extent to which gridlock really exists as more than simply a convenient description of institutional conflict. We need to question the extent to which gridlock will be reduced or eliminated when, as after the 2008 elections, the presidency and Congress are controlled by the same party.

## Federalism

The most fundamental division in American government traditionally has been *federalism,* or the constitutional allocation of governmental powers between the federal and state governments. This formal, constitutional allocation at once reserves all powers not specifically granted to the federal government to the states (Ninth and Tenth Amendments) and establishes the supremacy of federal law when there are conflicts with state and local law (Article 6). Innumerable court cases and, at least in part, one civil war have resulted from this somewhat ambiguous division of powers among levels of government.

By the first years of the twenty-first century, American federalism had changed significantly from the federalism described in the Constitution. The original constitutional division of power assumed that certain functions of government would be performed entirely by the central government, and other functions would be carried out by state or local governments. In this "layer cake" federalism, or separated powers model, the majority of public activities were to be performed by subnational governments, leaving a limited number of functions such as national defense and minting money as the responsibility of the federal government.[2]

As the activities of government at all levels expanded, the watertight separation of functions broke down, and federal, state, and local governments became involved in many of the same activities. The layer cake then was transformed into a marble cake, with the several layers of government still distinct but no longer horizontally separated from one another. This form of federalism still involved intergovernmental contacts through central political officials. The principal actors were governors and mayors, and intergovernmental relations remained on the level of high politics, with the representatives of subnational governments acting almost as ambassadors from sovereign governments and as supplicants for federal aid. Furthermore, in this form of federalism, the state government retained its role as intermediary between the federal government and local governments.

Federalism evolved further from a horizontal division of activities into a set of vertical divisions. Whereas functions were once neatly compartmentalized by level of government, the major feature of "picket fence" federalism is the development of policy subsystems defined by policy rather than level of government.[3] Thus, far-reaching decisions about health policy are made by specialized networks involving actors from all levels of government and from the private sector. Those networks, however, may be relatively isolated from other subsystems making decisions about highways, education, or whatever. The principal actors in these subsystems frequently are not political leaders but administrators and substantive policy experts. Local health departments work with state health departments and with the Department of Health and Human Services (HHS) in Washington in making health policy, and these experts are not dependent on the intervention of political leaders to make the process function. This form of federalism is as much administrative as it is political, and it is driven by expertise as much as by political power.

In many ways, it makes little sense to discuss federalism in its original meaning; it has been argued that contemporary federalism is as much facade as picket fence. A term such as *intergovernmental relations* more accurately describes the complex, crazy quilt of overlapping authority and interdependence among levels of government than does a more formal, constitutional term such as *federalism.*[4] In addition to being more oriented toward administrative issues than high politics, contemporary intergovernmental relations are more functionally specific and lack the coherence that might result if higher political officials were obliged to be involved in the principal decisions. Thus, as with much of the rest of American politics, intergovernmental relations often are without the mechanisms that could generate effective policy control and coordination.

Despite the complexity, overlap, and incoherence that exist in intergovernmental relations, one can still argue that centralization of control in the federal system has increased.[5] The degree of dependence of state and local governments on federal financial support for their services has varied over the past several decades. The Reagan administration reduced federal support for state and local activities, especially social services, but the level of federal support has been creeping back up (see Table 2.1). Along with financing has come increased federal control over local government activities. In some cases, that control is absolute, as when the federal government mandates equal access to education for those with disabilities or establishes water quality standards for sewage treatment facilities. In other instances, the controls on state and local governments are conditional, based on the acceptance of a grant: If a government accepts the money, it must accept the controls accompanying that money.

In general, the number and importance of mandates on state and local governments and the conditions attached to grants have been increasing. For example, the Department of Health and Human Services threatened to cut off funding for immunization and other public health programs in states that did not implement restrictions on procedures performed by doctors and dentists

TABLE 2.1    Changing Levels of Federal Grants-in-Aid to State and Local Governments

|  | *1970* | *1980* | *1985* | *1990* | *1995* | *2000* | *2007* |
|---|---|---|---|---|---|---|---|
| Total amount ($ millions) | 24,065 | 91,385 | 105,852 | 135,325 | 224,991 | 284,659 | 443,797 |
| Percentage of state and local expenditures | 29.1 | 39.9 | 29.6 | 25.2 | 31.5 | 31.3 | 31.9 |

*Source:* Historical Tables, *Budget of the United States Government* (Washington, DC: Office of Management and Budget, 2008).

with AIDS. Even the existence of many federal grant programs may be indicative of subtle control from the center, inasmuch as they direct the attention, and especially the money, of local governments in directions they might not otherwise have chosen.

In addition to controls exercised through the grant process, the federal government has increased its controls over subnational governments through intergovernmental regulation and mandating. Regulations require the subnational government to perform a function such as wastewater treatment, whether or not there is federal money available to subsidize the activity. These regulations are certainly intrusive and can be expensive for state and local governments. Even when the mandates are not expensive and are probably effective, such as the requirement that states raise the minimum drinking age to twenty-one or lose 5 percent of their federal highway money, they can still be perceived as "federal blackmail" of the states.[6]

One part of the "Contract with America" promoted by the incoming Republican majority in Congress in 1994 was to end unfunded federal mandates, and the assault on mandates was the first section of the "contract" enacted into law. In particular, the Unfunded Mandates Reform Act of 1995 requires the Congressional Budget Office to estimate the mandated costs of legislation reported out of committee in Congress. This provision by no means outlaws federal mandates, but it does require that members of Congress at least know what they are doing to the states and localities if they pass particular legislation. That measure did not in any way affect existing mandates, nor will the federal government have to pay the bill for those. Conservatives believe that in practice the legislation has been largely toothless,[7] while liberals believe that environmental and consumer standards are in danger of being undermined. The shift from mandates to the suggestions to control drunk driving that were part of the 1998 highways bill indicates something of a shift in attitudes about mandates—there is still some attempt to impose federal priorities but mostly through suasion rather than direct command. That said, the No Child Left Behind program of President George W. Bush imposed potentially huge costs on the states and localities (for testing and for supporting students in "failing schools") with little funding attached.

One factor complicating intergovernmental relations has been the proliferation of local governments in the United States. As fiscal constraints on local governments have caused problems for mayors and county commissioners, new local governments have been created to circumvent those restrictions. States frequently restrict the level of taxation or bonded indebtedness of local governments, but when a local government reaches its legal limit, it may simply create a special authority to undertake some functions that the general-purpose local authority formerly carried out. For example, as Chicago faced severe fiscal problems in 2005, it sold its Skyway toll road to a private contractor; it leased Midway Airport to combat the financial crisis of 2008.

An average of almost five hundred local governments is created every year, primarily special districts to provide services such as transportation, water, sewerage, fire protection, and other traditional local government services.[8] The new special-purpose governments multiply the problems of coordination and may frustrate citizens who want to control tax levels but find that every time they limit the power of one government, a new one is created with more fiscal powers. They also present problems of democratic accountability. The leaders of special-purpose governments often are not elected, and the public can influence their actions only indirectly through the general-purpose local governments (cities and counties) that appoint the boards of the special-purpose authorities.[9]

The economic circumstances of the late 1980s and early 1990s—rapidly mounting federal deficits and healthy state treasuries—tended to push power back toward the states.[10] The recession of the early 1990s ended public surpluses in almost all states and turned eyes in state capitals back toward Washington and the incoming Democratic administration. The Clinton administration, however, proved to be as decentralizing as most previous Republican administrations and perhaps even more so. For example, the welfare reform passed in 1996 was a major decentralization of power to the states, and the general pattern of policy change was to increase the powers of states and localities vis-à-vis Washington. Like President Clinton, President George W. Bush also had been a governor and brought a decentralizing agenda with him to the White House, but the September 11 attacks tended to move power back toward Washington more clearly than at any time since the 1960s. The Bush administration was, in fact, one of the most centralizing in recent American history and involved the federal government in local education, law enforcement, and health issues in ways that previous administrations had not thought appropriate. Some of the attempts at central control, such as using federal drug statutes to prevent Oregon from implementing its own "death with dignity" law, went too far even for a Supreme Court that seemed to accept greater centralization in issues such as gun control in the District of Columbia.[11]

Despite those earlier trends, the American federal system still centralizes power more than was planned when the federal system was formed. The grant system has been purchasing a more centralized form of government, although the shift in power appears to have come less from power hunger on the part of federal bureaucrats and politicians than from the needs to standardize many public services and to promote greater equality for minorities. Furthermore, even if federal programs are intended to be managed with no strings attached, there is a natural tendency, especially in Congress, to demand the right to monitor the expenditure of public funds to ensure that the money is used to attain the desired goals. In an era in which the accountability of government is an increasingly important issue, monitoring is likely to increase in intensity, even when Republican members of Congress stress the need to limit federal power.

The Obama administration has also tended to centralize, although without a few comments on the sort of federalism that it would find most congenial; in large part, this centralization has been the result of the fiscal crisis beginning in 2008 and the poor condition of state and local finances. For example, the Stimulus Package of 2009 provided billions of dollars to state and local governments to support infrastructure programs and some service delivery in areas such as education. Likewise, the passage of the health reform acts places the federal government in a much more central position in health care.

## Separation of Powers

The second division of American government exists within the federal government itself and, incidentally, within most state and local governments as well. The Constitution distributes the powers of the federal government among three branches, each capable of applying checks and balances to the other two. In addition to providing employment for constitutional lawyers, this division of power has a substantial impact on public policies. In particular, the number of "veto points" in the federal government alone makes initiating any policy difficult and preventing change relatively easy.[12] It also means, as I mentioned when discussing the incoherence of American public policy, that the major task in making public policy is forming a coalition across a number of institutions and levels of government. Without "legislating together" in such a coalition, either nothing will happen, or the intentions of a policymaker will be modified substantially in the policy process.[13]

The president, Congress, and the courts are constitutionally designated institutions that must agree to a policy before it can be fully legitimated. The bureaucracy, although it is only alluded to in the Constitution, is now also a force in the policy process with which elected politicians must contend. Despite its conservative and obstructionist image, the bureaucracy is frequently the institution most active in promoting policy change, as a result of government workers' close connections with the individuals and interests to which they provide services, as well as their own ideas about public policy.[14] The bureaucracy is also given latitude to elaborate congressional legislation, as well as to adjudicate the application of laws within each policy area.[15]

The bureaucracy—or, more properly, the individual agencies of which it is composed—has interests that can be served through legislation.[16] The desired legislation may only expand the budget of an agency, but it usually has a broader public policy purpose as well. Administrative agencies can, if they wish, also impede policy change or perhaps even block it entirely. Almost every elected or appointed politician has experienced delaying tactics by nominal subordinates who disagree with a policy choice and want to wait until the next election or cabinet change to see if someone with more compatible policy priorities will come into office. The permanence of the bureaucrats, along with their command of technical details and of the procedural machinery, provides bureaucratic agencies much more power over public policies than one would assume from reading formal descriptions of government institutions. It has become increasingly evident that agencies may drive the congressional agenda almost as much as Congress shapes the agenda of the agencies.[17]

The institutional separation in American government has led to a number of critiques based on the concept of divided government.[18] Those critiques argue that American government is incapable of being the decisive governance system required in the twenty-first century and that some means must be found of generating coherent decisions. This has been an issue especially when the presidency and Congress have been controlled by different political parties, as they were during the later part of George W. Bush's presidency, or the second half of President Obama's administration. In both cases, there were also divisions within their own parties that made policymaking difficult. Despite the impacts of divided government, David Mayhew, Charles O. Jones, and other scholars have argued that the system can govern effectively because it is capable of making decisions and even of rapid policy innovation.[19]

Whether the policymaking system is efficient or not, one principal result of the necessity to form coalitions across a number of institutions is the tendency to produce small, incremental changes rather than major revamping of policies.[20] This might be described as policymaking by the lowest common denominator. The need to involve and placate all institutions within the federal government—including the many component groups of individuals within each—and perhaps state and local governments as well means that only rarely can there be more than minor changes in the established commitments to clients and producer groups if the policy change is to be successful.[21] The resulting pattern of incremental change has been both praised and damned. It has been praised for providing stability and limiting the errors that might result from more significant shifts in policy. If only small policy changes are made and those changes do not stray far from previously established paths, then it is unlikely that major mistakes will be made.

The jiggling and poking of policies characteristic of incremental change is perfectly acceptable if the basic patterns of policy are acceptable, but in some areas such as health care and mass transportation, a majority of Americans have said (at least in polls) that they would like some significant changes from the status quo.[22] The existing system of policymaking appears to produce major desired changes only with great difficulty; the increasing partisanship in Congress has made change even more difficult. In addition, the reversibility of small policy changes, assumed to be an advantage of incrementalism, is often overstated.[23] Once a program is implemented, a return to the conditions that existed before the policy choice is often difficult. Clients, employees, and organizations are created by any policy choice, and they usually will exert powerful pressures for the continuation of the program.

The division of American government by the constitutional separation of powers doctrine creates a major institutional confrontation at the center of the federal government. Conflicts between the president and Congress over such matters as war powers, executive privilege, and the budget also test and redefine the relative powers of institutions. These conflicts became more apparent in 2005 with revelations of the use of presidential authority to wiretap Americans' phones without a judicial warrant, as well as other uses of the fight against terrorism to justify increased presidential action. Is the modern presidency inherently imperial, or is it still subject to control by Congress and the courts? Does too much checking by each institution of the others generate gridlock and indecision? Likewise, can the unelected Supreme Court have as legitimate a rule-making role in the political system as the elected Congress and president? Do the regulations made by the public bureaucracy really have the same standing in law as the legislation passed by Congress or decrees coming from the court system? These questions posed by the separation of powers doctrine influence substantive policy as well as relationships among the institutions.

## Subgovernments

A third division within American government cuts across institutional lines within the federal government and links it directly to the picket fence of federalism. The results of this division have been described variously as "iron triangles," "cozy little triangles," "whirlpools," and "subgovernments."[24] The underlying phenomenon that these terms describe is that the federal government rarely acts as a unified institution making integrated policy choices but tends instead to endorse the decisions made by portions of the government. Each functional policy area tends to be governed as if it existed in splendid isolation from the remainder of government, and frequently, the powers and legitimacy of government are used to advance individual or group interests in society, rather than a broader public interest.[25]

Three principal actors are involved in the iron triangles still so relevant for explaining policymaking in the United States. The first is the interest group, which wants something from government, usually a favorable policy decision, and must attempt to influence the institutions that can act in its favor.

Fortunately for the interest group, it usually need not influence all of Congress or the entire executive branch but only the relatively small portion concerned with its particular policy area. For example, farmers who want continued or increased crop supports need not influence the entire Department of Agriculture but only those within the Agricultural Stabilization and Commodity Service who are directly concerned with their crop. Likewise, in Congress, they need only influence the Commodities Subcommittee of the House Agriculture Committee; the Senate Subcommittee on Agricultural Production and Stabilization of Prices; and the Rural Development, Agriculture, and Related Agencies Subcommittees of the appropriations committees in the Senate and House. In addition to the usual tools of information and campaign funds, interest groups have an important weapon at their disposal: votes. They represent organizations of interested individuals and can influence, if not deliver, votes for a representative or senator. Interest groups also have research staffs, technical information, and other support services that, although their outputs must be regarded with some skepticism, may be valuable resources for members of Congress or administrative agencies seeking to influence the policy process.

The second component of these triangular relationships is the congressional committee or subcommittee. These bodies are designated to review suggestions for legislation in a policy area and to make recommendations to the whole Senate or House of Representatives. An appropriations subcommittee's task is to review expenditure recommendations from the president, then to make its own recommendations on the appropriate level of expenditures to the entire committee and to the whole chamber. Several factors combine to give these subcommittees substantial power over legislation. First, subcommittee members develop expertise over time, and they are often regarded as more competent to make decisions concerning a policy than the whole committee or the whole house.[26] Norms have also been developed that support subcommittee decisions for less rational, and more political, reasons.[27] If the entire committee or the entire house were to scrutinize any one subcommittee's decisions, it would have to scrutinize all such decisions, and then each subcommittee would lose its powers. These powers are important to individual Congress members because each wants to develop his or her own power base in a subcommittee or perhaps even the entire committee.[28] The time limitations imposed by the huge volume of policy decisions that Congress makes each year also mean that accepting a subcommittee's decision may be a rational means of reducing the workload of each individual legislator.

Congressional subcommittees are not unbiased; they tend to favor the very interests they are intended to oversee and control. The reason is largely that the Congress members serving on a subcommittee tend to represent constituencies whose interests are affected by the policy in question. As one analyst argued, "A concerted effort is made to ensure that the membership of the subcommittee is supportive of the goals of the subgovernment."[29] For example, in 2012, the members of the Energy and Mineral Resources Subcommittee of the House Resources Committee included representatives from the energy-producing states of Texas (2), California, Louisiana (2), West Virginia, Alaska, Pennsylvania, Ohio, and Oklahoma and from the mining states of Arizona, Colorado, and Nevada; there were representatives from Maryland and New Jersey. This pattern is not confined to natural resources. The Housing and Community Development Subcommittee of the House Banking, Finance, and Urban Affairs Committee has representatives from all the major urban areas of the United States.

These patterns of committee and subcommittee membership are hardly random; they enhance the ability of Congress members to deliver certain kinds of benefits to constituents, as well as the members' familiarity with the substantive issues of concern to their constituents. Subcommittee members also develop patterns of interaction with the administrative agencies over which they exercise oversight. Individual members of Congress and agency officials may discuss policy with one another and meet informally. As both parties in these interactions tend to remain in Washington for long periods, the same Congress members and officials may interact for many years. The trust, respect, or simple familiarity this interaction produces further cements the relationships between committee members and agency personnel, and it also tends to insulate each individual policy area from meddling by outside interests.

Obviously, the third component of the iron triangle is the administrative agency, which, like the pressure group, wants to promote its interests through the policymaking process. The principal interests of an agency are its survival and its budget. The agency need not be, as is often assumed, determined to expand its budget—it may wish merely to retain its fair share of the budget pie as it expands or contracts.[30] Agencies are not entirely self-interested; they also have policy ideas that they wish to see translated into operating programs, and they need the action of the congressional committee or subcommittee for that to happen. They also need the support of organized interests in the process.

Each actor in an iron triangle needs the other two to reach its goal, and the style that develops is symbiotic. The pressure group needs the agency to deliver services to its members and to provide a friendly point of access to government. The agency needs the pressure group to mobilize political support for its programs among the affected clientele. Letters from constituents to influential representatives and senators must be mobilized to argue that the agency is doing a good job and could do an even better job if given more money or a certain policy change. The pressure group needs the congressional committee again as a point of access and as an internal advocate in Congress. And the committee needs the pressure group to mobilize votes for its members and to explain to group members how and why they are doing a good job in Congress. The pressure group can also be a valuable source of policy ideas and research for busy politicians. Finally, the committee members need the agency as an instrument for producing services to their constituents and for developing new policy initiatives. The agency has the research and policy analytic capacity that Congress members often lack, so committees can profit from their association with the agencies. And the agency obviously needs the committee to legitimate its policy initiatives and provide it with funds.

All the actors involved in a triangle have similar interests. In many ways, they all represent the same individuals, variously playing the roles of voter, client, and organization member. Much of the domestic policy of the United States can be explained by the existence of functionally specific policy subsystems and by the absence of effective central coordination. This system of policymaking has been likened to feudalism, with the policies being determined not by any central authority but by aggressive subordinates—the bureaucratic agencies and their associated groups and committees.[31] Both the norms of policymaking and the time constraints of political leaders tend to make central coordination and policy choice difficult. The president and his staff (especially the Office of Management and Budget) are in the best organizational position to exercise such control, but the president must serve political interests, just as Congress must, and he faces an even more extreme time constraint. Thus, decisions are rarely reversed once they have been made within the iron triangle, except in a crisis. For example, following the 2001 terrorist attacks, there was pronounced movement toward greater presidential control over a range of organizations and less separation among the policy subsystems. That change was most pronounced in the area of homeland defense, but to some degree, all organizations in government have become less particularistic.

One effect of the subdivision of government into a number of functionally specific subgovernments is the incoherence in public policy already mentioned. Virtually all societal interests are served through their own agencies, and there is little attempt to make overall policy choices for the nation. These functional subgovernments at the federal level are linked with functional subsystems in intergovernmental relations—the picket fences described earlier. The result of this segmentation of decision making is that local governments and citizens alike may frequently receive contradictory directives from government and may become confused and cynical about the apparent inability of their government to make up its mind.

A second effect of the division of American government into a number of subgovernments is the involvement of a large number of official actors in any one policy area. The proliferation of actors is in part recognition of the numerous interactions within the public sector and between the public and private sectors, in the formulation and implementation of any public policy. For an issue area such as health care, the range of organizations involved cannot be confined to those labeled *health* but must expand to include consideration of the social welfare, nutritional, housing, educational, and environmental policies that may have important implications for citizens' health.[32] But the involvement of an increasing number of public organizations in each issue area also reflects the lack of central coordination, which allows agencies to gain approval from friendly congressional committees for expansion of their range of programs and activities.

From time to time, a president will attempt to streamline and rationalize the delivery of services in the executive branch, and in the process, he generally encounters resistance from agencies and their associated interest groups. For example, when creating the cabinet-level Department of Education, President Jimmy Carter sought to move the educational programs of the (then) Veterans Administration (VA) into the new department.[33] In this attempt, he locked horns with one of the best organized and most powerful iron triangles in Washington—the Veterans Administration, veterans organizations, and their associated congressional committees. The president lost. Subsequently, the veterans lobby was sufficiently powerful to have the VA elevated to a cabinet-level department. Presidents do not always lose: President Clinton was able to downsize or eliminate several organizations during implementation of his National Performance Review, including several that had substantial political clienteles.[34] George W. Bush also was successful in a massive reorganization to create the Department of Homeland Security, but that reform has not produced most of the results desired. It appears that there has been substantial internal conflict over policy and reduced effectiveness in some areas.[35] The administration of George W. Bush attempted to use performance management techniques to improve control over agencies, with at best limited success.[36]

As easy as it is to become enamored of the idea of iron triangles in American government—they do help explain many of the apparent inconsistencies in policy when viewed broadly—there is some evidence that the iron in the triangles is becoming rusty.[37] More groups are now involved in making decisions, and it is more difficult to exclude interested parties, leading Charles O. Jones to describe the current pattern as "big sloppy hexagons" rather than "cozy little triangles."[38] For example, debates over health care reform include not just representatives of the medical professions, the hospitals, and health insurers but also a range of other interests such as small business, organized religion, and organized labor. A simple Internet search on most any policy issue will reveal a wide range of groups expressing their views and attempting to influence public—and congressional—opinion.[39]

The concepts of *issue networks* and *policy communities* involving large numbers of interested parties, each with substantial expertise in the policy area, now appear more descriptive of policymaking in the United States as well as other

AP Photo/Jacquelyn Martin

*The economic crisis beginning in 2008 led to major policy interventions by the federal government attempting to stimulate the economy. These initiatives included support for public infrastructure, such as this project to replace a sidewalk ramp in Silver Spring, Maryland, and required the involvement of both the President and Congress to be enacted.*

industrialized democracies.[40] These structures of interest groups surrounding an issue are less unified about policy than were the iron triangles, and they may contain competing ideas and types of interests to be served through public policy—the tobacco subsystem may even be invaded by health care advocates. There has been some rusting of the iron in the triangles, but the indeterminacy and lack of coherence of networks make them less valuable in the day-to-day work of governing. As important as the network idea has been for explaining changes in federal policymaking, it does not detract from the basic idea that policymaking is very much an activity that occurs within subsystems.

American government, although originally conceptualized as divided horizontally into levels, is now better understood as divided vertically into a number of expert and functional policy subsystems. These virtually feudal subsystems divide the authority of government and attempt to appropriate the mantle of the public interest for their own more private interests. Few of the actors making policy, if any, have any interest in altering these stable and effective means of governing. The system is effective politically because it results in the satisfaction of most interests in society. It also links particular politicians and agencies with the satisfaction of those interests, thereby ensuring their continued political success.

The basic patterns of decision making in American politics are *logrolling* and the *pork barrel,* through which, instead of clashing over the allocation of resources, actors minimize conflict by giving one another what they want. For example, instead of contending over which river and harbor improvements will be authorized in any year, Congress has tended to approve virtually all proposals, so that all members can claim to have produced something for the folks back home. Or Congress members from farming areas may trade positive votes on urban development legislation for support of farm legislation by inner-city Congress members. This pattern helps incumbents to be reelected, but it costs taxpayers a great deal more than would a more selective system.

Although logrolling tends to spread benefits widely, being directly involved in the decision-making subsystem tends to produce more benefits for Congress members and their constituents. That could be seen easily in the distribution of funds from the 2005 SAFE Transportation Equity Act. This act provided a good deal of highway spending for all the American states but tended to favor the states and congressional districts represented on the transportation committees in both houses of Congress (see Table 2.2). The most famous example of this pork barrel spending was a bridge to a sparsely populated island in Alaska, which became a symbol of federal waste and congressional excess. Also, the adding of "earmarks," or special spending provisions for constituencies, to bills has come under increased scrutiny following the 2006 investigations of lobbying.[41] The Republican primary battles of 2011–2012 had all the candidates opposed to wasteful earmarking (which seemed to be earmarks to states other than their own).[42]

Logrolling and pork barrel policymaking are very effective as long as there is sufficient wealth and economic growth to pay for subsidizing large numbers of public programs.[43] Nevertheless, this pattern of policymaking was one (but by no means the sole) reason for the federal government's massive deficits in the 1980s and early 1990s, which have returned in recent years, and it appears that it can no longer be sustained comfortably. Various attempts at budget reform have endeavored to make pork barrel politics more difficult to pursue. In particular, the PAYGO system in Congress, by requiring consideration of alternative uses of money or an alternative source of revenue, made it more

TABLE 2.2    Per Capita Appropriations in Highway Bill of 2005, by Representation on Congressional Transportation Committees

| No representatives | One representative | Multiple representatives |
|---|---|---|
| $31.78 | $43.56 | $48.36 |

difficult, at least for a while, for Congress to spend (see chapter 7). Given the divisions within American government, however, it is difficult for the policymaking system as a whole to make the choices among competing goals and competing segments of society that would be necessary to stop the flow of red ink from Washington.

## Public and Private

The final qualitative dimension of American government that is important in understanding how contemporary policy is made is the increasing confusion of public and private interests and organizations. These two sets of actors and actions have now become so intermingled that it is difficult to ascertain where the boundary between the two sectors lies. The leakage across the boundary between the public and private sectors, as artificial as that boundary may be, has been occurring in both directions. Activities that once were almost entirely private now have greater public sector involvement, although frequently through quasi-public organizations that mask the real involvement of government. Functions that are nominally public have significantly greater private sector involvement. The growth of institutions for formal representation of interest groups and for implementation of policy by interest groups has given those groups perhaps an even more powerful position in policymaking than that described in the discussion of iron triangles. Instead of vying for access, interest groups are accorded access formally and can exert a legitimate claim to their position in government.

The other major component of change in the relationship between public and private has been the privatization of public activities.[44] The United States traditionally has had an antigovernment ethos; that set of values was articulated strongly, and the positive role of the federal government was minimized, during the 1980s.[45] At the state and local levels, a large number of functions—hospitals, garbage collection, janitorial services, and even prisons—have been contracted out or sold off as a way to reduce the costs of government.[46] In the administration of George W. Bush, the most evident privatization trend was the opening of federal land to private mining and forestry.

The blending of public and private is reflected to some degree in employment.[47] Table 2.3 shows public employment in twelve policy areas, as well as the changes that occurred from 1970 to 2000. By 1980, for example, only education comprised more than 80 percent public employees, and that percentage was dropping. Even two presumed public monopolies—defense and police protection—had significant levels of private employment. The two policy areas differ, however, in the form of private employment. Defense employment in the private sector is in the production of goods and services that the armed forces use, whereas in policing, a number of private police officers actually provide the service.

TABLE 2.3   Percentages of Public Employment in Selected Policy Areas, 1980–2005

| Policy area | 1980 | 1990 | 2000 | 2005 |
|---|---|---|---|---|
| Education | 85 | 83 | 82 | 80 |
| Postal service[a] | 73 | 70 | 62 | 63 |
| Highways[b] | 68 | 62 | 61 | 58 |
| Tax administration[c] | 57 | 55 | 40 | 37 |
| Police[d] | 60 | 56 | 55 | 56 |
| Defense[e] | 59 | 62 | 63 | 64 |
| Social services[f] | 35 | 32 | 23 | 22 |
| Transportation | 31 | 34 | 31 | 32 |
| Health | 30 | 37 | 33 | 34 |
| Gas/electricity/water | 27 | 24 | 17 | 13 |
| Banking[g] | 1 | 1 | 1 | 1 |
| Telecommunications | 1 | 1 | 1 | 1 |

*Sources:* Bureau of the Census, *Census of Governments,* quinquennial; Department of Defense, *Defense Manpower Statistics,* annual; Employment and Training Administration, *Annual Report.*

a. Private sector counterparts are employees of private services, couriers, etc.

b. Private sector counterparts are employed by highway construction contracting firms.

c. Private sector counterparts are tax accountants and staffs, H&R Block employees, etc., some only seasonal.

d. Private sector counterparts are security guards, private police, etc.

e. Private sector counterparts are employed by military suppliers.

f. Private sector counterparts are employed in social work and philanthropy, many only part-time.

g. In 2009 proportion will have increased because of bailout of banks.

The development of mechanisms for direct involvement of interest groups in public decision making is frequently referred to as *corporatism* or *neocorporatism.*[48] The terms refer to the representation in politics of members of the political community not as residents of a geographical area but as members of functionally defined interests in the society—labor, management, farmers, students, the elderly, and so forth. Associated with this concept of representation is the extensive use of interest groups both as instruments of input to the policy process and as means of implementing public policies. The United States is a less corporatist political system than most industrialized democracies but still has corporatist elements. Most urban programs mandate the participation of community residents and other interested parties in decision making. Crop allotment programs of the U.S. Department of Agriculture have used local farmers' organizations for monitoring and implementation for some time, and fishing quotas are negotiated with local fishery management councils.[49] County medical societies have been used as professional service review organizations for Medicare and Medicaid, checking on the quality and cost of services, and medical and legal associations license practitioners on behalf of government. In addition, as of the early twenty-first century, there were approximately 6,500 advisory bodies in the federal government, many containing substantial interest group representation.[50]

A number of other organizations also implement public policy. For example, when cabin attendants in an airplane require passengers to fasten their seat belts, they are implementing Federal Aviation Administration policies. Universities are required to help implement federal drug policies (by requiring statements of nonuse by new employees) and federal immigration policies (by requiring certification of citizenship or immigration status). Manufacturers of numerous products must implement federal safety and environmental standards (e.g., installing seat belts and pollution-control devices in automobiles), or they cannot sell their products legally.

The increasing use of quasi-public organizations, changes in the direction of a limited corporatist approach to governance in the United States, and privatization (largely through contracting) raises several questions concerning responsibility and accountability in government. These changes involve the use of public money and, more important, the name of the public by groups and for groups that may not be entirely public. In an era when citizens appear to be attempting to exercise greater control over their governments, the development of these forms of policymaking "at the margins of the state" may be an understandable response to financial constraints but may exacerbate underlying problems of public loss of trust and confidence in government.

## The Size and Shape of the Public Sector

We have looked at some qualitative aspects of the contemporary public sector in the United States. What we have yet to do is examine the size of that public sector and the distribution of funds and personnel among the various purposes of government. As was pointed out, drawing clear distinctions between public and private sectors in the mixed-economy welfare state is difficult, and growing more difficult, but we will concentrate on the expenditures and personnel that are clearly governmental. As these figures include only those expenditures and employees that are clearly public, they inevitably understate the size and importance of government in the United States. The understatement is perhaps greater for the United States than would be the case for other countries because of government's attempts to hide the extent of its involvement in the private sector.

Table 2.4 contains information about the changing size of the public sector in the United States since the post–World War II era and the changing distribution of expenditures and employment.[51] Most obvious in this table is that the public sector in the United States has indeed grown, with expenditures increasing from less than one-quarter to more than one-third gross national product. Likewise, public employment has increased from 11 percent of total employment to over 15 percent. The relative size of the public sector, however, has decreased from the mid-1970s, especially in terms of the percentage of employment. Although the number of public employees increased by over four million from 1994 to 2009, government's share of total employment declined slightly, despite the increasing employment at the state and local levels. There was a slight

TABLE 2.4    Growth of Public Employment and Expenditures, 1950–2009

| Year | Civilian public employment (in thousands) | | | Public expenditures (in thousands) | | |
|---|---|---|---|---|---|---|
| | Federal | State and local | Total | Federal[a] | State and local | Total |
| 1950 | 2,117 | 4,285 | 6,402 | $44,800 | $25,534 | $70,334 |
| 1960 | 2,421 | 6,387 | 8,808 | 97,280 | 54,008 | 151,288 |
| 1970 | 2,880 | 10,147 | 13,028 | 208,190 | 124,795 | 332,985 |
| 1980 | 2,876 | 13,315 | 16,191 | 576,700 | 432,328 | 1,009,028 |
| 1990 | 3,105 | 14,976 | 18,081 | 1,243,125 | 976,311 | 2,219,436 |
| 2000 | 2,799 | 17,506 | 20,305 | 1,689,300 | 1,720,899 | 3,420,200 |
| 2006 | 2,695 | 19,327 | 22,022 | 2,635,200 | 1,898,200 | 4,533,400 |
| 2009 | 2.824 | 19,809 | 22,632 | | | |

| Year | As percentage of total employment | | | As percentage of GNP | | |
|---|---|---|---|---|---|---|
| 1950 | 3.6 | 7.3 | 10.9 | 15.7 | 8.9 | 24.6 |
| 1960 | 3.7 | 9.7 | 13.4 | 19.2 | 10.7 | 29.9 |
| 1970 | 3.7 | 12.9 | 16.6 | 21.2 | 12.7 | 33.9 |
| 1975 | 3.4 | 14.2 | 17.6 | 22.5 | 14.4 | 36.9 |
| 1980 | 2.9 | 13.1 | 16.0 | 20.0 | 16.4 | 36.4 |
| 1990 | 2.6 | 12.5 | 15.1 | 23.2 | 18.2 | 41.4 |
| 2000 | 2.1 | 12.8 | 14.9 | 16.7 | 24.1 | 40.8 |
| 2006 | 2.0 | 13.4 | 15.4 | 17.0 | 23.7 | 40.7 |
| 2009 | 2.0 | 13.6 | 15.6 | | | |

*Source:* U.S. Census Bureau, *Statistical Abstract of the United States* (Washington, DC: GPO, annual).

a. Does not include federal monies passed through grant programs to states and localities for final expenditure at state and local levels.

increase at the end of this period, due in part to declining private employment in the recession. Government in the United States is large, but it does not appear to be the ever-increasing Leviathan that its critics portray it to be.[52]

It is also evident that growth levels of public expenditures are more than twice as large, relative to the rest of the economy, as public employment figures. Public expenditures as a share of gross national product have continued to increase slightly. The differences relative to the private sector and the differences in the patterns of change are largely the results of transfer programs, such as Social Security, which involve the expenditure of large amounts of money but require relatively few administrators. In addition, purchases of goods and services from the private sector (for example, the Department of Defense's purchases of weapons from private firms) involve the expenditure of large amounts of money (over $260 billion in 2006) but generate little or no employment in the public sector. In 1988, however, those purchases created approximately 2.1 million jobs in the private sector, a figure similar to the number of people then in the armed forces.[53] From these data it appears that some portions of "big government" in the United States are more controllable than others, even during the eight-year term of a popular president determined to reduce the size of the public sector.

The distribution of expenditures and employment among levels of government also has been changing. In 1950, the federal government spent 64 percent of all public money and employed 33 percent of all public employees. By 2006, the federal government spent approximately 60 percent of all public money but employed only 12 percent of all civilian public employees.[54] The remarkable shift in employment relative to a rather stable distribution of expenditures is again in part a function of the large federal transfer programs, such as Social Security. It also reflects the expansion of federal grants to state and local governments and the ability of the federal government to borrow money to meet expenditure needs, in contrast to the requirement that state and local governments balance their budgets.

In addition, the programs that state and local governments provide—education, social services, police and fire protection—are labor intensive. The major labor-intensive federal program, defense, had declining civilian and uniformed employment even before the apparent end of the Cold War in the late 1980s. These data appear to conflict somewhat with the popular characterization of the federal government as increasingly important, or intrusive, in American economic and social life. Although it is a large institution, employing over four million people when the armed forces are included, its level of employment actually had been declining, absolutely as well as relatively, and the major growth of government employment was occurring at the state and local levels. The increased emphasis on security, at home and abroad, in response to the terrorist attacks of 2001 is shifting more employment to the federal government, both in the military and in homeland security, but the major action in public employ-ment is at the state and local levels.

Another factor in the federal government's declining share of employment is the shift from defense programs toward social programs. In 1952, national defense accounted for 46 percent of all public expenditures and for 49 percent of all public employment. By 2009, defense had been reduced to 9 percent of all spending and less than 3 percent of public employment. By contrast, a panoply of welfare state services (health, education, and social services) accounted for 20 percent of public expenditures in 1952 and 24 percent of public employment. By 2009, these services accounted for 64 percent of spending and 57 percent of all public employment. Within the welfare state services, education has been the biggest gainer in employment, with more than seven million more employees in 2009 than in 1952. Social Security programs alone increased their spending by well over $400 billion during that time period. The United States is often described as a "welfare state laggard," but the evidence is that although it is still behind most European nations in the range of social services, a marked increase has been occurring in the social component of American public expenditures and employment.

It was argued that the landslide victories of the Republican Party in the presidential elections from 1980 to 1988, and even the narrow victories in 2000 and 2004, were a repudiation of that pattern of change and that they should have produced little increase, or actual decreases, in public spending for social pro-grams. There was a slight relative decrease in social spending from 1980 to 1992—in part a function of increasing expenditures for other purposes, such as interest on the public debt—but sustained decreases remain difficult to obtain. Most social programs are entitlement programs, and once a citizen has been made a recipient of benefits, or has made the insurance contributions to Social Security, future governments find it difficult to remove those benefits. This is especially true of programs for the retired elderly, as they cannot be expected to return to active employment to make up losses in benefits, and unfortunately for budget cutters, public expenditures are increasingly directed toward the elderly. For example, in 2009, approximately 53 percent of the federal budget went to programs (Social Security, Medicare, housing programs, and so forth) for the elderly. As the American population continues to grow older, spending for this social group will increase. What is true in particular for the elderly is true in general for all entitlement programs, and reducing the size of the government's social budget will be difficult indeed.

We have been concentrating attention on public employment and public expenditures as measures of the size of government, but we should remember that government influences the economy and society through a number of other mechanisms as well. For example, the federal government sponsors a much larger housing program through the tax system—through the tax deductibility of mortgage interest and property taxes—than it does through the Department of Housing and Urban Development (see Table 10.3, chapter 10). Government also provides a major educational program of guaranteed and subsidized student loans that shows up only indirectly in figures on public spending.

In the United States, because of the generally antistatist views of many citizens, regulation has been the major form of government intervention in the economy, rather than the more direct mechanisms used in other countries. The regulatory impact of government on the economy can be counted in the billions of dollars—one estimate was more than $21,000 per household in 2000.[55] Reliance on such indirect methods of influence was heightened by the conservative Congresses over the past fifteen years, although the George W. Bush administration eliminated a number of environmental and health regulations. The conservatives in Congress were, however, successful in creating requirements for government to report the estimated costs of its regulations.[56] As governments continue to find less intrusive ways of making and implementing policy—using loans rather than expenditures, for example—assessing the size, shape, and impact of government in the United States based solely on public spending figures and public employment becomes less and less accurate.

The first decade of the twenty-first century has been one of extremely dramatic change in the role of the public sector in the United States. The economic crisis created by the failures of a number of banks has produced the largest expansion of federal power, and spending, since Franklin Roosevelt's New Deal. The federal government has assumed effective ownership of a number of banks and has embarked on massive public spending in an attempt to revive the economy. This large-scale spending may undermine attempts to promote a national health program and to enhance the performance of the educational program.

## Summary

American government in the new century is large, complex, and to some degree unorganized. Each individual section of government, be it a local government or an agency of the federal government, tends to know clearly what it wants, but the system as a whole lacks overall coordination, coherence, and control. Priority setting is not one of the strongest features of American government. An elected official coming to office with a commitment to give direction to the system of government will be disappointed in the extent of his or her ability to produce desired results, by the barriers to policy success, and by the relatively few ways in which the probability of success can be increased. These difficulties, however, may be compensated for by the flexibility and multiple opportunities for citizen inputs characteristic of American government.

Despite the problems of coordination and control and the tradition of popular distrust of government, contemporary American government is active. It spends huge amounts of money and employs millions of people to perform a bewildering variety of tasks. These activities are not confined to a single level of government; all three levels of government are involved in making policy, taxing, spending, and delivering services. This activity is the reason why the study of public policy is so important. It is a means of understanding what goes on in the United States and why government does the things it does. The emphasis in the next portion of this book is on the processes through which policy is made. All governments must follow many of the same procedures when they make policy: identify issues, formulate policy responses to problems, evaluate results, and change programs that are not producing the desired results. American governments do all these things, but they do them in a distinctive way and produce distinctive results.

CHAPTER 3

# Explaining Policy Choices

MOST OF THIS BOOK describes the stages of the policy process and individual policy areas. In each of the descriptive components of the book, there are implied ways of explaining how decisions are made and why policies are adopted in the way that they are. The *stages model* of policy, for example, assumes that the process of making policy plays a significant part in determining the outcome. This simple explanation has a great deal of validity, given that at each stage of the process certain types of solutions will have a better chance than others of being successful. At the implementation stage, for example (see chapter 6), policies that require fewer independent decisions and that have more robust instruments available are more likely to be successful than more complex policies.

Although the stages model is a useful heuristic, it is but one of several explanations of how decisions can, and should, be made when making policy. Some of these models are based on economic reasoning and make strong assumptions about optimal policies. Optimality may not be achieved in the "real world" of making policy, but the optimal models are a useful standard against which to compare the results of actual policy processes. The majority of the models I will discuss, however, will be political models that attempt to explain how political forces and political institutions shape choices.

## Power and Public Policy

Power is fundamental to all models of policymaking, including the stages model. Many scholars would argue that the simplest way to understand policymaking or any other form of political activity is to understand who has the power to make things happen. So if we want to understand why a law is adopted in a particular manner in Congress or is implemented in a particular way within the bureaucracy, we need to identify who has the power and therefore can make other actors comply with their wishes. Although power is to some extent a function of formal positions in government—the presidency, for example—it also may be a function of the characteristics of the individuals themselves or a product of other resources, such as money, that enable them to be effective in politics.

Whatever the basis of the power, those who have it are able to overcome the opposition of others.[1] Power can be manifested in a number of ways in the policymaking process. The most obvious is when one actor is capable of getting what it wants in fights over legislation or regulations. In the United States, for example, it is often assumed that corporate interests have that capacity.[2] At other times, the exercise of power may be simply the power to prevent action or indeed to prevent some issues from ever being considered.[3] However power is manifested, it is a factor that always must be considered when examining the choices made by governments.

The policymaking process, especially in a complex setting such as U.S. government, involves countervailing power, with all the actors involved having some resources that they can bring to bear. Even individuals and groups outside the mainstream of political life can bring some resources, including moral claims, to bear on the final decision. Therefore, simply saying that policymaking is about the exercise of power is not sufficient, and we must attempt to understand how this fundamental resource for actors in governing is used.

## The Policy Process—The Stages Model

The study of public policy in political science has several important but somewhat disparate dimensions. The largest single body of research has been on the policy process.[4] This approach to policy is inherently political, arguing that the policy choices that governments make are primarily a function of the political process through which they are made and the institutions in which they are made. Most process models attempt to explain policy choices by understanding the actors who are involved at each stage, as well as understanding linkages among the stages. These models are, however, far more useful for describing the process than they are as means of explaining outcomes. We will deal with the stages model of policy in some detail in chapters 4–8, and I will not detail the assumptions of each of its aspects. That said, it is important to consider the way in which adopting a stages model of this type shapes thinking about policy in the United States and also some of the analytic issues raised by this approach.

The conventional process model of policymaking begins with agenda setting or problem definition; then it proceeds through a series of steps such as program design, legitimating, budgeting, and evaluation but typically does not make any strong assumptions about the political mechanisms that are used to manage that movement (see Figure 3.1). Although some elements within the general model,

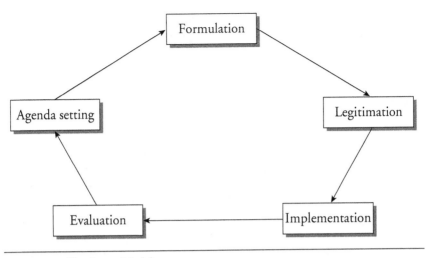

FIGURE 3.1    The Stages Model

such as agenda setting,[5] rely on policy entrepreneurs to provide agency within the process, the general models tend to be largely devoid of that animation. Especially in a political system with as many institutional "veto points" and "veto players" as that of the United States, we need to understand better how the process can be made to work and who drives the action of policymaking forward.[6]

The conventional stages model, as useful as it is, also tends to assume that the stages discussed come in the order laid out in the model and that the process is taking place anew, with relatively little concern for the past. In reality, however, both of those implicit assumptions tend to be incorrect. First, the order may be less linear in practice than it appears in the model. For example, the process of implementation often involves policy formulation because the administrative decisions needed to make programs work in essence transform the policy. Likewise, important policy issues often arise when other programs are being budgeted and it becomes clear that for a program to work other programs will need to be changed or perhaps given additional resources.

It is also important to remember that most policymaking is actually revising and—we hope—improving existing policies.[7] Some policy issues—for example, the budget—return to the agenda automatically, whereas others may remain dormant for some time. In both cases, however, policymaking involves working with existing programs. In some ways, this is an easier process for the political institutions, given that the basic parameters of public intervention have been determined and the involvement of the public sector has been legitimated. On the other hand, however, existing programs have clients and employees, and those groups may resist changes. Thus, the political coalition process may involve more overt conflicts than the relatively infrequent cases in which the public sector chooses to intervene for the first time.

That point raises the importance of conflict in understanding the policy process. The stages model as usually used in political science does not reflect the degree of conflict that may exist in these crucial political processes; rather, the process appears to move along smoothly to its conclusion. At each stage, and as programs and policies move from one stage to the next, there will be conflicts. Furthermore, each stage of the process may involve different sets of actors with different concerns about the programs. For example, as a program moves from formulation and legitimation on to the process of implementation, the state governments are likely to become involved, given that in the United States most federal programs require some state-level implementation. This may transform conflicts about policy substance into ones of funding for the state governments.

In summary, the stages model is a very useful heuristic device for mapping the route that policies take from being just a good idea to being a functioning program, but it provides little explanation for the choices that are made. Many of the stages of the process, such as agenda setting and implementation, have well-developed theoretical explanations for choices, but the links among the stages, and the overall model itself, lack such capacity for explanation. Other approaches in political science may be able to provide more compelling explanations for policy choices.

## Institutional Models of Policy

The stages model is based to some extent on the institutions that are involved in making policy; it tends to assume that certain institutions are associated with certain stages. For example, legislatures are generally crucial for legitimating policy choices and also for budgeting, and the bureaucracy is generally responsible for implementing policy. In addition to those specific institutional linkages, we should also consider a more general institutional model for making policy decisions. Institutions do matter, but we need to specify how they exert their influence.[8]

As the new institutionalism has become a major approach to contemporary political science, the role of institutions has become more clearly conceptualized.[9] Although there are several contending approaches to the role of institutions, they accept the general idea that institutions are crucial for understanding why the public sector functions as it does. New institutionalism emphasizes the normative elements of institutions and the "logic of appropriateness" that provides a guide for action to their members. From this perspective, individuals learn to behave in certain ways in organizations because of organizational values rather than because of the utilitarian consequences of the policies selected. For example, being a member of the U.S. Senate is learned, and members tend to become effective only after they have mastered the formal and informal rules of that institution.

Another way of thinking about the role of a logic of appropriateness is that organizational cultures shape the policies that the organization advocates and implements. The individuals who work in many agencies and departments have their own views of what constitutes good government and good policy and will attempt to have government implement those policies. Political leaders at times find it difficult to overcome these internal logics, for example, when more conservative administrations attempt to change the policy directions of the Environmental Protection Agency or when more liberal administrations confront the Department of Defense.[10]

Whereas such normative institutionalism assumes that policy choices are motivated by an internal logic of appropriateness, historical institutionalism emphasizes the importance of path dependency and the persistence of policy decisions once they are made. Whether simply because it is difficult to change ongoing programs or because of the positive reinforcement that programs receive, once they are initiated, they tend to be "path dependent"—in other words, they tend to follow the status quo—unless there is some sufficient external shock that can disrupt the stability and create a new equilibrium in the policy.[11]

The historical institutionalist perspective is very useful for describing what happens in the policy process, but it is less useful for explaining how choices are made and, more important, why change might occur. Persistence and inertia are rather standard stereotypes of the policy process and often do describe what is happening. We also need, however, means of understanding and explaining policy choices that move away from the status quo, that enable governments to reform and, one hopes, improve policy. Historical institutionalism has begun to think about these ideas of change,[12] but the underlying nature of the approach is to emphasize persistence and the continuity of policy.

Rational choice models of institutions assume that institutions are sets of incentives and rules that shape the rational actions of the individuals who operate within government.[13] These models address some classic problems in political science and policymaking, including the "tragedy of the commons," in which rational individual action leads to the exhaustion of common resources. Furthermore, institutions can help to create equilibrium in situations—legislatures, for example—in which cyclical majorities may make reaching a decision difficult.[14] Perhaps most important for policymaking, rational choice models of institutions have examined the difficulties that institutional design may pose for making decisions.[15] So, for example, the U.S. government, with its multiple institutions, presents special problems for decision making that may not be encountered in less complex systems of governing.

Finally, discursive models of institutions are founded primarily on the ideas and discourses that guide the institution.[16] In this perspective, similar to the normative institutionalism, the institution is shaped by the discussions that members use to persuade one another and to persuade the outside world about the actions undertaken by the institution. The discursive model, however, is not as stable as the normative approach, and the present configuration within the institution reflects a short-term equilibrium that will be altered through continuing debate and discussion.

## Advocacy-Coalition Framework

One important addition to process models of policy that contains the conflict missing in the stages model is Sabatier and Jenkins-Smith's advocacy-coalition framework (ACF).[17] This model is concerned explicitly with policy change and argues that policy change comes about through the clash of ideas, as manifested in an existing policy coalition and a potential replacement. In any policy subsystem, there are core beliefs, and those beliefs are supported by coalitions of actors—experts, interest groups, political parties. When these core beliefs are challenged, the conflicts can be worked out through bargaining, often generating a new synthesis about policy that will in turn be institutionalized and set the stage for the next round of policy change.

The advocacy-coalition framework was developed specifically to deal with issues in which there is substantial disagreement about values or feasibility—for example, the clash between environmentalists and industry. This disagreement is taking place in a policy subsystem that is at least partially insulated from the remainder of the political system. If a policy does not have those "wicked" characteristics, then perhaps it can proceed nicely through the path described by the stages model. Many policy proposals, however, involve major disagreements about both ends and means and therefore require some means of resolving the conflict.[18] The ACF is primarily about change and the need to move from one policy equilibrium to another, and to do so when there are some basic disagreements about the best policy.

Most policy subsystems, such as those described in the ACF, tend to be rather stable until they are confronted by some external shock or by an opportunity for learning from other successful cases. When such a disturbance occurs, different sets of perceptions and ideas are activated, and conflicts emerge over the reactions to the shocks and the need to create some new equilibrium. In the development of the new equilibrium, the contending parties are assumed to maintain their core beliefs, but at the same time, they can bargain over issues and options that do not directly threaten those core beliefs. So, for example, an environmentalist would not be expected to yield on his or her commitment to ecological values but might negotiate over acceptable levels of pollution or over the use of particular pieces of land, possibly achieving operational coalitions with industry representatives.

The advocacy-coalition framework model also provides a means of understanding how change may occur within the seemingly stable, path-dependent models of historical institutionalism. The ACF is a means of introducing conflict into those models and understanding the dynamics of policy change in the context of apparent stability.[19] This model emphasizes that a great deal of the change that occurs in policy is a function of clashes of ideas, as well as clashes of economic interests, as would be at the center of rational choice theories. In this perspective, sometimes the best ideas win, rather than the most powerful.

## Policy Causes Politics

Another strand of theorizing about policy in political science has to some extent reversed the logic of the stages model and argues that policy produces politics.[20] This model involves the assumption that four fundamental types of policy—distributive, regulatory, redistributive, and constituent—tend to be associated with certain types of political action. For example, redistributive policies such as Social Security are assumed to be associated with a type of politics in which political elites (often the president and his advisers in the private sector) create a policy and appeal to class divisions to build support for it. Salisbury and Heinz used a similar set of policy variables but related them more to the types of demands being placed on the policymaking system and the degree of the system's fragmentation.[21]

The model developed by Theodore Lowi has motivated a great deal of empirical research as well as a number of theoretical critiques.[22] Perhaps its most fundamental contribution, however, has been to make political scientists think about policies in more analytic categories. There is always the tendency to think about policies in terms of the names one finds on government buildings—agriculture, defense, and housing, for example. That manner of thinking is useful, but only up to a point, and it may mask some of the internal variations in individual policy areas.

A slightly different version of the "policy causes politics" approach is the argument made by Gary Freeman and others that differences across political systems are not as great as differences across policy areas. That is, the technical and political foundations of a policy area such as health may be more similar across countries than are those foundations for disparate policy areas within a single system. As policy ideas spread across national boundaries, the common aspects of policy may become more similar. Pressures from globalization and from Europeanization have tended to homogenize policy across national boundaries, further reinforcing Freeman's argument.[23]

## Policy Styles

To be able to understand public policy, it is important to consider the policy choices made by any one country (or subnational unit) and compare them with the choices made by other countries. That comparison could be done on a policy-by-policy basis, as described for the welfare state below, or we could typify a policymaking style for the political system in question. In this case, rather than politics being assumed to cause policy, policy is being used to characterize the political systems and as the lens through which to compare them.

Jeremy Richardson did the first major analysis of policy styles in western Europe, arguing that the policy styles in those countries could be characterized by two variables:[24] One was an active-reactive dimension, assessing the extent to which a country attempted to anticipate policy problems. The other dimension was the extent to which the political system operated by reaching consensus decisions versus the dominant political group—generally a party in control of government—being able to impose its view. So, for example, the need of the United States to create a consensus among multiple institutions and its general aversion to government planning would place it in one cell, while the United Kingdom might share the tendency to reactive solutions to problems but would have a stronger government, able to impose decisions.

Richardson's model is not the only approach to understanding policy styles. Frans van Waarden, for example, has been concerned with identifying the dimensions of policy styles that can be used to assess the capacity of political systems to make and implement policies effectively. His dimensions include such factors as links with society and legalism, which shape the politics of public policy. Interestingly, in this analysis, the presumably weak government of the United States appears to have the capacity to be much stronger than it is usually thought to be. The reactive policy style of the United States, therefore, may be a function more of its political culture and the long-standing laissez-faire tradition than of institutional factors within government itself.

For policymaking in a single country, such as the United States, the utility of the policy styles approach is to understand some of the implications of the manner in which policies are made and implemented in that country and what the options might be. For example, the reactive policymaking style of the United States has meant that the country does not anticipate major problems and therefore may have difficulty responding to problems such as floods, hurricanes, and declining infrastructure, as evidenced by Hurricane Katrina in New Orleans in 2005 and the collapse of Minneapolis's I-35W bridge in 2007. On the other hand,

© Joe Raedle/Pool/Corbis

*President Barack Obama visits the tornado-ravaged community of Joplin, Missouri, on May 29, 2011. A natural disaster such as a tornado always provokes some sort of policy response. The severity and immediacy of a crisis will cause governments to act quickly and decisively.*

as Frans van Waarden points out, the capacity to mobilize after recognizing problems helps to ameliorate conditions once the disasters occur.[25] The major question, then, is the extent to which citizens are willing to bear the costs and dangers of the reactive style.

Furthermore, there may be greater differences across policy areas in a single country than there are across countries.[26] For example, the United States may be very reactive in a policy area such as health care, except when policy windows open as one did for Medicare and Medicaid in the 1960s (see chapter 11), and as another did after the election of Barack Obama in 2008. But American government may be very active in foreign policy and some areas of education. The internal dynamics of these policy areas may be very different, with government having greater latitude for action without influence from interest groups in foreign policy than in most areas of domestic policy.[27]

### Policy Instruments

Implementation studies have been concerned with the ability to transform stated policies into effective action. The ability to make that difficult translation from law to action involves a number of components; an important one is the choice of one or more policy instruments.[28] The basic idea of policy instruments is that the public sector can achieve its goals using a variety of different types of programs—subsidies, regulation, vouchers, and so forth—and each of these will have different substantive and political characteristics that will influence the likelihood of success.

While it is common to think of these instruments in more or less technical terms, it is crucial to remember that they do have a strong political dimension. For example, as the politics of governing has changed to cast suspicion on direct public sector interventions, many of the conventional "command and control" instruments of the public sector, such as regulation, have been exchanged for softer instruments, such as recommendations and nonbinding agreements.[29] The choice of policy instruments may also reflect the need to build coalitions to have legislation adopted. For example, much of the federal support for university students in the United States has been provided through private bank loans guaranteed by government. Although it might be more efficient to have the loans managed through the universities, it was important to create a political ally in the banking industry.

The study of policy instruments leads to a number of other, even more difficult issues about public policy and the possibilities of effective public sector intervention. The most fundamental of these is that the choice of instruments raises the possibilities of policy design. Do policy analysts, whether in political science or not, have the ability to design better policies than those designed through political mechanisms? To do so requires some understanding of the causes of policy problems and the relationship of those problems to the instruments available to address them, and some normative basis to evaluate the outcomes of the policy intervention.[30] The design issue also raises the question of whether the simple functional categories we generally use for policy are sufficient to capture the complexity of the challenges of attempting to match instruments to policy problems.[31]

## Bounded Rationality, Multiple Streams, and Incrementalism

Economic models of policymaking stress the rationality of human action when humans act politically or use rational, economic criteria to assess the quality of decisions (see below). In the former case, rational choice models of politics argue that the best way to understand how politicians,[32] bureaucrats,[33] and interest groups,[34] among others, act when making policy is to consider those individuals as rational utility maximizers. People operate within the context of formal, legal institutions, but advocates of rational choice argue that we can best understand their behavior by beginning with those basic motivations.

Scholars have advanced any number of critiques of the rationalist model of policymaking. While still adopting some of the basic orientation toward rationality, scholars using the bounded rationality approach point to the extreme difficulty of making fully rational decisions and argue that rationality can best be seen as bounded by organizational, political, and cultural parameters that constrain the choices that an individual will have to make. This school of policy-making is based on the work of Herbert Simon and has continued through other literature that has emphasized the difficulties in depending on models that assume entirely rational decision making.

The garbage can model of organizational decision making is one of the important contributions of the bounded rationality approach.[35] The basic idea of the garbage can is that the multiple constraints on policy prevent real-world implementation of the rational model of policies to pursue goals. Rather, in the garbage can, streams of opportunities converge almost at random, so it is difficult to predict what policies will be adopted. For example, John Kingdon has discussed agenda setting in policy as the opening of windows of opportunity that present the opportunities to use solutions.[36] The confluence of those streams may mean that solutions pursue goals, rather than the usual assumption that programs are formulated to solve problems. This is often a function of the organizational nature of politics. Bureaucratic organizations have commitments to instruments and other "solutions" and hence may want to find ways of using their instruments. This behavior may be especially evident when the organization is threatened by termination or by other organizations competing for their turf.

The garbage can model has been generalized to the multiple streams approach to policymaking.[37] The logic of this approach is that three streams of factors—problems, politics, and policy characteristics—converge in more or less accidental manners. The substantive discussions of policy in chapters 9–16 point to a number of instances in which policy choices have been made through such a convergence. For example, the crumbling infrastructure in the United States might have continued to crumble if the economic crisis of 2009 had not provided an opportunity for funding public works to get people back to work.[38] This process is not entirely accidental, however; policy entrepreneurs play a crucial role in bringing together the various streams and in using, if not creating, windows of opportunity. Thus, although elements in the streams may emerge somewhat randomly, there is a need for some political or administrative actor to bring the streams together and produce effective action.

The logic of bounded rationality that rejects comprehensive rationality when considering policymaking appears also in the incrementalist approach to policy. *Incrementalism* has two distinct elements, but both support the basic logic that making comprehensively rational policy decisions is impossible and perhaps even unwise.[39] The empirical approach to incrementalism has examined repetitive policymaking—especially on the budget. Those studies have found that the volume and complexity of decisions lead decision makers to fall back on simple incremental rules of thumb rather than attempt to make perfect allocations of funds. The assumption is that by making a series of small adjustments over time, appropriate allocation of funds will be achieved.

The normative argument for incrementalism is that in the long run better decisions are made by "successive limited comparisons" of a policy choice to the status quo and by gradually adapting policies through trial and error and learning.[40] The argument is that this allows retreats if poor initial choices are made and prevents costly investments in poorly designed programs. On the other hand, incrementalism can be seen as excessively conservative, retaining existing policies for longer than might be justified and preventing significant reforms.

## The Private Sector, Iron Triangles, and Networks

The liberal, pluralist tradition of politics in the United States has provided the private sector a rather ambiguous position in policymaking. To some extent, the involvement of interest groups and other private actors in policy is illegitimate. The groups that gain access to policy often have a great deal of influence, and their actions are often hidden from public view. The increasing openness of the private sector to the media and other forms of scrutiny has made the involvement of those groups more obvious to the public and has often made policymaking appear even less "in the public interest" than it is meant to be.

Even in the absence of apparent corrupt practices, the interaction of the public and private sectors in the United States has been described as "iron triangles," in which there is a symbiotic relationship among interest groups, congressional committees and subcommittees, and administrative agencies.[41] The interest groups need access to Congress and to the administrative agencies who serve their members. The agencies need support (on their budgets and other legislation) from Congress, and they use interest group support to obtain it. Congress members want to be reelected and need effective programs that serve their constituencies, as well as support (including financial support) from interest groups. These three sets of actors have worked together effectively and are able to prevent interference in their cozy relationships.

The continuous expansion of interactions between citizens and government has to some extent eroded the exclusivity of the iron triangles and has produced important changes in the ways that private sector actors become involved in the public sector. In particular, networks of public actors have been formed around numerous policy areas that include a range of private sector actors who have some involvement with the policy. For example, the health summit that President Obama called early in his term involved a number of federal and state officials but was mostly populated by a range of medical professionals and insurance and other corporate executives. The conventional iron triangle description of American politics has been supplanted by an understanding of the complex networks that now surround many policy areas.[42] A growing body of literature on network theory points to the role of social actors in governing.[43]

## Optimal Decision Making

The models of policymaking presented thus far are politically driven, their motivations coming from the need to reconcile competing interests and political pressures. The outcomes of those processes are often very disappointing to the participants, but they do reflect the manner in which institutions function and their ability to begin with a contradictory set of values and interests and produce an outcome. Furthermore, these political models often can be illuminated by comparative analysis, using other cases to understand better how policies are made and how they may be improved.

Another approach to policy is to attempt to develop more abstract models of optimal policy processes and optimal policies. Whereas political models are driven by process, most economic models are driven by attempts to define optimal policy outcomes and to design institutional arrangements that may be capable of producing those desirable outcomes. While these optimal models may not be achievable in the real world of politics, they can function as a useful standard against which to compare "real" policy processes and policy outcomes. In addition, if the utilitarian assumptions are converted into measurements, the models can be used to advise policymakers about the best choices.

The starting point for economic analysis of policy is the justification for public sector intervention into the economy and society. If one believes that the market can produce optimal economic outcomes, then any interventions into that market must be justified by some form of market failure.[44] Public goods are one of the classic cases in which markets do not work effectively. Markets cannot efficiently produce goods such as national defense or public parks that, once created, are difficult to prevent all citizens' enjoying.[45] Therefore, these goods (and services) may have to be delivered through the public sector and financed through taxation. Markets may also fail because of externalities, meaning that the total social costs—for example, pollution—of some activities are not included in the market price of a product. And markets may also fail because the participants do not have adequate information and therefore cannot make optimal decisions. This is the (economist) justification for regulations that force producers to provide consumers information about risks of the products.

Economic models of policy also look at the capacity to change from one policy position to another, especially to find so-called Pareto optimal moves that make at least one person better off without harming anyone else. The problem is that few such opportunities present themselves in the real world of public policy, and most policy choices involve making choices that may benefit some people but at the same time make others worse off.[46] Similarly, optimal budget making in the public sector is supposed to be an allocation in which the marginal utility of a dollar spent for each and every activity covered by the budget is equal.

In addition to these more abstract economic models of policy, more applied approaches such as cost-benefit analysis (see chapter 17) apply the same utilitarian logic for thinking about public policy. In other words, the best policy is one that maximizes total utility, with that utility being considered in economic terms. Even attributes such as environmental quality are reduced to monetary values, so that the costs and benefits can be compared easily. Unlike Pareto optimal moves, however, this version of welfare economics accepts that decisions will have negative consequences for some people and assesses the balance between the positive and negative contributions to total social utility.

## Constructivist Models

I have argued above that one of the problems with the normative economic models of policymaking is that they do not have as close a connection with the complexities of reality as do the political science models. Constructivist, or argumentative, models of policy, on the other hand, argue that the reality of policymaking must be constructed through social and political processes. The existence and nature of some policy problems may be obvious—public pensions, perhaps—but most must be created and defined. Some policy problems—the environment or spousal abuse—may be excluded from the agenda of government until a policy entrepreneur or a confluence of events brings attention to them.

The logic of constructivism has been linked to the general problem of policy design.[47] That is, not only are policy problems constructed politically but so too are the overall patterns of the public sector's response to a problem once constructed. Just as ideas can be used to understand policy problems, they can also be linked to the solution of those problems, and solutions must also be constructed. The ideas used may be general orientations toward politics and governing—for example, limited government—or they may be more specific ideas about particular policies, such as Keynesian approaches to economics.

Drug policy has been one of the best examples of the constructivist logic in policy in the United States. Although few people would disagree that there is a real policy problem there, the question is what type of problem it is. The definition of the problem will influence the political forces that are brought to bear on it.[48] In the case of drugs, the policy has been constructed primarily as an issue of criminal justice, and therefore, law enforcement organizations have become central in implementation.[49] If, however, drugs had been considered more of a health issue or a social issue, then a very different set of organizations and different policy instruments would have been central to the solutions that government would have pursued.

The constructivist position in policy analysis has a close relationship to the agenda setting literature. If issues are to be placed on the agenda of the public sector, then they must be defined in a way that makes them acceptable to important political forces and that can be used to mobilize support. The constructivist position, therefore, is not a passive one but often depends upon active political intervention by entrepreneurs—organizations as well as individuals—to define the policy and make it function as intended. The constructivist position is also closely connected to the advocacy-coalition framework model, given that there may be several alternative conceptions of a policy and that different entrepreneurs will contend to have their own views dominate.

Deliberative policy analysis represents one variant of the general constructivist approach to policy. The logic of deliberative analysis is that better policies can be chosen through interactions of the affected actors, and even the interactions of ordinary concerned citizens, than through the imposition of more technocratic solutions by experts.[50] The logic is that there are a number of interests and points of view in society, and the policy process should not privilege one view or one set of actors. In the American context, the New England town meeting, with open discussions of policy, is used as a model of such deliberations, although organizing such discussions for larger political units and more complex issues is at best problematic.

The majority of thinking about public policy has been in a strongly objective model, attempting to measure policies as dependent variables and then finding the factors that explain those policy choices. Likewise, economic and utilitarian values tend to undergird much of this analysis, assuming that policies are best understood in terms of improving the economic well-being of those affected by them. One strand of reasoning in political science, however, argues that policy is best understood in more linguistic terms. The assumption of deliberative models is that the discourse surrounding a policy and conflicts among alternative discourses defines the ways in which policy choices are made.[51] Of course, utilitarian values is one discourse, but only one among many possible sets of values that can guide policy choices.

Discourse and deliberative models are often best applied in areas such as science policy and some aspects of environmental policy, where there are often widely diverging understandings of the nature of the policy. Herbert Gottweiss, for example, has examined the deliberative aspects of research on human biology, and there have been a number of analyses of environmental policy that apply the deliberative approach.[52] These studies have demonstrated the range of values that may be involved in complex policy issues, as well as something of the ways in which those almost inherent conflicts may be resolved.

## Summary

Policymaking is an extremely complex process, involving a wide range of actors and ideas. This chapter has been my attempt to provide some alternative approaches for understanding that process and evaluating the outcomes. Many of these themes are echoed in other parts of this book. For example, when discussing the agenda-setting process (see chapter 4), we can see the importance of framing issues and hence can see how constructivist approaches to policy can be used. Likewise, the discussion of the evaluation of policy (see chapter 8) is closely related to the normative economic models discussed in this chapter. It is important, therefore, not to separate policy analysis from the understanding of substantive policy dynamics.

It is also important not to separate conflict and political action from thinking about policy. Too often the search for optimal outcomes by policy analysts ignores the political debates and the deeply entrenched conflicts that define policymaking. Ultimately public policy is, as Harold Lasswell argued, concerned with "who gets what," and making those choices will provoke intense political activity.[53] The institutions and processes of policymaking help to channel the demands of groups into effective action and enable government to make decisions in the face of those competing demands.

Finally, these alternative conceptions of the policy process represent some of the richness of the discipline of political science, but they also represent some of the possible confusion. This is especially a problem if a student is seeking a single "right answer" and finds it frustrating that there may not be one. The availability of these multiple approaches does allow the student, or the policy analyst, to triangulate and to see what light each of several different approaches may shed on the policy process being researched. For example, institutions may matter, but the exercise of overt political power may matter as well. The use of these multiple lenses[54] provides a richer view of the reality and, while providing no simple answer, helps us to understand how policy is made and what its effects may be.

PART TWO
# The Making of Public Policy

CHAPTER 4

# Agenda Setting and Public Policy

TWO PARTS OF THE POLICYMAKING process that occur rather early in the sequence of decisions leading to the actual delivery of services to citizens are crucial to the success of the entire process—*agenda setting* and *policy formulation*. They are important because they establish the parameters within which any additional consideration of policies will occur. Agenda setting is crucial because if an issue cannot be placed on the agenda, it cannot be considered, and nothing can possibly happen in government. Policy formulation then begins to narrow and structure consideration of the problems on the agenda and to prepare a plan of action to rectify them. These two stages are also linked because it is often necessary to have a solution before an issue can be accepted on the agenda. Moreover, how a problem is defined as it is brought to the agenda determines the kinds of solutions that will be developed to solve it.

## Agenda Setting

Before government can make a policy choice, a particular problem in the society must have been deemed amenable to public action and worthy of the attention of policymakers. Government gives no consideration at all to many real problems, largely because the relevant political actors are not convinced that government has any role in attempting to solve them. On the other hand, once accepted as a part of the general, systemic agenda, problems tend to remain for long periods, although some of them do come on and off the active policy agenda.

One of the best examples of a problem being accepted as part of the agenda after a long period of exclusion is the problem of poverty in the United States. Throughout most of the nation's history, poverty was perceived not as a public problem but as merely the result of the (proper) operation of the free market. The publication in 1963 of Michael Harrington's *The Other America* and the growing mobilization of poor people brought the problem of poverty to the agenda and indirectly resulted in the launching of a wide-ranging effort to eradicate it.[1] Once placed on the agenda, poverty has remained an important public issue, although different administrations have given different amounts of attention to it. For example, the effects of the economic crisis since 2008 highlighted growing inequality in the United States and the return to higher levels of poverty (see chapter 9).

Another obvious case of external events contributing to setting the policy agenda is that the perceived poor quality of American elementary and secondary education, especially in science and technology, did not become an issue at the federal level until the Soviet Union launched *Sputnik I.* It has again become an issue as American children's test scores continue to be poor compared with those of children in many other countries in the world, especially those in Asia. Once cast as a national defense issue, education is now debated more in terms of economic competitiveness (see chapter 13). The attacks of September 11, 2001, and the Hurricane Katrina disaster in 2005 brought into focus the question of America's preparedness for disasters, as well as the general capacity of government at all levels to work effectively. In these cases, a dramatic public event awakened the populace to an existing social problem that needed to be addressed.[2]

The best example of an issue being removed from the policy agenda remains the repeal of Prohibition, by which the federal government said that preventing the production and distribution of alcoholic beverages was no longer its concern. Despite the end of Prohibition, all levels of government have nonetheless retained some regulatory and taxing authority over the production and consumption of alcohol, and of course governments have prohibition programs for a number of other drugs as well. The movement to privatize some public services (usually at the local level) also has removed some issues from direct concern in the public sector, although again a regulatory role usually continues.

What can cause an issue to be placed on the policy agenda? The most basic cause is a perception that something is wrong and that the problem can be ameliorated through public action. This answer in turn produces another question: What causes the change in perceptions of problems and issues? Why, for example, did Harrington's book have such far-reaching influence on the public, when earlier books about social deprivation, such as James Agee's *Let Us Now Praise Famous Men,* had relatively little impact?[3] Did the timing of the "discovery" of poverty in the United States result from the election of a young, seemingly liberal president (John Kennedy), who was succeeded by an activist president (Lyndon Johnson) with considerable sway over Congress? When do problems cease to be invisible and become perceived as real problems for public consideration?

Issues also appear to pass through an "issue attention cycle," in which they are the objects of great public concern for a short period and generate some

© Brooks Kraft/Corbis

*Although high gasoline prices depend upon many factors beyond the control of government, they do irritate citizens. That irritation, in turn, will produce government actions. The president and Congress cannot afford to ignore issues that affect so many people.*

response from government.[4] The initial enthusiasm for the issue is generally followed by more sober realism about the costs of policy options available and the difficulties of making effective policy. This realism is followed in turn by a period of declining interest, as the public seizes on a new issue. The histories of environmental policy, drug enforcement, and, to some degree, the women's movement illustrate this cycle very well. Also, after some honeymoon period, the political forces opposed to involvement in these policy areas have the opportunity to mobilize and to slow further initiatives.

Just as individual issues go through an issue attention cycle, the entire political system may also experience cycles of differential activity. One set of scholars has described this pattern as "routine punctuated by orgies."[5] A less colorful description, developed by Frank Baumgartner and Bryan D. Jones, is "punctuated equilibria."[6] Some time periods—because of energetic political leaders or large-scale mobilization of the public, or for a host of other possible reasons—are characterized by greater policy activism than others. Those periods of activism are followed by periods in which the programs adopted during the activist period are rationalized, consolidated, or perhaps terminated.[7]

In this chapter, I discuss how to understand, and how to manipulate, the public agenda. How can a social problem be converted into an issue and brought into a public institution for formal consideration? In the role of policy analyst, one must understand not only the theoretical issues concerning agenda setting but also the points of leverage within the political system. Much of what happens in the policymaking system is difficult or impossible to control: the ages and health of the participants, their friendships, constitutional structures of institutions and their interactions, and external events, to name but a few of the relevant variables. Some scholars have argued that agendas do not change unless there is an almost random confluence of events favoring the new policy initiative.[8] Such random factors may be important in explaining overall policy outcomes, but they are not the only pertinent factors to consider when one confronts the task of bringing about desired policy changes. Despite all the imponderables in a policymaking system, there is still room for initiative and for altering the political behavior of important actors.

It is also important to remember that social problems do not come to government fully conceptualized, with labels already attached. Policy problems need to have names if government is to deal with them, and labeling or framing is itself a political process.[9] For example, how do we conceptualize the problem of illegal drugs in the United States? Is it a problem of law enforcement, as it is commonly treated, or is it a public health problem, or a problem of education, or a reflection of poverty, despair, and social disorder?[10] Perhaps drug use indicates something more about the society in which it occurs than it does about the individual consumers usually branded as criminals. There are a number of possible answers to such definitional questions, but the fundamental point is that the manner in which the problem is conceptualized and defined determines the remedies likely to be proposed, the organizations that will be given responsibility for the problem, and the final outcomes of the public intervention into it.

## Kinds of Agendas

Until now, we have been discussing "the agenda" in the singular and with the definite article. There are, however, different agendas for the various institutions of government, as well as a more general agenda for the political system as a whole. The existence of these agendas also is to some degree an abstraction. Most agendas do not exist in any concrete form; they exist only in a collective judgment about the nature of public problems or as fragments of written evidence, such as legislation introduced, the State of the Union message of the president, or a notice of intent to issue regulations appearing in the *Federal Register*. On the other hand, cases appealed—and especially cases accepted for appeal—do constitute a clear agenda for the Supreme Court.

Roger Cobb and Charles Elder, who produced some of the principal writing on agendas in American government, distinguished between the systemic and institutional agendas. The systemic agenda consists of "all issues that are commonly perceived by members of the political community as meriting public attention and as involving matters within the legitimate jurisdiction of existing governmental authority."[11] This is the broadest agenda of government and includes all issues that might be subject to action or that are already being acted on by government. It is a definition, however, that implies a consensus on the systemic agenda that may not exist. Some individuals may consider a problem—abortion, for example—as part of the agenda of the political system (whether to outlaw abortion or to provide public funding for it), while others regard the issue as entirely one of personal choice. The southern states' reluctance for years to include civil rights as part of their agendas indicated a disagreement over what fell within the "jurisdiction of existing governmental authority." Setting the systemic agenda is usually not consensual, as it is a crucial political and policy decision. If a problem can be excluded from consideration, then those individuals and organizations that benefit from the status quo are assured of victory.[12] It is only when a problem is placed on the agenda and made available for active discussion that the forces of change have some opportunity for success.

The second type of agenda that Cobb and Elder discuss is the institutional agenda: "that set of items explicitly up for active and serious consideration of authoritative decision-makers."[13] An institutional agenda is composed of the issues on which the individuals in power within a particular institution actually are considering taking action. These issues may constitute a subset of all the problems they will discuss, as the complete set will include "pseudoissues" discussed to placate clientele groups but without any serious intention to make policy.[14] Actors within institutions run a risk, however, when they permit discussion of pseudoissues: Once they appear on the docket, something may actually be done about them.

A number of institutional agendas exist—as many as there are institutions—and there is little reason to assume any agreement among institutions as to which problems are the most appropriate for consideration. As with conflicts over placing issues on the systemic agenda, interinstitutional conflicts will arise in moving problems from one institutional agenda to another. The agendas of bureaucratic agencies are the narrowest, and a great deal of the political activity of those agencies is directed at placing their issues onto the agendas of other institutions. As an institution broadens in scope, the range of its agenda concerns also broadens, and those interested in any particular issue will have to fight to have it placed on a legislative or executive agenda. This is especially true of the conversion of *new problems* into active issues. Some older and more familiar issues will generally find a ready place on institutional agendas. Some older issues are *cyclical issues*: A new budget must be adopted each year, for example, and many other public programs are designed to include periodic reviews. There is a quadrennial defense review for national security policy.[15] Other, older agenda items may be *recurrent issues,* indicating primarily the failure of previous policy choices to produce the intended or desired impact on society. Even recurrent issues may not be returned easily to institutional agendas when existing programs are perceived to be "good enough," or when no new solutions are readily available. Indeed, the beneficiaries of a program may work hard to keep it off an active agenda, lest new legislation upset the existing policy.[16]

Jack Walker classes problems coming on the agenda in four groups.[17] Walker defines issues that are dealt with time and time again as either "periodically recurring" or "sporadically recurring" issues (similar to our cyclical and recurrent issues). He also examines the role of crises in placing issues on the agenda, as well as the difficulties of having new or "chosen" problems selected for inclusion on agendas. Within each institution, those interested in an issue must use their political power and skills to gain access to the agenda. The failure to be included on any one institutional agenda may be the end of an issue, at least for the time being.

Finally, we should note that these recurring issues also constitute an opportunity to open other issues that might otherwise not be so easy to address. For example, the return of the need to authorize increases in the public debt in 2011 gave conservatives in Congress an opportunity to force reductions in spending on social policy and domestic discretionary spending.[18]

## Who Sets Agendas?

Establishing an agenda for society, or even for one institution, is a manifestly political activity, and control of the agenda gives substantial control over the ultimate policy choices. Therefore, to understand how agendas are determined requires some understanding of the manner in which political power is exercised in the United States. The idea of a punctuated equilibrium may be a good description of the process of change, but it does not explain how the punctuations come about. The most important answer to that question is that political power is used to alter the agenda.[19] As might be imagined, there are a number of different conceptualizations of just how power is exercised. To enable us to understand the dynamics of agenda setting better, I will discuss three important theoretical approaches to the exercise of political power and the formation of policy agendas: *pluralist, elitist,* and *state-centric.*

### Pluralist Approaches

The dominant, though far from undisputed, approach to policymaking in the United States is pluralism.[20] Stated briefly, the pluralist approach assumes that policymaking in government is divided into a number of separate arenas and that the interests and individuals who have power in one arena do not necessarily have power in others. The American Medical Association, for example, may have a great deal of influence over health care legislation but little influence over education or defense policy. Furthermore, interests that are victorious at one time or in one arena will not necessarily win at another time or place. The pluralist approach to policymaking assumes that there is something of a marketplace in policies, with a number of interests competing for power and influence, even within a single arena. The competitors are conceived as interest groups competing for access to institutions for decision making and for the attention of central actors in the hope of producing their desired outcomes. The groups are assumed, much as in the market model of the economy, to be relatively equal in power, so that on any one issue any interest might be victorious. Finally, the actors involved in the political process generally agree on the rules of the game, especially the rule that elections are the principal means of determining policy. The principal function of government is to serve as an umpire in this struggle among competing group interests and to enforce the victories through public law.

The pluralist approach to agenda setting would lead the observer to expect a relatively open marketplace of ideas for new policies. Any or all interested groups, as a whole or within a particular public institution, should have the opportunity to influence the agenda. These interest groups may not win every time, but neither will they systematically be excluded from decisions, and the agendas will be amenable to adding new items as sufficient political mobilization occurs. This style of agenda setting may be particularly appropriate for the United States, given the multiple institutions and multiple points of access in the structure of the system.[21] Even if an issue is blocked politically, the courts can enable otherwise-disadvantaged groups to bring it into the policy process, as happened with civil rights and with some aspects of sexual harassment.

## Elitist Approaches

The elitist approach to American policymaking seeks to contradict the dominant pluralist approach. It assumes the existence of a power elite that dominates public decision making and whose interests are served in the policymaking process. In the elitist analysis, the same interests in society consistently win, and they are primarily those of business, the upper and middle classes, and whites.[22] Analysts from an elitist perspective have pointed out that to produce the kind of equality assumed in the pluralist model would require relatively equal levels of organization by all interests in society. They then point out that relatively few interests of working- and lower-class individuals are effectively organized; compared to many of its European counterparts, American labor is not particularly well organized or powerful. Although all individuals in a democracy certainly have the right to organize, elitist theorists point to the relative lack of resources (e.g., time, money, organizational ability, and communication skills) among members of the lower economic classes.[23] Thus, political organization for many poorer people, if it exists at all, may imply only token participation, and their voices will be drowned in the sea of middle-class voices described by E. E. Schattschneider.[24] The claims of elitism have been reinforced in 2011 and 2012 by increasing aware-ness of the economic and political power of the richest 1 percent of the Ameri-can population.[25]

The implications of the elitist approach are rather obvious. If agenda formu-lation is crucial to the process of policymaking, then the ability of elites to keep certain issues off the agenda is crucial to their power. Adherents of this approach believe that the agenda in most democratic countries represents not the competi-tive struggle of relatively equal groups, as argued by the pluralist model, but the systematic use of elite power to decide which issues the political system will or will not consider. Jürgen Habermas, for example, argues that the elite uses its power systematically to exclude issues that would threaten its interests and that those "suppressed issues" represent a major threat to democracy.[26] If too many significant issues are kept off the agenda, the legitimacy of the political system can be threatened, along with its survival in the most extreme cases.

Peter Bachrach and Morton Baratz's concept of "nondecisions" is important here. Bachrach and Baratz define a *nondecision* as a decision that results in the suppression or thwarting of a latent or manifest challenge to the values or inter-ests of the decision maker. More explicitly, nondecision making is a means by which demands for change in the existing allocation of benefits and privileges in the community can be suffocated before they are even voiced, or kept covert, or killed off before they gain access to the relevant decision-making arena—or fail-ing all else, maimed or destroyed in the decision-implementing stage of the policy process.[27] A decision not to alter the status quo is a decision, whether it is made overtly through the policymaking process or is the result of the application of power to prevent the issue from ever being discussed.

These issues may not remain suppressed forever, even in the face of powerful economic and political elites. For example, large-scale discontent with the bank-ing industry and business in general has placed on the agenda a number of issues that might have been unthinkable previously. These responses to economic crises have included placing caps on the salaries and bonuses of individuals in the private sector.

## State-Centric Approaches

Both the pluralist and elitist approaches to policymaking and agenda setting assume that the major source of policy ideas is in the environment of the policymakers—primarily interest groups or other powerful interests in the society. It is, however, quite possible that the political system itself is responsible for its own agenda.[28] In a state-centric analysis, the environment is not filled with pressure groups but with "pressured groups" activated by government. As governments become more interested in managing the media and in influencing public opinion, the state-centric view may be more viable.[29]

The state-centered concept of agenda setting conforms quite well to the "iron triangle" conception of American government but would place the bureaucratic agency or the congressional committee, not the pressure group, in the center of the policy process.[30] This approach does emphasize the role of specialized elites within government but, unlike elitist theory, does not assume that the elites are pursuing policies for their own personal gain. Certainly, their organizations may obtain larger budgets and greater prestige from the addition of new programs, but the individual administrators have little or no opportunity to appropriate any of that budgetary increase.

In addition, the state-centric approach places the major locus of competition over agenda setting within government itself, rather than in the constellation of interests in society. Agencies must compete for legislative time and for budgets; committees must compete for attention for their particular legislative concerns; and individual Congress members must compete for consideration of their own bills and their own constituency concerns. These actors within government are more relevant in pushing agenda items than are interests in the society. This competition may be not only about getting an issue on the agenda but also about framing it in a particular manner that will advantage one agency or another.

One interesting question arises about agenda setting in the state-centric approach: What are the relative powers of bureaucratic and legislative actors in setting the agenda? An early study by the Advisory Commission on Intergovernmental Relations argued that the source of the continued expansion of the federal government was within Congress.[31] The authors of that study argued that Congress members, acting out of a desire to be reelected or from a sincere interest in solving certain policy problems, have been the major source of new items on the federal agenda. The behavior of Congress in the early twenty-first century would seem to support that contention, given the number of programs initiated by Congress, even when the legislative branch presumably was dominated by conservatives from 2000 to 2006.[32] Other analyses have placed the source of most new policy ideas in the bureaucracy as much as, or more than, in Congress.[33] Also, the nature of American government requires that the president and Congress work together to set agendas and make policy, and presidents may have as much to do with the expansion of the public sector as does Congress.[34] Because the chain of events leading to new policies is complex, it may be difficult to determine exactly where ideas originated, but there is (at least in this model) no shortage of policy advocates.[35]

The agenda resulting from a state-centric process might be more conservative than one resulting from a pluralist process but less conservative than one from the elitist model. Government actors may be constrained in the amount of change they can advocate on their own initiative; they may have to wait for a time when their ideas will be acceptable to the general public. Members of Congress can adopt a crusading stance, but that is a choice usually denied to the typical bureaucratic agency. Except in rare instances—efforts by the surgeon general and the Food and Drug Administration to reduce cigarette smoking, perhaps—a government-sponsored agency may be ahead of public opinion but only slightly so.

When we consider a state-centric approach in the United States, we must also remember that state and local governments are often far ahead of the federal government in addressing issues. Historically, that was the case for issues such as Social Security and environmental regulation, and it is true at present for a number of more inclusive programs of health care. At least a dozen states have investigated implementing broader programs to address the health care needs of their citizens. For example, in 2006, Massachusetts enacted a health care reform law that mandated health insurance for all its residents and provided subsidies for those who could not afford to purchase it. State innovations like this one helped pave the way for the emergence of health care reform as a major point on President Obama's agenda (see chapter 11).[36]

Which approach to policymaking and agenda formation is most descriptive of the process in the United States? The answer is probably all of them, for the proponents of each can muster a great deal of evidence for their position. More important, one approach rather than another might better describe policymaking for particular kinds of problems and issues. For example, we would expect policies that are very much the concern of government itself (e.g., civil service laws or perhaps even foreign affairs) to be more heavily influenced by state-centric policymaking than other kinds of issues. Certain kinds of problems that directly affect powerful economic interests would be best understood through elite analysis. Energy policy and its relationship to the major oil companies might fit into that category. Finally, policy areas with a great deal of interest group activity and relatively high levels of group involvement by both clients and producers—education is a good example—might be best understood through the pluralist approach. Unfortunately, these categorizations are largely speculative, for political scientists have only begun to produce the kind of detailed analysis required to track issues as they move on and off agendas.[37]

## From Problem to Issue: How to Get Problems on the Agenda

Problems do not move themselves on and off agendas. Nevertheless, a number of their characteristics can affect their chances of becoming a part of an active, systemic, or institutional agenda. We should remember, however, that most problems do not come with these characteristics clearly visible to most citizens or even to most political actors. Agendas must be constructed and the issues defined by a social and political process in a manner that will make them most amenable to political action.[38] Furthermore, it usually requires an active policy entrepreneur to do the political packaging that can make an issue appear on an agenda.[39]

### The Effects of the Problem

The first aspect of a problem that can influence its placement on an agenda is whom it affects and to what extent. We can think about the extremity, concentration, range, and visibility of problems as influencing their placement on agendas. The more extreme the effects of a problem, the more likely it is to be placed on an agenda. An outbreak of a disease causing mild discomfort, for example, is unlikely to produce public action, but the possibility of an epidemic, life-threatening disease, such as AIDS, usually provokes some kind of public action. This is especially true for a disease such as avian flu, which unlike AIDS, tends not to have any stigma associated with it and which may be especially deadly for the elderly and the very young.[40] Although less extreme, the rapidly increasing prices for gasoline in 2008 produced a number of reactions from the public sector.

Even if a problem is not life threatening, a concentration of victims in one area may produce public action. The unemployment of an additional 50,000 workers, while certainly deplorable, might not cause major public intervention if the workers were scattered around the country, but it might well do so if the workers were concentrated in one geographical area. Most industries in the United States are concentrated geographically (automobiles in Michigan, aerospace in California and Washington, oil in Texas and Louisiana), and that makes it easier for advocates of assistance to any troubled industry to get the help they want from government. Even conservatives, who tend to oppose government intervention in the economy, usually appear happy to assist failing industries when it is clear that there will be major regional effects.

The range of persons affected by a problem may also influence the placement of an issue on an agenda. In general, the more people affected or potentially affected by a problem, the greater is the probability that it will be placed on the agenda. There are limits, however. A problem may be so general that no single individual believes that he or she has anything to gain by organizing political action to address it. An issue that has broad but only minor effects therefore may have less chance of being placed on the agenda than a problem that affects fewer people but affects them more severely.

The intensity of effects, and therefore of the policy preferences of citizens, is a major problem for those who take the pluralist approach to agenda setting.[41] Many real or potential interests in society are not effectively organized because few individuals believe that they have enough to gain from establishing or joining an organization. For example, although every citizen is a consumer, few effective consumer organizations have been established, whereas producer groups are numerous and are effective politically. The specificity and intensity of producer interests, as contrasted to the diffuseness of consumer interests, creates a serious imbalance in the pattern of interest group organization that favors producers. An analogous situation would be the relative ineffectiveness of taxpayers' organizations compared with organizations of clientele groups, such as defense industries and farmers, that are interested in greater federal spending. The organizational imbalance against consumers and taxpayers has been mitigated somewhat since the 1980s but still exists. The apparent increase in the power of lobbyists over the past decade contributes to the continuing imbalance in favor of producer interests.[42]

Finally, the visibility of a problem may affect its placement on an agenda as an active issue. This might be called "mountain climber syndrome." Society appears willing to spend almost any amount of money to rescue a single stranded mountain climber but will not spend the same amount of money to save many more lives by, for example, controlling automobile accidents or vaccinating children. Statistical lives are not nearly so visible and comprehensible as an identifiable individual stuck on the side of a mountain. Similarly, the risks of nuclear power plants have been highly dramatized in the media, while less visibly an average of 150 men die each year in mining accidents, and many others die from black lung disease contracted in coal mines. The existing environmental effects of burning coal, although certainly recognized and important, appear to pale in the public mind when compared to the possible effects of a nuclear accident. The Fukushima accident in Japan may have only reinforced this calculus of risk in the popular mind.

### Analogous and Spillover Agenda Setting

Another important aspect of a problem that can affect its being placed on an agenda is the presence of an analogy to other public programs. The more a new issue can be made to look like an old issue, the more likely it is to be placed on the agenda. This is especially true in the United States because of the traditional reluctance of American government to expand the public sector, at least by conscious choice. For example, the federal government's intervention into medical care financing for individuals with Medicare and Medicaid was dangerously close to the then-feared "socialized medicine."[43] It was made more palatable, at least in the case of Medicare, by making the program appear similar to Social Security, which was already highly legitimate. The administration of George W. Bush continued this pattern by making a program to support drug costs for the elderly a part of Medicare and using many existing private insurers, such as Blue Cross, to administer the plans.[44] If a new agenda item can be made to appear as only an incremental departure from existing policies, rather than an entirely new venture, its chances of being accepted are much improved.

Also, the existence of one government program may produce the need for additional programs. This spillover effect is important in bringing new programs onto the agenda and in explaining the expansion of the public sector. Even the best policy analysts in the world cannot anticipate the consequences of all the policy choices the government makes. Thus, the adoption of one program may soon lead to the adoption of other programs directed at "solving" the problems created by the first program.[45] For example, the federal government's interstate highway program was designed to improve transportation and to serve domestic defense purposes. One effect of building superhighways, however, has been to make it easier for people to live in the suburbs and work in the city. Consequently, the roads assisted in the flight to the suburbs of those who could afford to move. This, in turn, contributed to the decline of central cities, which created a need for the federal government to pour billions of dollars into urban renewal, Urban Development Action Grants, and a host of other programs for the cities. Although the inner cities would probably have declined somewhat without the federal highway program, the program certainly accelerated the process.

Policies in modern societies are now tightly interconnected, and they may have so many secondary and tertiary effects on other programs that any new policy intervention is likely to have results that spread like ripples in a clear lake. To some degree, the analyst should anticipate those effects and design programs to avoid negative interaction effects, but he or she can never be perfectly successful in doing so. Tax policies in particular tend to spawn unanticipated responses, as individuals and corporations seek creative ways of legally avoiding paying taxes and the Internal Revenue Service tries to close unanticipated loopholes.[46] As a consequence, "policy is its own cause," and one policy choice may beget others.[47]

### Relationship to Symbols

The more closely a problem can be linked to important national symbols, the greater is its probability of being placed on the agenda. Mundane programs may thus be wrapped up in rhetoric about freedom, justice, and traditional American values. Conversely, a problem will not be placed on the agenda if it is associated primarily with negative values. There are, of course, some exceptions: Although the gay community is not a positive symbol for many Americans, the AIDS issue was placed on the agenda with relative alacrity, even before its spread among other sectors of the population.[48]

There are several interesting examples of the use of positive symbols to market programs and issues that might not otherwise have been accepted on the agenda. Although American government has generally been rather slow to adopt social programs, those associated with children and their families have been more favorably regarded. Therefore, if someone wants to initiate a social welfare program, it is well to associate it with children, or, possibly with the elderly. It is perhaps no accident that the basic welfare program in the United States was long known as Aid to Families with Dependent Children. The reforms of the AFDC program used first "families" (Temporary Assistance to Needy Families, or TANF) and then "opportunity" (Personal Responsibility and Work Opportunity Reconciliation Act)—perhaps equally powerful symbols—to justify change. The 1994 crime bill contained a variety of social programs (the famous "midnight basketball" provisions) that might not even have made it to a vote if they were not attached to the symbolic issue of crime control.

Symbol manipulation is an extremely important skill for policy analysts. For example, creation of the label "death tax" for the inheritance tax had no small effect on the attempts at repeal in 2001. The symbolism helped to obscure the extremely regressive nature of the change in tax policy.[49] In addition to being rational calculators of the costs and benefits of programs, analysts must be capable of relating programs and program goals to other programs, of elucidating the importance of the problem, and of justifying the program to actors who may be less committed to it and its goals. Placing a problem on the agenda of government means convincing powerful individuals that they should make the effort necessary to rectify it. The use of symbols may facilitate that process when the problem itself is not likely to gain wide public attention.

### The Absence of Private Means

In general, governments avoid accepting new responsibilities, especially in the United States, with its laissez-faire tradition, and especially in a climate of budgetary scarcity (even when a balanced budget has been attained). The market, rather than collective action, has become the standard against which to compare good policy.[50] There are, however, problems in society that cannot be solved by private market activities alone. Two classic examples are social problems that involve either public goods or externalities.

*Public goods* are goods or services that, once produced, are consumed by a relatively large number of individuals and whose consumption is difficult or impossible to control—they are not "excludable." This means that it is difficult or impossible for any individual or firm to produce public goods, for they cannot be effectively priced and sold.[51] If national defense were produced by paid mercenaries, rather than by government, individual citizens would have little or no incentive to pay the group of fighters because citizens would be protected whether they paid or not. Indeed, citizens would have every incentive to be "free riders"—to enjoy the benefits of the service without paying the cost. Government has a remedy for such a situation: It can force citizens to pay for the service through its power of taxation.

*Externalities* are said to exist when the activities of one economic unit affect the well-being of another and no compensation is paid for benefits or costs created externally.[52] Pollution is a classic case: It is a by-product of the production process, but its social costs are excluded from the selling price of the products the manufacturer makes. Thus, social costs and production costs diverge, and government may have to impose regulations to prevent the private firm from imposing the costs of pollution—such as damage to health, property, and amenities—on the public. Alternatively, government may develop some means of pricing the effects of pollution and imposing those costs on the polluter.[53]

All externalities need not be negative. Some activities create public benefits that are not included in the revenues of those producing them. If a dam is built to generate hydroelectric power, the recreational, flood control, and economic development benefits cannot be included as part of the revenues of a private utility, although government can include those benefits in its calculations when considering undertaking such a project with public money (see chapter 17). Thus, some projects that appear infeasible for the private sector may be feasible for government, even on strict economic criteria.

Public goods and externalities are two useful categories for consideration, but they do not exhaust the kinds of social and economic problems that have a peculiarly public nature.[54] Of course, issues of rights and the application of law are considered peculiarly public. In addition, programs that involve a great deal of risk may require the socialization of that risk through the public sector. For example, lending to college students who have little credit record is backed by government as a means of making banks more willing to take the risk. These loans illustrate the general principle that the inability of other institutions in society to produce effective and equitable solutions may be sufficient to place an issue on the public agenda.

## The Availability of Technology

Finally, a problem generally will not be placed on the public agenda unless there is a technology believed to be able to solve it. For most of the history of the industrialized nations, people assumed that economic fluctuations were, like the weather, acts of God. Then, the Keynesian revolution in economics produced what seemed to be the answer to those fluctuations, and governments soon placed economic management in a central position on their agendas. In the United States, this new technology was reflected in the Employment Act of 1946, pledging the U.S. government to maintain full employment. The promise of fine-tuning the economy through Keynesian means, which appeared possible in the 1960s, has since become increasingly elusive. The issue of economic management, however, remains central to the public agenda, with politicians being evaluated very much on the economy's performance (see chapter 9). Subsequent governments have provided new technologies (e.g., *supply-side economics* during the Reagan years), but they have not been able to evade responsibility for the economy. Much of the debate in the primary campaign in 2012 has assumed, however, that the best technology for government to support for economic growth is to do little or nothing.

Another way of considering the role of technology in agenda setting is the "garbage can model" of decision making, in which solutions find problems, rather than vice versa.[55] A problem may be excluded from the agenda simply because of the lack of an instrument to do the job, and the example of economic management points to the dangers of the lack of an available instrument. If government announces that it is attempting to solve a problem and then fails miserably, public confidence in the effectiveness of government will be shaken. Government must then take the blame for failures along with the credit for successes. The garbage can model also illustrates the relationship between agenda setting and policy formulation because an issue is not accepted as a part of the agenda unless it is known that a policy has been formulated, or is ready on the shelf, to solve the problem. Solutions may beg for new problems, like a child with a hammer finding things that need hammering, and organizations that have a particular technology will attempt to use that technology to advance their own position in the political process.[56]

As with all portions of the policymaking process, agenda setting is an intensely political activity. Indeed, it may well be the most political aspect of policymaking because it involves bringing to the public consciousness an acceptance of a vague social problem as something government can, and should, attempt to solve. It may be quite easy for powerful actors who wish to do so to exclude unfamiliar issues from the agenda, making active political mobilization of the less powerful necessary for success. Rational policy analysis may play only a small role in setting the agenda for discussion; such analysis will be useful primarily after it is agreed that there is a problem and that the problem is public in nature. In agenda setting, the policy analyst is less a technician and more a politician, understanding the policymaking process and seeking to influence that process toward a desired end.[57] That involves the manipulation of symbols and the definition of often vague social problems. Nevertheless, agenda setting should not be dismissed as simply political maneuvering; it is the crucial first step on the road to resolving any identified problem.

## Policy Formulation

After the political system has accepted a problem as part of the agenda for policymaking, the logical question is what should be done about it. We call this stage of the process *policy formulation*, meaning the development of the mechanisms for solving the public problem. At this point, a policy analyst can begin to apply analytic techniques to attempt to justify one policy choice as superior to others. Economics and decision theory are both useful in assessing the risks of particular outcomes or in predicting likely social costs and benefits of various alternatives. Rational choice, however, need not be dominant; the habits, traditions, and standard operating procedures of government may prevail over rational activity in making the policy choice. But even such seemingly irrational sets of choice factors may be, in their way, quite rational: The actors involved have experience with the "formula" to be used, are comfortable with it, and consequently can begin to make it work much more readily than they could a newer instrument in which they may have no confidence, even if that instrument is technically superior.

The Clinton administration's formulation of its health care reform proposal demonstrates some of the pitfalls of rationalistic and expert policy formulation. Although the proposal may have been excellent technically, it simply did not correspond to the familiar political and administrative patterns of the United States. Likewise, the attempts of George W. Bush to privatize Social Security may have made sense to (some) economists but did not to citizens who were committed to the existing program. In a more general sense, the rationalistic appearance of the Obama administration's response to the economic crisis has been politically damaging to the administration.

The federal government has followed several basic formulas in attempting to solve public problems. In economic affairs, for example, the United States has relied on regulation more than on government ownership of business, which has been more common in Europe. In social policy, the standard formulas have been social insurance and the use of cash transfer programs rather than direct delivery of services. The major exception to the latter formula has been the reliance on education as a means of rectifying social and economic inequality. And finally, there has existed a formula of involving the private sector as much as possible in public sector activity through grants, contracts, and use of federal money as leverage for raising money from private sources and from state and local governments.

We should not be too quick to criticize the federal government for its lack of innovation in dealing with public problems. Most governments do not use all the tools available to them.[58] Also, there is very little theory to guide government policymakers trying to decide what tools they should use.[59] In particular, there is very little theory or practical advice that links the nature of public problems with the most appropriate ways of solving them. As a consequence, a great deal of policy formulation is done by inertia, by analogy, or by intuition.

## Who Formulates Policy?

Policy formulation is a difficult game because any number of people can and do play; there are few rules. At one time or another, almost every kind of policy actor will be involved in formulating policy proposals, although several kinds of actors are especially important. Policy formulation is also very much a political activity but not always a partisan activity. Political parties and candidates, in fact, are not as good at promulgating solutions to problems as they are at identifying problems and presenting lofty ambitions for society to solve them. Expertise begins to play a large role here because the success or failure of a policy instrument will depend to some degree on its technical characteristics, as well as on its political acceptability.

*The public bureaucracy.*   The public bureaucracy is the institution most involved in taking the lofty aspirations of political leaders and translating them into concrete proposals. Whether one accepts the state-centric model of agenda setting or not, one must realize that government bureaucracies are central to policy formulation. Even if programs are formally introduced by Congress members or the president, it is quite possible that their original formulation and justification came from a friendly bureau.

Bureaucracies presumably are the masters of routine and procedure. The commitment to procedures is at once their strength and their weakness. They know how to use procedures and how to develop programs and procedures to reach desired goals. Yet an agency that knows how to do these things too well may develop an excessively narrow vision of how to formulate answers for a particular set of problems. As noted earlier, certain formulas have been developed at the governmental level for responding to problems, and much the same is true of individual organizations that have standard operating procedures and thick rule books. Many of the administrative reforms undertaken during the 1990s sought to jog bureaucracies from those established routines, but old habits are difficult to break, and organizations often reverted to their old ways of doing business after the pressure of the reformers had been removed. Of course, some commitment to established programs and approaches may not be all bad, as it may complicate the task of reformers who want to embark on untried programs.[60]

Certainly, familiarity with an established mechanism can explain some of the conservatism of organizations in the choice of instruments to achieve their ends, and faith in the efficacy of the instrument also helps explain reliance on a limited range of policy tools. One important component of the restrictiveness of choice, however, appears to be self-protection. That is, neither administrators nor their agencies can go very wrong by selecting a solution that is only an incremental departure from an existing program. This is true for two reasons: (1) such a choice will not have as high a probability of failure as a more innovative program, and (2) an incremental choice will almost certainly keep the program in the hands of the existing agency. Hence, reliance on bureaucracy to formulate solutions may be a guarantee of stability, but it is unlikely to produce many successful policy innovations.

Also, agencies will usually choose to do *something* when given the opportunity or the challenge to do so. Making policy choices is their business, and it is certainly in their organizational self-interest to respond to a problem. The agency personnel know that if they do not respond, some other agency soon will, and their agency will lose an opportunity to increase its budget, personnel, and clout. Agencies do not always act in the self-aggrandizing manner ascribed to them,[61] but when confronted directly with a problem already declared to need solving, they will usually respond with a solution—one that involves their own participation.

There is one final consideration about bureaucratic responses to policy problems: An agency often represents a concentration of a certain type of expertise. Increasingly, this expertise is professional, and a growing percentage of the employees of the federal government have professional qualifications.[62] In addition to helping an agency formulate better solutions to policy problems, expertise narrows the vision of the agency and the range of solutions that may be considered. Professional training tends to be narrowing rather than broadening, and it tends to teach that the profession possesses *the* solution to a range of problems. Thus, with a concentration of professionals of a certain type, an agency will tend to produce only incremental departures from existing policies. For example, although both the Federal Trade Commission and the Antitrust Division of the Department of Justice are concerned with eliminating monopolistic practices in the economy, the concentration of economists in the former and lawyers in the latter may generate different priorities.[63]

The occupation of public manager itself is becoming more professionalized, so the major reference group for public managers will be other public managers, a factor that may further narrow the range of bureaucratic responses to policy problems. Much of the drive of the new public management,[64] however, has been to empower public managers to make more of their own decisions and to be more significant forces in implementing, if perhaps not making, public policy. Thus, senior bureaucrats may be expected to employ their professional expertise and that of their colleagues to develop new programs and strategies in addition to simply making programs perform well.

*Think tanks and shadow cabinets.*   Other sources of policy formulation are the think tanks that pervade Washington and state capitals around the country.[65] These are organizations of professional analysts and policy formulators who usually work on contract for a client in government, often an agency in the bureaucracy. We would expect much greater creativity and innovation from these organizations than from the public bureaucracy, but other problems arise in the types of policy options they propose. First, an agency may be able virtually to guarantee the kind of answer it will receive by choosing a certain think tank. Some organizations are more conservative and will usually formulate solutions relying more on incentives and the private sector, whereas other consultants may recommend more direct government intervention. Their reports are likely to have substantial impact, not only because they have been labeled as expert but also because they have been paid for and therefore should be used.

Another problem that arises is more a problem for the consultants in think tanks than for the agencies, but it certainly affects the quality of the policies they recommend. If the think tank is to get additional business from an agency, the consultants believe—perhaps rightly—that they have to tell the agency what it wants to hear. In other words, a consulting firm that says that the favorite approach of an agency is entirely wrong and needs to be completely revamped may be both technically correct and politically bankrupt. A problem of ethical judgment hence arises for the consulting firm, as it might for individual analysts working for an organization: What are the boundaries of loyalty to truth and loyalty to the organization?

Three particular think tanks have been of special importance in U.S. policy formulation. Traditionally, the two dominant organizations were the Brookings Institution and the American Enterprise Institute (AEI). During the Republican Nixon, Ford, and Reagan administrations, the Brookings Institution was often described as "the Democratic party in exile." The Clinton administration tapped a number of Brookings staff members for appointments, and Barack Obama followed a similar strategy, appointing former Brookings fellows Susan E. Rice as ambassador to the United Nations and Peter Orszag as director of the Office of Management and Budget. On the other side of the fence, the AEI has been the home of moderate Republican officials, although relatively few were tapped by the more conservative George W. Bush administration. Both of these think tanks support wide-reaching publication programs to attempt to influence elite public opinion, in addition to their direct involvement in government.

The third major think tank is the Heritage Foundation, which came to prominence during the Reagan years as an advocate of a number of neoconservative policy positions, especially privatization and deregulation.[66] It was less prominent in the George H. W. Bush administration than it had been during the Reagan years, but it was extremely prominent during the administration of George W. Bush, with its proposals central to policy formulation in some fields. The number of think tanks on the political right has been increasing, funded largely by industry and wealthy individuals. Prominent among them are the Cato Institute, Citizens for Tax Justice, and the National Center for Policy Analysis. There also has been some resurgence of think tanks on the political left, such as the Center for Budget Priorities. Perhaps most important, these developments demonstrate the continuing polarization of political ideas in the United States.

Universities also serve as think tanks for government, especially the growing number of public policy schools and programs across the country that, in addition to training future practitioners of the art of government, provide a place where scholars and former practitioners can formulate new solutions to problems. Robert Reich, for example, developed some of the ideas he later attempted to implement as secretary of labor while at the Kennedy School of Government at Harvard.[67] In addition to the policy programs, specialized institutes, such as the Institute for Research on Poverty, at the University of Wisconsin, and the Joint Center on Urban Studies, at Harvard and MIT, develop policy ideas in their specific policy areas.

It is sometimes difficult to determine where think tanks end and interest groups and lobbying organizations begin. The term *think tank* has a more positive connotation than does *interest group,* so lobbying groups have gone to some lengths to appear as if they were doing objective public policy research. If we go to the Internet and begin to look at the range of opinions that appear on any issue, we can find a number of "institutes," "centers," or "foundations" that are attempting to influence opinion; a careful analysis will reveal that these are really subsidiaries of interest groups.[68]

*Interest groups.* Another important source of policy formulation is interest groups, which must not only identify problems and apply pressure to have them placed on the agenda but also supply possible remedies. Those cures will almost certainly serve the interests of their group members, but that is only to be expected. It is the task of the authoritative decision makers to take those ideas about policy choices with as many grains of salt as necessary to develop workable plans for solving the problem. Given the continued existence of iron triangle relationships in many policy areas, a close connection is likely to exist between the policy formulation ideas of an agency and those of the pressure group. The policy choices that established pressure groups advocate will again be rather conservative and incremental; such groups rarely produce sweeping changes from the status quo in which they and their associated agency have a decided interest.

The public interest groups, such as Common Cause, the Center for the Public Interest, and a variety of consumer and taxpayer organizations, contradict the traditional model of policy formulation by interest groups. Perhaps the major task of these organizations is to break the stranglehold that the iron triangles have on policy and attempt to broaden the range of interests represented in the policymaking process. These groups are oriented toward reform. Some of the issues they have taken up are substantive, such as the strengthening of safety requirements for a variety of products sold in the marketplace. Other issues are procedural, such as campaign reform and opening the regulatory process to greater public input. In general, however, no matter what issue they decide to interest themselves in, these groups advocate sweeping reforms as opposed to incremental changes, and they are important in providing balance to the policy process, as well as providing a strong voice for reform and change.

*Members of Congress.* Finally, although we have previously tended to denigrate the role of politicians in formulating policy, a number of Congress members do involve themselves in serious formulation activities instead of just accepting advice from friendly sources in the bureaucracy.[69] Like the public interest groups, these senators and representatives are generally interested in reform, for if they were primarily interested only in incremental change, there would be little need for their involvement. Some are also interested in using formulation and advocacy as means of furthering their careers, adopting roles as national policymakers as opposed to the more common pattern of emphasizing constituency service.

Congress as an institution in the early twenty-first century is better equipped to formulate policy than it has ever been, even considering the policy challenges it faces. There has been a continuing growth in the size of congressional staffs, both the personal staffs of representatives and senators and the staffs of committees and subcommittees.[70] For example, in 1965 Congress employed just over 9,000 people; by 2000, the number had increased to over 31,000, and the number continues to increase slowly. These employees are on the public payroll at least in part to assist members of Congress in doing the research and drafting necessary for active policy formulation, and they are important in rectifying what some consider a serious imbalance between the power of Congress and that of the executive branch. For example, the Congressional Budget Office now shadows the Office of Management and Budget, providing an independent source of advice on budgeting and a range of other issues. The contemporary deadlock within Congress has tended to lessen the opportunities for congressional legislative action, but some policy entrepreneurs do remain.[71]

### How to Formulate Policy

The task of formulating policy involves substantial sensitivity to the nuances of policy (and politics) and a potential for the creative application of the tools of policy analysis. In fact, many of the problems that the government faces require substantial creativity because little is known about the problem areas. Nevertheless, governments may have to react to a problem whether or not they are sure of the best, or even a good, course of action. In many instances, the routine responses of a government agency to its environment will be sufficient to meet the problems that arise, but if the routine response is unsuccessful, the agency will have to search for a more innovative response and perhaps involve more actors in policy formulation. In other words, a routine or incremental response may be sufficient for most policy problems, but if it is not, the policymaking system must look for something else. Making policy choices that depart radically from incremental responses requires methods of identifying and choosing among alternatives.

Two major barriers may block government's ability to understand the problems it confronts. One is the lack of some basic facts about the policy questions at hand. The most obvious example is defense policy, in which governments often lack information about the capabilities and intentions of the opposing side. Indeed, since the end of the Cold War, it has become difficult even to identify the potential enemies, much less anticipate their actions. Similarly, in assessing risks from various toxic substances or nuclear power plants, there may not be sufficient empirical evidence to determine the probabilities of undesirable events occurring or their probable consequences.[72] Even more difficult for government is that frequently there are no agreed-on indicators of the nature of social conditions, and even widely accepted indicators for economic variables, such as gross national product and unemployment rates, are somewhat suspect.[73]

Perhaps more important, government decision makers often lack adequate information about the underlying processes that have created the problems they are attempting to solve. For example, to address the poverty problem, one should understand how poverty comes about and how it is perpetuated. But despite the masses of data and information that have been generated, there is no accepted model of causation for poverty. This lack of a causal model may be contrasted with decisions about epidemic diseases made by public health agencies using well-developed and accepted theories about how diseases occur and spread. Clearly, different decision-making procedures should be used to attempt to solve different kinds of problems.

Figure 4.1 demonstrates possible combinations of knowledge of causation and basic facts about policy problems. The simplest type of policymaking involves *routine* policy, such as Social Security. Making policy in such areas, with adequate information and an accepted theory of causation, primarily requires

*Knowledge of causation*

|  | *High* | *Low* |
|---|---|---|
| **High** | Routine | Conditional |
| **Low** | Craftsman | Creative |

*Information*

FIGURE 4.1    Kinds of Policy Formulation

routine adjustment of existing policies, and for the most part the changes made will be incremental.[74] This relative simplicity would be complicated if fundamental theories about creating a desirable retirement situation or the mechanism for financing such a system were seriously altered (see chapter 12).

*Creative* policy formulation lies at the other extreme of information and knowledge held by decision makers. In this instance, they have neither an adequate information base nor an adequate theory of causation. Research and development operations, such as those in the National Institutes of Health or in numerous agencies within the Department of Defense, provide important examples of policy formulation of this type.[75] Another example may be the formulation of policies for personal social services, such as counseling. In these instances, a great deal of creativity and care must be exercised in matching the particular needs of the individual with the needs of the agency for efficient management and accountability. Such policies require building in reversibility of policy choices, so that creative formulations that prove unworkable can be corrected.

In some situations, there may be sufficient information but an inadequate understanding of the underlying processes of causation. These policymaking situations require the formulation of *conditional* policies, in which changes in certain indicators trigger a policy response of some sort, even if only the reconsideration of the existing policy. It is possible that government can know that certain policies will produce desired results, even if the underlying processes are not fully understood. Following the general loss of faith in Keynesian theories of economic management, it may be that macroeconomic policy is made in this manner. There are several accepted indicators of the state of the economy—unemployment, inflation, and economic growth rates, for example—and changes in these indicators may trigger relatively standard reactions, even if the policymakers cannot always specify, or agree on, their underlying logic.[76] It is also generally advantageous to build a certain amount of automaticity into the policy response, or at least to provide some insulation against political delay or interference. In economic management, for example, countries with relatively independent central banks have been more successful than those with more politicized central banks, although most central banks have become more politicized after the beginning of the economic downturn in 2008.[77]

Finally, in some policy areas, governments may have a model of causation for the problem but lack sufficient information to be confident in any policy response they may formulate. Defense policies may fit this category of *craftsman* policies, for governments appear to understand quite well how to respond to threats and how to go to war, although they frequently have only limited, and possibly distorted, information about the capabilities and intentions of their adversaries. Formulating policies of this type depends on developing a number of contingencies and potential forms of response, as well as identifying means of assessing the risks of possible occurrences. The complex policy deliberations of the U.S. government concerning the possible nuclear capabilities of North Korea and Iraq illustrate the "craftsman" nature of defense and foreign policy. In other words, formulating such policies involves building a probabilistic basis for response, rather than relying on the certainty that might be taken for granted in other policy areas. The eventual discovery that Iraq did not possess weapons of mass destruction, as the Bush administration believed, demonstrates the potential risks of this approach to policy formulation.

These four categories of policymaking are important, but how a policy is defined is a political issue, and the clever policy formulator will attempt to define problems and issues so that they will fit into one category or another. For example, if a problem lies within an agency's range of action, it will attempt to keep it there by defining it as routine. Any agency or interest group that wants to shift the definition—whether to improve the policy or to increase its budget—will attempt to define it as requiring more of a craftsman or creative solution.

## *Aids for Policy Formulation*

Given the difficulties of formulating effective policy responses to many problems, it is fortunate that some techniques have been developed to assist in the task. In general, these techniques serve to clarify the consequences of certain courses of action and to provide a summary measure of the probable effects of a policy along a single scale of measurement, usually money, so that different policy alternatives can be more effectively compared with one another. I discuss two of these techniques only briefly here, reserving a more detailed exposition and discussion of cost-benefit analysis for chapter 17. It is important, however, to understand at this point in the discussion something about the considerations that one might take into account when selecting a policy alternative.

*Cost-benefit analysis.*    The most frequently applied tool for policy analysis is cost-benefit analysis. The utilitarian assumptions and methodology underlying this technique reduce all the costs and benefits of proposed government programs to a quantitative, economic dimension and then compare available alternative policies using that standard. In this mode of policy analysis, economic considerations are almost always paramount. As the methodology has been developed, attempts have been made to place economic values on factors that might be primarily noneconomic, but the principal means of evaluating programs remain utilitarian.[78]

Cost-benefit analysis is in some ways deceptively simple. The total benefits created by a project are enumerated, including those that would be regarded as externalities in the private market (amenity values, recreation, and the like). The costs of the program are also enumerated, again including social costs (e.g., pollution or inequalities). Long-term costs and benefits are also taken into account, although they may be discounted or adjusted because they will occur in the future. Projects whose total benefits exceed their total costs are deemed acceptable; then choices can be made among the acceptable projects. The general rule is to adopt the project with the greatest net total benefit for society (total benefits minus total costs) and then all others that fit within the total available budget.

Later, I will discuss some of the more technical problems of cost-benefit analysis. It is important here to talk about some of the ethical underpinnings of the technique, as they have a pronounced effect on the formulation of policy alternatives. The fundamental ethical difficulties arise from the assumptions that all values are reducible to monetary terms and that economic criteria are the most important ones for government when making policy. There may well be some values, such as civil liberties, human life, or the environment, that many citizens would not want reduced to dollars and cents.[79] Even if such a reduction were possible, it is questionable whether the primary goal of government should be maximizing economic welfare in the society.

*Decision analysis.*    Cost-benefit analysis assumes that certain events will occur: A dam will be built; it will produce $X$ kilowatts of electricity; $Y$ people from a nearby city will spend $Z$ hours boating and waterskiing on the newly created lake; farmers will save $Q$ dollars in flood protection and irrigation but lose $N$ acres of land for farming. Decision analysis, in contrast, is geared toward making policy choices under conditions of less certainty.[80] It assumes that in many instances government, having inadequate information, is making probabilistic choices about what to do—that, in fact, government may be almost playing a game, with nature or other human beings as the opponent. As pointed out, governments often do not have a very good conception of the policy instruments they choose, and that lack of knowledge, combined with inadequate knowledge about patterns of causation within the policy area, can be a recipe for disaster. However, if we have some idea about the probabilities of certain outcomes (even without a model of causation), there is a better chance of making better decisions.

Take, for example, a situation in which a hurricane appears to be bearing down on a major coastal city. On the one hand, the mayor of that city can order an evacuation and cause a great deal of lost production as well as a predictable number of deaths during the rush to escape the city. On the other hand, if he or she does not order the evacuation and the hurricane actually does strike the city, then a far larger loss of life will occur. Of course, the hurricane is only forecast to be heading in the general direction of the city, and it may yet veer off. What should the mayor do? How should he or she assess the risks and the possible outcomes of the decision?[81]

This decision-making problem can be organized as a "decision tree," in which the mayor is essentially playing a game against nature (see Figure 4.2). The mayor has two possible policy choices: evacuate or not evacuate. We can assign probabilities to the two potential occurrences in nature—hit or miss the city—based on the best information available from the weather bureau, and we have estimates of the losses that would occur as a result of each outcome. In this analysis, we assume that if the hurricane strikes, the loss of property will be approximately the same whether or not the city is evacuated. As the problem is set up, the mayor makes the smallest possible error by choosing to evacuate the city. By doing that, the mayor may cause an expected unnecessary loss of $7 million ($10 million multiplied by the probability of the event of $.70) if the hurricane does not hit, but there would be an expected unnecessary loss of $30 million if the evacuation was not ordered and the hurricane did actually strike. Such a simple decision will be easy to make if there is sufficient information available.

| Decision | Probability | Nature | Expected loss |
|---|---|---|---|
| Evacuate | –0.3 | Hurricane hits | $0 |
| | –0.7 | Hurricane misses (Loss = $10 million) | $7 million |
| Not evacuate | –0.3 | Hurricane hits (Loss = $100 million) | $30 million |
| | –0.7 | Hurricane misses | $0 |

FIGURE 4.2   A Decision Tree on Evacuation

In more complex situations, when many facts need to be considered simultaneously, the decision-making process becomes more difficult, especially when one faces a human opponent rather than nature. Even then, the technique, like cost-benefit analysis, is only an aid to decision making and policy formulation. Decisions still must be made by individuals, who will consider ethical, economic, and political factors before making a judgment about what should be done. And as the results of policy formulation will be felt in the future, the exercise of judgment is especially important. When an issue is newly placed on the agenda, the first formulation of a solution will to some degree structure subsequent attempts at solution. It therefore will have an enduring legacy that must be considered very carefully.

## Policy Design

All the aids that government can bring to bear when formulating policy still do not generate an underlying approach to policy design. That is, no technical means of addressing public problems relate the characteristics of those problems to the instruments that might be used to solve them or to the values that would be used to evaluate a policy's success.[82] Without such a comprehensive approach to design, much policy formulation in government is accomplished by intuition or inertia or by analogy with existing programs. The inertial pattern produces frequent mistakes and often much wasted time and effort. Thus, one of the many tasks of policy analysis is to develop a comprehensive approach to the problems of formulating effective policies—it requires not only some idea of what "good" policies are but also some strategies for developing processes that can produce desirable policies.

In the United States, any such comprehensive approach to policy design is likely to be resisted. In the first place, the generally antistatist values of U.S. politics make a planned, rationalistic approach unacceptable to many politicians and citizens. Second, as was pointed out earlier, for institutional as well as ideological reasons, American politics tends toward incremental solutions to problems rather than imposition of comprehensive frameworks or use of design concepts for policymaking.[83] Attempting to impose a design on a policy area may threaten the interests of agencies and committees that believe that they "own" the problem and that they have been responsible for the development of the existing policy over time. Third, there is as yet inadequate agreement on the nature of many of the most important policy problems that the U.S. government now faces, and even less on the nature of the solutions. Important policy problems such as poverty, crime, poor education, and the like still lack clear definitions of causes or solutions. These important political realities should not, however, prevent policy analysts from attempting to understand social problems in a less haphazard fashion than is sometimes encountered in government or from advocating innovative program designs for solving them.

## Summary

In this chapter, I have taken the policymaking process through its first stages: considering problems and then developing some mechanisms for solving them. Both activities—and indeed the entire activity of policymaking—are political exercises, but they also involve the application of techniques and tools for analysis. The tools for agenda setting are largely political, requiring the "selling" of agenda items to authorized decision makers, who may believe that they already have enough to do. Agenda setting also requires a detailed knowledge of the issue in question so that it can be related, first, to the known preferences of decision makers, and second, to existing policies and programs. Agenda setting is in some ways the art of doing something new so that it appears old.

The techniques that can be applied to policy formulation are more sophisticated technically, but they also require sensitive political hands that can use them effectively. To a great extent, the use of old solutions for new problems applies in formulation as well as in agenda setting. For both agenda setting and policy formulation, incremental solutions are favored in the United States. This incrementalism produces a great deal of stability in the policy process, but it makes rapid response to major changes in the economy and society difficult.

The solutions that emerge from these first stages of the policy process, then, are designed to be readily accepted by legislators and administrators who must authorize and legitimate the policies selected. A more comprehensive approach to design might well produce better solutions to problems, but it would face the barrier of political feasibility. The task of the analyst and advocate, then, becomes stretching the boundaries of feasibility to produce better public policies.

CHAPTER 5

# Legitimating Policy Choices

ONCE IT HAS BEEN DECIDED that a certain program is required, or is feasible, as a response to a policy problem, that choice must be defended as a legitimate one for government to make. No matter what course of action is decided on, it is almost certain that some citizens will believe themselves disadvantaged by the choice. At a minimum, any public program or project will cost money, and citizens who pay taxes and receive (or perceive) no direct benefits from it will frequently consider themselves to be harmed by the policy choice. Because policy choices inevitably benefit some citizens and not others, a great deal of attention must be given in a democratic government to the process by which decisions are made. It is by means of the official process of government that substantive policy decisions are legitimated; that is, the process attaches the legitimate authority of the state to the policy that is chosen.

*Legitimacy* is a fundamental concept in the discipline of political science, and it is important in understanding policymaking. Legitimacy is conventionally defined as a belief on the part of citizens that the current government represents a proper form of government and a willingness on their part to accept the government's decrees as legal and authoritative.[1] The vast majority of Americans regard the government of the United States as the appropriate set of institutions to govern the country. And most Americans consequently accept the actions of the government as authoritative (as having the force of law), as long as they are carried out in accordance with the processes established in the Constitution or by procedures derived from them. It is understood that all policies adopted must be within the powers granted to the federal government by the Constitution. The boundaries of the policies considered constitutional have expanded during the history of the United States, but the limits current at the time establish the boundaries of legitimate action. So, for example, the federal government in 2010 can become involved in economic policy areas that it could not have in 1910, although perhaps fewer than in the late 1960s or early 1970s.

Several things should be understood about legitimacy as it affects contemporary policymaking in the United States. First, legitimacy is largely a psychological property. Legitimacy depends on the majority's acceptance of the appropriateness of a government. A government may come to power by all the prescribed processes, but if the population does not willingly accept that government or the rules by which it gained power, then in practice it has no legitimacy. For example, many constitutions (including those of France and Britain) give government the right to suspend civil liberties and declare martial law, but citizens accustomed to greater freedom may find it difficult to accept decrees such as that,[2] unless a crisis such as the attacks of September 11, 2001, intervenes to expand the range of acceptable action. Changes in a government may cause some citizens to question the legitimacy of a new government's actions.

Legitimacy has substantive as well as procedural elements. It matters not only how issues are decided but also what is decided. The government of the United States might decide to nationalize all oil companies operating in the country. (It will not do this, but just imagine so for a moment.) The decision could be reached with all appropriate deliberation as prescribed by the Constitution, but it would still not be acceptable to the majority of citizens. A more realistic example is provided by the wars in Vietnam and then in Iraq, which were conducted according to the procedures of the Constitution but nevertheless rejected as illegitimate by a significant proportion of the population. As a consequence of the Vietnam War, Congress passed the War Powers Act, which changed the procedures by which the United States could become involved in any future foreign conflicts.[3] The substantive question of legitimacy therefore produced a procedural response, although the debate in 2002 and 2003 over the ability of President George W. Bush to attack Iraq demonstrated that the procedures are themselves far from clear. At a less dramatic level, the attempts on the part of Congress to increase its own pay during 1989 and 1990 were procedurally correct but raised such an outcry from the public that they could not be implemented; the American public clearly regarded the action as illegitimate. Congress has since changed the way its pay is determined, so increases automatically follow increases in the cost of living unless Congress acts to stop the increase, but even that automatic procedure has created questions with some voters.[4]

The limits of government activity became major political questions during the congressional elections of 2010, and those issues persisted into the 2012 presidential election. The rise of the Tea Party movement, opposed to most forms of government intervention into society, has placed the question of the limits of government more in the center of American politics.[5] While seeming radical after the expansion of American government since World War II, this movement is yet another manifestation of the populist tradition in American politics that rejects large institutions in social and political life and promotes ideas of individualism.

Legitimacy is both a variable and a constant—it differs among individuals and across time. Some citizens of the United States may not accept the legitimacy of the current government. For example, some African American activists rejected the legitimacy of the U.S. government and called for the formation of a separate African American nation within the country. On the other side, white supremacists and some religious sects have organized settlements in parts of the West that reject the authority of all the constituted governments, and they even have engaged in armed conflict with federal agents. Citizens also appear more willing to accept the actions of state and local governments than those of the federal government.

A general decline in confidence in American institutions has been occurring, and it has been especially pronounced for government institutions other than the military (see Table 5.1).[6] There was some upturn in confidence in the 1980s, but that has decayed, and Americans now have less confidence in government than they have had in the past. In particular, Congress now is one of the least-respected institutions in the United States. The various scandals during the second Clinton administration reduced citizens' confidence in the presidency. The first years of the George W. Bush administration seemed to restore legitimacy to the office, despite the extreme confusion of the 2000 election,[7] but scandals of another sort in 2005 and 2006 and failures in economic management reduced the president's approval ratings to the lowest point ever.[8]

The economic crisis beginning in 2008 has posed a major challenge to the legitimacy of American government. Although public confidence in government is to some extent an emotional attachment to the symbols of the system, another major part of legitimacy derives from the effectiveness of government.[9] Somewhat

TABLE 5.1    Confidence in American Institutions, 1983–2008 (combined percentages saying "Great deal" or "Quite a lot")

| | 2008 | 2006 | 2004 | 2002 | 1998 | 1996 | 1993 | 1990 | 1988 | 1985 | 1983 |
|---|---|---|---|---|---|---|---|---|---|---|---|
| Military | 71 | 73 | 75 | 71 | 64 | 66 | 68 | 68 | 58 | 61 | 53 |
| Organized religion | 48 | 52 | 53 | 53 | 59 | 57 | 53 | 56 | 59 | 66 | 62 |
| Supreme Court | 32 | 40 | 46 | 41 | 42 | 45 | 44 | 47 | 56 | 56 | 42 |
| Presidency | 26 | 33 | 52 | 50 | 22 | 39 | 43 | n.a. | n.a. | n.a. | n.a. |
| Public schools | 33 | 37 | 41 | n.a. | 37 | 38 | 39 | 45 | 49 | 48 | 39 |
| Newspapers | 24 | 30 | 30 | 16 | 31 | 32 | 31 | 39 | 36 | 35 | 38 |
| Organized labor | 20 | 24 | 24 | 11 | 26 | 25 | 26 | 27 | 26 | 28 | 26 |
| Big business | 20 | 18 | 24 | 16 | 22 | 24 | 22 | 25 | 25 | 31 | 28 |
| Congress | 12 | 19 | 30 | 22 | 28 | 20 | 22 | 24 | 35 | 39 | 28 |

*Sources:* Various Gallup Polls, CNN/Gallup Polls, and Harris Polls.

*Note:* n.a. = not available.

paradoxically, although most Americans say they do not want government heavily involved in the economy, when the economy has difficulties, government is blamed for its inaction. The latest economic crisis is no different and is perhaps even more destructive of legitimacy because it has undermined the housing market, which many people counted on as their major investment.[10]

In societies that are deeply divided ethnically or politically, the rejection of the sitting government by one side or another is a constant fact of life. Even a government that is widely accepted may lose legitimacy or strain its legitimate status through unpopular activities and leaders. The Vietnam War and the Watergate scandal illustrate the low point to which the legitimacy of even a widely accepted political regime may fall. Nevertheless, the American government was able to survive those problems, as well as such subsequent problems as the Iran-Contra controversy, several scandals during the Clinton administration, and failures in responding to Hurricane Katrina, and continue to govern with legitimate authority.

Because of the variability of legitimacy, a fully legitimated government may gradually lose its legitimate status over time. A series of blatantly unpopular or illegal actions may reduce the authority of a government, making it open to challenge, whether of a revolutionary or more peaceable nature. Or a government may lose legitimacy through incompetence rather than unpopular activities, as has been demonstrated in the handling of both Iraq and the economic problems beginning in 2008. Citizens in most countries have a reservoir of respect for government, and governments can add to or subtract from that stock of authority. As a result, governments are engaged in a continuing process of legitimation for themselves and their successors.

Finally, government must somehow legitimate each individual policy choice. No matter how technically correct a policy choice may be, it is of little practical value if it cannot be justified to the public. For example, the decision to correct the formula for indexing Social Security pension benefits, once it was discovered that the increases it produced were unjustifiably large, was absolutely correct. But it created a huge political controversy and a sense of betrayal among some elderly citizens (see chapter 12). Policy analysts, in their pursuit of elegant solutions and innovative policies, frequently forget this mundane point, and that forgetfulness can present a real barrier to their success.[11] To design a policy that can be legitimated, a policy analyst must understand the political process. That process will define the set of feasible policy alternatives in a more restrictive fashion than does the economic and social world—that is, more programs could work than could be adopted within the political values of the American system. Thus, the task of the policy analyst is to be able to "sell" his or her decisions to the individuals who are crucial to their being legitimated. That does not mean that the analyst must advocate only policies that fit existing definitions of

| | | Characteristics of decisions | |
|---|---|---|---|
| | | *Majoritarian* | *Nonmajoritarian* |
| *Range of actors* | *Mass* | Referendums | — |
| | *Elite* | Congress | Courts; Administrative regulations |

FIGURE 5.1    Modes of Legitimation

feasibility, but it does mean that the analyst must have a strategy for expanding that definition if a highly innovative program is to be proposed.[12]

In general, legitimation may be performed through the legislative process, through the administrative process designed for the issuing of regulations (secondary legislation), through the courts, or through mechanisms of direct democracy. As shown in Figure 5.1, these modes of legitimation can be seen as combining characteristics of decisions—majoritarian and nonmajoritarian—and the range of actors involved.[13] The nonmajoritarian mass cell is empty in the figure, but it might be filled by revolutionary or extremely powerful interest group activities. Indeed, the ongoing political controversy over abortion policy may fall into this cell, given that there is apparently no popular majority for the policies being pushed by an intense and active minority, although that minority has been successful in some states (see chapter 16). We will discuss each type of legitimation and its implications for the policy choices that might be feasible as a result of each process.

## Legislative Legitimation

In the United States, we traditionally have equated lawmaking with Congress, the principal legislative body at the federal level, or with similar bodies in the states. That notion is now excessively naive, for the workload and the technical content of many subjects on which decisions have to be made have overwhelmed Congress. The loss of capacity to legislate effectively has occurred despite the growth of legislative staffs and the increased availability of policy advice for legislators. Governments are simply too large and involved in too many issues to permit a large legislative institution, such as Congress, with all its intricate procedures, to make the full range of decisions required to keep the society functioning (from a public policy perspective). This problem was highlighted when it seemed that no members of Congress had read the 1,000-page economic stimulus bill that they voted on in 2009.

Of course, Congress remains the crucial source for primary legislation. That is, although administrative bodies are responsible for writing regulations in large numbers, Congress must supply the basic legislative frameworks within which the other bodies operate. Congress tends to pass legislation written in relatively broad language, allowing administrators latitude for interpretation. Thus, despite various attempts to reassert the authority of Congress in opposing the "imperial presidency," it is best to think about the legitimating role of Congress as the authorizing of relatively diffuse statements of goals and structures. Those broad statements are then made operational by the executive branch, which fills in the details by writing regulations and by the implementation process.

Congress also retains its supervisory powers—oversight—so that if the executive branch strays too far when writing regulations, Congress can reassert its intentions in constructing the legislation.[14] Until 1983, Congress had virtually unlimited power to pass "legislative vetoes," which required agencies issuing certain types of regulations to submit them to Congress for approval. Although the Supreme Court declared that the legislative veto is excessive meddling by one branch of government in the affairs of another and so is not constitutional,[15] Congress has nevertheless continued to use similar instruments in other policy areas.[16] If nothing else, Congress can always amend a law to clarify its intentions—or, if it must, even repeal the previous legislation.

Congress places great emphasis on procedural legitimation and has established elaborate procedures for processing legislation.[17] In fact, its institutions and procedures have become so well developed that it is difficult for legislation to be passed. Typically, a bill must be passed by a subcommittee, by a full committee, and by floor action in each house. And because one house is unlikely to pass a bill in exactly the same form as the other, conference committees are often necessary to reconcile the two versions. More arcane procedural mechanisms, such as filibusters, amendments, and recommitals, can slow down or kill legislation at a number of points if it fails to attract the necessary majority at the proper time. Or to put it the other way around, all that the opponents of a bill have to do is to muster a majority at one crucial point to prevent its passage.[18] Evidence from lobbying investigations in 2005 and 2006 also indicated the extent to which less formal rules permit Congress members to add money earmarked to benefit their constituents to legislation.[19]

Legislative procedures are important as mechanisms to prevent unnecessary or poorly formulated legislation from becoming law, but they can also frustrate good and needed legislation. The ability of the opposition to postpone or block civil rights legislation during the 1950s and 1960s demonstrated clearly the capacity of legislative procedures to thwart the apparent majority will of Congress. More recently, the continuing inability to produce a national health insurance bill, or to pass a strong bill to control tobacco, indicates the difficulties of passing legislation even when a significant portion of the population favors some change from the status quo.[20] Also, the threat of throwing the United States into default on its obligations in the debate on the debt ceiling was insufficient to prevent the use of an array of procedural devices.[21] A committed and well-supported minority is thus able to use legislative procedures to achieve its own ends.

Legitimation through the legislative process is majoritarian. It depends on building either simple or special majorities at each crucial point in the process. The task of the policy analyst or the legislative leader is to construct such majorities. In addition to appealing for support on the basis of the actual qualities of the proposed legislation, the analyst can form the needed majorities in several other ways. One method, which has been referred to as *partisan analysis*,[22] involves convincing members of Congress that the piece of legislation that the analyst wants is something that they want as well. The trick here is to design the legislation in such a way that it will appeal to a sufficient number of interests to create a winning coalition. For example, the National Defense Education Act of 1958, which still funds some international programs, was passed by a coalition of Congress members interested in education and in defense. The title of the bill indicates that it was intended to serve those two purposes and affect those two areas. It brought together liberals favoring a stronger federal role in education and conservatives favoring a stronger defense posture. More recently, some Democrats supported changes in Medicaid and Medicare that the George W. Bush administration favored as a strategy to prevent passage of more conservative legislation.

Another strategy for forming coalitions that is similar to partisan analysis is *logrolling*,[23] in which coalitions are formed not around a single piece of legislation but across a set of legislative initiatives. In the simplest example, Representative A favors bill A but is indifferent to bill B. Representative B, on the other hand, favors bill B but is indifferent to bill A. The logical thing for these two members to do is to trade their votes on the two pieces of legislation, with A voting for bill B and B voting for bill A. Several bills may be involved in vote trading over time. In some ways, logrolling is a rational activity because it allows the passage of legislation that some members of Congress—and presumably their constituencies—favor intensely but that might not otherwise be able to gain a majority. But logrolling also has the effect of bringing about the approval of a great deal more legislation than would otherwise be passed, thus boosting public expenditures and taxation. It enables relatively narrow interests in the nation to develop coalitions for their legislation that may not be justifiable in terms of the broader public interest.

As well as being a majoritarian body, Congress has universalistic norms that promote the spreading of government expenditures very broadly.[24] This is commonly referred to as *pork barrel legislation,* or as the parochial imperative, in

American politics. Pork barrel legislation often concerns capital expenditures, of which the classic examples are river and harbor improvements. Obtaining such capital projects for their home districts has become a measure of Congress members' success; some argue that "bringing home the bacon," instead of policymaking on broad national issues, has become the dominant activity of Congress.[25] The tendency in designing legislation of this kind is to spread benefits as broadly as possible geographically and to create a majority by benefiting virtually anyone who wants a piece of the "pork." As with logrolling, this pattern of decision making tends to increase the costs of government. Douglas Arnold pointed out that pork barrel legislation costs very little when compared with national defense or Social Security,[26] but it stands as an example of the way in which government misuses money by funding projects with relatively minor social benefit in order to ensure the reelection of incumbent members of Congress. Spending on pork barrel projects has increased, in part through earmarked expenditures.[27] The political importance of this style of decision making may outstrip the actual amount of money spent, as it has become a symbol of waste and abuse in government and was a target of reform for Barack Obama as he took office.

This description of legitimation through the legislative process does not paint the most favorable picture of Congress. Actually, a good deal of congressional decision making is based on the merits of legislation. To the extent that partisan analysis, logrolling, and pork barrel legislation characterize the actions of Congress, however, the legislative process has certain effects on the kinds of rules that can be legitimated. It can be argued that the process almost inevitably produces broad and rather diffuse legislation. The necessity of building a coalition requires that one take care not to offend potential members and that the proposed legislation produce benefits for individual legislators and their districts. As a consequence, a bill must be designed to be amenable to partisan analysis and must not be so clearly worded as to reduce the number of possible coalition members. This strategy of obfuscation allows administrators to make politically charged decisions on difficult issues by deflecting criticism from individual members of Congress.

Both logrolling and pork barrel legislation are related to the expansion of government beyond the bounds that could be set if there were no possibility of vote trading. The possibility of trading votes and building coalitions across pieces of legislation fuels a tendency to adopt public projects that are marginal in terms of social productivity. It is obvious that the world of policymaking is not perfectly rational, but these patterns of institutional decision making seem to exacerbate the irrational character of much of politics, producing programs that benefit the few at the expense of the many.[28] Logrolling and the pork barrel also make reducing the size of unneeded programs difficult. For example, the only effective way for Congress to accomplish the closing of redundant military bases in the early 1990s was to specify in advance that an independent commission would recommend closings, which would then be voted on as a group. Otherwise, logrolling might have prevented the closing of any bases at all. This self-denying restraint appeared to break down in 1998, when Congress demanded more influence in retaining bases that the Department of Defense itself wanted to close.[29] This process continued through summer 2005, when several apparently redundant bases escaped closure after coalitions to retain them were formed across partisan and geographical lines.[30] The proposed decline in defense spending after 2012 will again likely produce another round of debates over the geographical distribution of the losses.

These difficulties in congressional decision making suggest more general points concerning social decision making. In its simplest terms, the problem is, How can a set of conflicting social preferences best be expressed in a single decision? Congress faces this problem when it attempts to combine the preferences of its members and their constituents in a single decision whether or not to adopt a piece of legislation; the same general problem arises in clubs, committees, and college faculty meetings.

One underlying problem facing decision makers in legislatures and elsewhere is the varying intensity of preferences of the participants. We encountered this problem when discussing the logic of logrolling—in a majoritarian system, it may be possible to construct a majority composed of individuals who are not much interested in a proposal or do not feel intensely about it. This decision-making problem is in part a function of each legislator's having only one vote, whereas individuals in the market setting have more than one dollar and can apply their resources differentially depending on their preferences and the intensity of those preferences. Logrolling is one means of attempting to overcome the intensity problem, but it can be successful only in a limited set of circumstances with a certain distribution of preferences.

In majoritarian institutions with one vote per member, it is difficult to reflect accurately the preferences of the participants in a manner that creates their greatest net satisfaction. Generating such an optimal decision is made more difficult if in a number of successive decisions (e.g., voting on amendments), the order in which options are eliminated affects the final preferences.[31] In examining choices of this type, the economist Kenneth Arrow argued that it is impossible to devise a social-choice mechanism that satisfies the logical conditions for rationality.[32] The only way in which such decisions can be arrived at, in Arrow's framework, is to impose them, which he rejects on philosophical grounds. But the imposition of administrative regulations as another means of legitimating decisions has some characteristics of imposed solutions, although the procedures for adopting regulations have been sanctioned legally.

Once Congress has enacted legislation, it has played its major role in legitimating policy, but its involvement in the policy process is not over. We have already pointed out that the administrative agencies perform a major role in translating legislation into specific regulations. Congress then exercises some degree of oversight over the actions of the agencies.[33] The committees that initially approved the legislation monitor the way in which the agencies implement it and can act legislatively to correct anything the agencies may do incorrectly. Congress may not even have to do anything directly—often it can rely on its implicit authority over legislation and budgets to gain compliance from the agencies.

Oversight is in essence a second round of legitimation by Congress, which passes the initial legislation and then looks over the shoulders of the implementers to ensure that its intentions are followed. This oversight activity can be only so effective, however, because of the scarcity of time and the need of congressional actors to proceed with the next round of legislation. Furthermore, even the well-staffed U.S. Congress may lack the necessary expertise to judge the numerous, complex, and technical regulations that the administrative agencies issue and their even more numerous administrative decisions. This means that oversight tends to be more "fire alarm" (reaction to crises) than "police patrol" (routine scanning of the relevant environment).[34]

The divided government in the United States after the 2010 elections had led to a growth of oversight activities, especially over federal government responses to the economic crisis. Specific issues such as the huge financial losses of Fannie Mae (Federal National Mortgage Association) and Freddie Mac (Federal Home Loan Mortgage Corporation) provoked substantial congressional response, and policies such as the Troubled Asset Relief Program (TARP) also were targets for Congress, and especially congressional Republicans. More generally, Congress created the Congressional Oversight Panel in 2008, headed by Elizabeth Warren, to address some of these economic policy issues. These oversight opportunities, like many others, constitute both political and policymaking opportunities for Congress.

## Regulations and the Administrative Process

Most rulemaking in the United States and other industrialized societies is now done through the regulatory process.[35] I use the term *regulatory process* in a broad context, to include the rulemaking activities of executive branch agencies as well as those of independent regulatory commissions.[36] Administrative or independent regulatory bodies can issue binding regulations that are subsidiary to congressional legislation—these regulations are sometimes referred to as *secondary legislation*. Issuing such regulations is definitely a legislative or legitimating activity because it makes rules for the society, but the rules must be pursuant to primary legislation that Congress has already adopted.

The volume of regulation writing in the federal government is immense, as can be judged by the size of the *Federal Register,* a daily publication containing all regulations and proposed regulations (approximately 80,000 pages per year), and by the size of the *Code of Federal Regulations* (CFR), which contains all the regulations currently in force. An example of the volume of regulatory activity is provided by the Occupational Safety and Health Administration (OSHA) in the Department of Labor. OSHA, which has been a frequent target of the critics of government regulation, issued 4,600 regulations during the first two years of its existence and continues to issue hundreds of new regulations each year. As of 2010, these amounted to over 4,700 pages of rather fine print in the CFR. Taken together, three areas of public policy—agriculture, labor, and the environment—account for rules requiring approximately 25,000 pages in the *Code of Federal Regulations.*

Although conducted through a legal process, the decision making required for adopting regulations is not majoritarian. If it were, many of the regulations adopted by OSHA and other regulatory bodies might never be approved. Decision making in the regulatory process can be more technical and less tied to politics than is decision making in Congress, although political considerations cannot be neglected entirely, especially by agencies within executive branch departments. Executive branch agencies are directly responsible to the president and consequently are under pressure to issue regulations that address the president's political priorities. Recent presidents have taken greater pains than their predecessors to know what regulations are being issued and to ensure that they match presidential priorities. President George W. Bush, for example, pushed forward a number of regulations during the last days of his administration that President Obama promptly attempted to rescind.[37] Even the regulations issued by independent regulatory agencies cannot afford to stray too far from the basic political and ideological norms of the public; if they do, the agency threatens its own survival or at least its latitude to issue further regulations.

One way in which government has attempted to keep regulatory activity in check is through *regulatory analysis,* the attempt to apply cost-benefit analysis and other forms of economic analysis to regulations before they are adopted. President Reagan, for example, required executive agencies to submit all new regulations for review by the Office of Management and Budget (OMB) and later to report their plans for regulatory activity for the subsequent year. These regulatory reviews were as much political as economic, and they resulted in critics' referring to OMB as the "regulatory KGB."[38] The Republican Congress first elected in 1994 took regulatory analysis even further by mandating, through a formal regulatory review statute (Public Law [Pub. L.] 104-208), that OMB submit to Congress an economic impact assessment of each new regulation. Although the review of regulations by the president's Office of Management and Budget has in many cases been political and ideological, it also has served a legitimation function. In the first place, the elected presidency does have greater legitimacy than does the unelected bureaucracy, especially given the generally low opinion that Americans have of the bureaucracy. It can be further argued that because the techniques used in regulatory analysis are "rational," regulations that survive it may be more likely to make a positive contribution to the well-being of society.[39] That conception of positive contribution is primarily economic, however, rather than taking into account a broader range of concerns (see chapter 17).

Even by the time of the George H. W. Bush administration, some analysts were arguing that deregulation had gone too far, spurring a number of important new regulations, including significant new air pollution standards. The Clinton administration adopted a more activist position in environmental and economic regulation, but it attempted to include more public involvement and public disclosure in the writing of regulations, even though some of the tools of regulatory analysis remained in place.[40]

The George W. Bush administration placed a moratorium on regulation and in 2007 issued an executive order that greatly centralized regulatory power in the executive branch. Barack Obama promptly revoked that executive order and called on the OMB director to assist him in crafting a new plan for regulatory review. Although this came rather late in his administration, President Obama has undertaken some significant attempts at reforming regulation and making a number of administrative processes substantially easier for citizens and businesses.[41]

## Public Access to the Regulatory Process

The process of making regulations is open to the public's influence, as well as that of the president and OMB. The Administrative Procedures Act and several other laws affecting the issuing of regulations require that agencies accept advice and ideas from interested citizens as the process goes forward and that time be given at each stage for affected interests in the society to respond to agency initiatives.[42] For some segments of the economy, in fact, the regulatory process may be more democratic than decision making in Congress. The regulatory process permits affected interests to have direct access to decision makers. In deliberations in Congress, affected interests may be excluded from effective involvement, especially if they represent an interest not widely considered "legitimate" by Congress members. Furthermore, regulatory outcomes may be "in the public interest" to a greater extent than those Congress devises, given that special interest influences are funneled through an administrative process and frequently made subject to judicial review.[43]

Access to the regulation-writing process does not, of course, mean that the ideas of the affected interests or of public interest groups will dominate the decisions finally made. Simply granting access does not protect the interests of segments of the society that are not sufficiently well organized, or sufficiently alert, to make their presentations to the agency. Maintaining access to agency decision making is by no means cost free, so many less well-funded groups may be excluded. This has led some agencies, such as the Federal Trade Commission, to provide funding for interests that might not otherwise have the lawyers and other resources to participate effectively.[44] There are no guarantees of success, but the procedures do indicate the openness of the regulatory process to a range of ideas and opinions.

### The Processes of Writing Regulations

There are two principal ways in which regulation writers collect ideas and opinions. The first, *formal rulemaking,* appears somewhat like a court proceeding, with a formal hearing, the taking of oral testimony from witnesses, and the use of counsel.[45] Formal rulemaking is a time-consuming and cumbersome process, but it is deemed necessary when the social and economic interests involved are sufficiently important. Examples of formal rulemaking are the approval of new medications by the Food and Drug Administration and the licensing of nuclear power plants by the Nuclear Regulatory Commission. The written records generated in such proceedings are important, given that these rulings are important to many elements in society and may be the subject of subsequent discussion and litigation. The procedure for licensing nuclear power plants and the degree of public participation have slowed approval of these facilities and may be a barrier to building new ones (see chapter 14).

The second method of collecting inputs is *informal rulemaking,* which proceeds through several steps. First, the agency must publish in the *Federal Register* a notice of its intent to issue a certain regulation. A period of several months is specified, during which individuals and groups who believe themselves potentially affected by the rule can offer opinions and make suggestions about its content. After the designated time has passed, the agency may issue a draft of the regulation that it would ultimately like to be put into effect. The draft may be based on the suggestions received from affected interests, or it may be what the agency had been planning all along. Then, there is another waiting period for responses to the draft regulation, which may be made directly to the agency or submitted indirectly by having a friendly member of Congress contact the agency with proposed alterations. Then, based on these responses as well as its own beliefs, the agency issues the final regulation, which will have the force of law.

In addition to the two principal forms of rulemaking, administrative law has developed two other ways of adopting regulations. *Hybrid rulemaking* represents an attempt at compromise between the thoroughness of the formal process and the relative ease of the informal process.[46] Hybrid rulemaking came about in part because of the courts,[47] but it also was required by some acts of Congress, especially for environmental policy.[48] Although it does not entail full-scale judicial proceedings, it may require the opportunity to cross-examine witnesses, so as to create a full judicial record that can be the basis for an appeal if further judicial proceedings are demanded.

The other emerging form of rulemaking is *negotiated rulemaking*. Given the complexity of many of the policy areas into which government must now venture and the number of interests involved in each policy, it may be easier to negotiate rules than to attempt to make them administratively.[49] This process can save a great deal of future ill will among the affected interests, and it may actually create policies superior to those that might emerge from a more centrally directed process. Congress recognized the validity of this form of rulemaking by passing the Negotiated Rulemaking Act of 1990 to specify the conditions under which it can be used and the procedures required. Language about negotiated rulemaking has also been included in the authorizing legislation for several executive agencies.[50] While negotiated rulemaking is an attempt to open the process to a variety of actors and thus make it somewhat more democratic, there are also pressures to make the process more technocratic. In particular, there has been increasing interest in regulatory analysis.

The legitimate force of a regulation comes from passage of a statute by Congress and from correct procedures (as specified in the Administrative Procedures Act) in issuing the regulation. In general, issuing a regulation takes about eighteen months from beginning to end and allows for substantial representation of affected groups and individuals. Although the law makes some provision for emergency rulemaking by some agencies, attempts to short-circuit the process will probably result in a regulation's being rejected, no matter how reasonable on its face, if it is appealed through the court system.

The role assigned to affected interests in the regulatory process brings up another point about social decision making. In part as a means of justifying slavery, John C. Calhoun argued that a proper democracy would take into account not only the majority of individuals but also a majority of interests in society. His idea of "concurrent majorities" would have assigned greater importance to pressure groups than does most of American political thought and would have made the opinions of such groups more central in the process of writing regulations. The fundamental point is that a decision should reflect not a simple majority but rather a more complex agreement among a range of segments of society.

The role of interest groups in decision making about regulations is similar to the development of "neocorporatism" in western Europe.[51] The principal difference is that interest groups in the United States usually are not granted quasi-official status as representatives of an economic or social group, as they are in much of Europe. Affected U.S. interest groups are rarely brought together to negotiate a compromise decision, as they might be in many European systems.[52] The Clinton administration took such a step, however, in organizing a conference between logging interests and conservationists in the Pacific Northwest to discuss their differences over protection of the spotted owl.[53] The Bush administration involved industrial groups heavily in making decisions about energy policy, provoking challenges to the exclusivity of the process.[54] In the United States, decision making is still carried out largely within the agency itself, however, with interest groups involved primarily as sources of information. In addition to protecting the interests of their members, interest groups frequently make substantive points about proposed regulations and can help prevent agencies from making errors in their rules.

Finally, regulatory decision making is threatened by the classic problem of *agency capture,* in which agencies that regulate a single industry have tended to become advocates for their industries rather than impartial protectors of the public interest.[55] Capture results from the agencies' need to maintain political support when, especially in the case of independent regulatory commissions, the only logical source of such support is the regulated industry itself. The public is usually too amorphous a body to offer the specific support an agency requires to defend its budget, or even its very existence, before Congress. Thus, reforms intended to remove political pressures from regulatory decision making, by making the agencies independent, have succeeded only in making them independent of one source of political pressure but dependent on another. In Theodore J. Lowi's terminology, the public interest is appropriated for private gain.[56]

The capture argument is less applicable to newer regulatory agencies, which operate across a number of industries, than it is to single-industry regulatory bodies.[57] For example, both the Consumer Product Safety Commission (CPSC) and the Occupational Safety and Health Administration regulate virtually every industry in the country; their advocacy and protection of any one industry might only injure other industries. It is generally too difficult for an industry to capture these cross-cutting regulators, and they are therefore more likely to operate in the public interest—although an agency itself may be permitted to define the public interest. These organizations are not immune from political pressures, however. The George W. Bush administration quickly became embroiled in a conflict over its appointments to the CPSC when it attempted to make the organization more friendly to business in general than it had been during the Clinton years.

The economic crisis following 2008 has provoked a more aggressive form of economic regulation in the United States. In particular, the Obama administration created the Consumer Financial Protection Bureau as part of the

*Mark Wilson/Getty Images*

*The Consumer Financial Protection Bureau (CFPB) is one response of the federal government to the financial crisis beginning in 2008. The formulation of this policy response involved the White House and Congress in a substantial policy debate. President Barack Obama shakes hands with Richard Cordray (r), whom he nominated as director of the CFPB during a press conference on July 18, 2011.*

Dodd-Frank Act addressing the crisis. This bureau was designed to address some of the issues that had become apparent as the causes of the economic crisis became more apparent. This organization is given substantial powers to protect consumers against credit card and mortgage companies that were overcharging or deceiving their customers.

Regulation is a central process in the legitimation of policies, although it is one that many citizens would challenge. Many critics, both popular writers and academics, comment negatively on the making of laws by bureaucrats without the direct congressional involvement that they consider essential for legitimation.[58] These regulatory procedures are "due," however, and they have been ordained by several acts of Congress. Each regulation adopted must have a legislative peg to hang on, but unlike acts of Congress, regulations tend to make specific judgments and decisions, and by so doing, they affect individual interests more directly. Many regulations issued through this process have been criticized as impractical and unnecessary—everyone has his or her favorite silly regulation. Presidents have also been concerned about the effects of regulation on the economy and society and, in general, have sought to create more deregulation than regulation, although the recent economic crisis may alter that trend.[59] Although the regulatory process offers a possibility of greater objectivity and scientific rationality than the more politicized arena of Congress, the very attempt to apply such strict criteria for decisions is the source of many objections.

## The Courts

The courts provide another nonmajoritarian means of legitimating policies. Just as the administrative process has assumed an increasing role in legitimation, the courts have become increasingly involved in issuing authoritative policy statements. Some critics have argued that public policy in the United States is dominated by the court system, and not to the benefit of the types of policies generated.[60] Along with complaints against the administrative process, there have been complaints about judge-made law as a usurpation of congressional prerogatives. Of course, the courts have been involved in legitimating actions and issuing law-like statements in the United States for some time. However, perhaps because of increasing litigation involving social issues (such as gay marriage) and the willingness of the courts to make declarations about remedies to remove violations of the Constitution from federal laws, popular awareness of the role of the courts in making rules for society has grown.

The constitutional basis for the courts to make legitimating decisions is the "supremacy clause," which says that all laws and treaties made in pursuance of the Constitution are the supreme law of the land. In *Marbury v. Madison*, Chief Justice John Marshall decided that it was incumbent on the courts to decide whether or not a law conformed to the Constitution and to declare, if it did not, that the law was void. Following from that fundamental declaration of judicial power, the courts have been able to make rules based on their interpretation of the Constitution. Particularly crucial to their role in legitimating actions is their ability to accept or reject the remedies proposed by the parties to particular disputes. If an action is declared unconstitutional, the courts frequently become involved in determining the actions needed to correct that unconstitutionality.

The most obvious examples of courts prescribing remedies to situations they find unconstitutional have been in cases involving school desegregation and prison overcrowding. In several cases—for example, *Swann v. Charlotte-Mecklenburg Board of Education*—the courts declared that boundaries between school districts constituted intent on the part of local governments to maintain or create racial segregation of the schools and that cross-district busing was the logical remedy for the problem. In other cases, the courts declared that seriously overcrowded prisons constituted cruel and unusual punishment, violating the

Eighth Amendment to the Constitution. Judges then decided that they would take over the prison systems and run them directly to correct the situation, or they would make very specific policies that state administrators were obliged to follow.[61] These decisions represent greater involvement of the courts in mandating state and local government actions than many citizens consider proper.

The role the courts have assumed in legitimating action is twofold. In its simplest sense, the courts may further legitimate the actions of other decision makers by declaring that their actions are acceptable under the Constitution. As mentioned above, American society appears to be becoming increasingly litigious, so that more and more issues are not fully decided until they have been ruled on by the courts. Litigation presents an important means of protecting individual rights in the policymaking process, but it can also greatly slow the implementation of policy. Putting an issue into the court system is sometimes a means of winning a conflict simply by delay, as with the largely successful attempts to block construction of nuclear power plants.

In a second sense, the courts take part in policy legitimation by deciding that certain conditions that exist in society, especially if they are sanctioned by government, are in contradiction of the Constitution and then offering solutions to the problems. The role of the courts in school desegregation is an example of this kind of legitimation, and it occurred not only in busing cases but also in the entire process of desegregation, beginning with *Brown v. Board of Education* (1954). The courts have acted relatively independently of other political institutions and have been active in making decisions and offering remedies that they believed were derived from sound constitutional principles. Just as administrative agencies need a legal peg to hang their rulemaking on, so too do the courts need a constitutional peg on which to hang their interventions. Such terms as *due process* and *equal protection* are sufficiently broad to permit a wide scope for judicial involvement in legitimation activity. For example, the right to privacy was derived from other basic rights in the Constitution, and that right has been used to place limits on state laws outlawing abortion, a continuing policy debate in the United States (see chapter 16).

Because the role of the courts is to judge the constitutionality of particular actions and to protect individual liberties against incursions by government or other individuals, decision making in the courts can be expected to be different from decision making through a legislative body. In many ways, the decisions that courts make are more authoritative than other legitimating decisions, both because of the courts' connection to constitutional authority and because of the absence of any ready recourse once appeals through the court system are exhausted. The courts leave less room for compromise and vote trading than does a legislative body, and they have a less clearly defined constituency, if they have any constituency at all. Finally, a court decision is narrower, speaking to the particular case in question, rather than a general principle of policy to be implemented in other specific cases. Thus, court decisions legitimate certain actions but leave future decisions somewhat ambiguous, whereas decisions taken by both legislatures and administrative agencies are attempts to develop more general principles to guide subsequent actions and decisions.

## Popular Legitimation

The three methods of legitimation discussed so far share one common feature: They are all performed by elites through political institutions. A number of American states provide mechanisms for direct democracy that allow voters to legitimate policy decisions.[62] The referendum is in part a way for state legislatures to pass the buck to the people on issues that the legislators fear might be too hot for the good of their future political careers. Alternatively, in some instances, the public can use these mechanisms to bypass legislatures entirely or to prod them into action. Despite some agitation, direct democracy mechanisms have not been adopted at the federal level.

A *referendum* is a vote of the people on an issue put to them by the legislature or some other authoritative body. Approval by popular vote is required before the measure in question can become law. The majority of states in the United States employ referendums for some policy decisions—typically to pass bond issues and to change the state constitution—but some states use them to enact other legislation as well. An issue thought by the legislature to be sufficiently important, or highly charged politically, may be put to the voters for a decision. This practice certainly satisfies the tenets of democracy, but because voter turnout on referendums is low, it may lead to small numbers of relatively uninformed voters deciding issues of great importance that might be better left to more deliberative bodies. Furthermore, money for publicity campaigns is at least as important in referendums as it is in campaigns for office, so more powerful and affluent interests may be able to influence these elections significantly.

An even more extreme means of involving the public in policymaking is the *initiative*, which permits voters not only to pass on an issue put to them by government but also to place an issue on the ballot themselves. If the requisite number of signatures to a petition is obtained, an item can be placed on the ballot at the next election and will become law if approved by the voters. A number of significant policy measures—most notably the so-called Proposition 13, limiting property taxes and several important environmental laws in California—have been adopted through the initiative process. The initiative poses many of the same problems as the referendum. One difficulty is that important policy disputes, such as the use of nuclear power, become embroiled in political campaigns, so the complex issues involved become trivialized and converted into simple yes–no questions. The initiative provides an avenue for the expression of popular opinion, however, and it gives real power to the voters, who often think of themselves as absent from representative policymaking institutions.

Initiatives sometime are used to overcome legitimation activities by other actors, notably the courts. For example, in the 2008 elections, a number of popular referendums were used to overcome judicial decisions on social issues such as same-sex marriage.[63] Even then, however, the battles may not end because the courts may argue that even popular votes cannot override fundamental rights.

In addition to these established mechanisms for popular involvement, there are continuing calls for additional means of citizen involvement that would go beyond mere voting or public hearings. Such mechanisms are usually discussed under the term *deliberative democracy* or sometimes *strong democracy*.[64] The basic idea is that in a true democracy, the role of citizens would not be confined to selecting their leaders but would extend to the debate and selection of policies. This model has worked in the traditional New England town meeting, and the advocates of expanded participation would like to make it more general. The difficulty is in making it work in a country of 300 million people.

Even if it cannot work for such a large aggregation, deliberative democracy could perhaps be applied in smaller settings when making public policy. For example, there is a tradition of public hearings in the policy process at all levels of government in the United States. The typical pattern has been for citizens to make statements of their views to a decision-making body. In some areas, however, this pattern is being revised to allow citizens to discuss policy among themselves and perhaps even make the final decisions themselves. Ideas such as "citizens' juries" and "deliberative elections" are providing opportunities for increased participation by ordinary citizens.

## Summary

Legitimation is at once the most difficult and the simplest component of the policymaking process. It generally involves the least complex and technical forms of policy analysis, and the number of actors is relatively limited, except in initiatives and referendums. On the other hand, the actors involved are relatively powerful and have well-defined agendas of their own. Consequently, the task of the policy analyst seeking to alter perceptions and create converts to new policies at the legitimation stage is difficult. The type of formal evidence used at other stages of the process may not carry much weight at this stage, and political factors become paramount.

The barriers that the policy analyst faces in attempting to push through his or her ideas are sometimes individual and political, as when members of Congress must be convinced through partisan analysis or vote trading to accept the analyst's concept of the desirable policy alternative. Conversely, the task may be one of altering substantial organizational constraints or mediating turf wars on a decision that would facilitate the appropriate policy response to a problem. The problem may also be a legal one, of persuading the courts to respond in the desired fashion to a set of facts and to develop the desired remedy for the perceived problem. Or, finally, the problem may be a political one in the broadest sense—that is, to persuade the voters (through the political mastery of the analyst) to accept or reject a particular definition of an issue and its solution. This is a great range of problems for the analyst, and it demands an equally great range of skills.

No individual is likely to have all these skills, but someone must make strategic choices as to which skills are the most appropriate for a particular problem. If the problem is to get a dam built, then Congress is clearly the most appropriate arena. If the problem is a civil rights violation, the best place to begin is probably the court system. If the problem is a specialized environmental issue, then the regulatory process is the appropriate locus for intervention. Policies do not simply happen; they must be made to happen. This is especially true given the degree of inertia in American government and the number of points at which action can be blocked. It frequently occurs that the major task of the policy analyst is to define clearly the problem that must be solved. Once that is done, the solution may not be simple, but at least it is potentially analyzable, and a feasible course of action may become more apparent.

CHAPTER 6

# Organizations and Implementation

When people walk around Washington, D.C., they see a number of buildings with blue signs in front of them proclaiming that this is the home of the Department of Commerce, or the Federal Trade Commission, or any of a hundred other organizations. These buildings are the concrete (sorry for the pun) manifestation of the organizational basis of governing. Without these organizations, often collectively referred to as "the bureaucracy," very little will happen in government.

Once a piece of legislation or a regulation has been accepted as a legitimate public law, in some ways, the easiest portion of the policymaking process has already transpired; government must then put the legislation into effect. To do so requires developing organizations that will apply the principles of the legislation to specific cases, monitor the performance of the policies, and perhaps propose improvements in their content and administration. Even policies that are primarily self-administered or that rely on incentives rather than formal regulations require an organizational basis for administration, although the organizations can certainly be smaller than those needed to implement programs that depend on direct administration and supervision. For example, collecting the income tax, which is largely self-administered, requires many fewer people per dollar collected than collecting customs duties, even leaving aside the role of customs agents in controlling smuggling.

American political thinkers have generally denigrated the roles of public administrators and bureaucrats in policymaking. The traditional attitude has been that policy is made by legislatures, and that administrators merely follow the guidelines the legislation sets forth. Such an attitude fails to take into account the important role of administrative decision making, and especially the importance of decision makers at the bottom of the organization, in determining the effective policies of government.[1] The real criminal justice policy of a nation or city is to a great extent determined by the way the police enforce the laws, just as the real social welfare policy is determined by decisions made by caseworkers or even receptionists in social service agencies. We have noted that bureaucrats play an important role in interpreting legislation and making regulations to put it into effect; they also make important decisions while applying laws and regulations to individual cases.[2]

It is also customary to consider government as an undivided entity and to regard government organizations as monolithic. In fact, that is not the case at all. We have mentioned that American government is divided horizontally into a number of subgovernments and vertically into levels of government in a federal system. But within the federal bureaucracy, and even within a single cabinet-level department, there are a number of bureaus, offices, and sections, all competing for money, legislative time, and public attention. Each has its own goals, ideas, and concepts about how to address the public problems it is charged with administering. As in the making of legislation, those ideas will influence the implementation of legislation. Implementation often involves conflicts and competition, rather than neat coordination and control, and struggles over policy content persist long after Congress and the president have enacted legislation. Policies, as operating instruments, commonly emerge from those conflicts as much as they do from the initial design of legislation. Policies should not necessarily be designed to be implemented easily, but anyone interested in policy outcomes must monitor implementation as well as formulation.

## Dramatis Personae

The organization of the federal government is complicated not only because of the number of organizations it comprises but also because of the number of different kinds of organizations. There is no single organizational format for accomplishing the work of government, and the various organizations exist in different relationships to elective officials and even to government authority as a whole. In addition to the three constitutionally designated institutional actors—the president, Congress, and the courts—at least eight different organizational formats exist within the federal government (see Table 6.1).[3] One of these is a catchall category for organizations that are difficult to classify within the other major types.

The absence of a basic organizational format weakens central policy coordination and thus contributes to the incoherence of the policy choices the federal government makes. Moreover, the eight forms of organizations themselves have a great deal of internal variation. As Table 6.1 shows, the organizations differ greatly in size; they can also differ greatly in their internal organization. For example, the Department of Agriculture consists of almost fifty offices and bureaus, whereas the Department of Housing and Urban Development is structured around several assistant secretaries and their staffs, with few operating agencies within the department.

TABLE 6.1 Examples of Employment in Federal Organizations

| Kind of organization | Employment |
|---|---|
| Executive departments | |
| Department of Defense (civilian) | 675,700 |
| Department of Education | 4,331 |
| Executive Office of the President | |
| Office of Management and Budget | 482 |
| Council on Environmental Quality | 18 |
| Legislative organizations | |
| Government Accountability Office | 3,172 |
| U.S. Commission on International Religious Freedom | 17 |
| Independent executive agencies | |
| Social Security Administration | 62,400 |
| Appalachian Regional Commission | 9 |
| Independent regulatory commissions | |
| Nuclear Regulatory Commission | 3,713 |
| Commodity Futures Trading Commission | 442 |
| Foundations | |
| National Science Foundation | 1,350 |
| African Development Foundation | 29 |
| Public corporations | |
| U.S. Postal Service | 757,400 |
| Neighborhood Reinvestment Corporation (NeighborWorks) | 322 |
| Other | |
| Smithsonian Institution | 4,833 |
| Office of Government Ethics | 76 |

*Source:* Office of Personnel Management, *Federal Civilian Workforce Statistics, 2007.*

The most familiar forms of organizations are the fifteen *executive departments,* such as the Department of Defense and the Department of Health and Human Services. Each of those is headed by a secretary who is a member of the president's cabinet and who is directly responsible to the president. The executive departments should be regarded not as uniform wholes but as collections, or "holding companies," of relatively autonomous agencies and offices.[4] Departments vary in the extent to which their constituent agencies respond to central direction. Some, such as the Department of Defense, have relatively high degrees of internal coordination; others, such as the Department of Commerce, are extremely decentralized.[5]

Although the cabinet departments are important, in some instances, an individual agency may have more political influence than does the department as a whole. One such agency is the Federal Bureau of Investigation (FBI), which is part of the Department of Justice but often can operate as if it were independent. In some instances, it is not entirely clear why an agency is located in one department rather than another—for example, why the U.S. Forest Service is located in the Department of Agriculture rather than the Department of the Interior, or why the U.S. Coast Guard is now located in the Department of Homeland Security, rather than in Treasury, Commerce, Defense, or Transportation, where it has resided at various times in its history.

Although the executive departments are linked to constituencies and provide services directly to those constituencies, the organizations within the *Executive Office of the President* exist to assist the president in carrying out his tasks of control and coordination of the executive branch as a whole.[6] The most important units within the Executive Office of the President are the Office of Management and Budget (OMB), the Council of Economic Advisers, the National Security Council (NSC), the Domestic Policy Council, and the White House Office. The first two assist the president in his role as economic manager and central figure in the budgetary process. The NSC provides advice and opinion on foreign and defense issues, independent of that provided by the Departments of State and Defense, and the Domestic Policy Council performs a similar role for domestic policy. The White House Office manages the everyday complexities of serving as president of the United States and employs a number of personal advisers for the president. The units within the Executive Office of the President now employ roughly 1,800 people—an insignificant number compared with a total federal civilian workforce of more than two million but quite large when compared with the personal offices of the chief executives of other nations.[7]

Congress has also created organizations to assist it in policymaking. The three most important *legislative organizations* are the Government Accountability Office (GAO), the Congressional Budget Office (CBO), and the Congressional Research Service. Legislatures in democratic political systems generally audit the accounts of the executive to ensure that public money is being spent legally. The Government Accountability Office (formerly named the General Accounting Office) was strictly a financial accounting body for most of its existence but in the 1970s began to expand its concerns to the cost-effectiveness of expenditures.[8] For example, in one of its reports, the GAO agreed that the Internal Revenue Service (IRS) had been acting perfectly legally in the ways it sought to detect income tax evaders but recommended changing the IRS program to one the GAO considered more efficient. Few organizations in the federal government have escaped similar advice.[9] The CBO has its major policy impact on the annual preparation of the budget; its role is discussed thoroughly in chapter 7. The Congressional Research Service, located within the Library of Congress, assists Congress in policy research and prepares background material for individual members and committees.

In addition to the executive departments responsible to the president, there are a number of *independent executive agencies*. They perform executive functions, such as implementing a public program, but they are independent of the executive departments and generally report directly to the president. The independence of these agencies can be justified in several ways. Some, such as the National Aeronautics and Space Administration (NASA), are mission agencies created outside departmental frameworks so as to have greater flexibility in completing their mission. Others, such as the Environmental Protection Agency (EPA) and the Small Business Administration, are organized independently to highlight their importance and in recognition of the political power of the interest groups supporting them. Moving the Social Security Administration out of the Department of Health and Human Services in March 1995 was recognition of the importance and size of that organization, which spends close to one-quarter of the federal budget. Other organizations such as the General Services Administration and the Office of Personnel Management provide services to a number of government departments, so locating them in any one department might create management difficulties.

The fifth form of organization is the *independent regulatory commission*. Three such organizations are the Federal Trade Commission, the Federal Energy Regulatory Commission, the Consumer Product Safety Commission, and the newly created Consumer Financial Protection Bureau. These commissions are different from independent executive agencies in that they do not perform executive functions but act independently to regulate certain sectors of the economy.[10] Once the president has appointed the members of a commission, the formulation and application of its regulations are largely beyond his control. The absence of direct political support often results, however, in the "capture" of the regulatory commissions by the interests they were intended to regulate.[11] Over time, lacking ties to the president or Congress, the independent agencies may seek the political support of the regulated interests to obtain their budgets, personnel, or legislation from the other institutions in government. The tendency toward capture is not so evident in agencies that must regulate several industries—the Federal Trade Commission or Consumer Product Safety Commission, for example.[12] Not all economic regulation is conducted through the independent commissions, and some important regulatory agencies, such as the Occupational Safety and Health Administration (OSHA) and the Food and Drug Administration (FDA), are in executive departments—OSHA in the Department of Labor and the FDA in Health and Human Services.

There are also several *foundations* within the federal government, the principal examples being the National Science Foundation, the National Endowment for the Humanities, and the National Endowment for the Arts. The foundation format is intended primarily to separate the organization from the remainder of government because of a justifiable fear of creating a national orthodoxy in the arts or in science and thereby stifling creativity. Again, the foundation's relative autonomy enables government to support the activities while being removed from the decisions. The independence of the foundations is far from complete, however, for Congress has not been reluctant to intervene in their decisions, for example, by criticizing projects supported by the National Endowment for the Arts that conservatives alleged were "pornography."[13] The NEA responded with a "general standard of decency" for projects it funds, a provision that the Supreme Court said did not violate the First Amendment.[14] The president can also attempt to influence the foundations, primarily through the appointment of directors and board members.

The government of the United States has generally avoided becoming directly involved in the economy other than through regulation, but there are a number of *public corporations* in the federal government.[15] For example, since 1970, the U.S. Postal Service has been a public corporation rather than part of an executive department, as it was before. That one public corporation employs over 750,000 people, or almost one-third of all federal civilian employees. Another public corporation, the Tennessee Valley Authority, has about 6 percent of the total electrical generating capacity of the United States. There are also some very small public corporations, such as the Overseas Private Investment Corporation, which employs less than 200 people.

A public corporation is organized much like a private corporation, with a board of directors and stock issued for capitalization. The principal difference is that the board members are all public appointees and the stock is generally held entirely by the Department of the Treasury or by another executive department. There are several reasons for choosing the corporate form of organization. One is that these organizations provide marketed goods and services to the population and hence can be better managed as commercial concerns.[16] This is also a means of keeping some government functions at arm's length, so the president and Congress are not held directly responsible for the actions of the organizations.

In addition to the wholly owned government corporations, there is a group of organizations described as "quasi-governmental," or in the "twilight zone." Examples of these are the National Railroad Passenger Corporation (Amtrak), the Corporation for Public Broadcasting, and the Federal Reserve Board. These organizations have some attributes of public organizations—most important, access to public funding—but they also have some attributes of private organizations. They are similar to public corporations except that a portion of their boards of directors is appointed by private sector organizations; the board of Amtrak is appointed in part by the member railroad corporations. Also, some of their stock may be owned by the cooperating private sector organizations. Employees of these quasi-governmental organizations generally are not classified as public employees, and they generally are not subject to other public sector regulations, such as the Freedom of Information Act.

The justification for the formation of quasi-governmental organizations such as these is again to permit government to become involved in a policy area without assuming any real or apparent direct control. The federal government subsidizes certain activities—passenger railroad service would almost certainly have vanished from the United States without Amtrak—but its intervention is not as obvious as other forms of public sector involvement in the economy. Intervention by a quasi-governmental organization also gives the public a greater role in decision making and provides greater representation of private interests such as affected corporations. And as with the Corporation for Public Broadcasting, this form of organization permits the federal government to become involved in an area from which it has traditionally been excluded.

It is important to understand just how vital these quasi-governmental organizations are to the federal government. For example, the Federal Reserve Board fits comfortably into this twilight zone, given its isolation from executive authority and its relationship to its member banks. But the Federal Reserve Board is responsible for making monetary policy for the United States and thereby has a significant—probably now the most significant—influence on the nation's economic conditions.[17] Similarly, the Corporation for Public Broadcasting is a significant complement to commercial radio and television broadcasting, although Congress often fails to support public broadcasting with anything like the funds available to commercial broadcasting.[18]

The quasi-governmental organizations in the federal government have been in the public eye during the 2008 and 2009 economic crisis more than they might have liked. Two of these organizations, the Federal National Mortgage Association (Fannie Mae) and the Federal Home Mortgage Corporation (Freddie Mac), were government-sponsored corporations that served as a secondary market for mortgages, enabling private banks to make more home loans than they might otherwise. In the process of performing this task, however, these two organizations came to hold a number of almost worthless subprime mortgages and were so threatened that the federal government had to buy, and in essence nationalize, them.[19] The economic crisis also led to the partial inclusion of several banks and insurance companies into this quasi-governmental arena of government.

Finally, there is the catchall category *other organizations,* which contains several regional commissions that coordinate economic or environmental policy in parts of the country. Various claims commissions, the Administrative Office of the United States Courts, and the Sentencing Commission operate on the fringes of the judicial process. And organizations such as the Smithsonian

Institution, the National Academy of Sciences, and the American Red Cross are mentioned in federal legislation and receive subsidies, but they are far removed from the mainstream of government action.

We should note several other points about the complexity of the structure of the federal government. One is the redundancy built into the system. First, both Congress (through the Congressional Budget Office) and the Executive Office of the President (through the Office of Management and Budget) have organizations to deal with budgeting and with many other economic aspects of government. Because of the doctrine of separation of powers, such duplication makes a great deal of sense, but the overlap still conflicts with conventional managerial thinking about eliminating duplicative organizations.

Second, we have seen that some units in the Executive Office of the President duplicate activities of the executive departments. Most notably, presidents appear to demand foreign policy advice other than that provided by the Departments of State and Defense, and they get it from the National Security Council. This demand may be justified, as the executive departments have their own existing policy commitments and ideas, which may limit their ability to respond to presidential initiatives in foreign policy. But during at least every administration since Richard Nixon's, conflicts have arisen between the two sets of institutions, and the management of foreign policy may suffer as a result. In most instances, the conflict has been perceived as one between the experienced professionals in the Department of State and committed amateurs in the National Security Council. Such conflicts were evident at the outset of the Iraq War and have persisted to some extent throughout the conflict.

In other policy areas, several federal organizations may regulate. For example, both the Federal Trade Commission and the Antitrust Division of the Department of Justice are concerned with antitrust policy and monopolies.[20] Some redundancy in this activity can be rationalized as a means of limiting error, as well as providing alternative means for accomplishing the same tasks and even alternative definitions of the issues.[21] If the redundant institutions are occupied by ambitious men and women, however, the potential for conflict, "gridlock," or excessive regulation is substantial.[22]

It is also interesting that not all central fiscal and management functions of the federal government are located in the Executive Office of the President. Several important management functions—monetary policy, personnel policy, debt management, and taxation—are controlled by agencies outside the president's office, one by an organization in the twilight zone. This diffusion of duties and responsibilities limits the president's ability to implement his policy priorities and consequently to control the federal establishment for which he is held accountable politically and to some extent legally. Reactions to the fiscal crisis in 2008 and 2009 indicate that these organizations can work together effectively when necessary, but in more normal times, they will operate quite separately.[23]

Third, we have mentioned variations in the "publicness" of organizations in, or associated with, the federal government. Some organizations are clearly public: They receive their funds from the federal budget; their employees are hired through public personnel systems; and they are subject to legislation such as the Freedom of Information Act, which attempts to differentiate public from private programs.[24] Other organizations appear tied to the private sector as much as to government: They receive some or all of their funds as fees for services or interest on loans; they have their own personnel policies; and they are only slightly more subject to normal restrictions on public organizations than is Starbucks. For a president—who will be accountable to voters and to Congress for the performance of the federal government—this presents an immense and perhaps insoluble problem. How can the president really take responsibility when so many of the organizations charged with implementing his policies are beyond effective control? This is but one of many difficulties a president encounters when attempting to put his policies into effect, and it is a bridge to our discussion of implementation.

The issue of the publicness of organizations arose in a particularly controversial form in President George W. Bush's proposal to use "faith-based organizations" to deliver a range of social services.[25] The organizations involved are primarily private, and the tradition of the separation of church and state in the United States makes their affiliation with government more suspect than would be the case with other private organizations. Many citizens expressed concern about the possibility that the organizations would proselytize recipients of their services or make religious adherence a criterion for receiving them. Some of the organizations themselves expressed doubts about closer involvement in the public sector, fearing that entanglement with government would reduce their capacity to maintain religious and programmatic freedom. All of that said, President Obama announced his own attempts to involve faith-based organizations in delivering public services.

## Implementation

All the organizations we have been discussing are established to execute legislation or to monitor that execution. Once enacted, laws do not go into effect by themselves, as was assumed by those in the (presumed) tradition of Woodrow Wilson, who discussed "mere administration."[26] In fact, one of the most important things to understand about government is that it is a minor miracle that implementation is ever accomplished.[27] There are so many more ways of blocking intended actions than there are of making results materialize that all legislators should be pleased if they live to see their pet projects not only passed into law but also actually put into effect. Although this is perhaps an excessively negative characterization of implementation, it should underline the extreme difficulties of administering and implementing public programs.

A large number of factors may limit the ability of a political system to put policies into effect. Rarely will all the factors affect any single policy, but all must be considered when designing a policy and attempting to translate it into real services for citizens. Any one of the factors may be sufficient to cause the failure or suboptimal performance of a policy, and all may have to be in good order for the policy to work. In short, it is much easier to prevent a policy from working than it is to make it effective.

### The Legislation

The first factor that affects the effective implementation of a policy is the nature of the legislation that establishes it. Laws vary in their specificity, clarity, and the policy areas they attempt to influence, as well as in the extent to which they bind the individuals and organizations charged with implementing them to perform in the way the writers intended. Unfortunately, both legislators and analysts sometimes overlook the importance of the legislation. Laws that are easier to implement are, everything else being equal, more difficult to pass. Their specificity may make it clear who the winners and losers are and thus complicate the task of building the political coalitions necessary for passage.

### Policy Issues

Legislators frequently choose to legislate in policy areas where they lack sufficient information about the causes of problems to enable them to make good policy choices. If we refer to the four kinds of policy formulation discussed earlier (see Figure 4.1), we can estimate the likelihood of effective implementation of a policy. We anticipate that the highest probability of effective implementation will occur with both sufficient information about the policy area and adequate knowledge of the causes of the problems. In such situations, government can design legislation to solve, or at least ameliorate, the problem. On the other hand, effective implementation is not likely in policy areas where there is inadequate information and little knowledge about problem causes.

The other two possible combinations of knowledge of causation and information may differ very little in their likelihood of effective implementation, although we would expect a somewhat better probability when there is knowledge of the patterns of causation, as opposed to more basic information. If the underlying process is understood, it would appear possible to formulate policy responses based on available information, however poor the information may be. When there is inadequate information, policy responses involve a certain amount of excessive reaction, or overkill. If the underlying process is misunderstood, or is not understood at all, there is little hope of effectively implementing

*President Lyndon Johnson and his wife, Lady Bird, center left, leave the home in Inez, Kentucky, of Tom Fletcher, a father of eight who told Johnson he'd been out of work for nearly two years, on April 24, 1964. The president visited the Appalachian area in eastern Kentucky to see conditions firsthand and announce his War on Poverty from the Fletcher porch.*

a policy except by pure luck. In such instances, governments often wind up treating symptoms, as they do with the problems of crime and delinquency, instead of dealing with the underlying social processes.

Perhaps the best example of a large-scale policy formulation and implementation in spite of inadequate knowledge of patterns of causation was the War on Poverty in the United States during the 1960s. There were (and are) as many theories about the causes of poverty as there were theorists, but there was little real understanding even of the basics of the economic and social dynamics producing the problem.[28] War was thus declared on an enemy that was poorly understood. Sen. Daniel P. Moynihan put it this way:

> This is the essential fact: The Government did not know what it was doing. It had a theory. Or rather a set of theories. Nothing more. The U.S. Government at this time was no more in possession of a confident knowledge as to how to prevent delinquency, cure anomie, or overcome that midmorning sense of powerlessness than it was the possessor of a dependable formula for motivating Vietnamese villagers to fight Communism.[29]

Not only was it a war, but it was also a war based on something approaching a dogma about the plan of attack—for example, using large-scale and rather expensive programs involving direct services to clients. Arguably, the programs were doomed to fail because they were based on dubious assumptions about the society and the mechanisms for approaching such problems. But the interventions, if misguided, had the political appeal and visibility that smaller-scale efforts would have lacked.

A more recent example of a policy made without adequate knowledge was the Strategic Defense Initiative and subsequent attempts to build an antimissile defense during the George W. Bush administration. These policies "forced" the development of technologies that would be at least as important for domestic as for defense purposes.[30] The Bush administration's stress on alternative power sources for automobiles is another recent example of technology forcing (see chapter 14).[31] The Obama administration's agreement with automobile manufacturers to increase the gas mileage of their products significantly will also depend upon developing new technologies.[32]

Technology forcing is an interesting if somewhat novel approach to designing public programs, but it is not one that can be recommended as a strategy for policymaking. It has been successful in some policy areas, in part because the problems being dealt with were aspects of the physical world rather than the more complex social and economic realities that governments often face.[33] The potential difficulties should not be taken to mean that governments should just keep to their well-worn paths and do what they have always done in the ways they always have. Instead, they should caution that if one expects significant results from programs based on insufficient understanding of the subject matter, those expectations are likely to be dashed.

## Political Setting

Legislation is adopted through political action, and the political process may plant within legislation the seeds of its own destruction. The very compromises and negotiations necessary to pass a bill may ultimately make it virtually impossible to implement. An example is the thousand-page stimulus bill adopted in early 2009. The speed with which it was drafted and the compromises contained within it began to produce implementation problems almost as soon as it was adopted.

The effects of the political process on legislation are manifested in different ways. One is vague language: Lack of clarity may be essential to develop a coalition for passage, as every time a vague term is made specific, potential coalition members are lost. But by phrasing legislation in vague and inoffensive language, legislators risk leaving their intent unclear to those who must implement the law, thus allowing the implementers to alter the meaning of the program substantially. Phrases such as "maximum feasible participation," "equality of educational opportunity," "special needs of educationally deprived students," and that favorite vague concept "public interest" are all subject to various interpretations, many of which could betray the true intent of the legislators. Even words about which most citizens can agree may produce problems during implementation, as when the Reagan administration attempted to define ketchup as a "vegetable" under the School Lunch Program, and more recently, the tomato sauce on pizza also was considered to meet the criterion of a vegetable.[34]

In addition to coalitions formed for the passage of a single piece of legislation, other coalitions may have to be formed across several pieces of legislation—the classic approach to logrolling. To gain support for one favored measure, a coalition-building legislator may have to trade his or her support on other measures. In some instances, this may simply increase the overall volume of legislation enacted. In others, it may involve passing legislation that negates, or decreases the effects of, desired legislation. Some coalitions that must be formed are regional, so it may become virtually impossible to give one region an advantage, even one justified by economic circumstances, without making commensurate concessions to other regions, thereby nullifying the intended effect. It is also difficult to make decisions that are redistributive across economic classes—either the legislation will be watered down to be distributive (everyone gets a piece of the pie) or additional legislation will be passed to spread the benefits more broadly. A good deal of the politics of taxation exemplifies this tendency in writing legislation.[35]

Similar problems of vagueness and logrolling can occur when other institutions make rulings that must be implemented. In a number of instances, a judicial decision intended to mandate a certain action has been so vague as to be difficult or impossible to implement. One of the best examples of this lack of clarity is the famous decision in *Brown v. Board of Education,* which ordered schools to desegregate with "all deliberate speed." Two of those three words, *deliberate* and *speed,* appear somewhat contradictory, and the decision did not specify exactly what the phrase meant. Similarly, the police are prohibited from searching an individual, an automobile they stop, or a home without "probable cause," but that phrase was left largely undefined until a series of cases required the courts to be clearer. The process of writing regulations in administrative agencies, intended to clarify and specify legislation, can itself create ambiguities, which require more regulations to clarify and cause more delay in implementation.

In summary, politics is central to the formulation of legislation, but the results of the political process often are such that legislation cannot be implemented effectively. The compromises necessitated by political feasibility may result in just the reductions in clarity and purpose that make laws too diffuse to be implemented so as to have a real effect on society. The vagueness of legislation may make room for another type of politics dominated more by interest groups than by elected officials.

## Interest Group Liberalism

Theodore J. Lowi's concern about government involvement in the more abstract aspects of human behavior helps illuminate some of the problems of vagueness in legislation.[36] Lowi's argument is that the United States has progressed from concerted and specific legislation, such as the Interstate Commerce Act of 1887, which established clear standards of practice for the Interstate Commerce Commission, to abstract and general standards, such as "unfair competition" in the Clayton Act of 1914. The tendency has been extended through even more general and diffuse aspects of human behavior in the social legislation enacted after the 1960s to regulate what Lowi refers to as the "environment of conduct." It is simply more difficult to show that a person has discriminated against another person on the basis of race, color, or sex than it is to show that a railroad has violated prohibitions against discriminatory freight rates.

Lowi believes that the problems arise not from the commendable intentions of these vague laws but from the difficulty of implementing them. The diffuseness of the targets specified and the difficulty of defining standards subject policies for regulating those behaviors to errors in interpretation during implementation. It also becomes more difficult to hold government accountable when it administers ambiguous legislation. The "interest group liberalism" inherent in U.S. politics, in which the public interest tends to be defined in terms of many private interests, and especially the private interests of better-organized groups, means that the implementation of a piece of legislation will generally differ greatly from the intentions of those who framed it. Implementation will be undertaken by agencies that are themselves tied to clients and to particular definitions of the public interest, and which will not want to be swayed from their position. Problems of accountability created by the deviation of policies in practice from the intentions of their framers can only alienate the clients and frustrate the legislators, and perhaps the administrators as well.

## The Organizational Setting

As noted earlier, most implementation is undertaken by organizations, especially organizations in the public bureaucracy. Given the nature of public organizations, and of organizations in general, the probability that one of them will effectively implement a program is not particularly high. The reason is not moral failings on the part of the bureaucracy but simply the internal dynamics of large organizations, which often limit their ability to respond to policy changes.

To begin to understand what goes wrong when organizations attempt to implement programs, a model of "perfect" administration may be useful. Christopher Hood proposes five characteristics of perfect administration of public programs:

1. Administration would be unitary; it would be one vast army all marching to the same drummer.
2. The norms and rules of administration would be uniform throughout the organization.
3. There would be no resistance to commands.
4. There would be perfect information and communication within the organization.
5. There would be adequate time.[37]

Clearly, these conditions are often absent in organizations, and almost never are all of them present. Because governments depend on large organizations to implement their policies, difficulties inherent in large organization—public or private—arise. The difficulties need not be insurmountable, but they need to be understood and anticipated if possible, if successful implementation is to occur. Just what characteristics and difficulties in organizations lead to difficulties in implementation?

### *Organizational Disunity*

Organizations are rarely unitary administrations—indeed, a number of points of disunity almost always exist in organizational structures. One is the disjunction between the central offices of organizations and their field staffs. Decisions may be made by politicians and administrators sitting in national capitals, but those decisions must be implemented by people in the field who may not share the values and goals of the administrators in the home office.

The disjunction of values may take several forms. A change in central values and programs may occur as a result of a change in presidents or in Congress, and the field staff may remain loyal to the older policies. For example, the Clinton administration inherited a government shaped in most areas by twelve years of Republican presidents. The George W. Bush administration, in turn, had to deal with the residual organizational values from the Clinton years.[38] After eight years of Republican dominance, the Obama administration expressed some concerns about the reliability of some public organizations. Problems with field staff over policy changes produce frustration for politicians nominally in control of policymaking and make implementation of policies that violate the norms of the existing field staff extremely difficult.

A more common disparity between the goals of field staffs and those of the home office may occur as the field staff is "captured" by clients. Field staff members are frequently close to their clients, and they may adopt their clients' perspective in their own relationships with the remainder of the organization.[39] This can happen when the clients are relatively disadvantaged and the organization is attempting either to assist them or to exercise some control over them. The identification of staff members with their clients is fostered by frequent contact, sympathy, empathy, and quite commonly genuine devotion to a perceived mission that is in contrast to the mission fostered by the central office. This pattern of conflict between central and field staffs emerged when welfare reform (see chapter 12) began to have negative impacts on recipients and social workers attempted to protect their clients.[40] Whatever the cause, this identification makes implementation of centrally determined policy difficult.

Field staffs may also find that if they are to perform their tasks effectively, they cannot follow all the directives coming to them from the center of the organization. In such instances, to obtain substantive compliance, the organization members may not comply with procedural directives. For example, in a classic study of the FBI, Peter M. Blau found that field agents frequently did not comply with directives requiring them to report the offering of a bribe by a suspect.[41] The agents had found that they could gain greater cooperation from a subject by using the threat to have the person prosecuted for offering the bribe at any time. Their performance of the task of prosecuting criminals was probably enhanced, but it was done at the expense of the directive from the central office.

Eugene Bardach and Robert A. Kagan have argued that regulatory enforcement in the United States could be improved if field staffs were granted greater latitude for independent action.[42] They believe that rigidities resulting from strict central controls actually produce less compliance with the spirit of regulations than would a more flexible approach. This interest in enhancing regulatory latitude can, however, be contrasted with the continuing (and strengthening) interest in control over bureaucracies, especially regulatory bureaucracies. Congress is concerned with efficient enforcement, but it is often more concerned with ensuring that what is being implemented corresponds with its intentions.[43] In attempting to design programs to ensure compliance, lawmakers paradoxically may limit enforcement.

### Standard Operating Procedures

Organizations develop standard operating procedures (SOPs). When a prospective client walks into a social service agency, the agency follows a standard pattern of response: Certain forms must be filled out, designated personnel interview the prospective client, and specific criteria are applied to determine the person's eligibility for benefits. Likewise, if a blip appears on the radar screen of a defense installation, a certain set of procedures is followed to determine if the blip is real and, if so, whether it is friendly or hostile. If it should be hostile, further prespecified actions are taken.

Standard operating procedures are important for organizations because they reduce the amount of time spent processing each new situation and developing a response. The SOPs are the learned response of the organization to particular problems; they represent to some extent the organizational memory in action. SOPs may also be important for clients, as they are adopted at least in part to ensure equality and fairness. Without SOPs, organizations might respond more slowly to each situation, they might respond less effectively, and they would probably respond more erratically.

Although SOPs are generally beneficial for organizations, they can also constitute barriers to good implementation. This is most obvious when a new policy or a new approach to an existing policy is being considered. An organization is likely to persist in defining policies and problems in the standard manner, even when the old definition or procedure no longer helps it fulfill its mission. For example, when Medicare was added to the responsibilities of the Social Security Administration, the agency faced an entirely new set of concerns in addition to its traditional task of making payments to individuals. In particular, it assumed responsibility for limiting the costs of medical care. It chose to undertake that responsibility in much the same way that it would have attempted to manage problems arising from pensions—by examining individual claims and denying those that appeared to be unjustified. It took the Social Security Administration some time to focus attention on more fundamental and systemic problems of medical cost inflation and to develop programs such as diagnostic-related groupings (see chapter 11). The agency took some time even to cope with adding the Supplemental Security Income program, which was much closer to its original portfolio of income maintenance policies but more similar to a means-tested program than to a social insurance program.[44]

There is thus a need to design public programs and administer organizations that will consistently reassess their goals and the methods they use to reach them. In some instances—for example, correlating the number of births and the future need for schools—the response should be programmed to be almost automatic; other situations will require more thought and greater political involvement. Organizations do not like to perform such reassessments, which may threaten both the employees of the organization and its clients. One reason for creating organizations with standard operating procedures is to ensure some stability and predictability, but that stability can become a barrier to success when problems and needs change.

Standard operating procedures also tend to produce inappropriate or delayed responses to crises. The military, perhaps more than any other organization, tends to employ SOPs and to train its members to carry them out in the absence of commands to the contrary. The brief invasion of Grenada in 1983 encountered difficulties when the communication SOPs of the navy and army did not correspond, so the soldiers on the island could not communicate with the ships providing them support. Soldiers found that the best way to communicate was to use their telephone credit cards to call the Pentagon, which would then communicate with the navy. The response of the air force to the airplanes aimed at New York and Washington on 9/11 was slowed because they were conditioned to think of threats coming from across the borders of the United States, not from within. Like the military, fire and police units develop standard operating procedures, and some of those routines—and the consequent inability to recognize the novelty of new events—appear to have contributed to the huge loss of life among firefighters when the World Trade Center collapsed.

A standard means of avoiding the constraining effects of SOPs is to create a new organization to run a new program. When the Small Business Administration was created in 1953, Congress purposely did not locate it in the Department of Commerce, whose SOPs tended to favor big business. The Office of National Drug Control Policy was established within the Executive Office of the President to ensure both its priority and its independence from other organizations such as the Drug Enforcement Administration and the Customs Bureau. There are, of course, limits to the number of new organizations that can be set up, for the more that are created, the greater the chance that interorganizational barriers to implementation will replace the barriers internal to any one organization. Drug policy suffers from coordination problems among the numerous agencies—the three just mentioned, as well as the Coast Guard, the Department of Defense, the FBI, and numerous state and local authorities, among others—involved in the policy area. This lack of coordination is evident even after the creation of a national "drug czar" to provide direction to the programs.

SOPs aid in the implementation of established programs, whereas they are likely to be barriers to change and to the implementation of new ones. Procedures may be too standardized to permit effective response to nonstandard situations or nonstandard clients; they may create rigidity and inappropriate responses to novel situations. Established procedures often prompt organizations to try to classify new problems as old ones for as long as they can and to continue to use familiar responses even when the problems appear demonstrably different to an outsider.

## Organizational Communication

Another barrier to effective implementation is the improper flow of information within organizations. Because government organizations depend heavily on the flow of information—just as manufacturers rely on the flow of raw materials—accurate information and the prevention of blockages of information are extremely important to their success. Unfortunately, organizations, and particularly public organizations, are subject to inaccurate and blocked communication.

In general, information in bureaucracies tends to be concentrated at the bottom of the hierarchy.[45] Field staffs are in closer contact with the organization's environment, and technical experts tend to be clustered at the bottom of organizations, with more generalist managers concentrated at the top. This pattern means that if the organization is to respond to changes in its environment and if it is to make appropriate technical decisions, then information at the bottom must be transmitted to the top, and then directions must be passed back down to the bottom for implementation. Unfortunately, the more levels through which information has to be transmitted, the greater is the probability that it will be distorted when it is finally acted on.

The distortion in communications may result from random error or from *selective distortion,* as when officials at each stage of message transmission attempt to transmit only the information that they believe their superiors wish to hear or that they think will make them look good to their superiors. The superiors, in turn, may attempt to estimate what sort of distortion their subordinates may have introduced and try to correct for it.[46] The result of the transmitting of messages through a hierarchical organization thus is frequently rampant distortion and misinformation that limit the organization's ability to make effective decisions.

Some characteristics of an organization may improve the transmission of information through its hierarchy. If organization members share a common technical or professional background, their communication with one another should be less distorted. But a common language can also prevent an organization from responding to new situations or producing innovative solutions and diminish its ability to communicate effectively with other organizations. Attempts by the organization to create internal unity through training and socialization should improve internal patterns of communication.[47] And the "flatter" the organization is—the fewer levels through which communication must go before being acted on—the less distortion is likely to occur.[48]

Another way to improve communication in organizations is to create more, and redundant, channels. President Franklin Roosevelt developed personal ties to lower-level members of federal organizations and placed his own people in organizations to be sure that he would receive direct and unvarnished reports from the operating levels of government.[49] A president or manager might also build in several channels of communication to make them function as checks on one another. Again, Roosevelt's frequent development of parallel organizations (e.g., the Works Progress Administration and the Public Works Administration) provided him with alternative channels of information about the progress of his

New Deal. In more contemporary times, the creation of several channels of advice and communication to the president about national security policy and drug policy may be a way of ensuring that the information he receives is both accurate and complete.

A particularly interesting threat to effective organizational communication is secrecy.[50] Although a certain level of secrecy is important for some government organizations, it can inhibit both communication and implementation. Secrecy frequently means that a communication cannot be shared because it has been classified; other parts of the organization or other organizations are consequently denied what they need to know. The Cuban missile crisis provides numerous examples of how the military's penchant for secrecy can prevent a rapid response to situations. Secrecy can produce inefficiency, as when FBI agents had to spend time reporting on one another when they infiltrated subversive organizations, such as the Ku Klux Klan. To make themselves more acceptable to the organizations they had infiltrated, the agents tended to be among the most vociferous members, and consequently, they became the subjects of a disproportionate share of reports by other agents. More recently, the Central Intelligence Agency's (CIA) identification of spies in its midst was slowed because parts of the organization were unwilling to share information with other parts of the public sector. Secrecy may be counterproductive even when it is justified. For example, one argument holds that the interests of military deterrence are best served by informing an adversary of the full extent of one's arsenal instead of masking its strength, since uncertainty may create a willingness to gamble on the strength of the opponent, whereas openness may prevent war.

In modern organizations, knowledge is power, and the inability of an organization to gather and process information from its environment will harm its performance. Clearly, the management of communication flows within an organization is an important component of taking raw information and putting it into action. Most organizations face huge problems in performing even this simple (or apparently simple) task and as a consequence do not implement their programs effectively. Their internal hierarchical structures, differential commitment to goals, and differences in professional language all conspire to make organizational communication more difficult than it may appear from the outside.

### Time Problems

Hood points to two time problems that inhibit the ability of public organizations to respond to situations in their policy environments. One is a linear time problem, in which the responses of the organization tend to lag behind the need for the response.[51] This often happens in organizations that have learned their lessons too well and that base their responses on previous learning rather than on current conditions. The problem is similar to what occurs with standard operating procedures, but it has less to do with processing individual cases than with designing the mechanisms for putting new programs into effect. Organizations frequently implement programs to deal with a crisis that has just passed rather than with the crisis they currently face or might soon face. To some degree, the U.S. armed forces in Vietnam used the lessons they had learned, or thought they had learned, in World War II and the Korean conflict. Unfortunately for them, a highly mechanized, technologically sophisticated, and logistically dependent fighting force broke down in a tropical guerrilla war. Lessons presumably learned from the Gulf War proved to be something of a problem in the Iraq War.

Government also has at times failed to respond even to obvious social changes, such as demographic ones. The fact that newborn babies will five or six years later require places in public schools sometimes seems to amaze public officials. Governments have not prepared well for the baby boomer generation that will begin to reach retirement age around 2012 but have allowed this large population to proceed through the life cycle without making adequate plans for the burdens it will impose on the Social Security retirement system and on health care (see chapters 11 and 12).

Other time problems are cyclical, and delay in acting can contribute to their persistence and severity. This is especially important in making and implementing macroeconomic policy, in which, even if the information available to a decision maker is timely and accurate, any delay in response may exaggerate economic fluctuations. If a decision maker responds to a threatened increase in inflation by reducing money supplies or reducing spending, and if that response is delayed for a year, or even for a few months, it may only accelerate an economic slowdown that has emerged in the meantime from other causes. Thus, it is not sufficient merely to be right; an effective policy must be both correct and on time if it is to have the desired effect.

### Horseshoe-Nail Problems and Public Planning

The final organizational problem in implementation arises when organizations plan their activities incompletely or inaccurately. Hood calls these "horseshoe-nail" problems because failure to provide the nail results in the loss of the horse and eventually the battle.[52] And because government organizations often must plan for implementation with limited information, problems of this kind are likely to arise in the public sector. Examples abound: passing requirements to inspect coal mines but failing to hire inspectors, as emerged after several mine disasters in Pennsylvania and West Virginia; requiring clients to fill out certain forms but neglecting to have the forms printed; forgetting to stop construction of a $160 million highway tunnel that leads nowhere once the plan to build the rest of the highway is abandoned. There are countless examples of this political and policy version of Murphy's law.[53]

To ensure effective management and implementation, planners must identify the crucial potential blockages in their organization and allow for them in their planning. With a new program or policy, such planning may be extremely difficult; the problems that will arise may be almost impossible to anticipate. Some planners use these difficulties to justify incremental or experimental approaches when introducing new policies. Instead of undertaking large projects with the possibility of equally large failures, they may substitute smaller projects whose failure or unanticipated difficulties would impose minimal costs but would help prepare the organization to implement full-scale projects. The problem, of course, is that such programs often are not permitted to grow sufficiently to reach an effective level but may remain small and "experimental."

Some programs will be effective only if they are comprehensive and implemented on a large scale. Paul Schulman's analysis of the National Aeronautics and Space Administration points out that a program such as the space program designed to reach a major goal within a limited time and with engineering as opposed to a pure research focus—must be large in scale to be effective.[54] It has been argued that the War on Poverty, instead of being the failure portrayed in the conventional wisdom, actually was never tried on a scale that might have made it effective. In contrast, the so-called "war on cancer" was implemented in the 1970s as if it were a program that required a centralized mission format, whereas in reality, it required a more decentralized structure to allow scientific research to pursue as many avenues as possible.[55] Those who design programs and organizations must be very careful to develop them to match the characteristics of the problem and the state of knowledge about the subject. Even if objectively correct, a strategy may still provoke political criticism, as the failure to launch a "war on AIDS" did in many circles.[56] The "war on terror" may be better fought by a collection of largely autonomous and decentralized, albeit coordinated, organizations than by the comprehensive and hierarchically organized program that is the presumed purpose of the Department of Homeland Security.

## Interorganizational Politics

Few policies, if any, are designed and implemented by a "single lonely organization."[57] Although individual organizations have their problems, many more difficulties are encountered in the interactions among several organizations attempting to implement a policy. The problems of organizational disunity and communication become exaggerated when the people involved are not bound even by a presumed loyalty to a single organization but have competing loyalties to different organizations, not all of them interested in the effective implementation of a particular program.[58] The tendency may be exaggerated when a central element in implementation is private contractors, whose goals of profit and contract fulfillment conflict with goals of service delivery and accountability in the public sector.[59]

Jeffrey L. Pressman and Aaron Wildavsky, who popularized the concern for implementation several decades ago, speak of the problems of implementing policies through a number of organizations (or even within a single organization) as problems of "clearance points"—defined as the number of individual decision points that must be agreed to before any policy intentions can be translated into action.[60] Even if the decision makers at each clearance point are favorably disposed toward the program in question, there may still be impediments to reaching agreement on implementation. Some problems may be legal, some may be budgetary, and others may involve building coalitions with other organizations or interests in the society.

Statistically, one would expect that if each decision point is independent of the others and if the probability of any individual decision maker's agreeing to the program is 90 percent (.9), then the probability of any two agreeing is 81 percent (.9 × .9). For three points, the probability would be 73 percent (.9 × .9 × .9), and so forth. Pressman and Wildavsky determined that there were at a minimum seventy clearance points in the implementation of the Economic Development Administration's decision to become involved in public works projects in Oakland, California.[61] With this number of clearance points, the probability of all of them agreeing, given an average probability of 90 percent for each clearance, would be less than one in a thousand. Only if there were a probability greater than 99 percent at each clearance point would the odds in favor of implementation be greater than fifty-fifty. Of course, implementation is not just a problem in statistics, and the political and administrative leaders involved in the process can vastly alter the probabilities at each stage. With so many independent clearance points and limited political resources, however, a leader may well be tempted to succumb to the inertia inherent in the implementation system.

Judith Bowen has argued that the simple statistical model that Pressman and Wildavsky propose may understate the probability of successful implementation.[62] Bowen points out that if persistence is permitted and each clearance point can be assaulted a number of times, the chances for successful implementation increase significantly. She also explains that the clearance points may not be independent, as assumed, and that success at one clearance point may produce increased probability of success at subsequent ones. The clever implementer can also make strategic choices about which clearance points to try first and how to package the points so that some success can be gained even if the whole campaign is not won. Thus, although successful implementation is still not perceived to be a simple task, it is subject to manipulation, as are other stages of the policy process. The clever policy analyst can improve his or her probabilities of success by understanding how to intervene most effectively.

The administrative reforms of recent decades have tended to exacerbate the problems of implementation by including more actors in the process, especially private sector (both for-profit and not-for-profit) organizations. A common admonition now is that governments should "steer but not row"[63]—that is, governments should make policy but depend on other organizations that may be more efficient for the actual implementation. This strategy is presumed both to reduce costs (and public employment) and to boost the quality of the services delivered to citizens. Whether those goals are achieved or not, it is clear that the new style of administration builds in more clearance points and hence more opportunities for policies to go astray in the implementation process.

### Vertical Implementation Structures

One problem in implementation occurs vertically within the hierarchical structures of government. I have described some problems of intergovernmental relations in the United States that are associated with the several levels of government. The impact of intergovernmental relations is especially evident with federal social and urban legislation, in which all three levels of government may be involved in putting a single piece of legislation into effect. For example, the welfare reforms of the 1990s depended on the actions of state governments, local governments, and private contractors to move poorer citizens off public assistance and into productive work, and that has produced an immense implementation problem.[64] Some of the failures to rebuild quickly in the Gulf states following Hurricane Katrina can be linked to the complexity of the implementation structures.

A vertical implementation structure gives rise to several possibilities for inadequate implementation or none. One source of such problems is simple partisan politics, when state or local governments and the federal government are controlled by different political parties and consequently have different policy priorities. Localities may for other reasons have different policy priorities than the federal government and may choose to implement programs differently than the federal government desires. Two good examples of such differences can be seen in the resistance of local governments to federally mandated scattering of public housing in middle-class neighborhoods and in the resistance of most state and local governments to federal proposals to locate nuclear waste disposal facilities in their territory. The state of Nevada, for example, fought the federal government for more than twenty years over the proposed location of a repository for nuclear waste at Yucca Mountain.

Even if local governments want to do what the federal government would have them do, they sometimes lack the resources to do it. Local governments have attempted to resist various federal mandates, such as day care quality standards, claiming they lacked the funds to meet the standards imposed.[65] States and localities sometimes have few incentives to comply with federal directives. For example, in the Elementary and Secondary Education Act of 1965 the states were to receive their grants merely for participating in the program, without having to do anything in particular to improve education.

The increasing emphasis on the use of the private sector to achieve public purposes means that implementation is increasingly being performed by private groups as well as by subnational governments. For example, tenants organizations have begun to manage public housing projects, and churches and other charitable organizations became contractors for services under the AmeriCorps volunteer program in the Clinton administration. This pattern of implementation can easily create the problems of capture described earlier. For instance, some attempts to regulate the amount of fish that can be caught in the Atlantic have been implemented by the affected parties (fishermen and processors, among others) through eight management councils, with the result that overfishing has been permitted and fish stocks have been seriously depleted.[66]

## Horizontal Implementation Structures

In addition to problems incurred in achieving compliance across several levels of government, difficulties may occur in coordinating activities and organizations horizontally. That is, the success of one agency's program may require the cooperation of other organizations, or at least the effective coordination of their activities. As one simple example, the Department of Agriculture has assisted the Department of Health and Human Services in implementing the Women, Infants and Children's (WIC) nutrition program by bargaining to keep the price of infant formula lower, so that the funds provided by WIC to women can go farther.

Coordination can break down in several ways. One is through language and encoding difficulties. Individual agencies hire certain kinds of professionals and train all their employees in a certain manner. As a result, the Great Society–era Model Cities Program's housing experts decided that the problems of residents resulted from substandard housing, whereas employment experts thought that the problems arose from unemployment, and psychiatric social workers perceived them as resulting from personality problems. Each group of professionals, in other words, was oblivious to the perspectives of the other groups and consequently found it difficult to cooperate in treating the "whole client"—one of the stated objectives of the Model Cities Program. This was strongly demonstrated in the pattern of referrals among agencies. The vast majority of referrals of clients from one agency to another occurred within policy areas, rather than across policy areas.[67] Clients who visited an agency seeking health care would frequently be referred to another agency, most commonly another health care agency rather than a social welfare agency that might help them receive enough money to obtain better nutrition, which might have been as effective as medical care in improving their health.

Sometimes, the objectives of one organization conflict with those of other organizations. At a basic level, an organization may be unwilling to cooperate in the implementation of a program simply because the success of another agency may threaten its own future prospects. On a somewhat higher plane, organizations may disagree about the purposes of government or about the best way to achieve the goals on which they do agree. Or an agency may want to receive credit for providing a service that inevitably involves the cooperation of many organizations, and its insistence on receiving credit may prevent anything from happening. For example, several law enforcement agencies knew about a major drug shipment, but they allowed it to slip through their fingers because they could not agree on which of the "cooperating" agencies would make the actual arrest and receive the media attention.

Even a simple failure to think about coordination and to understand linkages among programs may prevent effective implementation. Most citizens have heard their share of horror stories about the same streets being dug up and repaired in successive weeks by different city departments and private utilities. Equally dismaying stories are told of reporting requirements issued by a variety of federal agencies that require contradictory definitions of terms or that involve excessive duplication of effort by citizens. Corruption is rarely at the root of these problems, but that neither prevents the loss of efficiency nor makes citizens any happier about the problems of management in their government.

Coordination of programs appeared to become more difficult during the 1990s, and the problems become more important every day. As the federal government began to rely more on the private sector and on state and local governments to deliver public programs, it became more difficult to provide integrated services. This remains true despite widespread pressure to make the public sector more "user friendly" and "customer oriented."[68] Effective coordination is increasingly important as the interactions among various program providers become more evident. For example, social programs are increasingly dependent on effective job training programs, and economic success is increasingly dependent on educational policy. The demands of homeland security require a number of organizations to coordinate and cooperate in ways that previously have not been considered.

## From the Bottom Up?

Scholars have argued that many implementation problems are a function of their being considered from a top-down perspective.[69] That is, the person evaluating implementation looks at what happens to a law and considers that the bureaucracies have failed because they have not produced outcomes exactly like those intended by the framers of the legislation. The assumption here, rather like Hood's, is that bureaucracies should march to a single drummer and that the drummer should be Congress or the president. Anticipating such an orderly approach may be expecting too much from the U.S. government, given its complexity and the multiple and competing interests organized within the system. Indeed, the appropriate questions may be, In what policy areas can we accept slippage between goals and outcomes? and, What can be done to produce greater compliance in the most sensitive areas?[70]

An alternative to the top-down perspective is to think of implementation from the bottom up, or through "backward mapping."[71] This approach holds that the people who design public programs should think about the ease, or even the possibility, of implementation during the development stage. Programs should consider the interests of the lower echelons of the bureaucracy, their contacts with the program's clients, and indeed the values and desires of the clients themselves. With these factors in mind, policymakers should then design policies that can be readily implemented. The program may not fulfill all the original goals of the policy formulators, but it will be able to gain a higher degree of compliance than a program based on strict legal norms of compliance and autonomy of policy formulators.

The bottom-up concept of implementation and program design is appealing, for it promises rather easy victories in the complicated wars involved in making programs work. Even if those promises could be fulfilled, however—and there are reasonable doubts—there are important problems with the approach. The most important is the normative problem that political leaders and their policy advisers have the responsibility (and usually the desire) to formulate programs that meet their political goals and fulfill the promises made in political campaigns.[72] Programs that are implemented easily may not meet those goals. That is perhaps especially true when conservative administrations attempt to make changes in social programs through field staffs committed to more liberal goals or when liberals attempt to carry out expansionary economic policies through more conservative economic institutions inside and outside government. Governments may wind up doing what they can do, or what they have always done, rather than what they want to do.

In addition, the ability of agency field staffs to define what is feasible may allow them substantially greater control over policy than is desirable within a democratic political system. Their definition of *feasibility* may be excessively conservative, limiting the options that might be available with proper design. Indeed, there may be little reliable evidence about what really is feasible in implementation and what is really impossible.[73] Too-facile definitions of feasibility may undervalue the abilities and leadership of politicians and administrators alike.

### The Third Generation?

After the original top-down and bottom-up implementation studies, and some attention to political factors in implementation, there might be said to be a third generation of thinking about the problem.[74] It attempts to replace these relatively simple models with more complex descriptions of the relationships that exist in the process of implementation. Much of the earlier literature on implementation tended to provide a single answer, regardless of the question. The third wave, on the other hand, tends to show answers to most questions about implementation with the accurate if somewhat unsatisfying, "It depends."

The real task for understanding implementation, then, is to identify what factors serve as contingencies for success or failure. Some of the factors are expressly political, and others are a function of the type of policy being implemented. Still others may be a function of the organizations that are used as the agents of implementation. Specifying why a program succeeds or fails involves the identification and interaction of all these factors. That is a complex research task, just as it is a complex practical task to design an implementation structure that can actually make a program function in something close to the manner intended by the people who designed it.

The study of interorganizational politics has been extended to cover more completely the organizations in the private sector.[75] These organizations add to the complexity of implementation, but they also add to the capacity of the public sector to make its programs work, and work efficiently.

### Summary

American government is a massive, complex, and often confusing set of institutions. It contains numerous organizations but lacks any central organizing principle. Much of the structure of American government was developed on an ad hoc basis to address particular problems at particular times. Yet even with a more coherent structure, many of the same problems might still arise in the implementation of programs. Many problems are inherent in any government but are exacerbated by the complex and diffuse structure of government in the United States. For public policy, implementation is a vital step in the process of governing because it involves putting programs into action and producing effects for citizens. The difficulty of producing desired effects, or indeed any effects, means that policy is a much more difficult commodity to deliver to citizens than is commonly believed. The barriers to effective implementation often discourage individuals and organizations from engaging in the activities devised for their benefit. Public management then becomes a matter of threatening or cajoling organizations into complying with stated objectives or of convincing those organizations that their goals can best be accomplished through the programs that have been authorized.

CHAPTER 7

# Budgeting:
# Allocation and Public Policy

IMPLEMENTING PUBLIC POLICIES requires money as well as institutional structures. The budget process provides the means of allocating the available resources among numerous competing purposes. In principle, all resources in the society are available to government, although in the United States, a politician who openly expressed such a position probably would not last beyond the next election. Moreover, almost all the purposes for which politicians and administrators wish to spend public money have some merits. The question is whether those merits are sufficient to justify using the resources in the public sector instead of in the private sector. Finding answers to such questions requires economic and analytical judgment, as well as political estimates of the feasibility of proposed policies.

When President Barack Obama assumed office in 2009, he faced a number of significant budget issues. He inherited a large deficit from the Bush administration, and the economic crisis was adding to it at an unprecedented rate. Furthermore, during the campaign, Obama had made a number of commitments to health care, education, and the environment. He had also pledged to attack pork barrel spending and entitlement programs. But it was not clear how much could be saved through those means.[1] In short, President Obama had major budget problems. The battles with Congress over the budget in the time since his election have demonstrated not only the extent of those problems but also the central political position of the budget.

For any president, two aspects of budgeting sometimes merge. The question of system-level allocation between the public and private sectors is the first. How many activities or problems justify government intervention into the economy for the purpose of taxing and spending?[2] Could the best interest of society be served by keeping the money in the hands of businesses or individuals for their investment decisions, thereby allowing some potentially beneficial programs in government to go unfunded? Or do the equity, equality, and economic growth potentially produced through a public project justify officials' expending political capital to pass and collect or increase a tax? The system-level questions also include the proportion of its expenditures government should finance through taxes and fees; in other words, how large a deficit could the United States afford to run?[3]

The second aspect is how available public sector resources should be allocated among competing programs. When they devise a budget, decision makers function within resource constraints—they must base their decisions on the assumption that no more revenue will come in (or that no larger deficit will be accepted). Decision makers must therefore attempt to allocate available money for the greatest social, economic, and political benefit. Doing that is not an easy task, of course, because of differing opinions about what uses of the money would be best. Decision makers also are often constrained by commitments to fund existing entitlement programs before they can begin to allocate the rest of the funds to other worthy programs.[4] Because money can be divided almost infinitely, however, it offers a medium for resolving social conflicts that indivisible forms of public benefits, such as rights, often do not. Therefore, although there are a number of possible justifications for budgetary decisions, we must be aware that political considerations tend to dominate and that many of the most effective arguments revolve around votes and coming elections.

## Characteristics of the Federal Budget

Before discussing the *budget cycle,* through which the federal budget is constructed each year, we should explain several of the budget's fundamental features. These features are in some ways not only beneficial to decision makers but also serve to constrain them and at times help create undesirable outcomes; the format of the budget is not politically neutral but directly affects the outcomes of the process. The frequent attempts to reform almost all features of the budgetary process thus encounter resistance from the interests advantaged by the status quo, so the process as well as the content of budgeting become part of the political debate.

### An Executive Budget

The federal budget is an executive budget, prepared by the president and his staff, approved by Congress, and then executed by the president and the executive branch. That has not always been the case. Before 1921, the federal budget was a legislative budget, prepared almost entirely by Congress and then executed by the president. One major tenet of the government reform movement of the early twentieth century was that an executive budget was a necessity for more effective management.[5] According to that doctrine, no executive should be required to manage a budget that he or she had no part in planning or preparing.

The Budget and Accounting Act of 1921 marked a new stage in the conflict between the executive and legislative branches over their respective budgeting powers.[6] In general, budgetary power has accumulated in the executive branch and in the Executive Office of the President, in large part because of the analytical dominance of the Office of Management and Budget (OMB; it was called the Bureau of the Budget until 1971). The excesses of the Nixon administration—and to some degree those of the Johnson administration during the Vietnam War— led to the establishment of the Congressional Budget Office (CBO) in a provision of the Congressional Budget and Impoundment Control Act of 1974. The CBO gives Congress much of the analytical capability that the executive branch has. The budget committees in both houses also give Congress greater control over budgeting than before passage of the act. Congress played an active part in the 1997 budget settlement that contributed to attaining a balanced budget as early as fiscal year 1998.[7] Nevertheless, Congress remains in the position of primarily responding to budgetary initiatives from the White House, rather than initiating the budget.

### The Line Item

Despite several attempts at change, the federal budget remains a *line-item* budget. That is, the final budget document allocates funds into categories—wages and salaries, supplies, travel, equipment, and so forth—for specific purposes within an agency. These traditional categories give Congress some control over the executive branch, allowing the legislature, through the Government Accountability Office (formerly the General Accounting Office), to make sure that the money is spent under legal authority. It is more difficult, however, to determine if it is being spent efficiently and effectively. The rigidities of the line-item budget may actually inhibit the effectiveness of good government managers by limiting how they can spend the money. For example, it may be that more equipment and fewer personnel could do the same job better and/or more cheaply, but managers generally are not given that option.

Input controls, such as line-item budgets, are now considered inefficient means of control over public organizations and their managers. Critics have argued that it would be better to give a manager a relatively unrestricted budget and then judge him or her on the achievement of program goals. Congress, however, tends to want to maximize its oversight over the executive instead of allowing managerial flexibility. Through the Government Performance and

Results Act of 1993, Congress attempted to overlay the fundamental line-item structure of the budget with a more performance-based system of assessment and allocation, thus using output controls to replace the input controls.[8] That system has had some success, but the older patterns of emphasizing financial control rather than performance may come to dominate even a reformed budget process.

## An Annual Budget

The federal budget is primarily an annual budget. Agencies now must submit five-year forecasts for each of their expenditure plans, but they are used primarily for management purposes within OMB. The budget presented to Congress and the appropriations bills that Congress eventually adopts together constitute only a one-year expenditure plan. The absence of a more complete, multiyear budget makes planning difficult for federal managers, and it does little to alert Congress to the long-term implications of spending decisions made in any one year. A small outlay in one year may result in much larger expenditures in subsequent years, and it may create a clientele that cannot be eliminated without significant political repercussions. In other cases, a project that would have to run for several years to be truly effective may be terminated after a single year. Many state and local governments in the United States now operate with multiyear budgets, but the federal government still does not. OMB's annual advice to the agencies serves as a guide for preparing budgets and provides some information about expectations for five years, but the information for the four "out years" is speculative at best.

One of the several recommendations of the Gore commission (the National Performance Review) was to move the federal government toward a biennial budget to enable organizations to plan more effectively and deliver services more efficiently.[9] Such a reform might also allow Congress to reduce the amount of time that it must devote to the budget process, freeing it to spend more time addressing its other legislative duties. Again, however, Congress does not appear to favor this reform, largely because it might lessen congressional control over the executive branch. Neither has there been much enthusiasm for capital budgeting or better identification of the investment aspects of federal expenditures.[10]

## The Budget Cycle

The annual, repetitive nature of the budget cycle is important, for agency officials might behave differently if they did not know that they have to come back year after year to obtain more money from the same OMB officials and members of Congress. In addition to the emphasis that repetition places on building trust and a reputation for dependability, it allows policy entrepreneurs multiple opportunities to build their case for new programs and changes in budget allocations. Preparing the budget is an extremely long, deliberative process, requiring a year or more to complete and allowing for a great deal of analysis and political bargaining among the many parties involved.[11]

### Setting the Parameters: The President and His Friends

Most of this chapter pertains to the microlevel allocation of resources among programs, rather than the setting of broad spending and economic management policy. It is necessary, however, to begin with a brief discussion of the initial decisions concerning overall levels of spending and revenue, which will influence subsequent decisions about programs. Inevitably, changes in particular programs and in socioeconomic conditions (wars, recessions, and the like) influence the total spending levels of government, so this stage mostly involves setting targets rather than making final decisions.

The first official act of the budget cycle is the development of estimates of the total size of the federal budget to be prepared for the fiscal year, the so-called spring review. Although agencies and OMB will already have begun to discuss and prepare expenditure plans, the letter from the president through OMB (Circular A-11, usually issued in June) is an important first step in the formal process, providing a statement of overall presidential budgetary strategy and of the financial limits within which agencies should begin to prepare their budgets. In addition to setting the overall parameters, the letter presents some detail on how the parameters apply to individual agencies. Naturally, the past experience of budgeting officials in each agency gives them some further sense of how to interpret the general parameters. Defense agencies, for example, knew after the inception of the war on terror that they were not necessarily bound by the parameters, whereas planners of domestic programs with little client support and few friends on Capitol Hill could only hope to do as well as the letter had led them to believe they might.

The overall estimates for spending are prepared some sixteen months before the budget goes into effect. For example, the fiscal year 2010 budget went into effect on October 1, 2009, but the planning for that budget began in June 2007 or even earlier. For any budget, this means that the economic forecasts on which spending estimates are based may be far from the prevailing economic reality when the budget is actually executed. Any deviation from those economic forecasts is important for the outcomes of the budget. The recession of 2008–2009, for example, will mean a reduction in revenues and an increase in expenditures—people who are out of work do not pay income or Social Security taxes, and they demand unemployment insurance payments and, perhaps, welfare.

*The budget is a central political event each year. The importance of the budget has been emphasized by the continuing debates over deficits and debt in the federal government. Vice President Joe Biden and President Barack Obama (center) meet with House Speaker John Boehner (left) and House Majority Leader Eric Cantor (right) in the Oval Office to discuss the debt limit and deficit reduction on July 20, 2011.*

Those important economic forecasts are not entirely the product of technical considerations; they are also influenced by political and ideological considerations. For example, the Reagan administration's belief that "supply-side" economics would produce larger revenues through increased economic activity led to a serious overestimation of the amount of revenue. The choice of that approach to public finance began the large federal deficits that characterized U.S. public finance for over fifteen years (see chapter 9).[12]

The preparation of economic and expenditure estimates is the result of the interaction of three principal actors—the Council of Economic Advisers (CEA), OMB, and the Treasury—which are collectively referred to as the "troika."[13] The CEA is, as the name implies, a group of economists who advise the president. Organizationally, they are located in the Executive Office of the President. The role of the CEA is largely technical, forecasting the state of the economy and advising the president on the basis of the forecasts. Its economists also mathematically model the probable effects of budgetary choices on the economy. Of course, the economics of the CEA must be tempered with political judgment, for mathematical models and economists do not run for office—but presidents must. One former chair of the Council of Economic Advisers said that he relied on his "visceral computer" for some of the more important predictions.[14]

Despite its image as a budget-controlling organization, OMB comes as close to a representative of the expenditure community as exists within the troika. Even though the agencies whose budgets OMB supervises find it difficult to perceive OMB as a benefactor, some of its personnel may be favorably disposed toward expenditures. They see the huge volume of agency requests coming forward and are aware of a large volume of uncontrollable expenditures, such as Social Security benefits, that will have to be funded regardless of changes in economic circumstances.

The Treasury represents the financial community, and historically it has been the major advocate of a balanced budget within the troika, for it must cover any debts created by a budget deficit by issuing government bonds. The principal interest of the Treasury in troika negotiations often is to preserve the confidence of the financial community at home and abroad in the soundness of the U.S. economy and the government's management of it. Some particular (and increasing) concerns of the Treasury may regard relationships with international financial organizations, such as the International Monetary Fund, that are important for maintaining international economic confidence. The increased role of the Federal Reserve in the economic policy process and in financing the deficit has made it more of a player in the budget than it had been in the past.

The Federal Reserve has to some extent begun to play part of the role that the Treasury had typically played in the budget process. Because of the importance of monetary policy in economic policy in general and the particularly important role in the economic recovery, the Federal Reserve has moved into a more central role in the budget process. This central role for the "Fed" has helped to integrate monetary and fiscal policy (see chapter 9) but also undermines its political independence that has been important for maintaining its legitimacy.

Even at this first step in the budgetary process, a great deal of hard political and economic bargaining occurs among the participants. This bargaining will be more intense in a period of economic crisis. Each member of the troika must compete for the attention of the president as well as protect the interests of the particular professional, organizational, and political community it represents in budgeting. But the bargaining is just the beginning of a long series of political debates and bargains as agencies attempt to get the money they want and need from the budgetary process.

### Agency Requests

As in so much U.S. policymaking, government agencies are central actors in the budget process.[15] Whether independent or within a cabinet-level department, the agency is responsible for the initial preparation of estimates and requests for funding and working with OMB, and, if applicable, the agency's executive department budgeting personnel. OMB provides guidance and advice about total spending levels and particular aspects of the agency's budget. The agency may have to coordinate with other agencies within the department where it is located. Accomplished through a departmental budget committee and the secretary's staff, this coordination is necessary to ensure that the agency is operating within presidential priorities and that the secretary will provide support in defending the budget to OMB and Congress.

The agency must be aggressive in seeking to expand its own expenditure base while recognizing that it is only one part of a larger organization.[16] In other words, the agency must be aggressive but reasonable, seeking more money but realizing that it operates within the constraints of what the federal government as a whole can afford. The executive department must recognize its responsibilities to the president and his program, as well as to the agencies under its umbrella. The cabinet secretary must be chief spokesperson for his or her agencies at higher governmental levels, although agencies often have more direct support from interest groups and perhaps from Congress than does the department as a whole. Thus, a cabinet secretary may not be able to go far in following the president's program if that program seriously jeopardizes ongoing programs, and their clienteles, in his or her department. This problem reflects the general fragmentation of U.S. government, which places much of the power and the operational connections between government and interest groups at the agency, rather than the department, level.

An agency may employ a number of strategies in seeking to expand its funding but is restrained by the knowledge that budgeting is an annual cycle. Any strategic choice in a single year may preclude the use of that strategy in later years and, perhaps more important, may destroy confidence that OMB and Congress have had in the agency.[17] For example, an agency may employ the "camel's nose" or "thin wedge" strategy to get modest initial funding for a program, knowing that it will have rapidly increasing expenditure requirements. Even if that strategy is successful once, however, the agency may be assured that any future requests for new spending authority will be carefully scrutinized. Agencies are well advised to pursue careful, long-term strategies and to develop trust among the political leaders who determine their budgets.

## Executive Review

After the agency has decided on its requests, it passes them on to the Office of Management and Budget for review. OMB is a presidential agency, one of whose principal tasks is to amass all the agency requests and conform them to presidential policy priorities and to the overall levels of expenditure desired. That may make for a tight fit, as some spending programs are difficult or impossible to control, leaving little space for any new programs the president may consider important. Even recent conservative presidents have found it difficult to make overall spending levels conform with their view that government should tax and spend less.

After OMB receives the estimates, it passes them on to its budget examiners for review. In the rare case in which an agency has actually requested the same amount, or less, than OMB had planned to give it, there is no problem. In most cases, however, the examiners must depend on their experience with the agency in question, as well as whatever information about programs and projected expenditures they can collect, to make a judgment concerning the necessity and priority of requested spending increases.

On the basis of agency requests and the information developed by the examiners, OMB holds hearings, usually in October or November, at which each agency must defend its requests. Although OMB sometimes seems to be committed to cutting spending, several factors prevent it from wielding its axe with excessive vigor. First, it is frequently possible for an agency to execute an end run around the hearing board by appealing to the director of OMB, the president, or ultimately to its friends in Congress. Also, some budget examiners come, over time, to favor the agencies they are supposed to control, so they may become advocates of an agency's requests rather than the fiscal controllers and financial conservatives they are expected to be, a pattern similar to regulatory capture.

The results of the hearing are forwarded to the director of OMB for the "director's review," which involves the top staff of the bureau. At this stage, through additional trimming and negotiation, the staff attempts to pare the final budget down to the amount desired by the president. After each portion of the budget has passed through the director's review, it is forwarded to the president for final review and then sent on for compilation into the final budget document. This stage necessarily involves final appeals from agency and department personnel to OMB and the president, as well as last-minute adjustments to take into account changes in economic forecasts and desired changes in the total size of the budget. The presidential budget is then prepared for delivery to Congress within fifteen days after it convenes in January each year. Presidents differ in the amount of time they devote to budgeting, but the budget is perceived as a statement of the priorities of the president and his administration, even if it is really prepared largely by the public servants at OMB.

In this way, the presidential budget is made ready to be reviewed through the appropriations process in Congress, but the two branches of government will already have begun to communicate about the budget. By mid-November each year, the president must submit to Congress the "current services budget," which includes "proposed budget authority and estimated outlays that would be included in the budget for the ensuing fiscal year . . . if all programs and activities were carried on at the same level as the fiscal year in progress."[18] This is a form of volume budgeting, for it posits a constant volume of public services and then determines the price. During a period with rapidly rising inflation, such as the 1970s and early 1980s, this constant-service budget can give Congress an early warning about current expenditure commitments if they are extended. But the estimates are subject to substantial inaccuracy, either purposive or accidental, so they provide a rough estimate for planning purposes, but only that.

## Congressional Action

Although the Constitution specifically grants it the powers of the purse, by the 1960s and 1970s, Congress had ceased to be dominant in budgetary decisions. Congress attempted a counterattack, largely through the Congressional Budget and Impoundment Control Act of 1974 described above, which established the budget committees in each house of Congress. These committees develop two concurrent resolutions each year outlining spending limits, much as the troika does in the executive branch. As mentioned, the act also established the Congressional Budget Office to give the budget committees a staff capacity similar to what OMB provides for the president.[19] This enhanced analytic capacity is important for Congress in understanding its budgetary activity, but the need to implement somewhat more immediate and less analytic expenditure reforms has tended to make the changes less important than they might have been.

Decisions on how to allocate total spending among agencies and programs are made by the appropriations committees in both houses.[20] These committees are extremely prestigious and powerful, and those serving on them generally are veteran members of Congress. Members tend to remain on these committees for long periods, developing not only budgetary expertise but also political ties with the agencies they supervise as well as with their own constituencies.[21] The two committees—and especially the House Appropriations Committee—do most of their work through subcommittees, which may cover one executive department, such as Defense; or a number of agencies, such as Housing and Urban Development and independent executive agencies; or a function, such as public works. Most important, the whole committee does not closely scrutinize the decisions of its subcommittees, nor does the House of Representatives as a whole frequently reverse the decisions of its appropriations committee.

Scrutiny by the whole House has increased, however, in large part because of the general opening of congressional deliberations to greater "sunshine," or public view. In addition, the politics of deficit reduction has tended to place greater restraints on committee and subcommittee autonomy. The committees must now submit appropriations levels that correspond to the total spending levels permitted under the previously enacted joint resolutions on taxing and spending. Provided that the committees can keep their appropriations within those predetermined levels, they can have substantial autonomy; once an agency's budget has been accepted by a subcommittee, that budget has, in all probability, been decided.[22]

Beginning with the presidential recommendations, each subcommittee develops an appropriations bill, or occasionally two, for a total of thirteen or fourteen bills each year. Hearings are held, and agency personnel are summoned to testify and justify the size of their desired appropriations. After those hearings, the subcommittee will "mark up" the bill—make such changes as it feels are necessary from the original proposals—and then submit it, first to the entire committee and then to the House of Representatives. In accordance with the Congressional Budget Act, appropriations committees are expected to have completed markups of all appropriations bills before submitting the first for final passage, so that members have a better idea of the overall level of expenditure that would be approved. The Senate follows a similar procedure, and differences between the two houses are resolved in a conference committee.

This procedure in Congress needs to be finished by September 15 for the budget to be ready to go into effect on October 1, but the Congressional Budget Act also requires the passage of a second concurrent resolution setting forth the budget ceilings, revenue floors, and overall fiscal policy considerations governing the passage of the appropriations bills. Because there will undoubtedly be differences in the ways in which the two houses make their appropriations figures correspond with the figures in the concurrent resolution, the *reconciliation bill*, in which both houses agree on the spending totals, must be passed by September 25.

Although the reconciliation bill appears to be a technicality, it has been used to impose great effects on the budget; for example, Congress used reconciliation bills to enact three significant tax cuts during the George W. Bush administration. The need to pass a single reconciliation bill tends to move power away from the appropriations committees and subcommittees and to centralize it in the leadership, especially in the House of Representatives.[23] After all the stages have been completed, the budget (in the form of the various appropriations bills) is then ready to go to the president for his signature and execution. Although the process has clear deadlines, they are often missed, and as this has occurred in most years since 2002, Congress frequently must pass continuing resolutions to maintain funding for programs until the appropriations bills are finally passed.[24]

Although this congressional procedure is the formal means through which the budget should be adopted, in practice it has not been effective over most of the past decade. The political process has become so contentious, and the magnitude of the budget so great, that the reconciliation process has largely broken down. Through the use of continuing resolutions and the eventual passage of appropriations acts, the federal government continues to function, but the intention of the legislation to provide a more coordinated and coherent style of budgeting has not been achieved.[25] Perhaps at the extreme, the budget for the Federal Aviation Administration has not been passed (as of February, 2012) for some sixteen months, with the agency having to rely on continuing resolutions that have prevented it from pursuing its goals of modernizing the air traffic control system.[26]

It is difficult to overstate the extent to which the budget and public finance in general in the United States has become politicized, and especially so in Congress. When President Obama introduced his budget for fiscal 2013 in February 2012, the Republican leadership said that it was basically dead on arrival. The bargaining and compromise that had characterized budgeting (and other aspects of congressional action) has been replaced by opposition and stalemate.

## Budget Execution

Once Congress has appropriated money for the executive branch, the agencies must develop mechanisms for spending it. An appropriations warrant, drawn by the Treasury and countersigned by the Government Accountability Office, is sent to each agency. The agency makes plans for its expenditures for the year on the basis of the warrant and submits a plan to OMB for apportionment of the funds. The funds appropriated by Congress are usually made available to the agencies on a quarterly basis, but for some agencies, there may be great differences in the amounts for each quarter. For example, the National Park Service spends a very large proportion of its annual appropriation during the summer because of the demands on the national parks at that time. Quarterly funding provides greater control over spending and prevents an agency from spending everything early in the year and then requiring a supplemental appropriation. Such overspending may still happen, but apportionment helps to control potential profligacy.

The procedures for executing the budget are relatively simple when the executive branch actually wants to spend the money appropriated; they become more complex when the president decides he does not want to spend the appropriated funds. Prior to the Congressional Budget Act of 1974, a president had at least a customary right to impound funds—that is, to refuse to spend them.[27] Numerous impoundments during the Nixon administration—as when half the money appropriated for implementing the Federal Water Pollution Control Act Amendments of 1972 was impounded from the 1973 to 1975 budgets—forced Congress to take action to control the executive and to reassert its powers over the purse.

The Congressional Budget and Impoundment Control Act of 1974 was designed to limit the ability of the president to use impoundment as an indirect means of overruling Congress when he was not able to do so through the normal legislative process (the water pollution control legislation had been passed over a presidential veto). The 1974 act defined two kinds of impoundment. The first, *rescissions,* are cancellations of budgetary authority to spend money. If he decides that a program could reach its goals with less money, or simply that there are good reasons not to spend the money, the president must send a message to Congress requesting rescission. Congress must act positively on this request within forty-five days; if it does not, then the money is made available to the agency for obligation (see Table 7.1). Congress can also rescind money on its own by passing a resolution in both houses withdrawing the agency's authority to spend.

*Deferrals,* on the other hand, are requests merely to delay making the obligational authority available to the agency. In this case, the deferral is granted unless either house of Congress exercises its veto power. The comptroller general (head of the Government Accountability Office) has the power to classify specific presidential actions, and at times, the difference between a deferral and a rescission is not clear. For example, attempting to defer funds for programs scheduled to be phased out is, in practice, a rescission. These changes in the impoundment powers of the president have substantially increased congressional leverage over how much money the federal government will spend each year.

Although he used the impoundment mechanism only once during his term of office, President George W. Bush proposed an "enhanced rescission authority" as a means of creating a version of a line-item veto and controlling the budget more directly at its execution.[28] Under his proposal, the authority would have

TABLE 7.1   Rescissions Proposed and Enacted, by President

| President | Number proposed | Number accepted | Amount proposed (millions) | Amount enacted (millions) |
|---|---|---|---|---|
| Ford | 152 | 52 | $7,935.0 | $1,252.2 |
| Carter | 89 | 50 | 4,608.5 | 2,116.1 |
| Reagan | 602 | 214 | 43,436.6 | 15,656.8 |
| Clinton | 186 | 103 | 9,557.7 | 4,318.6 |
| Bush | 1 | 0 | 23,000.0 | 470.0[a] |
| Obama | 0 | 0 | 0 | 0 |

*Sources:* General Accounting Office, *Frequency and Amount of Rescissions*, OGC–7–9 (Washington, DC: U.S. General Accounting Office, September 26, 1997); calculated from Office of Management and Budget, *Budget of the United States* (annual).

a. Not technically a rescission under the terms of the Impoundment Control Act, but funds were withheld.

extended to tax expenditures as well as to specific projects, and Congress would have been forced to make an up or down decision rather than simply ignoring the president's message. Such an enhancement of the rescission authority, as well as a constitutional amendment permitting a line-item veto, remains under consideration, although there has been little congressional action. The proposal for "enhanced rescission" authority resurfaced in 2010, but again with little action in Congress.[29]

### Budget Control

After the executive branch spends the money Congress has appropriated, Congress must check to be sure that the money was spent legally and properly. The GAO and its head, the comptroller general, are responsible for a postexpenditure audit of federal spending. Each year, the comptroller general's report to Congress outlines deviations from congressional intent in the ways government agencies have spent their money. Requests from individual Congress members or committees may produce earlier and perhaps more detailed evaluations of agency spending or policies. Each year, the GAO provides Congress and the interested public with hundreds of evaluations of expenditures, as well as general audit reports on federal spending.

The Government Accountability Office has undergone a major transformation from a simple accounting organization into a policy-analytic organization for the legislative branch.[30] It has become concerned not only with the legality of expenditures but also with the efficiency with which the money is spent. Although GAO reports on the efficiency of agency expenditures have no legal standing, any agencies wishing to maintain good relations with Congress are well advised to take those findings into account. Congress will certainly be aware of any adverse reports when it reviews agency budgets the following year and may expect to see some changes in the way in which the agency conducts its business. The GAO recommendations also form one part of the ongoing process of congressional oversight of administration. The problem with GAO controls—whether accounting or policy analytic—is that they are largely ex post facto, meaning that the money will probably have been spent long before the conclusion is reached that it has been spent either illegally or unwisely.

### Problems in the Budget Process

As we have seen, a long and complex process, taking almost eighteen months to complete, is required to perform the difficult task of allocating federal budget money among competing agencies. The process involves substantial bargaining and analysis, from which emerges a plan for spending billions of dollars. But even this complex process, complicated by numerous reforms of congressional budgeting and deficit-fighting procedures, cannot control federal spending as completely as some would desire, nor can it provide the level of fiscal management that may be necessary for a smoothly functioning economic system. Because budgeting is inherently political as well as economic, the process may never be as rational as some would like, but there are identifiable problems that cause particular difficulty.

The major problems arising in the budget process of the federal government affect the fiscal management function of budgeting, as well as the allocation of resources among agencies. It is difficult, if not impossible, for any president or any session of Congress to make binding decisions as to how much money will be spent during any one year, or even who will spend it for what purposes, and this absence of basic controls makes the entire process subject to error. Those elected to make policy and control spending frequently find themselves incapable of producing the kinds of program or budgetary changes they campaigned for, and that can result in disillusionment for both leaders and citizens.

## The Deficit

It would be difficult to follow American politics as it moved toward the election of 2012 without becoming aware of the issue of the budget deficit. The existence or prospect of a deficit has been a major force driving budget reform in the United States, for deficits and public debt are very negative symbols in the country's political discourse.[31] As the substantial budget surplus of the early twenty-first century changed to a deficit, politicians again became concerned about charges of fiscal irresponsibility. Because of the ideological baggage associated with deficit and debt, it has been difficult at times to discuss them rationally. The definition of a *federal deficit* is itself something of an artifact of a number of decisions made about the nature of the public sector and its budget. We tend to discuss the federal budget in isolation from state and local government spending and revenues, but given the ability of the federal government to shift some of its financial burdens to lower levels of government, looking at only one level of government may give a false impression of the state of public finance (see Table 2.4).

A less obvious problem in calculating the federal deficit is the part that Social Security funds play in reducing it. At present, the Social Security Trust Fund is receiving substantially more (roughly $30 billion per year) in tax income than it is having to pay out to retirees, but that began to change rapidly around 2010, when large numbers of baby boomers begin to retire. In the meantime, that extra income enabled the Clinton administration to balance the budget (see Table 7.2).[32] Defining the budget as including Social Security funds helps government leaders present balanced budgets in the short term, but it creates immense long-term

TABLE 7.2    Estimated Federal Budget Balances with and without Social Security (in billions of dollars)

| Year | With Social Security | Without Social Security |
|------|----------------------|--------------------------|
| 1997 | −22 | −103 |
| 1998 | −10 | −106 |
| 1999 | 10 | −96 |
| 2000 | 8.5 | −105 |
| 2001 | 28 | −94 |
| 2002 | 90 | −45 |
| 2003 | −226 | −378 |
| 2004 | −256 | −412 |
| 2005 | −255 | −427 |
| 2006 | −242 | −414 |
| 2007 | −162 | −349 |
| 2008 | −267 | −458 |
| 2009 | −1,285 | −1,413 |
| 2010 | −1,216 | −1,293 |

*Source:* Calculated from Office of Management and Budget, *Budget of the United States* (annual).

challenges to maintaining the soundness not only of the retirement system (see chapter 12) but also of the budget system. The federal government also controls public employee retirement funds, which it has at times manipulated to keep the deficit figure lower than it would otherwise be.[33]

Government accounting standards are being strengthened to take account of obligations such as unfunded pensions, but room remains for manipulating figures for political advantage.[34] For example, Social Security, Medicare, the federal debt, and civil service retirement obligations are all well known, but the budget has no clear mechanism for funding them.[35]

Another, related aspect of the deficit problem comes from the federal government's retaining what is called a "cash accounting system," rather than looking at the obligations being created for the future.[36] When a program is passed, it has future consequences that can be predicted, and it can be argued that government has accrued those future costs with its current decision.[37] Likewise, tax decisions have long-range revenue consequences that an annual budget may not capture.

The absence of a separate capital budget is another less obvious definitional problem. All state governments in the United States save one must, according to their state constitutions, have balanced budgets. But the states separate out their capital projects—roads, bridges, schools, and the like—into separate capital budgets, and they can borrow money, by issuing bonds, to build them. The federal budget does not separate capital from current expenditures. A good deal of federal borrowing is for projects for which borrowing is reasonable. Even good fiscal conservatives borrow money to buy a house or an automobile. With that in mind, the usual (if inaccurate) analogy between government and private household budgeting can be maintained even if government borrows extensively. If we took the spending that reasonably could be labeled *capital* out of the total budget, the federal government could be seen to have run a surplus, or at least a much smaller deficit, for a number of years. The deficits since 2002, however, have been so massive that the separation of capital spending would make little difference other than to make the nature of public spending more transparent.

This discussion of Social Security funds and capital budgeting should make it clear that many of the terms used in public policy have no single, accepted definition. Instead, *definitions*, like all other parts of the process, are constructed politically. It pays for incumbent politicians to calculate the deficit with Social Security revenues counted in, although some fiscal conservatives argue that this is actually a misuse of the funds and that the entire system should be privatized to prevent just such "abuses."

These technical issues about the budget deficit should not blind us to the increasingly politicized discussion of deficits and debt. The debate over raising the debt ceiling in 2011 demonstrated the intensity of the political commitments and also provided an opening to address other issues about public expenditure, such as entitlement commitments.[38]

### Uncontrollable Expenditures

Much of the federal budget is uncontrollable in any one year (see Table 7.3). Many federal spending programs cannot be controlled systematically without making policy changes that would be politically unpalatable.[39] For example, a president or Congress can do very little to control spending for Social Security

TABLE 7.3 Changes in "Uncontrollable" Federal Expenditures (in percentages)

| Type of Expenditure | 1976 | 1980 | 1990 | 1992 | 1995 | 2000 | 2003 | 2006 | 2010 |
|---|---|---|---|---|---|---|---|---|---|
| Controllable | 63.7 | 46.8 | 40.0 | 38.7 | 34.6 | 33.2 | 31.7 | 29.4 | 30.3 |
| Uncontrollable | 36.3 | 53.2 | 60.0 | 61.3 | 65.4 | 66.8 | 68.3 | 70.6 | 69.7 |

*Sources:* Office of Management and Budget, *Special Analyses of the FY 1995 U.S. Budget* (Washington, DC: U.S. Government Printing Office, annual); subsequent years calculated from discretionary and nondiscretionary expenditure totals.

in any one year without changing the criteria for eligibility or altering the formula for indexing (adjustment of the benefits for changes in consumer prices or workers' earnings). Either policy choice would produce a major political conflict that might well make it impossible. Some minor changes, such as changing the tax treatment of Social Security benefits for beneficiaries with other income, may be entertained, but the vast majority of outlay for the program is essentially uncontrollable.

The most important uncontrollable expenditures are the large entitlement programs, such as Social Security, Medicare, and unemployment benefits.[40] They cannot be readily cut, and government cannot accurately estimate, while planning the budget, exactly how much money will be needed for them. President Obama has promised to reform these entitlements but will face very strong pressures for maintaining commitments.[41] Actual spending will depend on levels of inflation, illness, and unemployment, as well as on the number of eligible citizens who actually take advantage of the programs. Outstanding contracts and obligations also constitute a significant share of the uncontrollable portion of the budget, although these can be altered over several years, if not in a single year. The major controllable component of the federal budget is the defense budget. The end of the Cold War made defense a particularly attractive target for budget cutting, but the apparent shift from large strategic forces to tactical (personnel-intensive) forces reduced the overall savings, and the big shift toward defense spending in the George W. Bush administration increased the discretionary budget, which has persisted under President Obama.[42]

The uncontrollable elements of the budget mean that even a president committed to reducing federal expenditures and producing a balanced budget (without figuring in a short-term Social Security surplus) will find it difficult to determine where reductions will come from. Congress has begun to grapple with controlling these expenditures but finds the political forces supporting entitlements difficult to overcome.[43] Some discretionary social expenditures have been reduced over the past decade, but the bulk of federal expenditures have increased (see Table 2.4) and likely will continue to do so.

## Backdoor Spending

Linked to the problem of uncontrollable expenditures is *backdoor spending*—spending decisions that are not made through the formal appropriations process. These expenditures to some degree reflect an institutional conflict within Congress between the appropriations committees and the substantive policy committees. They also reflect the difficulties of making the huge number of spending decisions that must be made each year through formal and somewhat recondite procedures. There are three principal kinds of backdoor spending.

*Borrowing authority.* Agencies are sometimes allowed to spend public money not appropriated by Congress if they borrow that money from the Treasury—for student loan guarantees, for instance.[44] It has been argued that these are not actually public expenditures because the money will presumably be repaid eventually. In many instances, however, federal loans have been written off, and even if the loans are repaid, the government may not know when that repayment will occur because students do not begin paying off loans until they complete their education.[45] The ability of government to control spending for purposes of economic management is seriously impaired when the authority to make spending decisions is so widely diffused.

The presence of myriad loans, loan guarantees, and other contingent obligations is becoming more evident to government, and it reduced some of the glee about the apparent end of the federal deficit during the last years of the Clinton administration.[46] There are few effective controls over loans, loan guarantees, or insurance obligations. For example, there are a dozen major federal insurance programs with authority to borrow over $60 billion,[47] and although some decision makers would like to impose firmer budget ceilings on them, finding the way to do so and preserve all their insurance coverage is difficult.

*Contract authority.* Agencies also may enter into contracts that bind the federal government to pay a certain amount for specified goods and services without going through the appropriations process. Then, after the contract is let, the appropriations committees are placed in the awkward position of either appropriating the money to pay the obligation or forcing the agency to renege on its debts. This kind of spending is uncontrollable in the short run, but any agency attempting to engage in such circumvention of the appropriations committees probably will face the ire of those committees when attempting to have its next annual budget approved. Congress has been developing rules that make spending of this type increasingly difficult for agencies. Still, the general shift toward implementation of public programs through third parties makes contracting a more important part of the process of governing.

*Permanent appropriations.* Certain public programs have authorizing legislation that requires the agencies responsible to spend money for designated purposes almost regardless of other conditions. The largest expenditure of this kind is payment of interest on the public debt; in 2010, this payment totaled over $350 billion, more than 12 percent of total federal spending that year.[48] Federal support of land grant colleges is a permanent appropriation that began during the administration of Abraham Lincoln. In the case of a permanent appropriation, the appropriations committees have relatively little discretion (other than to add to the spending) unless they choose to renege on standing commitments.

## The Overhang

Money that Congress appropriates for a fiscal year need not actually be spent during that fiscal year; it must only be *obligated*. That is, the agency must contract to spend the money or otherwise make commitments about how it will be spent, and the actual outlay of funds can come some years later. In 2007, there existed a total budget authority of about $2.79 trillion (see Figure 7.1), with only $2.2 trillion appropriated during that year.[49] Thus, the "overhang" was almost one-fourth as large as the amount of money Congress appropriated during that fiscal year. The president and the executive agencies could not actually spend all that overhang in the single fiscal year—a good deal of it was in long-term contracts—but it represented a substantial amount in unspent obligations for the agencies and the government as a whole.

The overhang makes it difficult for a president to use the budget as an instrument of economic management. A principal component of economic

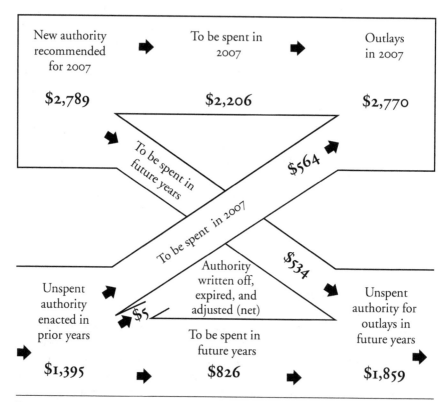

FIGURE 7.1    Relationship of Budget Authority to Outlays, Fiscal Year 2007 (in billions of dollars)

management, even in a post-Keynesian era, is the amount of public spending; because of the overhang, the president and Congress cannot always control the actual outlay of funds. The agencies may have sufficient budget authority, convertible into actual outlays, to damage presidential forecasts of spending. They might do that, not out of malice, but out of a perceived need to keep their programs operating as they think best, especially if the president were seeking to restrict the creation of new obligational authority.

### Intergovernmental Budget Control

Just as a president cannot control the overhang within the federal government, he cannot control the taxing and spending decisions of thousands of state and local governments, making it impossible to exercise the kind of fiscal management he might like. In 2008, the federal government itself spent only a little over half of the total amount of money spent by governments in the United States. Although it has the capacity to stimulate state and local governments' expenditures through matching grants, encouraging reductions in their expenditures is more difficult. The federal government has even less control over revenue collection. For example, in 1963, the Kennedy administration pushed through a tax cut at the federal level, only to have nearly the entire effect negated by state and local tax increases. The Bush tax cuts of 2001 and 2003 suffered a similar fate, as states enacted a variety of spending and revenue programs in their wake.

The principles of federalism appear to reserve to state and local governments a perfect right to decide on their own levels of revenues and expenditures. However, in an era in which the public budget is important for economic management as well as for the distribution of funds among organizations, there may be a need for greater overall control. This control need not be imposed unilaterally by the federal government but could perhaps be decided by "diplomacy" among representatives of the several levels of government, as it is in Germany and to some extent in Canada.[50] The potential effects on economic performance of uncoordinated fiscal policies were to some degree demonstrated by the large state and local government surpluses of the mid-1980s, at the time that the federal government was running large deficits.[51] Depending on one's point of view, that was either a good thing (helping to reduce total public borrowing) or a bad thing (counteracting the economic stimulus of the deficit). In either case, it represented the absence of an integrated fiscal policy in the United States.

### Reprogramming and Transfers

The first four problems we have identified in the federal budgetary process primarily affect the total level of spending. The next two problems, reprogramming and transfers, affect levels of spending by individual agencies and the purposes for which the agencies spend their money.

*Reprogramming* refers to the shifting of funds within a specific appropriations account. A congressional appropriations bill contains a number of appropriations accounts, which in turn contain a number of program elements. For example, the appropriations bill for the Department of Agriculture contains an appropriations account for crop supports, which is subdivided into separate program elements for cotton, corn, wheat, and so on. Reprogramming involves shifting obligational authority from one program element to another. Procedures for making reprogramming decisions have been thoroughly developed only in the Department of Defense. In general, there is a threshold (variable by agency) below which agencies are relatively free to reprogram funds but above which they must obtain approval from an appropriations committee or subcommittee, although not from the entire Congress. There are also requirements for reporting reprogramming decisions to the appropriations committees.[52]

*Transfers* are more serious actions, for they involve transferring funds from one appropriations account to another. In the Department of Agriculture bill referred to above, a transfer might involve shifting funds from crop supports to the Farmers Home Administration or to rural electrification. As with reprogramming, outside the Department of Defense, few established procedures exist for controlling the transfer of funds, other than specific prohibitions in the cases of certain functions.

Both reprogramming and transfers of funds are important in providing the executive branch with some flexibility in implementing its programs and in using public funds more effectively. These activities have been the subject of many abuses, however, and are ripe for reform and improvement. In particular, they frequently allow an agency to circumvent the judgment of the entire Congress through an appeal to the appropriations committee, or perhaps even to its chair. In the institutional battles for control over the budget, this is an area where Congress may want to be more active.

### The Defense Budget

In principle, budgeting for defense should present relatively few problems. The defense budget is huge, and it involves a number of complex programs and the purchase of very expensive equipment, but so do a number of other parts of the federal budget. Two major problems, however, have become apparent during the past several years. One is the continuing problem of secrecy. Part of total defense spending is not subject to the usual controls in Congress but goes through a more limited review because of fears of revealing secrets to potential enemies. One estimate is that almost $32 billion was allocated in this manner in 2008.[53] Secrecy also may make it easier for Congress members to hide pork barrel projects.

The second problem in the defense budget is that the George W. Bush administration financed the military operations in Iraq and Afghanistan through emergency supplemental appropriations rather than through the regular defense budget. Critics argue that these expenses were not surprises, like Hurricane Katrina, but were foreseeable and should have been debated as part of the normal budget process.[54] The need to include Iraq and Afghanistan was especially evident given that supplemental and emergency appropriations do not receive the scrutiny that the regular appropriations acts do (see below). Upon taking office in 2009, Barack Obama departed from this strategy and included war funds in the overall defense budget.

## Supplemental Appropriations

Agencies may also require supplemental appropriations, made outside the normal budget cycle, to cover shortfalls during the fiscal year. Agencies sometimes simply run out of money, either because of improper management or, more often, because of changes in the demand for services or poor estimates of demand for a new service. For example, during a recession, the demand for unemployment assistance will naturally increase, and supplemental funding will be required. Likewise, a year of poor weather may force additional funding for crop insurance in the Department of Agriculture. Or a new program, such as food stamps, may acquire more clients than anyone anticipated during the early years of its existence.

Supplemental appropriations are not insignificant amounts of money. In 1996, $3.52 billion was appropriated through supplementals. The figure ballooned to over $5 billion in 2002 with the impact of terrorism. Although a few supplemental actions reduced the amounts appropriated, additions to agency obligational authority ranged from $1.8 million for land acquisition for the U.S. Fish and Wildlife Service to almost $500 million for the Department of Defense for additional expenses incurred in operations in Somalia and Bosnia. There was also $225.5 million for the Soil Conservation Service, to aid recovery from disastrous floods in the Midwest. Deficit reduction strategies (discussed later in this chapter) have changed budget procedures and reduced the size of supplemental appropriations, but they are still an avenue for additional spending.

Requests for supplemental appropriations may be a useful strategy for agencies attempting to expand their funding. An agency may be able to initiate a program with minimal appropriations through the usual budgetary process, anticipating wide acceptance of its program by prospective clients, and then return to Congress for supplemental appropriations when clients materialize and demand benefits. Supplementals frequently are not scrutinized as carefully as regular appropriations, and their relative invisibility may permit friendly Congress members to hide a rapidly expanding program. Scrutiny of supplementals has increased because of the requirement that expenditure proposals be "deficit neutral," but they still are usually easier to push through Congress than regular appropriations. Obvious and frequent abuse of the supplemental appropriations process will damage the relationship between an agency and Congress, however, and that may hurt more than help the agency in the long run.

## Earmarks

The deficits in the federal budget have not been lessened by the increasing use of so-called earmarked appropriations added to appropriations bills.[55] Members of Congress who want to create special benefits for individuals in their constituencies are able to do so by adding riders to bills, generally after they have already gone through the appropriations committees. Once these provisions are part of the final act, Congress members are reluctant to overturn them because they want to ensure that their own earmarks are not eliminated. There were 587 earmarks in the defense appropriations bill in 1994; there were 2,837 in 2006.[56] In all, there were more than 15,000 of these earmarks in 2006, although this had dropped to slightly less than 10,000 by 2010.[57]

Providing benefits for their constituencies is one way that incumbent Congress members are able to stay in office. But the lack of scrutiny of these expenditures eliminates an important function of Congress in maintaining fiscal responsibility. Spending money for pork barrel projects may also leave less money for general public services, even in crucial areas such as defense.[58] Some analysis indicates that pork barrel programs are used to build coalitions for broader public goals.[59] Earmarks have become more visible after several scandals and allegations of congressional corruption in providing earmarked funds to campaign contributors.[60]

President Obama has promised to reduce the use of earmarks, but the absence of a line-item veto makes this task difficult (see below).[61] Spending bills come to the president with all the earmarks attached, meaning that he must sign the entire bill or veto it. Not signing an appropriations bill will mean that many public programs will have no funding, so presidents tend to sign them. Unless some negotiations with Congress can restrain the use of earmarks, this practice is likely to continue to be a problem for budgeting.

## Assessing the Outcomes: Incrementalism or What?

A standard term used to describe changes in budget allocations in the United States is *incremental.* Any number of meanings are attached to this word.[62] Broadly, *incrementalism* means that changes in an agency's budget from year to year tend to be predictable, but the word has taken on several additional, more specific interpretations. First, incremental decision making is described as a process that is not "synoptic," or not fully rational[63]—that is, incremental decision making does not involve examining sweeping alternatives to the status quo and then making a decision about the optimal use of budgetary resources. Rather, incremental decision making involves "successive limited comparisons," or the sequential examination of marginal changes from the status quo and decisions about whether to make those marginal adjustments to current policies.[64] An incremental decision-making process builds on earlier decisions, seeking means to improve the existing situation rather than altering current policies or budgetary priorities completely. In budgetary terms, this means that an agency can expect to receive in any year approximately what it received the previous year, plus a little more to adjust for inflation or expanded services.

Advocates of incremental decision making argue that it is actually more rational than the synoptic method. Because it provides an experiential base from which to work, the incremental method offers a greater opportunity to make good policy choices than does the apparently more rational synoptic method. In addition, errors made in an incremental decision-making process can be more easily reversed than can major changes made in a synoptic process. In many ways, incremental decision making is a cost-minimizing form of rationality rather than a benefit-maximizing approach. Incrementalism reduces costs, first, by limiting the range of alternatives and thereby limiting the research and calculation costs for decision makers, and second, by reducing the costs of change, particularly of error correction. Because in an incremental world few choices involve significant deviations from existing policies or appropriations, there is little need to make major adjustments either in the actual programs or in the thought patterns of decision makers about the policies. Given the limited calculating capacity of human beings—even with the aid of modern technology—and the resistance of most individuals and organizations to change, incrementalism can be argued to be a rational means for making choices.

*Incrementalism* also is used to describe the pattern of outcomes of the budgetary process. In particular, Otto A. Davis, M. A. H. Dempster, and Aaron Wildavsky demonstrated that there is a great deal of stability in the increase in agency appropriations from year to year.[65] The changes in budgets are not only small but also quite stable and predictable, so the best estimate of an agency's budget in one year is the previous year's budget plus a stable percentage increase. Some agencies grow more rapidly than others, but each exhibits a stable pattern of growth.

Several factors contribute to incremental budgeting in the United States. One is that such a large percentage of the budget is uncontrollable that few significant changes in appropriations can be made from year to year. Also, most empirical examinations of incremental budgeting have been made during periods of relative economic stability and high rates of economic growth. As less favorable economic conditions became more common in the United States, the incrementalism appropriate for rich and predictable budgeting systems diminished.[66] These changes in the economic climate of budgeting are to some degree reflected in the reform efforts I will describe later in the chapter.

Most important, the repetitive and sequential nature of budgeting tends to produce incremental budget outcomes. A budget must be passed each year, so minor adjustments can be made from year to year as the need arises, thus avoiding the need to attempt to correct all the problems of the policy area at once. The annual cycle prevents an agency from trying to "shoot the moon" in any one year—to expand its budget base greatly, perhaps with flimsy evidence. The sequential nature of the process requires several actors to make their own decisions one after another, and many bargains must be struck. The incremental solution not only provides a natural choice but also helps minimize the costs of bargaining among institutions. Once the precedent of a certain percentage increase for a particular agency each year has been established, it is far simpler to honor that rule than to seek a better decision for one year and then have to do the same hard bargaining and calculation in each subsequent year.

## Critiques of Incrementalism

A number of criticisms have been leveled at incrementalism, both in its prescriptive capacity (decisions should be made incrementally) and in its descriptive capacity (decisions are made incrementally). The basic argument against incrementalism as a prescription for policymaking is that it is excessively conservative—the status quo is perpetuated long after better solutions are available. This is true for some program decisions as well as for spending decisions. Incrementalism may be a perfectly rational means of policymaking so long as all parties agree that a policy or program is functioning well and is well managed. But how many policies currently fall in that happy category in the United States? In addition, even the incrementalist might agree that at times (e.g., during periods of crisis) nonincremental decisions are required, but the approach provides no means of identifying when and how those nonincremental decisions should be made.[67] If one uses the incremental approach to provide a prescriptive model for governmental decision making, then one must be able to specify what a "big" change would be, when it would be appropriate, and how it might be made.

Several problems also relate to incrementalism as a description of budgetary decision making. In the first place, the majority of empirical examinations of incremental budgeting have been performed at the agency level. That is certainly justifiable, given the importance of those organizations in U.S. public policy, but it is perhaps too high a level of aggregation for examining incremental budgeting.[68] When other researchers have disaggregated agency budgets into program-level budgets, they have found a great deal of nonincremental change—although, as pointed out, it is sometimes difficult to define just what is or is not an incremental change.[69] Although public organizations may have a stable pattern of expenditure change, the managers of the organizations can drastically alter priorities among the operating programs within the agency and produce more rapid change.

In addition, when the uncontrollable elements of public expenditures are removed from the analysis, the pattern of expenditure change for the controllable portion is anything but incremental.[70] As budgets have been squeezed by inflation, by citizen resistance to taxation, by presidents committed to reducing the public sector, and by large tax cuts, budgetary increments have not been granted as usual, and at times, the base has also been cut—that is, there have been real reductions in agencies' new obligational authority compared with the preceding year. Incrementalism may therefore now be descriptive only of certain kinds of expenditures and not of the budget process as a whole. Of course, since uncontrollable expenditures accounted for approximately 70 percent of total federal expenditures in 2006, the incrementalist approach may still be a useful description.

Incrementalism may apply only to certain kinds of agencies and programs such as those whose existence has been fully accepted as a part of the realm of government activity; it may not apply to newer or more marginal programs. For example, the budgets of programs such as food stamps are always more subject to change than are programs such as veterans benefits or Social Security, although all would be broadly classified as social service expenditures. The food stamp program has been in existence for a number of years but still does not have the legitimacy that other programs have developed, as evidenced by the ease with which it has been reduced in the past several budgets. Incrementalist theory also does not explain how and when programs experience big gains or big losses in their appropriations. Even if it explains a great deal of the variance in normal times, it seems incapable of explaining the most interesting and most important aspects of budgeting—who wins and who loses.

The prescriptive appeal of incrementalism is based in part on the reversibility of small changes, but in the real world of policymaking, many changes are not reversible.[71] Once a commitment is made to a client, or a benefit is indexed, it is difficult to go back and take it away. This is especially true of programs that have a "stock" component—that is, that involve the development of a capital infrastructure or a financial base.[72] Once a program such as Social Security is introduced, individuals covered under the program take the benefits into account when making their financial plans for retirement; any reduction or elimination of benefits may therefore create a hardship.

Despite these critiques, incrementalism has certainly become the conventional description of the U.S. budget process and its results. And that presumed incrementalism has prompted a number of proposals for reform of the budget process to make it more rational and to try to reduce the tendency for programs, once authorized, not only to remain in existence forever but to receive steadily increasing appropriations. It is to those attempts at reform that we now turn our attention.

## Reforming Budgeting: Large-Scale Approaches in the 1960s and 1970s

For most of contemporary history, criticisms of the U.S. budget process have focused on its incremental, "irrational," and fragmented character. More recently, however, the focus has shifted from imposing rationality toward finding somewhat simplistic means of correcting the negative results of the process, including huge federal deficits. At first, several methods sought to make the consideration of expenditure priorities more comprehensive and to facilitate government's making the best possible use of its resources. The two most important budgeting reforms of that type were program budgeting and zero-base budgeting. We discuss those two reforms briefly, for even though they were implemented several decades ago, the ideas behind them remain important. After that, we turn to the less rational but perhaps more effective reforms of the 1980s and 1990s.

### *Program Budgeting*

Program budgeting was largely a product of Lyndon Johnson's administration, although it had been tried previously in some agencies. Whereas traditional budgeting allocates personnel costs, supplies, equipment, and so forth among organizations, program budgeting allocates resources on the basis of the activities of government and the services that government supplies to society.[73] It also places a pronounced emphasis on the analysis of programmatic expenditures and the most efficient use of scarce resources.

Underlying program budgeting—or, more specifically, the planning, programming, budgeting system (PPBS)—is a systems concept. It is assumed that the elements of government policy are closely intertwined, so a change in one type of policy affects all others. For example, if one wants to improve the health of citizens in the United States, it may be more efficient to improve nutrition and housing than to invest money in medical care. Program budgeting was always looking for interactions among policy areas and for means of producing desired effects in the most efficient manner.

There were six basic characteristics of PPBS as practiced in the federal government. First, the major goals and objectives of government were to be identified; it was necessary to specify what government was attempting to do, but this identification was to be made high in the hierarchy of government, usually by the president and Congress. Whereas traditional line-item budgeting is initiated by the agencies, the concept of program budgeting began with a specification of the central goals and priorities of government, which could be supplied only by the principal political leaders.

Second, programs were to be developed according to the specified goals. How would government attempt to attain its goals? Programs were analytically defined and might not exist as organizational entities. For example, the strategic deterrence program in the Department of Defense was spread among three services: The air force had its manned bombers and some missiles, the navy had Polaris submarines, and the army had intermediate-range ballistic missiles located in Europe. *Strategic deterrence* described a set of activities of the defense establishment, but no organization was specifically responsible for it.

Third, resources were to be allocated among programs. Although many traditional line items were used in developing the program budget, the final budget document was presented as overall costs for the achievement of certain objectives. Those costs would then be justified as efficient and effective means of reaching the desired goals. PPBS thus emphasized the costs of reaching certain objectives, whereas line-item budgeting emphasizes the costs of keeping organizations or programs in operation.

Fourth, organizations were not sacrosanct in program budgeting, and there was no assumption that each program would be housed within a single agency or that each agency would provide only a single program. As in the defense example, program budgeting attempted to expand the framework of budgeting to include all the actors who contributed to the achievement of the goals. This was a realistic attitude toward the interaction of activities and organizations in producing the final effects on the society, but it made budgeting more difficult in an environment composed of many organizations, each attempting to sustain its own interests.

Fifth, PPBS extended the time limit on expenditures found in line-item budgeting, attempting to answer questions about the medium- and long-term implications of programs. Programs that appeared efficient in the short run might actually be less desirable when their long-term implications were considered. For example, most publicly supported health care programs concentrate on curative medicine, whereas it may be more efficient in the long run to emphasize prevention.

Sixth, alternative program structures were systematically analyzed in an effort to find more effective and efficient ones. Agencies were expected to present justifications for programs—to show, in other words, that the chosen program was superior to the alternatives investigated. This aspect of program budgeting relates to our previous discussion of policy formulation, for agencies were expected to develop alternatives and to examine their relative merits, using techniques such as cost-benefit analysis.

*Criticism of program budgeting.*   Advocates of program budgeting pointed with pride to the enhanced rationality and analytic rigor associated with it and to the way that it could break down organizational control over budgetary outcomes. Despite these apparent advantages, PPBS was not especially successful in most of its applications. There were some technical reasons for the apparent failures, but the most severe problems in implementing program budgeting were political.

Technically, applying PPBS successfully required a great deal of time and effort, as well as an almost certain knowledge of unknown relationships of spending to program success. The systems concept inherent in the method implies that if one aspect of the system is altered, the entire system must be rethought. That may mean that program budgeting actually institutionalizes the rigidity that it was designed to eliminate. Also, it is difficult if not impossible to define programs, measure their results, and evaluate the contributions of individual agencies and activities to the achievement of those results. The difficulty of measuring the effects of government is one of the major problems in public policy analysis, and such measurement occupies a central place in program budgeting.[74]

Program budgeting also had several political disadvantages. First, as mentioned, the method forced decisions to a higher level of government.[75] Agencies disliked this centralizing tendency, as did Congress members who had invested considerable effort in developing relationships with clientele groups supporting agencies. Moreover, the assumption that organizations are not the most appropriate objects of allocation ran counter to all the folkways of American government. Finally, the need to analyze systematically alternative strategies for achieving ends forced agencies to expose their programs to possible attack, as they might develop and eliminate alternative programs that others might prefer, and the explicit nature of the process brought those alternatives up for active consideration.

In short, PPBS was a dagger pointed at the central role of the agency in policymaking, and it should not have been expected to succeed, except perhaps in organizations such as the Department of Defense. That organization had a strong leader committed to the concept of program budgeting, and it produced extremely nebulous results that could be tested only against simulations or scenario-building exercises; it also had few potent political enemies. For other agencies, with much greater political opposition and with real clients demanding real services, PPBS was doomed to failure from the beginning.

*The rebirth of program budgeting.*   Although it has been declared dead as a formal device for allocating resources, the ideas of program budgeting continue to appear in thinking about the budget process, and especially in thinking about reforms. The basic idea of making the most efficient allocation of money among competing resources is an extremely alluring one, and politicians and analysts will attempt to pursue that rationalistic goal even in the face of massive evidence that it may not be attainable in the rough world of politics.

The Government Performance and Results Act of 1993 (GPRA) represented the rebirth of the fundamental idea of making the allocation of funds more rational.[76] The principal concept underlying this legislation was to shift the focus in assessing organizations in the budget process away from inputs and toward outcomes and "results." Thus, each organization in the federal government has been required to develop a strategic plan and a set of operational indicators of attaining the goals specified in that plan. The degree of success or failure in attaining the goals then plays a significant role in determining the budgetary success of the organization. This process involves neither the direct linkage to expenditures nor the level of analysis inherent in program budgeting, but it does depend on some of the same assumptions.

One of the consequences of this more rationalist style of budgeting was that there was much greater emphasis on identifying what government was attempting to do and assessing how well the goals were being achieved.[77] This style of budgeting can be done without tampering with the agency basis of budgeting or developing a systems framework for policy. However, even fifteen years after the adoption of this legislation, the difficulties of measurement and implementation are only beginning to be overcome.

The administration of George W. Bush extended the idea of performance budgeting to include an assessment of the progress that organizations were making in implementing a range of goals, such as "e-government," improved financial management, and use of private contractors when possible. Called "PART" (Program Assessment Rating Tool), this addition to the GPRA process evaluates every program but provides relatively weak measures of performance.[78] It tends to emphasize the management of the programs rather than the services provided to clients, and hence, efficiency may dominate effectiveness and equity considerations.

### Zero-Base Budgeting

If program budgeting required an almost superhuman analytical capability and rafts of data, the conceptual underpinnings of zero-base budgeting (ZBB) are extremely simple. Whereas traditional incremental budgeting operates from the assumption that the previous year's budget (the "base") was justified and so increments are all that need examination, ZBB holds that a more comprehensive examination of all expenditures should be conducted. That is, there should be no base, and the entire spending plan should be justified. It was assumed that weaker programs that were being extended largely through inertia would be terminated, or at least severely cut, and more meritorious programs would be fully funded.

Zero-base budgeting was carried out during Jimmy Carter's administration on the basis of *decision units,* which might be agencies but frequently were smaller components such as operating programs within an agency. Each budget manager was expected to prepare a number of "decision packages" to reflect his or her priorities for funding. These packages were to be presented in rank order, beginning with a "survival package" that represented the lowest level of funding on which the unit could continue to exist. On top of the survival package, additional decision packages were to reflect, first, the continuation of existing programs at existing levels of service and then expansions of service. Each decision package was to be justified in terms of the services it would provide at an acceptable cost.

Decision packages prepared by lower-level budget managers were passed up the organizational hierarchy to higher-level managers, who prepared consolidated decision packages ranking priorities among the several decision units that they might supervise. These rankings were then passed up and consolidated further, ending in the Office of Management and Budget. All the rankings from the lower levels were passed along with the consolidated packages, so higher levels could examine lower-level managers' preferences and their justifications. Like program budgeting, ZBB was geared toward multiyear budgeting to better understand the implications of budget choices made during any one budget cycle.

Zero-base budgeting, again like program budgeting, had several apparent advantages. Obviously, the method would eliminate incremental budgeting. The agency's base is no longer protected but must be defended—although in practice the survival level might function as a base. Also, ZBB focused on cost-effectiveness in the justifications of the rankings of decision packages and even of the survival level of funding. A chief advantage of zero-base budgeting was the involvement of managers at relatively low levels of the organization in the consideration of its priorities and goals. Also, the method considered the allocation of resources in package terms, whereas the incremental budget assumes that any additional money can be effectively used. It makes substantially greater sense to think of increments of money that can produce additional services than simply to add more money without regard for the threshold values for service provision and efficiency.

Nevertheless, there were a number of glaring difficulties with zero-base budgeting. For example, implementing it threatened the existence of some agencies. In practice, a number of factors such as powerful clientele groups and uncontrollable expenditures could negate the concern that many administrators might have had about ZBB, but it was nevertheless clear that its intent was to question the existence of each program every year.

Additionally, there was simply no means by which OMB, held to a reasonable size, or a Congress with its other commitments, could carefully consider the entire budget each year. Instead, there would be either a superficial analysis of each program under the guise of a zero-base review—probably with incremental results—or a selective review of a number of more controversial programs. Either would be an acceptable means of reducing the workload, but neither would constitute a significant departure from the incremental budget or justify the massive effort required to prepare the necessary documents.

In addition, ZBB threatened established programs by reopening political conflicts during each budget cycle. It is a virtue of traditional incremental budgeting that once a program has been agreed to, it is accepted and is not subject to significant scrutiny unless there are major changes in the environment or serious administrative problems in the agency. With zero-base budgeting, however, the existence of a program was subject to question each year, and the political fights over authorizing its existence might have to be fought again and again. Of course, this presented no problem for well-established and popular programs, but it was certainly a problem for newer and more controversial ones. ZBB also tended to combine financial decisions with program decisions, placing perhaps an excessive burden on budgetary decision makers.

## From Scalpels to Axes: Budget Reform from the 1980s to the 2000s

Incrementalist budgeting patterns have been more seriously challenged by the government's continuing fiscal problems than by the analytic methodologies proposed in program budgeting and (to some extent) zero-base budgeting. Those persistent fiscal problems have spawned a number of proposed solutions,[79] some of which have been implemented, including the Gramm-Rudman-Hollings Act (technically the Balanced Budget and Emergency Deficit Control Act of 1985), the budget agreement between Congress and President George H. W. Bush in 1990, and the Balanced Budget Act of 1997. Other proposals include a balanced budget amendment to the Constitution and the partially implemented line-item veto. Most of these are simply incrementalism turned around—they share incrementalism's tendency to substitute minimization of decision-making costs for maximization of benefits from expenditures. They are for the most part "no-think solutions," just as incrementalism has been a nonanalytic means for making budgetary decisions. But whereas incrementalism has been successful and acceptable, these methods for dealing with a complex problem have been proposed just because of their simplicity. Simple policies are perhaps only rarely the best solutions for complex problems, but they are often the most acceptable in the political world.

### Gramm-Rudman-Hollings

As the deficits created by the Reagan tax cuts grew during the 1980s, Congress began to look for means to stanch the budgetary hemorrhaging. This was difficult to do by traditional means because of the logrolling and pork barrel legislative styles so typical of Congress. Congress therefore adopted a method, commonly referred to as "Gramm-Rudman-Hollings," after its sponsors, that removed some of its discretion and forced spending reductions in cases where Congress and the president could not reach agreement. Initially, it aimed to reduce the federal deficit to zero within five years (by fiscal year 1991). That target was indicative of the totemic status of a balanced budget in American thinking about public finance, but it soon proved to be an unattainable and perhaps unwise target.[80]

The idea behind Gramm-Rudman-Hollings was that to meet the declining deficit target in any year, Congress and the president could cut spending, raise taxes, or use some combination of the two. If no agreement could be reached on those actions, however, automatic cuts in spending (called *sequestrations*), half taken from defense and half from domestic programs, would be imposed. Certain types of expenditures, including interest on the federal debt, Social Security, veterans benefits, and the like, were excluded, so the automatic reductions would have to come from only 30 percent of the budget. That meant that the cuts would have to be severe.

The initial scorekeeper in the process was to be the General Accounting Office, but the Supreme Court ruled that the GAO, a legislative organization, could not perform the executive act of ordering budget cuts for specific executive agencies.[81] The scorekeeper role was then reassigned to the Office of Management and Budget, despite Congress's fears that its interests might be slighted by the change. Other changes to the act followed in 1987–1988. First, the time for reducing the deficit to zero was extended to fiscal 1993. Second, most of the truly significant cuts were postponed until after the 1988 presidential and congressional elections, thereby confirming the adage that future budget cuts are always more acceptable than current ones, especially for incumbents. Congress attempted to restore deficit reduction to its original trajectory after the election but was deterred by economic and political circumstances.

The principal factor keeping the president and Congress from reaching their targets was a sluggish, then decelerating, economy. President George H. W. Bush proposed a budget that would meet the Gramm-Rudman-Hollings target of a $64 billion deficit for fiscal 1991, but as the budget process progressed during 1990, it became clear that the actual deficit would be closer to $300 billion because of the slowed economy. The sense of crisis emerging from the negotiations then produced a new program for deficit reduction, or at least deficit management. Adopted as the Budget Enforcement Act of 1990 (BEA), it provided for the following:

1. Separation of mandatory spending from discretionary spending
2. Differentiation of three types of discretionary spending: defense, international, and domestic, with separate spending targets for each
3. A "pay-as-you-go" plan for mandatory spending and revenues so that any increase in spending or reduction in revenue required a spending reduction or tax increase elsewhere, to keep the package deficit-neutral
4. Elimination of overoptimistic or unrealistic targets for deficit reduction
5. Inclusion of loan programs in the budget calculations (they had been excluded previously)
6. The Office of Management and Budget as scorekeeper[82]

Gramm-Rudman-Hollings, like other legislative attempts at fiscal control, represents a major effort at reform of the budget process to eliminate the deficit and force government to live within its revenues. It also points to the extreme difficulties of making and implementing such an agreement. Not only were unrealistic targets set and then dismissed, but also important segments of federal financial operations, such as credit (initially) and the savings and loan bailout, were ignored. Furthermore, the automatic cuts were imposed on a relatively small proportion of the budget and therefore fell very heavily in those areas.

The other effect of Gramm-Rudman-Hollings and its sequels was to add a new level of analysis to the budget process. One crucial element of budgeting introduced in the 1990s is scorekeeping in the pay-as-you-go—or PAYGO— system. Any spending bill had to be scored to determine whether it was revenue-neutral—that is, whether it provided sufficient revenues or savings from other programs to cover the costs of the new program. Legislation not meeting that fiscal neutrality criterion had to be redesigned so that it would do so. Making the determination of neutrality is by no means simple, for it often involves a number of economic assumptions and a variety of ways to do the calculations; politics enters here as well, as in the rest of the budget process.[83] In many ways, the Gramm-Rudman-Hollings and BEA enterprises helped add to the already high level of cynicism of Americans about government.[84]

In early 1993, the incoming Clinton administration used the provisions of the Budget Enforcement Act to begin to implement its own budgetary and economic strategy. The first Clinton budget proposed a very modest increase in expenditures but a much larger increase in revenues, thereby producing some reduction in the deficit, which continued for several years.[85] But by 2003, the Budget Enforcement Act was allowed to lapse. President Bush argued unsuccessfully for continuing the PAYGO principle for discretionary spending but not for tax legislation. The logic of the BEA had been reasonably successful in restraining spending, but its constraints were not impossible to elude, and the desire of the president and Congress to pursue tax reductions, combined with the need to spend heavily on the war on terror, Iraq, and growing entitlements, led to the end of the BEA.

The deficit and debt debate in 2010 and after provoked several responses to the problem. The Budget Control Act of 2011 contained several instruments for attacking the deficit. One was to attempt to address the problem by political negotiations, through the so-called Super Committee—the Joint Select Committee on Deficit Reduction. This committee was composed of equal numbers of Democrats and Republicans and was meant to reduce the deficit by $2 trillion to match the projected amount of borrowing needed. This committee, however, was not successful in reaching an agreement and disbanded with no recommendations.[86]

The second reaction of the deficit and debt problem contained in this act was to provide for automatic sequestration of funds if Congress and the president were incapable of reducing the deficit. In this plan, if the target figure is not reached, the amount needed would be automatically taken from spending, half from defense and half from domestic discretionary expenditures. This would protect major entitlement programs, such as Social Security, but unlike many budget plans, it did also threaten the defense budget (see below).

### The Balanced Budget Amendment

Among the most commonly discussed solutions to the federal budget deficit has been a balanced budget amendment to the Constitution. It would require Congress to pass a balanced budget each year unless an extraordinary majority declared that an economic emergency existed sufficient to justify running a deficit.[87] Somewhat like the PAYGO budgetary process, such an amendment would force a more explicit comparison of revenues and spending, and it would further require those involved in the budget process to be responsible for the amount of money that they appropriate. The difference, of course, is that the arrangement would be constitutional and therefore permanent.

A balanced budget amendment has had substantial political appeal and has gained some support. When it was voted on in 1993, it came close to receiving enough votes in Congress to send it to the states for ratification. Like many simple solutions to complex problems, however, it has some major shortcomings. First, as already noted, the planning for a budget begins over a year before it goes into effect and more than two years before the completion of the budget year. Both the revenue and expenditure projections on which a budget is based are influenced by the condition of the economy and its projected condition during the time the budget is to be executed.[88] It is easy to get the projections wrong—over the past twenty-five years, the official figures have overestimated revenues by an average of 3.5 percent and underestimated expenditures by an average of 3.9 percent.[89] Even if Congress acted in good faith in attempting to comply with the spirit of such an amendment, it could easily miss the target of a balanced budget badly—by an average of almost 8 percent.

In addition to potential economic problems from an unplanned deficit, a deficit might appear to be a violation of the Constitution and thus further undermine already weakened public respect for Congress. A more cynical scenario would have Congress passing a budget that, although balanced on paper, it would know had little chance of being balanced when executed. In either case, there could be substantial political damage to the legitimacy of Congress and government as a whole. The difficulties already encountered in applying Gramm-Rudman-Hollings to limit spending give some idea of how a balanced budget agreement would, or would not, work.

Deficits are not necessarily a public evil. When deficits are adopted for economic reasons—not created by political unwillingness to impose the true costs of government on citizens—they can be an important tool of economic management, following the Keynesian tradition. Passing a balanced budget amendment would only remove that management tool from the federal government without any certainty of generating economic benefits sufficient to justify the loss.

### The Line-Item Veto

In his 1985 budget submission, President Ronald Reagan proposed that a presidential line-item veto be adopted, especially for appropriations bills. He was not the first president to make the recommendation—Ulysses Grant had done so— nor was he the last. Similar to powers already invested in governors in forty-three states, the line-item veto would allow the president to veto a portion of a bill while permitting the rest to be put into effect.[90] Bill Clinton also advocated this instrument of presidential power, and it had been one part of the Republicans' Contract with America. Congress, seemingly against its own institutional interests, passed legislation in 1996 giving the president the line-item veto.[91]

This selective veto is seen as a weapon to deal with Congress members' tendency to add pet projects to appropriations bills, placing the president in the awkward position of having to refuse money for a large segment of the federal government as the only way to prevent the funding of one or two small, often wasteful, projects. The proliferation of these pork barrel provisions and earmarking in the early twenty-first century is making the line-item veto appear all the more desirable.[92] Some attempt to strengthen the rules against earmarking have, despite the rhetoric against earmarking, created a good deal of consternation among members of Congress.[93]

Although justified as a way to attack the problem of growing federal deficits, the veto cannot be applied to many uncontrollable programs, such as debt interest and Social Security. Using his powers of rescission, the president can achieve some of the same ends, although he needs the agreement of Congress. In 1992, President George H. W. Bush attempted to rescind $7.9 billion, but by the time Congress had finished with the proposal, it was a rescission of $8.2 billion that contained few of the cuts the president had proposed.[94] Despite continuing to press for the line-item veto, President George W. Bush used his rescission powers only once while in office. Congress would have the option of overriding a presidential line-item veto, first by a simple majority and then by a two-thirds majority if the president maintained his convictions about eliminating the expenditure.

The line-item veto might actually encourage Congress to add more pet projects onto appropriations acts, placing the onus on the president to remove them. Indeed, in his first use of the veto (before the courts intervened), President Clinton singled out some spending items that apparently were pork, concentrated in a few congressional districts.[95] The line-item veto might also give the president independent power over public spending not intended by the framers of the Constitution or desired by the public.

The first use of the line-item veto brought several lawsuits from affected parties and members of Congress. The courts ruled that it was unconstitutional because it violated the separation of powers provisions of the Constitution by conferring legislative powers on the president in enabling him to make selective decisions about what would be spent and what would not. The Constitution gives the president the veto, but over entire bills and not over the particular parts he dislikes. Although subsequent attempts to revive the line-item veto have proved futile, the debate over it is likely to continue, especially given the recent backlash against earmarks. As with the balanced budget amendment, the episode shows that there are few magic solutions for solving budget problems, but there is a continuing need for political will and courage to solve them.

The enhanced rescission authority sought by President George W. Bush and then President Obama is an attempt to have a line-item veto that would be constitutional.[96] In this proposal, the president would have forty-five days after signing a piece of spending legislation to send to Congress a statement about which parts of the spending he would rescind (not spend). Congress would then have twenty-five days to vote on this, without amendments. This would preserve the separation of powers, while still giving the president greater powers over selecting what to spend and what not to spend.

## Decrementalism

The preceding discussion of the balanced budget amendment and the line-item veto is indicative of the general problem facing American government: the control of public expenditures. While *incrementalism* has become the conventional description of budgeting, many politicians are looking for means of forcing *decrementalism,* or the gradual reduction of expenditures, on government.[97] The majority of them are on the political right—as exemplified by Republicans in the House of Representatives during the Obama administration—but even some on the left are seeking to reduce spending while hoping to be able to maintain levels of public service.[98]

In addition to the rationalistic approaches to budgeting and the Gramm-Rudman-Hollings machinery, other, somewhat blunter, instruments have been employed to try to reduce federal expenditures. One was the president's Private Sector Survey on Cost Control (the Grace Commission) in the early 1980s. That survey, similar to ones that had been conducted in most state governments, brought to Washington some 2,000 volunteers from business and other private sector organizations to examine the management of the federal government. The volunteers prepared 2,478 distinct recommendations, which were projected to save the government $424 billion a year if all were implemented.[99] Other efforts at controlling the costs of government have been even cruder, including across-the-board reductions in staffing levels and budgets and moratoriums on new programs and regulations. President Reagan and his advisers attempted to reduce the pay of public employees to 94 percent of that earned by comparable employees in the private sector—the 6 percent difference theoretically made up by the greater job security and fringe benefits associated with federal employment.[100] The Clinton administration had few proposals for changing the mechanisms for budgeting, other than the familiar arguments for a line-item veto and the proposals for a biennial budget contained in the National Performance Review.[101] The George W. Bush administration offered some ideas about cash management but little in the way of fundamental change in the budget process.

As discussed above, the United States has entered an era in which decrementalism appears to be more central to budgeting. The emphasis on reducing the federal debt has placed the need to cut expenditures more in the center of political discussion, especially given the reluctance of many involved to cut taxes. Attempts at more rationalistic procedures, such as the Budget Supercommittee, have again failed, so the latest version of across-the-board cuts—the Budget Control Act of 2011—is currently the only means available to manage the political difficulties associated with budgeting.[102]

Reaction to those proposals has been almost the opposite of that to proposals such as program budgeting and zero-base budgeting. The more recent across-the-board reform exercises have been criticized as mindless and as simply attacking government without regard to the real benefits created through some agencies and the real waste created by others. Such simplistic strategies contrast with the large-scale analytic exercises that would be required to implement PPBS or ZBB. Perhaps sadly, across-the-board exercises, such as the Budget Control Act of 2011, have a much greater chance of being implemented than do the more analytic methods.

## Summary

All the attempts at budget reform described here have had some impact on the way in which the federal budget is constructed. Both program budgeting and zero-base budgeting were significant rationalistic efforts at reforming the budgetary process. Although both had a great deal to commend them, neither was particularly successful in changing the behavior of budget decision makers. The less rationalistic methods, such as Gramm-Rudman-Hollings, have had a somewhat greater impact, in part because they did not attempt to change the basic format.

Why does the traditional, line-item, incremental budget persist despite the real shortcomings of both the process and the outcomes?[103] One reason is that the traditional budget gives the legislature an excellent means of controlling the executive branch. It allocates funds to identifiable organizations for identifiable purposes (personnel, equipment, etc.), not to nebulous programs or decision units. The political and administrative leaders who manage the real organizations to which the funds are allocated can then be held accountable for how they spend the money appropriated to them. Blunt instruments tacked onto the process, such as the Budget Enforcement Act, enhance the control elements of the budget process without altering it fundamentally.

More important, although the benefits promised by both PPBS and ZBB were significant, so too were the costs, in terms both of the calculations required to reach decisions and of the political turmoil created. Incremental budgeting provides ready guidelines for those who must make budget decisions, minimizing the necessity for them to engage in costly analysis and calculation. In addition, as most political interests are manifested through organizations, the absence in incremental budgeting of threats to those organizations means that political conflicts can be confined to marginal matters instead of repeated battles over the very existence of the organizations.

In short, although incremental budgeting does nothing very well, neither does it do anything very poorly. Incrementalism is a convenient means of allocating resources for public purposes. It is not an optimal means of making policy, but it is a means that works. It is also a means of making policy in which policymakers themselves have great confidence. These factors are not in themselves sufficient to explain the perpetuation of the incremental budget process in the face of so many challenges by presumably superior systems. There are always proposals for change, but there is rarely sufficient agreement on which of the possible changes to make to move the system away from the status quo. There have been some improvements, but the system remains firmly incremental.

CHAPTER 8

# Evaluation and Policy Change

THE FINAL STAGE of the policy process is to assess what has occurred as a result of the selection and implementation of a public policy and, if necessary, to change the current policy. Critics of government believe that these evaluative questions are extremely easy to answer, that the activities of government are rather simple, and that inefficiencies and maladministration could be corrected easily if only government really wanted to do so. This chapter will point out, however, that producing a valid evaluation of government programs is a difficult and highly political process in itself. It is much more difficult than evaluating most activities in the private sector.[1] Furthermore, if the evaluation determines that change is necessary or desirable, making the change is perhaps even more difficult than policy initiation—the first adoption of a policy. Government organizations have a number of means to protect themselves against change, and attempts to alter existing policies and organizations are almost certain to engender conflict.

Nevertheless, we should not be too quick to assume that government organizations are always wedded to the status quo. Change is threatening to any organization, public or private, but most organizations also know their own strengths and weaknesses and want to correct the weaknesses. The difficulties that organizations encounter in producing change arise as often from the rules imposed by Congress and from the demands of the organizations' clients as they do from internal conservatism. Most organizations, public as well as private, are engaged in continuous evaluation of their own performance, and changes in their management implemented over the past several decades have made public organizations even more conscious of how well they are doing.[2] What they must find is the means to produce effective change in that performance when they detect shortcomings.

## Problems in Evaluating Public Programs

Evaluation is an important requirement for programs and organizations in government. Like other organizations, they need to know how they are performing.

In its simplest form, evaluating a public program involves cataloging its goals, measuring the degree to which the goals have been achieved, and perhaps suggesting changes that might bring the organization's performance more in line with the stated purposes of the program. Although these appear to be simple things to do, it is actually very difficult to measure the performance of a public organization unambiguously.[3] Several barriers stand in the way.

## Goal Specification and Goal Change

The first step in an evaluation is to identify the goals of the program, but even that seemingly simple task may be difficult, if not impossible.[4] The legislation that establishes programs or organizations should be the source of goal statements, but we have already seen (in chapter 5) that legislation is frequently written in vague language to avoid offending potential members of the coalition necessary to pass it. As a result, it may be difficult to attach readily quantifiable goals to programs or organizations. The goals specified in legislation may be impossible or even contradictory. For example, one program had as its goal to raise all students to the mean reading level (think about it); the expressed aim of one foreign aid program was to assist the nations in greatest need, provided that they were the most likely to use the money to produce significant developmental effects. When an organization is faced merely with impossible goals, it can still do something positive, but when it is faced with contradictory goals, its own internal political dynamics become more important in determining ultimate policy choices than any legislative statement of purpose. As organizations do not function alone in the world, contradictions existing across organizations—as when the federal government continues to subsidize tobacco production and simultaneously discourages tobacco consumption—make identification of the goals of government as a whole that much more difficult.

Of course, internal political dynamics are still important in organizations whose enabling legislation states clear and unambiguous goals. A statement of goals may be important in initiating a program, but once the program is in operation, its goals may be modified. The changes may be positive, as when programs adapt to changing environmental conditions to meet new societal needs. Positive goal changes have been noted most often in the private sector, as when the March of Dimes shifted its goal from serving victims of polio to helping children with birth defects, but they also occur in the public sector.[5] For example, the Bureau of Indian Affairs has been transformed from an organization that simply exercised control over Native Americans into one that now frequently serves as an advocate for their rights and interests.[6] The Army Corps of Engineers transformed its image from one of gross environmental disregard to one of environmental sensitivity and even environmental advocacy.[7] Several organizations that were moved into the Department of Homeland Security—for example, the Coast Guard—have had to modify their goals to meet new international challenges.

Goal transformations may also be negative. The capture of regulatory bodies by the industries they regulate is a commonly cited example of negative goal change.[8] The failures of economic regulation that became apparent in 2008 may be a function of the regulators being too close to the regulated industries. More common is "displacement of goals" among the employees of an organization who, although they may have been recruited on the basis of public service goals, over time become more focused on personal survival and aggrandizement.[9] Similarly, the goals of the organization as a whole may shift toward its own maintenance and survival. Anthony Downs describes organizations (as well as individuals within them) as going through a life cycle, beginning as zealots or advocates of certain social causes but over time becoming more interested in surviving and maintaining their budgets than in serving clients.[10] In such instances, the operating goals of a program deteriorate, even if the stated goals remain the same. The organization may not even realize that the change has occurred, but its clients almost certainly will.

Among the managerial changes in the public sector over the past several decades has been an attempt to develop ways to prevent goal displacement. A common change has been to make managers more directly responsible for the performance of their organizations, with rewards for those whose organizations perform well and possible dismissal for the managers of poorly performing organizations.[11] At lower levels, performance pay schemes are designed to produce similar responsibility for performance.[12] A variety of mechanisms have been developed to make the public sector more "consumer driven" by permitting clients and the general public to know what is going on in organizations and to have some influence over outcomes.[13]

Even when goals are clearly expressed, they may not be practical. The Preamble to the Constitution, for instance, expresses a number of goals for the U.S. government, but few, if any, are expressed in concrete language that would enable a researcher to verify that they are or are not being achieved. Specifying such goals and putting them into operation would require further political action within the organization or the imposition of the values of the researcher to make it possible to compare performance with aspiration. For example, the Employment Act of 1946 pledged the government of the United States to maintain "full employment." At the time the act was passed, full employment was declared to be 4 percent unemployment. Over time, the official definition crept upward to 4.5 percent and then to 5 percent unemployed, and some economists have argued that 6 percent is an appropriate level. In the context of 2012, 6 percent would appear a marvelous achievement for government. Obviously, political leaders want to declare that full employment has been achieved, and to justify the claim, they apply pressure to change the definition of full employment. In this case, an admirable goal has been modified in practice, although the basic concept has remained a part of the policy statement. This is one instance of government playing the "numbers game" to attempt to prove that goals have been reached.[14]

Most public organizations serve multiple constituencies and therefore may have different goals for those different groups. For example, the Supplemental Nutrition Assistance Program, or SNAP program (formerly Food Stamps), performs several different functions for different groups. For the less affluent members of society, it is a means of nutritional support. For farmers, it is a means of increasing demand for their products and thereby raising prices and ensuring higher sales. For the Department of Agriculture, it enables them to become more involved in urban areas, thus expanding their constituency and perhaps also their political support. In general, the goals of these groups align well, but other programs may not be so fortunate.

Finally, it should be noted that goals may be either straitjackets or opportunities for an organization. In addition to telling an organization what it should be doing, specific goal statements tell it what it is not supposed to be doing. That may serve as a powerful conservative force within the organization and limit its creativity. The specification of goals can limit the efficiency and effectiveness of government as a whole. Any one statement of goals may divide responsibilities in ways that are less meaningful for citizens and policymakers in general than different statements might, especially if an expansion of knowledge or a change in social values occurs. So, for example, locating the U.S. Forest Service in the Department of Agriculture may mean that trees are treated more as a crop than as a natural resource, as they might be if the agency were located within the Department of the Interior. Giving any one program or organization a goal may mean that other, more efficient means of delivering the same service will not be explored or that existing duplications of service will not be eliminated.

## Measurement

Once goals have been identified and expressed in clear, concrete language, the next task is to devise a means to measure the extent to which they have been attained. In the public sector, measuring results or production is frequently difficult. In fact, one fundamental problem that limits the efficiency and effectiveness of government is the absence of any ready means of judging the value of what is being produced.[15]

One of the best examples of the measurement problem occurs in one of government's oldest functions: national defense. The product called "defense" is, in many ways, the failure of real or potential enemies to take certain actions.

Logically, the best defense force would never do anything, for there would be no enemy willing to risk taking offensive actions. In fact, if a defense force is called into action, it has to some degree already failed. But measuring nonevents and counterfactual occurrences is difficult, so defense is frequently the object of surrogate measures. Thus, the megatonnage of nuclear weapons available and capable of being launched in fifteen minutes and the number of plane-hours of flight time logged by the Strategic Air Command have been used as measures of defense. In a post–Cold War era, at least until the Iraq War, the indicators of an effective defense policy were even less clear, involving as much the capacity to enforce peace settlements as the ability to wage war.[16]

The illustration from defense policy helps make the point that activity measures are frequently substituted for output measures when attempting to evaluate performance in the public sector. Some scholars, as well as some politicians and analysts, despair of finding more adequate means to measure the benefits of many public sector programs. For example, I. C. R. Byatt argues that "It is not possible to measure benefits from defense by any known techniques, nor is it easy to even begin to see how one might be developed." He goes on to say that "It is quite impossible to allocate costs to the final objectives of education."[17] He might well have extended the list to include most of the functions of the public sector. That is especially true for the federal government, which delivers few identifiable services to the public, and it explains in part why the federal government is often evaluated as the least effective of the three levels of government in the United States.

Scholarly pessimism aside, the perpetuation of activity measures serves the interests of existing organizations. First, such measures can shield them from stringent evaluations on nonprocedural criteria. Perhaps more important, action becomes equated with success, and that will have the predictable effect of raising levels of funding. It may also have the less obvious effect of giving incentives to program personnel to keep their clients in a program when its benefits are no longer needed. Despite skepticism and organizational politics, governments continue to express interest in measuring what their organizations actually deliver for the public, and reforms in recent years have attempted to focus more clearly on the impacts of government.

Several factors inhibit adequate measurement of government performance. One is the time span over which the benefits of many programs are created. For example, although the short-term goal of education is to improve reading, writing, and computation, its ultimate and more important goals can be realized only in the future.[18] They cannot be measured or even identified during the time a child is attending school. Among other things, education is supposed to increase the earning potential of individuals, make society more stable, and generally improve the quality of life for the individuals who receive it. These are elusive qualities when an evaluation must be done quickly. The time problem in evaluation is illustrated by Lester Salamon's analysis of the "sleeper" effects of New Deal land reform programs in the rural South. It was widely believed while the programs were in operation that they were failures, but significant results such as those of the new landowners' involvement in the 1960s civil rights movement became apparent thirty years after the programs were terminated.[19]

The other side of the time problem is that any effects a program produces should be durable.[20] Some programs may produce effects only after they have been in existence for years, whereas others produce demonstrable results in the short term but have no significant effects in the long run. It has been argued that the latter is true of the Head Start program. Participants in the program tend to enter school with skills superior to those of non–Head Start children, but after several years, no significant differences can be discerned. It seems that without reinforcement in later years, the effects of Head Start decay.[21] The program per se, therefore, may not be unsuccessful or ineffective; it may simply not have been carried through for a sufficient amount of time.[22]

The time element in program evaluation also produces significant political difficulties. The individuals responsible for making policy decisions are often short of time, and they must produce results quickly if their programs are to be successful. Representatives in Congress have terms of only two years before facing reelection, making it necessary that any program they advocate show some "profit" before those two years have passed. The policy process thus tends to favor short-term gains, even if they are not durable, over long-term successes. Some actors in the policy process, notably the permanent public bureaucracy, can afford to take a longer perspective, but most politicians cannot. Thus, time itself is crucial in evaluation.[23] The policymaking cycle is largely determined by the political calendar, but the effects of policies have their own timetables. Part of the job of the analyst and evaluator is to attempt to make the two coincide.

The evaluation of public programs is also confounded by other factors in the environment that affect the people to whom the programs are addressed. For example, if we try to evaluate the effectiveness of a health program for a poor population, it may be difficult to isolate that program's effects from those of a nutrition program or a housing program. In fact, several programs may be related to any observed changes, so it becomes difficult to determine which is the most efficient means of affecting the health of that community. We may be able to isolate the effects of an individual program with a more controlled social experiment, but few people would want to be the subjects of such an experiment.[24] It is difficult to hold constant all the social and economic factors that might affect the success of a public program independent of any policy; health may have improved because more people are employed and can afford more

Joe Raedle/Getty Images

*The continuing economic slowdown in the United States has forced increasing numbers of people to rely on public sector programs such as SNAP (Supplemental Nutrition Assistance Program) as well as on private food banks. Cordahlia Ammons (right) speaks to social worker Kethia Dorelus (left) to sign her son Zach Ammons up for SNAP at the Cooperative Feeding Program in Fort Lauderdale, Florida.*

nutritious food for their families. These problems illustrate that measurement in policy analysis is not as simple as the measurement that a scientist can make of a passive molecule or an amoeba.

Measurement of the effects of a public program can also be confounded by the histories of the program and of the individuals involved.[25] Few truly new and innovative policies are initiated in industrialized countries, such as the United States, and programs that have existed in the same policy area for some years may jeopardize the success of any new ones. Clients may well become cynical when program after program promises to "solve" their problems. Likewise, administrators may become cynical and frustrated after changing the direction of their activities several times. Any number of policy areas have gone through cycles of such change and contradiction, with inevitable effects on the morale and cooperation of clients and administrators alike. The numerous attempts to solve the problems of the poor offer the best example of endless change and confusion. In addition to creating frustration over the inability of government to make up its collective mind, a new policy may not be successful after another policy has been in place. For example, if a regime of lenient treatment and rehabilitation is tried in a prison, it may be difficult for jailers to return to more punitive methods without disruption. Interestingly, the reverse may also be true.

Another problem is that the organizational basis of some evaluations excessively limits the scope of the inquiry, so that many unintended consequences of a program are not included. For example, highway engineers probably regard the Interstate Highway System as a great success. Many miles of highways were built in a relatively short period, and they have saved many lives and many millions of gallons of gasoline—assuming that Americans would have driven the same number of miles if the superhighways had not been built. The mayor of a large city or members of the Department of Energy, however, may regard the program as a colossal failure. They realize that building highways in urban areas facilitated urban sprawl and the flight of the middle class to the suburbs, which reduced the tax base of the cities and caused social and economic problems, in addition to raising the costs of urban programs, while the surrounding suburbs grew affluent. The rapid automobile transportation that the highways promised encouraged people to move to the suburbs and consequently to consume millions of gallons of gasoline each year in commuting. Furthermore, as gasoline has become more expensive and urban living more popular, the suburbs may become the new slums, with the more affluent moving back into the cities.[26] This one program and its widespread effects demonstrate that measures that any single agency uses to evaluate its programs may be too narrow to detect many unintended social or economic consequences.

If experimentation is used to try to ascertain the utility of a program, the danger that the "reactive effects of testing" will influence the results becomes an important consideration.[27] That is, if citizens are aware that a certain policy is being tried "as an experiment," they may behave differently than they would if it were declared to be a settled policy. Those who favor the policy may work especially hard to make the program effective, whereas those who do not support it may attempt to make it appear ineffective. Even those who have no definite opinions on the policy may not behave as they would if the policy were thought to be a true attempt at change instead of an experiment. For example, if a voucher plan for educational financing is being tried, neither parents nor educational providers are likely to behave as they would if a voucher plan were stated to be fully in operation. Parents may be reluctant to place their children in private schools for fear that the voucher program will be terminated, and providers are unlikely to enter the marketplace if the number of parents capable of paying for their services is likely to decrease soon.

The simple knowledge that a policy initiative is considered to be a test will alter the behavior of those involved and consequently influence the results of the experiment, or quasi-experiment. There have been some very successful experimental evaluations of programs, such as the New Jersey Income Mainte-nance Experiment, but most have required some strong incentives to gain the effective participation of the subjects.[28] Researchers then may have difficulty knowing whether the participants are behaving "normally" or simply responding to the unusual, and often exciting, opportunity to be a guinea pig.

In evaluation research, problems are also encountered with research designs, experimental or not, that reduce the analysts' ability to make definitive state-ments about the real worth of policy. The importance and expense of public programs have led to more experimental evaluations of programs before they are implemented.[29] The experiments are concentrated very heavily in the area of social policy, in part because of the controversy surrounding many of those pro-grams, and they are expensive, though perhaps not as expensive as implementing a poorly designed program. Conversely, not using an experimental method means that a large number of mainly unmeasured social and economic factors, not the program in question, may be the cause of any observed effects on the target population.

## Targets

Identifying the targets of a program may be as difficult as identifying goals.[30] It is important for the evaluator to know not only what the program is intended to do but also whom it is intended to affect. Programs that have significant effects on the population as a whole may not have the desired effects on the more spe-cific target population. For example, the Medicare program was intended, in part, to benefit less affluent older people, although all the elderly are eligible for it. However, although the health of the elderly population in general has improved, probably at least in part as a result of Medicare, the health of the need-iest elderly has not improved commensurately. And as the program has been implemented, substantial coinsurance has been required, along with substantial deductibles if the insured enters a hospital, so that it is difficult for the neediest elderly citizens to participate.

A similar problem has been developing with the Head Start program. Con-ceived as a component of the War on Poverty, Head Start was primarily intended to serve lower-income families and to enable their children to participate and learn effectively once they entered school. Head Start is, however, only a part-day program, whereas in most low-income families, all the adults who can do so will be working all day, and they therefore need day care for the full day. The educa-tional qualities of Head Start are largely absent from such day care programs, but the parents must go to work. As a result, Head Start tends to be used by higher-income families, and the target population has been largely missed or, at a mini-mum, has been underserved.[31]

One problem in defining a target population and measuring a program's success in reaching it is that participation in many programs is voluntary and depends on individuals who are potential beneficiaries taking up the benefit. Voluntary programs directed at the poor and the less educated members of society frequently face difficulties in making their availability widely known among the people they aim to serve. Even if it is made widely known to potential beneficiaries, factors such as pride, real and perceived administrative barriers, and real difficulties in using the benefits offered may make a program less effective than intended. An extreme example may be taken from the United Kingdom's experience with its National Health Service (NHS). One ostensible purpose of the NHS was to equalize access to medical care among members of all social classes, but the evidence after more than four decades of its existence did not indicate that such equalization had taken place.[32] The disparities in health status that existed before adoption of the NHS, and that in fact existed in the early twentieth century, had not been narrowed by an almost completely free system of medical care. Noneconomic barriers such as lack of education, transportation, free time, and simple belief in the efficacy of medical care served to ensure that although there was a general improvement in health status among the British population, little or no narrowing of class differentials occurred. The less affluent simply were not availing themselves of the services offered to the extent that they might, especially given their relatively greater need for medical services. Although the evidence is less dramatic, it appears that social programs in the United States have suffered many of the same failures in equalizing access to, and especially use of, some basic social services.

A program may create a false sense of success by "creaming" a segment of the population it serves.[33] That is to say, programs with limited capacities and stringent criteria for eligibility may select clients who actually need little help instead of those with the greatest need. This can make the programs appear successful, although those being served did not need the program in the first place, while a large segment of the neediest goes unserved. This pattern has been observed, for example, in drug treatment programs that take addicts who are already motivated to rid themselves of their habits. Likewise, some of the early successes of welfare reform in the United States may reflect that clients with the greatest motivation entered training first and got jobs—but would they have done so anyway, without the program?[34] Such programs can show success when they argue for additional public funding, but their success is actually limited. It would be a mistake for policymakers to generalize from the "successes" of such programs and assume that similar programs would work if applied to a general population with lower motivation. Of course, negative results may be produced by including too many subjects, many of whom may be inappropriate, in the population selected for treatment.[35]

As with so much of policy evaluation, defining the target population is a political exercise as much as an exercise in rational analysis. As we noted when discussing legitimation, one tendency in formulating and adopting policies is to broaden the definition of the possible beneficiaries and loosen eligibility requirements for a program. Although it helps to build the political coalition necessary for approval, this political broadening frequently makes the program's target population more diffuse and consequently makes the program more difficult to evaluate. It is therefore often unfair to blame program managers for failing to serve the target population when those who constructed the legislation have provided broad and unworkable definitions of that target. With the increasing strains on the public budget, it may become more politically feasible to target programs more tightly simply to reduce program costs.

## Efficiency and Effectiveness

A related problem is the search for the philosopher's stone of efficiency in government, a search that often leads up a dead-end street. Measuring efficiency requires relating the costs of efforts to results and then assessing the ratio of the two. We have noted that measuring results is difficult in many policy areas; it is often equally difficult to assign costs to particular results, even if the results are measurable. For much the same reasons, equal difficulties may arise in attempting to measure effectiveness. Surrogate measures of the intended results are frequently developed for public programs and policies, but all require the suspension of disbelief to be accepted as valid and reliable descriptions of what is occurring in the public sector.

As a consequence of these difficulties in measuring the substantive consequences of government actions, much of the assessment of performance in government depends on the evaluation of procedural efficiency. That is, what is assessed is not so much what is produced as how the agencies go about producing it. Some of this proceduralism depends on the legal requirements for personnel management, budgeting, and accounting, but attempts to assess procedural efficiency go beyond those formal requirements. The efficiency of public agencies may be assessed by determining the speed with which certain actions occur or by ensuring that every decision goes through all the appropriate, specified procedural stages. The important point here is that goals may be displaced when evaluations are made on such a basis, as the process itself, rather than the services that the process is intended to produce, becomes the measure of all things.[36] The concern with measuring efficiency through procedures may, in fact, actually reduce the efficiency of the process in producing results for citizens because of the proliferation of procedural safeguards and their associated red tape.

## Values and Evaluation

The analyst who performs an evaluation requires a value system to enable him or her to assign valuations to outcomes. But value systems are by no means constant across the population or across time, and the analyst who evaluates a single program may perceive very different purposes and priorities within its policy area. Thus, there may be no simple means of determining the proper valuation and weighting of the program's outcome. That is especially true when the program has significant unintended effects (usually negative) that must be weighed against the intended ones.[37] For instance, how do we compare the lives saved because of the greater safety of the interstate highways against the social and economic problems of center cities that the highway program may have exacerbated?

One point for consideration is that the analyst brings his or her own values to the evaluation. Despite their rational and neutral stance, most analysts involved in policymaking have proceeded beyond the "baby analyst" stage to the point at which they have values they wish to see achieved through public policy.[38] And as the analyst is in a central position in evaluation, he or she may have a substantial influence over the final evaluation of outcomes. However, the analyst's values will be but one of several sets of values involved in making that final assessment. The organizations involved will have their own collective values to guide them in evaluating outcomes, or at least their own activities. The professions with which members of the organization or external service providers identify will also provide sets of well-articulated values that may affect the assessment. Frequently, these different sets of values conflict with one another or with the values of clients or of the general public. Assessing a policy is thus not a simple matter of relating a set of known facts about outcomes to a given set of values. As in all aspects of the policy process, the values themselves may be the major source of conflict and rational argumentation and policy analysis merely the ammunition.

## Politics

We must always remember that evaluations of public programs are performed in a political context. There may well be a sharp difference between the interpretation that an analyst might make about the success or failure of a program and the conclusion that political officials might draw from the same data. Most evaluation schemes, for example, may be based on total benefits for the society, but political leaders may be interested only in benefits created for their constituents; if that narrow range of benefits is significant, the overall inefficiency of a program may be irrelevant. The increasing use of pork barrel legislation to fund projects in the constituencies of individual members of Congress (see chapter 2) is a clear case in point. Political leaders may also be supportive of programs that their constituents like, whether or not the programs have any real impact on the social problems that they address.

It is also important to remember that evaluations may be done not for the purpose of evaluating a program but to validate a decision that has already been made for very different reasons. Thus, evaluations are often performed on very short notice, and the evaluators may be given little time to do their work. The purpose then may be simply to produce some sort of a justification for public consumption, not to produce a genuine answer about the quality of the program. That is, in part, why institutionalized and impartial forms of evaluation, such as those by the Government Accountability Office, are so important in the public sector. Their stability and relative impartiality offer some guarantee of the quality of the assessment made. For example, the evaluations of the Missile Defense System by the Department of Defense were quite positive, whereas the GAO found that the "successes" of the program were extremely questionable.

### Increasing Requirements for Evaluation

One component of the wave of managerial change that has swept government over the past several decades is a focus on the outputs of government as opposed to the inputs (budgets, personnel, etc.).[39] The conventional means of controlling organizations in the public sector is to control their budgets and their personnel allocations stringently (see chapter 6). Evaluations based on outputs, on the other hand, examine what government organizations do and the effects of their programs. This approach to evaluation is presumed to be a superior means of understanding the programs' real contribution to public welfare.

In 1993, Congress passed the Government Performance and Results Act (GPRA), the basic idea of which was to appraise government organizations on the basis of their strategic plans and on the quantitative indicators that were developed as components of those plans.[40] As noted earlier, this legislation was an attempt to make programs justify their existence on the basis of the outputs they produced and to use changes in those outputs to judge the organizations' performance. This emphasis on outputs would, of course, enhance the need for evaluation within the federal government. The danger, as with many other exercises in evaluation, was that Congress would focus attention on a few simple, quantitative indicators and fail to understand the complexities of both the evaluation process and the programs that were being evaluated.

Other initiatives in the federal government also require increased evaluation. The National Performance Review, led by Vice President Al Gore and later renamed the National Partnership for Reinventing Government, contained some of the same emphasis on outputs as the GPRA. The Bush administration also instituted the Program Assessment Rating Tool (PART) to hold public programs accountable for their results (see chapter 7).[41] Regulatory review requires the economic evaluation of all new regulatory initiatives, although that would only touch the surface of the kind of evaluation that would be required to fully understand the impact of these rules on the economy and society. The continuing debates over educational quality also appear to require an extensive effort at evaluation, although again the effort seems to be narrowing to simple standardized tests rather than a broader assessment of quality in education.[42] The George W. Bush administration's efforts to punish poorly performing schools were based on these rather simplistic measures of progress, creating the additional risk that all schools would focus on their children's ability to pass the tests rather than on learning at a more fundamental level.

## Summary

Policy evaluation is a basic political process, and although it is also an analytic procedure, the central place of politics and value conflict cannot be ignored. As increasing pressures are brought to bear on the public sector to perform its role more effectively and efficiently, evaluation will probably become an even greater source of conflict. Negative evaluations of a program's effectiveness and efficiency now will be more likely to lead to the program's termination than in more affluent times. The content of an evaluation, the values that are contained in it, and even the organization performing the evaluation will all affect the final assessment. Evaluation research is now a major industry involving numerous consulting firms ("Beltway bandits"), universities, and organizations within government itself. These evaluative organizations will have their own perspectives on what is right and wrong in policy and will bring those values with them when they perform an analysis.

The latter point is demonstrated clearly by the evaluation of a Comprehensive Employment and Training Act (CETA) program performed some years ago by both the John F. Kennedy School of Government at Harvard University and the School of Public Policy at the University of California, Berkeley. The two schools stressed different values and approaches. The JFK School researchers concentrated on the costs and benefits of the program in strict economic terms, reflecting more utilitarian values. They found the program to be failing, its costs surpassing the value of the benefits created. The Berkeley researchers, in contrast, stressed the political and participatory aspects of the program.[43] They found the program to be a great success, with the participants pleased with the outcomes and more involved in society. The difficulty is, of course, that both sets of evaluators were correct.

## Policy Change

After evaluation, the next stage of the policy process is policy change. Rarely are policies maintained in exactly the same form over time; instead, they are constantly evolving. Sometimes, they evolve as the direct result of an evaluation, but more often change comes in response to changes in the socioeconomic or political environment, learning on the part of the personnel administering the program, or simple elaboration of existing structures and ideas. A great deal of policymaking in industrialized countries, such as the United States, is the result of attempts at policy change, rather than of new issues coming to the public sector for the first round of resolution.[44] Most policy areas in industrialized democracies are already populated by a number of programs and policies, so what is usually required is change rather than creation of totally new policies. Policy succession, or the replacement of one policy by another, is therefore an important concept in examining the development of contemporary public policies.

When a policy or program is reconsidered or evaluated, three outcomes are possible: policy maintenance, policy termination, or policy succession.[45] *Policy maintenance* occurs rarely as a conscious choice but happens rather as a result of simple failure to make decisions. It is possible, but unlikely, that a policy will be considered seriously and then maintained in exactly the same form. In the first place, politicians make names for themselves by advocating new legislation, not by advocating the maintenance of existing programs. Less cynically, few policies or programs are so well designed initially that they require no changes after they are put into operation. The implementation of programs frequently demonstrates weaknesses in the original design that require modification. Through what might be considered almost continuous experimentation, programs can be made to match changes in society, in the economy, and in knowledge and can thus be made to work more effectively.

It is also unlikely that many public programs will be *terminated.* Once begun, programs have a life of their own—they develop organizations, which hire personnel, and they develop a clientele, who come to depend on the program for certain services. Once clients use a service, they may find it difficult ever to return to the market provision of that service or to do without. This is especially true for programs that create a "stock" of benefits, as opposed to those that are merely a flow of resources. For example, Social Security created a stock of future benefits for its clientele, so once the program was initiated, future recipients began to plan differently for their retirement; any reduction in benefits would thus create severe hardships that the participants in the program could not have anticipated. Programs such as welfare or food stamps, which involve no planning by recipients, also create hardships if they are reduced, but the planning, or stock, element is not involved, and so it may be possible to move clients back into the market system. Public programs, policies, and organizations may not be immortal, but relatively few are ever fully terminated.[46]

Dismissing the other two options leaves *policy succession* as the most probable outcome for an existing policy or program. Policy succession may take several forms:

1.  *Linear.* Linear succession involves the direct replacement of one program, policy, or organization by another or a change in an existing program's location. The replacement of the Aid to Families with Dependent Children welfare program by the Personal Responsibility and Work Opportunity Reconciliation Act of 1996 was an example of a linear succession, as was replacing Food Stamps with Supplemental Nutrition Assistance Program (SNAP) in 2008.

2.  *Consolidation.* Some successions involve placing several programs that have existed independently into a single program. Moving numerous protective services into the Department of Homeland Security was to some extent a consolidation.

3.  *Splitting.* Some programs are split into two or more components in a succession. For example, the Atomic Energy Commission was split in 1974 into the Nuclear Regulatory Commission and the Energy Research and Development Agency, reflecting the contradictory goals of regulation and support of nuclear energy that had existed in the earlier organization.

4.  *Nonlinear.* Some policy and organizational successions are complex and involve elements of other kinds of succession. The multiple changes involved in creating the Department of Energy from existing programs (including the two nuclear energy agencies mentioned above) are an example of nonlinear succession.

Although they entail much of the same process described for making policy (see chapters 4–7), policy successions are processed in a distinctive manner. First, the agenda-setting stage is not so difficult for policy succession as it is for policy initiation. The broad issue has already been accepted as a component of the agenda and therefore needs only to be returned to a particular institutional agenda. Some issues such as debt ceilings and annual reauthorizations of existing programs automatically return to an agenda every year or even more frequently. More commonly, dissatisfaction with the existing program returns an issue for further consideration, but returning an issue to the institutional agenda is easier than its initial introduction because there are organizational manifestations of the program and identified clients who are in a better position to bring about the consideration. Furthermore, once organizations exist, it is more likely that program administrators will learn from other, similar programs and find opportunities for improving the program, or that they will simply think of better solutions to problems.

The legitimation and formulation processes will also be different from those employed in policy initiation. But instead of fewer obstacles, as in agenda setting, there are likely to be more. As noted, the existence of a program produces client and producer interests that may be threatened by a proposed policy change. This is especially true if the proposed succession involves "policy consolidation" (combining several programs) or a change in the policy instrument delivering the program in a direction that will demand less direct administration. For example, using policy consolidation to combine a number of categorical grants into block grants during the Reagan administration provoked outcries from both clients (primarily big-city mayors) and producers (administrators who managed the categorical programs). And part of the conflict over the negative income tax proposed in President Nixon's Family Assistance Plan, as well as that over some of President Carter's welfare reforms, concerned changes in the instruments used to deliver benefits, as well as ideological conflicts over the level of benefits.[47]

Thus, once a policy change of whatever kind enters an institutional arena, it is quite likely to encounter severe resistance from affected interests. That may be true even if the threat to those interests is not real—the mere prospect of upsetting established patterns may be sufficient to provoke resistance. For example, the numerous discussions on "reforming" entitlements in the budget debates of 2011 and 2012 have created anxiety among people who depend upon those programs for some or all of their income.

Of course, some policy successions may be generated within an organization rather than imposed from the outside. An array of external political forces may be strong enough to produce the change, so the organization and the clientele will gladly accede and possibly even publicly cosponsor the change. Although most public bureaucrats tend to be risk avoiders, some program managers may be risk takers, willing to gamble that a proposed change will produce greater benefits for the organization, and feel no need to attempt to hang onto what they have. Some programs may have expanded too far; their personnel may wish to pare off some of the peripheral programs to target their clientele more clearly and protect the organizational "heartland."[48] The pared-off programs will not necessarily be terminated; they may only change organizational location.

Clientele groups may seek to split a program from a larger organization to develop a clearer target for their political activities. Pressures from the National Educational Association and other educational groups to break up the Department of Health, Education, and Welfare (HEW) and establish an independent Department of Education illustrate this point. It was argued that HEW did not give educational interests the direct attention they deserved and that because the educational budget had the greatest flexibility of all the budgets in HEW (the remainder being primarily entitlement programs), any budget cutting was likely to be in education.[49]

Forming a coalition for policy change requires careful attention to the commitments of individual Congress members to particular interests and to ongoing programs. As with the initial formulation and legitimation of a policy, an attempt at policy succession requires use of the mechanisms of partisan analysis, logrolling, and the pork barrel to deliver change (see chapter 5). Again, this stage of the policy process may be even more difficult than policy initiation. Although the implications of a new policy are often vague, the probable effects of a change in an existing policy are likely to be more readily identifiable. It may be easy to persuade legislators of the benefits of a new policy on the basis of limited information, but once a program has been running for some time, information will become available to legislators that makes it much more difficult to persuade them to change a program that is "good enough."

There may, however, be many clients, administrators, and legislators dissatisfied with a program as it is being implemented, and those individuals can be mobilized to advocate change. A coalition of this kind may involve individuals from both the right and left who oppose the existing policy. The coalition built around the 1996 welfare reform illustrates this type of process—it combined liberals who wanted more funds for social programs and conservatives who wanted greater work incentives for aid recipients. Trying to bring about a policy succession by organizing such a broad coalition carries the risk that termination of the policy may be the only alternative to the status quo on which the coalition can agree. Before beginning the process, therefore, it is crucial for the analyst to have in mind the particular policy succession that he or she would like to see occur. Otherwise, allowing political forces to follow their own lead may threaten the existence of the program.

Putting any policy into effect in the intended manner is problematic at best, but several features of policy succession may make it even more difficult. First, it is important to remember that organizations exist in the field as well as at headquarters.[50] People working in the field may have policy preferences as strong as those of the home office workers, and they may not be consulted about proposed changes. Yet the field workers are the ones who must put the policy change into effect and ultimately decide the real consequences of the change. If policy change does not involve significant and clear modification of the existing policies, the field staff may well be able to continue doing what they were doing before and so subvert the intention of the succession legislation. This subversion need not be intentional; it may be only the result of inertia or inadequate understanding of the intentions of headquarters or of the legislation.

In this context, it is important to remember that organizations do not exist alone in the world, nor do policies. Each organization exists within a complicated network of other organizations, all of which must cooperate if any of them is to be successful.[51] A change in the policies of one organization may reduce the ability of other organizations to fulfill their own goals. Education and job training may now be as important for economic performance, especially in the long run, as is formal economic policy. This interaction is perhaps especially evident in the field of social policy, where a variety of programs are necessary to meet the many and interrelated needs of poor families and in which changes in any one policy or program may influence the success of all the programs. Terminating food stamps, for example, would mean that welfare payments would not be sufficient for families to buy the amounts of food they used to buy. As a consequence, housing, education, and even employment programs would be adversely affected by increasing demands. The reform of welfare during the Clinton administration changed eligibility for food stamps, but it did so in the context of a general weakening of the social safety net and a greater emphasis on employment.

As government shifts its focus from directly providing services to "new governance," in which it operates through a variety of third parties and indirect mechanisms, associating particular outcomes with particular programs may become even more difficult. Generating change in this setting implies changing not only the public sector programs and their intentions but also the network that will become responsible for delivering programs.[52] Dependence on a network for service will further complicate the process of policy change, given the resilience that characterizes the behavior of both public and private organizations.

Implementing policy succession is almost certain to be disappointing. The massive political effort required to bring about policy succession is unlikely to be rewarded in the first month, or even the first year, after the change. That is likely to create disappointment in the new program and perhaps cynicism about the policy area. As a consequence, one policy succession may generate enough disruption to engender a rapid series of changes. Once a stable set of policies and organizations has been disturbed, there will no longer be a single set of entrenched interests with which to contend, so forming a new coalition for policy change or termination may be easier. Advocates of policy change must be aware that they may produce more change than they intended once the possibility of reform becomes apparent to participants in the policy area.

Since we now understand that implementing policy succession will be difficult, we should address the problem of designing policy changes for easier implementation. The ease with which change can be brought about is a function at least in part of the design of previous organizations and programs. In an era of increased skepticism concerning government and bureaucracy, policies are being designed with built-in triggers for evaluation and termination.[53] The interest in sunset laws means that any administrator joining an organization with such a provision, or any client becoming dependent on its services, has reason to question the stability of the arrangement.[54] If the declining sense of entitlement to either employment or benefits from an organization can make future policy successions more palatable to those already connected with a program, then one major hurdle to policy change will have been overcome. However, that declining sense of entitlement may be related to a declining commitment of workers to the program, which can have negative consequences for the organization that exceed the costs of change.

It is not possible to reverse history and redesign programs and organizations that are already functioning without such built-in terminators. The analyst or practitioner of policy change must therefore be prepared to intervene in existing organizations to produce the smooth transition from one set of policies to another. One obvious trigger for such change would be a change in the party in office, especially in the presidency. Before the Reagan presidency, however, the alternation of parties in office had produced little significant policy change. The Clinton administration in many ways represented a return to that earlier pattern, for "New Democrats" seemed very similar to a moderate Republican like George H. W. Bush. The initial emphasis of the George W. Bush administration seemed to be on the downsizing of programs, but the pursuit of homeland security produced greater policy change than might have been anticipated from the campaign rhetoric. The Obama administration appears likely to produce even greater transformations than have previous administrations.[55]

Rapid changes in demand and environmental conditions may also trigger attempts at policy succession, but organizations have proved remarkably effective in deflecting attempts at change and in using change for their own purposes. At present, it is fair to say that there is no readily available technology for implementing policy succession, just as there is no reliable technology for implementation in general. A common finding is that organizations are able to interpret new policy initiatives in ways that fortify their current approaches. As with the discussion of the social construction of issues on the agenda (see chapter 4), organizations also socially construct the meaning of policy and law and do so in ways that will benefit themselves.

## Summary

Policies must be evaluated, and frequently policies must be changed. But neither task is as easy as some politicians, and even some academicians, make it appear. Identifying the goals of policies, determining the results of programs, and isolating the effects of policies from the effects of other social and economic forces all make evaluating public policies tricky and at times impossible. The surrogate measures that must frequently be used may be worse than no measures at all, for they emphasize activity of any sort rather than actions performed well and efficiently, placing pressure on agencies merely to spend their money rather than always to spend it wisely.

Evaluation frequently leads to policy change, and the process of producing desired changes and implementing them in a complex political environment will tax the abilities of the analyst as well as the politician. All the usual steps in policymaking must be gone through, but they must be gone through in the presence of established organizations and clients. The implications of proposed policy changes may be all too obvious to those actors, and they may therefore resist strenuously. As often as not, the entrenched forces will be successful in deflecting pressures for change. Without the application of significant and skillful political force, then, American government often is a great machine that simply proceeds onward in its established direction. Those whose interests are already being served benefit from this inertia, but those on the outside may continue to be excluded.

# 3 The President's Toolkit

*The real organization of government at higher echelons [is] how confidence flows down from the President.*

—Secretary of State Dean Rusk[1]

*"Not this one, Mr. President, your helicopter is over there,"* said the Army sergeant.

*Replied Lyndon Johnson, "Son, they're all my helicopters."*

The Framers took only 223 words to describe the powers of the president:

> The President shall be Commander in Chief of the Army and Navy of the United States, and of the Militia of the several States, when called into the actual Service of the United States; he may require the Opinion, in writing, of the principal Officer in each of the executive Departments, upon any Subject relating to the Duties of their respective Offices, and he shall have Power to grant Reprieves and Pardons for Offences against the United States, except in Cases of Impeachment.
>
> He shall have Power, by and with the Advice and Consent of the Senate, to make Treaties, provided two thirds of the Senators present concur; and he shall nominate, and by and with the Advice and Consent of the Senate, shall appoint Ambassadors, other public Ministers and Consuls, Judges of the supreme Court, and all other Officers of the United States, whose Appointments are not herein otherwise provided for, and which shall be established by Law: but the Congress may by Law vest the Appointment of such inferior Officers, as they think proper, in the President alone, in the Courts of Law, or in the Heads of Departments.
>
> The President shall have Power to fill up all Vacancies that may happen during the Recess of the Senate, by granting Commissions which shall expire at the End of their next Session. (Art. I, Sect. 2)

They added a requirement for the president "from time to time" to give Congress "Information on the State of the Union" and permission to recommend measures for consideration. They also made him the point of

54

contact for foreign governments by saying "he shall receive Ambassadors and other public Ministers." They saw little need to elaborate on the "Executive Power" that they "vested" in the president in part because they saw him as the agent of the legislative branch, implementing their laws, and in part because they trusted the likely first president, George Washington.

Presidents have built on these formal powers a strong and flexible set of tools to shape and carry out foreign policy. Several tools are centered in the White House: the President, the staff, the National Security Council (NSC) system. These tools can be used at the president's discretion and in numerous ways, from informal conversations to formal executive orders. (See Table 3.1.) The president can also order use of the key institutions for foreign policy making that are discussed in later chapters. The president may choose to use any or all of government's capabilities—the diplomatic instrument managed by the State Department, the economic instruments available to several other government agencies, the military instrument operated by the Defense Department (DOD), the secret intelligence instruments, the homeland security instrument, or even international organizations. But first, it is important to understand the way the president as a person and the presidency as an institution use their powers.

# Presidential Power

Many laws passed by Congress over the past two centuries have added specific requirements and authorities for the president. Even when lawmakers expect a cabinet officer to use the authority, they often assign it to the president to establish the highest level of accountability. For example, the basic foreign aid law stipulates the following: "The President shall withhold assistance under this Act to the government of any country that provides assistance to the government of any other country" on the list of terrorist supporters. Another section of that law demands that "the President shall assist American small business to participate equitably in the furnishing of commodities, defense articles, and services (including defense services) financed with funds made available under this Act."[2]

Longstanding law requires a cutoff of aid when U.S. property abroad is nationalized or seized by the local government and adequate compensation is not promptly provided. Laws also may assign authority to the president. For instance, a 1998 law imposing sanctions on individuals found trying to circumvent the Chemical Weapons Convention says, "The President shall take all steps necessary to block any transactions in any property subject to the jurisdiction of the United States" of such individuals.[3] Congress wanted the ball in the president's court even if he chose to pass it to a cabinet department.

Laws without enforcement mechanisms may not be effectively implemented. The War Powers Resolution, PL 93–148, tried to force an end to military operations not specifically authorized by Congress. Section 5(b)

| Table 3.1 | The Presidential Toolkit Brief | |
|---|---|---|
| **TOOL** | **ADVANTAGES** | **DISADVANTAGES** |
| **People** | **Greater credibility because of closeness to the president** | **Enormous time constraints on senior leaders** |
| President | No higher authority | Limited time and focus |
| Vice president | High authority if seen as close to the president | Spread thinly over domestic and foreign policy |
| National security adviser | Authoritative conduit | More time but still limited |
| NSC staff | Loyal, attuned to White House moods | May have own agendas |
| Special envoys | Manage major issues across agencies | Actual power limited if not Senate-confirmed |
| **Processes** | **Allows issue resolution at the lowest possible level** | **Time-consuming, not usable in crises** |
| Principals Committee (PC) | Avoids overreaction to presidential signals | Requires president to resolve conflicts |
| Deputies Committee (DC) | Workhorse of NSC process | Overburdened from above and below |
| Interagency Policy Committees (IPC) | Venue for interagency coordination | Leader may lack clout with bureaucratic equals |
| **Presidential actions** | **Greater authority from White House actions** | **Legal and political limitations often apply** |
| Personal contact | Conveys presidential views directly; gets responses | Personal chemistry may hurt as well as help |
| Public statement | Clarity and transparency | Hard to satisfy multiple audiences |
| Executive order | Force of law; hard to change | Needs careful drafting; hard to change |
| International agreement | Many models: private understanding, agreed statements, executive agreements, treaties; the more formal, the more binding | The more formal, the more time-consuming for senior leaders |
| Allocation of funds | Gives specific resources for policy actions | Many funding actions require notification or approval by Congress |
| Order to departmental instruments | Delegates action to presumed experts with authority to act | Reduces White House supervision and control; agencies may pursue separate agendas |

There are numerous resources available to the president in making foreign policy, including people, processes, and actions. The president relies on people he trusts to serve as his advisers and bring high-level issues to him with their recommendations. Through the process of delegation, the president allows committees to resolve low-level issues. The actions the president takes, from signing international agreements to making public statements, have the weight of authority, though they may still be constrained by political and legal limitations.

required: "Within sixty calendar days after a report is submitted or is required to be submitted pursuant to section 4(a)(1), whichever is earlier, the President shall terminate any use of United States Armed Forces with respect to which such report was submitted (or required to be submitted), unless the Congress" has acted. This mandate left action up to Congress. It had no teeth other than the willingness of Congress to punish noncompliance with a cutoff of funds—something Congress historically has been unwilling to do during ground combat.

The chief executive also has discretion over carrying out the laws because of their inherent vagueness or generality. For example, one of the laws passed by the First Congress in 1789 authorized the president to summon militia from the several states "for the purpose of protecting the inhabitants of the frontiers of the United States from the hostile incursions of the Indians." The lawmakers left the decisions on how to do this up to President Washington. In 1798, Congress empowered the president "to instruct and direct the commanders of the armed vessels belonging to the United States to seize, take, and bring into any port . . . any such armed vessel which . . . shall be found hovering on the coasts" that threaten U.S. merchant ships.[4]

Even today, the law often gives broad discretion to the president. A 1996 law, noting the threat from terrorists using weapons of mass destruction, contained this order to the chief executive: "In light of the potential for terrorist use of weapons of mass destruction against the United States, the President shall take immediate action . . . to enhance the capability of the Federal Government to prevent and respond to terrorist incidents involving weapons of mass destruction."[5]

In practice, presidential power and influence are derived from more than those legal authorities. As Richard Neustadt argued, presidents ultimately have only the power to persuade others to do what he asks because they conclude it is in their own interests. In addition to their formal authorities, presidents have certain levels of public prestige, measured in approval ratings by opinion polls, that strengthen or weaken their persuasiveness. They also develop professional reputations within the Beltway among the political and media elites that attract or repel allies and potential adversaries.[6]

## Legal Constraints

The chief executive is, of course, bound to follow the law and stay within the limits set by the Constitution, but he can also hire lawyers. Lyndon Johnson (LBJ) reportedly once asked a new staff member whether he was "a yes lawyer or a no lawyer." The president obviously wanted permissive legal advice rather than obstruction. Franklin Roosevelt (FDR) worried about how to help British Prime Minister Winston Churchill by transferring 50 older U.S. destroyers until his attorney general provided a legal opinion blessing the deal—notwithstanding some obvious obstacles in existing law. Dwight Eisenhower twice sought prior congressional approval of military commitments to Formosa (now called Taiwan) and Lebanon in part because of legal doubts but also to secure congressional support for the policy.

In recent decades, conservative legal scholars have elaborated a theory of the *unitary executive*. They argue that the Constitution permits full presidential control of the executive branch, including over appointees and so-called independent agencies and regulatory commissions. They supplement this notion of executive power with a very broad reading of presidential power over national security. This view, most strongly expressed in Justice Department opinions after the 9/11 attacks, admits virtually no limits on presidential actions in wartime or in defense of the United States.[7]

Congress passed the War Powers Resolution of 1973 over Richard Nixon's veto, but no subsequent president has acknowledged its constitutionality or binding validity. Instead, presidents have sidestepped the law's conditions by reporting military deployments consistent with the law but never pursuant to its requirements. Despite much bluster, lawmakers failed to make presidents comply fully with the act. In practice, there have been notifications and consultations as envisioned by the law, and until the 9/11 attacks, most military operations were designed to be completed within the law's 90-day time limit.

Leaving aside the legal questions surrounding war powers, it is clear that presidents feel some constraints on their ability to employ the military instrument and on their freedom of action on other foreign policy matters. No White House counsel would likely recommend actions to diminish executive power, such as accepting the validity of the War Powers Resolution. Even if a new president previously criticized an earlier president's behavior, most would be reluctant to toss away a tool that might be useful to him as well. For example, Senator Obama criticized the George W. Bush administration's use of *signing statements,* indicating a refusal to abide by a provision of law deemed unconstitutional, but as president, Obama has found it useful to issue a few such statements himself.

### Political Constraints

Most presidents treat legal constraints as political ones, raising the costs of taking controversial actions but not preventing choices that can be popularly defended. Political constraints can limit a president's actions. They can be imposed by the president's political party or come from opposition parties. They can be molded by public opinion as well as international influences. The Reagan executive order prohibiting assassinations of foreign officials remains on the books, for example, but the post-9/11 determination to attack terrorists has made targeted drone strikes politically legitimate.

The more significant political constraints are those imposed by public opinion and by the strength and motivations of the president's adversaries and supporters. As Kennedy aide Theodore Sorensen once stated, or perhaps understated, "Politics pervades the White House without seeming to prevail." He called it an "ever-present influence—counterbalancing the unrealistic, checking the unreasonable, sometimes preventing the desirable, but always testing what is acceptable."[8] Presidents and their White House staffs always follow public opinion polls closely in part as a barometer of the success of their messaging and in part to learn of warning flags regarding particular policy choices. They know that to go against solid public opinion on a matter has high risks, while framing a policy in terms of public preferences has benefits.

The domestic political context usually imposes significant constraints on presidential foreign policy actions unless they can be carried out in secret. The president's political supporters need to be consulted and persuaded to fall in line. Meanwhile, his political adversaries stand ready to pounce on unpopular or unsuccessful moves. Even if they support the announced policy, they feel free to criticize the way it is implemented. When the opposition party controls one or both houses of Congress, the incentives to criticize and investigate and even obstruct presidential policies are usually too attractive. Presidents can ignore such opposition, at least for a while, but they need to work to reassure the public and to achieve some examples of progress.

## Other Constraints on Presidential Choice

Newly elected presidents do not enter office with a blank slate for foreign policy. They have to deal with the world as it is, not as they might prefer. They face geopolitical contexts that often have long histories and numerous precedents in U.S. policy. Accordingly, their ability to change existing policies is limited. For example, in 1992, three weeks before leaving office, President George H. W. Bush gave Serbian president Slobodan Milosevic the "Christmas warning" that Serb military action against the ethnic Albanian majority in Kosovo would lead to an American military response against Serbia. In stating its position, the incoming Clinton administration reiterated the warning. The response was reflexive, not based on a calculated policy review, but it locked Clinton into a policy that made the 1999 bombing of Serbia practically inevitable.

Campaign themes also limit presidential flexibility, even if they were chosen for competitive advantages or in search of favorable publicity rather than as part of a planned international strategy. For example, George W. Bush's criticism of nation building by the Clinton administration made it harder for his administration to embrace nation-building programs when they were required to stabilize Afghanistan and Iraq. Similarly, Bill Clinton's campaign attacks on President Bush the elder for coddling the "Butchers of Beijing" made it difficult for him to decouple human rights concerns from broader economic and strategic interests when dealing with China, a change that took more than 18 months and was met with predictable sharp criticism. Ronald Reagan also spent several years as president criticizing the Soviet Union as an "evil empire" before changing his approach in response to changed leadership in the Kremlin and their promising initiatives.

Personnel choices also have a powerful influence in predetermining future policies. Woodrow Wilson chose a three-time Democratic presidential nominee and party luminary as his secretary of state only to discover that William Jennings Bryan had his own Christian pacifist views of what

American foreign policy should be. Dwight Eisenhower admired John Foster Dulles's diplomatic skills, but he also had to work around the Presbyterian moralism that made Dulles inflexible in dealing with some Cold War issues. Ronald Reagan fired his first Secretary of State, Alexander Haig—one of the few such officials to be ousted in modern times—because of the secretary's differing views and abrasive style on foreign policy issues.

Presidents select their national security teams only partly with regard to compatibility of views. They also may want symbolism from the nominee's prior roles, political base, or race or gender. President Truman chose Louis Johnson as his second secretary of defense because of personal friendship, recognition of Johnson's well-regarded earlier service in the War Department, and his political standing as former head of the American Legion. But, Johnson's budget-cutting zeal became a political liability when Truman had to change course in his military policy and rearm troops to fight in the Korean War. Lyndon Johnson expected that longtime friend and adviser Clark Clifford would be a loyal defender of the Vietnam War when he was named to replace Robert McNamara as secretary of defense, but Clifford soon became a critic and the architect of a radical change in policy.

Senior officials often have their own agendas—personal or political—that may conflict with the president's or drive policy along unintended paths. Madeleine Albright's Czech background made her especially concerned about Eastern Europe. Caspar Weinberger's romanticizing of Winston Churchill made him uncompromising on defense issues either with congressional leaders or his Reagan administration colleagues. Faced with a cabinet officer's separate agenda, the president usually acquiesces unless or until the policy becomes a political problem because the consequences of firing the person would likely be more harmful as that would call into question the president's judgment in nominating the official in the first place.

## Historical Consensus and Dissensus

There are other important givens that limit presidential flexibility on national security policy, especially patterns of historical consensus and dissensus that have existed for several decades. For example, U.S. political leaders almost without exception strongly support Israel diplomatically and financially. Many feel it would be political suicide to be seen as critical of Israeli policies. There have, of course, been occasions when U.S. officials have openly opposed some Israeli positions, such as on control of West Bank territories captured in 1967 and the expansion of settlements there, but on many occasions, pro-Israeli members of Congress rejected executive branch policies seen as adversely affecting Israel.

Another area of broad consensus has been on policy toward Europe. Support for the North Atlantic Treaty Organization (NATO) as an institution and for NATO expansion by adding nations formerly under the domination of the Soviet Union have been bipartisan policies since the 1950s. This favorable attitude still allows criticism of particular European policies and insistence that Europeans do more burden sharing with the United States, but it is unlikely that any president could easily withdraw from NATO or America's European commitments.

There are also areas of shared antipathy, such as bipartisan demonization of certain regimes, that limit presidential flexibility to engage with them. This has been the case with Castro's Cuba since 1961 and with the Islamic regime in Iran since 1979. The same hostility dominated U.S. policies toward Libya until that nation openly showed a willingness to make amends for its pariah behavior. The few friendly gestures tried by recent presidents toward Cuba or Iran have been quite limited and still politically painful.

On the other hand, certain policy areas have long been shackled with dissensus and caught up in perennial debates. One of the most significant was policy toward the Soviet Union and now toward Russia. Some U.S. political leaders favored steadfast hostility, while others sought engagement on matters that seemed reasonable and resolvable. This dissensus also affected arms control issues, with anti-Soviet advocates doubting the wisdom of any agreement with Moscow and pro-arms control advocates fighting an uphill battle to obtain limits on Soviet capabilities, which arguably were more significant than those on U.S. forces. The same black–white divide has existed since the 1970s on programs for national missile defense, with one group embracing successive technological approaches and the other doubting the need, the effectiveness, or the cost estimates.

China policy has also often been politically contested since the 1940s. Richard Nixon changed his own views and, as president, changed China policy—and was praised for it. His successors, however, have been sharply criticized when they seemed to move closer to Beijing. In the 21st century, a new faction has emerged in U.S. policy making, linking those who want to contain China as basic strategy with U.S. critics of China's economic policies and human rights practices.

While there is strategic consensus on opposing China's neighbor North Korea and especially its nuclear weapons programs, there is sharp tactical disagreement on what can and should be done to thwart the hermit kingdom. Presidents who campaign and govern as opponents of dealing with major adversaries find it hard to make exceptions when that seems opportune, and those who campaign and govern in support of engagement find it hard to shift gears when the engagee acts nasty.

The prospects of political disagreement, either by going against established consensus or by trumpeting a firm position where there is dissensus, tend to limit presidential choice, usually to baby steps, symbolic measures, or reversible policies.

# Presidential Management Styles

How presidents organize the White House and the national security system of the government depends a lot on their individual personalities and management styles. If the president chooses a compatible design for the system to make use of foreign policy tools, the system should function well. If not, flawed processes are likely to lead to flawed policies. Most advisers want to fit the system to the president rather than trying, and probably failing, to fit the president to an existing system. A talented executive can overcome a poorly organized system at least on some important issues, and a good system can reduce the number of errors by an inexperienced or unskilled manager. There are always trade-offs.

One analytic approach identified three organizations models used by recent presidents: competitive, formalistic, and collegial. Alexander George acknowledged trade-off dilemmas with each system but recommended a process of "multiple advocacy" to obtain the best decisions.[9] Thomas Preston developed a typology based on two personality characteristics—presidential need for control and involvement in the policy process and prior policy experience or expertise. In terms of the need to control the policy, he built a matrix of four types: director, magistrate, administrator, and delegator. In terms of prior experience and need for information, his matrix included navigator, observer, sentinel, and maverick.[10] While these scholarly insights are illuminating, most presidents blur the lines in practice, depending on the particular issue and its political context as well as their basic personalities and managerial tendencies. Moreover, these typologies are better used for retrospective analyses than for implementation by an incoming administration, where so many personal, political, and organizational factors need to be weighed and balanced and there is so much uncertainty about each of them.

Some presidents want some advisers to advise, others to debate, and still others to simply validate their own predilections. Some encourage disagreement; others want to avoid it. Bill Clinton enjoyed debate in front of him; Richard Nixon hated it. Some presidents want to feel that they alone are making decisions; others want to ensure group support. George W. Bush proudly called himself "the Decider." McGeorge Bundy, national security advisers to Presidents Kennedy and Johnson, said that LBJ treated his senior officials as if they were senators whose votes he needed.[11] Each approach has its pluses and minuses. Demanding consensus can result in the president's receiving a single option, perhaps including ambiguous compromises. Demanding options can force the president to choose among advisers, perhaps undermining their morale, as Henry Kissinger suggests. (See Box 3.1.)

## Sources of Information

Presidents need information and a system for obtaining it, especially once they enter the security bubble that surrounds them in order to protect the chief executive. Normal human contact is highly restricted. White House lawyers don't want presidents to have private e-mail accounts or diaries because of legal requirements that all official actions be documented and subject to possible subpoena.

---

| Box 3.1 |

## Inside View: Henry Kissinger on How Presidents Decide

Presidents get a lot of advice on what to do, often conflicting. Their advisers are bright people who can be very persuasive and thus are influential in the decision-making process. In choosing among alternatives for policy or action, presidents have to recognize that they are leading teams where morale is also an important factor.

Henry Kissinger aptly described how presidents make up their minds when they are confronted by so many supplicants with reasonable-sounding ideas.

*Before I served [in government], I had believed, like most academicians, that the process of decision-making was largely intellectual and that all one had to do was to walk into the President's office and convince him of the correctness of one's views. This perspective I soon realized is as dangerously immature as it is widely held. . . .*

*A President's schedule is so hectic that he has little time for abstract reflection. Almost all of his callers are supplicants or advocates, and most of their cases are extremely plausible—which is what got them into the Oval Office in the first place. As a result, one of the President's most difficult tasks is to choose among endless arguments that sound equally convincing. The easy decisions do not come to him; they are taken care of at lower levels.*

*As his term in office progresses, therefore, except in extreme crisis a President comes to base his choices more and more on the confidence he has in his advisers.*

*A Presidential decision is always an amalgam of judgment, confidence in his associates, and also concern about their morale.*

*Source:* Henry A. Kissinger, *White House Years* (New York: Little, Brown, 1979), 39–40.

---

To gauge public opinion, presidents used to rely on newspaper editorials and letters to the White House. Now, they can draw on instant public polls as well as privately commissioned ones. Nevertheless, each White House monitors carefully the volume and tone of incoming letters and messages and provides frequent reports to the president and senior officials.

In order to get "unvarnished" advice, especially on things that a president doesn't really want to hear but needs to be told, they rely on old friends outside the White House as well as longtime colleagues who get appointed to the staff. Each president builds a core staff of people he can trust with the most sensitive matters, often those who were in the campaign trenches, suffering the political highs and lows and learning how to deal with the boss. This reciprocal trust and loyalty explain why presidents tend to ignore their cabinet officials and work with and through their inner circles. Too much use of people not in the chain of command, however, can undermine the processes of government and limit the necessary sharing of information. When Henry Kissinger and Richard Nixon conspired to exclude the secretary of state from key decisions, the whole State Department was less effective as a consequence.

Presidents also need official information, reports on government activities for which he is ultimately responsible as well as secret information developed by the intelligence community (IC). For that, there are regular channels that ultimately funnel into the Situation Room. (See Box 3.2.)

---

## Box 3.2

## The White House Situation Room

The president receives information from sources far and wide. This information contributes to how foreign policy gets made. In the old days, before personal computers, video conferences, or even fax machines, couriers would bring paper copies of a selection of overseas cables and intelligence reports to the White House, where they could be distributed to the president and his senior aides. After the failed Bay of Pigs operations in 1961, President Kennedy asked his national security adviser, McGeorge Bundy, to get simultaneous copies of these messages in the White House. He wanted to know what State, Defense, and the CIA knew as soon as they knew it. An old White House bowling alley was replaced with the Situation Room.

In fact, the "room" is a set of rooms in the basement of the White House, including work stations for the staff, secure telephone booths, video facilities, and the main conference room where the president can meet with his advisers during crises. The situation room is a communications, intelligence, and operations complex, staffed around the clock by about 30 people organized into 5-person watch teams. They gather classified and unclassified reports and prepare morning and evening summaries of the most significant items. They also provide breaking news information to senior officials, serving as a constantly streaming source of information. Another major duty is arranging for secure presidential calls to foreign leaders. The staff also maintains constant communication with Air Force One when the president is traveling.

Movie sets intended to show the situation room usually have more high-tech gear and a larger facility than the real thing. The main conference room seats only a dozen people around its table, and there's room for only another dozen against the walls. Only in 2007 were the cathode ray video displays replaced with six flat screens, along with other upgrades of the 1985-era computers, phones, and faxes.

The real impact of having the situation room was not that it was more secure and better wired for meetings than the Oval Office or the cabinet room. Its communications capabilities and access to reports to State, Defense, and the CIA gave NSC staff the ability to centralize real-time control over national security information and operations inside the White House. The Situation Room complex increased the power of the president's staff, who were no longer dependent on what those couriers brought them, eventually, from distant buildings. They could get the president to act immediately without waiting for advice from subordinate officials and their departments.

---

*Sources:* "Situation Room," www.whitehousemuseum.org/west-wing/situation-room .htm; Michael K. Bohn, Nerve Center (Washington, DC: Brassey's, 2003).

A president's most valuable, and inevitably limited, resource is time. He needs time to think, to read, to talk with others, to sleep, and to get away from the pressures of the Oval Office. Those who serve him, therefore, are sensitive to the time constraints as they decide what information to provide, when, and in what form. George W. Bush was famously told in August 2001 that Osama Bin Laden was likely to strike in the United States, but the information wasn't specific enough to be actionable. Bush himself reportedly congratulated the intelligence briefer for protecting his own backside by conveying the warning.

Some presidents seek out information, occasionally by calling experts in the bowels of the bureaucracy. But normally, they are passive recipients of what subordinates choose to share with them. Just as they rely on certain people to cover certain policy areas, the rest of the government relies on those same people to keep the boss informed and, if the circumstances require it, advised regarding possible courses of action. Advisers, however, can offer conflicting advice, and in the end, the president must face difficult choices for high-level decisions. (See Box 3.1.)

## Creation of the White House-Centered National Security Council System

Presidential personalities and management styles can make big differences on all aspects of government, but in foreign policy, there is now a regular, proven system for advice and decision making. The modern president relies on a system of national security advisers not available to his early predecessors. The NSC evolved out of the need to close or minimize gaps in information—necessary for the best presidential decision making nationally and internationally. Roosevelt's successors built on the foundations of his Joint Board of the Army and Navy to create the NSC system in place today.

Franklin Roosevelt came to office in 1933 to lead a government much larger than the one originating with George Washington, yet Roosevelt's immediate resources were in many ways similar to the first president's. Despite the increased responsibilities of the job, Roosevelt ran his ever-growing executive branch with just a handful of aides. Only in 1939, in response to a commission saying "the president needs help," did Congress approve funds for six assistants, who formed the core of the new Executive Office of the President (EOP). They were sufficient, however, because Roosevelt empowered them by supporting their actions when challenged by others. His management style of dealing one-on-one with his aides and giving them sometimes overlapping areas of responsibility greatly frustrated many senior officials. Even a loyal admirer like Secretary of War Henry Stimson confided to his diary in 1943, "But the President is the poorest administrator I have ever worked under in respect to the orderly procedure and routine of his performance. He is not a good chooser of men and he does not know how to use them in coordination."[12]

Despite Stimson's impressions, Roosevelt strengthened his ability to manage national security affairs by bringing into the EOP—two months before the start of war in Europe—the only body in use that forced the military services to work together, the Joint Board of the Army and Navy. The Joint Board provided staff for what later became the Joint Chiefs of Staff (JCS). Two months before Japan attacked Pearl Harbor, FDR began regular meetings with a new war council, composed of the chiefs of staff and the secretaries of war, navy, and state. After Pearl Harbor, however, he stopped inviting the secretary of state to the meetings and ran the war without formal diplomatic input. He tended to deal directly with the military chiefs, taking them and personal aides like Harry Hopkins, but no other civilian officials, to the key wartime conferences with Churchill and Stalin.

Those conferences exposed U.S. military leaders to the well-oiled British chiefs of staff system and the cabinet-level coordinating body, the Committee on Imperial Defence. A senior American army planner complained that "we lost our shirts" at the 1943 Casablanca conference because the U.S. delegation had not developed coordinated proposals.[13] Out of necessity, therefore, the JCS adopted the British structure and improved their own coordination as a result.

After the war, many officials wanted to codify the best practices, such as a permanent JCS supported by a joint staff. They also wanted to overcome what a major study for the navy called "serious weaknesses in coordination," which had occurred during the war. That study cited "gaps between foreign and military policy—between the State Department and the Military Establishments. Gaps between strategic planning and its logistical implementation—between the Joint Chiefs of Staff and the military and civilian agencies responsible for industrial mobilization. Gaps between and within the military services . . ."[14] To narrow these gaps, many officials wanted to try to force the president to listen to alternative views and to give clear strategic guidance. While the idea of creating an NSC was broadly supported, its strongest advocate, Navy Secretary James Forrestal, viewed it as a substitute for what he vehemently opposed—unifying control of the armed services under a single secretary of defense.

The end result in the landmark National Security Act of 1947 was a compromise. The post of secretary of defense was created, but he had little real power and had to work through the separately managed army, navy, and air force departments. The law also created the NSC as a group "to advise the President with respect to the integration of domestic, foreign, and military policies relating to the national security."[15]

FDR's successor Harry Truman distrusted Forrestal's intentions, thinking he wanted to create a British-style cabinet government and fearing that the NSC could undermine the authority of the president. As a result, Truman remained aloof from the NSC for the first few years. But, when the Korean War broke out in June 1950, he saw the value of a formal advisory group and began regular meetings.

Dwight Eisenhower was even more comfortable with a strong staff system given his army experience, so he turned the NSC and its staff into the primary body for developing and implementing basic national security policy. Despite the differences in their specific structures and utilization, each president since the 1930s has seen the value of some mechanisms under White House control that would provide the chief executive with information and advice and channels for implementing decisions.

# The National Security Council and Staff

Several major distinctions need to be kept in mind while studying presidential control of foreign policy. First is the difference between the NSC as a list of key stakeholders in national security matters and the NSC as a formal advisory body. Second is the difference between NSC meetings and the numerous other sessions the president has with key officials and those they have among themselves. Third is the difference between the NSC group and the supporting NSC staff.

The membership of the NSC was intended to include those officials most knowledgeable and most responsible for national security matters and those most necessary for coordinating policy implementation. For nearly 60 years, the formal membership remained unchanged despite its inclusion of some officials whose posts were eliminated in the 1950s, such as the mutual security director and national security resources board chairman. The current members include: the president, the vice president, the secretary of state, and the secretary of defense. The chairman of the JCS and the director of national intelligence (formerly the director of central intelligence) are statutory advisers to the council. In 2007, Congress added a little-noticed provision making the secretary of energy a formal member.

Membership confers status and prestige, hence the desire to add particular officials as formal members. Recent presidents have issued formal orders conferring standing invitations to attend NSC meetings for several other cabinet-level officials and some senior White House staff. The secretary of the treasury has been a regular participant most of the time since the 1950s. Other White House aides handling economic and trade issues have been included when their issues were under review. Often, the attorney general or FBI director has been included as well as the U.S. ambassador to the United Nations and the director of the Office of Management and Budget (OMB). Recent presidents have added their chiefs of staff and even their political advisers to the list. These lists signify prestige but not power. Power depends, as Dean Rusk noted at the start of this chapter, on the official's personal relationship with the president and the confidence the chief executive has in his subordinate.

Despite its legal mandate, the NSC doesn't really function as an advisory body. It doesn't decide matters; only the president decides. It doesn't vote on policy questions; only the president's vote matters. It's also hard to see how the president as chairman of the NSC can advise himself. All presidents need a process to give them time-urgent information and at least partially considered and vetted policy recommendations. They tend to seek information and advice from people they trust, whether those individuals are part of the formal system or not.

Being on the attendee list does not even guarantee access to the president or attendance at key policy meetings because they may not be formal NSC meetings. Presidents have frequent meetings with their secretaries of state and defense and other key officials where they can discuss and maybe resolve policy matters. Calling a formal NSC meeting, however, has broader consequences. It may be done as a signal to the press and public that major issues are being seriously reviewed at the highest level of government. It may be done to give officials a formal opportunity to express their views on a pending crisis. But, it also raises the bureaucratic need for formal documentation, both for guidance to the rest of the executive branch and for the historical record.

In fact, other than President Eisenhower, most presidents have held few formal NSC meetings. Even if they start off with a burst of activity, the tendency is to drop off thereafter. President Nixon held 27 during his first six months, but only 10 during the following six months. President Carter held only 10 during his four years in office. President George H. W. Bush held only six during his last two years in the White House. President Clinton held only eight during his first year.[16]

A major reason for the decline in formal NSC meetings is the fear of leaks. After some news reports in the summer of 1969, Richard Nixon told his chief of staff, "No more NSC meetings. Result of leak. Can't trust to papers. Will make decisions privately with K[issinger]."[17] In fact, Nixon did not halt all NSC meetings, but he relied more frequently on his single channel to Henry Kissinger. A similar incident early in the Clinton administration led to an end to formal NSC meetings for several months, as a staffer explained, "So we wouldn't have to do a memo that might be leaked."

Instead, each administration has established multiple, regular, informal meetings of the president with key advisers and among those advisers. LBJ had *Tuesday lunches* with his national security adviser and the secretaries of state and defense. He added the chairman of the JCS only in 1967 when Congress began exposing military criticism of his Vietnam strategy. Jimmy Carter had *Friday breakfasts* with the same troika of civilian officials. Ronald Reagan had *family group* lunches with the same group plus the Central Intelligence Agency (CIA) director, his longtime friend William Casey. George Bush the elder convened the traditional three officials in inner circle meetings and occasionally broadened them to *Big Eight* meetings, adding the vice president, JCS chairman, White House counsel, and deputy national security adviser. Bill Clinton had informal meetings with varied sets of advisers, and the three senior officials—state, defense, and national security adviser—convened in regular lunches and breakfasts. George W. Bush had some informal meetings, and his key officials often had daily phone calls for coordination.[18] The Obama administration also had frequent meetings among senior officials and between them and the president in addition to the regularly scheduled sessions. These numerous informal channels demonstrate why one must look outside the formal NSC box to understand how U.S. foreign policy is made.

Although the NSC as an institution is mostly symbolic, its staff is a powerful instrument for the president. That staff grew significantly during the Nixon administration and then again under Clinton and Bush the younger. The hundred or so professional staff members are backed by another hundred support personnel. (See Figure 3.1.)

The NSC staff is its own small bureaucracy divided into directorates with specific portfolios. For issue management, George W. Bush divided his NSC apparatus into 6 regional and 11 functional interagency committees. The Obama administration had a similar arrangement of 8 regional and 11 functional groups. Obama also merged the Bush administration's Homeland Security Council staff with the NSC staff. (See Figure 3.2.)

These staff members are the president's issue experts for the huge variety of national security policy matters. They get the same field reports as their departmental counterparts. They are responsible for convening meetings of stakeholders to discuss developments in their domains and to prepare

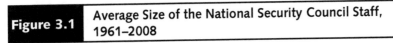

| Figure 3.1 | Average Size of the National Security Council Staff, 1961–2008 |

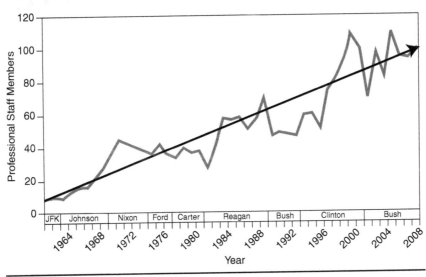

The NSC staff, with the resources and information it has access to, is a powerful tool for the president. The growing importance of the NSC staff to the president is evident in its growth over time. The larger numbers allow the White House to cover more policy areas and convene interagency meetings regularly and frequently.

*Source:* From Jeffrey Gelman, Ivo Saalder, and I. M. Destler, Brookings Institution NSC Project, in *Project on National Security Reform,* "Forging a New Shield," November 2008, 142, fig. 9. Reprinted with permission of the Brookings Institution Press.

69

## Figure 3.2  National Security Staff Organizational Chart

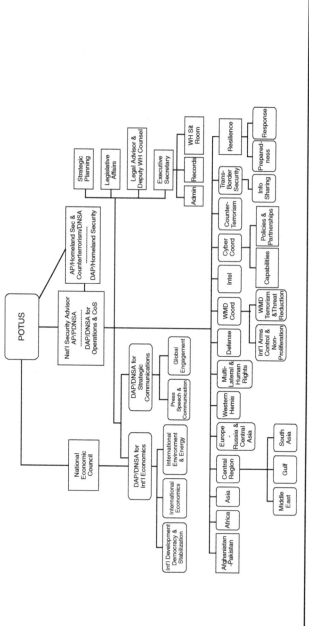

Though the formal NSC is comprised of a small number of advisers, the NSC staff has grown extensively over the years to gather information and report on a number of areas, from geographic regions to terrorism to human rights. Each of these units is supposed to be the coordinator for interagency planning in its area. In addition to the regional units, note the large number of offices dealing with various new threats like terrorism, cybersecurity, and homeland security ("resilience").

*Source:* Alan G. Whittaker, Shannon A. Brown, Frederick C. Smith, and Ambassador Elizabeth McCune, "The National Security Policy Process: The National Security Council and Interagency System, Appendix D," National Defense University, Industrial College of the Armed Forces, August 15, 2011, 69, at www.ndu .edu/icaf/outreach/publications/nspp/docs/icaf-nsc-policy-process-report-08–2011.pdf.

70

materials for meetings of higher-level officials. They head the assistant secretary-level Interagency Policy Committees (IPCs) that form the lowest rung of the interagency policy process. Most are detailees from their home agencies sent to work in the White House for a grueling couple of years, bringing their knowledge of their own departments and their capabilities as well as a roster of contacts to get information and pass along informal guidance.

## Role of the National Security Adviser

In charge of the NSC staff is the national security adviser, now often abbreviated as the NSA, although the official title is assistant to the president for national security affairs. Since 1953, the NSA has usually been seen as the most important foreign policy adviser to the president, usually given cabinet rank, although the position does not require Senate confirmation or confer directive authority over departmental officials. Their offices are traditionally in the West Wing not far from the Oval Office, and that proximity gives power. The adviser is also influential because he or she is often the first and last to discuss any policy matter with the president and can put a cover memo on documents from cabinet secretaries that colors the president's own reading.

NSAs tend to follow one of two basic models for the position. One is that of policy advocate, using NSC-level meetings and other devices to push for attendees to adhere to a particular policy that is encountering some resistance. This could be the NSA's own preferred approach or what he or she believes the president wants the rest of his foreign policy team to accept. The second model, more widely praised by outside observers, is that of *honest broker,* the person who makes sure that the president hears all relevant views and who conducts the policy process in a collegial and transparent way. Brent Scowcroft articulated this model and practiced it when he was NSA for President Bush the elder.[19]

Most NSAs develop close relationships with their presidents and succeed when they adapt the NSC staff to the president's operating style. McGeorge Bundy gave John F. Kennedy the small, informal, fast-acting policy team Kennedy favored; he found it hard to adjust to LBJ's more demanding and demeaning style. Henry Kissinger was the skilled consigliere who gave Richard Nixon a tightly controlled operation, filled with secrecy and surprises, that allowed the pair to craft grand strategy, often deliberately excluding the secretaries of state and defense. Zbigniew Brzezinski gave Jimmy Carter the assertive, moralistic policies he favored. Ronald Reagan subordinated his NSA and the NSC staff, not even granting the NSA routine direct access to the Oval Office. He wound up with a rogue staff that got him into the Iran-Contra scandal. Brent Scowcroft gave George Bush the elder the smooth-running and collegial process both men strongly favored, while Tony Lake and Sandy Berger worked diligently to keep the interagency process in tune with Bill Clinton's changing priorities and enthusiasms. Condoleezza Rice and Steve Hadley gave George W. Bush opportunities to set bold goals in the way he favored. Jim Jones gave Barack Obama a well-organized system in keeping with his pragmatic style. Tom Donilon proved himself as an energetic deputy NSA for Obama and was rewarded with the top spot.

### Other White House Operatives

The NSA and NSC staff are not the only ones working with and for the president on national security matters. The vice president often has the stature and experience to play a major role, as George Bush the elder, Al Gore, Dick Cheney, and Joe Biden have done. (See Box 3.3.) The president's chief of staff can also be a major player, both in giving advice with a political perspective and in enforcing the president's wishes on a recalcitrant administration. Many presidents hate to disagree with their loyal appointees and find it even harder to discipline them. Those tasks are often left to the chief of staff. For example, Richard Nixon had a recurrent pattern when someone got into the Oval Office and got him to agree to take some action that the president later regretted. He would call in Chief of Staff Bob Haldeman, tell him he had no intention of doing what he had agreed to, and insist that the subordinate never be allowed to see him alone again.[20]

---

**Box 3.3**

## Who Makes Foreign Policy: The Special Role of the Vice President

As the only prescribed duties for the vice president are to preside over the Senate and cast tie-breaking votes, he has lots of time for other things if the president wants to give him work. For much of U.S. history, vice presidents were political hacks, chosen for their electoral help and then banished from the White House. Richard Nixon, for instance, was allowed only a peripheral role in the Eisenhower administration, which he later avenged by treating his own vice presidents the same way. Vice presidents often traveled abroad on the principle of "You die, I fly" but rarely other than to show the flag.

Starting with the Carter administration, however, presidents chose running mates with congressional and foreign policy experience and gave them fuller access to the national security policy process, thus making them more influential in the foreign policy-making process. Walter Mondale asked for and received from Jimmy Carter several opportunities to be a much more substantive player in both domestic and foreign policy. He had on office in the West Wing and weekly private lunches with the president. He got to see the paperwork going to and from the president. And, he got a budget for his own staff. Later vice presidents were also granted such access, thus allowing them to partially institutionalize the office.

Some vice presidents preferred to be close advisers, often reserving their personal views for private meetings with the president. Others took on delegated tasks, such as Al Gore's supervisory role over U.S. policy with Russia, which became formalized in twice yearly meetings between him and the Russian premier. They all knew that their influence depended on maintaining close, personal relationships

*(Continued)*

(Continued)

with the president and that they might see their clout wax and wane depending on other political developments.

George H. W. Bush as vice president had a staff for foreign policy of about 10 professionals. Gore had about eight, but his own national security adviser was an active member of the DC. Dick Cheney greatly expanded and changed the vice presidential national security operation by hiring at least 14 professionals, many of whom were political appointees rather than agency detailees, as in previous administrations. Other estimates, including consultants and other seconded individuals, put the Cheney foreign policy staff at an unprecedented 35.

With so many people, Cheney was able to send agents to almost any interagency meeting that might be convened and thus monitor closely any issue he chose. He personally also was actively involved, such as by attending Principals Committee (PC) meetings and by meeting with CIA analysts to discuss their findings prior to the Iraq war.

Cheney would have had enormous influence in the Bush administration simply because of his broad experience—former White House chief of staff, secretary of defense, and deputy Republican leader in the House of Representatives—but he was even more powerful because of his staff support. News reports tended to call him *Bush's CEO* or *prime minister.*

President Obama chose Joe Biden as his vice president with full knowledge of the Delaware senator's long background and interest in foreign policy matters. He also delegated some key issues to him, including supervision of Iraq policy. And, insider reports suggest that Biden was willing to speak up with differing views in interagency meetings rather than reserving them for private sessions with the president. He appeared to make full use of the tools of the vice presidency to shape policy.

*Sources:* Jack Lechelt, *The Vice President in Foreign Policy: From Mondale to Cheney* (El Paso, TX: LFB Scholarly Publishing, 2009); Rothkopf, 421–422.

Because White House aides have predetermined loyalty to the president and the proximity that makes them easily accessible, they can be called on for a variety of tasks, domestic and international. In recent years, presidents have given special portfolios to some of these aides or have named officials to report directly to them, although they are based elsewhere. Harry Hopkins was in effect the deputy president for foreign affairs during World War II. L. Paul "Jerry" Bremer headed the U.S.-run Coalition Provisional Authority in Iraq and dealt frequently with President Bush, though he was nominally under Secretary Rumsfeld. President Obama made Richard Holbrooke his special representative for Afghanistan and Pakistan and former Senator George Mitchell as special representative for Middle East peace issues. While such appointments allow the president more direct control over particular policy matters, they also can undermine the interagency process by circumventing its normal procedures and protections.

As economic policy matters have gained in priority for presidential attention, White House economic advisers have been drawn into the NSC process. Bill Clinton created a separate, NSC-like National Economic Council (NEC) to coordinate administration economic policy, a body continued by his successors, though with varying effectiveness. Often, the NEC personnel for international economic issues including trade were dual-hatted with the NSC staff assigned those subjects.

As the Presidential Toolkit Brief (Table 3.1) shows, the chief executive has a number of people in the EOP to use for foreign policy missions as well as a number of possible actions even before turning matters over to one of the established departments or agencies. The president can engage in personal diplomacy by phone calls or face-to-face meetings with foreign leaders, or he can use people seen as close to him—especially the vice president, NSA, or special envoys—as instruments to convey messages and seek mutual agreements. While such actions have important advantages, they must be used sparingly because of the enormous demands on the limited time of senior officials.

Presidents also can use the White House *bully pulpit* to promote their foreign policies, though they must recognize that everyone can hear what they say, and not all overseas audiences will react the same. Presidents have legal powers to implement some policies by the stroke of a pen, such as by signing an executive order forbidding assassinations or authorizing a CIA covert operation. And within some limits, depending on the purpose and size of the sums involved, they can allocate funds to special activities without further action by Congress.

As chief diplomat, the president can conclude international agreements directly, ranging from agreed statements to formal documents to treaties that require Senate approval. More often, of course, the negotiations are delegated to other government officials, subject to presidential review and endorsement.

While America's foreign policy instruments are numerous and diverse, as later chapters will detail, presidents may choose to keep the action close to the White House either for secrecy or urgency.

## National Security Council System: The Scowcroft Model

Former Air Force Lt. Gen. Brent Scowcroft was promoted by President Ford to be NSA and then was brought back to that post by President Bush the elder. In 1987, he was one of three members of the Tower Commission investigating the Iran-Contra scandal for President Reagan, where he learned how dysfunctional the NSC staff had become in the Reagan years. Scowcroft and Bush formed a solid team of shared views and created the NSC system that remains essentially unchanged to this day. Some features had been used by earlier administrations, but Scowcroft organized and codified them into an elegant whole.

At the top is the formal NSC, used sparingly. Scowcroft added a venue—called the Principals Committee or PC—for senior officials to meet without the president. The PC could be used to develop recommendations or options for the president, and their deliberations could occur without the jockeying that might take place as members reacted to presidential comments or body language. This can work for several different operating styles—those presidents who want an agreed consensus as well as those who want discrete options to decide on.

Beneath the PC, the real workhorse for the interagency process was the DC, the Deputies Committee, consisting of the number two officials in most departments. They would meet frequently to "tee up" matters for the PC and the president.

Below them would be the issue groups at the assistant secretary level, called variously Policy Coordinating Committees (Bush) or Interagency Policy Committees (Obama). These would be the standing panels to meet and prepare materials for meetings at higher levels. The key political issue for members was who had the authority to convene a meeting, that is, to elevate a particular matter for interagency consideration. In some administrations, that power rested solely with the NSC staff; in others, some groups were chaired by departmental assistant secretaries.

Scowcroft also argued that the NSA should play the honest broker role and that the NSC staff should avoid getting involved in operational activities. That approach worked well in the first Bush administration because of the extraordinary collegiality of the senior officials. Secretary of State Baker and Defense Secretary Cheney had known and worked well with Bush and Scowcroft in earlier administrations, and they remained determined to keep their deliberations out of the newspapers and their staffs collaborative. Those conditions did not prevail in subsequent administrations.

Despite broad agreement that the Scowcroft model was best, his successors have failed to recreate it. Bill Clinton had a more fluid if not undisciplined management style, and he broadened the number of members of advisory groups, thus sacrificing efficiency for inclusion. George W. Bush named NSAs that were unable to corral the vice president and defense secretary. One high-level participant said that "the Pentagon had their thumb on the scales" and that the vice president created his own parallel system that short-circuited the regular process.[21]

On taking office, President Obama's NSA, retired Marine Corps General Jim Jones, issued a formal memorandum to national security policy makers that implicitly overturned many Bush administration practices. Jones declared that the president wanted an interagency process that was "strategic, agile, transparent, and predictable." He also promised that policy papers would be circulated 48 hours in advance of meetings, that there would be a "regular announced schedule" of meetings; an agreed agenda; and that "every meeting will end with clear agreement on what was decided and *what may not have been decided.* Such an ending will also include the delegation of responsibilities for implementation." Jones also insisted that "agency representatives must be able to speak for their agency."[22] The extent to which the Obama administration met these standards is unclear.

# National Security Council Culture

Whether there is a distinctive NSC staff culture is a matter of debate. One scholar says no organization culture develops because most NSC staff stay no longer than a president's term of office, that the staff consists of "an ever-changing mix of officials" of diverse backgrounds, and that detailees from other agencies are chosen carefully but asked to set aside their bureaucratic loyalties for the duration.[23] On the other hand, former staff report that they become immersed in the rhythms of the White House and are acutely sensitive to the personal and political moods of the president. In short, their culture is that of the White House, where political considerations are omnipresent, and policy success often depends on presidential success. Condoleezza Rice underscored the same point by telling her staff, "Your first responsibility is to staff the president." Their second responsibility, she said, was "to make sure that when he wants to move an agenda in a particular direction that you can get this huge ship of state turned around and moved in the direction he wants to go."[24]

This psychological as well as physical proximity to the president and other senior White House officials sets norms of responsiveness as well as a kind of authority to command others in the interagency process. *The president wants this* is about as close to a command as any bureaucrat would expect to hear, and it implicitly demands compliance and warns of punishment of resistance. NSC staff are loyal to the president as a man and to the presidency, rarely in a partisan way but in an institutional way.

# The Paper Flow[25]

Disappointing as it may be to acknowledge, even the biggest national security issues get resolved through a mundane process of meetings and policy papers. In the George W. Bush administration, the PC, with cabinet members and maybe the vice president but excluding the president, met once or twice a week. In the first year or so of the Obama administration, there were often several meetings in a week. These formal sessions were supplemented in both administrations by regular informal lunches or breakfasts as well as telephone and video conferences. The role of the PCs is to develop coordinated consensus recommendations for the president or at least to highlight options when the principals disagree.

The DC is supposed to review issues papers and policy options provided by the subordinate IPCs and decide what should go forward to the PC. During the Bush administration, at least two DC meetings were scheduled each week, and sometimes more were held. In the first year or so of the Obama administration, the DC met almost daily, sometimes in person but also via teleconferences. In addition, some issues get handled without formal meetings but through a *paper PC* or *paper DC* process of circulating documents for review and approval. There are often four or five paper DC documents circulating at any one time.

The IPCs are organized regionally and functionally. They meet at the call of the chair. NSC staff directors often oversee three to five IPCs at the same time. The committees are supposed to do the heavy lifting of policy analysis and the formulation of viable options, which then go forward to the deputies. Sometimes agreement is easy, as on routine matters. At other times, however, differing ideas or departmental equities lead to sharp clashes, the most likely result of which is indecision and delay—doing nothing for now. When they act, the IPC is supposed to draft integrated policy options papers including the basic strategy, assignment of responsibilities among agencies, the resources and mechanisms to be used, and metrics for evaluating the policy.

All of this work must be highly condensed into crisp prose. The typical paper submitted for presidential decision is only a couple of pages in length. Integrated policy options papers are only a few pages longer, no matter how complex the issue. (See Box 3.4.)

---

### Box 3.4

## Inside View: Keep Memos to the President Short

Robert Gates worked on the NSC staff in several administrations before he became CIA director and later secretary of defense. He describes his actions as deputy national security adviser in the G. H. W. Bush administration. His role as a senior adviser to the president gives an inside view into how someone in this position serves as an intermediary and gatekeeper for the president and aids in the policy-making process.

*More than sometimes, I frequently would send it [the memos] back. One of the common faults, even at the NSC level, is that experts think that Presidents cannot conceivably understand an issue unless it covers several pages. One of our jobs in that front office was to protect the President. So one of my tasks was to make sure not only that the stuff was clear, but that it was concise. And I've been doing this my whole career, chopping things down to a page or a page and a half for senior officials, and that's what I did. Sometimes I'd make them do it, sometimes I'd do it myself. But also it was questions of clarity, questions of whether it had been properly coordinated, whether other affected members of the NSC had seen a piece of paper.*

*Everybody tries to slip their stuff through without having to share it with anybody else and play these games and we, I think, put a discipline in the process that after a few months became less and less necessary because they understood it wasn't going through if it hadn't been properly coordinated. So all the paper came through me. A lot of it went back to be worked on or re-worked. A lot of drafts would come over. And I spent a lot of time just sitting with NSC staffers. They would just come in and talk.*

*Source:* From the oral history for the G. H. W. Bush administration, interview with Robert Gates at http://millercenter.org/president/bush/oralhistory/robert-gates.

# Crisis Management

The process is often different in short-fuse crises. (See Box 3.5.) The news report of a military incident or a sudden change of government abroad forces the government into crisis mode. That means urgent meetings that may drag on for hours and subordinates drafting options papers in another room with little guidance from their bosses. It may mean seat-of-the-pants judgments without fuller consideration of alternatives. Critics of groupthink point to the tendency of policy makers under stress to agree to the first reasonable-sounding proposal. Critics of reasoning by analogies point to the habit of policy makers to try to compare one situation to a past event despite the inevitable differences. Many officials looking at Vietnam saw "another Munich," while only a few said "it's another Korea, an unwinnable ground war." On the other hand, rapid agreement may be better than prolonged debate while the situation deteriorates. And, the right analogy can expedite a selection of good choices. The Kennedy administration reached a better decision by taking time for deliberation in the Cuban missile crisis instead of immediately launching air strikes, as some recommended. And, international support to drive Iraqi forces from Kuwait in 1991 was stronger because there was a clear invasion across an internationally recognized border, a stop-Hitler-now situation.

In such crises, presidents usually turn to informal processes to handle the issue. They usually rely on a very small circle of key advisers both because of the urgency of the situation and the need for secrecy, especially if use of force could be involved.[26] They have to decide whether or when to include congressional leaders in the discussion. Bringing them in raises the risks of leaks and political opposition; excluding them raises the risks of anger and fractured unity in the face of threats.

# Process Matters

Does the process really matter? Can it shape the substance of policy choices in subtle and perhaps nonrational ways? Yes it can and sometimes does. Part of the policy process is defining the participants—the stakeholders who deserve to have a seat at the table when matters affecting their responsibilities are discussed. When Dwight Eisenhower included his treasury secretary in NSC meetings, he forced all participants to avoid the argument often used in defense discussions: if we need it, we should pay whatever the cost. John F. Kennedy included his brother the attorney general in the Cuban missile crisis discussions, and at other times, he added someone who made significant and influential comments that drove other participants to a different outcome than they otherwise seemed likely to recommend. When Richard Nixon regularly excluded his secretaries of state and defense from key discussions, he avoided their insights and thus felt more confident in his own decisions. When Ronald Reagan subordinated his NSA to other White House staff, he made it easier for them to run their own

---

| Box 3.5 |

## How Foreign Policy Is Made: Crisis Day at the National Security Council

When a crisis erupts, the NSC system goes into a 24/7 mode. Participants are pulled away from their normal activities and forced to focus on a single, major problem. Participants say that such events "suck the oxygen" out of their departments and agencies as lesser matters get postponed and senior officials are preoccupied with crisis matters. A National Defense University study of the NSC during crises such as the 1991 Gulf War, 1999 Kosovo crisis, the aftermath of the terrorist attacks on September 2001, and the conduct of military operations in Afghanistan and Iraq, described how hectic a typical day was for senior policy makers.

- Departmental meetings with Secretaries or Deputy Secretaries in the early morning to review developments, responsibilities, taskings, and policy issues of concern to the mission of each department.
- In mid-morning, the DC (Deputies Committee) meets, sometimes conducted via secure teleconferencing with senior staff and area/functional experts, to develop interagency positions on developments and new policy issues. This DC meeting might be followed immediately by a meeting of the DC senior members (without supporting staff) to discuss sensitive intelligence or policy issues.
- In late morning or early afternoon, the PC (Principals Committee) meets to discuss the results and unresolved issues of the DC, consider strategic policy directions, and determine what issues need to be brought to the attention of the President. PC members may then meet with the President (who usually receives updates on the crisis situation from the National Security Advisor throughout the day).
- In mid or late afternoon, the DC again meets to discuss the implementation of decisions reached by the PC and President, and discuss the results of IPC [Interagency Policy Committees] meetings that have been held throughout the day (individual IPCs may meet more than once a day during crisis periods).
- Individual members of the DC are likely to have a late afternoon meeting with their principals to confer about developments of the day, and a subsequent meeting with their staffs to discuss the day's decisions, developments, and next steps. Depending upon the circumstances of the day, the PC may have an additional evening meeting and subsequent consultation with the President.
- This kind of high operational tempo may persist for several weeks or months, depending upon the duration of the crisis and the need to involve the President and cabinet level officers on a daily basis.

---

*Source:* Alan G. Whittaker, PhD, Frederick C. Smith, and Ambassador Elizabeth McKune, "The National Security Policy Process: The National Security Council and Interagency System," Annual Update: October 8, 2010, NDU paper at www.ndu.edu/icaf/outreach/publications/nspp/docs/icaf-nsc-policy-process-report-10–2010.pdf.

unsupervised foreign policies. When NSA Tony Lake deliberately scheduled meetings when Richard Holbrooke could not attend, he avoided whatever wisdom or problems the assertive Holbrooke might have brought to the table. When Vice President Cheney sat in on PC meetings and sent his aides to most lower-level NSC staff meetings, he intimidated discussion, just as he intended to. When Barack Obama skipped General Jones to deal with his longtime aide Denis McDonough, he weakened the presumed influence of his NSA.

The process also establishes who can delay or object to clearance of a proposed statement or policy. Can a subordinate act for his principal? Can a senior NSC staffer override the request of a secretary of state or defense? Protocols have to be established, and whoever truly has veto power gains enormous leverage over the process. Even within the White House, rules have to be established. One frequent area of conflict is between cabinet department heads and presidential speech writers. CIA Director George Tenet objected to President George W. Bush's mention of Iraq seeking uranium from Africa in a State of the Union speech only to be overruled by Condoleezza Rice and the speechwriters.[27] What gives a speech punch may be what the diplomats want to avoid.

The policy process also creates action channels for implementation of presidential decisions. When DOD received formal responsibility for preparing for Phase IV of the Iraq war—the post-hostilities situation after the defeat of Saddam Hussein—State Department experts on those matters were excluded from the minimal planning that took place. When White House speechwriters are making last-minute revisions to a presidential statement, they may not have time or inclination to check with an issue expert in a cabinet department who may have valuable advice.

Another way process can affect substance is when the face of the issue—the apparent matter up for decision—is different from its broader or more appropriate context. A request from the president of Taiwan to visit his college reunion in America became a major foreign policy problem for the Clinton administration when Chinese officials objected to this action as a kind of diplomatic recognition of the Taiwanese government. When the United Nations (UN) Security Council was debating how to respond to an ambush killing 24 Pakistani peacekeepers in Somalia during the Clinton administration, the face of the issue was how to keep the UN operation from falling apart rather than the broader issue of the U.S. military role in Somalia. General Colin Powell learned of the U.S. vote while exercising on his treadmill. Similarly, Rumsfeld's creating the notion of a Global War on Terror (GWOT) automatically redefined issues that might have been treated as minor incidents or criminal matters as part of the GWOT channel, thereby adding some bureaucratic elements and excluding others from policy deliberations.

Secretary of State Powell was also excluded from many important Bush administration meetings because of what his aides deemed a refusal by other officials to follow the "regular order" of interagency policy discussions.

Time and again, Vice President Cheney or Defense Secretary Rumsfeld got the president to agree to some national security matter without involving the State Department.

As the below case study on Obama's Afghanistan Policy Review demonstrates, the president can insist on a thorough process, but that takes time and is subject to leaks intended to influence the ultimate decision. Yet, such a process can also lead to a narrowing of differences and even consensus in support of the policy.

The absence of a regular process satisfactory to the participants leads to one-off deals with the president and only narrowly considered policies. That was what Nixon realized had occurred and which he tried to stop by further isolating himself from many of his advisers. On the other hand, FDR relished conducting policy that way. The value of vetting ideas is that mistakes and unintended consequences are more likely to be avoided. The costs of vetting are delays and possible unwanted disclosures of matters under discussion. There's no way to avoid these dilemmas and trade-offs. The process can shape the substance of policy.

## Foreign Policy Is a Never-Ending Process

Despite the finality of announcements that the president has decided on some new policy, the reality is what former Secretary of State George Shultz complained about. "Nothing ever gets settled in this town, a seething debating society in which the debate never stops, in which people never give up, including me. And so that's the atmosphere in which you administer." His comments point to two realities: first, big issues are perennial issues; second, each big decision requires numerous subsequent decisions on implementation. How to deal with a rising China won't be settled by a single policy paper. Whoever loses the policy fight in round one may scheme to win in round two and may even stir up a new issue to provoke a second round. That has been the story, for example, of policy toward North Korea, where new accusations of cheating on earlier agreements resurrects the policy debate. Even when there is a settled policy—like President Obama's December 2009 on Afghanistan—practical questions arise each month afterward that can lead to tweaks or revisions, such as further troop deployments that later occurred. Issues are settled only when no one has any reason to disagree any more. And even those may require additional confirming decisions.

New presidents inherit the NSC process, but they don't inherit the files. In fact, NSC materials are trucked away to the departing chief executive's presidential library on Inauguration Day, leaving the files empty and thus imposing an immediate loss of institutional memory.[28] In fact, of course, some staff serve before and after January 20, and cabinet departments have their own files. But, the system imposes a blank slate event that exaggerates the freedom of maneuver of a new administration.

# Critiques of the Current National Security Council System

The president can change the NSC system, and each does to some extent. While the Obama administration was reacting to perceived flaws of the Bush system, it stopped short of adopting changes suggested by outside analysts. Among the frequent recommendations are to have a robust strategic planning cell and to empower issue team leaders by giving them staff, directive power over other agencies, and even some budget authority. While Bush and Obama both endeavored to do more strategic planning, they encountered problems that are probably inherent in trying to get people nearly overwhelmed by immediate problems to think long range.[29]

Empowering issue team leaders, as might have been done for Richard Holbrooke or George Mitchell, requires legislation, which the administration did not request. In fact, the NSA has no legal standing or authority because the post is not Senate confirmed, and thus the NSA cannot be an officer of the United States with any directive authority. Requiring confirmation, of course, would give the Senate a veto over the president's preferred adviser and subject the nominee to testify before Congress, a task now avoided by presidential order and long-standing precedents.

Some analysts consider the NSC staff too large, others too small. That of course depends on what one expects the staff to do. More people creates a larger staff to manage, only a few of whom would ever come in contact with the president. Fewer people might leave some issues unwatched at the White House level, thus freeing the operating agencies to do more smart or dumb things on their own. There are always these trade-offs.

Presidents can learn too. They can change the way they do business if they have incentives to change—either policy failures or new opportunities—and if they can find the right people and an effective mechanism to do the job. Most organizations innovate not by radically changing what everybody does but by empowering a new entity to do the new tasks. There are many ways a president can add to his foreign policy toolkit or find new ways of using the existing ones.

* * *

The president has enormous discretion over which tools to use to carry out his foreign policies and how to use them. There are some legal constraints and often even stronger political constraints from public opinion and Congress. Since the 1960s, the president has had a White House-centered information and advisory system based on the NSC and its staff. But, the president can also make use of the vice president, other White House officials, and special envoys. The process of cabinet-level, deputy secretary-level, and assistant secretary-level committees has been largely the same since 1989, but in crisis situations, most presidents turn to much smaller groups of trusted advisers.

While there is a tendency to focus on specific presidential announcements and actions as definitive, the policy process in fact is ongoing, never ending, and frequently revisiting and changing what had been decided earlier.

# Case Study: Obama's Review of Afghanistan Policy

This case shows how one president used his foreign policy advisory system in a lengthy and deliberate way to review a major issue and devise a new strategy. President Obama had the luxury of time in which to conduct his reassessment. He also had a mostly unified national security team—unlike George W. Bush, who in 2006–2007, relied on outside advocates and disagreed with the recommendations of his senior military advisers regarding a U.S. troop surge for Iraq.

Barack Obama campaigned for the presidency as a critic of the war in Iraq, but he supported the fight against the Taliban and al Qaeda in Afghanistan, calling it a *war of necessity*. On January 21, 2009, the day after his inauguration, he held his first NSC meeting and was told of a pending military request to send an additional 30,000 U.S. troops to Afghanistan, nearly doubling the existing 38,000 who were there along with 29,000 from NATO countries. He ordered a 60-day policy review.

His new team included Defense Secretary Robert Gates, who had led the Pentagon for the previous two years under George W. Bush, Secretary of State Hillary Clinton, National Security Adviser General Jim Jones, and his special representative for Afghanistan and Pakistan, former Ambassador Richard Holbrooke.

Sensing resistance, military planners scaled back their request to 27,000 troops. On February 13, with the policy review just starting, Obama held an NSC meeting that considered whether to postpone action on the troop request until completion of the review, or to send 17,000 troops immediately and consider the rest later, or to send the entire 27,000. As often happens, Obama chose the middle option.

The new policy was announced on March 27. The president declared a goal to "disrupt, dismantle, and defeat al Qaeda and its safe havens" and said an additional 4,000 U.S. troops would be sent, along with the 17,000 announced earlier, in order to accelerate the training of Afghan security forces. The classified policy paper included 20 recommendations and 180 subrecommendations for action.

On May 11, Secretary Gates, seeking fresh thinking and new military leadership, replaced the U.S. commander in Afghanistan with Gen. Stanley McChrystal. In his Senate confirmation hearing, McChrystal said he might need more troops than had already been sent.

The troop increase question led to renewed tension between the president and some of his civilian advisers and senior military leaders. People in the White House thought that the troop issue had been settled for the rest of the year and resented the pressure to revisit Obama's decision. The military had meanwhile translated the policy into one of defeating the Taliban as well as al Qaeda and thought the mission was inadequately resourced.

At the end of August, Gen. McChrystal sent a 66-page classified assessment of the problems his command faced and what was needed to carry out the announced policy. He warned that "the status quo will lead to failure" and said much had to be done promptly to avoid "strategic defeat." At Gates's request, there were no troop increase numbers in the report. They were provided on September 25—a three-option proposal for 10,000 or 40,000 or 80,000 more U.S. troops.

Obama began another formal and extensive policy review on September 13. He spent more than 25 hours in 10 meetings over the next three months. Gen. Jones later said that "none of us ended up where we started." The president ran the meetings with a lot of questions. He forced the group to consider what goals were achievable given the bleak military and political situation. By October 9, the group consensus was to change the explicit goal from *defeating* to *degrading* the Taliban, thus prompting suggestions for lower troop numbers.

Vice President Joe Biden was the most vocal opponent of substantial troop increases, calling instead for what he labeled counterterrorism plus. He worked back channel with the vice chairman of the JCS, Gen. James Cartwright, to develop a 20,000-troop plan, but it was opposed by Gates, Clinton, and others. Obama later said that he particularly wanted to be sure that he maintained Gates's support for his strategy.

Obama continued to express frustration in several NSC meetings during October because he didn't feel he had been given real options. "We don't have two options yet," he complained. "We have 40,000 and nothing." On October 30, Gates responded with an Option 2A, calling for 30,000 to 35,000 more troops.

Obama welcomed the sign of flexibility and even told his November 11 meeting that he supported a *surge* of troops into Afghanistan, using the term for a similar policy he had opposed in Iraq. He also began pushing back on the deployment timetable. "Why can't we get them there faster?" he asked. He then seized on Gates's willingness to start troop reductions after 18 to 24 months in order to pressure the Afghan government.

The remaining debates in November focused on the precise troop number, the speed of their deployment, and the possible timetable to start withdrawals. The sizable surge pleased the military, the planned withdrawals pleased the skeptical civilians, and the accelerated deployments pleased everybody.

On November 29, Obama met with his advisers, told them he would approve 30,000 troops plus no more than 10 percent more for trainers. He insisted on a July 2011 deadline to begin withdrawals but agreed that the pace of reductions would depend on conditions. He also told his generals, "Don't clear and hold what you can't transfer [to the Afghans]." He asked for and received formal support for the plan. He even took the unusual step of getting them to endorse a six-page terms sheet that he had drafted, laying out the new strategy.

While not part of the Afghanistan policy review, though it was at the back of everyone's mind, was what to do in Pakistan. In October, the president approved increased secret operations in Pakistan, including more drone strikes against terrorists there.

Obama announced his Afghanistan policy in a nationally televised address delivered to cadets at West Point on December 1.

While other aspects of Afghanistan policy had been considered earlier, this case focuses on the question of how to use the military instrument. The president used his NSC advisory system to discuss and debate policy options. The process was disrupted by press reports of leaked information. Eventually, the president obtained formal assent from his advisers before announcing his policy publicly.

*Sources:* Peter Baker, "How Obama Came to Plan for 'Surge' in Afghanistan," *The New York Times,* December 5, 2009; Anne E. Kornblut, Scott Wilson, and Karen DeYoung, "Obama Pressed for Faster Surge," *Washington Post,* December 6, 2009; Bob Woodward, *Obama's Wars* (New York: Simon & Schuster, 2010).

## Selected Resources

The current White House website is at www.whitehouse.gov/. There are also archived presidential websites for earlier presidents:

George W. Bush—http://georgewbush-whitehouse.archives.gov/

Bill Clinton—www.clintonlibrary.gov/archivesearch.html

The best recent description of the White House staff is in Bradley H. Patterson, Jr., *To Serve the President: Continuity and Innovation in the White House Staff* (Washington, DC: Brookings, 2008).

Historical studies of the NSC and the ways different presidents have used the NSC and its staff can be found in: Peter W. Rodman, *Presidential Command* (New York: Knopf, 2009); David Rothkopf, *Running the World* (New York: Public Affairs, 2005); Ivo M. Saalder and I. M. Destler, *In the Shadow of the Oval Office* (New York: Simon & Schuster, 2009); and John P. Burke, *Honest Broker? The National Security Advisor and Presidential Decision Making* (College Station, TX: Texas A&M University Press, 2009).

Historical collections of presidential documents and other information are available through The American Presidency Project at the University of California, Santa Barbara, www.presidency.ucsb.edu/ and the CB Presidential Research Services site, Presidents of the United States, www.presidentsusa.net/.

# 4

# Congress's Toolkit

*If we cannot inquire into the state of the Army, it follows that the Army belongs to the President and not to the nation.*

—Nathaniel Macon (D-NC), three-term speaker of the house, 1810

*I don't care to be involved in the crash-landing unless I can be in on the take-off.*

—Harold Stassen, later frequently repeated by Senator Arthur Vandenberg

*We don't need 535 secretaries of state.*

—Vice President Dick Cheney, April 13, 2007

Congress is rarely in the driver's seat for U.S. foreign policy, but it fuels the car, sometimes tries to navigate from the front seat, and often complains from the backseat. It also has its own hand brake to use in emergencies. Needless to say, the vehicle goes farthest and fastest when Congress and the president agree on the route forward.

The Constitution gives Congress its own set of powers over foreign policy, including most notably the powers to appropriate funds and to write the laws governing executive departments. The Senate has the additional right to advise and consent to nominations and treaties. These powers can be abused, but they also can be left dormant or delegated. History has examples of each. Sometimes over the course of U.S. history, Congress has been assertive and influential in foreign policy matters. At other times, lawmakers have been deferential toward the executive branch or cowed by strong presidents.

This chapter describes the legislative tools that Congress has—summarized in the Toolkit Brief (See Table 4.1)—and gives examples of how and when lawmakers have used them. While the formal tools of the legislative process are the most powerful, the most influential tools are often the less visible ones—the informal contacts, the framing of issues, and the law of anticipated reactions that often limit presidential options. Congress is a political institution, not only in the sense of being influenced by partisan and electoral considerations but also as it competes with the executive branch for power over domestic and foreign policy.

86

| Table 4.1 | The Congressional Toolkit Brief | |
|-----------|--------------------------------|--|
| **ACTION** | **ADVANTAGES** | **DISADVANTAGES** |
| Substantive legislation | Binding law; limits presidential discretion | Harder to pass; much harder to change |
| Procedural legislation | Puts onus on president | Can be evaded |
| Advisory legislation | Easier to pass | Can be ignored |
| Appropriations | Unchallengeable as grants or denials of funds | Many hurdles to approval; some loopholes to denials |
| Oversight (hearings, investigations, reports) | Dramatizes issues; gains information | Time-consuming; can be abused |
| Informal contacts | Easy; less confrontational | Can be ignored |
| Delay or rejection of nominations | Gains attention and leverage over issue | Limits presidential choice and actions |
| Delay or rejection of treaties | Gains attention and leverage over issue | Can damage relations with other nations |
| Framing issues | Rewards for early action | Many potential competitors |

Congress has several means at its disposal to use to influence foreign policy making, including the passage of legislation, use of appropriations, oversight, and delaying or rejecting nominations and treaties. While each of these provide advantages to Congress, such as setting limits on presidential actions, they also hold drawbacks, including the potential to damage U.S. relations with other countries through inaction or inconsistency. Congress used its legislative tools in 1947 to provide a new instrument of foreign policy to the executive branch when it created the Central Intelligence Agency (CIA), the National Security Council (NSC), and what became the Department of Defense (DOD).

# How Congress Acts

The formal legislative process—how a bill becomes a law—explains only partly how Congress influences U.S. foreign policy. There are occasions when a member introduces a bill, watches a committee hold hearings and report it, debates it on the floor, and succeeds in getting it passed, only to await similar action by the other chamber until the measure is sent to the president for signature. More often, foreign policy legislation is attached to broader bills that are expected to be passed, sometimes with little or no consideration by the relevant committees or foreknowledge by the executive branch. Sometimes, the new law is the product of months of negotiations among interested officials. Other times, it may be a quick response to that day's news.

Congress can also influence presidential actions without actually passing a law. The threat of passage, or even a narrow defeat, can persuade senior policy makers to alter course. Consultations might actually change minds. Suggestions from lawmakers might be adopted by the administration. A scheduled hearing can force a divided executive branch to make up its mind.

A required report on human rights or religious liberty can give U.S. diplomats leverage over another nation that hopes to get a favorable comment.

Simply by drawing attention to a foreign policy issue—the plight of Soviet Jews in the 1970s, starvation in Somalia in 1992, ethnic conflict in the Balkans in the 1990s, genocide in Sudan in the 2000s—Congress can force a reluctant administration to fashion a policy and take action abroad. By their speeches and activities, lawmakers can frame issues for public debate, pushing secondary issues like drug trafficking or terrorism to the front burner. The most powerful tools, however, are the regular ones that are part of the constitutional system.

## The Legal Tool

The legislative process can create instruments for the executive branch in foreign policy by creating the agencies and giving them authorities, responsibilities, and capabilities. There was no secretary of defense until Congress created the post in 1947. In fact, there was no DOD until two years later. The first secretary had only coordinating powers over the long-established service bureaucracies. The 1947 law also created the CIA and gave statutory standing to the Joint Chiefs of Staff (JCS).

The Marshall Plan to rebuild war-ravaged Europe required an agency to administer it. Congress created that bureaucracy and later broadened its mandate to other foreign aid programs. Over the decades, lawmakers have frequently changed foreign aid agencies, often by adding new and separate entities like the Millennium Challenge Corporation and by giving new mandates such as combating HIV/AIDS.

Although it stopped short of creating a Department of Trade, Congress did create the post of U.S. trade representative (USTR), the official charged with negotiating trade agreements, located it in the Executive Office of the President (EOP), and made it equal in rank to any cabinet officer. As discussed in Chapter 7, this made the USTR more an arm of Congress than a subordinate to the president.

When Congress wanted to push the executive branch toward greater efforts at nuclear arms control, it created the Arms Control and Disarmament Agency in 1961. Nearly four decades later, Congress reversed course and abolished the agency.

Similarly, to increase military capabilities for special operations and counterterrorism, Congress created a separate combatant organization, the Special Operations Command (SOCOM) and protected its budget by segregating it from the rest of Pentagon spending. After the 9/11 attacks, Congress and President George W. Bush sparred over how to strengthen the government's capacity for homeland security. The president favored informal coordination but was ultimately forced by Congress to accept a full-fledged department for that task.

Once created, these national security organizations depend on financial and human resources to do their assigned jobs. Sometimes that comes easily, as when Congress mandated increases in the army and marine corps in 2004. Other times, there is resistance, as there has been to proposals to increase the civilian capacity of the U.S. government for post-conflict stabilization missions in Iraq and Afghanistan.

Congress can also pass laws changing the rules under which agencies operate. Policies followed in international family planning programs have been reversed and re-reversed by changing congressional provisions related to domestic disputes. Likewise, the nature of military leadership has been changed by legislation like the Goldwater–Nichols Defense Reorganization Bill of 1986, which forced military officers seeking to become generals or admirals to serve an assignment in a so-called joint post that would give them familiarity with other armed services. Congress also wrote new rules into the laws underpinning the foreign aid programs, such as the numerous provisions requiring cuts in assistance to countries that abuse human rights or help terrorist organizations or suffer military coups against democratically elected governments.

## Substantive Versus Procedural Laws

There are two basic models of foreign policy laws. One approach, substantive legislation, sets forth policy principles and administrative tasks. The other, procedural legislation, establishes a series of steps the executive branch must take before it has the authority to act abroad. Sometimes, Congress stops short of binding laws and passes *sense of Congress* measures that are merely advisory, however strongly felt.

Laws with teeth include embargos against trade and other relations with Fidel Castro's Cuba, imposed by executive order in 1962 and codified in law in 1992 (PL 102–484). Another example of substantive legislation was the 1986 law, passed over President Reagan's veto, prohibiting new U.S. investment in South Africa as well as trade in agricultural products, steel, and nuclear supplies. As discussed in the accompanying case study, bipartisan majorities demonstrated their opposition to South African apartheid policies. During the early 1980s, Congress also wrote a series of laws trying to constrain Reagan administration policies toward Central America. A ban on aid to the Nicaraguan contras, who sought to overthrow the leftist government there, was passed 10 times during the 1980s.[1] In another example, the Nuclear Non-Proliferation Act of 1978 (NNPA) revised the laws controlling the export of nuclear-related materials and mandated renegotiation of existing cooperative agreements with other countries. It also imposed sanctions on countries that conducted nuclear tests or failed to sign on to the Non-Proliferation Treaty.

On occasion, tough laws have unintended consequences. In 1981, Congress waived provisions of the NNPA that would have required cuts in U.S. aid to Pakistan because lawmakers wanted to help that nation in its efforts to undermine the Soviet invasion of Afghanistan. In 1985, in order to head off even tougher provisions, Congress approved an amendment allowing aid so long as the president could certify that Pakistan did not possess a nuclear device. By 1990, however, the first President Bush could no longer make such a certification, and arms sales were abruptly halted.[2] What was sold as a way to deter a Pakistani nuclear capability created major diplomatic problems when it failed. Lawmakers granted further exemptions for Pakistan in the mid-1990s, but the experience has had a lasting impact on U.S.–Pakistani relations. Even as Pakistan has been a major recipient of U.S. aid since 2001, both civilian and military leaders in Islamabad have expressed distrust of U.S. motives and anger at U.S. policies in the region.

When President Jimmy Carter established full diplomatic relations with the People's Republic of China and abrogated the 1954 Mutual Defense Treaty with the government on Taiwan, new legislation was required. Conservatives in Congress challenged the legality of Carter's treaty action, which was ultimately upheld by the courts. They also tried to mandate U.S. military support for Taiwan in case of an attack from the mainland. The final version of the bill contained rhetorical provisions sympathetic to Taiwan and declared that the United States would continue to provide defense articles and services "to enable Taiwan to maintain a sufficient self-defense capability." Other provisions established unusual arrangements for unofficial, quasi-diplomatic relations (PL 96–8). This is an instance in which Congress sought to first reverse and then strictly limit the impact of the president's policy change.

The second basic model of foreign policy law, procedural legislation, is commonly used to establish tough principles but then allow the president discretion in implementing the provisions. Most mandatory sanctions carry waivers allowing the president to avoid imposing them by submitting some certification to Congress. Aid to El Salvador in the 1980s, for example, followed this pattern—requiring presidential certification that the Salvadoran government was complying with human rights, making political and economic reforms, and preventing torture by its armed forces. When this was attested by President Reagan, U.S. aid was allowed to be given. Other waivers are tied to presidential declarations that important national security interests require the law to be set aside. Such a waiver allowed President Clinton to suspend a section of the 1996 Helms–Burton law that would have allowed U.S. nationals to sue foreign companies that did business with Cuba.[3]

Starting during the 1970s, Congress passed a series of major foreign policy laws creating procedures for handling important issues. The War Powers Resolution is a prime example. It allows presidential decisions to use military force but tries to limit the duration of combat operations and allows Congress to revisit the decision later. The Arms Export Control Act sets rules and conditions for arms sales but gives Congress a right to review and veto them. Fast-track provisions allowing the United States to enter into trade negotiations, now called *trade promotion authority (TPA)*, establish procedures leading ultimately to non-amendable bills with guaranteed single up-or-down votes in the Senate and House. These examples illustrate the ways in which Congress can restrain presidential action and help guide policy as well as ways that Congress seeks to allow itself flexibility to change decisions later.

Lawmakers have also built procedural remedies for opponents of certain trade practices. The International Trade Commission is an independent, quasi-judicial agency that has been empowered to administer trade remedy laws. It hears complaints of unfair trade practices by foreigners, such as the *dumping* of commodities at prices below those at home, and makes recommendations for presidential actions. Another trade law created the interagency Committee on Foreign Investment in the United States (CFIUS) to make findings on whether a planned foreign investment in an American company would have adverse national security risks.

Procedural legislation has numerous advantages for the executive and legislative branches. From the president's standpoint, it allows some discretion as he determines whether the specified conditions apply or whether a waiver is justified. Yet, the threat of sanctions gives the administration leverage over foreign nations in pressing for policy changes. The advantage for lawmakers is that they can trumpet their stances on principle yet distance themselves from the consequences and place any blame on the president if things go badly.

## The Money Tool

Congress frequently uses its appropriations bills to shape and direct U.S. foreign policy. As Chapter 5 discusses in more detail, lawmakers boost aid to favored nations and restrict it to those that fall out of favor. They also demand that the executive branch seek agreements with others, such as in sharing military burdens and in joining sanctions against misbehaving states. At various times, Congress has used its money tool to forbid certain military operations, as in parts of Southeast Asia during the Vietnam War, or to oppose certain military capabilities desired by the Pentagon, including antisatellite weapons and certain kinds of missile defense systems. Even routine buy-American provisions can cause foreign policy problems for the U.S. government.

Current practice also gives congressional committees leverage over other foreign policy transactions. They must be notified in advance of proposed arms sales and aid disbursements and transfers of funds between accounts above certain thresholds.

America's foreign aid programs are also tightly constrained by earmarks—where lawmakers assign funds for specific countries, thereby limiting executive branch discretion or flexibility in changed circumstances. About three fourths of the Foreign Operations Appropriations Bill has been routinely earmarked in recent years. Theoretically, earmarks in committee reports are not legally binding, though those in law are. Even so, bureaucrats are reluctant to disregard committee wishes, fearing retaliation the following year.

While substantive and procedural legislation may contain ambiguities or loopholes that allow for presidential discretion or even evasion, the money tool is unchallengeable. No president has claimed the right to ignore congressional denial of funds for foreign policy activities. Even Richard

Nixon ended U.S. combat operations in Southeast Asia when Congress cut off funds.

### The Treaty Tool

The Senate can influence foreign policy through its special power to advise and consent to treaties with other nations. The president, of course, can decide how closely to consult with senators or whether to accept their advice. George Washington's experience led to a distancing rarely closed in the past two centuries. (See Box 4.1.)

---

### Box 4.1

## Who Makes Foreign Policy: George Washington Gives Up on Advice and Consent

The Constitution allows the president to conclude treaties and nominate officials "with the advice and consent" of the Senate. George Washington thought that that provision meant that he was to consult with senators in advance so that he could receive their advice. His first attempts to do so, however, created more problems than they solved.

From the start of his presidency, Washington was scrupulous in following the intent of the framers as he performed his duties. He was greatly offended, however, when the Senate for the first time rejected one of his nominees, Benjamin Fishbourn, to be a naval officer assigned to the port of Savannah, Georgia. Fishbourn was the only one of 102 nominees for various posts to be voted down. On August 5, 1789, the president stormed into the Senate chamber, surprising its members, and demanded an explanation for the rejection. He also suggested that the senators should have told him of their problems with his nominee before actually taking a vote. One of the Georgia senators outlined his own opposition but noted that the Senate was not obligated to give any reasons. This marked the beginning of *Senatorial courtesy*, which allowed lawmakers to block appointments of federal officials in their own state.

Washington calmed down and submitted an alternate nominee, who was quickly approved. Meanwhile, the Senate voted to establish a committee to work out "the mode of communication proper to be pursued between him and the Senate" in appointment and treaty matters. Some members suggested that Senate advice and consent should be given in the presence of the president, but Washington said he preferred written communications as a general rule. He said he didn't want to inhibit free discussion by the lawmakers.

On Saturday, August 22, by prior arrangement, Washington again went to the Senate, accompanied by Secretary of War Henry Knox, this time to seek its advice and consent on plans to negotiate some Indian treaties. He handed the vice president his message and took his seat. Noisy carriages outside drowned out the first reading of the president's message, so it had to be read again. It explained his plans and asked the Senate's advice on a series of seven questions related to the negotiations.

Senators started discussing the first question, then postponed action until the following Monday in order to get more information. They started to discuss the

---

(Continued)

second question, and agreed to postpone it as well, but continued to argue over the issue. Some members favored creation of a special committee to consider the message. Washington then rose "in a violent fret." He complained, "This defeats every purpose of my coming here."

Washington eventually agreed to the delay, returned on Monday, and stayed during the long session while Senators argued and voted on the seven questions. He then left and never again returned in person to seek the Senate's advice and consent, nor did any of his successors.

Washington's troubled experience seeking Senate advice led later presidents to restrict consultation to informal soundings and private conversations. The consultation tool has been used much less frequently than the framers probably expected.

*Sources:* Annals of Congress; David P. Currie, *The Constitution in Congress: The Federalist Period* (Chicago: University of Chicago Press, 1997), 21–26; Ron Chernow, *Washington: A Life* (New York: Penguin Press, 2010), 590–593.

---

The constitutional requirement for a two-thirds vote for approval makes any treaty an easy hostage for any groups of senators who object to its provisions or want other matters settled to their satisfaction. The historical record misleadingly suggests that treaty ratification is common. In its first 200 years, the Senate voted in favor of more than 1,500 treaties, about 90% of those submitted. Moreover, only 21 treaties were actually rejected by the Senate, and only three of these defeats occurred since the 1930s. (These were the Law of the Sea convention in 1960, the Montreal aviation protocol setting new limits on damage awards in plane crashes in 1983, and the Comprehensive [nuclear] Test Ban Treaty in 1999.)

But, the threat of defeat or of indefinite delay led many presidents to resort to executive agreements that do not require Senate approval. Since the start of World War II, the United States has concluded approximately 16,500 executive agreements and only about 1,100 treaties.[4] When Congress learned of secret agreements concluded in the 1950s and 1960s, it passed the Case Act (1 USC 112b[a]) requiring congressional notification of all such agreements within 60 days.

What's the difference between a treaty and an executive agreement? Basically, if the deal is called a treaty, it requires a two-thirds vote; if it's not called a treaty, no vote is necessary. The State Department has published criteria separating the more technical agreements from the policy-significant matters that could become treaties, including a provision calling for consultations with the Senate on the matter. Sometimes, it's a close call. In 2002, the Russians insisted that the Strategic Offensive Reductions Treaty (SORT) be considered a treaty and sent to the Senate a for approval, a demand probably made to force the Bush administration to defend its Russia policy just six months after the president announced that the United States would withdraw from the 1972 Anti-Ballistic Missile Treaty, which the Russians wanted to preserve.[5] The 2007 security agreement with Iraq became less controversial when it imposed a deadline for U.S. troop withdrawals favored by antiwar congressmen, who dropped their insistence on considering it a treaty.

Treaties need to run the Senate's legislative gauntlet like any other bill. They are all referred to the Foreign Relations Committee, where hearings are usually held. A favorable vote there reports a resolution of ratification, which is what needs the two-thirds vote. During its consideration, the Senate may amend the treaty itself as well as the resolution of ratification, but any treaty amendment has to be accepted by other signatories. Such proposals are often *killer amendments* that can defeat the treaty under the guise of strengthening or clarifying it. If a treaty is not acted on in the first year or so, it goes back on the calendar, where it can languish until there are enough votes for passage. The Genocide Convention stayed on the Senate calendar for 40 years before finally being approved in 1988.

Noncontroversial treaties, like bilateral tax conventions, are often approved by voice vote. Controversial ones, however, can tie up the Senate for weeks and lead to complex maneuvering. The 1977 Panama Canal treaties were debated for six weeks and were ultimately approved only after the Panamanian leader accepted an actual amendment to the treaty text.

The Senate can attach reservations to the resolution of ratification that may or may not require consent by other signatories, depending on their substance. One of the more famous measures was the *Connally Reservation* to the treaty establishing the International Court of Justice to bar the court from having jurisdiction over domestic matters "as determined by the United States." In addition to reservations, the Senate sometimes adds *understandings* that are binding only on the United States, and *declarations* that are rhetorical and advisory. In 2010, action on the new START nuclear arms treaty with Russia, the Senate used a different formulation. Instead of reservations, it attached *conditions* that it said were "binding upon the [U.S.] President." In that case, the conditions included increased spending on programs to maintain the effectiveness of U.S. nuclear weapons capabilities.[6]

During treaty consideration, the Senate leadership often negotiates with the executive branch in order to win acceptance of such additions to the resolution of ratification precisely in order to build bridges for skeptical senators to cross over from opposition to support. The sponsors of amendments can then claim that they improved the treaty and thus justify their votes. This process is another way for the Senate to influence foreign policy.

### The Nomination Tool

The Senate takes seriously its *advice and consent* power over nominations. From the earliest days of the republic, Senators told presidents whom they favored for various administration jobs. Proposed nominations are often quietly vetted with key senators, especially the chairman and ranking member of the committee with jurisdiction over the nomination. And senators are quite willing to give advice to nominees during their confirmation hearings on how they should perform their jobs.

The path to Senate confirmation is often long and difficult. The average time from inauguration to confirmation of senior officials has more than tripled since the 1960s, from less than three months in the Kennedy administration to more than eight months for recent presidents. Some of those delays are the fault of the White House, which can be slow to pick people and which requires personal background checks by the FBI and lengthy financial and other reports. The Senate then adds its own delays and a different set of required reports. In order to avoid possible conflicts of interest, the Armed Services Committee has long required senior Pentagon officials to divest themselves of stocks in defense companies and to recuse themselves from decisions involving companies they worked for. Delays in handling Pentagon civilian nominations have become so persistent that about 20% of political appointee posts are vacant at any one time.

The number of officials requiring confirmation has grown in recent years—to the point that there is now a push in the Senate to reduce that number. Currently 115 officials in national security positions—plus more than 120 ambassadors—require Senate confirmation. There are 44 in the State Department, 45 in the Defense Department, 8 at CIA, and 18 in Homeland Security. As recently as 1994, there were 27 in State, and in 1977, there were only 31 in DOD. Several senior members of the White House staff—though not the chief of staff or the national security adviser (NSA)—also require confirmation, including the budget director, the science adviser, the members of the Council of Economic Advisers, and the U.S. trade representative.

Lawmakers look at more than the nominee's qualifications for the job. They also consider the person's views on the programs they will administer and their willingness to support ideas favored by Congress. Since the 1950s, senior military officers have been required to promise to come before Congress and give their personal and professional views on military issues, even if those views are different from the president's.

Sometimes senators abuse their power over nominations by taking hostages, usually by placing a *hold* on a nomination until some demand is met. These holds were completely secret until 2007, but a new law trying to ban anonymous holds has been only partially effective. The demand might be for information, or for a certain policy decision, or for something totally unrelated to the responsibilities of the nominee facing delay. An Alabama senator blocked action on over 70 nominations in several departments in an effort to prevent budget cuts affecting his state. He eventually backed down. A Louisiana senator delayed action on the budget director pending an administration decision on offshore oil drilling. In 2011, the Senate adopted a minor reform to end secret holds on nominations but still allowing acknowledged holds.

---

| **Box 4.2** |

## Inside View: Senators Are Human; Not All Are Trustworthy

Congress has many means at its disposal to influence foreign policy, and one of its main vehicles for doing so is via the Senate Foreign Relations Committee. Established in 1816, this standing committee has considered a range of issues over the course of U.S. history. Committee members thus play integral roles in the development of U.S. foreign policy, and the committee can be equally influential on other members of Congress, though it is not without its own internal politics. Carl Marcy, chief of staff of the Senator Foreign Relations Committee from 1955 to 1973, describes some of the men he worked with and some of their personality quirks.

*One of the most effective senators on the Committee during the time that I was there was Senator (Jacob) Javits (R-NY). He was effective because he had an organized mind. He could organize the miscellany of conversations that went on. As you will have seen from the transcripts of executive and mark-up sessions, a lot of things are thrown on the table and then usually the discussion would get to the point where the chairman (William Fulbright, D-AK) would turn to me and say, "Well, Carl, write it up," or "include it in the report." And it was very confusing to know what in the dickens the Committee had really done! Often times Senator Fulbright was more considerate of me and would ask Senator Javits to summarize the discussion, put it in a form that could be used. Javits was very good at that. . . .*

*This business of the powerful chairman of the Foreign Relations Committee, implying that the chairman was a tyrant who controlled everything, when would the Committee meet, what subjects would come up, how people would act, what would come out. He wasn't that kind of person at all. He listened, he'd try to educate. At some point I remember Senator (Stuart) Symington (D-MO) coming to me after he had changed his attitude with respect to our involvement in Vietnam and said something to general effect that "Carl, I've changed my position, and the reason was because Bill educated me. I've learned." For a former secretary of the Air Force to have been exposed to the Fulbright school of foreign policy and admit that it had an impact on him, says much about Fulbright-Symington is not the kind of person anyone would be inclined to whip around at all; Senator Al Gore (Sr., D-TN) was very much the same way. What happens in a committee, or happened in that Committee, was that judgments are developed about how particular people, how senators will act in given situations.*

*Senator Fulbright at one point said to me, "You can't count on Frank Church (D-ID). You can count on Senator Gore, you can count on Senator Symington." What he meant was that if Symington or Gore or (Bourke) Hickenlooper (R-IA) said they were going to do so-and-so, they'd do it. They would support him on the floor on an amendment or whatever it might be. Fulbright was never sure of Senator Church. Always the implication being, without his every [sic] having said it, that Senator Church was a bit of an opportunist. If that meant that he had to change his position or create a doubt about something maybe Fulbright had been led to believe he was firm on, he'd shift. I don't think of any others.*

---

*Source:* Senate oral history, Carl Marcy, SFRC chief of staff 1955–1973, 175, 178 at www.senate.gov/artandhistory/history/resources/pdf/Marcy_interview_5.pdf.

### Oversight Tools

Lawmakers also gain leverage over senior officials by their power of oversight. While no committee has jurisdiction over multiagency operations as such, each panel jealously guards its rights to investigate the departments within its purview. The defense committees oversee the Pentagon; the foreign policy committees oversee the State Department and foreign aid agencies; the intelligence committees oversee the intelligence community (IC); and the appropriations subcommittees oversee the spending by their respective agencies.

Since 1946, every congressional committee has had a requirement to "exercise continuous watchfulness" over programs and agencies within their jurisdiction. Oversight is usually defined as the review, monitoring, and supervision of federal agencies, programs, activities, and policy implementation. The ideal, at least to political scientists, is continuous and comprehensive oversight for purposes of better governance and not merely reelection or intimidation of the bureaucracy being overseen. It should be ongoing and thorough, forward-looking (anticipatory) as well as retrospective, with a focus on big, strategic issues and not merely minutiae. Lawmakers should uncover problems and legislate solutions rather than punishments. They should look beyond compliance issues and try to create incentives and rewards for better performance as well as developing organizational capacities to cope with emerging problems. Members should subordinate scoring political points to promoting better governance. And, of course, the executive branch should be fully forthcoming in providing information.

Besides uncovering past misdeeds, checking up on agencies can also help to prevent future ones. As former Congressman Lee Hamilton has said, "Congressional oversight helps keep federal bureaucracies on their toes."[7]

In practice, however, much oversight is of the *fire-alarm* type, responding to scandals and crises, rather than the regularized *police-patrol* variety. Oversight is a political act. Lack of oversight is also a political act. Everything Congress does or chooses not to do is suffused with political considerations and pregnant with political consequences. Political motivations take many forms—personal power and reelection, notably, but also the institutional power of a committee or a legislative chamber as well as partisan, ideological, or regional power. Even when committees investigate programs to determine their efficiency, effectiveness, and compliance with existing law, how and when they act have political consequences.

Studies have found that congressional oversight—especially measured in terms of frequency of hearings—is most active when the congressional body differs politically with the president.[8] Party loyalty, on the other hand, can mute investigative tendencies. During the Vietnam War, for example, the Foreign Relations Committee under Chairman J. William Fulbright (D-AR) held hearings critical of the conflict, while an Armed Services Committee panel gave military officers a chance to criticize restrictions on the air campaign against North Vietnam.

Lawmakers have several tools to conduct oversight. The most notable are committee hearings and investigations. Sometimes, special committees are established for the purpose, such as the joint panel created to review the Iran-Contra scandal during the Reagan administration, the joint hearings held into the firing of General Douglas MacArthur in 1951, and the 1930s hearings into *merchants of death* involvement in World War I. High-profile investigations of the IC by the Church and Pike Committees in 1975 and 1976 led to the establishment of permanent intelligence oversight committees in both the House and Senate.

At other times, the regular committees of jurisdiction investigate waste, fraud, and abuse in programs they authorize. Routine program hearings and crisis briefings by senior officials can all be occasions for productive oversight, even if that is not the formal purpose of the event. Committees can also request formal reviews by the Government Accountability Office (GAO) or other legislative support organizations. Since the 1940s, the House Appropriations Committee has had a surveys and investigations staff for detailed but quiet oversight. Congress has also created independent inspectors general in most departments and is a ready recipient for their reports.

Another tool for Congress, much resented by the executive branch, is a requirement for reports, one-time or regular, on a vast array of topics. The Pentagon complains that it has to submit more than 700 annual reports to Congress. The State Department says that it has to prepare 310 separate reports each year and that there is a lot of overlap, redundancy, and duplication among those reports. From the congressional perspective, such requirements may be a way of focusing attention on a problem area in order to stimulate the department to devise a better approach. Or, it may be an alternative to an immediate change in the law favored by other lawmakers.

For example, since 1986, the president has been required to submit a comprehensive report on national security strategy each year at the same time the presidential budget is submitted. Few presidents met the annual requirement, and Congress has held no hearings specifically on the content of the report in part because the official responsible for the report, just below the president, is the NSA, who by custom, is not allowed to testify before Congress. Nevertheless, the report forces action and policy coordination within the executive branch and provides Congress with a formal policy statement to use in evaluating administration programs.

## Informal Tools

While hearings gain the most publicity—and are often designed for that purpose—Congress is also very influential over executive agencies by means of less formal devices, such as contacts by members and staff and the resulting meetings and briefings. Outside of the glare of cameras, legislators and administrators can share ideas and information and sometimes make deals separate from what the White House might want. Some observers see an *iron triangle* linking officials in the two branches of government with outside interest groups in cooperation, or collusion, over policy.

Congress also influences policy by raising issues to public consciousness and thus forcing the executive branch to respond with some kind of policy. What happens in medical research—where celebrities are recruited to publicize diseases and lobby for funds—also occurs on foreign policy issues when other celebrities draw attention to human rights issues in particular countries or to savage conflicts that don't receive daily news coverage.

Raising and framing issues occur in both branches, sometimes collaboratively, sometimes competitively. Members of Congress worked with some allies in the executive branch to focus attention on Soviet Jews in the 1970s, Bosnia and then Kosovo in the 1990s, and on the southern Sudan in the 2000s.

Consultations between senior officials and lawmakers occur all the time. Sometimes, they are used to float trial balloons or to try to obtain advance support for measures to be announced. Members routinely demand consultations prior to decisions, and they complain about being informed after the fact. As former Minnesota Governor Harold Stassen and Senator Arthur Vandenberg repeatedly said regarding Roosevelt and Truman foreign policy, "I don't care to be involved in the crash-landing unless I can be in on the take-off."

Perhaps the greatest congressional influence over executive branch decisions comes by way of the *law of anticipated reactions,* where expectations of opposition on Capitol Hill can sidetrack certain policy options in favor of steps that would not be opposed by lawmakers. In 2007, for example, General Peter Pace was denied a second two-year term as chairman of the JCS because lawmakers indicated that he would be sharply criticized in his confirmation hearing. Bill Clinton ruled out the use of ground troops in the conflict with Serbia over Kosovo because of a fear that ground combat would be strongly opposed on the Hill.

While Congress gets regularly praised—or blamed—for its efforts to influence, or meddling, in U.S. foreign policy, its impact has been broader and more significant than the typical examples of the Vietnam War and Cuba. (See Box 4.3.)

# Congressional Culture

Members of Congress are politicians with all that implies. They thrive on confrontation and publicity and so are quite willing to turn minor misunderstandings into major clashes, either among themselves or with the executive branch. Senior members have relatively safe seats, freeing them somewhat from the shifting sands of public opinion but also allowing them to pursue their fixed ideas and bumper-sticker slogans. Seniority is rewarded with power in both chambers, especially committee chairmanships. But, that seniority often reflects issue involvement and familiarity far in excess of what political appointees bring to their positions. Long-serving members and staff are quite willing to remind the new secretaries and assistant secretaries that the big ideas they advocate were actually tried and failed two decades before.[9]

---

**Box 4.3**

## Additional Examples of Congressional Impact on National Security

In addition to the high-visibility actions relating to war and peace and U.S. relations with Russia, China, and the Middle East, Congress has succeeded in influencing U.S. policies on many of the major national security issues since the 1940s:

- Framed the debate and urged the creation of NATO
- Originated ideas for what became the Peace Corps
- Provided aid to Franco's Spain to reduce its alienation from the West
- Created rules for high technology trade with communist nations that led to the creation of the Coordinating Committee for Multilateral Export Controls (COCOM)
- Elevated the policy priority of human rights issues
- Banned military assistance to Augusto Pinochet's regime in Chile
- Aided mujaheddin fighting in Afghanistan
- Pressured U.S. citizens to stop funding the Irish Republican Army
- Pressured the administration to intervene to protect Bosnian Muslims
- Pressured the administration to recognize Vietnam
- Urged the overthrow of the Saddam Hussein regime in Iraq
- Banned trade in *conflict diamonds*

---

*Source:* Ralph G. Carter and James M. Scott, *Choosing to Lead: Understanding Congressional Foreign Policy Entrepreneurs* (Durham, NC: Duke University Press, 2009), 3–5.

---

Party identification and loyalty are the basis for congressional organization. The parties decide who sits on which committees and who gets punished for breaking with the leadership on a key vote. In recent decades, the Democratic and Republican members of Congress have become increasingly polarized with fewer centrists and more frequent party-line votes even on relatively minor issues. While there is a tradition of saying that "politics stops at the water's edge," the historical practice has varied widely, from the cooperation in containing communism in the 1940s to the bitter fights over the Vietnam War and relations with Russia in later years. Despite all the incentives for party loyalty, some members, especially the more senior ones, become institutionalists, staunch defenders of congressional prerogatives even against presidents of their own party.

Legislators are deal makers, not managers or decisive executives. Former governors who go to Congress regularly lament their inability to get things done quickly. The default position in a legislature is often to study the matter further, sometimes in a search for more definitive information that would make their choices easier, sometimes in the hope of avoiding an action that may prove unpopular. Politicians may be even more risk averse than the citizenry as a whole. Deal makers thrive on compromise, so they hedge their positions as long as possible and try to avoid outcomes that anger sizable segments of voters. They prefer both/and results to either/or; they enjoy addition more than subtraction, especially when it comes to budgets.

Members are often very jealous of their constitutional powers. As the statement by Speaker Nathaniel Macon quoted at the head of this chapter indicates, Congress believes it is essential to civilian control of the military and of the president's use of force. They also insist on consultation, not just being informed of presidential actions on foreign policy, for they share the view of Harold Stassen and Arthur Vandenberg, also quoted at the start of this chapter, that Congress wants to be in on the policy takeoff and not called only just before a crash-landing.

Congress is torn between assertiveness and deference to the president on foreign policy. As former Congressman Lee Hamilton (D-IN) has said, "Its tendency too often has been either to defer to the president or to engage in foreign policy haphazardly."[10] Humorist Will Rogers, writing in the 1930s, had another explanation: "If you don't scare Congress, they go fishing; if you do scare them, they go crazy."

## House Culture

Party differences are especially evident in the House of Representatives, which runs by strict majority rule. The speaker's party almost always gets its way, not least because the Rules Committee can change the rules on any measure by simple majority vote, thereby structuring the legislative process so that the majority party wins.

Representatives are on fewer committees than senators, and they usually become quite knowledgeable on the matters within their jurisdictions. House culture supports cosponsorship of legislation as a means of issue promotion in contrast with the more individualistic Senate.

Their two-year terms also mean that members are continuously in campaign mode, raising money, listening to voters, and trying to appeal to their constituents. Representatives have even greater incentives than senators to be partisan and confrontational.

On national security and other foreign policy matters, the House is more closely attuned to whatever the current public sentiments are regarding those issues—critical of the Pentagon sometimes and quite deferential at other times; ready to endorse the most extreme but popular measures against overseas adversaries; sometimes quite parochial in support of local ethnic interests, such as whether to condemn Turkish genocide of Armenians a century ago.

## Senate Culture

Senators have the luxury of six-year terms, giving them more time and political freedom to develop issue expertise in areas they deem important. They also have greater prestige and media attention, especially on foreign policy questions. As a result, every senator hires staff and uses opportunities to express positions on the broad range of national security issues, whether or not they serve on one of the committees with formal jurisdiction.

Senate rules give enormous power to individual members. Most legislative action is based on *unanimous consent* agreements. These understandings do not require agreement on all matters of substance but rather on the process to be followed on a given measure, particularly the offering of amendments and the length of debate. Without prior agreement, bills and nominations can be debated forever unless and until 60 Senators vote to end debate, called *cloture.*

Prolonged debates, called *filibusters,* have been used more frequently in recent years on all kinds of measures. Even the threat of a filibuster can force the leadership to sidetrack a bill or change an amendment. Efforts in 2011 to modify the filibuster rules fell short when the party leaders, each worried about setting precedents that might hurt them after the next election, agreed only to minor rules changes and a nonbinding gentleman's agreement to show more restraint. It is noteworthy that it took a foreign policy dispute to force the Senate into adopting its first rule allowing the cutoff of debate. When a handful of senators successfully blocked a bill to arm U.S. merchant ships threatened by German submarines in 1917 only a few days before the United States declared war on Germany, the outcry was so strong that the Senate adopted the original version of Rule XXII allowing cloture by a two-thirds vote.

Unlike the House, the Senate has no *germaneness rule* except in limited circumstances. What that means in practice is that any subject can be brought up at any time. Foreign policy measures can be offered whenever the proponent gets recognized, even if the pending bill deals with education or agriculture or commerce. That allows the Senate to be responsive to fast-breaking events but also creates legislative confusion.

While the Senate has been less partisan than the House, that seems to be changing with changes in the national parties and the election to the Senate of former House members, who are more comfortable with partisan clashes and less deferential to civility traditions.

## Committee Cultures and Dynamics

Most congressional action on foreign policy is handled by committees of jurisdiction, especially the defense, foreign policy, and appropriations committees, plus the intelligence and trade committees for those issues. By long-standing precedents, however, several other committees also have control over other legislation affecting U.S. foreign policy, including agricultural exports, exports of security-related items, foreign direct investment in U.S. firms, the EOP and NSC, and government reorganization and reform.

Whatever their jurisdictions, committee chairs are extraordinarily turf conscious and defensive of their prerogatives. It took an unusual degree of comity for the House Foreign Affairs and Armed Services Committees to work together in overseeing the combined civil–military provincial reconstruction teams in Iraq and Afghanistan in 2007–2009. It was surprising in 2009–2011 to have both Secretary of State Hillary Clinton and Secretary of Defense Robert Gates appear together before committees that nominally have jurisdiction only over one of them. Even though executive branch foreign policy making is done jointly through the interagency NSC process, congressional committees still largely refuse to work together on interagency matters because of their jurisdictional jealousies.

Committees act when the chairs want them to act and thus in response to the chairs' interests and political objectives. Rules do give the minority some say in naming witnesses, but only the chair can decide whether to hold a hearing on a given issue. Senator John Warner (R-VA), chairman of the Senate Armed Services Committee, held six hearings on the Abu Ghraib prison scandal, but his House counterpart held only one, saying he didn't want to undermine public support for the war in Iraq by holding more sessions.

The defense committees frequently fight over particular programs and occasional policies like allowing gays in uniform, but they have united each year since 1961 to produce a defense authorization bill and shepherd it through floor debate and conference with the House. The House Armed Services Committee has long had a combined staff, while most congressional committees have clearly defined majority and minority staff.

Because foreign policy committees have weak records of producing actual legislation—no foreign aid authorization bill has been enacted since 1986, for example—they have less experience with compromising to produce a single major bill. The chairs and ranking members of the Senate Foreign Relations Committee (SFRC), however, have traditions of cooperating on a wide range of issues and trying to minimize their differences on other foreign policy questions.

A major tool of member education and oversight is overseas travel. Congressional delegations (CODELs) are often feared by embassy staff, who worry about catering to the egos and demands of lawmakers, and criticized by the media as *junkets*. While some congressional travel seems wasteful or at least questionable, visits to war zones in recent years have given a great many lawmakers invaluable firsthand knowledge of the conflicts in the Middle East. Congressional visits may also help U.S. diplomacy by letting lawmakers play *bad cop* to foreign governments reluctant to believe the seriousness of American demands for changed policies.

## Why Congress Acts That Way

These are the ways Congress acts to shape U.S. foreign policy. The results can be criticized and defended, depending on one's perspective. Lee Hamilton, former congressman and longtime House Foreign Affairs Committee chairman, acknowledges the legislative branch's deficiencies in dealing with foreign policy. "Congress often fails to act in a constructive manner, views foreign policy through domestic political lenses, acts unilaterally or at the instigation of special interest groups, and shirks many of its foreign policy responsibilities."[11] But, he also notes the strengths of Congress in representing the diversity of views and interests of the American people and serving as a prod and check on the president.

In fact, congressional weaknesses in foreign policy mirror those of any democracy, as Alexis de Tocqueville noted in the 1830s. "Foreign politics demand scarcely any of those qualities which are peculiar to a democracy; they require, on the contrary, the perfect use of almost all those in which it is deficient. . . . [A] democracy can only with great difficulty regulate the details of an important undertaking, persevere in a fixed design, and work out its execution in spite of serious obstacles. It cannot combine its measure with secrecy or await their consequences with patience."[12]

Yes, indeed, Congress is shortsighted, erratic, prone to changes of course in the face of problems, congenitally unwilling to keep secrets, and impatient of results. Presidents, except in reelection years, are a little less subject to these pressures. They can have slightly longer time horizons, maintain steady courses despite problems, impose secrecy, and wait more patiently for favorable results.

The fundamental explanation for congressional behavior is politics and the dynamics of the American political system.

## Member Motivations

Members of Congress are human beings engaged in the very public realm of politics. (See Box 4.2.) They are diverse in background and experience, but most share an ambition to promote good policies and to be recognized for that work. As scholar David Mayhew has written, "With the member's job goes a license to persuade, connive, hatch ideas, propagandize, assail enemies, vote, build coalitions, shepherd coalitions, and in general cut a figure in public affairs."[13] Most want to be reelected, and they work hard to make that possible and to avoid actions that would make it more difficult. But, electoral motivations are only part of the story, sometimes a misleading part.[14]

Working on foreign policy issues is sometimes hard to justify to the voters back home. Senator Charles Percy (R-IL) attributed his defeat to an opponent who said that Percy was "more interested in the Middle East than the Middle West."[15] But another Midwesterner who served as chairman of the Foreign Relations Committee, Richard Lugar (R-IN), had little trouble winning reelection five times—until his 2012 defeat—in spite of his extensive work on foreign policy issues.

Lawmakers have freedom to choose how to spend their legislative time. They have to raise money, of course, and stay in touch with the voters, but what issues they dig into and what committees they serve on are within their choice. They may be interested in Israel because they are Jewish, or many of their constituents are, or they have visited the area, or they see Israel as a key to U.S. security and Middle East peace—for any or all of these reasons. They may be interested in childhood diseases in Africa because of medical training, or travel there, or membership in a nongovernmental organization

(NGO) that has programs there, or because they know some constituents active in those issues. They may be interested in better equipment to protect troops from improvised explosive devices (IEDs) because of their own prior military service, or because of bases or contractors in their districts, or because they believe the issue deserves more attention.

The nature of contemporary U.S. politics makes them, as Tom Mann and Norm Ornstein say, "independent entrepreneurs, each with an autonomous electoral base, who will not allow other members, even leaders, an excessive degree of control over their careers."[16] Candidates for Congress may receive some money from official party sources, but they largely have to rely on their own efforts. Once in office, they chart their own courses, whether to be party loyalists or mavericks, mirrors or leaders of public opinion.

## Public Opinion

With rare exception, the only public views that really matter to any lawmaker are those of the voters back home. And, few of them have much interest in most national security and foreign policy issues. Former Congressman Steve Solarz (D-NY) reported the typical experience when he spoke to a black church group. Afterward, they gently reminded him, "What you said about South Africa was well and good, but we mostly care about what's going on in Coney Island."[17]

War and peace issues are more salient to the public than, say, policy toward Burma or counterdrug programs in South America. But even there, as Bruce Jentleson discovered long ago, Americans are "pretty prudent" in judging military actions in terms of their primary objectives. The U.S. public generally views use of force as a last resort after diplomacy, economic pressure and sanctions, and military aid and arms sales to possible surrogates. Americans also prefer limited operations and air strikes to ground combat forces. They are willing to support use of force to stop aggression and provide humanitarian aid but not to bring about internal political change.[18]

On the other hand, one of the greatest constraints on lawmakers who favor an active, civilian-led foreign policy is the overwhelming public opposition to foreign aid, which many people think consumes up to 20% of the U.S. budget when the actual figure is 1%.

Lawmakers may point to public opinion to justify some of their positions, but legislative activists are more concerned with shaping public views than reacting to them. Only a relatively small number of members tend to be active on foreign policy issues, but they are policy entrepreneurs who really care about their causes and can't wait for the administration to act. Ralph Carter and James Scott say these members are expert and persistent and are not especially driven by constituent pressures. These entrepreneurs tend to be from the party opposite the president, and they tend to serve on the defense, foreign policy, or intelligence committees.[19] It is often easier for senators to be active on foreign policy issues because of the fewer constraints in the Senate rules.

# Congressional Inputs to the National Security Council System

Congress created the NSC and the NSC system in 1947 and has continued to try to influence national security policy by legislative action ever since. One key purpose of the original act was to force the executive branch to integrate and coordinate all of its activities—military, diplomatic, and economic—that affected national security. As is often the case, lawmakers thought that was best achieved by giving designated stakeholders seats at the table next to the president so that their points of view would not be overlooked.

That pattern has been followed in recent years as Congress added statutory members to the NSC and to the JCS and created the Homeland Security Council. It was echoed in other advisory panels that Congress created or supported with funding, such as the National Economic Council (NEC), the president's Foreign Intelligence Advisory Board, and second-opinion panels reviewing the Pentagon's Quadrennial Defense Review.

Just as Congress hoped to impose a particular decision process on the president by establishing the NSC, it tried to structure the processes for national security strategy, defense planning, arms sales, treaty commitments, intelligence operations, and even international economic transactions. Some have been followed, others mostly ignored.

Congress also forced structural reforms on the executive branch. First, it created and later disbanded the Arms Control and Disarmament Agency to give bureaucratic voice to arms control proposals. Later, it created SOCOM in order to build a counterterrorist capability that was a low priority for the Pentagon. The reforms of the 1986 Goldwater–Nichols Act were as steadfastly opposed by many in the Pentagon as the original 1947 act was. The navy and its friends especially feared that greater central control would weaken its independence. Lawmakers created the CIA in large part to avoid another Pearl Harbor, and when the CIA failed to prevent the 9/11 attacks, Congress created a superior office, the director of National Intelligence, to prevent another 9/11. Congress also forced a reluctant executive branch to establish a new Department of Homeland Security (DHS) for the same purpose.

In addition to these structural changes, Congress has also tried to reform some of the processes used for particular national security issues. One of the most significant reforms was the 1974 Hughes–Ryan amendment on covert operations by the CIA. Prior to its enactment, presidents could *plausibly deny* that they had any personal knowledge of CIA operations that ranged from dirty tricks to the overthrow of governments. Oversight by Congress was weak, with many lawmakers willing to be kept in the dark. Responding to disclosures of long-secret CIA operations, the Hughes–Ryan amendment required the president personally to approve the activity in what is called a *finding* and to promptly notify the relevant congressional committees. The amendment was recodified in 1990 with provisions for notifying only eight members of the congressional leadership in special circumstances. This basic process has been acceptable to both branches.

### The Effort to Legislate War Powers

Despite the clear language of the Constitution giving Congress the power to declare war, lawmakers over the years have varied in their interpretations and assertions of congressional war powers. Congress has actually declared war in only five major conflicts, though it has authorized the use of force an additional 15 times. (See Table 4.2.) Lawmakers also tolerated and funded numerous presidential military operations without raising war powers issues.[20]

Prior to the availability of jet aircraft, ballistic missiles, and nuclear weapons, getting into war was a slow-motion process, requiring the mobilization and dispatch of soldiers and sailors. The United States and other nations felt few restraints on using military force to solve diplomatic and economic problems without triggering major combat. While some lawmakers criticized U.S. military interventions in Central America and the Caribbean in the late 20th century, Congress as an institution went along, as it did with the suppression of rebels in the Philippines at the start of the 20th century.

After 1945, however, lawmakers generally agreed that the president needed to be able to act quickly to defend the nation, perhaps within the half-hour flight time of a nuclear armed missile from the Soviet Union. They supported the development of warning radars and other technologies

| Table 4.2 | Congressional Authorizations of the Use of Force, 1798–2011 | |
|---|---|---|
| **YEAR** | **ENEMY/OBJECT** | **PROVISIONS** |
| 1798 | France | "Subdue, seize, and take any armed French vessel" on the high seas |
| 1802 | Tripoli | "Subdue, seize and make prize" of Tripoli's ships and goods |
| 1812 | Britain | Declaration of war: The president "authorized to use the whole land and naval force" of the United States |
| 1815 | Algeria | Allowed "acts of precaution or hostility" |
| 1846 | Mexico | Declaration of war: The president "authorized to employ the militia, naval and military forces" and accept volunteers |
| 1858 | Paraguay | Authorized "such measures and use such force" as may be necessary to obtain "just satisfaction" in a dispute |
| 1861 | Confederacy | To enforce the laws and suppress rebellion |
| 1898 | Spain | 1) Authorization of force issued against Spain; 2) Declaration of war: The president "directed and empowered to use the entire land and naval forces" of the United States |

*(Continued)*

| Table 4.2 | (Continued) | |
|---|---|---|
| **YEAR** | **ENEMY/OBJECT** | **PROVISIONS** |
| 1914 | Mexico | "President is justified in the employment of the armed forces of the United States to enforce his demands" |
| 1917 | Germany, Austria–Hungary | Declaration of war: The president "authorized and directed to employ the entire naval and military forces" and "resources of the government" |
| 1941–1942 | Japan, Germany, Bulgaria, Hungary, and Romania | Declaration of war: The president "authorized and directed to employ the entire naval and military forces" and "resources of the government" |
| 1955 | Defense of Formosa (Taiwan) | The president authorized to use force "as he deems necessary for protecting the security of Formosa" |
| 1957 | Threats to Middle East | To preserve independence and integrity, the United States is "prepared to use armed forces to assist [nations facing] armed aggression from any" communist-controlled country |
| 1962 | Cuba | United States is "determined to prevent by whatever means may be necessary, including the use of arms" threats by Cuba |
| 1964 | Defense of Southeast Asia Treaty Organization (SEATO) nations | United States is "prepared, as the President determines, to take all necessary steps, including the use of armed force" to assist SEATO members "in defense of freedom" |
| 1983 | Defense of Lebanon | Authorized U.S. forces in UN peacekeeping mission for 18 months; they "will not engage in combat" but can take "protective measures" |
| 1991 | Iraq | Force authorized to obtain compliance with United Nations Security Council (UNSC) resolutions, but the president must determine that all peaceful means had been used and more would not be successful |
| 2001 | 9/11 attackers | Authorized "all necessary and appropriate force against those [who] planned, authorized, committed, or aided" the 9/11 attacks |
| 2002 | Iraq | The president "authorized to use the [U.S.] armed forces" to "defend [U.S.] national security . . . against the continuing threat posed by Iraq" and to enforce UNSC resolutions |

While Congress has declared war in only 5 conflicts, it has authorized the use of force on 15 additional occasions. In most cases, the congressional action was at the request of the president. In some cases, however, Congress took the initiative, and the president acquiesced: the first authorization of force against Spain in 1898 (later followed by a requested declaration of war); Cuba, 1962; and Lebanon, 1983. Many lawmakers felt that Lyndon Johnson (LBJ) had abused his authority under the 1964 Tonkin Gulf resolution, and they fashioned the 1973 War Powers Resolution to create a regular process for congressional involvement in use of force decisions.

*Source:* Charles A. Stevenson, *Congress at War: The Politics of Conflict Since 1789* (Washington, DC: Potomac Books, 2007), 30–31.

allowing the United States to have a hair-trigger defense capability. They abandoned their reluctance to have a large standing army and put the United States on a permanent war footing with a large army, navy, marine corps, and air force. Congress also created a diverse, if not duplicative, nuclear weapons capability deployed on aircraft, ships, submarines, and underground.

In response to presidential requests, Congress also approved laws authorizing force in certain contingencies. This was done in 1955 for Formosa (Taiwan) and in 1957 for the Middle East, where troops were later sent to Lebanon. Lawmakers also approved contingent force measures against Cuba in 1962 and Vietnam in 1964 (the Tonkin Gulf Resolution).

But, when the Vietnam war involved more than half a million American troops, many of them draftees, Congress began rethinking what it had done in 1964 and searching for a way to avoid a repetition of what by then was considered a mistake. Leading members of the Senate and House drafted bills codifying a new war powers procedure and ultimately approved a compromise, the War Powers Resolution, that became Public Law 93–148 despite President Nixon's veto.

The law insists that "the President in every possible instance shall consult with Congress before introducing United States Armed Forces into hostilities or into situations where imminent involvement in hostilities is clearly indicated by the circumstances." It also requires a report to Congress within 48 hours when U.S. troops "equipped for combat" are sent abroad in large numbers or into hostile situations. Recent presidents have generally followed these provisions, although the reports have been submitted *consistent* with the War Powers Resolution rather than *pursuant* to it, a lawyerly distinction denying that the reports were legally required but suggesting that Congress ought to be happy with receiving them anyway.

A compromise most troubling to some members who felt that Congress should approve any major military operation in advance except time-urgent self-defense was that the War Powers Resolution allowed the president to use force for 60 days pending a congressional vote to authorize the operation. If Congress failed to act, he could still take another 30 days if the president declared an "unavoidable military necessity."

What greatly undermined the act's effectiveness, however, was a Supreme Court decision in 1983 (*INS v. Chadha,* 462 U.S. 919) outlawing the use of legislative vetoes that were not subject to presidential vetoes, thus requiring reliance on a two-thirds vote to override the chief executive. The original War Powers Resolution had provided for a concurrent resolution of both houses, requiring only majority votes, as sufficient to force the withdrawal of combat troops. No sitting president since 1973 has ever declared that he considered the law binding on his administration, further weakening the act. Efforts to amend the law have been unsuccessful, as were proposals to repeal it. The most widely discussed alternative is a new law simply requiring presidential consultation.

It's clear now that the 1973 law was based on a faulty assumption that Congress would be willing to vote to stop an unpopular war, either immediately or after 60 days. While theoretically possible, it has not been true historically. The vote cutting of funds for the Vietnam War applied only to air operations and only after ground combat troops had been withdrawn. The cutoff of funds for operations in Somalia merely codified a presidential commitment to complete withdrawals within six months. The more relevant example is the war with Mexico in 1846. Although both houses voted overwhelmingly for a declaration of war, many members opposed the conflict on strategic grounds but said that they couldn't bring themselves to vote against sending guns and bullets to General Taylor's troops, who were already engaged in battle.

The War Powers Resolution was an effort to limit presidential warmaking while preserving a role for Congress. It tried to balance recognition of some need for immediate military action with the constitutional requirements for congressional authorization. The law, however, was weakened by presidential refusal to concede its force and effect despite the submission of reports and by Congress's own unwillingness to insist on compliance.

### Inconsistency in Practice on War Powers

With the law still on the books, Congress has reacted inconsistently to various uses of force in recent decades. As Lee Hamilton explained, "Congress frequently prefers to play Monday morning quarterback, letting the president make the tough military decisions, then criticizing or praising him depending on the results."[21] Put another way, Congress and the American people like short, successful wars but do not like any operation that is prolonged or unsuccessful.

Another variation in congressional behavior is that members of the president's party tend to argue for executive discretion and members of the opposition repeat the arguments about congressional war powers. There have been some exceptions, like Senator Robert C. Byrd (D-WV), who regularly argued that only Congress could authorize major military operations. But, most members tended to defer to the president on substantive and practical grounds or criticized his actions only when problems arose.

The only times Congress has approved the use of force abroad in advance as envisioned by the War Powers Resolution, and with presidential endorsement, were for peacekeepers in Lebanon in 1983, to drive Iraqi forces from Kuwait in 1991, for action against those involved in the 9/11 attacks in 2001, and for war on Iraq in 2002.

Congress failed to pass measures on Somalia in 1993–1994 until it wrote into law President Clinton's pledge to remove U.S. troops by a certain date. It took many votes but failed to enact legislation on Haiti in 1994 or Kosovo in 1999 or Libya in 2011. In 1995, Congress was on the verge of passing a bill supporting military action against Serbia over President Clinton's veto when peace talks were started and proved successful.

In fact, the War Powers Act has had a major impact on presidential behavior despite its uncertain legal standing and inconsistent legislative support.

Almost every major military operation since 1973 has been designed and conducted within the 60-day limits—except for the conflicts specifically authorized by Congress. No president has initiated prolonged combat operations without seeking or at least welcoming congressional support.[22]

### Tying the President's Hands

Congress has also asserted itself in setting war aims and restrictions on combat in those measures it has passed. The 1983 war powers authorization for Lebanon was limited to 18 months, and troops were allowed only a defensive mission of backstopping the Lebanese army and protecting themselves. After the tragic barracks bombing that killed 241 marines, President Reagan decided to withdraw the troops prematurely.

The 1991 authorization for war against Iraq was limited to enforcing various UNSC resolutions, which only required a withdrawal from Kuwait, not regime change in Baghdad.

In 2001, the White House sought language that would have authorized preventive attacks against any and all terrorists. Congress refused to go along with that blank check and limited the authorization of force to people and nations involved in the 9/11 attacks.

An effort to limit the 2002 authorization for renewed war against Iraq failed, but the final bill did require regular reports as well as a presidential certification that "diplomatic or other peaceful means" had failed.[23]

Congress has tried to tie the president's hands on other occasions as well. Lawmakers declared war on Spain in 1898 but prohibited annexation of Cuba, as detailed in the case study for this chapter. They limited U.S. arms sales in the 1930s until Germany's Adolph Hitler launched an all-out war. They barred Franklin Roosevelt (FDR) from sending draftees outside the Western hemisphere—until war was declared after Pearl Harbor. They prohibited U.S. ground combat operations in Laos or Thailand after 1969 but neglected to include Cambodia, which Nixon invaded in 1970 until forced to withdraw by another law. After U.S. combat troops were largely withdrawn from Vietnam, Congress set a deadline for the end of all U.S. bombing raids in Southeast Asia. Congress also prohibited U.S. military operations in Angola in 1975 and tried to ban aid to the Contras in Nicaragua in the 1980s.[24]

While these examples demonstrate congressional willingness to limit presidential options and otherwise guide U.S. policy, they contrast with the usual practice of allowing presidents broad freedom of action in foreign policy. Only occasionally, and for reasons that may be political rather than substantive, does Congress actively fight what the president wants to do. Of course, it always reserves the right to kibbitz and criticize.

## Should Politics Stop at Water's Edge?

Bipartisanship seems to be the last refuge not of scoundrels but of beleaguered presidents and their supporters. Calls for suspending the usual political infighting when it comes to foreign policy are usually made when a policy is under attack, not before it is crafted and announced. In short, saying politics should stop at the water's edge is primarily an argument to suppress dissent.

On the other hand, there is no doubt that a nation is stronger when it speaks with a single voice. The absence of dissent suggests that a policy will be sustainable over time and that corollary actions can follow logically. Unity of purpose and unity of action can lead to successful outcomes.

How to get from disagreement to consensus, from uncertainty to clarity of purpose, from political gamesmanship to genuine collaboration, is an art, not a science. The U.S. political system has more incentives for conflict than for cooperation, especially in Congress. Foreign policy is not exempt from debate, for members remember well Professor Edward Corwin's famous observation, "The Constitution . . . is an invitation to struggle for the privilege of directing American foreign policy."[25]

✳ ✳ ✳

Congress has many tools to shape U.S. foreign policy, most notably the power of the purse through appropriations but also by writing legislation with substantive requirements, procedural rules, or advisory opinions. Lawmakers also influence policy by raising issues for public debate and by investigating U.S. programs. The Senate's special powers over treaties and nominations give it tools to obstruct or delay presidential plans. Congress has been inconsistent in exercising its war power. While formally authorizing the use of force on at least 20 occasions, it has often failed either to support or oppose many military operations in recent decades.

## Case Study: Congress and Cuban Independence, 1898

This case tells of a Congress eager for war and a reluctant president. It also shows how Congress can set war aims that affect the conduct of military operations and the ultimate peace settlement. Congress used its formal legislative tools to make war inevitable, to condition how it was fought, and to limit what America gained as a result. The president abided by those conditions as commander-in-chief.

Congress pushed President William McKinley into war with Spain in 1898. He hoped to avoid war until the very last minute but could not resist the public and political pressures to fight.

A rebellion against Spain and for independence began in Cuba in 1895. When the Cleveland administration sided with Spain, congressional Republicans responded by passing nonbinding resolutions urging recognition of the insurgent government. Both Republican and Democratic conventions in 1896 approved platforms favoring the Cubans, with the Republicans calling for U.S. efforts to secure Cuban independence. The popular press had aroused U.S. public opinion in support of the Cuban insurgents and against the repressive acts by Spain. Politicians of both parties echoed a romantic view of the rebels and the virtues of independence from Spain.

McKinley won the White House, and the Republicans retained control of Congress. No action on Cuba occurred for several months, however, because House Speaker Thomas Reed (R-ME) strongly opposed Cuban independence. By early 1898, rioting in Havana and brutal repression by Spanish soldiers brought the issue back onto the front pages of American newspapers. On February 14, both houses of Congress passed resolutions calling on the president to publish the reports of the U.S. consuls in Cuba—reports that the foreign policy committee members already knew depicted the suffering of the Cuban people and the failures of the Spanish military.

Two days later, an explosion on the U.S. battleship *Maine* killed 266 soldiers. The ship had been sent to Havana harbor in case it might be needed to evacuated U.S. citizens. Later analysis determined that the damage came from an internal explosion rather than from a Spanish mine or torpedo, but suspicions at the time put added pressure on McKinley to act. In early March, he told lawmakers that America was not prepared for war and that he needed money and time to get ready.

On March 7 and 8, with great enthusiasm but virtually no debate, Congress voted $50 million for national defense, giving the president full discretion on how to spend it. This was a staggering 60% increase above what had been voted for the army and the navy only a few months before. McKinley's supporters called the funds a *peace measure.*

Still the president hesitated. Though he drafted a message to Congress, he locked it in his safe to allow more time for diplomacy. Meanwhile, backbencher Republicans talked with Democrats about joining to declare war regardless of McKinley's position. This forced the president to send his message on April 11.

The message did not satisfy lawmakers. It criticized the Spanish for their military actions and described the suffering of the Cuban people. But, it did not call for war. It even opposed Cuban independence, arguing that that would limit U.S. freedom of action. Instead, McKinley said, "I ask the Congress to authorize and empower the President to take measures to secure a full and final termination of hostilities between the Government of Spain and the people of Cuba, and to secure in the island the establishment of a stable government, capable of maintaining order and observing its international obligations, insuring peace and tranquillity [sic] and the security of its citizens as well as our own, and to use the military and naval forces of the United States as may be necessary for these purposes."

Democrats in the House responded with a resolution recognizing Cuban independence, but the Republican majority voted to authorize the president to use U.S. forces "to intervene at once to stop the war in Cuba" and seek to establish "a stable and independent government" by the free action of the Cuban people

The Senate took six more days to debate and vote on its alternative, which became, with some minor changes, the final version sent to the president. A key provision added by the Senate was the amendment of the silver Republican from Colorado, Henry Teller, that declared that the United States would not seek to annex Cuba. Although many interventionists, including businessmen eager to protect their investments in Cuba or to import Cuban products tariff free, favored eventual U.S. control, others strongly opposed annexation. Southerners did not want to grant citizenship to the nonwhite, non-English-speaking people of the island. Lawmakers like Teller, from sugar beet growing areas, did not want competition from Cuban sugar, which then was under a stiff tariff. Another argument against annexation was the concern that the United States might incur the obligation to repay the $400 million bond issue Spain used to finance its military efforts, pledging Cuban revenues.

The law signed by McKinley on April 20 called for the recognition of Cuban independence, using language from the Declaration of Independence: "[T]he people of the Island of Cuba are, and of right ought to be, free and independent." The measure demanded an end to the Spanish government and "directed and empowered [the president] to use the entire land and naval forces of the United States . . . to carry these resolutions into effect." It also included the Teller amendment denying any intent to control Cuba after pacification.

Despite his earlier reservations, McKinley signed the joint resolution and notified Madrid. When the Spanish government, as expected, rejected the U.S. demands, Congress voted a formal declaration of war on April 25.

The war ended quickly, with Spanish surrender of Cuba on July 17 and of the Philippines on August 13. The peace treaty, signed on December 10, gave Cuba independence but gave the United States control of Puerto Rico and the Philippines. Many in Congress, especially anti-imperialist Democrats, had second thoughts about the war and its consequences. The peace treaty was approved in the Senate by only a two-vote margin on February 6, 1899. Congress had succeeded in limiting U.S. war aims but had not fully realized that America would now face the burdens of empire.

This case shows Congress taking the initiative on a major foreign policy matter, passing a huge bill for unspecified military expansion, forcing the president to act prematurely, and then limiting the war aims of the conflict. It also shows both parties maneuvering for political advantages with an aroused public. A Congress determined to act, and able to pass binding legislation, can dominate a hesitant president.

Sources: Ernest R. May, *Imperial Democracy* (New York: Harcourt, Brace, 1961); Paul S. Holbo, "Presidential Leadership in Foreign Affairs: William McKinley and the Turpie-Foraker Amendment," *The American Historical Review*, vol. 72, no. 4 (July 1967), 1321–1335; *The Congressional Record*.

# Case Study: Congress Struggles With Apartheid and South Africa

In this case, bipartisan majorities in Congress forced a major change in the administration's foreign policy, going so far as to override a presidential veto. Lawmakers chose moral concerns over strategic arguments and insisted on prompt action against a pariah regime rather than sustained pressure and the hope of eventual change.

Starting in 1948, the South African government imposed racial separation—*apartheid* in Afrikaans—in a series of laws. Among other things, those laws imposed official racial identity on all citizens, prohibited mixed-race marriages, set aside geographic zones where designated groups could reside, and segregated schools and public transportation. Later on, separate Bantu Homelands were created, and blacks were allowed into white areas only as temporary guests.

U.S. policy makers largely ignored the racial repression in South Africa because the white minority government was an anticommunist bulwark on a continent where the Soviet Union and its allies were supporting nationalist independence movements. Newly inaugurated President Ronald Reagan reflected this attitude in a 1981 interview: "Can we abandon a country that has stood by us in every war we've ever fought, a country that strategically is essential to the free world in its production of minerals we all must have and so forth?"

Reagan's predecessor Jimmy Carter had condemned apartheid and ordered compliance with the arms embargo voted in 1977 by the UNSC, but his administration resisted efforts by the UN and the U.S. Congress to impose economic sanctions. The only restriction voted into law was a 1978 amendment requiring U.S. firms seeking Export-Import Bank (Ex-Im) financing to demonstrate that they followed "fair employment practices" in South Africa.

The Reagan administration adopted a policy labeled *constructive engagement* that avoided public pressure but sought to encourage reform by the South African government. The U.S. government relaxed the terms of the Carter arms embargo by allowing sales of some nonlethal items like food, clothing, computers, and chemical and transportation equipment. And the P.W. Botha government in South Africa made some modest reforms, such as including colored and Asian representation in a tricameral parliament that still excluded blacks. Protests erupted in black townships starting in September 1984 and were brutally suppressed in full view of the international news media.

Congress had been under pressure from antiapartheid activists for several years, but the uprisings in South Africa and a July 1985 declaration of a state of emergency spurred lawmakers to action. As freshman Senator Mitch McConnell (R-KY) said, "The apartheid issue made civil rights black and white again. It was not complicated." Across the United States, 13 state governments, 11 city governments, and 102 colleges and universities had by 1985 adopted measures divesting themselves of investments linked to South Africa.

In April 1985, the Republican-controlled Senate approved a resolution condemning apartheid by a vote of 89–4. The Democratic-controlled House of Representatives developed and passed on June 5 a different measure that would have banned U.S. bank loans to the South African government and businesses, barred new U.S. business investment there, and prohibited importation of the gold coins called Krugerrands. The vote was a veto-proof 295–127, with 56 Republicans joining 239 Democrats. In July, the Senate adopted (80–11) a more limited measure that banned bank loans to the South African government and barred sales of nuclear and computer equipment. In conference committee, the two sides agreed to the Krugerrand ban but dropped the immediate ban on new investments. The revised version passed the House 380–48 on August 1.

Senate Republicans wanted to support the president, who threatened a veto of the bill, but many also wanted some action on South Africa. They launched a filibuster that delayed action until after the August recess. On September 9, President Reagan tried to preempt legislation by issuing Executive Order 12532, banning most new loans, Krugerrand imports, and computer and nuclear-related sales. This satisfied enough Republicans that they joined the filibuster in order to prevent an embarrassing defeat for the president. When sanctions supporters pressed for another vote to halt debate, Senate Republican leaders then took the extraordinary step of removing the formal copy of the conference report from the Senate chamber and locking it in a safe in the Foreign Relations Committee. Under Senate rules, no consideration of the conference report could occur in the absence of the signed conference report. The document was returned two weeks later, but Senate willingness to push for a final vote had subsided. No further legislative action occurred until 1986.

Racial violence continued in South Africa, leading to another state of emergency in June. That month, the House debated a new and broader sanctions bill. House Republicans, apparently calculating that an extreme measure was doomed to defeat, allowed an amendment to pass by voice vote that would have suspended virtually all trade with South Africa and force U.S. businesses to leave within 180 days. They then allowed the amended bill to pass by voice vote.

Senators now felt under pressure to pass something tough. Foreign Relations Committee Chairman Richard Lugar (R-IN) was no longer willing to defend the administration's position. He had concluded that "the president's normal passion for democracy and freedom seemed to diminish when Africa came into view." Lugar persuaded his committee to pass a bill that rejected the more extreme measures in the House bill and accepted some minor amendments by conservatives. The measure, which ultimately passed the Senate 84–14, banned new U.S. business investment in South Africa as well as trade in agricultural products, steel, and nuclear supplies. It threatened additional sanctions in a year if South Africa failed to make "substantial progress" in eliminating apartheid. The bill also put into permanent law the sanctions in Reagan's executive order the year before. The measure also gave the president authority to lift or modify the sanctions if some of five specified conditions were met, including the release from prison of Nelson Mandela and the repeal of the laws on population registration and residency restrictions. Lugar successfully insisted that the House adopt the Senate version of the bill in order to avoid any filibuster, and representatives did so by a 308–77 vote.

President Reagan vetoed the bill on September 26, arguing that sanctions would be counterproductive, hurting blacks more than the white minority government. But, the large majorities held firm, and the veto was overridden by the House 313–83 (with 81 Republicans joining 232 Democrats in the majority) and by the Senate 78–21 (with 31 Republicans joining all 47 Democrats). This was one of the rare cases in American history when Congress overrode a presidential veto on a major national security issue.

The Comprehensive Anti-Apartheid Act of 1986 (Public Law 99–440) did not lead to an immediate end of apartheid in South Africa, but it put the United States and its economic and moral power on the side of political reform and added to the external pressures on the white minority government, which released Nelson Mandela in 1990 and negotiated power-sharing arrangements and a gradual dismantling of apartheid. Multiracial elections were held in 1994.

As this recounting indicates, there were important policy differences over how to deal with South Africa, but there was also sufficient bipartisan consensus in favor of tough action that many Republicans were willing to oppose their popular president. For several weeks, Republicans tried to support the administration by legislative tactics in the House and Senate, filibustering in the Senate to buy time for the president and in the House allowing passage of a more extreme measure so that a veto might be sustained. But ultimately, they felt compelled to join with Democrats to be sure some law was passed in response to the situation in South Africa. Lawmakers wanted to be on the right side of history.

Sources: Congressional Quarterly Almanacs; Alex Thomson, *U.S. Foreign Policy Towards Apartheid South Africa, 1948–1994* (Palgrave Macmillan, 2008); Peter J. Schraeder, *United States Foreign Policy Toward Africa: Incrementalism, Crisis and Change* (Cambridge University Press, 1994).

## Selected Resources

The gateway congressional website is at http://thomas.loc.gov/home/thomas.php.

Valuable books on the history of Congress include: Julian E. Zelizer (ed.), *The American Congress* (Houghton Mifflin, 2004); Julian E. Zelizer, *Arsenal of Democracy* (Basic Books, 2010); Robert David Johnson, *Congress and the Cold War* (Cambridge University Press, 2006); James M. Lindsay,

*Congress and the Politics of U.S. Foreign Policy* (Johns Hopkins University Press, 1994).

The Center on Congress at Indiana University has a useful website for information on Congress at http://congress.indiana.edu/.

CSPAN, in addition to live coverage of congressional debates and many hearings, has its own website with other links and resources at http://www.c-span.org/.

# 6 The Diplomatic Instrument

*The State Department is a bowl of jelly. It's got all those people over there who are constantly smiling.*

—President John F. Kennedy to reporter Hugh Sidey in 1961[1]

*[My] one legacy is to ruin the foreign service. I mean ruin it—the old foreign service—and to build a new one.*

—Richard Nixon to Henry Kissinger, November 13, 1972[2]

While the president is the chief diplomat because of his constitutional duties to receive foreign ambassadors and appoint American ones, the State Department is the primary tool for U.S. diplomacy. The secretary of state holds the most prestigious cabinet post and is fourth in line of succession to the presidency after the vice president and two congressional leaders. The secretary is also viewed as the primary spokesperson to explain and defend U.S. foreign policy.

Despite the professionalism of the foreign service, presidents of both parties, as quoted at the start of this chapter, have often distrusted the State Department. They often turned instead to White House-based people for key diplomatic missions. Nevertheless, the bulk of U.S. diplomatic activities, and the infrastructure and procedures for them, are handled by the State Department. As with all of the foreign policy instruments, Congress can play a role along with the president. While the president can use officials from anywhere in government and sometimes even private citizens for diplomatic activities, most diplomacy in conducted by or through the State Department, the principal focus of this chapter. (See Table 6.1.)

## The Nature of Diplomacy and the Diplomatic Mission

Despite the comment by the English diplomat Sir Henry Wotton (1568–1639) that an ambassador is "an honest man sent to lie abroad for the good of his country," diplomacy is a long-respected profession. Every country uses ambassadors (the highest formal rank) and other envoys to represent its interests in dealing with other governments. Diplomats are protected

141

| Table 6.1 | The Diplomatic Instrument Brief | |
|---|---|---|
| **PEOPLE** | **ADVANTAGES** | **DISADVANTAGES** |
| Secretary of state | Authoritative, powerful | Limits on time, multiple demands |
| U.S. ambassadors | Empowered heads of country teams | Uneven in skills and host-country influence |
| Foreign service | Professionals | Subject to instructions |
| **ACTIONS** | | |
| Engagement | Allows broad exchanges of views | Multiple voices, sometimes confusing or discordant |
| Negotiations | Can achieve definitive agreements | Often time-consuming, subject to domestic pressures |
| Public diplomacy | Nonthreatening, potential long-term benefits | Slow, hard to judge effectiveness |
| **ROLE OF CONGRESS** | Independent voice; can play "bad cop" | Can confuse others regarding U.S. positions |
| **CULTURE** | Professional, high value on negotiations, comfortable with ambiguity | Resists ruptures in relations |

The diplomatic instrument of foreign policy consists of people—U.S. government officials—and actions they can perform. Those actions can be broadly grouped in the categories of engagement, negotiations, and public diplomacy. Diplomats, however, have a special culture that shapes how they operate.

against local arrest by international conventions, thus allowing them to disregard parking and speeding tickets and to avoid jail for even more serious crimes. Misbehaving diplomats can be declared *persona non grata,* however, thereby forcing recall to their home countries.

Traditionally, diplomacy has been seen as *the art and practice of conducting negotiations between nations,* but scholars now distinguish between formal intergovernmental relations, called *Track One,* and numerous additional tracks for conflict resolution, including nongovernmental contacts by professionals, businesspeople, academics, and religious organizations. While these private organizations may consult and collaborate with governments, our focus here is on the formal channels the president can use to conduct American foreign policy.

Modern American diplomats perform many functions besides negotiating with established governments. They represent the United States to foreign publics. They help U.S. citizens overseas, including Americans in trouble and businesses seeking markets. They analyze and report on developments abroad from grand strategy and economic trends to cultural changes and leadership gossip. They carry out the duties assigned by various laws from assessing the qualifications of people seeking visas to helping Afghans and

Iraqis build new institutions. And, they are the experts who advise in the development of new policies.

The State Department is the lead agency for U.S. diplomacy, but officials from other departments often meet with foreign officials on matters related to their responsibilities. Sometimes, the disparate perspectives and concerns of different U.S. agencies leave outsiders confused about American policy despite the best efforts of the State Department to have Americans speak in a single voice. In foreign capitals, however, the U.S. ambassador heads *the country team* of American personnel and is empowered to enforce a common strategy.

The diplomatic instrument already exists, ready for the president to use. The United States is caught in a web of international agreements and organization memberships. Many of them have regular meetings or prepare regular reports that can be used for discussions, negotiations, and actions—the United Nations Security Council (UNSC) and General Assembly, the North Atlantic Treaty Organization (NATO) Council, ad hoc groups such as those convened to discuss aid to Afghanistan and contact with anti-Qaddafi Libyan rebels.

Deciding to use diplomacy is only the first step, raising further issues of when, with whom, where, and how. Any new initiative has to be put in the mix with ongoing interactions and other issues where there may be agreements or disagreements. The president and subordinate officials need to determine which matters have priority, which have deadlines, and which have the greatest promise of success. Every time the president or secretary of state meets with a foreign official, someone has to decide which handful of the many issues that could be raised for high-level discussion actually will be raised in the limited time available. Diplomacy isn't just talking, much less negotiating, but rather involves pursuing particular goals in the context of overall foreign policy.

## Growth and Professionalization of the State Department

In creating the State Department in 1789, Congress made clear that it was an instrument for the president by reiterating four times that it was subordinate to the chief executive. The secretary was to "perform and execute such duties as shall from time to time be enjoined on or entrusted to him by the President" and was required to conduct departmental business as the president "shall from time to time order or instruct." Current law has similar phrasing.[3]

Thomas Jefferson, the first secretary, was paid $3,500 (equivalent to about $85,000 today) and had three clerks, an interpreter, a doorkeeper, and a messenger.[4] In the first few years, the new nation had small diplomatic missions abroad in London, Paris, Lisbon, Madrid, and the Hague. As there were only two other executive departments in the early years of the republic—War for military affairs and Treasury for raising revenue and managing government accounts—State functioned as the department of everything else. State managed the mint and issued patents; it oversaw U.S. marshals and conducted the census; it supervised territorial affairs and collected immigration data. It kept and used the Great Seal of the United States and served as the repository for official documents. These collateral duties explain why the department was named State instead of just Foreign Affairs. As other departments were established in subsequent decades, most of those domestic duties were transferred away from State.

The department grew as the nation grew and expanded as America increased its dealings with the rest of the world. As Tables 2.1 and 6.2 show, personnel figures stayed below 1,000 until the 1890s and surged again only during and after World War II. The number of major diplomatic posts abroad was small until the 1830s, then doubled after the Civil War, and continued to climb with America's rise as a global power. The number of consular posts, however, was large by the middle of the 19th century as America saw the need for agents to promote commerce and protect American ships and crews. After 1945, many of these smaller posts were upgraded to full embassies.

One factor aiding the professionalization of the department and continuity in foreign policy was the presence of long-serving officials. Only three men held the top career post from 1841 to 1924, providing institutional memory and establishing a distinctive style to American diplomacy. And despite the use of political patronage in most presidential appointments, many highly-regarded 19th-century diplomats were retained in their posts through several changes of administration and party.

Grover Cleveland instituted written examinations and language tests for subordinate officials in 1895, and Congress combined the diplomatic and consular services into a single foreign service in 1924, with salaries and benefits creating opportunities for those with less wealthy backgrounds. While no career officers served as chief of mission before 1920, the figure rose to 30% after 1924 and to 55% by World War II.

These changes and subsequent ones gave America a professional foreign service of skilled practitioners diverse in background and well trained to deal with the complexities of modern international affairs. The department also reorganized periodically to cope with the emergence of new states and the rise of new problems.

American foreign policy changed more gradually, with periods of isolation from many of the rest of the world's diplomatic and security controversies even as the United States expanded its overseas economic activities and foreign trade. In the early years, American diplomacy sought to assert and protect its new nationhood, a goal endangered by the European wars after the French Revolution and America's still-unresolved problems with Great Britain. The mid-19th century saw the resolution of America's borders through a combination of threats, proposals, negotiations, and even limited war. The Union won the Civil War in part because of deft diplomacy that limited outside support to the Confederacy.

| Table 6.2 | Department of State Personnel and Foreign Missions, 1950–2010 | | | | | | | |
|---|---|---|---|---|---|---|---|---|
| **Personnel** | | | | | | | | |
| 1950 | 1955 | 1960 | 1965 | 1970 | 1975 | 1980 | 1985 | 1990 |
| 24,628 | 27,495 | 37,983 | 40,656 | 39,753 | 30,376 | 23,497 | 25,254 | 25,288 |
| 1995 | 2000 | 2005 | 2010 | | | | | |
| 24,859 | 27,983 | 33,808 | 39,016 | | | | | |

| **Foreign Missions** | | | | | | | |
|---|---|---|---|---|---|---|---|
| Year | 1950 | 1960 | 1970 | 1980 | 1990 | 2000 | 2010 |
| Diplomatic Posts | 74 | 99 | 117 | 133 | 145 | 160 | 184 |
| Consular Posts | 179 | 166 | 122 | 100 | 97 | 92 | 84 |

This series of tables shows the expansion of the State Department during the 1960s and the reductions following the Vietnam War that were reversed only after the 9/11 attacks. The number of overseas missions has steadily expanded with the creation of new foreign governments and international organizations.
*Sources: Statistical Abstract of the United States;* Department of State, Office of the Historian.

By the start of the 20th century, the United States had acquired overseas territories, which it was unwilling to call colonies, and a sense that it had political, security, and economic interests that required global engagement with other powers. Despite a retrenchment after World War I, President Franklin D. Roosevelt (FDR) pushed and pulled the United States into a leadership role even before Pearl Harbor. Later presidents used diplomacy and other instruments in their foreign policy toolkits to prevail in the Cold War and to cope with the newly emerging major powers and security threats of the 21st century.

The State Department today employs about 12,000 people in the foreign service plus about 9,000 in the civil service. It maintains 260 embassies, consulates, and other posts in 180 countries. Support staff of foreign nationals at these posts totals 37,000. State's operational budget, not counting foreign assistance or contributions to international organizations, was $11.4 billion in 2011. While these figures have been growing in recent years, driven especially by the need for safer embassies and for civilian activities in Iraq and Afghanistan, deficit reduction pressures may limit or reverse these trends.

# Organization

The diagram of the State Department (Figure 6.1) is misleading because it shows connections rather than power. Each node is equal-sized on the chart, despite wide variations in personnel, resources, and influence in practice. Nevertheless, it demonstrates that State has a section for every major issue

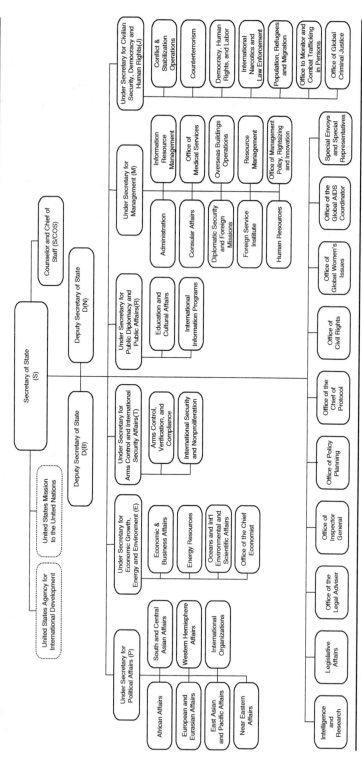

**Figure 6.1** U.S. Department of State Organizational Chart

It's important to note in this chart how many special offices report directly to the secretary rather than through other channels. Whether these units are strong or weak depends on the personal preferences of the secretary. The middle and right portions of the chart show the many functional offices in State, but the real power historically has been in the regional bureaus headed by the under secretary for political affairs, usually seen as the number three at State.

*Source:* U.S. Department of State.

146

seen to be facing the department and the nation in its international dealings. Each office has a special shorthand designation, rooted in the distant past and often with no obvious connection to the title or subject matter, such as "T" for arms control, "R" for public affairs, and "H" for legislative affairs.

The secretary is at the top of the State Department, as law and tradition require. Next are two deputy secretaries, one as the alter ego of the secretary and the other as the chief manager of the department, especially of its budget and personnel processes. Nestled near the top and reporting directly to the secretary is the executive secretariat (S/ES), which functions as the secretary's right arm—coordinating the work of the department, dealing with the White House and other agencies, and running the 24-hour operations center. The S/ES also polices the flow of paperwork to the secretary, particularly to ensure that all the proper clearances have been obtained from stakeholding offices.

Curiously off to the side are the administrator for foreign aid programs, the U.S. permanent representative to the UN, and the counselor. It's easy to explain the counselor's role as an adviser on various topics who frequently gets special assignments from the secretary, thus removing the position from the regular bureaucratic hierarchy. Similarly, the ambassador to the UN is often a person with independent political standing, sometimes with cabinet rank, perhaps even a rival to the secretary, and thus not necessarily a true subordinate. The head of the Agency for International Development (AID), while dual-hatted as a State Department official, has separate legislated responsibilities, and the AID budget is only coordinated with State rather than determined by the senior department.

At the bottom of the chart are the many offices allowed to report directly to the secretary rather than through the regular bureaus. The important offices include the department's intelligence unit, Intelligence and Research (INR); the Office of Legislative Affairs (H), which handles congressional relations; the legal adviser; and small, specialized offices given special status often for symbolic reasons.

The Office of Policy Planning (S/P) has a celebrated history (George Kennan and Paul Nitze were its first two directors), a talented staff of both career and political appointees, and a mandate to think big thoughts, look ahead, and avoid trivia. S/P houses the secretary's speechwriters, who can shape policy by the simple words they choose. It also wields enormous bureaucratic power because its clearance is required on all policy papers going to the secretary from other offices.

There are five functional units and one regional one, each headed by an under secretary, but they vary widely in power. The under secretary for management (M) runs day-to-day operations as well as personnel management and training. It is also responsible for developing the department's budget but from a much less powerful position than, for example, the Pentagon, where budgets are a major tool of policy making as well as management. The under secretary for public diplomacy and public affairs (R) is the residual presence of what used to be the U.S. Information Agency until it consolidated with and subordinated to the State Department in 1999. In addition to normal public and media relations, R runs the educational and cultural programs that sends U.S. musical groups abroad and brings future leaders on visits to America.

The remaining three functional groups—Economic Growth, Energy, and the Environment (E), Arms Control and International Security Affairs (T), and Civilian Security, Democracy, and Human Rights (G)—all struggle to bring their concerns to bear on the policies largely formulated and implemented by the regional bureaus and the under secretary for political affairs (P), historically the third or fourth highest post in the department, just below the deputies. The regional bureaus house the *country desks,* which are the focal points for messages going to and from overseas posts.

Foreign policy tends to be made on a regional or country basis because that is the way diplomats think and work. Issues that cut across regional compartments are often harder to visualize and even harder to coordinate. Who has the lead in responding to Chinese arms sales to Africa, the China desk or the affected African desk officer? Who at State should be responsible for following Iranian-Venezuelan cooperation on oil and arms? The functional bureaus may weigh in with their concerns and recommendations, but the channels for policy development and action tend to be in and through the regional bureaus. Thus, even within State, there is a need for coordination and compromise in the carrying out of U.S. diplomatic activity.

## The Country Team

Overseas, each embassy staff constitutes a country team for conducting American foreign policy. Achieving genuine teamwork, however, is a difficult process. As many as 30 different U.S. agencies may have people assigned to a given embassy. At the larger posts, State Department people may account for only one third of U.S. personnel.[5] Among the other agencies sending large numbers of people abroad are: DOD, with its military attachés; the United States Agency for International Development (USAID), to run assistance programs; Agriculture (USDA), with its Foreign Agricultural Service; Commerce, with its Foreign Commercial Service; Justice, with its legal liaison, drug enforcement, and Federal Bureau of Investigation (FBI) representatives; Treasury, with its attachés; the Peace Corps, with its volunteers; the Department of Homeland Security (DHS), with its immigration, customs, and transportation security offices; and the intelligence community (IC), with its spies.

These agency representatives perform important services for the United States as well as for their home departments. The defense attachés often develop close relationships with host country military leaders that can be helpful in crises. The agricultural representatives provide export services to U.S. producers and administer food aid and technical assistance to locals. The commercial attachés help U.S. businesses establish local markets and contacts. FBI and Drug Enforcement Administration (DEA) agents work with their foreign counterparts to combat crime. Treasury representatives provide on-scene expertise that helps the U.S. government and permits close collaboration with local financial authorities. As these examples illustrate, U.S. foreign policy activities have a wide reach and cover areas that many in the public, who associate American diplomacy more with the secretary of state and U.S. ambassadors, may not expect.

The chief of mission (usually the ambassador) has formal authority over all the people assigned to the embassy, though not over military personnel under the command of the regional combatant commanders. Each chief of mission receives a formal letter from the president designating him or her "the personal representative" of the president and assigning "full responsibility for the direction, coordination, and supervision of all United States government executive-branch employees." The chief of mission also has the right to see all communications to and from embassy officials. While the chiefs of mission can veto the assignment of particular people from the various agencies and insist on the recall of objectionable ones, they do not write the performance reports on those from outside State—and in practice they cannot really oversee the communications that go directly to and from agency home offices, bypassing State's channels.[6]

The presidential letter clearly provides *de jure* authority to the ambassador, but the chief of mission may lack *de facto* authority because the separate agencies often feel free to pursue their own agendas. The non-State people often view the ambassador as representing his or her department rather than the president, a point of view reinforced by the fact that most communications go *through* the secretary of state and most official guidance is developed under State's leadership even if there is interagency coordination.[7]

Each of the agencies sending people abroad has its own programs, goals, and priorities, and these may clash with the overarching goals established by the ambassador and coordinated with policy makers in Washington. The highest priority for the commercial attaché, for example, might be to secure some U.S. export, but that could conflict with embassy efforts to avoid questionable business practices or enriching certain host country officials. The ambassador's efforts to maintain cooperative relations with the national leader may conflict with military or intelligence programs that help political rivals. Former Ambassador Robert Oakley describes the many simultaneous challenges facing an embassy staff: "In Moscow, the Country Team must promote democratic reform efforts while enhancing opportunities for U.S. businesses in a dynamic emerging market, as well as improve nuclear security initiatives and monitor avian flu. It must do this while working on global and regional energy problems as well as traditional diplomacy."[8]

Ideally, potential conflicts should be worked out in Washington or in the local embassy. But, that requires timely communication and sometimes compromise, all of which can be hard to achieve in chaotic circumstances. That Moscow embassy has about 400 Americans plus another 665 local employees. The embassy in Afghanistan has over 800 U.S. personnel spread throughout the country. With the withdrawal of U.S. military forces from

Iraq in 2011, the U.S. embassy in Baghdad was scheduled to take over 310 of the 1,000+ tasks the Pentagon had been performing. Along with about 650 diplomats, the embassy was slated to oversee 17,000 people—about 1,000 from other government agencies, with the rest being mostly third-country nationals working as life support and security contractors. Security and budget concerns led the State Department in 2012 to review those plans, seeking significant cuts.[9]

Various studies have urged changes in the ways embassies operate. Most call for increased personnel and resources. Many envision the use of new technologies even to the point of virtual presence posts. Some call for better management training for senior officials so that they can better oversee and coordinate the multitude of activities underway by the various U.S. agencies. Both Secretary Condoleezza Rice's Transformational Diplomacy and Secretary Hillary Clinton's Quadrennial Diplomacy and Development Review (QDDR) contained new initiatives to strengthen civilian activities abroad.

### Leadership

The secretary of state has the preeminent position in the president's cabinet and in the public eye on matters of foreign policy. (See Box 6.1.) Throughout history, some of America's most distinguished political figures have held that post. Recent decades have witnessed the first female secretaries of state—Madeleine Albright, Condoleezza Rice, and Hillary Clinton—and the first African-American Secretary, Colin Powell.

There are two contrasting operating styles among State's leaders. Most tend to run the department with a small circle of advisers, often long-time friends or associates. This was the model, for example, followed by James Baker, Madeleine Albright, Condoleezza Rice, and Hillary Clinton. The other approach, followed by George Shultz and Colin Powell, utilized the full professional hierarchy of the department, empowering subordinates by regularly including them in decision processes. There are pros and cons to each model. The small circle is good for loyalty, speed, political sensitivity, and consistency. The empowered bureaucracy is good for departmental

---

| Box 6.1 |

### Secretary of State . . . and President?

Thomas Jefferson was the first of six presidents who had previously served as secretary of state, the most prestigious cabinet post for most of U.S. history. Jefferson, Madison, Monroe, John Quincy Adams, Van Buren, and Buchanan all got significant government and foreign policy experience in that job. Another eight political leaders served as secretary but were defeated in their quests for the White House: Henry Clay, Daniel Webster, John C. Calhoun, William H. Seward, James G. Blaine, William Jennings Bryan, Charles Evans Hughes, and Edmund Muskie.

---

**Box 6.2**

## Who Makes Foreign Policy: The Busy Secretary of State

The secretary of state hardly ever has a day off. White House meetings have been held once or twice a week in the Bush and Obama administrations. In addition, the secretary has to travel abroad for face-to-face meetings with foreign leaders and for international conferences. Secretaries Condoleezza Rica and Hillary Rodham Clinton each averaged about 250,000 miles per year in foreign travel. In 2010, for example, Secretary Clinton visited 54 countries and spent 81 days away from Washington.

---

*Source:* U.S. Department of State.

---

morale, professionalism, subordinate buy-in, and fuller consideration of alternative views.[10]

Whether secretaries of state are powerful within the government as a whole, however, depends on their relationships with the president. When presidents rely on others for key foreign policy advice—as Richard Nixon did on Henry Kissinger and George W. Bush did on Vice President Cheney and Defense Secretary Rumsfeld—the State Department suffers a loss of power, influence, and morale. As former Secretary Dean Rusk, who served two quite different presidents, acknowledged, "The real organization of government at higher echelons [is] how confidence flows down from the President."

Any secretary of state is enormously busy, as Box 6.2 indicates. They all have to travel widely and frequently. They appear on Capitol Hill regularly to explain and defend U.S. policy. And as members of the National Security Council (NSC), they are summoned to numerous White House meetings. In fact, the entire State Department is very busy. (See Box 6.3.)

The State Department itself is a large bureaucracy. There are 44 positions important enough to require Senate confirmation in addition to the more than 100 ambassadorial appointments. While most of these officials work in hierarchical channels, some 45 different people are formally authorized to report directly to the secretary—far more than any good manager could handle.[11] Many of these posts are traditionally given to career foreign and civil service personnel, thus enhancing the institutional memory and professionalization of the department. In contrast to DOD, where no career civilian has ever been appointed to a post requiring Senate confirmation, the State Department typically appoints career foreign service officers (FSOs) to half of the assistant secretary posts and to 85% of the deputy assistant secretary positions.[12]

Ambassadorships are awarded to both political appointees and career officials. Some presidents—and host countries—prefer envoys who are personally close to the White House despite their diplomatic inexperience. Some presidential friends and major contributors welcome the prestige of an

---

| Box 6.3 |

# Who Makes Foreign Policy: A Day in the Life of the State Department

Every day, U.S. diplomats are busy around the globe, gathering information, consulting with foreign officials, attending international conferences, urging actions in support of American policies and interests. Some days are busier than others, of course, but here is a sample of the publicly announced activities of senior State Department officials based in Washington on a fairly typical day. While many more meetings are not announced publicly, and those may be even more significant for foreign policy, the breadth of diplomatic engagement shows that the United States must deal simultaneously with dozens of countries and hundreds of issues. When the president chooses to use the diplomatic instrument for a particular foreign policy goal, that action must be integrated with the many ongoing diplomatic interactions.

## On May 18, 2011

- The Secretary of State met with a Chinese general; met with the U.S. ambassador to India; met the Icelandic foreign minister; met with the Secretary of Defense and the National Security Adviser.
- The senior Deputy Secretary of State was in Bahrain, heading a U.S. delegation that met with local government officials.
- The junior Deputy Secretary met with the Tunisian finance minister and attended a meeting at the White House.
- The USAID Administrator met with the Israeli ambassador; met with three U.S. ambassadors; attended a meeting in the Senator's Dining Room in the Capitol.
- The Under Secretary for Political Affairs spoke at the opening of a historical exhibit at the State Department and met with a U.S. Senator.
- The Under Secretary for Economic, Energy, and Agricultural Affairs gave speeches to a presidential science advisory group and a study group on the U.S. and Chinese economies.
- The Under Secretary for Arms Control and International Security Affairs traveled to Moscow for meetings with Russian officials.
- The Assistant Secretary for International Narcotics and Law Enforcement Affairs was in Accra, Ghana, discussing the West Africa Citizen Security Initiative.
- The Assistant Secretary for East Asian and Pacific Affairs was in Singapore during a trip to Southeast Asia and Japan.
- The Assistant Secretary for Economic, Energy, and Business Affairs met with the Paraguayan Ambassador and the Paraguayan Vice Minister of Economic Relations.
- The Assistant Secretary for European and Eurasian Affairs testified before the Senate Foreign Relations Committee.
- The Assistant Secretary for Population, Refugees and Migration participated in an intergovernmental consultation on migration, asylum, and refugees held in Miami.

*(Continued)*

(Continued)
- The Assistant Secretary for Educational and Cultural Affairs met with the Panamanian Ambassador.
- The Ambassador-at-large and Coordinator for Counterterrorism met with an official from the British ministry of foreign affairs.
- The Special Representative for North Korea Policy held meetings in South Korea.
- The Ambassador-at-large to monitor and combat trafficking in persons spoke to a conference in Rome on modern day slavery.
- The Ambassador-at-large for global women's issues met with a delegation of Pakistani female entrepreneurs.
- The Special Representative for Global Intergovernmental Affairs was in Nigeria meeting with Nigerian governors.
- The Special Envoy for climate change was in Mexico City for a meeting of the U.S.-Mexico Bilateral Framework on Clean Energy and Climate Change.

*Source:* U.S. Department of State, www.state.gov/r/pa/prs/appt/2011/05/163617.htm.

ambassadorial title, especially if they can serve in a less stressful post with good weather. In recent decades, with minor variations, careerists have held about 70% of the ambassadorial slots, with about 30% political. Virtually all Caribbean posts go to political appointees, while most African and Middle Eastern positions go to careerists.[13]

# The Changing Foreign Service

Until the creation of the permanent career foreign service in 1924 and the establishment of professional pay, housing allowances and other benefits, and retirement pensions, most U.S. officials abroad had to be independently wealthy. Until World War II, most American diplomats were white males, mostly Anglo-Saxon Protestants, and often with Ivy League degrees. Much of the time, the work wasn't very hard and the parties were fun. A career officer who was then ambassador to Poland, Hugh Gibson, told Congress in 1924, "You hear very frequently about the boys with the white spats, the tea drinkers, the cookie pushers, and while they are a very small minority, they make a noise entirely disproportionate to their numbers." He urged professionalization of the foreign service in order to "crowd out those incompetents and defectives."[14] In some circles, diplomats are maligned with such stereotypes.

The road to diversity was uphill and slow. By 1970, the foreign service was still 95% male and 99% white. Women could serve, but they had to resign if they married. Lawsuits forced changes in these practices and opened more opportunities during the 1970s, and the Foreign Service Act of 1980 specifically declared that "the members of the Foreign Service should be representative of the American people."[15]

The foreign service today is much more diverse, both in the backgrounds of people recruited and in the range of assignments they perform. As of 2011, two thirds of the total (including FSO generalists and specialists) were male and one third female. African-Americans constituted 7.0%, Hispanics 5.0%, and Asian-Americans 6.8%; the overwhelming majority of 80.6% were white. Of the total foreign service, over half (about 6,800) are generalists, the people who perform the key diplomatic tasks, and the remainder (about 5,000) are the specialists who handle daily operations of office management, security, technical equipment, health, and other support services. Overseas posts also employ about 38,000 foreign service nationals, local citizens who are support staff to U.S. personnel.[16]

The core of America's diplomatic instrument, foreign service generalists, is outnumbered by many measures in the Pentagon. There are more Pentagon lawyers than FSOs, more colonels (and navy captains) than in all ranks of the foreign service, and more members of military bands than FSOs.

The generalist FSOs enter one of five career tracks. Political officers deal directly with host governments and report on policy developments. Economic officers work on economic, trade, energy, and related issues. Consular officers provide citizen services to Americans abroad, such as facilitating adoptions as well as screening visa applicants. Public diplomacy officers—successors to the once-separate U.S. Information Agency—run educational and cultural exchange programs as well as efforts to explain America and its policies to others. Management officers specialize in budgets and embassy management. While any of these tracks could lead to senior posts and satisfying careers, the political officers are generally seen as the diplomatic elite.

In addition to FSOs, who typically spend two thirds of their careers overseas, the department employs 9,300 civil service careerists, mostly in Washington. These people have professional or scientific backgrounds and perform legal, research, administrative, or management duties. One key disparity is that few FSOs want to serve in the functional bureaus because such assignments are viewed as less career enhancing than in the regional bureaus, so they are largely staffed by civil service personnel.[17]

Although some presidents have had low regard for the State Department and the foreign service, former secretaries have much more positive views. As Henry Kissinger wrote: "Several Secretaries have begun their tours of office with that expressed determination [to 'clean out' the department]. I know of none that left office without having come to admire the dedicated men and women who supply the continuity and expertise of our foreign policy. I entered the State Department a skeptic, I left a convert."[18]

On the other hand, former Secretary Alexander Haig called the service "an asteroid, spinning in an eccentric orbit, captured by the gravity of its procedures and its self-interest, deeply suspicious of politicians who threaten its stability by changing its work habits." And James Baker, while praising

FSOs for talent and loyalty, also noted their tendency "to avoid risk taking or creative thinking."[19]

# State Department Culture

There is a dominant culture in the State Department, quite distinctive from those in the other major institutions of American foreign policy. A colonel at the Army War College contrasted the military culture with that of diplomats in his 1998 paper, "Defense Is From Mars, State Is From Venus." While sometimes snarky and condescending—"Venutians frequently find that explaining what they do for a living is met with blank stares"—the colonel also has valuable insights based on scientific evidence. [20]

It so happens that both State and DOD make extensive use of the Myers-Briggs Type Indicator (MBTI) personality evaluation tests, and that the characteristics of people in each department are sharply different. Myers Briggs analyzes people on four contrasting pairs: extroversion (E) versus introversion (I); intuition (N) versus sensation (S); thinking (T) versus feeling (F); and judging (J) versus perceiving (P). There are thus 16 possible combinations.

Both military personnel and FSOs are overwhelmingly introverted, thinking, and judgmental, but uniformed officers tend to rely on sensation, while the diplomats rely on intuition.

Nearly half (47%) of FSOs have the INTJ personality type, compared to only 1% of the general population.[21] Such people, according to the analysts, "convey confidence, stability, competence, intellectual insight, and self-assurance." They are also "intensely individualistic. Stimulated by difficulties, and most ingenious in solving them. Motivated by inspiration." They tend to see the world as a chessboard and like to act independently. Teamwork is hard for them. They embrace theory but avoid long-range planning as they see each problem as unique. They have a much higher tolerance for ambiguity and uncertainty than their military colleagues.

In practice, these differing personality styles help explain why interagency coordination is difficult. But, they also point out State's strengths at seeing the forest as well as the trees and at finding ways to bridge what to others appear to be irreconcilable points of view. Diplomats negotiate. Successful negotiation means reconciling differences, often by compromises that have to be face-saving in order to be durable.

The downside to this way of thinking, however, is that it presumes that blacks and whites can always be combined into a comfortable gray, that artful ambiguity can paper over wide differences, that searching for an agreement is almost always better than giving up, especially if the likely alternative is war. To have to suspend talks, to halt contacts, especially to have to close an embassy because of fundamental disagreements, is a diplomat's worst failure.

Similarly, a diplomat's special skills—the ability to understand foreign governments and cultures, to empathize with them in order to craft agreements—can lead to *clientitis,* that bureaucratic disease that makes foreign concerns seem more important than American ones. Senator Jesse Helms (R-NC), a longtime critic of the State Department, used to complain, "There's no American Desk at the State Department." And, former Secretary George Shultz used to meet with newly named ambassadors and ask them to point on a globe to their country. Almost invariably, they indicated their new postings. The secretary corrected them by pointing instead to the United States. He wanted to inoculate them against that clientitis.

President John F. Kennedy distrusted the State Department because he believed it was too conservative. Richard Nixon distrusted it because he considered it too liberal. Former Speaker of the House Newt Gingrich criticized the department for being insufficiently loyal to President George W. Bush and said that Secretary Colin Powell had "gone native" by adopting departmental views. The common thread in these comments is that State, like all bureaucracies, is fundamentally a force for continuity, and its perspective is necessarily different from that of the White House, where domestic political pressures are most acute.

## Representation and Engagement

The State Department's people and organizations form the primary instrument of diplomacy. They are actually used in a wide variety of activities, with specialized skills and responsibilities. Foremost, of course, is representation of the United States, both symbolically and as a point of contact for foreigners. Representation also entails communicating and advocating American policies.

Presidents often deal directly with foreign leaders and frequently use other officials and even private citizens as emissaries to foreign governments. (See Box 6.4.) National Security Advisers (NSAs) Henry Kissinger, Zbigniew Brzezinski, and Brent Scowcroft were each sent on sensitive missions to Beijing to resolve issues in U.S.–China policy. President Bill Clinton used former President Jimmy Carter, Senator Sam Nunn, and then retired General Colin Powell to persuade the Haitian military government to surrender power in order to avoid a U.S. military invasion. Former New Mexico Governor Bill Richardson—who also has been a member of Congress, a cabinet officer, and UN ambassador—has frequently traveled to North Korea to convey messages and resolve particular problems.

These people were not part of the State Department hierarchy, but they often were advised and supported by foreign service personnel in Washington and abroad. Their activities demonstrate the flexibility of America's diplomatic instrument, while the State Department remains the principal agent for international diplomacy.

The Obama administration made even greater use than its predecessors of special representatives or envoys for various foreign policy issues,

---| Box 6.4 |---

# Inside View: The State Department Outnumbered

In the George W. Bush administration, the national security policy process was dominated by Defense Secretary Rumsfeld in collaboration with Vice President Cheney. The State Department was frequently bypassed by those senior officials, who went directly to the president, or outnumbered in meetings that were held including the diplomats. The State Department's director of the policy planning staff explained how things worked.

*In this administration, the process didn't work nearly as well [as when Bush's father was president] for several reasons. . . . One is that [the Joint Chiefs of Staff] had a lot less voice in this administration. The Pentagon in previous administration really had two voices. Not in this administration. It was just Rumsfeld. Second of all, the vice president's office has become the equivalent of a separate institution or bureaucracy. When I was in the White House in [Bush] 41, the vice president had one or at most two people doing foreign policy. . . . In this administration, the vice president has his own mini-NSC staff. And at every meeting they had a voice and a vote. The vice president ended up getting, from what I could tell, three bites at the apple. He had his staff at every meeting. He would then come to the principals meetings. And then he'd have his one-on-ones with the president. And given the views that came out of the vice president's office, it introduced a certain bias to the system. As a result, I felt that at just about every meeting, the State Department began behind two and a half to one.*

Source: Policy Planning Staff Director Richard Haass, quoted in David J. Rothkopf, *Running the World* (New York: Public Affairs, 2004), 407–408.

some two dozen by 2010. Former Ambassador Richard Holbrooke was the Obama administration's special representative to Pakistan and Afghanistan. Former Senator George Mitchell was special envoy for Middle East Peace. Retired General Scott Gration was special envoy to Sudan. And there were also special advisors for nonproliferation, North Korea policy, Guantanamo, climate change, and various energy issues. Such arrangements have their own strengths and weaknesses. It helps to have a single point of focus and responsibility for issues that cut across usual bureaucratic borders, provided that person can build a competent team and receive the necessary support from his or her superiors and colleagues. But, such a post can easily be orphaned by higher-ranking officials or policy priorities as few have the legal standing to control their own budgets or give orders beyond their own offices.

Regular diplomatic personnel spend most of their time in the representation function, meeting with foreign officials and reaching out to others on behalf of the United States. They explain and advocate U.S. policies and seek agreement and support from the host governments. Sometimes they cajole; sometimes they threaten; sometimes they deliver dollars or deals; sometimes they deny what the host government most desperately wants.

## Negotiations

The most dramatic aspect of international engagement is summit diplomacy. Presidents regularly travel to multinational meetings of organizations like NATO, Asia-Pacific Economic Cooperation (APEC), the G-8 and G-20 economic summits, and the annual session of the UN General Assembly. They also travel abroad for bilateral meetings with foreign leaders and high-profile public events. This is not surprising because the president is the chief diplomat. But behind the scenes, U.S. officials from the White House and State Department frequently lay the groundwork and negotiate the communiqués and agreements announced during these meetings.

Ambassadors and special envoys also negotiate but only subject to guidance and approval from Washington. That guidance can be very specific and constraining, such as on nuclear weapons matters, or it can be more general and flexible. Negotiating teams are also dispatched to major international conferences, some of which last for weeks, months, and even years. For example, negotiations for a follow-on arms control agreement with Russia—called New Strategic Arms Reduction Treaty (START)—began in 2006 and continued for four years under two different presidents.

Negotiations can take numerous forms—informal, highly secret, indirect through third parties, formal meetings and conferences, bilateral and multilateral, and so forth. While the sides may make formal proposals, diplomats often use the device of a *nonpaper*, a proposal not officially attributable to a particular government on blank paper rather than letterhead. In 2006, for example, the Iranian government sent a nonpaper to the United States via a European diplomat suggesting ways for the United States and Iran to engage in diplomatic talks.[22]

## Analyzing and Reporting

What Washington wants most from the field, and what FSOs spend most of their office time doing, is crafting brilliant analyses of host country policies, politics, and personalities. Many a young diplomat dreams of writing a new *long telegram*, George Kennan's broad and deep analysis of the sources of Soviet conduct that led to a Washington consensus on the policy of containment and a prestigious job as first head of the new policy planning staff. Short of that, embassy officials hope that they can put daily events into a broader context and that their inside sources can provide more significant information than journalists can obtain.

FSOs get chosen in part on the basis of their analytical and writing skills. They get promoted in part on how well they report on developments in their overseas posts. There are frustrations, of course. Much reporting is to answer the mail to Congress with required reports on human rights and drug enforcement and so forth or to check the box on a required annual survey of key economic sectors or social trends. Only rarely can their reports justify high levels of classification, yet they know that people in Washington tend to read only top secret messages, saving the unclassified ones for the free time that never comes. (See Box 6.5.)

Overseas messages are called cables, echoing the time when they traveled undersea at high cost and were often written in truncated form, combining words and omitting articles in order to minimize per-word pricing. Now, they arrive on secure computer terminals but are still formatted so that anyone will know who cleared it and who gets to see it. By convention, all outgoing cables are signed with the secretary's name, even if he or she never sees it, and incoming ones carry the ambassador's name, regardless of who authored it.

As a result of the flood of diplomatic messages leaked to the news media, the rest of us can see examples of routine analysis and reporting from U.S. embassies. Many are dull; some are clever; few even begin to approach the Kennan model.

## Public Diplomacy

Although what we now call public diplomacy was an essential part of the State Department at least since World War II, it had a separate bureaucratic existence until 1999, when it was merged with the department. Many insiders claim that the merger downgraded their programs and weakened America's ability to maintain prestige and influence abroad. Recent studies and statements by Secretaries Rice and Clinton have urged greater emphasis on public diplomacy as a tool of foreign policy.

Some public diplomacy is short-term public relations—seeking publicity of U.S. policy statements and favorable coverage of events in the United States. But, some of the most effective work pays out only in the long term. Cultural exchanges nurture public understanding and appreciation between Americans and foreigners. Sending musicians and other performers abroad adds to American *soft power*. Bringing future leaders to extended visits around the United States, and not just to Washington, makes them more realistic and perhaps more sympathetic about America than if they were dependent on their local media. As these benefits are slow to accrue and hard to quantify, it's easy to cut back when cuts are required.

## Citizen Services

Consular officers probably do more to help or hurt America's image abroad, or public approval of the State Department at home, than U.S. ambassadors. They are in the receiving line of those seeking U.S. visas. They help Americans in trouble while traveling as well as facilitate adoptions and business contacts. Their work puts them in danger but also gives them unique insights into the thinking of local people. Their job of assessing visa applicants also puts them in the front line of defense against terrorists. Despite these invaluable functions, consular officers are peripheral to what we usually think of as *doing diplomacy*.

Surprising as it may seem, the United States has embassy-like operations in countries with which it has no formal diplomatic relations. They are used to perform citizen services rather than regular diplomacy. Since 1977, there has been a U.S. interests section in the Swiss Embassy in Havana and a similar Cuban presence in Washington. Switzerland also houses a U.S. interests section in Iran, while Pakistan has one for Iran in Washington. Sweden represents several western countries in North Korea. There is a different arrangement in Taiwan, where the U.S. has a *de facto* embassy, which is technically a private organization staffed by career diplomats who are formally on leave.

## Other Operations

Increasingly, State Department personnel are being used to run programs in the field very operationally. While USAID personnel and others in the embassy have long been operational, this is a change for many in the political and economic sections, who were used to working close to the capital wearing business dress. This activity has been most evident in Iraq and Afghanistan, where civilians from State worked alongside U.S. military personnel in the provincial reconstruction teams (PRTs) in their efforts to advise and assist local communities and officials. The teams arranged community meetings, advised local officials on procedures for activities like elections and budgeting, helped facilitate funding for local projects, and myriad other tasks. As forward-deployed Americans, they were also well positioned to report on political and security developments. When the teams were less successful, it was usually because the security situation was too perilous for them to move about easily.

Secretary Rice began a process of shifting several hundred positions out of Washington and Europe in order to put more people in more difficult strategic posts in the Near East, Asia, Africa, and Latin America. Many were sent to Iraq and Afghanistan but also to India, China, Indonesia, and Venezuela.

## Policy Making

Diplomats don't just execute foreign policy; they also work to develop it through a sometimes somewhat cumbersome process. Ambassadors routinely conclude their reports on foreign developments with recommendations for actions. Policy planners write options papers and circulate them to other offices for clearance to send the documents to more senior officials. Every day, desk officers draft *talking points* for official spokespeople to use in responding to media inquiries. Speechwriters use public appearances and congressional testimony by senior officials to announce policies in the most persuasive language. Reports to Congress and self-initiated policy reviews may conclude with major policy announcements.

Policy is more than statements of goals and intentions; it's also what governments do. And when what the government says is different from what it does, that suggests that policy is not very well coordinated.

Policy papers may recommend actions in the form of statements—"Let's criticize this example of Chinese abuse of human rights"—or in the form of tangible measures—"Let's halt aid to that corrupt government." State mandates a careful review of such proposals from the country desk to the regional bureau and then to senior leaders. All potentially interested offices should be asked to comment and ultimately to *clear*—that is to approve sending the paper forward. This process is policed by the S/ES, which has a formal handbook outlining the procedures to be followed. One of the special powers of the policy planning staff is that its clearance is required on all policy papers submitted to the secretary, ostensibly to ensure consistency with other established policies.

Multiple veto points can slow the process down or lead to more ambiguous language or less radical departures from current policy. Bureaucracies, after all, are a predictable force for continuity. On major issues, the paper—with its recommendations or options or key talking points—may go to the secretary for decision.

---

### Box 6.5

## Inside View: The Clearance Process

Almost every document going to the secretary of state and other senior officials has to be seen and approved by several subordinate officials. The same is true for official "cables" sent to U.S. embassies abroad, all of which are nominally issued in the secretary's name. This clearance process can be very time-consuming, and dissenting officials can insist on changes to satisfy some of their concerns. The process often involves intense negotiations over what words to use and what positions to take. The bureaucratic hoops are spelled out in this excerpt from the handbook from the office that polices the clearance process.

*Write concisely; if you don't, your Principal may not have time to read the memo. Present the facts clearly and in an organized manner; make sure the analysis holds. Give sufficient detail to offer a sound basis for a decision, but don't overwhelm the Principal with minutiae. . . . If there is a difference of opinion within the Department, don't obfuscate—make that difference clear.*

*It is the drafting officer's responsibility to clear memos involving the interests of other bureaus or agencies with those bureaus or agencies. **Neither the Secretary nor USG policy interests can be well-served by uncleared talking points, recommendations, or briefing materials.** It is important that the Secretary or other Principal be confident that the memo has been vetted, that its contents is accurate, that the downsides of a policy decision or discussion are clear, and that any recommended course of action is legal.*

*Don't let disagreement on substantive recommendations hold up a memorandum's progress; where differences exist, craft the memo to highlight clearly the bureaus' differing views and the full range of reasonable options available. Although memoranda must be cleared fully, drafters should avoid unnecessary clearances. One clearance per bureau is generally sufficient, provided the person clearing has sufficient knowledge of the bureau's interest and the authority to represent it.*

---

*Source: The Executive Secretariat Handbook, 2000, U.S. Department of State.*

As the most important foreign policy matters need to be vetted through an interagency process usually run by the NSC staff, State personnel have an incentive to draft the first paper on an issue because that can frame the matter in a way that points to its favored outcome. And when that first paper arrives from another agency, State may have to raise objections or delays to obtain changes.

## Bureaucratic Rivalries Among State, Defense, and the National Security Council

In the interagency process, State is often literally outgunned. What Defense Secretary Robert Gates has called "the defense 800 pound gorilla" tends to dominate foreign policy discussions that have any kind of security component, as most do. If State wants to back diplomacy with the threat of force, the Pentagon insists that that force be ready and credible and usable without interfering with other DOD activities. DOD also represents capabilities for immediate action—aircraft, people, tents, and radios—that no other department has, especially not State.

Whatever deference may be given to State as the lead agency on foreign policy may be insignificant when someone asks, "Who's going to pay for this?" There was a time, the golden year of 1950, when State's budget equaled half the Pentagon's budget. In recent years, the ratio has been more like 1 to 20.

Nevertheless, State brings analytic and diplomatic skills to interagency discussions, so its views can get a fair hearing. The NSC staff, however, has even greater advantages: proximity to the president, access to all of the most sensitive intelligence, and the right to call—or cancel—interagency meetings and set the agenda.

While the formal processes tend to be dominated by the NSC and the Pentagon, there are also informal processes that give State more equal standing. In most administrations, there are regular face-to-face meetings over breakfast or lunch for the secretaries of state and defense and the NSA. These are in addition to the numerous formal NSC-level meetings and permit out-of-channel exchanges: "We're thinking of doing this." "Can you help us resolve this problem our subordinates are having?" In addition to these cabinet-level sessions, departmental deputies also meet frequently both formally and informally and can use those venues to settle disputes. Some analysts believe that the widespread use of informal channels is the result of officials trying to work around a weak and ineffective formal system.[23]

Within State, there are other rivalries that can impede effective action. The regional bureaus have more prestige and people than the functional bureaus, and State's processes channel most activities on a bilateral or regional track. The foreign service similarly tends to dominate civil service personnel on policy questions. And USAID remains in an uncertain status, not fully subordinate to State but not really independent either.

# Congress and the State Department

Congress manages and oversees the State Department with a great tangle of frayed ropes. Most basic foreign policy law is contained in the Foreign Assistance Act of 1961, a 400-page measure that has not been substantially amended since 1985. As a result of patchwork changes over the years, the law contains a bewildering array of 33 goals, 75 priority areas, and 247 directives.[24] No State Department authorization bill has been enacted since 2002. Even when the foreign policy committees produce legislation widely viewed as necessary for enactment, individuals and groups may seek to add controversial measures that prolong debates and may undermine support for the basic legislation. The net result of this failure to pass basic legislation is a weakening of the authorizing committees compared to the appropriations committees and thus a weakening of the policy perspectives and basic guidance that those committees are supposed to provide.

Nor has Congress provided funds for international activities in a timely manner. Neither of the appropriations bills for the State Department and foreign operations has been passed before the end of the fiscal year since 1996. Only four times in the past 20 years has the Foreign Operations Bill been passed on time. The figure for State Department funding is only three times. Even worse, four times in the past 10 years, neither bill passed until January or February.

There is no strong domestic constituency for foreign policy funding. Surveys find that a large number of Americans think that foreign aid takes up close to one fifth of the federal budget, when in fact, all international affairs programs, including the State budget, amount to only 1%. Defense programs produce jobs at home; foreign policy programs don't, except to a very minor degree.

As a consequence, Congress feels freer to cut international programs (budget function 150) than defense (budget function 050). Lawmakers routinely cut presidential requests for international affairs programs, often by percentages 5 to 10 times greater than legislative cuts in defense spending. For example, in the Reagan administration, Congress reduced defense requests by an average of 2.73% while cutting international affairs by 7.07%. In the G. H. W. Bush administration, function 050 was cut an average 2.08% each year, while function 150 was slashed by 12.62%. In the Clinton administration, Congress added an average 1.55% to 050 while cutting 150 by 14.49%. In the George W. Bush years, Congress added 0.4% to basic (nonemergency) defense requests on an average annual basis while cutting international affairs by 2.0%.[25] (See Figure 6.2.)

The State Department has many critics and few defenders on Capitol Hill. The two foreign policy committees—Senate Foreign Relations and House Foreign Affairs—offer few political benefits to members. They may gain attention during international crises but get criticized back home for foreign travel. They gain firsthand knowledge of foreign leaders, but can't

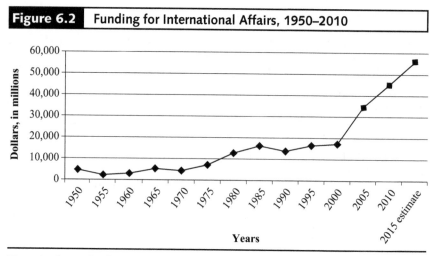

| Figure 6.2 | Funding for International Affairs, 1950–2010 |

The major factors for changing funding levels were increased aid to nations in the Middle East after the 1978 Camp David agreements, cutbacks as the Cold War ended, and then the surge of spending after 2001 relating to counterterrorism and the war in Iraq. Costs also climbed as the U.S. added posts in newly independent countries and built more secure embassies. Despite these increases, total spending on international affairs-related programs has remained as only about 1% of the total federal budget.

*Source:* Office of Management and Budget, Historical Statistics, Table 3.1 Outlays by Function and Superfunction: 1940–2016, www.whitehouse.gov/sites/default/files/omb/budget/fy2012/assets/hist03z1.xls.

accept campaign contributions from foreigners. On the other hand, some members have been effective issue entrepreneurs, becoming key players on particular issues, like Senator Richard Lugar (R-IN) on Soviet nuclear dismantling, or Senator James Webb (D-VA) on Burma, or Congressman Tom Lantos (D-CA) on human rights issues.

Congress treats foreign aid programs the way it handles much domestic legislation, earmarking funds for favored countries and imposing sanctions on miscreants. Programs with strong political support—such as aid to Israel or measures to combat HIV/AIDS—get robust funding, while less favored activities get squeezed for funds. Under Secretary Colin Powell and his successors, the State Department won added funds to increase personnel after years of restraint and even hiring freezes. More recent political pressures for budget cuts may curtail such growth.

Congress tends to prefer procedural legislation to substantive policy laws. For example, it has written laws imposing sanctions on nations supporting terrorism or abusing human rights but gives the president discretion to make such findings—and usually even to waive the sanctions for a higher national security interest. (One reason sanctions on dealings with Castro's Cuba are so hard to change is that they were written into permanent law without the waiver provisions now commonly included.) Similarly, the law requires reports on foreign arms sales and the right to pass legislation vetoing particular sales. Even the War Powers Act, arguably a delegation of Congress's power to declare war, merely requires reports from the president and timely procedures to pass restraining legislation. Observers can debate whether this approach is in recognition of the need for executive discretion or a way of permitting criticism while avoiding congressional accountability.

While it is difficult to pass binding, substantive legislation, Congress often resorts to symbolic gestures, such as a sense of Congress resolutions praising or condemning foreign leaders or their actions. Legislation condemning Ottoman Turkey for "genocide" of Armenians has come close to passage several times, pushed by Armenian-Americans and their friends in Congress, despite warnings that this would cause serious problems for U.S. relations with modern Turkey.

The Senate, with its constitutional powers to advise and consent to nominations to ambassadorships and other senior positions and to approve treaties by a two-thirds vote, plays a special role in foreign policy, sometimes abusing its privileges by delaying or denying votes on noncontroversial nominees in order to gain leverage on some other matters or by complicating treaty consideration with unrelated political issues. In recent decades, the executive branch has tried to get around the treaty hurdles by concluding agreements with other nations that are not labeled treaties and thus do not have to be submitted for the two-thirds vote of approval.

While Congress is usually willing to defer to the executive branch in crisis situations, it has jealously guarded its power of the purse when asked for contingency funds. For example, a small ($25 million) contingency fund for unanticipated opportunities was reduced and then eliminated from the Foreign Operations Appropriations Bill in the 1970s after it was used to pay for a helicopter for a visiting foreign leader. On the other hand, Congress has also been willing to fund over $1.3 billion in annual funds for certain specific contingency situations, including disaster and famine aid, refugee assistance, and peacekeeping operations.[26] It's worth noting, however, that in an era of greater legislative-executive cooperation on foreign affairs, and less virulent partisanship (1960–1961 in particular), Congress was willing to give the president a yearly overseas contingency fund equal to $1 billion to 1.5 billion in current dollars.

As will be clear in Chapter 7, many committees have jurisdiction over matters that affect U.S. foreign policy. The foreign policy committees have primary jurisdiction on, say, policy toward China, but the defense committees can hold hearings and write legislation that relates to Chinese military capabilities and strategy. The trade committees (House Ways and Means and Senate Finance) can set tariffs or authorize trade agreements, but the banking committees can write laws on China's currency. The judiciary committees can write laws on intellectual property rights after looking into China's software piracy activities. Other committees could write consumer laws forbidding importation of Chinese products containing lead or other dangerous products. And, the appropriations committees can condition money for any federal agency on some aspect of relations with China.

There is no requirement—or easy mechanism—for Congress to fashion a comprehensive and consistent grand strategy for China or any other major nation or issue. Political incentives push members toward *ad hoc* responses and prevent much collaboration across party or committee lines. On occasion, Congress has been a strong supporter of the State Department and its people and programs, but more often, it is a fair-weather friend.

\* \* \*

The diplomatic instrument with its many channels and venues is always available to the president. The State Department manages the infrastructure for international engagement, though other officials may be tasked for particular issues. The real choice for senior policy makers is rarely whether to talk to foreign officials but rather which issues to raise, and when and how, in the context of all issues that may be relevant and outstanding.

## Case Study: Building the Gulf War Coalition, 1990

Routine diplomacy involves meetings, conferences, exchanges of views, and occasionally negotiations of international agreements. This is a story of extraordinary diplomacy, when the secretary of state traveled widely and engaged numerous foreign leaders in an urgent effort to build a coalition to challenge Saddam Hussein's invasion of Kuwait. It shows that personal diplomacy can make a difference.

Secretary of State James Baker was in Siberia, talking and fishing with Soviet Foreign Minister Eduard Shevardnadze, when he learned of Saddam Hussein's imminent invasion of Kuwait on August 1, 1990. He told his Soviet counterpart, who checked with Moscow and told Baker not to worry. When confirmation of the invasion came a few hours later, Shevardnadze was angry and embarrassed. Baker seized the opportunity to press for a joint statement condemning the attack and demanding an immediate withdrawal as well as halting arms shipments. Because the USSR was a major weapons supplier and diplomatic supporter of Iraq, Baker saw cooperation with Moscow as the linchpin for building an international coalition against Saddam Hussein. The two sides decided to discuss the matter further.

Baker left for a preplanned visit to Mongolia. Shevardnadze called from Moscow and said it might be difficult to reach agreement on a joint statement. A State Department team in Moscow found Soviet officials opposed to tough language and recommended against a Baker visit. But, the secretary decided he could succeed if he put American prestige—and prospects for further U.S.-Soviet cooperation on other issues—on the line in a face-to-face meeting. The two foreign ministers met and issued a strong statement calling upon the rest of the international community to join in an international cutoff of all arms supplies to Iraq.

President George H. W. Bush had been conducting his own personal diplomacy, calling the leaders of Egypt, Jordan, and Saudi Arabia, and meeting with British Prime Minister Margaret Thatcher. After an NSC meeting, he sent Defense Secretary Dick Cheney to seek Saudi permission to send U.S. troops to help defend that nation.

While the UNSC approved Resolution 661 imposing severe economic sanctions on Iraq, Bush and Baker believed they needed to continue pressing other nations for tough enforcement and for possible additional steps to pressure Iraq. On August 9, Baker headed to Turkey, the first of 20 nations he would visit during the crisis. Turkish President Ozal agreed to halt shipments of Iraqi oil through a Turkish pipeline but sought and received from Baker a pledge for World Bank loans of $1.5 billion to offset lost revenues.

In September, despite five more UN resolutions, Baker began what he called his "tin cup trip" to get financial support for what had become Operation Desert Shield defending Saudi Arabia and preparing for a possible move back into Kuwait. Baker got pledges of $15 billion from the Saudi king and from the emir of Kuwait. He got Egypt to commit some of its troops in return for forgiveness of $7.1 billion in U.S. loans. He secured a troop pledge from Syria and a squadron of fighter planes from Italy. Germany pledged another $2 billion. Ultimately, the U.S. cost of Operations Desert Shield and Desert Storm totaled $61 billion, of which $54 billion was supplied by other nations.

When President Bush decided at the end of October to double the U.S. troop commitment and prepare for war, he also decided to try to get another UNSC resolution authorizing the use of force. Baker undertook a new mission. "I was determined to meet personally with the head of state or foreign minister of every Council member in the weeks before the vote." He also wanted the foreign ministers present for the vote—the first UN authorization of force since Korea in 1950.

During November 1990, Baker visited 12 countries in what he called "an intricate process of cajoling, extracting, threatening, and occasionally buying votes." The Chinese indicated they wouldn't veto a resolution but wanted to arrange a high-level visit. Turkey pledged support. French President Francois Mitterrand agreed that war was necessary. Ethiopia was supportive. Zaire (previously and now again called Congo) complained about a congressional cutoff of military aid, which Baker promised to try to reverse. The secretary also promised to try to get additional debt forgiveness for Ivory Coast. Romania, recipient of $80 million in humanitarian assistance only a few months earlier, offered no objections. Yemen's leader said no, but Colombia's president gave his support. Malaysia's foreign minister was noncommittal. After a final flurry of talks just before the UNSC vote on November 29, Baker presided as the members voted 12 to 2 (Cuba and Yemen), with the Chinese abstaining, for Resolution 678 authorizing "all necessary means" to get Iraq to withdraw from Kuwait. The deadline was January 15, 1991.

Despite the international support for possible military action, public opinion in the United States was less enthusiastic. Baker joined in the administration effort to build public support but in a way that backfired. Critics had been saying, "No war for oil," and Baker only reinforced that connection when he told reporters that the global economy would be threatened by allowing Saddam Hussein to control substantial oil reserves. "If you want to sum it up in one word, it's jobs," he declared. That led many in Congress to demand a vote on whether or not to go to war.

Congress ultimately approved a resolution authorizing force but only after Baker went the last mile in a search for peace by meeting with the Iraqi Foreign Minister Tariq Aziz in Geneva on January 9, 1991. The diplomats spent nearly seven hours exchanging points of disagreement then parted. Coalition forces began their war on January 16, and Iraq was driven from Kuwait and ready to conclude a cease-fire on February 28. The coalition that James Baker, President Bush, and other diplomats had built held firmly together through the conflict.

This case shows the value of personal diplomacy by the secretary of state but also the enormous time required on this single issue. It also shows that, although the United States was already engaged with the members of the UNSC, building a coalition required special negotiations with foreign leaders to gain their support for U.S. proposals.

By contrast, in 2002 and 2003, the George W. Bush administration secured UNSC approval, by a unanimous vote, of Resolution 1141. That measure was admittedly ambiguous. It declared Iraq in "material breach" of its obligations under earlier UNSC resolutions, called for renewed international inspections, and warned that Iraq "will face serious consequences as a result of its continued violations of its obligations." After dramatic testimony by Secretary of State Colin Powell, the Bush administration determined that it could not win a second UNSC resolution formally authorizing the use of force and thus never pushed it to a vote.

Sources: James A. Baker, III, *The Politics of Diplomacy: Revolution, War, and Peace, 1989–1992* (New York: G.P. Putnam's Sons, 1995); Condoleezza Rice, *No Higher Ground* (New York: Crown Publishers, 2011).

## Selected Resources

The main Department of State website is at www.state.gov/.

Sites that follow State Department activities, policies, and budgets include: www.usglc.org/, http://thewillandthewallet.squarespace.com/, http://thecable.foreignpolicy.com/, http://news.yahoo.com/blogs/envoy/.

What it's like in an embassy abroad is detailed in Robert Hopkins Miller, *Inside an Embassy: The Political Role of Diplomats Abroad* (Washington, DC: Institute for the Study of Diplomacy, 1992). A more recent publication on the same topic is Dorman, Shawn, ed., *Inside a U.S. Embassy: How the*

*Foreign Service Works for America* (Washington, DC: American Foreign Service Association, 2005).

The Institute for the Study of Diplomacy has reports and case studies at http://isd.georgetown.edu/.

The Association for Diplomatic Studies and Training also has background information on diplomacy and diplomats at www.usdiplomacy.org/index.php.

# 7 The Economic Instruments

*Foreign economic policy in the United States is shaped not systematically, but almost by accident. It is a least common denominator, worked out, as some have so aptly put it, by a kind of guerrilla warfare among the Departments of State, Treasury, Agriculture, the Federal Reserve Board, and a whole host of other Executive Branch agencies.*

—former Senator and Treasury Secretary Lloyd Bentsen[1]

Most of the instruments of national power are controlled by the U.S. government. The armed forces are controlled by the president all the time, and he can federalize the national guard as needed. Diplomacy is a federal function, except for those local communities that try to have their own foreign policies on boycotts, human rights, or immigration. Nongovernmental organizations gather information abroad, including news and satellite imagery, but only the intelligence agencies have the resources and the mandate to break foreign laws if necessary to get the desired information.

The economic instruments of national power, however, are nested in a much larger market economy, which itself is subject to international legal and market forces beyond the day-to-day control of the national government. They can be used for national security purposes but only with collateral consequences and with less precision compared with the other instruments.

The president has a broad array of economic tools to support U.S. foreign policy. (See Table 7.1.) The toolkit is not well organized, however, because different institutions control different instruments and there is only a weak coordinating mechanism in the White House. Those institutions have their own cultures and core missions, which can easily come into conflict. The Department of Commerce, for example, may want to promote exports of high-tech devices that the Defense Department (DOD) fears might lead to a loss of U.S. technology. The State Department may want to give aid to a country for political reasons that the Agency for International Development (USAID) views as wasteful or inefficient. Moreover, there is often a domestic component of economic policy that the foreign policy experts are ill-equipped to assess.

170

| Table 7.1 | The Economic Instruments Brief | | | |
|---|---|---|---|---|
| ACTION | EXECUTIVE AGENT | ADVANTAGES | DISADVANTAGES | CONGRESSIONAL ROLE |
| Sanctions | President, Department of the Treasury, Office of Foreign Assets Control (OFAC) | Highly punitive when supported by others | Unintended consequences, often ineffective if unilateral | Set by general or country-specific law |
| Capital flows; currency support | Department of the Treasury, Federal Reserve (the Fed) | Few restraints on action | Limited impacts in global economy | International Emergency Economic Powers Act, money laundering laws, International Monetary Fund contributions |
| Foreign direct investment | Committee on Foreign Investment in the United States reviews; OFAC enforces sanctions | Assures control | Political pressures frequent | Broadened Committee on Foreign Investment in the United States (CFIUS) |
| Exports | 19 agencies promote; Dept. of State runs munitions list; Dept. of Commerce runs commerce control List; OFAC issues licenses | Popular support for export promotion with minor controls | Little coordination, complaints on arms limits | Review of major arms exports, basic law expired, no consensus on renewal |
| Imports | Department of Commerce; Customs; International Trade Commission (ITC) review | ITC review can reduce political pressures | Reduced presidential discretion | Tariffs; quotas; other restrictions |
| Trade agreements | U.S. Trade Representative (USTR) negotiates: tariffs, quotas, non-tariff barriers; ITC review of alleged violations | Important outcomes when achieved | Authority limited; lengthy negotiations | Grants negotiating authority; single vote on trade agreements |
| Military aid | Department of State; Department of Defense | Valued support to allies | Unintended political consequences | Appropriations; many earmarks |

(Continued)

171

**Table 7.1** (Continued)

| ACTION | EXECUTIVE AGENT | ADVANTAGES | DISADVANTAGES | CONGRESSIONAL ROLE |
|---|---|---|---|---|
| Economic aid | Department of State; U.S. Agency for International Development; Department of Defense; + 22 others | Appreciated economic support | May not be effectively used | Appropriations; many earmarks |
| Development aid | Department of State; U.S. Agency for International Development; Millennium Challenge Corp. + 22 others | Noncontroversial aid | Slow to achieve results | Appropriations; many earmarks |
| Humanitarian | Department of State; U.S. Agency for International Development; Department of Defense | Noncontroversial aid | Some unintended consequences | Appropriations; many earmarks |
| Multilateral | Department of the Treasury votes at International financial institutions (IFIs) | Professional | Little U.S. political benefit | Approves contributions |
| Culture | Each agency distinctive | Good at core competencies | Hard to coordinate | Tends to view economic instruments through domestic lens |

There are many quite different economic instruments in the foreign policy toolkit. Congress plays an active role in some, but many are within the discretion of the president. In the executive branch, there are often overlapping authorities, making it hard to achieve a coordinated foreign policy. Some of the economic tools are quick acting, while others are very slow; some are direct, while others are indirect. A further complication is that these tools operate in a globalized economy, where private sector forces can overwhelm or offset whatever a government may try to do.

172

# Carrots and Sticks

Economic statecraft is conducted with various carrots and sticks—some provide incentives and rewards for other nations; others impose punishment or pressure on those who are not cooperating. Among those carrots are favorable tariff and tax treatment, direct monetary aid and guarantees, subsidies and licenses for imports and exports, and helpful capital flows and foreign investment. Some of these measures are conducted directly by the U.S. government, while others benefit and are used by the private sector for its own profit-making purposes.

The sticks can be heavy and painful. Sanctions can be used to cut off aid and other favorable treatments as well as private sector sales and investments. Exports can be restricted and imports banned. Assets of countries, companies, and even individuals can be seized or denied access to U.S. financial institutions. These penalties can be imposed quickly by presidential order.[2]

What complicates things is how these instruments affect other economic activities and other foreign policy goals. Forbidding sales of U.S. oil drilling equipment, as has been done at different times to punish Libya, Iran, and Iraq, hurt American companies even as it demonstrated a foreign policy principle. Limiting food aid to North Korea for important security goals may hurt the Korean people more than its leaders. Or as one analyst has said, "America continues to place far greater emphasis on bribing nondemocratic states than on promoting their democratization."[3] The challenge for the president is to balance these domestic and foreign policy concerns.

# A Disorganized Toolkit

In the U.S. government itself, the economic tools are dispersed and disorganized. Except for the agencies handling foreign assistance, the agencies with responsibilities for international economic policy have a primarily domestic focus. Treasury worries about the strength of the dollar and the U.S. economy as a whole. Commerce wants to help U.S. businesses and domestic markets. Even the U.S. trade representative (USTR) negotiates trade agreements in order to help domestic companies and industries, as the Korea Free Trade Agreement case study makes clear. Several of the important institutions are not under direct presidential control, including the Fed, the International Trade Commission, the Export-Import Bank (Ex-Im), and the Overseas Private Investment Corporation (OPIC).

If the White House wanted to convene an interagency meeting to harmonize export strategy, they would have to invite at least 19 different agency heads, who have mandates to promote U.S. exports along with other responsibilities. A meeting of those involved in providing development assistance would have to include 26 different institutions. Each of those bureaucratic entities has its own laws, often written by different congressional committees to serve different purposes. Unlike most countries with large economies, the United States does not have a department of trade or even a truly central bank.[4] This multiplicity of agencies with similar activities prompted President Obama in 2012 to seek reorganization authority—subject to a congressional veto—to consolidate several organizations that help U.S. businesses at home and abroad.

Foreign assistance is also dispersed among several agencies. About 20% of development aid is administered by the Pentagon. USAID has its own bureaucratic competition from the Millennium Challenge Corporation (MCC) and the U.S. Trade and Development Agency.

Exports of military or potentially military *(dual-use)* equipment and technologies often have to pass muster with DOD, State, and Commerce. Imports of different kinds may be subject to review and limitations by Treasury, Commerce, DOD, Transportation, and even the Fish and Wildlife Service (which administers the endangered species list).

Americans wishing to invest abroad may be limited by rules from Treasury, which administers financial and trade sanctions and maybe the Securities and Exchange Commission (SEC). Foreigners wishing to invest in U.S. companies might also need permission from Treasury and perhaps other departments as well.

The laws are complex. The bureaucracies are numerous. It is very hard for the United States to pursue a consistent and well-coordinated strategy using international economic policy instruments. As Stephen D. Cohen has written, "International economic policies serve as important means to the end of achieving domestic and external political and economic goals that the official sector has determined would enhance the country's national interests. . . . All too often, however, it is an either/or case, and considerations of global efficiency are unceremoniously brushed aside by perceptions of domestic or international political necessity."[5]

## The Globalized Economy

Even if agencies and actions were fully integrated, they would still be subject to larger forces both domestically and internationally. The federal government accounts for only 20% of the gross domestic product (GDP), and its revenues are crucially dependent on the health of the other 80%. Foreign trade accounted for nearly 33% of the economy in 2011, and daily currency transactions totaled $2 trillion. Currency controls are still at least theoretically possible, but electronic transfers in nanoseconds could sink a troubled economy before most could kick in.[6]

International organizations like the International Monetary Fund (IMF), World Bank, and the G-20 have become crisis managers, weighing in with advice and assistance on matters far beyond the control of any small handful of countries. Apart from the governments, multinational corporations dominate the global economy, and they often have great flexibility in choosing the tax and legal regimes to which they subject themselves.[7]

| Table 7.2 | U.S. Net Economic Engagement With Developing Countries, 2009 | |
|---|---|---|
| **SOURCES OF ECONOMIC ENGAGEMENT** | **BILLIONS OF DOLLARS** | **PERCENT OF ENGAGEMENT** |
| U.S. official development assistance | $28.8 | 13% of overall engagement |
| U.S. private philanthropy | 37.5 | 17% of overall |
| Foundations | 4.6 | 12% of private sources |
| Corporations | 8.9 | 24% of private |
| Private and voluntary organizations | 12.0 | 32% of private |
| Volunteerism | 3.0 | 8% of private |
| Universities and colleges | 1.8 | 5% of private |
| Religious organizations | 7.2 | 19% of private |
| U.S. remittances | 90.7 | 40% of overall |
| U.S. private capital flows | 69.2 | 31% of overall |
| Total U.S. economic engagement | $226.2 | 100% |

Within the developing world, the amount of U.S. government support is dwarfed by the private sector. Remittances sent to home countries by foreign workers in the United States alone amount to triple official government assistance.

*Source:* The Index of Global Philanthropy and Remittances, 2011, Hudson Institute.

In addition to the numerous financial transactions for profit-making purposes, there are sizable private transactions. (See Table 7.2.) Foundations, corporations, religious organizations, universities, and private and voluntary organizations gave nearly 40% more than official U.S. development assistance. Individual remittances totaled three times the official government total.[8] Thus, whatever government may be doing, the private sector is doing much more and for its own purposes, which may or may not be in sync with U.S. government policy. Government rules can limit or shape many of these private actions through tax treatment and prohibitions to enforce sanctions, but it is harder to direct these resources as a conscious instrument of U.S. policies. Only the institutions of government can reliably be used for that.

## Key Institutions

While the president usually orders the use of the economic instruments, the implementation of those orders is done through and by different organizations within the U.S. government. Table 7.3 lists the major institutions and their key responsibilities relating to foreign economic policy along with the organizational culture that dominates them.

| Table 7.3 | Key Institutions in U.S. Economic Foreign Policy | |
| --- | --- | --- |
| **INSTITUTION** | **ECONOMIC ACTIVITIES** | **CULTURE** |
| National Economic Council (NEC) | Coordinates administration of domestic and international policies; provides collective advice to the president | White Houser-centric, supports the president |
| Federal Reserve | Independent status; crafts U.S. monetary policy; works with foreign central banks | Conservative bankers |
| Department of Treasury | Administers economic sanctions; monitors foreign investments in the United States; safeguards the financial system from foreign threats; advisers and attachés overseas work with communities and local governments | Conservative bankers plus law enforcement |
| U.S. Trade Representative (USTR) | Advises on trade policy and negotiates trade agreements when the president has the requisite authority from Congress; reports directly to the president, yet often mediates between both branches | Trade deals are us |
| Department of Commerce | Enforces import regulations and some export laws; runs the U.S. Commercial Service to help American businesses sell in global markets | Supports U.S. business |
| Department of State | Develops foreign aid programs for recipient countries, especially security-related assistance; oversees rules and processes for the export of military goods and services | Promotes U.S. foreign policy |
| U.S. Agency for International Development (USAID) | Manages American foreign aid programs concerned with economic development and improved living conditions | Helps the needy abroad |
| Department of Defense (DOD) | Manages foreign military grant and loan programs and foreign military sales programs; oversees counterterrorism training and postconflict stabilization programs as well as some humanitarian assistance | Strengthens military ties and improves capabilities of friends |
| Department of Agriculture (USDA) | Promotes exports of U.S. agricultural products with subsidies, export credit guarantees, and food aid | Keeps U.S. agriculture strong and prosperous |

*(Continued)*

| **Table 7.3** (Continued) | | |
|---|---|---|
| **INSTITUTION** | **ECONOMIC ACTIVITIES** | **CULTURE** |
| Other Organizations | Partner with foreign governments to help shift former weapons scientists into nonmilitary research (Department of Energy); work with other nations on container security and law enforcement training (Department of Homeland Security, DHS); liaise abroad on legal issues and counterterrorism and counternarcotics programs (Department of Justice) | Promotes core mission by overseas activities |

While Table 7.1 shows the types of economic instruments and the roles of the president and Congress over them, here we highlight the major institutions that have responsibilities over those instruments. You can see from this summary of activities how responsibilities, goals, and actions may overlap across the different institutions.

### National Economic Council

The NEC was established by executive order under President Bill Clinton and has been retained by his successors. In theory, the NEC is supposed to coordinate administration domestic and international economic policies and provide collective advice to the president. Its success as a coordinating body has depended on the personal skills and relations of the chairman, for it has no substantive authority. Its membership includes most of the members of the cabinet as well as the senior people in the Executive Office of the President (EOP). Day-to-day operations are handled by National Security Council (NSC)-like committees of lower-ranking officials.

The NEC staff of about 20 people typically run dozens of meetings and conference calls each week to discuss policy matters. A decision paper might require 200 to 300 hours of preparation for a 45-minute meeting with the president.[9]

International economic issues may be handled by the NEC, but its staff also tend to be dual-hatted as NSC staff, so the venue can change. The NEC has been used for some trade issues like North American Free Trade Agreement (NAFTA) under Clinton and for some international economic crises in later years.

Because the NEC is based on an executive order rather than a statute and its leadership is not confirmed by the Senate, it has only informal dealings with Congress. Unlike the NSC, which has a 65-year track record and an established process that departments can rely on, the NEC is an organization-in-waiting, dependent on support and taskings from the president.[10]

### Federal Reserve

Also called the Fed, the Federal Reserve is a key player in the U.S. economy at home and abroad, but it has an independent status that allows it to act on its own. It does not participate in NEC deliberations. The members of the board of governors have long-term presidential appointments, while the heads of the 12 regional banks are chosen locally. The Fed system was created by Congress in1913 in order to have an "elastic currency" and better supervision of U.S. banking. In 1978, Congress gave the Fed a broad and difficult mandate to promote "the goals of maximum employment, stable prices, and moderate long-term interest rates."[11]

While its most visible role is in monetary policy—setting interest rates and trying to limit inflation—it is in regular contact with foreign central banks and regulates the U.S. activities of foreign banks. It also carries out foreign currency operations that affect exchange rates. In the 2007–2008 global financial crisis, and again in 2010–2011, the Fed established swap arrangements with foreign central banks to help provide liquidity.

When finance ministers gather to discuss crisis responses or general international economic policies, the Fed chair and Treasury secretary usually attend for the United States. While legally independent, their institutions are expected to harmonize their activities.

The Fed culture is a banker's culture—conservative, concerned with stability, worried about inflation, viewing international and domestic policies through an economic lens. These are not the hedge fund high fliers but the sober, risk-averse bank managers, skeptical of optimistic forecasts and concerned about collateral for loans. The international economy is seen as a dark forest of wild beasts that can sometimes only be tamed by heavy doses of austerity medicine. The banker's culture is willing to protect the system as a whole but hard-nosed toward any individual country or institution.

As a result, the Fed can be quick to join efforts to provide liquidity to U.S. banks and companies, as it did in 2008–2009, and to help the international system cope with the sovereign debt crisis more recently. But, it is much more cautious of using monetary tools for foreign policy objectives. Fed Chairman Ben Bernanke did call the Chinese currency undervalued, but he avoided endorsing punitive actions favored by many in Congress.

Congress is the only overseer of the Fed as it writes the laws giving its authorities and responsibilities, and the Senate can block appointments to the board. But in general, lawmakers have stood in awe of the Fed chairmen, even as they tried to elicit comments helpful to their own agendas.

### Department of the Treasury

The Treasury Department, second oldest in the government, was created to handle federal finances—collecting revenues, paying bills, and managing the public debt. It now has broad responsibilities to promote economic prosperity and ensure the nation's financial security. In international affairs, it administers economic sanctions of foreigners, monitors foreign investments in the U.S., and works to safeguard the financial system from foreign threats.

Although the State Department was historically the primary institution to craft U.S. foreign economic policy, Treasury has gained a preeminent role since the 1960s, reinforced by the increase in political and economic importance of international economic issues and the need to balance domestic and foreign policy concerns.[12] It also represents the United States in the international financial institutions like the IMF and the World Bank. As a consequence, Treasury votes for the U.S. on which assistance programs run by the multilateral development banks go to which countries. Treasury also runs the debt relief program for poor countries with a budget of about $100 million per year.[13]

Treasury has two offices headed by under secretaries that deal with international policies—the Office of International Affairs (OIA) and the Office of Terrorism and Financial Intelligence (OTFI). OIA handles the traditional portfolios of economic issues with regional and functional bureaus for matters like debt, trade, and energy. It also heads CFIUS, the interagency panel that reviews possibly troublesome investments in American companies. OTFI, which was established only in 2004, houses OFAC, which enforces economic and trade sanctions. Another office works with law enforcement agencies domestically and abroad to combat financial crimes. An office of intelligence and analysis is Treasury's subsection of the intelligence community (IC).

Overseas, Treasury has attachés in 16 major posts who relate primarily to foreign finance ministries and central banks. It also has technical advisories in about 40 countries, helping them develop human and institutional capacities for their governments. The State Department also has economic specialists in its embassies, but the Treasury people are often the best connected with the local financial community.

The senior officials at Treasury have the banker's culture—concerned with the health of the dollar and the domestic economy and conservative in approach with a focus on macroeconomic and systemic issues. The people at OIA, OFTI, and OFAC are more often economists and lawyers, trying to use their professional tools to advise on policies and enforce the laws.

Congressional oversight of Treasury is mainly by the tax committees, House Ways and Means and Senate Finance, and their focus is more on domestic than foreign issues. Those committees also handle trade policy, however, but their focus there is on the USTR.

## United States Trade Representative

Congress created the post of USTR in 1962 because it didn't trust any other part of the American government to handle what became the Kennedy round of multilateral trade negotiations. Lawmakers wanted someone reporting directly to the president. The system worked well enough that, in 1974, Congress made the post permanent and gave it cabinet rank.

As a creature of the Congress, despite its bureaucratic placement in the EOP, USTR feels a dual responsibility to both branches and often ends up negotiating with one on behalf of the other. The trade representative chairs

19-member interagency committees on trade policy and is on the board of directors of the MCC, OPIC, and Ex-Im.

The primary USTR missions are to advise on trade policy and to negotiate trade agreements when the president has the requisite authority from Congress—something Bill Clinton was denied and George W. Bush was granted for only five years.

The culture of USTR is that of deal makers balancing multiple clients and feeling constant cross-pressures from within and outside the government while they advocate for U.S. interests with foreigners. In their interagency roles, USTR people are the voice for trade as an instrument for various domestic and foreign policy goals.

### Department of Commerce

The Department of Commerce is a collection of disparate bureaus with what it calls "cross-cutting responsibilities in the areas of trade, technology, entrepreneurship, economic development, environmental stewardship and statistical research and analysis."[14] It includes the Census Bureau, a Bureau of Economic Analysis, the patent and trademark office, the National Oceanic and Atmospheric Administration, and the National Institute of Standards and Technology. Its key international activities are enforcing import regulations, issuing export licenses and enforcing export laws, and running the U.S. commercial service, which has offices in more than 100 U.S. cities and 80 countries to help American businesses sell in global markets.

Commerce has a probusiness culture overall, though its export and import offices have a law enforcement focus. Its International Trade Administration is primarily concerned with advocating for U.S. businesses that want to export than with other aspects of trade. Congress, over the years, has shifted functions into Commerce when lawmakers felt that another department was ineffective in fulfilling its assigned missions. Commerce reclaimed the commercial service from State in 1978 when lawmakers concluded that diplomats weren't especially interested in promoting U.S. businesses. Commerce gained enforcement of the dumping and countervailing duty laws in 1980 when Treasury was viewed as more interested in macroeconomic issues than in responding to the grievances of individual companies and industries.[15]

Commerce's role may change if the Obama administration's National Export Initiative results in a consolidation of exporting activities in a single organization. In 2012, the president sought reorganization authority to combine the business-related components of Commerce with the USTR, the Small Business Administration, the Ex-Im, and OPIC. Any such changes require congressional approval.

### Department of State

The State Department has a bureau for Economic Growth, Energy, and the Environment and numerous economic officers posted abroad, but its primary role in international economic policy involves developing and implementing foreign aid programs for recipient countries, especially security-related assistance. State also oversees the rules and processes for the export of military goods and services.

As discussed in Chapter 6, State is better at diplomacy than program management. It rewards individual accomplishments more than teamwork. Its culture relies on engaging foreigners more than punishing them. In contrast to the more domestically oriented departments of the U.S. government, State tends to "give top priority to foreign policy considerations because they view international economic policy as being mainly the economic aspect of the pursuit of a stable, friendly, and prosperous global environment. Hence, economic considerations should be subordinate to the primary objective of good relations with other nations."[16]

For Congress, State is the perennial whipping boy on the whole range of foreign policy issues, including softness toward bad guys and mismanagement of the limited funds provided. Lawmakers reflect the public mood that historically has wanted to cut foreign aid more than any other activity by the government.

## United States Agency for International Development

USAID, as the agency likes to be called, is the primary manager of American foreign aid programs that are concerned with economic development and improved living conditions. It coordinates with State on those programs but has the lead for policy implementation.

Foreign aid programs are governed by the lengthy, complex, and somewhat inconsistent provisions of the Foreign Assistance Act of 1961, which has not been substantially amended since 1985. USAID currently has a checklist of 65 statutory provisions that must be considered when determining country eligibility and budget amounts as well as funding allocations.[17]

Congress complicates USAID programs by earmarking the bulk of foreign assistance for a handful of countries, forcing restraint on more modest and long-term development programs.

## Department of Defense

The Pentagon currently manages more than one fifth of the funds that count as overseas development assistance, mainly because of huge programs in Iraq and Afghanistan. But, there has also been a major increase in other DOD-run programs since the 9/11 attacks. The Pentagon launched programs in counterterrorism training and postconflict stabilization and became a major player in humanitarian assistance. In Iraq and Afghanistan, it provided substantial economic assistance through the Commander's Emergency Response Program (CERP) and led most of the interagency provincial reconstruction teams (PRTs).[18]

For several decades, the Pentagon has managed the foreign military grant and loan programs as well as the foreign military sales programs, albeit with inputs from the State Department, which sets guidelines for these programs and must approve all sales and transfers. DOD personnel, however, are usually the ones working with local militaries and developing program requests. DOD has a Defense Security Cooperation Agency (DSCA) for these activities. That agency also manages the International Military Education and Training (IMET) program that brings foreign military personnel into U.S. programs. In 2009, for example, approximately 69,500 students from 159 countries participated in such training.

The defense committees of Congress have supported these DOD activities, but the foreign policy committees have sometimes criticized them, complaining that the Pentagon puts too much of a military face on U.S. foreign policy.

### Department of Agriculture

Besides running domestic government farm programs, the USDA has long been active in promoting exports of U.S. agricultural products with subsidies, export credit guarantees, and food aid.[19] Although USAID now administers much of *Public Law 480,* the 1954 measure that created the Food for Peace program, the impetus behind it has always been agricultural interests and their congressional allies. They succeeded magnificently, for agriculture now accounts for 6% of U.S. exports of goods and supports nearly one million jobs in the United States. Market access for U.S. agricultural products is often a key sticking point in negotiating trade agreements.

### Other Organizations

Several other parts of the U.S. government run programs that provide security assistance abroad. The Department of Energy has a Nonproliferation and International Security Program costing over $1 billion annually that partners with foreign governments and helps shift former weapons scientists in Russia and elsewhere into nonmilitary research. State and DOD also run related programs with nonproliferation goals. DHS has international programs working with other nations on container security and law enforcement training. The Department of Justice and the Federal Bureau of Investigation (FBI) both send people abroad for liaison on legal issues and counterterrorism and counternarcotics programs.[20]

Other agencies also run their own economic assistance programs. The Department of Health and Human Services (HHS) has numerous programs in the Centers for Disease Control and Prevention (CDC). The Food and Drug Administration (FDA) and National Institutes of Health (NIH) have technical assistance and training programs abroad, as does the Environmental Protection Agency (EPA). The Department of Education has foreign study grants and runs language study centers.[21]

# Key Processes

As Table 7.1 shows, many of the economic tools have shared or overlapping control in the bureaucracy. The processes for sanctions and trade agreements, for example, are narrowly held. But, imports and exports and foreign direct investments are overseen by many different agencies, often for differing purposes. Foreign assistance also comes in many varieties, each managed by separate organizations with differing core missions. Even a determined president and an unusually effective White House will have difficulty integrating these disparate organizations into a coherent policy.

## Sanctions

One of the most powerful tools of foreign economic policy is the threat or use of economic sanctions. These are from the bag of sticks, seeking to punish objectionable behaviors or to coerce a change in behavior. The president has several legal authorities to use against other nations, and even against individuals and private entities.

The broadest law is the International Emergency Economic Powers Act (IEEPA) of 1977 (PL 95–223, 50 USC 1701 et seq.), which allows the president "to deal with any unusual and extraordinary threat, which has its source in whole or substantial part outside the United States, to the national security, foreign policy, or economy of the United States." If he declares a national emergency, the president can then "investigate, regulate, or prohibit" foreign exchange transactions, banking credits or payments, and importing or exporting of currency or securities. Any such emergency, however, must be renewed annually in order to remain in effect.

IEEPA was enacted to regularize the use and impact of national emergency declarations, some of which dated to the depression and World War II. It also narrowed the 1917 Trading With the Enemy Act to apply only in wartime.

The president also has more specific authorities to control imports and exports of certain goods to or from specific countries, discussed below. But, the limits on financial transactions can be sufficient to block trade in goods.

In addition to trade and financial sanctions, the president can cut off U.S. government assistance to targeted countries and institutions—both direct funding programs and access to programs like loan guarantees. The executive branch can also use its regular discretionary authority to impose very specific sanctions against foreign officials and their families, such as denying them travel visas. These are viewed as *smart sanctions* that try not to punish ordinary citizens for their governments' actions.

Congress has also legislated a large array of sanctions[22] that are supposed to be applied when the president determines that certain conditions exist. In most cases, the law allows the president to waive enforcement for national security interests.

Long-standing law prohibits U.S. assistance to "communist" countries. A related measure, the Jackson–Vanik amendment of 1974, bars most-favored nation trade status and U.S. trade credits to nonmarket economy countries that try to prevent emigration—a provision credited with forcing the Soviet government to permit emigration of Soviet Jews.

Another law requires a cutoff of economic aid to any country whose democratically elected leader is deposed by a military coup. Various laws prohibit U.S. aid to countries that seize ownership or control of American-owned property without paying adequate compensation.

Human rights violators are subject to another set of laws, including bans on security and other assistance and mandates to vote against multilateral aid to such countries. Nations that fail to cooperate with U.S. counternarcotics efforts are supposed to lose their economic aid.

Several laws require sanctions for nations that provide nuclear technology outside of international controls or that test nuclear weapons. A 1998 law imposes sanctions against countries engaged in a pattern of religious persecution.

Long before the 9/11 attacks, Congress passed laws prohibiting aid to governments that support international terrorism. A 1976 law requires the secretary of state to maintain a list of terrorist-supporting countries to which various sanctions should be applied. A 1985 law permitted the president to restrict or ban imports from countries on that list. A 1996 law banned financial transactions with nations on the list. The USA PATRIOT Act in 2001 added provisions prohibiting money laundering that helps terrorists and requiring more extensive reporting and record keeping.

In addition to these more generic statutes, Congress, over the years, has enacted country-specific laws with sanctions against Cuba, South Africa, Iran, Libya, Syria, and Burma. These were typically designed to limit presidential discretion in order to ensure tough policies against the pariah regimes. Congress usually preferred to impose drastic sanctions and get public credit for them, even while allowing the president to set most of the provisions aside if he submitted the required finding. One provision that Congress likes but executive branch officials regularly oppose because of the foreign policy problems it would cause is one with *extraterritoriality*—trying to prevent foreign companies from ignoring U.S. sanctions by allowing actions against them in U.S. courts.

Most of these various laws remain on the books as powerful sticks to use against violators. It would take a new law, not just presidential waivers, for example, to reduce the sanctions currently applied to Cuba, Iran, and North Korea.

Most studies of sanctions conclude that their effects are greatest when they are broadly applied by the international community, especially pursuant to a United Nations Security Council (UNSC) order, rather than by single countries, even ones as powerful economically as the United States. Unless there is broad support, nonsanctioning nations can easily supply what the United States denies.[23]

The key issue for a president to decide is whether the sanctions can be effective or at least whether they punish the target more than they hurt Americans. Once imposed, and especially if they do not seem to be effective, the White House faces the agonizing choice of persisting in futile and perhaps counterproductive gestures or admitting defeat. Sanctions against Iranian nuclear programs, while not effective in stopping them, have set an otherwise encouraging example of increased tightening with UN support in part because U.S. officials identified shell companies and other arrangements that could be targeted, and even international companies decided it was in their own interests to cease operations in Iran.

## Trade

As an instrument of policy—in order to persuade other nations to act in particular ways—trade is most powerful when used negatively through restrictions or suspensions. But, trade relationships are also positive forces for political cooperation and economic growth. The United States seeks trade agreements both for economic benefits and for the political goodwill that can accompany good trading arrangements. On the other hand, trade disputes can exacerbate tensions in other areas, especially because trade is, for many nations, a leading foreign policy concern.

Congress is a necessary player for trade to be a policy instrument. The legislative branch sets tariffs and special trade preferences as well as authorizing negotiations for multilateral agreements. Protrade lawmakers endorse the idea that freer trade has economic benefits for all nations, but they are often held in check by legislators concerned about job losses and industrial decline in their home areas. These parochial concerns, understandably, have weakened some of the political benefits of trade deals as Americans resisted threats to domestic textile and steel companies, for example, and Koreans resisted threats to their automobile and cattle producers.

Trade preference laws are a major way of promoting economic growth in less-developed countries by allowing certain specified imports into the United States. The 1974 Generalized System of Preferences (GSP) provides benefits to more than 130 less-developed countries. Under GSP, the president can grant duty-free status to selected imports from qualifying nations. Certain conditions apply, such as reasonable market access, worker rights, support for U.S. antiterrorism programs, and not engaging in practices that would harm U.S. economic interests. Many agricultural, textile, apparel, and import-sensitive products are excluded. In addition to GSP, several regional trade preference programs have been adopted in recent decades, including ones for the Caribbean Basin, Central America, Andean nations, and Africa. Each law has to be extended periodically.[24]

Free trade agreements (FTAs), regional and bilateral, have been used frequently in recent years both for their economic benefits and for the associated political benefits. The negotiations generally seek to eliminate tariffs and nontariff barriers on trade in goods and services. Collateral agreements on investment, intellectual property rights, labor practices, and environmental protection are often demanded by Congress and become part of the negotiating agenda. FTAs have been negotiated by the USTR under time-limited power given by Congress to the president, originally called *fast track* and now renamed Trade Promotion Authority (TPA). From Congress's perspective, TPA is a self-denying process where legislators surrender their tariff-setting power in order to avoid dismemberment of multilateral agreements by parochial amendments. Under TPA, Congress allows only an up-or-down vote on the package. But, the trade committees insist on, and have been granted by USTR, close consultations during the negotiations process, so they can raise concerns and try to forestall objectionable outcomes.

When major international talks on trade liberalization have stalled, U.S. administrations rushed to sign bilateral or regional free trade agreements. America currently has such pacts in force with Israel, Canada, Mexico, Jordan, Australia, Singapore, Morocco, Oman, Bahrain, Chile, Peru, Dominican Republic–Central America, and—in 2011—Colombia, Panama, and South Korea. The most recent three agreements were stalled for more than four years until the Obama administration agreed to revisions demanded by congressional Democrats. More details on the diplomatic and political processes are in the case study on the Korean FTA at the end of this chapter.[25]

To reduce domestic opposition to liberalized trade relations, Congress has established various trade remedy devices. Trade adjustment assistance has been made available since 1974 to workers, firms, farmers, and communities hurt by shifts in trade. For example, workers can get job training, search, and relocation benefits as well as up to 130 weeks of income assistance equal to what they would get as unemployment compensation. Firms can get technical assistance on how to be more competitive. Farmers can get technical assistance and training as well as some financial grants. And, communities can get redevelopment assistance.[26]

Congress has also created a quasi-judicial International Trade Commission (ITC) to investigate and make recommendations in cases where foreign products are subsidized at home and cause economic injury in the United States. Countervailing duties can be imposed if the ITC finds in favor of the complainant. ITC also hears cases under the antidumping laws and can recommend punitive duties. The Commerce Department is also involved in these investigations and determinations. ITC has a culture of professionalism in conducting its investigations despite the enormous political pressures to make judgments in favor of American industries.

Presidents thus have numerous trade tools to pursue their foreign policy goals, but they also face domestic pressures to use trade measures for local benefits. Executive action is also severely limited by the actual authorities granted by Congress.

While trade negotiations are handled by the USTR, and USTR chairs interagency panels on trade policy, the Obama administration has dropped hints that it might propose a consolidated trade department, combining the trade activities now in Commerce with the USTR duties, plus perhaps some of the separate export promotion entities. This might be opposed by congressional trade supporters who want to keep the function in the EOP and by defenders of Commerce who don't want to see its other activities subordinated to trade missions.

## Exports

Export promotion is as American as apple pie. In fact, there are at least 19 federal agencies that have that goal as one of their mandates. President

Obama in 2010 announced a National Export Initiative (NEI) to double U.S. exports by 2015. The NEI hopes to increase access to export financing mechanisms already run by the government, such as the Ex-Im and OPIC, and to increase trade missions and commercial advocacy by government agencies. There is little opposition to such activities in principle, but agencies and their congressional overseers may resist particular changes in their established ways of doing business.

Parallel to the NEI is an administration effort to rewrite the laws and reorganize the processes for commercial export controls. An administration review in 2010 concluded that the existing system was overly complicated, had too many redundancies, and tried to protect too much. Defense Secretary Gates spearheaded the reform effort, calling for "a higher fence around a smaller yard." Currently, there are two different control lists, one managed by the State Department covering military items (the munitions list) and one by the Commerce Department (the commerce control list) for commercial items with possible dual use as military items. There are three agency licensing systems that don't tell each other of their decisions and have incompatible information technology systems. In addition to licenses by State and Commerce for items on their respective lists, Treasury licenses items subject to trade sanctions and embargoes. This stovepiped system somehow issues about 130,000 licenses each year.

Each agency tends to apply its own culture and perspective to its licensing system. State, in consultation with DOD, wants to limit exports that might benefit adversaries, except in those cases where it wants to reward cooperative regimes. Commerce wants to say yes to exports wherever possible. And, Treasury wants to apply the rules strictly but professionally.

The Obama administration wants to develop a single control list managed by a single licensing agency using a single IT system and relying on a single primary enforcement coordination agency. This would require legislation passed by Congress.

Congress's record on export controls is not very encouraging. The basic Export Administration Act, first passed in 1949 and then thoroughly revised in 1979, expired in 1989. It has been resuscitated for short periods in later years and remains operative only because of annual presidential declarations under the International Emergency Economic Powers Act. Efforts to extend or amend the basic law have foundered on political and policy disagreements among lawmakers over whether the new law should be more restrictive or more permissive. It doesn't help the process that two quite different committees have jurisdiction over the legislation—the House Foreign Affairs Committee and the Senate Banking Committee.

Export restrictions are allowed for various specified purposes. For national security reasons, restrictions are allowed on items that would significantly improve the military capability of countries that pose a threat to the United States. For economic reasons, restrictions are allowed where items are in short supply or might have harmful impact on U.S. industry or economic performance. Numerous foreign policy concerns can also be used to justify restrictions: regional stability, human rights, antiterrorism, missile technology, nuclear nonproliferation, and chemical and biological warfare.

An additional process is required for exports of major defense equipment valued at $14 million or more and for sales of defense articles or services totaling $50 million. Under the 1976 Arms Export Control Act (PL 90–629), the president must notify Congress of such proposed sales, and Congress then has 45 days to consider passing a resolution of disapproval. Supreme Court rulings on legislative vetoes suggest that such a measure would be subject to a presidential veto and thus would require two-thirds votes for enactment. But, the threat of congressional debate and criticism of the recipient country still can be factors in the diplomacy surrounding arms sales.

Exports are thus an instrument with two sharp edges. They can cut policy makers when they are used and when they are withheld. While export promotion serves mainly domestic American economic goals, it can come in conflict with various foreign policy objectives. The president may thus face conflicting advice from his cabinet on whether to allow certain kinds of exports either in general or to particular countries. Foreign leaders may seek specific items from the United States both to help their nations economically and as evidence of American diplomatic support. The president has to balance the various pressures and considerations. Selling Pakistan military helicopters to allow the army to conduct flood relief operations has humanitarian and political benefits, but such sales may also lead the Pakistani military to discount U.S. pressures related to terrorist networks or better relations with India.

## Imports

American laws restrict imports in various direct and indirect ways—thus potentially causing foreign policy problems with the countries wishing to sell restricted items. Basic tariffs limit imports. Eliminating tariffs is the standard practice of free trade agreements. Those measures may also deal with nontariff barriers such as copyright protections for intellectual property or environmental restrictions.

Imports may also be barred by buy-American provisions in law since the Great Depression, which have regularly added to federal spending programs for highways and other infrastructure. The president also has long-standing authority under a 1962 law to restrict imports that "may threaten to impair national security" (19 USC 1862).

As discussed in the trade section, import relief in the form of countervailing duties or other penalties may be imposed by the president after findings by the ITC.

Import quotas apply to certain categories of goods. Sugar and dairy products are subject to quotas that allow a lower tariff for importers with licenses limited to the quota and higher tariffs for any other importers. There are also some absolute limit quotas on some clothing and textiles. Sometimes, nations get others to impose voluntary export restraint as Japan did on its auto exports to the U.S. for several years in the 1980s.

U.S. laws and regulations impose import restrictions on a broad array of goods. For example, imported cars must meet U.S. fuel emission and safety standards; biological specimens require permits from USDA or CDC; items derived from endangered species, as set by the Fish and Wildlife Service, are banned; most merchandise from embargoed countries (Cuba, Iran, Burma, and most of Sudan) cannot be imported.

Import issues can be foreign policy bones of contention that influence the handling of other foreign policy issues. Presidential decisions thus have to balance diplomatic concerns against the domestic economic and other factors that led to the import limitations.

## Foreign Assistance

One of the most visible economic tools in foreign policy is government-provided assistance to other nations. (See Table 7.4.) These are actions the president can turn off quickly, if he chooses, or turn on, though at a much slower pace because of the need for congressional approval and contracting procedures. Accumulated controversies over the years have tangled foreign aid programs in a web of restrictions and conditions. The basic 1961 law, now more than 500 pages in length and not significantly amended since 1985, has 33 goals, 75 priority areas, and 247 directives.[27]

Overall, some 26 agencies and offices have foreign assistance programs. In addition to the major organizations—State, USAID, DOD, USDA, Commerce, Justice, and Health & Human Services/CDC—there are foreign programs in the EPA, the Forest Service, the Patent and Trademark Office, National Science Foundation, and National Oceanic and Atmospheric Administration.[28] One study concluded, "At any given time, in any particular developing countries, any or all of over fifty separate government units could be operating separate aid activities with distinct objectives, implementing authorities, and local points of contact."[29]

Some of these smaller programs are technical assistance—sharing best practices of a U.S. agency with a foreign counterpart. But, several large programs have been created in recent decades deliberately outside the State–USAID core. The collapse of the Soviet empire prompted creation of the Support for Eastern European Democracies (SEED) program and the Freedom Support Act and the Nunn–Lugar program for cooperative threat reduction. Under the G. W. Bush administration, Congress created the MCC and the President's Emergency Plan for AIDS Relief (PEPFAR).

Creating new stand-alone programs serves many bureaucratic purposes: It allows greater visibility and budget protection for the effort; it attracts fresh, high-energy personnel in contrast to the established bureaucracies; and it allows officials and lawmakers chances to brag about their farsightedness and accomplishments. On the other hand, the proliferation of special programs leads to coordination problems, conflicts over priorities, and dilution of the assistance effort.

Secretary Hillary Clinton tried to reduce these problems by her 2010 Quadrennial Diplomacy and Development Review (QDDR). On paper, the

| Table 7.4 | Top Recipients of U.S. Foreign Assistance, 1980–2010, in millions | | | |
|---|---|---|---|---|
| | 1980 | 1990 | 2000 | 2010 |
| 1 | Israel $1,868 | Egypt $4,977 | Israel $4,069 | Afghanistan $2,624 |
| 2 | Egypt 1,470 | Israel 4,454 | Egypt 2,028 | Israel 2,220 |
| 3 | Turkey 538 | Poland 919 | Colombia 899 | Pakistan 1,457 |
| 4 | Taiwan 388 | Philippines 566 | West Bank and Gaza 485 | Egypt 1,295 |
| 5 | Mexico 180 | Pakistan 524 | Jordan 428 | Jordan 542 |
| 6 | United Kingdom 178 | Turkey 367 | Russia 195 | Colombia 512 |
| 7 | Bangladesh 175 | El Salvador 303 | Bolivia 194 | West Bank and Gaza 502 |
| 8 | Spain 159 | Greece 282 | Ukraine 182 | Iraq 466 |
| 9 | Zaire 148 | Philippines 260 | Peru 120 | Haiti 363 |
| 10 | Indonesia 137 | Zaire 241 | Kazakhstan 112 | Lebanon 238 |

The changing priorities of U.S. aid policy in recent decades are evident in the amounts of foreign assistance provided. While the Middle East, and especially Israel and Egypt, have been major recipients, Latin American countries have risen or fallen in priority in response to changing local threats.

*Source:* Statistical Abstracts of the United States, U.S. Department of State.

QDDR claimed to resolve long-standing disagreements over the roles of State and USAID by saying they would be integrated and coordinated but that USAID would remain bureaucratically separate and would be given increased personnel and resources. It left precise delineation of activities to a midlevel panel, however, and many of the QDDR recommendations also required new legislation from a Congress not especially warm to foreign aid.[30]

While the Bush and Obama administrations gave rhetorical support to the idea of making development equal to diplomacy, their proposed budgets fell far short of that goal. And, there remains a profound disagreement among practitioners—in the government and in the nongovernmental organization (NGO) community that runs assistance programs—over whether and how to separate diplomatic goals from purely developmental ones. Even politically motivated aid can achieve developmental goals; even humanitarian relief can serve diplomatic-political objectives. The overlaps just lead to more disagreements over priorities.[31]

There are three broad types of foreign assistance programs in terms of what they provide: military, economic, and development aid. The State Department is the primary agency for all three, at least in terms of selecting recipient countries and persuading Congress to go along. The Pentagon, however, actually manages the military assistance programs, and USAID runs most of the development programs. The MCC is legally independent.

Opinion polls ever since the 1950s have shown that foreign aid is the least popular program in the U.S. government, the one people are most eager to cut and cut deeply. While every president has supported significant aid programs, they have usually depicted the assistance as an alternative security measure to the use of U.S. military forces or as a humanitarian effort to relieve widespread poverty and disease. Aid advocates are also sharply divided between those who favor programs based on economic and humanitarian needs and those who want aid to serve U.S. foreign policy goals and interests.

Current U.S. assistance is 17.5% military, 27.1% economic for political reasons, 35.5% for bilateral development aid, 14.4% for humanitarian aid, and 5.5% through multilateral organizations, to use the figures for 2009. These figures do not include, however, Pentagon-run programs in Iraq and Afghanistan. Within the regular State–USAID programs, the share of military aid has declined since the 1990s, and the portion for development has increased because of anti-AIDS and other health programs and the new MCC. Total U.S. spending for foreign aid dropped steadily during the 1990s but surged after the 9/11 attacks mainly because of programs in Afghanistan, Pakistan, and Iraq.[32]

In order to use the aid tools, the president needs to be sure he has the authority and the resources. What used to be broad discretionary authority has been whittled down by Congress, which doesn't like contingency funds because they allow spending without congressional guidance or necessary approval. Under Presidents Eisenhower and Kennedy, there was a foreign policy contingency fund equal to $1.5 billion in current dollars. After some questionable expenditures in the 1970s, Congress cut the fund to its current $25 million. In 2009, Congress approved a massive, five-year aid authorization for Pakistan (PL 111–73), but it still requires annual appropriations, which can get caught up in current controversies and budget freezes. In 2011, lawmakers considered a special fund to help Egypt after the resignation of longtime President Mubarak in the wake of proreform demonstrations. Meanwhile, the State Department announced a "reprogramming of $150 million" for Egypt. This turned out not to be new money, however, but funds previously appropriated for Egypt, some in earlier years, but not yet spent. In 2012, however, Congress created a $200 million Global Security Contingency Fund to be jointly managed by State and DOD and subject to advance notifications to Congress.[33]

Most aid programs require advance notification to congressional committees and, in some cases, committee approval before the funds can be spent. The system is confused by the many pots of money created by different sections of the law and the lack, in contrast to the Pentagon, of a clear, consolidated system for Hill consultations on fund transfers.

Military aid programs are often based on collaboration between U.S. defense attachés and the host government military leaders. There are many potential benefits from such collaboration, including deeper knowledge of the military leaders and the capabilities of their forces, adoption of U.S.

equipment and doctrine that can make future cooperation easier, and sometimes reduced costs for U.S. forces because of foreign sales. Grant military aid, called Foreign Military Funding (FMF), helps to finance purchases of American equipment and services. Most FMF goes to Israel and Egypt. Cash sales go through the Foreign Military Sales (FMS) program, where major sales are subject to a potential congressional veto.

The major economic aid program with a clear political purpose is the Economic Support Fund (ESF) that runs about $6.5 billion per year, 77% of which currently goes to friendly countries in the Middle East: Israel, Egypt, Jordan, Afghanistan, Pakistan, Lebanon, and Iraq. While this money may be *projectized,* its real purpose is budgetary support for favored nations. Other politically driven aid goes for counternarcotics programs, nonproliferation programs, and democracy promotion efforts in Eastern Europe, the former Soviet Union, and parts of the Middle East.[34]

Development aid takes many forms and is delivered by many different providers. In addition to the programs for economic growth, the United States has specially targeted programs for countries in transition to democracy and for high-priority health programs, such as the PEPFAR. The programs run by MCC are specifically linked to host government performance in terms of noncorrupt rule-of-law governance, adequate social services, and economic freedom. It spends a bit over $1 billion yearly in countries that work to be eligible for the program funds.[35]

Since the 9/11 attacks, DOD has undertaken several major foreign assistance programs. It has *train-and-equip* programs in Afghanistan and Iraq as well as in other countries helping the United States combat terrorism. It also has *coalition support funds* to reimburse or reward nations like Pakistan and Jordan for logistical and military support for the wars in Iraq and Afghanistan. Especially valued by the U.S. military is CERP, which lets military units provide local assistance without the paperwork and other requirements of a regular aid program.[36] The $11.3 billion for these programs in 2010 equaled 25% of total U.S. foreign assistance that year.

### Financial Flows

As long as the United States has a large economy and is heavily involved in foreign trade and investment, the government has to worry about the value of the dollar and the smooth functioning of the international financial markets. America dominated the Bretton Woods system from 1945 until 1971, pumping out dollars to rebuild war-torn economies and then working with others to expand international trade and finance. As the global reserve currency, the United States was largely able to avoid having to make domestic economic policy changes to protect its international role. By August 1971, however, the dollar was under severe pressure because of domestic inflationary pressures and the first U.S. trade deficit in the 20th century. President Nixon abandoned the Bretton Woods system of fixed exchange rates, de-linked the dollar from gold, and imposed immediate 10% surcharges on Japanese and German imports to force them to revalue their currencies.[37]

The Economic Instruments

---

## Box 7.1

# Inside View: Treasury Versus State During the Asian Financial Crisis

Former Treasury Secretary Robert Rubin describes how policy to handle the 1997 Asian financial crisis was made by an interagency conference call on Thanksgiving Day. Local currencies and then stock markets began collapsing throughout Asia in the summer of 1997, with Thailand, Indonesia, and South Korea most adversely affected. By mid-1998, months after the rescue engineered by Rubin and the IMF, GDP had dropped over 34% in much of the region. Rubin notes that the concerns of Treasury were quite different from the concerns of the State Department and Pentagon, highlighting one of the key challenges faced by the White House when crafting a consistent foreign economic policy.

*On Thanksgiving Day . . . I spent much of the day and evening on a series of urgent conference calls with Treasury and Fed officials, the President, the national security advisor, and the Secretary of State. . . . For understandable reasons, we at Treasury and the foreign policy people in the administration looked at the issue from somewhat different perspectives. Madeleine [Albright] and the other foreign policy advisers on the phone were mainly worried about our relationship with a crucially important military ally, as well as national security issues. They thought any instability in South Korea might encourage a reaction from the North, where some troops had reportedly gone to some heightened state of alert. Their view was that we economic types were insufficiently focused on geopolitical concerns and that the United States needed to move quickly to show support for South Korea through the IMF and a backup loan from the ESF, as we had just done for Indonesia—what we were now calling a "second line of defense." I felt strongly that if economic stability wasn't reestablished, our geopolitical goals wouldn't be accomplished either. . . . Committing the IMF and ourselves to a show of financial support for South Korea without an adequate commitment to reform might even make it less likely that South Korea would get back on track, because providing money without strong conditions would reduce our leverage in getting the country to adopt a program that would work.*

Treasury worked with the IMF, which a few days later, announced its largest-ever assistance package—$55 billion—and which also had obtained the reluctant endorsement of reform measures by all three leading candidates for president of South Korea. Treasury and the Fed also worked out arrangements with major banks for a voluntary rollover of their loans. The final deal was announced on Christmas Day. As this chapter shows, the different agencies involved in crafting U.S. economic policy on an international scale often have overlapping areas of interest and differing perspectives on situations. Consequently, they may clash regarding their goals and approaches. In this case, Treasury wanted an economic solution, while State emphasized foreign policy concerns. The United States also enlisted the IMF to leverage its own economic support.

*Source:* Robert Rubin, *In an Uncertain World* (New York: Random House, 2003), 232–233.

Oil shocks in 1974 and 1979 forced the leaders of the major economic powers to recognize their interdependence and work together to solve problems. Annual financial summits began in 1975 and have continued to today. In the early years, the participants were usually the Group of Seven (G-7) economic powers, but in the 21st century it has been expanded to G-8 with the addition of Russia and the G-20, which was the principal forum for handling the global financial crisis starting in 2007.

Major nations liberalized their banking systems in the 1980s and 1990s, and the Europeans created a widely shared common currency. The IMF got increased resources and became actively involved in coordinating responses to the inevitable currency crises—in Mexico, Asia (see Box 7.1), and Russia, and more recently among Western European countries. Globalization has removed many of the long-standing tools government had to manage to protect domestic economies. Nations may still try to impose currency controls and restrictions on capital flows, for example, but with foreign exchange markets having an average daily turnover of around $4 trillion, some restrictions may be too little and too late, at least in the short run.

What this means for the U.S. foreign policy process is that the president is regularly engaging with foreign leaders on economic issues. The strength of the economy and of the dollar are important foreign policy concerns. The situation is complicated, however, because the president can give orders only to the secretary of the treasury. The Fed chair has enormous financial powers and tries to cooperate with Treasury, but their perspectives may diverge.

Both Treasury and the Fed have ways to help in currency crises. Treasury can draw on an Exchange Stabilization Fund with over $100 billion in 2009 and vote for action as the U.S. representative on the IMF. The Fed can work out swaps and other arrangements with other central banks. The president, under IEEPA, has broad powers to impose restrictions on economic transfers.

There are large capital flows in portfolio investments above and beyond trade in goods and services.[38] There are also large amounts of nongovernmental foreign assistance by private voluntary organizations, foundations, and religious groups, as Table 7.2 shows. Remittances to families back home total more than $90 billion per year, triple actual U.S. foreign development aid. In 2011, foreigners held 48% of U.S. debt, with China holding almost 12% and Japan nearly 10%.

One of the most important areas for policy action in recent years has been attempts to prevent money laundering by terrorist groups or illegal drug cartels. In 1998, IMF estimated that $800 million to $2 trillion was laundered each year. The laws then required banks to report any transaction of $10,000 or more and suspicious transactions of lower amounts. After the 9/11 attacks, the USA PATRIOT Act extended reporting requirements to securities dealers, casinos, and car dealers, among others. The attorney general also got powers to demand additional information on foreign accounts. These legal measures have been supplemented by efforts to cooperate and coordinate with foreign law enforcement and intelligence agencies abroad.[39]

The Securities and Exchange Commission (SEC) has even expanded its efforts, under congressional pressure, to make judgments about the impact on stocks of various foreign policy problems. It created an Office of Global Security Risk, which among other things, requires companies to disclose whether they are doing business with nations on the supporting terrorism list.[40]

## Foreign Direct Investment

Acquisition of foreign companies and real estate is called foreign direct investment (FDI) and is distinguished from the ebb and flow of portfolio investments discussed above. Most countries practice some forms of economic nationalism, although the trend in recent years has been more favorable to foreign investors. Formal restrictions are usually limited to complying with antitrust and competition rules, but governments can use informal pressures to encourage or discourage particular investments.[41]

Because FDI is done by the private sector, the government role is only negative—blocking investments that conflict with other policies. Even so, those blockages raise foreign policy issues that have to be weighed with other economic goals.

U.S. companies had invested more than $3.5 trillion abroad as of 2009, with new investments that year of $269 billion. About 70% of U.S. investments were concentrated in highly developed countries. There has been a shift since the 1990s from extractive and basic manufacturing activities in the less-developed world and toward high technology, finance, and service industries in economically advanced nations. American FDI abroad has averaged about double foreign FDI in the U.S. at least since 2001.[42]

FDI in the United States totaled about $2.3 trillion in 2009, mostly (95%) from developed economies. About one third of this investment is in manufacturing and one sixth in banking and finance. Already on the books are laws restricting foreign investment in the maritime industry and the aircraft industry. Only U.S. citizens or people in the process of acquiring citizenship can buy mining rights on U.S. lands. Only citizens or U.S. corporations can obtain licenses for power plants and transmission. There are also restrictions on foreign ownership of mass communications media. And, buy-American provisions are a standard feature of federal contracts, though they often have to be waived for practical reasons.[43]

Concerns over foreign acquisition of technologies or companies affecting national security led President Ford to create CFIUS by executive order. After a decade of limited activity by this Treasury-led panel, Congress passed the Exon–Florio amendment to codify the CFIUS process and strengthen the president's hand in blocking foreign acquisitions that might impair U.S. national security. While Treasury chairs CFIUS, its other members include representatives from State, DOD, Commerce, DHS, Justice, USTR, and presidential advisers for science, economics, and national security.

Congress amended the law further in 2007 by adding impacts on economic security and critical infrastructure to the established defense criterion.

The new law also requires more regular reporting to Congress on implementation of its provisions. President G. W. Bush took issue with some of the reporting requirements in a signing statement that said some information might be withheld for reasons of foreign policy or executive privilege.

The CFIUS process has been most influential in its preliminary informal phase, when companies report planned acquisitions and the staff raises questions and concerns. Between 1988 and 2005, CFIUS received more than 1,500 notifications of acquisitions and conducted full investigations in only 25 cases. Of those, 13 transactions were withdrawn when the formal review was launched and the remaining 12 were sent to the president. Only one of those was prohibited. Since the law was changed in 2007 through 2010, CFIUS received 451 notices, of which 57 were withdrawn during subsequent review, and no cases went to the president.[44]

Despite the CFIUS process in the executive branch, Congress has weighed in with statements, hearings, and amendments on some controversial cases. In 2005, the Chinese National Offshore Oil Corporation (CNOOC), a government-owned firm, announced a bid to buy Unocal, an American oil and gas company. A firestorm of criticism on Capitol Hill, culminating with passage of an amendment that would have delayed any acquisition pending additional cabinet-level studies, led CNOOC to withdraw its bid. In 2006, an effort by Dubai Ports World to acquire a British company that operated several U.S. ports led to renewed controversy and passage of amendments to block the deal. Faced with that, the company pledged to divest the U.S. operations to an American company within six months.[45]

China poses a special set of problems for use of the economic instruments of U.S. policy. With the world's second-largest economy and huge bilateral trade with America, China is regularly caught up in trade disputes, some of which have gone to the World Trade Organization (WTO) for adjudication. With large, state-owned companies and sovereign wealth funds, China is seeking foreign investments that are bound to raise concerns. It doesn't help that China is the one major U.S. trading partner that is viewed more as an adversary and potential threat than as a steady ally.[46] In recent years, China has complained about the denial of several investments it sought in the United States on security grounds. Whatever the merits of these cases, similar disputes are likely to continue as part of the complex U.S.–China relationship and must be sorted out through the various economic instruments and processes.

* * *

Each of the economic instruments in foreign policy can be used only in particular circumstances and only for specific purposes. Some can be used actively in support of foreign policy, while others must be used reactively and defensively. Some of the instruments can be used unilaterally by the president, while others require congressional approval, and still others necessarily involve the private sector. Many of the departments and agencies that are part of the toolkit have domestic economic responsibilities and constituencies that may conflict with their foreign policy roles. There is no simple coordination mechanism available to the president. But, the array of tools is ample and diverse. This chapter provides a scorecard of players and their regular positions.

# Case Study: The Korean-U.S. Free Trade Agreement

While sanctions are the most powerful negative economic tool for U.S. foreign policy, free trade agreements are one of the most powerful, positive instruments for economic and political linkage. The United States has entered into 20 such agreements with various countries since 1985, mostly with nations with far smaller economies. This is the story of the lengthy struggle to negotiate and approve a free trade agreement with the Republic of Korea, whose strong and emerging economy was the seventh-largest export market for the United States as well as the seventh-largest supplier of imports. The Korean–U.S. free trade agreement, called KORUS FTA in shorthand, was the most economically significant since the 1992 NAFTA linking Mexico, Canada, and the United States.

President George W. Bush gained approval from Congress in 2002 for TPA, the fast-track procedure forcing Congress to act by up-or-down votes within 60 days of submission of completed agreements. The votes were close, however. The House approved fast-track bills by one- and three-vote margins because of overwhelming opposition by Democrats. The Senate was more supportive—66–30—but Democrats were evenly divided. Supporters envisioned expanded export opportunities. Opponents feared the loss of U.S. jobs from foreign competition and outsourcing of production.

The Bush administration, after completing several smaller agreements, began negotiations with South Korea in February 2006. Seoul initiated the talks, feeling competitive pressures from Japan and China and wanting free trade deals with both the United States and the European Union (EU). Korea most wanted changes in U.S. antidumping rules and preferential treatment of products made at the Kaesong Industrial Complex, a joint South–North Korean facility inside North Korea and employing North Korean workers.

American negotiators were keen on improving access for exports of U.S. agricultural products, especially beef, rice, pork, and dairy items; of cars and trucks; and of U.S. financial and professional services and foreign investment. Other U.S. interests chimed in with proposals that would benefit their sectors or companies.

Negotiations proceeded steadily during 2006, with 17 negotiating groups and two *working groups* handling specific issues. They broke down in December 2006 over antidumping rules and rice.

Facing a deadline of July 1, 2007, when the TPA fast-track law would expire, the two sides made significant compromises in order to sign an agreement on June 30. The United States dropped its demands for rice exports and agreed to simpler procedures for dealing with antidumping cases. The two sides agreed to set up a panel to consider particular products made in Kaesong. There were complex agreements on a wide range of other trade issues, including several *snapback* provisions allowing temporary tariffs to offset unexpectedly large imports of some Korean products.

Two issues, however, remained inadequately resolved from the U.S. perspective. Korea kept restrictions on U.S. beef imports because of concerns over mad cow disease. And, U.S. automakers opposed the deal as insufficient. These matters caused enough opposition among Democrats, newly in control of both houses of Congress, that President Bush decided not to send the KORUS FTA to the Hill.

A major agreement between President Bush and congressional leaders on May 10, 2007, paved the way for more favorable consideration of all remaining trade agreements. The president agreed to include labor standards provisions, to enforce multilateral environmental agreements with trade partners, and to add provisions on generic pharmaceuticals, port security, and foreign investor rights. In the case of Korea, the Bush administration also reached an agreement in 2008 for a gradual expansion of U.S. beef exports.

The Obama administration sought changes in the KORUS FTA to make it more palatable to congressional Democrats, especially with regard to the auto provisions, pork, and dairy products. On December 3, 2010, the two sides announced an agreement on modifications. The changes in tariff phaseouts and other provisions relating to cars and trucks were sufficient to win the support of the Ford Motor Company and the United Auto Workers union. Agricultural interests were pleased by more favorable provisions for pork, oranges, and domestic cheeses. Financial services investors were also pleased with the revised deal. The steel and textile industries voiced their opposition.

Under congressional pressure, the Obama administration demanded that approval of three major FTAs, with Korea, Colombia, and Panama, be linked to an expansion of Trade Adjustment Assistance (TAA), the program to help U.S. workers displaced by foreign trade. The House and Senate trade committees held *mock mark-up* sessions in July 2011, when they considered advisory proposals to the administration before final submission of the FTA. The Republican-controlled House panel approved the FTA but not TAA, while the Senate panel approved both items on a party-line vote.

President Obama waited until October 3, 2011, when he received assurances that the House would pass TAA as well as the FTA. He then sent the three major agreements to Congress and started the clock running on the fast-track vote. The real deadline for congressional action, however, was the pending state visit and speech to Congress of South Korean president Lee Myung-bak on October 13. The day before, both chambers approved the KORUS FTA. The House voted 278–151 (with 21 Republicans and 139 Democrats in opposition) and the Senate 83–15 (with 14 Democrats and 1 Republican in opposition).

The long delay in final approval demonstrated the contentiousness of trade issues and the need for a broad coalition of supporters. While there were strong geostrategic arguments for close relations with South Korea—not least the U.S. defense commitment and deployment of 28,500 troops as well as the importance of cooperation on dealing with North Korea—the trade agreement depended on domestic economic support for its approval. The economic instrument of trade may serve foreign policy goals, but it also has to satisfy domestic interests. This case shows how domestic political and economic considerations intersected with and influenced the development and approval of an important foreign economic policy goal.

*Sources:* Congressional Research Service, *Reports to Congress* and *CQ Weekly Reports.*

## Selected Resources

Each of the following government agencies has a website with more information about its activities.

Committee on Foreign Investment in the United States, www.treasury.gov/resource-center/international/Pages/Committee-on-Foreign-Investment-in-US.aspx

Export-Import Bank, www.exim.gov/

International Trade Commission, http://usitc.gov/

Office of Foreign Assets Control, http://www.treasury.gov/resource-center/sanctions/Pages/default.aspx

Overseas Private Investment Corporation, www.opic.gov/

U.S. Agency for International Development, www.usaid.gov/

U.S. Department of Commerce, International Trade Administration, http://trade.gov/

U.S. Department of Defense, www.defense.gov/; Defense Security Cooperation Agency, www.dsca.osd.mil/

U.S. Department of State, www.state.gov/

U.S. Department of the Treasury, www.treasury.gov/

U.S. Trade Representative, www.ustr.gov/

The most thorough discussion of sanctions can be found in Gary Clyde Hufbauer et al., *Economic Sanctions Reconsidered, Third Edition* (Washington, DC: Peterson Institute for International Economics, 2009).

An excellent overview of this topic is in Benn Steil and Robert E. Litan, *Financial Statecraft* (New Haven, CT: Yale University Press, 2006).

# 8    The Military Instrument

"Long before September 11, the U.S. government had grown increasingly dependent on its military to carry out its foreign affairs. . . . The military simply filled a vacuum left by an indecisive White House, an atrophied State Department, and a distracted Congress."

—*Washington Post* reporter Dana Priest[1]

"The Department is run by intimidation, not by control, when you get right down to it. You have to intimidate people to get anything done."

—Deputy Secretary of Defense John Hamre (1997–1999)[2]

The largest, most capable, best-funded instrument in the foreign policy toolkit is the U.S. military. The Department of Defense (DOD), headquartered in the Pentagon, organizes, trains, and equips the armed forces and, through the military chain of command from the president, controls their conduct in peace and war. Paradoxically, the military is both the sharpest and the bluntest instrument, with stiletto-like capabilities for some missions, yet cumbersome to move about and difficult to use without causing broad and unintended consequences.

Military forces are a tool of foreign policy in many ways: They can back diplomatic and economic policies with the threat of violence and punishment; they can deter hostile actions against America and its interests; they can destroy units and weapons that threaten the United States or its allies; they can train and equip foreign militaries for combined operations. (See Table 8.1.) The United States has large, expensive, and ever-changing military capabilities, populated by an all-volunteer force equipped with technologically advanced weaponry. Pentagon leaders are key players in the interagency process advising the president and implementing presidential orders. This chapter highlights the strength and diversity of the military instrument and the organizational and political challenges it faces.

## Nature of the Military Instrument

The instrumental purpose for using military force for broader strategic goals is clear in current U.S. military doctrine: "The chief principle for employment of US forces is to achieve national strategic objectives established by the

200

| Table 8.1 | The Military Instrument Brief | |
|---|---|---|
| **PEOPLE** | **ADVANTAGES** | **DISADVANTAGES** |
| Secretary of Defense | Authoritative, powerful | Limits on time, multiple demands |
| Joint Chiefs of Staff (JCS) | Symbolic, best for dealing with other officers | Only advisory power in U.S. |
| Combatant Commanders (COCOMs) | Seen as pro-consuls, large staffs | Overshadow nonmilitary instruments |
| Special Operations Forces (SOF) | Secretive, highly capable | May produce blowback |
| **ACTIONS** | | |
| Presence | Symbol of commitment and support | Costly over time |
| Engagement and training | Symbolic, builds relations for future | U.S. may be blamed for repressive governments |
| Contingency planning | Allows prompt action in crises | Planning may create false expectations regarding war |
| Warfighting | Can achieve decisive results | Costly, many uncertainties, often unpopular over time |
| **ROLE OF CONGRESS** | Supporter and enabler, alternative source of civilian control | Micromanager |
| **CULTURE** | Can-do spirit, wants clear guidance and timely decisions | Tends to dominate, resists coordination with civilians; sees issues in black-and-white terms |

There are three separate groups of people who are most influential in shaping and using the military instrument, plus the increasingly important SOF, which have become a major foreign policy tool. Each of the components of the military performs four major activities under the direction of the president and subject to various actions by the Congress, thus assuring civilian control. The military's can-do culture makes it a reliable and effective instrument for foreign policy, provided that policy makers can deal with the political and diplomatic consequences of using deadly force.

President through decisive action and conclude operations on terms favorable to the United States."[3] That same doctrine recognizes a wide range of actions that armed forces may be called upon to perform:

The United States employs its military capabilities at home and abroad in support of its national security goals in a variety of operations. These operations vary in size, purpose, and combat intensity within a range of military operations that extends from military engagement, security cooperation, and deterrence activities to crisis response and limited contingency operations, and if necessary, major operations and campaigns.[4]

These statements mark a shift from what had been traditional American military thinking that proclaimed a narrower goal: "The purpose of the Armed Forces is to fight and win the Nation's wars."[5] While many officers still repeat that slogan without qualifications, U.S. military leaders now acknowledge that they will be called upon for more tasks than simply fighting and often with objectives less concrete than "winning" what are called "wars."

After a long tradition of following military theorists who concentrated on the operational level of war, U.S. military leaders now acknowledge the wisdom of the Napoleonic era writer, Carl von Clausewitz, who stressed that war should be judged in terms of its strategic role. Perhaps his most famous statement in *On War* is this: "We see, therefore, that war is not merely an act of policy but a true political instrument, a continuation of political intercourse, carried on with other means."[6]

The U.S. experience in World War II, which had a clear and simple objective—"unconditional surrender" by Germany and Japan—and which was followed by a forceful occupation of enemy lands, along with rewriting their basic laws and reshaping their political institutions, made it hard for many Americans to accept limited wars, where the means used and the goals sought fell short of total war or an unambiguous victory. The wars in Korea and Vietnam, and more recently in Afghanistan and Iraq, lost popular support in part because they were pursued for less ambitious and less satisfying goals and with far more restraints on the use of force than public opinion preferred.

From Vietnam into the 1990s, U.S. military leaders repeatedly argued that force should be used only for vital interests, and then only in an overwhelming way. They used a disparaging term for lesser conflicts: Military Operations Other Than War—MOOTW or *moot-wah*. By the 21st century, however, military leaders and civilians agreed on the need to conduct *stability operations,* and in 2005, this capability was made equal in importance to major wars.[7]

The U.S. military is not always comfortable with the limits that limited war entails, but official doctrine currently lists 20 different types of military operations for which it must prepare. (See Box 8.1.)

Note that only a handful of these operations necessarily involve the use of lethal force. The problem for the military, however, is that any of them could. And, that fact raises the risks for political leaders considering use of the military instrument.

Civilian leaders are also sometimes uncomfortable with the proliferation of missions the U.S. military now undertakes. They see a vicious circle in which civilian capacities are inadequate for urgent tasks, the military comes to the rescue, and the civilians are pushed aside and denied resources to regain their normal roles. Many officials also believe in the just war tradition of exhausting all other means before resorting to the use of force, a

---

| **Box 8.1** |

## How Foreign Policy Is Made: Types of Military Operations

Here is the Pentagon's list of the types of operations the U.S. military trains to conduct. As you can see, many of them are directly part of U.S. foreign policy and only indirectly related to national defense. Assistance and training of foreign forces (including tasks like combating terrorism, counterinsurgency, and nation assistance) are a major use of U.S. forces for foreign policy purposes. The U.S. military also works with U.S. civilians in humanitarian assistance, peace operations, and recovery operations. The list also makes clear that the military can help insurgents and counterinsurgents, depending where U.S. interests dictate. The ability to conduct raids, strikes, and shows of force allows the United States to back its diplomacy with the threat of force. The very diversity of capabilities makes use of the military a valuable instrument for more than killing and destroying enemy forces.

| | |
|---|---|
| Major operations, such as war | Nation assistance |
| Arms control and disarmament | Noncombatant evacuation operations |
| Homeland defense | Peace operations |
| Civil support | Protection of shipping |
| Combating terrorism | Raids |
| Consequence management | Recovery operations |
| Counterinsurgency operations | Routine, recurring military activities |
| Enforcement of sanctions | Show of force |
| Foreign humanitarian assistance | Strikes |
| Freedom of navigation | Support to insurgency |

*Source:* Joint Operations, August 11, 2011. Figure I-2. Types of Military Operations from JP 3–0, I-3 at www.dtic.mil/doctrine/new_pubs/jp3_0.pdf.

---

notion that treats war as a binary choice where the diplomats turn out the lights and leave subsequent decisions solely to the military.

Whether one believes in the moral traditions of just war doctrine or in international law, which has been more aspirational than truly binding on nations, it is hard to justify the killing of others or the deaths of one's soldiers for lesser purposes than national survival. These moral qualms work to make any use of military force a painful and difficult choice for national leaders. (See Table 8.2.)

There are risks of combat and deaths even when military units are used to deter actions by others by making clear that a hostile move could be countered by significant force, as the effectiveness of such threats depends on the credibility of their actual use. Commanders abhor empty, symbolic gestures. And, U.S. presidents have learned that troops sent on peacekeeping missions and even disaster relief operations can come under fire and suffer casualties.

| Table 8.2 | Major U.S. Military Operations and U.S. Battle Deaths, 1775–2011 | |
|---|---|---|
| CONFLICT/OPERATION | NUMBER SERVING | BATTLE DEATHS |
| Revolutionary War (1775–1783) | Estimated 184,000–250,000 | 4,345 |
| War of 1812 (1812–1814) | 286,730 | 2,260 |
| U.S.–Mexican War (1846–1848) | 78,718 | 1,733 |
| Civil War (Union only)** (1861–1865) | 2,213,363 | 140,414 |
| Spanish–American War (1898) | 306,760 | 385 |
| Philippine insurgency (1898–1902) | 126,468 | 1,108 |
| World War I (1914–1918) | 4,734,991 | 53,402 |
| World War II (1941–1945) | 16,112,566 | 291,557 |
| Korean War (1950–1953) | 5,720,000 | 33,741 |
| Vietnam (1964–1975) | 8,744,000 | 47,424 |
| Lebanon UN Peacekeeping (1983) | 1,800 | 256 |
| Urgent Fury, Grenada (1983) | 1,900 | 18 |
| Just Cause, Panama (1989) | 27,000 | 23 |
| Desert Shield/Storm (1990–1991) | 2,225,000 | 147 |
| Restore Hope, Somalia (1992–1994) | 30,000 | 29 |
| Enduring Freedom, Afghanistan* (2001–present) | 1,353,627 (combined) | 1,850 |
| Iraqi Freedom, Iraq* (2003–2011) | 1,353,627 (combined) | 4,408 |

*As of January 3, 2012

**Confederate figures are estimated to be about 850,000 to 900,000 serving, and about 75,000 battle deaths.

Modern weapons and modern medicine have reduced U.S. battle deaths in recent wars. The reliance on volunteers since 1973 has also seen a reduction in the number of Americans who have served in combat operations.

Source: Department of Defense; Congressional Research Service at http://fpc.state.gov/documents/organization/139347.pdf.

They have also learned to distrust advisers who claimed that "surgical" strikes could achieve quick and lasting success.

These experiences have made U.S. political leaders cautious about the use of force but not unwilling to order operations. The growing use of unmanned aerial drones, especially under President Obama, shows the attractiveness of military actions that reduce the risks of American casualties.

## Growth and Professionalization of the Military

While the United States has always had an active diplomatic instrument for foreign policy, the development of the military instrument has been much more episodic. For the first 150 years of the republic, except for the Civil War and four short-duration declared wars, the armed forces were small in size and cost, a cheap insurance policy in case of hostile attacks or threats to commercial freedom of the seas. See Table 2.2 for the details. The framers of the Constitution, mindful of English history, opposed the idea of a large standing army and planned to rely on local militias for defense.

The U.S. Army in 1789 was a small force of 718 men, headed by Secretary of War Henry Knox and a single clerk. The navy and marine corps were not reconstituted after the Revolutionary War until 1794. The army was expanded in the 1790s, first to deal with frontier threats from Indians and then to prepare for a possible war with France. The navy got its first new warships, and marines to sail with them, in response to threats from the Barbary pirates and later also to prepare for a possible war with France.

Thomas Jefferson saw the army less as a tool for military action than as a force for civic improvement. In 1802, he worked to create the U.S. Military Academy at West Point, which was to train officers primarily as engineers. The navy did not get its own service academy until 1845 at Annapolis. These measures helped to professionalize military service by creating a corps of well-trained officers schooled in military tactics and in the operation of military equipment.

Limits on the size of the forces, however, kept promotions slow, and the lack of retirement benefits kept many senior officers on active duty long beyond their best days. In 1860, for example, 19 of 33 army officers at the rank of colonel or higher were veterans of the war of 1812, nearly a half century earlier.

U.S. leaders followed the practice of expanding the military only when combat seemed imminent. Shortly before declaring war in 1812, Congress voted a 25,000-man increase in the army for a 5-year enlistment, including a bounty of $16 and a promise, upon honorable discharge, of 3 months' pay and 160 acres of land. A few months later, lawmakers sought another 15,000 men for 18 months.[8] Congress approved fewer ships than Madison proposed, and none was completed in time to join the fight. After the war ended, the forces shrank below their prewar numbers.

In 1846, Congress voted to raise 50,000 volunteers to supplement the regular forces already fighting Mexico. When that proved insufficient, lawmakers added bonuses in 1847. The navy was not expanded, and the army was cut to prewar levels after the war.

The Civil War saw almost 3 million men under arms during its four bloody years, about 2 million for the Union and another 900,000 for the Confederacy. For the first time, men were drafted into service, though with exceptions for those who could hire a substitute or pay a commutation fee of $300. Despite the need for personnel for reconstruction duties in the South, the size of the U.S. Army dropped steadily in the decade after 1865. The late 19th century army was garrisoned on the frontier and used against Indians until the war with Spain in 1898.

The navy in 1865 was one of the largest in the world, with 471 warships, but its force was designed mainly for coastal and riverine operations. Few ironclads were kept in service after the war. Instead, the navy remained tangled in tradition, still preferring sails and wooden hulls until the 1880s. By 1890, the navy's 44 ships ranked America 12th in naval power, below Turkey and Austria–Hungary. By 1898, however, the navy ranked 6th and had its first battleships.[9]

In 1898, Congress approved an additional force of 200,000 men for the army, a fivefold increase, and nearly doubled the size of the navy and marine corps to about 26,000 total. The army remained about 100,000 thereafter, and the navy grew steadily in quantity and quality of its ships in the years leading up to World War I.

To raise the army to join the fight in World War I, which in 1918 had more than 2.3 million Americans in uniform, Congress again enacted a draft. The navy and marine corps were also greatly expanded, but all the forces fell to prewar levels during the isolationist 1920s.

While constrained in size, the U.S. military used the interwar years to pioneer many innovative approaches to future conflict. Both the army and navy developed air forces, the former to conduct strategic bombing and the latter to sink enemy ships at great distances from their own. Some in the army, but far too few at the time, saw that tanks could be used as primary attack weapons and not just mobile artillery for infantry troops. And in a forerunner to the challenges he would face mobilizing 12 million men and women after Pearl Harbor, General George C. Marshall was deeply involved in the recruitment, training, and use of 2.5 million jobless men who joined the Civilian Conservation Corps.

As war began in Europe, President Franklin Roosevelt (FDR) overcame isolationist resistance and persuaded Congress to increase weapons production for U.S. forces, to aid allies fighting Hitler, and even to institute the first peacetime draft in 1940. While programs for atomic weapons, jet airplanes, and other advanced weaponry did not reach the front lines until later in the war, the foundation was laid for the scientific–industrial–military complex, which flourished after 1945.

## Consolidation, Nuclear Weapons, and Jointness

In an effort to improve the process for developing and carrying out national security policy—seen as a combination of foreign, military, and economic policy—Congress enacted the National Security Act of 1947. This law created the job of secretary of defense (but didn't create the actual Department of Defense, DOD, until 1949), codified the Joint Chiefs of Staff (JCS), created an independent air force, created the Central Intelligence Agency (CIA), and created the National Security Council (NSC). In fact, the NSC was proposed by the navy as an alternative to a unified military establishment, but its value was recognized by people on all sides of the question.

A separate law created the Atomic Energy Commission, devised so that the development of nuclear weapons would remain in civilian control. (President Truman was unwilling to turn actual custody of the bombs over to the military until war broke out in Korea in 1950. For their part, military leaders like General Curtis LeMay devised nuclear war plans out of sync with civilian guidance.) The American nuclear monopoly ended in 1949 with the first test of a Soviet A-bomb, and the Cold War race to build bigger and better bombs and delivery systems continued into the 1970s, when the first limits were imposed by U.S.–Soviet agreements. Modernization and worst-case fears about what the other side might do in a crisis persisted until the fall of the Soviet Union in 1991. Changes in the size of the armed forces since 1950 are shown in Table 8.3.

Interservice rivalry between the U.S. armed forces led each component to try to develop capabilities to fight the USSR on its own. Each service thought deterrence of Soviet attack depended on matching Soviet offensive capabilities more than building actual defenses against its missiles and bombers. Each nation based threat assessments on what the other might be able to do in the future and rushed to exceed that capability. In practice, however, both sides showed enormous restraint in readying the weapons

| Table 8.3 | U.S. Armed Forces, 1950–2010 | | | | |
|---|---|---|---|---|---|
| | Numbers by Service, End Strength in Thousands | | | | |
| Fiscal year | Army | Navy | Marine Corps | Air Force | Total* |
| 1950 | 593 | 381 | 74 | 411 | 1,459 |
| 1955 | 1,109 | 661 | 205 | 960 | 2,935 |
| 1960 | 873 | 617 | 171 | 815 | 2,476 |
| 1965 | 969 | 672 | 190 | 825 | 2,656 |
| 1970 | 1,322 | 692 | 260 | 791 | 3,066 |
| 1975 | 784 | 535 | 196 | 613 | 2,129 |
| 1980 | 777 | 527 | 188 | 558 | 2,063 |
| 1985 | 781 | 571 | 198 | 602 | 2,207 |
| 1990 | 751 | 583 | 197 | 539 | 2,144 |
| 1995 | 509 | 435 | 174 | 400 | 1,583 |
| 2000 | 482 | 373 | 173 | 356 | 1,449 |
| 2005 | 492 | 362 | 180 | 352 | 1,455 |
| 2010 | 468 | 271 | 181 | 263 | 1,183 |

*Includes full-time national guard and reserve personnel where applicable.

Military force levels have experienced ups and downs throughout American history. Since 1950, the greatest changes have occurred in the ground combat services during and after major combat operations and steady reductions after the end of the Cold War in 1991. Conscription from 1948 to 1973 allowed rapid expansion of the force for the Korean and Vietnam wars, but it has been all-volunteer since the draft law expired. The services also worked to reduce human resource needs with technological improvements in weaponry.

Source: DOD.

for use. Starting in the 1960s, U.S. and Soviet leaders welcomed a *hotline* between Moscow and Washington and negotiated an incidents-at-sea agreement to reduce the dangers of accidental war.

U.S. military doctrine changed under different leaders. President Eisenhower reduced conventional forces and tried to reduce some of the interservice duplication of efforts. President Kennedy and Defense Secretary Robert McNamara limited the U.S. nuclear arsenal, imposed tighter civilian controls, and changed deterrence doctrine by developing precise damage expectancy criteria. President Nixon agreed to forego national ballistic missile defenses. President Reagan resurrected the idea of missile defenses, which President George W. Bush favored to the point of abrogating the Nixon Antiballistic Missile (ABM) treaty.

Military commanders fought the Vietnam War the way they fought World War II and Korea—with large force movements aimed at reducing and defeating enemy forces. At the same time, American advisors tried to build South Vietnamese units into an effective fighting force. There were some programs like what we now call counterinsurgency, aimed at winning civilian loyalty and providing local security, but most of these were not significant until the final period of U.S. military involvement in the early 1970s. When the war ended, the U.S. military tried to forget Vietnam and especially counterinsurgency operations.

Military misadventures—such as the ill-fated attempt to rescue American diplomatic personnel held hostage by Iranians in 1980 and the nearly bungled invasion of Grenada in 1982—led Congress to impose requirements for better military coordination of the armed forces, labeled *jointness* by the Goldwater–Nichols Defense Reorganization Act of 1986. The following year, Congress passed another law creating the Special Operations Command for counterterrorist missions, a capability deemed inadequately developed in the services. Jointness improved over the following decades not only operationally but also in terms of doctrine and management. A provision requiring, as a precondition for promotion to one-star general or admiral, that the officer serve in a multiservice job, such as in a combatant command or the joint staff, led to higher-quality people in those jobs. For that assignment at least, they were *purple suiters*. As a result, senior officers had some familiarity and experience with the capabilities and operations of other services.

The first Gulf War of 1991 demonstrated the apparent success of traditional U.S. military doctrine as well as improved jointness. Main battle units won a quick and decisive victory by destroying and defeating similar enemy units. No effort was made, however, to conquer and occupy Iraq. When that was done in 2003, it rapidly became apparent that the United States had no ready plans or capability to occupy and rebuild the war-torn country.

The minor conflicts of the Clinton years—the botched intervention in Somalia, the collapsed opposition to intervention in Haiti, and the military operations followed by successful negotiations in the Balkans—left U.S. military planners confident that they had learned all the right lessons from the past. They also believed that, by exploiting new information technologies and the realm of space with what they called the *revolution in military affairs,* they could sustain American military superiority for the foreseeable future.

Then came the 9/11 attacks and the search for ways to defeat an elusive but determined enemy comfortable in caves in rugged mountains. This was followed by the invasion of Iraq and the long struggle to build a viable successor government. The ground forces were called into action, and the air and sea forces shifted into supporting roles. The 21st century was starting to look a lot like the start of the 20th. With the withdrawal of U.S. forces from combat activities in Iraq and Afghanistan, the U.S. military faced a readjustment of strategic focus as well as strong pressures to cut spending to help reduce budget deficits.

---

### Box 8.2

### Secretary of Defense: A Hard Job to Keep

The secretary of defense has to confront daunting challenges almost daily: managing the sprawling Pentagon, obtaining military hardware at reasonable cost, planning and executing military operations, advising the president and NSC, and winning support from Congress for military programs.

The job is almost impossible to do well. In fact, more than one man in three who has held the post was fired or forced to resign. Ironically, most lost their jobs not because they failed to manage DOD but rather because they lost the confidence of the president or Congress or caused major political problems for the administration.

- James Forrestal (1947–1949) lost the confidence of President Truman, began behaving strangely, and later committed suicide.
- Louis Johnson (1949–1950) lost the confidence of President Truman and was sacrificed in recognition of U.S. military unpreparedness at the start of the Korean War.
- Charles Wilson (1953–1957) became a political embarrassment to President Eisenhower.
- Neil McElroy (1957–1959) lost the confidence of President Eisenhower.
- Robert McNamara (1961–1968) lost faith in his own Vietnam War and lost the confidence of President Johnson.
- James Schlesinger (1973–1975) irritated and caused political problems for President Ford.
- Caspar Weinberger (1981–1987) lost the confidence of Congress and caused political problems for President Reagan.
- Les Aspin (1993–1994) lost the confidence of President Clinton and was sacrificed after military problems in Somalia.
- Donald Rumsfeld (2001–2006) lost the confidence of Congress and caused political problems for President Bush.

---

*Source:* Charles A. Stevenson, *SecDef: The Nearly Impossible Job of Secretary of Defense* (Washington, DC: Potomac Books, 2006).

# Leadership

The person in charge of the Pentagon is the secretary of defense, known in bureaucratic shorthand as the SecDef. The top official has ample authority to meet his responsibilities. As with the secretary of state, the SecDef is an instrument of the president. (See Box 8.3.) As the basic law says, "The Secretary is the principal assistant to the President in all matters relating to the Department of Defense. Subject to the direction of the President and to [other laws], he has authority, direction, and control over the Department of Defense" (10 USC 113b). He is also supposed to be "appointed from civilian life" rather than directly from the senior officer ranks, as in many other countries. In fact, this law had to be specifically waived by Congress when President Truman wanted to name retired General George C. Marshall as SecDef at the start of the Korean War.

Originally, the job was much less powerful than it is now. The very first Secretary, James Forrestal, was increasingly frustrated in the post. He called it "probably the greatest cemetery for dead cats in history." He also concluded that "the peacetime mission of the Armed Services is to destroy the Secretary of Defense."[10] They succeeded. Forrestal was fired, showed signs of mental illness, and jumped to his death from the 16th floor of the Bethesda naval hospital.

The law was changed in later years to give the secretary more power over the armed services. The first man to exploit it to the full was Robert McNamara, who served under Presidents Kennedy and Johnson. McNamara dominated the Pentagon through a series of processes, all of which went directly through his office. The most powerful was the budget process, which McNamara—and all of his successors—used to set the size of the forces, their military missions, their capabilities, and their research and development (R&D) efforts for the future. Any change in previously approved programs had to be approved by his office, and only on the basis of elaborate justifications, including future year costs.

McNamara ultimately failed, however, when he tried to impose his accounting metrics—and his intrusive personality—on the men fighting the war in Vietnam. The boss wanted numbers, so he was given numbers in accordance with the military maxim, "if you want it bad, you'll get it bad."

Many Pentagon chiefs practiced leadership by intimidation, as former Deputy Secretary John Hamre recommended in the quotation at the start of this chapter. Others, the ones generally judged more favorably by history, listened as well as talked and sometimes even accepted the advice of their subordinates. The quiet successes included men like Melvin Laird under Richard Nixon and William Perry under Bill Clinton.

It's hard to succeed as boss of the Pentagon. (See Box 8.2.) Of the 21 men who have served as SecDef, at least 8 were fired or forced to resign. Most lost the confidence of the president or caused him major political problems. Several also lost the confidence of the defense overseers in the Congress, endangering Pentagon programs and causing additional political problems.

---

**Box 8.3**

## Who Makes Foreign Policy: The Very Busy Secretary of Defense and Chairman of the Joint Chiefs of Staff

Besides the demanding requirements of running the Pentagon and attending White House meetings to advise the president, the secretary of defense has to travel widely to oversee military operations, deal with foreign officials on security issues, and attend conferences with allies. In 2010, for example, Defense Secretary Robert Gates spent 67 days away from Washington on foreign travel, visiting 25 different countries, several more than once. During his four and a half years in office, Gates was away from the Pentagon 282 days, visited an average of 33 countries each year and traveled over 664,000 miles.

The chairman of the JCS also has to travel widely, visiting U.S. forces and conferring with foreign military leaders. In 2010, Admiral Mike Mullen traveled abroad 72 days, visiting 26 countries, several more than once. During his four years in office, he averaged visits to 39 countries each year, traveling 78 days. His four-year total was 157 country visits and 313 days of travel.

Both officials used their travel for diplomatic activities and military consultations as well as overseeing U.S. forces, thus demonstrating how important they are as part of a foreign policy team.

*Source:* DOD.

---

Success requires the trust and support of the president, collaborative relations with the military leadership in the JCS, and at least a tolerable working relationship with the rest of the administration's national security team. Failure in any of those roles puts the secretary on the exit ramp.

The senior military leader is the Chairman of the JCS (CJCS). The JCS used to be a consensus-based advisory committee whose advice was often slow to come and opaque in form. The 1986 Goldwater–Nichols law gave the chairman special status and allowed him to offer independent advice without logrolling and compromise among the chiefs. This is one of the CJCS's few powers. He is not in the chain of command to warfighting forces and cannot give orders to subordinate commanders. But, his public and private advice is frequently sought and carries great weight throughout government. The JCS still perform important roles as representatives of their service in Pentagon policy making. And while they hold formal sessions in their *tank*, the chairman may also consult them informally, as Admiral David Jeremiah reports. (See Box 8.4.)

The COCOMs in charge of U.S. forces in various regions and for particular missions like the use of strategic nuclear weapons and SOF are independently powerful because of their warfighting responsibilities. They are directly under the secretary in the chain of command and share their war plans with the JCS only as a matter of courtesy rather than law. In planning for the Iraq war, for example, Secretary Rumsfeld and Central Command

---

**Box 8.4**

## Inside View: Joint Chiefs of Staff Meet in the Kitchen

Admiral David Jeremiah, vice chairman of the JCS, 1990–1994, describes how the JCS Chairman, Gen. Colin Powell, scheduled formal meetings but did most work in informal ones. The use of informal meetings and processes is common in government, but it makes it harder for outsiders to know what is happening. Formal sessions require paperwork before and afterward and stimulate interest among subordinates. Informal sessions allow franker exchanges and fewer leaks. That makes it easier for the president to feel comfortable with the advice on the use of the military instrument that the chiefs are established to provide.

*We scheduled—historically, the Chiefs would go in on, say, Tuesdays, Thursdays, maybe Wednesday, and they'd have tank sessions. Tank sessions were wonderful theater. Coffee or tea or seltzer water or whatever the drink of choice was, a candy jar with whatever the candy of choice was, in the old days an ashtray with cigar or whatever. Beautiful. Everybody sat down, everybody had their staff position, and they would settle up defending their staff position that had been worked up through their individual service staffs . . .*

*The product was not of any particular consequence. . . . We met in the tank a lot but we met in [Gen.] Colin [Powell]'s kitchen a lot, sometimes in my kitchen, sometimes in other places, often in the office. Get the Chiefs down, everybody popping in, and we'd talk. He would tell the Chiefs what was going on, what the issue was. What do you think about it? He pretty well knew what he wanted to do. Let's talk about it. Sometimes it got vectored a little bit differently, but when it came out it didn't take up a lot of staff time trying to fool around with the issue. If the issue required a lot of staff time, the staff ought to take care of it. If you really wanted to know something about it and do something about it, then we should be able to deal with it at the service chiefs' level without having to mess around with the whole process.*

*[Powell's approach was:] I think we need a meeting on that, do you? Yes. Makes sense. Get some comments, get the Chiefs together. Or, you just came from the White House and this is what the deputy said to say? Let's get the Chiefs down and you tell them what's going on, where it's headed, something like that.*

Source: Oral history for the G. H. W. Bush Administration, Admiral David Jeremiah at http://millercenter.org/president/bush/oralhistory/david-jeremiah.

---

(CENTCOM) Commander General Tommy Franks collaborated together and allowed little input from the JCS.

The U.S. military fully embrace the notion of civilian control, but they sometimes chafe at its practice. They prefer to design and execute military operations based on clear, strategic guidance, yet presidents and SecDefs over the years have tended to give only vague guidance and then to insist on close tactical oversight. Military officers tend to resent any civilian intrusion into what they see as their domain, yet with few historical exceptions, they will loyally carry out even orders they think unwise.

Scholar–practitioner Peter Feaver has said that, in the American system of civil–military relations, "The civilians have the right to be wrong." And another professor–policy maker, Eliot Cohen, has recommended regular civil–military consultations, even though it is necessarily an unequal dialogue. Professor Richard Betts has noted that, except for the 1983 intervention in Lebanon, no major military operation in the latter half of the 20th century was conducted when more than one of the JCS was strongly opposed. One might now add another possible exception—the "surge" of additional troops to Iraq in 2007. But I think the evidence there, and elsewhere in the historical record, points to a different conclusion. The U.S. military, because of the enormous deference given them by the public and political leaders, have an implicit veto over the use of force in major operations. They never use the veto as such; they never refuse to follow orders, but they do insist on and obtain terms and conditions that limit the way force is used.[11]

Civil–military relations in the United States have been tense for several decades despite the best efforts of many leaders to build bridges of understanding. Many military officers believe that civilian officials "lost" a war in Vietnam that might otherwise have been "won" because of poor strategy and intrusions into the military domain. Many officers in the 1980s and 1990s objected to being sent on *nation-building* missions because they believed the military should be held in reserve for major, nation-threatening conflicts. Many officers resented Bill Clinton as commander-in-chief because he had avoided the draft during Vietnam. Some senior officers spoke out against Secretary Rumsfeld's intrusive management of the Pentagon.

Rumsfeld managed by *snowflakes*, personal memos raising questions and offering ideas sent at the rate of hundreds per week. "I want to run this department from my outbox, not my inbox," he explained.[12] He also bullied his subordinates but yielded to unshaken and persuasive responses, as described in Box 8.5. He was often quite willing to impose his ideas contrary to military advice, even going as far as demanding changes in the complicated and long-planned timetables for shipping equipment and personnel for the Iraq war. (See Box 8.5.)

Rumsfeld's successor, Robert Gates, had a quite different style and was unusually successful as secretary of defense. He won the confidence of Congress and two different presidents while managing two difficult wars. Gates challenged the status quo in the Pentagon in numerous ways. He enforced accountability on senior officials who made mistakes or were too slow to accept changed approaches to major policy issues. For example, he replaced the secretary of the army, the secretary of the air force, the chairman of the JCS, the air force chief of staff, the commander of CENTCOM, and two U.S. commanders in Afghanistan.

Gates also forced the Pentagon to give priority to ongoing wars and overrode bureaucratic emphasis on future weapons development. For example, he ordered accelerated production and delivery of the mine-resistant, ambush-protected (MRAP) armored trucks that were saving lives in the war

---

| Box 8.5 |

## Inside View: Rumsfeld's Assertive Style

Defense Secretary Donald Rumsfeld intimidated his subordinates, even those he admired, according to one of his senior staff, the Defense Department Comptroller Dov Zackheim. He challenged them but appreciated those who had cogent arguments and stood their ground.

*Rumsfeld's style also confused many senior people inside the Pentagon. He would not hesitate to vent his annoyance when he felt a briefer was unprepared or when he perceived that someone had not done his or her homework. Many of us were on the receiving end of comments like 'a trained ape could do better than that,' and not everyone grasped that Rumsfeld was not being personal.*

*[One day Rear Admiral Stan Szemborski] had been called into the secretary's office to outline how efficiencies could reduce the defense budget by 15 percent. . . . Stan told the boss flatly that it couldn't be done. Rumsfeld was outraged. It was not what he had expected to hear; it confirmed his worst suspicions about the pedestrian nature of the military and its adherence to 'old think.' But Stan stood his ground in the face of Don's displeasure. Rumsfeld finally stormed out of the conference room back to his office. The rest of us stared at one another in silence as embarrassment blossomed among us. Finally, I remarked to Stan, 'He really likes you.'*

---

*Source:* From Dov S. Zackheim, *A Vulcan's Tale* (Washington, DC: Brookings Institution, 2011), 59, 60.

---

zones. Within two years, the number of such vehicles with U.S. forces in Iraq and Afghanistan surged from 64 to more than 13,000. Similarly, he compelled the air force to greatly expand its number and use of unmanned aerial vehicles (drones) in combat areas.

He patiently used Pentagon processes to obtain military concurrence in budget cuts and program changes and even to support repeal of the law banning service by gays and lesbians. He arranged for a thorough study of the Don't Ask, Don't Tell law that answered many criticisms and secured the support of most senior military commanders for repeal, which passed Congress in 2010. Gates probably ranks as the most effective and highly regarded secretary of defense in history.

### People in Many Uniforms

There are almost 3 million men and women who are the human factor behind the military instrument of national power. Some 736,000 are civilians, and the remaining 2.252 million (1.4 million on active duty, 846,000 in the reserves) are in one of many different uniforms. All share, however, a military ethos of order, sacrifice, loyalty, and other important virtues. All of the people in uniform are volunteers, either for active duty or for reserve assignments that in recent years have included many months in Iraq and

Afghanistan. The draft ended in 1973 and, with it, the incentive to volunteer for safer assignments than combat infantry.

The all-volunteer force is diverse in composition but not a demographic mirror of American society. Whites represent 79.4% of the general population and 70.7% of the armed forces, according to a survey in 2008. Blacks are 12.8% of the population but account for 16.5% of the military. Hispanics are 15.8% of the population and 10.6% of those in uniform. Women are 50.4% of the population but only 14.3% of the active-duty personnel.[13]

Southern states have accounted for a disproportionate share of military recruits throughout the all-volunteer force, from about one third during the 1970s and 1980s to 42% since the early 1990s. The number of enlistees from New England and the Middle Atlantic states is significantly below the national average. While about 30% of the new accessions come from urban areas, nearly half come from relatively small towns and rural areas.[14]

The quality of the armed forces is generally quite high because virtually all enlisted personnel are high school graduates or the equivalent and most officers eventually obtain master's degrees.

The risks of military service are obviously high, but benefits have steadily increased in order to sustain a volunteer force and avoid a draft. For example, men and women serving in Afghanistan or Iraq or some nearby countries could also qualify for hostile fire pay, hardship duty pay, a family separation allowance, and a per diem—with most or all of these payments excluded from federal taxes. Military personnel and their dependents also receive generous health care benefits while on active duty, and they qualify for veterans' benefits and a special retiree health care program more generous than Medicare.

In addition to the active forces, there are over 1 million men and women in the reserve component forces. The army, navy, marine corps, and air force reserve units are designed as replacements or supplements for regular forces if needed. The national guard is different, the modern equivalent of the militia that the framers preferred to a standing army. Unless called to federal duty by the president, the guard belongs to the governor of the state where it was recruited and trained. Even if given advanced weapons and training for ground combat, the guard is used locally mainly for disaster relief and riot control. In recent years, about 6,000 guard personnel have been federalized for border security missions along parts of the U.S.–Mexican border. This is an example of the use of military forces for a domestic homeland security mission that also has significant foreign policy consequences for U.S. relations with Mexico. The president has to weigh both domestic and foreign policy factors before using such an instrument.

The reserve forces used to be a convenient way for people to continue military service, get a little money and eventual retirement benefits, and provide backup skills in case of a major war. As reservists were embedded in civilian life and often community leaders, presidents were very reluctant to call upon the reserves during the Cold War. As the Vietnam War was ending, General Creighton Abrams restructured the army so that large deployments could not occur without calling up reservists. Many police, medical, and transportation units—so-called combat service and combat service support units—were put in the reserves. It was Abrams's way of making sure that future presidents would think twice about major military operations and that civilian society would share in the costs and disruption.[15]

In fact, the numbers of reservists recalled to active duty were low and the domestic political impact small until the post-2001 wars in Iraq and Afghanistan, which became unpopular for many reasons, including the disruptions caused by the use of large numbers of guard and reserve personnel. Reservists were called to active duty frequently during the 1990s and since the 9/11 attacks. Nearly a quarter of a million were activated during the Persian Gulf War of 1990–1991; more than 6,000 were recalled for duty in Haiti during 1994–1996; more than 31,000 were used to support peacekeeping missions in Bosnia after 1995; another 11,500 were used in Kosovo after 1999. About 700,000 reservists have been activated for the wars in Afghanistan and Iraq. Air national guard units have provided about 30% of the aircraft used by U.S. forces in Iraq and Afghanistan. More than one fourth (28%) of the forces deployed to Iraq and Afghanistan during 2001–2007 were from the guard and reserves.[16] In 2011, Congress voted to make the chief of the National Guard Bureau a formal member of the JCS.

## Organization

The 2.1 million people regularly in the DOD (civilians and active duty military) pose a major management challenge. As the organization chart shows, DOD is divided into three military departments, 18 defense agencies, 10 combatant commands, 10 field activities, and several other organizations, including the important and powerful Office of the Secretary of Defense (OSD) and the Joint Staff. (See Figure 8.1.) There are about 2,000 people working in OSD and another 1,600 on the Joint Staff.

The military departments organize, train, and equip the armed forces, but most are assigned to the combatant commands for military operations. The defense agencies have special, department-wide tasks, like accounting and payroll, auditing, logistics, and various intelligence activities. The JCS, aided by the Joint Staff, provide advice to the secretary and the NSC, but they do not command any operating forces. OSD is the secretary's management device, with five under secretaries and numerous other officials reporting to him.

The deputy secretary has traditionally been the chief operating officer of DOD, the one managing the major processes of budgeting and weapons acquisition, facing inward, while the secretary is the public face and spokesperson on defense issues. For foreign policy matters, as well as for civilian control of military strategy, the under secretary for policy is the key official. Each secretary chooses which processes and issues deserve personal attention and which can be delegated to the experienced bureaucracy of the Pentagon. Secretary Rumsfeld reached far down the chain of command with

## Figure 8.1 U.S. Department of Defense Organizational Chart

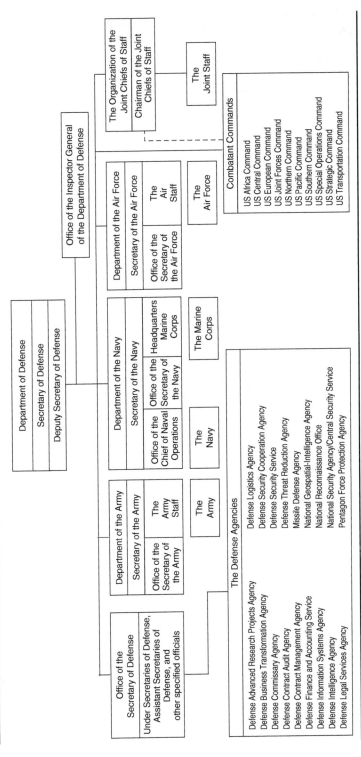

Note the complexity of DOD organizations, the services separate from the combatant commands, and the many defense agencies separate from both. Yet, all funnel into the OSD for management and decisions. On the other hand, the diversity and specialization of DOD organizations has made it easier to militarize foreign policy because the Pentagon usually has people and resources ready to use, and the civilian agencies do not.

Source: DOD, 2010.

217

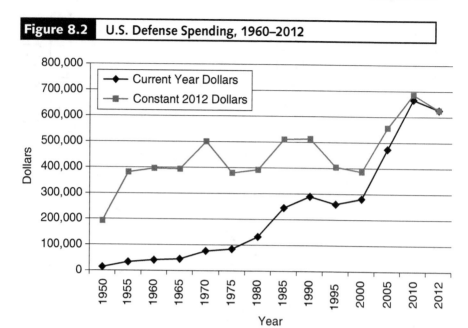

**Figure 8.2**  U.S. Defense Spending, 1960–2012

There are many different ways to measure military spending. This chart shows the actual budget outlays in current year dollars and in constant dollars, factoring out inflation. As you can see, in constant dollars, recent budgets have been about as high as during the Vietnam War and the mid-1980s military buildup. And even with congressionally mandated cuts during 2012–2017, spending should remain above the Cold War average.

*Source:* National Defense Budget Estimates for FY 2012, Office of the Under Secretary of Defense, 2011, 141–146 at http://comptroller.defense.gov/defbudget/fy2012/FY12_Green_ Book.pdf.

questions and guidance. Secretary Gates relied more on the formal processes that routinely bring matters for high-level decision.

While the budget is the primary process for managing and controlling the Pentagon (see Figure 8.2), the secretary is also at the pinnacle for other processes. The acquisition process supplements the budget process but allows the secretary to reshape the capabilities of the armed forces, sometimes giving them new missions and weaponry, other times denying them the desired but far too costly system they were hoping to acquire. The personnel system gives him, with presidential concurrence, the chance to pick civilian officials and the senior military officers. Some secretaries made a practice of interviewing several candidates for key posts, thus providing them a cadre of loyalists who shared his vision of what should be done and how. The public affairs process allows the secretary to shape the message of the Pentagon to friends and enemies at home and abroad. Rumsfeld's pronouncements about the Global War on Terror, which typically was quickly shortened to GWOT, were an effort to frame how to view the threats from loosely organized but violent groups. The legislative affairs process helps the secretary build a partnership with Capitol Hill, using devices such as classified briefings, locally helpful contracts, and occasional free trips home and abroad on military aircraft. Each of these tools can strengthen a SecDef's power and influence.

# The Culture of the Pentagon

There is a distinctive organizational culture in the Pentagon, widely shared by civilians and military alike. In terms of the Myers–Briggs typology, about 90% of military personnel test as thinking and judging, traits related to being logical, firm but fair, goal-oriented, decisive, and organized. Some 30% are introversion–sensation–thinking–judging (ISTJ), compared to only 6% in the population as a whole. ISTJs "have a keen sense of right and wrong," believe in punctuality, are "factual, dedicated, thorough, systematic, steadfast, practical, organized, realistic, duty bound, sensible, painstaking, and reliable."[17] Just listing those words calls to mind warriors.

These personality traits also infuse organizations with an insistence on careful planning, seeking clear goals, and timely decisions. The elaborate DOD processes for budgeting and weapons acquisition are mirrored in war planning by the combatant commands. This culture also focuses on enemy capabilities, which seem measurable, rather than intentions, which can be vague, uncertain, and changeable. It also considers worst-case analysis as reasonable and necessary.

A vivid example of the military can-do spirit is what the author observed in a visit years ago to a live-fire exercise at Fort Benning, Georgia. Seeing M60 tanks crossing a small lake with their turrets open in order to attach flotation gear, he asked a young major, "Can they fire while in the water?" "Yes, sir," the major replied, "once." He explained that the recoil would make the tank take on water, but before sinking, it could contribute one shell to the fight.

All these characteristics make the Pentagon different from the other national security organizations, where multiple objectives (e.g., trade, human rights, support against pariah states) have to be balanced and prioritized and where the planning culture has not taken root. In interagency meetings, it's usually the Pentagon representatives who ask, "What are we really after, not just how do we solve today's problem?"

While the military ethos is widespread, each service has its own individual culture, reflecting its history and the way it views its core competencies. As Carl Builder and others have noted, the army views itself as the servant to society, and it emphasizes cooperation and coordination. Army units have to know who is on each side of them and what each is planning to do in battle. The navy honors its traditions, including the independence of the captain at sea. It also enforces a different standard of accountability, punishing the captain for errors by the crew, while the other services tend to look for the precise locus of error. The marine corps, lean and mean throughout history, has always stressed its willingness and readiness for almost any mission it might be assigned. When army leaders in the 1990s opposed nation-building and stabilization missions, saying "We don't do windows," the marines said they would do them. Despite easy political victories when civilians have tried to disband the corps—as Teddy Roosevelt and Harry Truman learned to their regret—the marines still feel embattled and threatened. The air force, the newest service that achieved independence only after a long struggle, emphasizes technology and the superiority of air power for most military tasks. [18]

There is one curious fact that makes DOD different from the State Department and other national security institutions and which may explain the dominance of the military mind-set: Most of the senior civilian officials in OSD are outsiders, political appointees. Very few careerists have ever been appointed to positions requiring Senate confirmation—in contrast to the State Department, where typically half the assistant secretaries and 85% of the deputy assistant secretaries are career foreign service officers (FSOs). This has numerous pernicious effects. Few talented DOD civilians can be motivated and rewarded by promotion to top posts. There is high turnover of political appointees, weakening institutional memory and learning. And, incoming officials distrust the loyalty of their new subordinates.[19]

## Use of the Military Instrument

Current military doctrine sets four strategic goals for the Pentagon, three for security purposes and one for management. They are these: Win our nation's wars; deter conflict and promote security; defend the homeland; and integrate business operations.[20] Plans and budgets are linked to those goals much more specifically than in other departments and agencies. The three security goals are also foreign policy goals that military forces help the United States to achieve.

When it comes to actual use of military capabilities, there is a tight system of civilian control. The secretary of defense may consult with the chairman or the JCS as a body, but only he can give direct orders to the COCOM to engage in military operations. Only he can approve war plans or assign troops to one command rather than another. In fact, the secretary personally must sign any deployment order sending military units abroad, except for small numbers of people sent on temporary duty for nonoperational support tasks.[21]

Within the United States, the limits on the use of the regular armed forces are even more restrictive. As part of the political settlement that ended Reconstruction and led to the withdrawal of federal soldiers from the former Confederacy, Congress passed a *never again law* forbidding the use of troops to enforce domestic law. This is called The *Posse Comitatus* Act (18 U. S. C. 1385), using the common-law phrase for a sheriff's power to call upon local citizens to help maintain law and order. There are some technical exceptions—the law doesn't apply to the navy or marine corps; the coast guard has explicit law enforcement duties; troops may still be used to suppress insurrections and repel invasions. But, the practical result is that the law prevents soldiers from arresting people or conducting searches and seizures to aid civilian law enforcement.

The law also imposes a strong psychological barrier against using troops domestically. For example, only in the 1980s did Congress enact provisions allowing military aircraft to pass along surveillance information that could be used to interdict drug smugglers. Officials reluctant to seek or use military personnel in some domestic matter raise the *posse comitatus* law as a first line of argument. Since 2006, national guard troops have been deployed along the southwest border with Mexico to supplement the activities of the border patrol. About 30,000 men and women have participated in this activity, called Operation Jump Start. They are paid for by the federal government but under the control of the respective state governors. And, they are limited to supporting local authorities, stopping short of actual arrest or search and seizure.[22]

Presidents are sometimes limited by law in their use of force abroad, though some lawyers dispute the validity of such limits. Nevertheless, Congress has passed and presidents have complied with numerous restrictions on troop deployments and warfighting. For example, President McKinley abided by a ban on the annexation of Cuba in the Spanish–American War. FDR agreed, prior to Pearl Harbor, not to send draftees outside the Western hemisphere. President Nixon complied with congressional bans on sending U.S. troops into combat in Laos or Thailand and on conducting bombing raids anywhere in Southeast Asia after August 15, 1973. President Reagan agreed to limit U.S. troops in Lebanon to a self-defense mission. President Clinton complied with troop limitations for Somalia and Rwanda. And, President George W. Bush accepted a ceiling on U.S. military personnel in Colombia.[23] Congress has imposed, and various presidents have grudgingly accepted, other limits on foreign policy activities using armed forces.

## Warfighting

The pointy end of America's military instrument is the combat force deployed abroad, armed and trained to fight, kill, and destroy hostile forces, weapons, and supporting elements. Staffs at each of the combatant commands, under presidential directives, prepare contingency war plans and variations to deal with crisis situations in their areas. These can be reviewed by a handful of senior DOD civilians and are periodically updated. See the case study at the end of this chapter showing the planning process followed before the start of the Iraq war in 2003.

In their regions, the COCOMs (formerly called CINCs) are powerful and prestigious. These four-star officers are often treated as American equivalents of ancient Roman proconsuls and are used for diplomatic missions even more than the State Department's ambassadors and assistant secretaries. The COCOMs also have the very practical advantage of dedicated aircraft to expedite their travel.

The regional commanders control all of the air, naval, and ground forces assigned to their regions, regardless of their own particular service backgrounds. They also coordinate with host country civilian and military leaders and are supposed to work collaboratively with the U.S. ambassadors in their areas as well. Sometimes, the civilian and military chiefs work well together, as did General David Petraeus and Ambassador Ryan Crocker in Iraq. Sometimes, the pair are in constant tension, as was the case between General Stanley McChrystal and Ambassador Karl Eikenberry in Afghanistan.

The Special Operations Command (SOCOM) is in charge of warriors who depend on stealth, surprise, and speed. They aren't designed for sustained combat. The 9/11 attacks prompted a rapid increase in SOF, from 35,000 in the late 1990s to about 66,000 in 2013, along with a tripling of its budget.[24] The SOF have land, sea, and air units used primarily to deter, disrupt, and defeat terrorists and their networks. As of 2010, 86% of deployed SOF personnel were in the CENTCOM region including Afghanistan and Iraq, but about 3,000 people were also routinely deployed in more than 75 countries, where they conduct training, advisory, or unpublicized missions.

Congress created an independent SOCOM in 1986, giving it an independent budget so that its capabilities would no longer be treated as an underfunded stepchild of the established armed services. In operations in CENTCOM, however, its forces often are dependent on the regular forces for mobility and some support functions. There are often tensions between the COCOM's chain of command and the somewhat autonomous line of authority for the SOF.

Separate from the uniformed military are the CIA's paramilitary forces, which since the Korean War era, have conducted clandestine operations both to gather intelligence and to pursue other goals. CIA operatives, for example, commanded the forces used in the failed Bay of Pigs attack on Cuba in 1961 and for secret operations in Laos against the North Vietnamese. CIA units have been active in Afghanistan since even before the 9/11 attacks. The president ultimately controls all of these supersecret military units, but the 9/11 Commission recommended moving the CIA paramilitary forces under the command of the Pentagon. Instead, Congress has endorsed closer coordination between the forces.[25]

### Engaging With Foreign Governments and Militaries

In recent years, the bulk of U.S. combat forces have been deployed in or near Iraq and Afghanistan. But, there are also substantial numbers of military personnel afloat on naval ships or deployed to other countries. In 2009, for example, the Pentagon had 20,000 men and women on the high seas and 52,000 in Germany, 36,000 in Japan, 25,000 in South Korea, more than 9,000 in Italy, and a similar number in the United Kingdom. Sizable contingents of more than 1,000 people were also in Bahrain, Belgium, Djibouti, Spain, and Turkey.[26]

Some of these people were in support of long-standing treaty obligations for mutual defense. Others were engaged in particular missions to advise or train local forces. Such deployments have long been an important tool of foreign policy, for they integrate local forces in common defense efforts; help to develop an affinity for American people, practices, and equipment; and provide invaluable contacts with those who are often the most powerful individuals in their respective nations.

Since the 9/11 attacks, DOD has undertaken a large share of U.S. security assistance, funneling more than $60 billion mainly to Iraq, Afghanistan, and nearby countries. DOD gained control of these programs because it was viewed as more agile and flexible than the State Department and its rigid legal authorities. The Pentagon also dominates the planning for foreign military sales and financing programs because its people develop the recommendations for recipient countries, which are then reviewed by the State Department. The regional military commanders often have their own resources—like the Commander's Emergency Response Program (CERP)—that supplement regular foreign assistance programs with flexible funds for small-scale civil and humanitarian projects.[27] As Dana Priest argues in the quotation at the start of this chapter, these many Pentagon activities have led to military dominance over much of U.S. foreign policy.

## The 911 Force

The U.S. military is a 911 force—large enough, diverse and redundant enough in capabilities, and trained and ready to be used in almost any way a president might wish. In recent years, U.S. military personnel have been sent to help deal with natural disasters like the Indian Ocean tsunami of 2004 and the 2010 earthquake in Haiti as well as domestic American missions after Hurricane Katrina and for wildfire suppression.

Military aircraft can speed supplies and people to far parts of the globe in a few hours. Military medical personnel can supplement overwhelmed local people. Military bulldozers can clear streets filled with rubble, and engineers can install temporary bridges in flood-ravaged countries. These capabilities bring prestige and soft power to the United States and are often welcomed for providing operational experience for military personnel.

## Planning and Policy Making

Crisis needs may be surprising, but they are rarely unanticipated in the Pentagon. Military planners may not know precisely where an incident may occur that may lead to a U.S. military response of some kind, but they know that certain kinds of activities will likely be necessary, so they plan, and budget, and train, and practice for them. Since the 1990s, Congress has required DOD to perform a Quadrennial Defense Review (QDR), a regular assessment of defense strategy and force structure that leads to changed priorities and new requirements to deal with current and expected developments.

The secretary of defense leads the QDR process, and it often is the central focus of Pentagon leadership during the first year after each presidential election. Secretary Rumsfeld tried to use the process to encourage a defense transformation toward more high-technology weaponry and other systems, but he was forced to devote more effort to the conflicts in Iraq and Afghanistan. Secretary Gates used the process to shift emphasis from future war planning to meeting urgent needs of deployed forces, especially those in the war zones. Secretary Panetta used the QDR as the baseline for analyzing reductions required by congressional budget ceilings and for planning the *pivot* or *rebalance* to the Asia–Pacific region.

In addition to these long-range, strategic plans, the Pentagon follows an elaborate process for all important policy decisions. Stakeholders at middle levels are convened to discuss and prepare options papers for high-level officials. Coordination is attempted across service or functional or regional lines as necessary. Senior leaders can reach down to force consideration of matters they deem important, or their subordinates can bring issues to their attention for decision and guidance. This is all routine and bureaucratic but fits well within the military's planning culture.

## Recurring Tensions

As in any diverse bureaucracy, there are in the Pentagon numerous rivalries and recurrent tensions that can affect the use of the military instrument. Foremost is that between civilians and the military. While the uniformed officers accept civilian control, they prefer that it be gentle and respectful without intruding on their professional expertise. For their part, the civilians want loyalty and obedience, and they get upset when the career military don't adopt the broader and more political perspective they have.

A revealing example of a legitimate disagreement is on the Rules of Engagement, the orders commanders give prescribing when force can and cannot be used in specified circumstances. From the military perspective, these are operational questions they should resolve, given their knowledge of military training and capabilities. From the civilian perspective, tactical matters can have strategic consequences and thus should be subjected to civilian review. Both sides want to protect the lives of Americans, for example, but they may disagree on which measures have collateral effects that undermine the war effort. When enemy soldiers appear to be firing from in or near a mosque or school, for example, the rules need to balance protection of civilians and friendly forces with steps to eliminate the threat. Similarly, the air force makes elaborate calculations of the potential blast effects of hitting certain targets in order to minimize collateral damage. These are not easy questions.

Another tension, quite evident in the Iraq war, is that between the JCS and the COCOMs. The chiefs are the leaders of their services concerned with its long-term capabilities, both human and material. The commanders, especially when engaged in a shooting war, care primarily about today and tomorrow, not next year, and doing whatever can be done to accomplish their missions. Each side has a legitimate perspective, and the policy process tries to balance the conflicting demands. Secretary Gates, much more than his predecessors, emphasized immediate requirements over future programs.

Interservice rivalry has been strong throughout U.S. history and was only slightly diminished by the recent emphasis on jointness. The air force wants the latest and best aircraft; the navy wants a number of aircraft carriers; the marines want to stay at three divisions; and the army wants next-generation weaponry even as it is stretched thin by current wars. It took civilian pressure to acquire airlift and sealift because those assets were going to be used to transport army people and equipment. It took civilian pressure to create the SOF because the regular forces viewed that as a minor mission, last in line for funding and promotions. It took civilian pressure to build up a force of unmanned aerial vehicles because as the military sees it, "real men should be in cockpits, not at computer terminals."

Still unresolved is the perennial conflict between the active forces and the reserves. Despite the valiant performance of reserve units in Iraq and Afghanistan, some senior officials still doubt their capabilities and insist on preserving full active-duty strength. Budget officials recognize the strong political support for the reserves on Capitol Hill and routinely omit full funding of particular programs in expectation of congressional add-ons. For its part, the national guard has embraced the homeland security mission, hoping to grow in size and capability as a consequence.

## The Pentagon in the Interagency Process

As Secretary Gates acknowledged, DOD is an "800-pound gorilla" when dealing with others. As a result, the military instrument is the default option even for many nonmilitary tasks, including a large share of U.S. foreign aid. Another consequence is that Pentagon views get special deference from presidents and other cabinet officials. Especially since the Goldwater–Nichols Act, the uniformed military have had their own seat in interagency planning meetings, thus giving military concerns a strong double voice in debates. Pentagon officials are used to careful planning and rapid responses. They can do the *first paper on the block* to frame issues for interagency discussion.

Conversely, when the Pentagon holds back, the whole interagency process comes to an abrupt halt. Two long-serving DOD officials, Frederick C. Smith and Franklin C. Miller, document this effect during Secretary Rumsfeld's tenure. Rumsfeld, they note, had "an abiding animosity" toward the interagency process. Especially in planning for the Iraq war, DOD officials failed to attend meetings or sat in but failed to share information.[28] Other participants have said that Rumsfeld insisted that his subordinates not deal with others on issues until DOD had a position, and then they were not supposed to agree to any alternatives. Such sabotage of the policy process probably contributed to shortcomings immediately after the invasion of Iraq in 2003.[29] Secretary Gates and Secretary Panetta were much more willing team players in the interagency process.

# Congress and the Pentagon

Congress shares control of the military through its constitutional powers to raise and support an army, provide and maintain a navy, organize the militia, and "make Rules for the Government and Regulation of the land and naval Forces" (Art. I, sect. 8). It also has functioned historically as an escape valve during civil–military tensions as people in uniform could freely complain to lawmakers, who often were happy to help them for personal or political reasons. Members of defense committees often challenge executive branch policies because of such back-channel reports from dissenting officials.

Key oversight is performed by the House and Senate Armed Services Committees. Most members represent states or districts with major military installations or defense contractors, and they necessarily view their jobs as protecting and enhancing those sources of local jobs. Many members also have personal backgrounds, such as prior military service, that give them expertise and affinities that influence their actions. Former marines are particularly supportive of their service, which is generally regarded to be the most effective on the Hill. Senior lawmakers often have far more experience with specific military issues than their three- and four-star witnesses, who rotate through jobs every two or three years. They can recognize the newly reinvented wheel that was tried but failed a decade or two earlier.

Congress has long insisted on its prerogatives in asserting civilian control over the military. Lawmakers want to hear from military officers and not just from their civilian superiors in the executive branch. For their part, senior officers use formal and informal access to Congress to provide back-channel information and complaints about presidential policies. In 1949, Congress passed a law giving the JCS the right to "make such recommendations to Congress" as they consider appropriate, after first informing the secretary of defense. Starting in the 1950s, the Senate insisted that all senior officers pledge, as a condition of confirmation, that they will provide Congress with their personal and professional judgments when asked. President Eisenhower called this whole system *legalized insubordination,* but it remains a key guarantor of civilian control.

The nature of congressional representation makes committee members more attuned to parochial concerns, like jobs and contracts, than grand strategy or innovative management. They are also steady advocates of military personnel benefits. For a half century, the armed services committees have produced an annual defense authorization bill, one of the *must-pass items* in the opinion of most members of Congress. This measure, now more than 900 pages long, sets personnel ceilings for each of the armed forces and adjusts military pay and benefits. It also authorizes weapons procurement, research and development programs, and military construction projects. Each year, the committees also request numerous reports on defense activities as part of their oversight process.

Actual funding for the Pentagon comes in the Defense Appropriations Bill from the appropriations committees, but the outlines are set in the authorization bills, and only those measures can contain the basic laws on the organization and operation of DOD.

While the committees responsible for the Pentagon tend to be parochial, they have on occasion had major impacts on national security strategy. It was the armed services committees that wrote the landmark National Security Act of 1947 and its later amendments strengthening the secretary of defense and his civilian control. Those committees also enacted the Goldwater–Nichols reforms in the face of vigorous Pentagon opposition. They have also tried to force the executive branch to frame its own grand strategy. A 1986 provision requires the president to develop and submit a national security strategy review that is used as the capstone document for all subordinate national security planning throughout the government. The committees also mandated the QDR—and usually added a requirement for a second opinion by a distinguished panel of outside experts.

In short, Congress, drawing on its own perspectives and prejudices, helps to build and shape the military instrument that is available to the president.

\* \* \*

The military instrument is well trained and equipped for use as the president may direct. The armed forces are especially good at planning complex actions and then carrying them out. But, the use of force raises moral, legal, and political concerns and often entails enormous and unanticipated consequences for those involved and the policy objectives being sought. The United States in recent decades has been more successful in the operational aspects of the use of force than in translating those actions into strategic victories.

# Case Study: Planning for the 2003 Iraq Invasion

Modern armed forces plan carefully for combat. Planning is their everyday business until the battle starts, so they are quite skilled at it. But since war is conducted for political purposes, as Clausewitz argued, political leaders have to be deeply engaged in the process. This case illustrates the lengthy and complex process followed to plan for the 2003 war against Iraq. It shows that two individuals—a determined secretary of defense and a stubborn combatant commander—can shape a war plan to fit their personal views.

Even after the Gulf War ended in 1991, the United States conducted regular military operations against Iraq and kept revising plans for major war. No-fly zones were established over northern and southern Iraq, and by 2002, more than 300,000 sorties had been flown. In 2002 alone, Iraq attacked coalition aircraft 500 times, leading to 90 retaliatory air strikes.

When Iraqi leader Saddam Hussein expelled United Nations (UN) monitors in December 1998, the United States responded with three days of bombing and cruise missile strikes in what was called Operation Desert Fox. CENTCOM Commander General Tony Zinni also revised the contingency war plan for a possible invasion of Iraq. His OPLAN 1003–98 envisioned using 380,000 troops.

Many officials joining the George W. Bush administration in 2001 regretted not finishing the job by removing Saddam Hussein in 1991. At the very first NSC meeting, the new president ordered his Pentagon leaders to "examine our military options" in Iraq. In July, Defense Secretary Donald Rumsfeld urged "a more robust policy" against Saddam Hussein.

Immediately after the 9/11 attacks, despite the lack of any evidence linking al-Qaeda to Iraq, Rumsfeld and his Deputy Paul Wolfowitz urged attacks on Iraq. Although Bush deferred that topic, on September 29, Rumsfeld told the incoming Chairman of the Joint Chiefs of Staff, General Richard Myers, to begin preparing military options for Iraq to achieve "regime change" and the location and destruction of Iraqi weapons of mass destruction (WMD).

By the end of November, with the Taliban government in Afghanistan overthrown, Bush ordered a new look at the Iraq war plan. Over the next 16 months, Rumsfeld worked closely and directly with the CENTCOM Commander, General Tommy Franks, supplementing frequent briefings and meetings with his snowflakes and memos. The previous practice had been for defense secretaries to work through the JCS chairman to the combatant commander, but Rumsfeld largely sidelined the chiefs and the Joint Staff. They were not formally briefed on the war plan until September 2002.

During the planning process, the defense secretary was "like a dentist's drill that never ceased," according to Franks. His staff faced a "daily barrage of tasks and questions [that] was beginning to border on harassment." Franks himself objected to JCS oversight of his planning or even participation in his video teleconferences with Rumsfeld. Two days before the start of the war, Franks sent a formal *letter of concern* to the Pentagon leadership. Though politely phrased, the point of his message was this: "Leave me the hell alone to run the war."

What Rumsfeld wanted was a lightning-fast attack followed by a rapid handover of power to Iraqis. He kept pressing Franks to reduce the number of troops needed. On at least six occasions during the course of the planning, Rumsfeld insisted on further cuts in ground troops. The final version called for 140,000 troops, compared to Zinni's 380,000. The secretary also wanted *off ramps* to divert unneeded troops if the battle went better than expected. From the start, the objectives remained unchanged: regime change and location and destruction of the WMDs. Franks never presented options short of major war, such as creating enclaves, supporting a guerrilla war, or limiting combat to airpower and SOF.

According to U.S. military doctrine, the plan had four phases: I, preparation; II, shape the battlespace; III, decisive operations; IV, posthostility operations. CENTCOM had responsibility for all phases but gave scant attention to Phase IV. Franks estimated he might need 250,000 troops for occupation and security duties but did not know how long they might be needed. While most of the military planners expected a quick victory, they shared other assumptions that proved to be incorrect. For example, most military officials believed that U.S. forces would be welcomed as liberators, that the Iraqi people yearned for democracy, that Iraqi could finance its own reconstruction, and that the professionalism of the Iraqi police, army, and government ministries would lead them to help coalition forces establish control and competent governance.

Just as Rumsfeld largely excluded the JCS and Joint Staff from detailed war planning, he also tried to limit the involvement of other departments. Civilian planners were not briefed on war plans until the summer of 2002. Rumsfeld then got Bush to sign a presidential directive in October 2002 giving DOD authority over postwar planning, but the office to do the job was not established until January 20, 2003, just two months before the start of the war. Staff from that office were then delayed in getting into Baghdad until mid-April, when they found that 17 of the 23 ministries they had hoped to restore under new leadership were gone, with the buildings looted and the workers fled. The widespread looting after the fall of Baghdad—which Rumsfeld dismissed as a sign of liberation: "Freedom's untidy," he said—was allowed because U.S. troops had not been given orders to prevent or stop it, and there were probably too few troops to have much success had they tried.

The JCS did influence some aspects of U.S. policy during the development of the final war plan. When civilians pressed for an earlier start to the U.S. attacks, the chiefs sided with Franks in urging more time and better weather. They also reportedly urged that congressional approval be sought for the attack—a position consistent with the U.S. military's post-Vietnam conditions for the use of major force.

Rumsfeld insisted on delaying mobilization deployment orders for some military forces because they were likely to become public. He also tinkered with the complex deployment plans that were designed to bring men and equipment together at the few available ports and airfields with the greatest efficiency. These actions caused enormous disruptions in the field.

In the final weeks before the start of the war, the president met with the JCS and heard their general support for the war plan despite some service-specific concerns. Retaliatory bombing raids were being directed against targets that would have been hit early in the ground combat phase. The battlespace had been prepared. Sufficient troops were in place, and follow-on units were en route. The president decided that diplomacy had failed and it was necessary to employ the military instrument of national power. Major combat began on March 19, 2003.

While tactical military success was achieved quickly and the Iraqi government overthrown, the failure to make adequate plans for the next phase of the operation led to numerous problems and additional years of combat. The war met its immediate military objectives but fell short of accomplishing its broader objectives, which included the creation of a stable, friendly, and democratic government in Baghdad. The military instrument, by itself, was insufficient to attain America's strategic goals.

---

*Sources:* Joseph J. Collins, "Opting for War: An Analysis of the Decision to Invade Iraq," *Project on National Security Reform, Case Studies, Vol. 1*, 9–58, accessible via www.pnsr.org.

Douglas J. Feith, *War and Decision* (New York: Harper, 2008).

General Tommy Franks, *American Soldier* (New York: Regan Books, 2004).

Richard Myers, *Eyes on the Horizon* (New York: Threshold Editions, 2009).

Michael R. Gordon and General Bernard E. Trainor, *Cobra II* (New York: Pantheon, 2006).

Bradley Graham, *By His Own Rules* (New York: Public Affairs, 2009).

Ron Suskind, *The Price of Loyalty* (New York: Simon & Schuster, 2004).

Bob Woodward, *Bush at War* (New York: Simon & Schuster, 2002).

Bob Woodward, *Plan of Attack* (New York: Simon & Schuster, 2004).

## Selected Resources

The main DOD website opens the door to a broad range of additional sites at www.defense.gov/.

Military doctrine is especially well outlined by these JCS publications:

Jt Pubs: interagency capabilities, www.dtic.mil/doctrine/new_pubs/jp3_08v2.pdf

Jt Ops 3–0, www.dtic.mil/doctrine/new_pubs/jp3_0.pdf

Jt Pub 1, www.dtic.mil/doctrine/new_pubs/jp1.pdf

Think tanks with excellent coverage of defense issues include: The Center for Strategic and Budgetary Assessments, www.csbaonline.org/; The Center for a New American Security, www.cnas.org/; the Center for Strategic and International Studies, http://csis.org/; the Rand Corporation, www.rand.org/; the Federation of American Scientists, www.fas.org/; and the International Institute for Strategic Studies, www.iiss.org/.

There are numerous scholarly and historical works on U.S. civil–military relations, including: Richard H. Kohn and Peter Feaver, *Soldiers and Civilians: The Civil–Military Gap and American National Security* (MIT Press, 2001); Peter Feaver, *Armed Servants: Agency, Oversight, and Civil-Military Relations* (Harvard University Press, March 2003); Charles A. Stevenson, *Warriors and Politicians: U.S. Civil–Military Relations Under Stress* (London: Routledge, 2006); Richard K. Betts, *Soldiers, Statesmen, and Cold War Crises* (Columbia University Press, Morningside edition, 1991).

# 9 The Secret Intelligence Instruments

*Policymakers crave certainty and abhor surprise. They come to office with more or less defined policy objectives that they hope to attain. They want to work on their priority agenda, not be sidetracked or deflected by unanticipated events. They look to the permanent civil service bureaucracy of government, including the intelligence community, to help them achieve those goals and feel let down that they do not get more help.*

—Deputy Secretary of State James Steinberg[1]

*Perhaps the most important thing to understand about covert action is that it is not a routine mission of the CIA, such as foreign intelligence collection or counterintelligence operations. Rather, covert action is very much an element of American presidential statecraft, joining the more familiar components of American foreign policy . . .*

—former CIA operative William J. Daugherty[2]

There are 16 members of the *intelligence community (IC),* responsive to presidential directions but largely hidden from public view. While much about their activities is broadly known, even more is suspected. The picture that emerges from declassified materials is of a set of large, well-funded organizations that do many things well and some things poorly. They are regularly blamed for alleged failures but cannot disclose many of their successes.

As reporters Dana Priest and William Arkin argue, "The CIA is the president's personal sword of power in foreign lands if all else fails, one he can use without asking Congress first."[3] Their comment applies to the entire IC, for presidents use the intelligence instruments to gather information not otherwise attainable, to analyze all available information, and to conduct activities that need to be kept secret. (See Table 9.1.) Intelligence organizations are thus key tools for U.S. foreign policy, gaining and providing analysis to aid decision making and then conducting operations when ordered. Each one has its own special capabilities and associated culture, though all share a preoccupation with secrecy.

231

| Table 9.1 | The Secret Intelligence Instrument Brief | |
|---|---|---|
| **ACTIONS** | **ADVANTAGES** | **DISADVANTAGES** |
| Collection | Multiple, highly specialized organizations | Competition for resources |
| Analysis | Professionalism | Resistance to information sharing |
| Operations | Highly secret | Subject to congressional oversight and blowback |
| **ROLE OF CONGRESS** | Overseer, policy legitimator | Leaks and criticism |
| **CULTURE** | Very secretive | Resists sharing information |

The nature of the IC's work leads to high competition, secrecy, and a reluctance to share, making each agency in the IC very protective of its independent roles.

## Secret Tools

Intelligence activities are cloaked in secrecy for many reasons. Collecting information abroad often requires breaking laws, stealing secrets, and bribing officials to betray their own nation's secrets. Governments do not like to acknowledge those truths. And, they certainly don't want their own spies to be jailed or executed for what they do.

Intelligence operatives want secrecy also in order to protect their sources and methods. Disclosure of information that could only have come from a clandestine listening device could lead to its destruction. Reporting information known only to a handful of people could jeopardize the life of the secret source.

Sometimes, governments want to do things without admitting any involvement, such as supporting a rebel group or financing a friendly foreign political party, where publicity could damage foreign relations or undermine the success of the enterprise.

Of course, secrecy can also be used to hide mistakes and misbehavior or simply to avoid political embarrassment. At least in the United States, there are laws and processes in place to reduce the abuse of secrecy, particularly through congressional oversight.

Secrecy is at the core of the IC's culture, separating members from the rest of the government and binding them together but still separated by *the need to know*. Intelligence personnel are adamant about secrecy when other officials are more relaxed. Confirming what is already reported in newspapers seems reasonable to political appointees used to living in the public sphere but still treasonable to those whose careers require secrecy. As former Director of Central Intelligence (and later Secretary of Defense) Robert Gates has written, "[T]he work of spies makes risk routine and danger the companion of every day's work. For them secrecy is not a convenience or a bureaucratic matter, but the essential tool of their craft."[4]

Most governments concentrate control over secret instruments in very few hands. In the United States, only the president can activate and use the most sensitive tools, and only the president can override the secrecy classifications imposed by subordinates.

# The Long History of Secret Programs

The men who won the revolution and created a national government for the United States knew the value of spies and secret dealings. The very First Congress passed a law allowing the president to spend $40,000 per year "for the support of such persons as he shall commission to serve the United States in foreign parts." And despite the Constitution's clear requirement for disclosure of a "statement and account" of expenditures of public money, lawmakers allowed secrecy in this case.[5]

The United States paid spies and gathered intelligence throughout the 19th century, but the effort was small and sporadic, except for wartime increases. The army and navy created military intelligence units in the 1880s. The U.S. government also played a not-very-covert role in the 1903 rebellion of Panama from Colombia, thereby allowing a canal to be built and enabling Theodore Roosevelt to boast, "I took Panama."

Despite U.S. code-breaking successes during World War I and the naval conferences in the 1920s, incoming Secretary of State Henry Stimson cut off his department's funding of the State–Army cryptanalysis office in 1929, famously saying, "Gentlemen do not read each other's mail." He had a different view when he was secretary of war during World War II.[6]

Secret operations peaked in World War II with the building of atomic bombs, very successful code breaking, and the intelligence operations of the Office of Strategic Services (OSS), the direct predecessor of the Central Intelligence Agency (CIA). Although Harry Truman disbanded the OSS at the end of the war, he agreed to the creation of the CIA as part of the National Security Act of 1947.

The new CIA was limited to overseas activities because lawmakers feared creating an American "Gestapo." But, Congress also wanted to prevent another Pearl Harbor, where intelligence was not shared or well coordinated, leading to the devastating surprise attacks of December 7, 1941. From the start, the new agency combined the talents of well-schooled analysts and gung-ho spies.

Throughout the 1950s and 1960s, the CIA and other components of the IC expanded their capabilities of technical collection—such as the high-flying U-2 spy plane and space satellites—and put their human agents to work overthrowing governments in Iran and Guatemala, tried to do so in Cuba and Indonesia, and also worked to prop up friendly governments in Western Europe and South Vietnam.

In the early 1970s, however, disclosures of some of these activities and other questionable ones, like assassination attempts on Fidel Castro, led to a public outcry and major congressional investigations. As a result, Congress created special committees to conduct regular oversight of intelligence activities, and later presidents issued executive orders limiting what intelligence operatives were allowed to do. Special committees were established in the executive branch to review and monitor covert operations.

The 9/11 attacks prompted a reexamination of the IC's structure and processes. As in the case of Pearl Harbor, there was a surprise attack that might have been prevented if those with bits and pieces of information had shared them with others and if senior leaders had responded more forcefully to the warnings they were given. The 9/11 Commission documented the failure and recommended the creation of a stronger central manager, a director of national intelligence (DNI), separate from the head of the CIA. The 2004 law creating the DNI fell short of giving him full directive and budget authority over the members of the IC, however, because of Pentagon resistance. Nor did Congress go along with the commission's recommendation of a single joint intelligence panel on Capitol Hill with both authorization and appropriations power.

# Major Institutions

While the components of the IC share a concern for secrecy and are supposed to work together, they have separate and distinct capabilities that they contribute to intelligence products and activities. (See Figure 9.1.) The president has to understand what each can do and what each does well in order to allocate budget resources and to assign special tasks.

### Office of the Director of National Intelligence

The IC today is headed by the DNI and a large staff, estimated to be 1,700 federal workers and 1,200 private contractors. Critics of the Direct of Central Intelligence (DCI) system argued that the DCI spent too much time overseeing the CIA and had too little power to direct the rest of the IC. The DNI was made the principal intelligence adviser to the president and the NSC. The official oversees and directs the NIP, which in 2011, was $54.6 billion, but the MIP of $24 billion remains under the control of the Pentagon. The NIP includes activities responding to the needs and priorities of national policy officials, while the MIP is focused on the needs and priorities of DOD and the armed services. These figures are said to be two and a half times the size of the IC budget at the time of the 9/11 attacks.[7]

The law creating the DNI position was a compromise. The DNI was given some added authorities over budget development and for transfers of people and resources but not full hire-and-fire or budgeting power. In fact, lawmakers included a provision demanded by the Pentagon that cautioned the DNI to use his authorities "in a manner that respects and does not

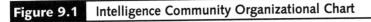

**Figure 9.1** **Intelligence Community Organizational Chart**

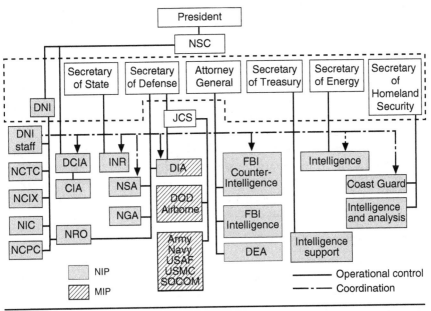

The DNI has direct operational control over only a few components of the IC and relies on coordination with the rest. The congressional intelligence committees oversee the National Intelligence Program (NIP), while the armed services committees oversee the Military Intelligence Program (MIP).

*Source:* Mark M. Lowenthal, *Intelligence: From Secrets to Policy,* Fourth Edition (Washington, DC: CQ Press, 2009). Used with permission of Mark M. Lowenthal.

abrogate the statutory responsibilities of the heads of the departments of the U.S. government."[8]

As a result, the assessments of the effectiveness of the Office of the Director of National Intelligence (ODNI) are mixed. A congressional research service summary in 2010 found lawmakers unwilling to undo creation of ODNI but also unwilling to create a fully empowered Department of Intelligence. An official who served in one of the top ODNI positions, Thomas Fingar, concluded that the impact of the office on the IC had been "limited by ambiguity, ambivalence, and animosity." He also says, "Key elements of the IC continue to resist that vision [of a single integrating enterprise], view colleagues as competitors, and disparage the work of fellow professionals."[9]

Former CIA Director Robert Gates, who turned down the DNI job before later becoming secretary of defense, said, "My view is that the compromises that were made in passing the Intelligence Reform Act really inhibited the ability of the DNI to carry out what most people thought the DNI should do. He has authorities and he has power, but at the end of the day, he's got to sort of lead and persuade people to follow in all these disparate organizations."[10]

Further evidence of the uncertain standing of the DNI comes from the fact that the first director quit after two years to take a lesser-ranking post at the State Department. His successor complained that he was only the coordinator and not really director of national intelligence. And, President Obama's first nominee for the post was fired after repeated conflicts with the CIA director and other missteps.[11]

ODNI runs several important units, including the National Counterterrorism Center (NCTC), the National Intelligence Council (NIC), and centers for counterproliferation and intelligence coordination. One of its major outputs is the President's Daily Brief (PDB), the highly classified intelligence summary circulated each day to a handful of senior officials.

Observers say the ODNI has not developed its own integrating culture. It "has no hoary traditions, limited staff loyalty, and few routinized procedures."[12] Only half its workforce are permanent staff. The remainder rotate in and out from IC components and thus are expected to show primary loyalty to their home organizations.

## Central Intelligence Agency

The CIA is no longer central, but it is still large, skilled, and important. The agency has three core missions: all-source analysis; managing human intelligence (HUMINT) operations, that is, recruiting and running spies; and conducting covert operations.[13]

The CIA has gained a host of critics and defenders over the years. Most of them clash over what the agency has done, especially in the realm of covert actions against foreign governments and whether the acts were effective and morally defensible. Some critics argue that agency analysts made wrong judgments, particularly on Soviet military spending and capabilities. Even former DCI Robert Gates acknowledged that CIA underestimated the pace of Soviet military programs in the 1960s and overestimated them in the 1980s and that it overestimated the size of the Soviet economy and underestimated the burden of military spending on that economy and its people. But, he says actual estimates of current Soviet military strength were quite good.[14]

Some critics say that the agency has become too cautious, perhaps because of disclosures of secret activities or because of past criticism from Congress and the media. Richard Clarke, who was the NSC staffer for counterterrorism under Presidents Clinton and Bush, complained about CIA reluctance to do more in Afghanistan, labeling the agency *risk averse*. He also quotes former Secretary of State Madeleine Albright's observation that CIA acted in a passive-aggressive way, as if "it has battered child syndrome." A retired CIA analyst counters, "What critics call risk aversion, professionals call common sense or good political judgment."[15]

CIA has about 20,000 people and four directorates, each drawing on quite different people and skill sets. The Directorate of Intelligence (DI) does the analysis and prepares the reports. The Directorate of Science and Technology (DS&T) exploits science to improve collection of information and protection of assets. The Directorate of Support (DS) manages the facilities, communications, payroll, and logistics for the agency.[16]

Most notable, or notorious, is the Directorate of Operations (DO), now renamed the National Clandestine Service (NCS). These are the spies abroad and the covert operators whose exploits, real or imagined, are the stuff of thrillers. While the analysts and scientists would not be out of place in a university, the NCS operatives are a separate guild, often recruited from the military and business worlds and trained separately from other agency personnel. They have a can-do culture and an obsession with secrecy.[17]

Agency observers say that the NCS culture dominates the CIA, reinforcing the need for secrecy and the protection of people, sources, and methods. The analysts have their own subset culture, adding commitments to professionalism and objectivity. They like to quote Sherman Kent, an OSS veteran who headed the DI in the early years. He said intelligence officers are supposed "to stand behind [policy makers] with the book open at the right page, to call their attention to the stubborn fact they may be neglecting, and—at their request—to analyze alternative courses without indicating choice."[18]

CIA personnel do feel that they are *the president's own,* on call to the chief executive for analysis and action and responsive to his orders. Often, CIA people are detailed to the NSC staff, and that staff regularly consults with agency people and asks for briefing memos that can be part of NSC submissions to the president. Vice President Dick Cheney developed his own agency contacts and pressed them for information related to his policy interests.[19]

The creation of ODNI posed various challenges to the CIA, once its director was no longer the overall IC director and no longer the daily briefer of the president. President Obama's appointees to the CIA and DNI slots reportedly clashed over who got to assign the top U.S. intelligence official in overseas embassies and other bureaucratic issues. In that case, the CIA won, but turf issues remain unresolved in the IC.

### Pentagon Management

Historically, those intelligence activities not assigned to the CIA fell under the control and management of DOD. The armed services had their own intelligence units for tactical and operational needs, and military planners had their own requirements for information about potential enemies and their capabilities.

The Pentagon also had the processes left over from World War II for secret budgets and programs as well as operational units that gathered electronic and signals intelligence. Consequently, the funds for much of the IC's activities are concealed within the DOD budget and ultimately controlled by the secretary of defense. Four major components of the NIP are DOD run: Defense Intelligence Agency (DIA), National Security Agency (NSA), National Reconnaissance Office (NRO), and National Geospatial-Intelligence Agency.

**Defense Intelligence Agency.** The DIA was created in 1961 in order to corral service intelligence activities and provide coordinated, all-source analyses of matters of interest to the Pentagon and the armed forces. The mission of its 16,500 people is to "provide timely and objective military intelligence to warfighters, policymakers, and force planners." The army, navy, air force, and marine corps retain units for tactical and operational intelligence for their service. But, DIA runs the defense attachés posted to U.S. embassies.[20]

The wars in Iraq and Afghanistan have placed extraordinary demands on military intelligence that sometimes conflict with priorities outside the war zone. One reason Congress limited the DNI's ability to direct DOD-run organizations was precisely the concerns about wartime requirements.

**National Security Agency.** The NSA was secretly established in 1952 as the principal agency for collection of signals intelligence (SIGINT) and code-breaking. SIGINT includes both communications intelligence (messages between individuals) and electronic intelligence (from electronic signals like radar). NSA is also responsible for information assurance, meaning creating the codes and communications procedures for government agencies with national security responsibilities. Long known as No Such Agency, its 20,000 personnel can now admit they work there.[21]

**National Reconnaissance Office.** The NRO's existence was not officially declassified until 1992, although it had been in existence since 1961, when it was created as an Air Force–CIA umbrella organization in charge of the U-2 spy planes and intelligence-gathering satellites. NRO has about 3,000 people and spends a lot of money developing, launching, and operating reconnaissance satellites for what is called *imagery intelligence* (IMINT).[22]

**National Geospatial-Intelligence Agency.** The National Geospatial-Intelligence Agency began in 1996 as the National Imagery and Mapping Agency. It has 8,500 people whose basic job is to turn imagery intelligence into maps and other depictions of geographical spaces that can be used for analysis and operations.[23] They can develop products that overlay terrain features with intelligence reports and weather data. Such information has been used for military operations, humanitarian relief, and support for diplomatic negotiations where terrain issues arise.

**State Department's Bureau of Intelligence and Research.** The Bureau of Intelligence and Research is the State Department's CIA, its own 300-person office providing all-source analyses on matters of special interest to the secretary, the department, and embassies overseas. Its staff produce regional and functional reports and participate for State in the NIC.[24]

### Other Intelligence Community Components

Several other cabinet departments have intelligence units that are part of the IC but are focused on the special responsibilities of their respective departments. The Justice Department has two components—the Federal

Bureau of Investigation's National Security Branch, which has responsibilities for counterintelligence and counterterrorism, and the Drug Enforcement Administration (DEA), which follows drug-trafficking organizations and provides other drug-related intelligence to IC members. The Department of Homeland Security (DHS) has a special Office of Intelligence and Analysis (OIA) to provide intelligence to state and local governments and private-sector partners on homeland security issues. The coast guard, now part of DHS, has long had its own intelligence units, which are now focused on counter-narcotics, port security, and immigrations interdictions. The Department of Energy has intelligence units focused mainly on other nation's nuclear capabilities. And the Department of the Treasury has an office of intelligence and analysis under the office of terrorism and financial intelligence.[25]

One emerging issue is the increased use of contractor personnel in intelligence jobs. In 2008, an official said that the roughly 100,000 government employees in the IC were assisted by 36,000 people on contract. About 22% of those contracted people did computer or information technology work, but 19% were involved in analysis. Some 27% were said to be involved in intelligence collection and operations.[26]

While many of these people were added to handle the informational and operational demands of the Iraq and Afghanistan wars and counterterrorism, the large numbers raised questions of government accountability and a brain drain of experienced people seeking higher salaries.

# Major Processes

The intelligence process is often described as a predictable sequence from requirements to collection to processing and exploitation to analysis to dissemination to consumption. In practice, there is regular feedback and often backtracking in order to make adjustments before proceeding forward.[27] For our purposes, it is useful to look at the three major processes where the president plays a role: collection, analysis, and operations.

### Collection

Several parts of the IC are specialized for collection of particular kinds of intelligence. The CIA has the lead for HUMINT, or old-fashioned spying. NSA is the principal organization for SIGINT, which includes intercepting communications and electronic emissions like weapons telemetry. NRO builds and operates satellites that gather various types of intelligence. NGA acquires geospatial intelligence (GEOINT), including photographic and other imagery intelligence linked to terrain—and processes it with SIGINT from NSA. NGA and DIA are the agencies principally responsible for measurement and signatures intelligence (MASINT), involving identifying and analyzing environmental byproducts of activities like weapons tests and the uses of industrial facilities.[28]

Intelligence collectors are professionals and are proud of their work. But, they may also develop stovepiped thinking that makes it hard for them to acknowledge the value of other collectors, especially if the issue is where to assign the marginal budget dollar when resources are tight.

In order to capture this intelligence, the government needs the collection capabilities and associated people—and then it needs to decide to target particular places and subjects. That means deciding in advance what images or emissions or other intelligence will be important tomorrow and next week and next year, for collection assets have to be assigned, and more focus on one area means less on another. As an example, journalists Dana Priest and Bill Arkin report that collection systems at the NSA intercept and store 1.7 billion e-mails, phone calls, and other types of communications every day and then sort a fraction of those into 70 separate databases.[29]

Starting in the Clinton administration, the president issued a formal order, called a Presidential Policy Directive (PPD) that established a tier system for intelligence collection. As described by the Federation of American Scientists:

> Tier 0 is warning and crisis management. Tier 4 is countries that are virtually of no interest to the United States. The PDD specifically identifies targets that the US intelligence community will not collect against. Under PDD 35 the highest priority is assigned to intelligence Support to Military Operations (SMO). The second priority is providing political, economic, and military intelligence on countries hostile to the United States to help to stop crises and conflicts before they start. Third priority is assigned to protecting American citizens from new trans-national threats such as drug traffickers, terrorists, organized criminals, and weapons of mass destruction. High priority is also assigned to Intelligence support to activities addressing counterproliferation, as well as international terrorism, crime and drugs. The Directive increased the priority assigned by the intelligence collection and analysis capabilities to the proliferation threat.[30]

The G. W. Bush administration developed an elaborate priority system that is now a matrix of functional issues plotted against nations and other groups. It gets reviewed every six months, and the decision makers have to make hard choices whether to reduce priority for some once-important issues in order to increase attention to something else.[31]

### Analysis

Instead of a case study on how intelligence products are developed, we have included in this chapter several declassified documents showing what senior officials were told by the IC. There are, however, numerous public accounts of how the Special National Intelligence Estimate (NIE) on Iraq was fashioned in 2002.[32]

Collected intelligence needs to be processed and evaluated then sent on for further analysis and incorporation into the reports and estimates that are the chief products of the IC. As former DCI Richard Helms wrote, "Casting aside the perceived—and I must admit the occasionally real—excitement of secret operations, the absolute essence of the intelligence profession rests in the production of current intelligence reports, memoranda, and National Estimates on which sound policy decisions can be made."[33]

The culture of analysts is that of skepticism. As former CIA official Mark Lowenthal notes, "Their training teaches them to question and to doubt. Although they may see an optimistic outcome to a given situation, they also see the pessimistic outcomes and likely feel compelled to analyze them as potential outcomes."[34]

Analysts are also human and therefore subject to human frailties. Lowenthal says analysts sometimes are guilty of adopting various mind-sets that shape their analyses. One is mirror-imaging, presuming that other leaders or nations share motivations similar to their own. Another flaw is clientism, when they have become so immersed in a subject that they lose perspective and "go native." Analysts may also commit layering, when they draw upon earlier work and fail to include the assumptions and uncertainties that may have influenced those judgments. Lowenthal also notes that the all-source analysts at CIA, DIA, and the State Department's INR can fall into analytical stovepipes where they disparage the work done elsewhere.[35]

Another flaw, noted by former DCI Robert Gates, is that "the CIA knew how foreign policy was made in every country of the world but one—our own." Analysts didn't realize how the president's schedule of meetings with foreign leaders, overseas trips, or current issue discussions would affect his need for information from the IC.[36]

Still another flaw is the politicization of analysis, where analysts tailor their reports to be consistent with the views and policy preferences of the president and other senior officials. A former senior CIA analyst describes the process as a *joust*. Paul Pillar writes, "Policymakers . . . would press intelligence officers—always in one substantive direction, never in the other—and keep pressing as long as sought-after conclusions were not yet forthcoming. They would stop short of blatant arm twisting to maintain the appearance that the analysts were only being healthily challenged, not pressured. Intelligence officers would cope with the pressure while trying to remain consistent with common standards of analytic tradecraft and objectivity. The joust typically would conclude with inventive wordsmithing that met each side's minimum requirements in the competition."[37] Analysts also know that their careers would be helped by praise from above and could be derailed if superiors concluded they were not team players.

Analysts prepare numerous reports and give briefings on demand, but its premier product is the PDB, the highly classified summary of information deemed most urgent and important for the president to know. (See Box 9.1.) Only a handful of copies of the PDB are circulated to senior officials; other less-sensitive but still highly classified reports get wider circulation in the Worldwide Intelligence Review (WIRe). Since 2004, preparation of the PDB has been done by the newly created DNI's office. At times, depending on the preferences of the president, the DCI or DNI personally briefed the chief executive. At other times, a designated briefer, often accompanied by

---

| Box 9.1 |

# How Foreign Policy Is Made: Examining the President's Daily Brief, April 1, 1968

Very few PBDs have ever been declassified, but the example here from the Lyndon Johnson (LBJ) administration during the Vietnam War gives you a flavor of what gets included. Note how short the items are. The in-person briefers can supply longer background materials if requested, but presidents have very limited time.

The PDB leads with the most important information from the war zone but also includes entries on other countries. This PDB addresses North and South Vietnam, Panama, Brazil, Cyprus, and Egypt. Aside from the Vietnam coverage, these are not really breaking-news items but teasers on other developments the analysts want to flag for the president's attention.

On Vietnam, the PDB warns the president that Hanoi is planning a summer offensive and that 17,000 North Vietnamese troops have been discovered moving south. The document also tells the latest in the power struggle among generals in South Vietnam. Neither report could have given the president much confidence about progress in the war.

The PDB alerts the president to unrest in Latin America. It suggests that a political dispute in Panama will lead to a military takeover. And in Brazil, it says that the military dictatorship there is unhappy with the government's handling of student demonstrations, which have "widespread sympathy" among the public but are now being led by "extremists."

The PDB also mentions a couple of developments in order to say that they are not significant—talks in Cyprus aren't likely to lead to anything, and Egyptian President Nasser's political reform promises won't amount to much.

If you received this PBD, what follow-up questions would you ask? What taskings, if any, would you send to your advisers and cabinet members?

\* \* \*

SANITIZED

The President's Daily Brief

1 April 1968

1. North Vietnam    [████] Hanoi reports the Vietnamese Communists are organizing a broad offensive to take place in South Vietnam this summer. [████] Hanoi expects the offensive to set the stage for a settlement on Communist terms and that the US will accept an "armistice" by early next year. [██] report that a special mobilization of manpower is under way in North Vietnam to provide large numbers of new forces for the South.

\* \* \*

What appear to be eight more infiltration groups were discovered [████] over the weekend, raising the number of units en route through central North Vietnam in March [████] More than 17,000 troops could be involved.

2. South Vietnam    Vice President Ky, chief of the Joint General Staff Vien, and at least three of the four corps commanders plan to submit their resignations en masse unless Thieu resolves certain doubts and agrees to consult them closely on

(Continued)

policy, according to [████] These doubts include rumors that Thieu is embarking on wholesale personnel changes which would revive the influence of the Dai Viet party at the expense of the military hierarchy.

The commanders are already disturbed by Thieu's recent provincial appointments which they see as a substitution of Thieu's followers for their own protégés or as creating unrest among province chiefs and military officers in general.

3. Panama  The Supreme Court will reconvene today to decide on the constitutionality of the Assembly's impeachment of Robles. No matter how the court rules, the situation is likely to deteriorate further.

The people around Arnulfo Arias are now working on more legal moves against the government, and are also keeping pressure on Robles and the National Guard through demonstrations and disorders. If the court invalidates the impeachment, Arias and company are prepared to impeach the court.

Pro-Arias demonstrators plan to be in the streets "to create an atmosphere of tension" while the court is deliberating. Influential families on both sides are becoming more and more convinced that a takeover by the guard is the only solution . . .

*Source:* The PDB, CIA, April 1, 1968.

---

an issue expert on the day's major topic, would perform that task.[38] To see the sorts of things included in a PDB, look at the copy of one of the few ever declassified.

The PBD document and knowledgeable briefers go to the president every day. (See Box 9.2.) In the Obama administration, the regular briefing usually included the vice president, the White House chief of staff, the NSA, and the deputy for homeland security. The sessions ranged from getting presidential directions for work on particular issues to what was called *blue sky* thinking on policy development. Presidents often raise questions or make comments that lead to additional activities by the IC. Those questions, of course, indicate areas of presidential interest or inquiry, creating valuable feedback to analysts preparing the next day's PDB and future activities. Throughout the process, analysts and senior officials recognize that the president is *the first customer,* and that intelligence materials have to be suited to his needs. This process of daily production creates a sense of urgency and time pressure. One analyst comments that he had not joined a university so much as a government-run newspaper business.[39]

Longer-term and broader focus intelligence studies include the all-source, all-community NIEs that may take months to prepare under the direction of specialists on the NIC. (See Box 9.3.)

From the standpoint of senior policy makers, there are two key problems with current intelligence analysis. There are too many reports: The sheer size of the IC probably involves a proliferation of reports that may overwhelm the intended recipients. Priest and Arkin estimate that more than 50,000 intelligence reports are published each year under 1,500 titles. The number

---

**Box 9.2**

## Inside View: The President's Daily Intelligence Briefing

Former DCI George Tenet describes his regular morning sessions in the Oval Office with an oral version of the PDB. He shows how much personal chemistry and management style mattered. These briefings remain the most important way a president can give the IC guidance and taskings.

*Around 8:00 A.M., the briefer and I would go across the street to the West Wing of the White House and troop up the back stairs to the Oval Office. The actual briefing would generally take between thirty and forty-five minutes—an hour when things were really busy. The vice president, Dick Cheney; Condoleezza Rice, then national security adviser; and Andy Card, the president's chief of staff, always sat in unless they were out of town. The briefer would usually 'tee up the piece,' explaining each PDB article's background or context, and then hand each item to the president to read. Often there would be additional material to flesh out the story—the nitty-gritty on how we had stolen the secrets contained in the item, and the like. Everyone loves a good spy story. More important, it was an opportunity to pull back the curtain, to talk to the president about a sensitive source or a collection method. The written items were generally short, and the president would read them carefully. Sometimes he would start tossing out questions before getting to the bottom line . . .*

*Source:* George Tenet, *At the Center of the Storm* (New York: HarperCollins, 2007), 32.

---

is so large that, in 2010, a new online newspaper, *Intelligence Today*, was created to summarize the greatest hits appearing elsewhere.[40]

The second problem is that the products often fail to give officials the certainty and clarity they most want, as indicated by Jim Steinberg's quote at the start of this chapter. Analysts respond that they live in a world of uncertainty and can only try to manage it. They also argue that prediction is not the best way to judge intelligence products because it performs so many other functions—identifying trends, documenting threats, listing possibilities and even likelihoods—that are helpful to policy makers even if they do not predict the timing of particular events.[41]

### Operations

Various activities are conducted to collect intelligence, some of them illegal in the places they are carried out. That's what espionage historically involves. It takes people with certain mind-sets and skill sets to run agents and steal secrets successfully. Collection in denied areas like the Soviet-era Kremlin or behind enemy lines in war zones also requires skill and bravery. Observers have noted that this operational culture pervaded the upper ranks of the CIA for many years, not only in the clandestine service.[42]

Since the 1970s, Congress and the president have made an important legal distinction between operations to gather intelligence and operations

---

| **Box 9.3** |

## How Foreign Policy Is Made: Key Judgments From a National Intelligence Estimate, Saddam Hussein, June 18, 1992

A year after the end of the first Gulf War, the IC produced this National NIE on Saddam Hussein's hold on power in Iraq. Policy makers wanted to know how viable the regime was and what might lead to its overthrow. While many senior officials had expected Saddam Hussein to be ousted after losing the war, the NIE judgment was that he had grown stronger in the past year and that the greatest threat to him was a military coup, not a popular revolt.

Policy makers also wondered whether international sanctions were being effective. The NIE's judgment pointed to two effects: increased public disaffection with his leadership but also increased popular resentment toward the West. Analysts said Saddam Hussein probably concluded that international support for continuing the sanctions was lessening, so he had weathered the storm.

One immediate policy question facing the George H. W. Bush administration was whether to continue Operation Provide Comfort, the U.S. flights enforcing a no-fly zone over northern Iraq. The NIE does seem to support the operation as it warns that, otherwise, the Iraqi leader would likely act to suppress the Kurds if Operation Provide Comfort were halted.

If you were a senior official receiving this report, how would it influence your policy choices for Iraq? Would you favor continued sanctions or other courses of action?

\* \* \*

Key Judgments

Saddam Husayn [sic]: Likely to Hang On▮▮▮

Saddam Husayn is likely to survive the political and economic challenges of the next year. Although he is significantly weaker than he was before the Gulf war, he appears stronger than he was a year ago. The only real threat to Saddam remaining in power over the next year is from a sudden, violent effort to remove him by one or more people with access to him.

▮▮▮▮

If we are wrong in our judgment about Saddam's survival, it is most likely in underestimating the current degree of unhappiness in the military and in the Sunni core that have provided Saddam's base of power. Important individuals in the inner circle and in the Republican Guard might be ready to mount a coup against Saddam. A popular revolt is much less likely. ▮▮▮

Saddam will continue to use the Army, the Republican Guard, and intelligence and security forces to stifle dissent, reassert his control over Iraq, and prevent the emergence of any potential rival. The resumption of Air Force fixed-wing flight activity in April probably added to public perceptions that the regime is growing stronger and that citizens are powerful to bring about change ▮▮▮

Economic sanctions alone are not likely to bring about Saddam's removal, but they will contribute to public disaffection with his leadership. Sanctions may also

*(Continued)*

(Continued)

be increasing popular resentment toward the West. Despite sanctions, Saddam has managed his core support group by providing goods and services not available to the masses. Saddam probably believes that Iraq has withstood the brunt of the sanctions and that international support for sanctions is flagging. [██]

Saddam will continue to test coalition resolve by using economic pressure and increasingly intimidating military positioning against the Kurds in northern Iraq. Should Provide Comfort not be extended, he would be freer to expand his operations in the north—and may hope for Turkish collusion in suppressing the Kurds. He will also be more likely to act against the Kurds if he thinks they are acquiring attributes of statehood. In addition, his success in restricting international attention to the plight of the Shias in the marshlands of southern Iraq permits him to carry out a ruthless, but probably only partially effective, military campaign against them. [████]

*Source:* DCI, NIE: Saddam Husayn: Likely to Hang On, NIE 92–7, June 18, 1992.

for certain other purposes. These latter are called *covert actions* or *special activities* and are subject to careful presidential review and approval. President Reagan issued Executive Order 12333, still in effect, that defined covert actions as "special activities conducted in support of national foreign policy objectives abroad which are planned and executed so that the role of the United States Government is not apparent or acknowledged publicly" but are not intended to influence domestic U.S. policies or public opinion.[43]

Congress enacted a similar definition in 1991 in setting forth a process for conducting such operations. It says: "Covert Action is an activity or activities of the United States Government to influence political, economic, or military conditions abroad, where it is intended that the role of the United States Government will not be apparent or acknowledged publicly." This law also excluded intelligence acquisition or counterintelligence activities, "traditional diplomatic or military activities," and law enforcement activities.[44]

Simply put, these definitions make clear that covert actions are to influence foreigners secretly in support of American foreign policy goals. The techniques involved are usually labeled propaganda, political action, paramilitary activities, and information warfare.[45]

Propaganda is said to be the most extensive type of covert action, spreading messages to support U.S. policy through various overt and covert channels. In the early years of the Cold War, the CIA secretly funded Radio Free Europe and Radio Liberty to broadcast programs behind the Iron Curtain.

Political actions are used to influence the political situation in a foreign country. Starting with efforts to build up anticommunist parties in Italy and France after World War II, money, advice, and equipment to support political movements and candidates are the typical tools for political action. In the 1990s, the CIA gave support to Iraqi dissident groups. CIA personnel were reportedly sent to Libya in 2011 to give certain kinds of assistance to anti-Qaddafi rebels.[46]

Paramilitary operations can secretly train foreign military and security forces. This was done on a large scale in Laos in the 1960s and more modestly in Persian Gulf states in the 1980s. CIA support to U.S. military operations was a major activity in Somalia and Bosnia in the 1990s. CIA-run paramilitary operations were significant in Afghanistan after the 9/11 attacks and have continued in recent years in Iraq, Afghanistan, and Pakistan.

Information warfare now includes hacking and full-scale cyberwar where the purpose is to hinder a target's capabilities and not merely obtain intelligence. The IC is only one part of the diverse U.S. government array of agencies involved in cybersecurity, both offensive and defensive, as discussed further in Chapter 10.

Close cooperation between CIA paramilitary forces and regular American special operations forces (SOF) is highly valued but hard to achieve. Many of their missions overlap. Both can conduct and train others in unconventional warfare, foreign internal defense, information warfare, and psychological operations. Yet, both value their independence, especially their freedom from a heavy, bureaucratic chain of command. Some analysts contend that Defense Secretary Rumsfeld's promotion of DOD-run SOF and his resistance to the use of CIA paramilitary forces in Afghanistan was driven both by a determination to win credit for the Pentagon and avoid the process of notifying Congress that is required for covert action missions.[47]

Notifying Congress was a special requirement added by the Hughes–Ryan Amendment in 1974 and revised to be more specific in the 1991 legislation. In response to news articles disclosing CIA covert operations in earlier years, Congress adopted the Hughes–Ryan Amendment to (1) require the president personally to approve all such operations and (2) require notification of the appropriate committees of Congress of all covert actions not merely to collect intelligence. In 1991, Congress revised the law to cover ambiguities exposed in the Iran-Contra scandal. The still-current law requires a presidential finding in writing in advance of the operation with a specification that the action is "necessary to support identifiable foreign policy objectives," with a list of all participating U.S. government entities, followed by notification to Congress within 48 hours. The law allows the president, in "extraordinary circumstances," to limit notification to the House and Senate leadership and the four senior intelligence committee members—sometimes called "the gang of eight."[48]

To comply with the law, subsequent administrations established a careful process, starting with a presidential request to the CIA to begin planning a covert action. The CIA has review groups to process the paperwork, including the required finding that the president must sign. Those materials go to the NSC staff, which moves it from the lowest interagency committee on intelligence matters to the deputies committee and then to the president and full NSC.[49] One of the few declassified presidential findings is the one by President Reagan on Nicaragua. (See Box 9.4.)

---

┤ **Box 9.4** ├

## How Foreign Policy Is Made: Presidential Finding for Covert Action: Nicaragua, September 19, 1983

Congress passed a law in December 1982 forbidding support for the antigovernment contras in Nicaragua "for the purpose of overthrowing the government of Nicaragua or provoking a military exchange between Nicaragua and Honduras." The Reagan administration claimed that it was abiding by the law, but some intelligence committee members believed it wasn't. To help calm fears and win support for its covert action, the president signed a new finding governing the operation on September 19, 1983, and informed the intelligence committees, as required by law.

As you can see from the provided excerpt, the finding says that the "goal" is persuading the Sandinista government to have "meaningful negotiations" with its neighbors and to end their support for regional insurgencies. It says that U.S. agents will train paramilitary units to attack various targets in order to "raise the price" for Cuban and Sandinista forces. It also reports that "financial and material" support will be given to opposition leaders in Nicaragua, including support for propaganda efforts. The cost is estimated to be $33 million. On the basis of this finding and assurances from the CIA director, the intelligence committees voted to allow the program but capped its cost at $24 million.

If you were on the intelligence committee receiving this finding, would you be reassured that the law was being followed? What questions would you raise in a classified hearing?

### SCOPE OF CIA ACTIVITIES UNDER THE NICARAGUA FINDING

The Finding replaces the 1 December 1981 Finding which authorized certain covert action programs in Nicaragua and Central America. This program remains a critical element of U.S. policy in the region which recognizes that Nicaragua's Sandinista regime, with Soviet and Cuban active support, is implementing a strategy of full support for insurgent elements whose aim is the overthrow of democratic governments in the region. The political and paramilitary pressures created by this program are linked and are essential (1) to enable friendly Central American nations to strengthen democratic political institutions and achieve economic and social development, free from Soviet, Cuban, and Sandanista interference and (2) to induce a negotiated political resolution of international tensions in Central America.

This Finding authorizes the provision of material support and guidance to Nicaraguan resistance groups; its goal is to induce the Sandinista government in Nicaragua to enter into meaningful negotiations with its neighboring nations; and to induce the Sandinistas and the Cubans and their allies to cease their provision of arms, training, command and control facilities and sanctuary to regional insurgencies. This support is to be provided [■] in cooperation with others, as appropriate. The provision of political support and funding to opposition leaders and organization [■] in order to maintain their visibility is also authorized.

**POLITICAL ACTION:** Financial and material support will be provided to Nicaraguan opposition leaders and organizations to enable them to deal with the Sandanistas

*(Continued)*

(Continued)

from a position of political strength and to continue to exert political pressure on the Sandanistas to return to the original premises of the revolution—free elections political pluralism, basic human rights and a free press.

**PARAMILITARY ACTION**: Arms and other support will be provided to Nicaraguan paramilitary forces operating inside Nicaragua for the purpose of pressuring the Sandanista government and its Cuban supports to cease their support for regional insurgencies. [■■] instructors will train these forces to attack targets in Nicaragua in order to deny facilities, interrupt support networks and to raise the price the Cubans and Nicaraguans and their allies must pay for continued support of insurgent groups elsewhere in Central America. [■■■]. . . .

**FUNDING REQUIRED**: $19,000,000 is included in the Fiscal Year 1984 CIA budget for this program. Additional funding requirements, to be determined by developments in the area, could be as much as $14,000,000. Any such additional funding will have to come from the Agency's Reserve for Contingencies or other authorized sources . . .

*Source:* Presidential Finding for Covert Action, Scope of CIA Activities under the Nicaragua Finding, September 19, 1983.

Covert actions are deliberate tools of presidential statecraft, as former CIA operative William Daugherty argues at the start of this chapter. Congress insisted on undeniable presidential approval, and presidents realized that it was in their own best interests to keep a close eye over operations that could inflict political and diplomatic damage on their presidencies. Despite the high risks and heavy secrecy, however, covert actions are reportedly only a small fraction of CIA activities and budgets. One estimate is that, while as much as half the CIA budget went for covert actions in the 1950s and 1960s, since the Kennedy years, the figure has been 5% or below. In the 1990s, the figure was said to be more like 1%.[50] Perhaps it's just harder to be covert or less important to preserve the secrecy in many cases.

# What Presidents Want

If the president is first customer of intelligence products and the necessary decision maker on covert actions, what is it that presidents want from the IC? George Tenet says that presidents like to hear the spy stories and they like to ask follow-up questions. Robert Gates says that presidents and their senior advisers "usually are ill-informed about intelligence capabilities." As a result, "they have unrealistic expectations about what intelligence can do for them." When they do learn the limitations, Gates says, "they are inevitably disappointed. Presidents usually learn the hard way that, although intelligence can tell them a great deal, it only rarely—and usually in crises involving military forces—provides the kind of unambiguous and timely information that can make day-to-day decisions simpler and less risky." Nevertheless, Gates says, presidents keep the CIA around and budget large sums for intelligence because they want "the politician's mother's milk of factual, accurate information" and they like to retain the option of using covert action in dealing with some problems abroad.[51]

James Steinberg, deputy national security adviser under Clinton and deputy secretary of state in the Obama administration, says "policymakers crave certainty and abhor surprise." He admits that policy makers "harbor unrealistic expectations" of the IC, hoping for omniscience. Policy makers also tend to view the analytic community as "cautioners" or naysayers rather than supporters of administration policy. Senior officials can rarely say "too hard." They have to make choices despite the uncertainties. Many policy makers, Steinberg says, feel that analysts are too insulated from the "on the ground reality" that they have experienced in their professional lives, such as direct interactions with foreign leaders.[52]

Former intelligence officials see the same cultural divide. Former Deputy Director of CIA John McLaughlin says that policy makers tend to have a "culture of optimism." They "live in a world heavily influenced by political considerations, and intelligence is only one factor weighing in their decision calculus." Of course, some officials cannot tolerate analysis or reporting that disagrees with their own views.[53]

Mark Lowenthal also says policy makers are optimists. "They believe they can make things happen for the better." Intelligence officers have different motivations. "What [they] want more than anything else is access. They want to know what policies are being developed so they can focus their analysis on these areas and thus contribute to the policy process. They want policymakers to read their analysis. They want to brief senior policymakers, which is the ultimate form of access."[54]

To bridge this cultural divide, analysts say participants on both sides need to understand the perspectives and expectations of each other. For policy makers, what they want most from intelligence professionals is accuracy, clarity, timeliness, and a willingness to revise their judgments. For intelligence professionals, the big red line is any answer to "what should we do?" They can assess the consequences of different actions but are culturally barred from making recommendations. They also want to avoid being blamed for judgments made under acknowledged uncertainty that turn out to be wrong. Former officials like John McLaughlin also point to *warning fatigue,* when policy makers stop listening because they want something harder and more actionable than just a warning of a likelihood.[55] In other words, cries of "wolf" are most valuable and most likely to be heeded when the animal has been spotted and is within range.

Over time, presidents learn the strengths and weaknesses of the intelligence tool, ideally without making any catastrophic decisions as they go through that learning process. The IC is big, costly, responsive, effective at many things, and pretty good at much else, but still far from perfect in its estimates or its operations.

President Obama fired his first DNI after only 15 months, reportedly because he wanted the DNI to be more a coordinator and manager rather than a kind of czar imposing his will on the entire IC. The president was said to be unhappy with the bureaucratic conflicts between the DNI and the CIA director. Obama subsequently expressed some dissatisfaction with perceived intelligence failures at the time of the December 2009 underwear bomber and in advance of later turmoil in Egypt and elsewhere in the Middle East. Such reactions are not unusual. Presidents want the IC to help and forewarn, not cause problems for the administration.[56]

Policy makers want intelligence instruments to make a difference for them, to make their jobs easier, yet there are numerous examples where intelligence assessments have been ignored. Sometimes, senior officials have fixed ideas about other nations or strategic principles, or they may think their policies can change the situations reported to them. As Paul Pillar sadly concluded, "Notwithstanding some instances (such as with terrorism) of intelligence enlightening policy, the overall influence—for good or ill—of intelligence on major decisions and departures in U.S. foreign policy has been negligible. Most notorious intelligence failures have similarly had almost no effect on U.S. policy or U.S. interests."[57]

# Congressional Oversight

Congress created the IC, regularly funds it in the multibillions of dollars, and frequently criticizes its performance. Some insiders claim that congressional investigations in the 1970s and since have weakened the intelligence instruments and made them less effective. What every president needs to know is that Congress claims coequal jurisdiction over intelligence activities, regardless of how skilled lawmakers are at their jobs.

Until 1974, only a handful of senior lawmakers on defense appropriations knew details of the intelligence budget, and many of them didn't really want to know. The 1976 Church Committee concluded that prior congressional oversight had been "more perfunctory than rigorous." And, some members declined to be briefed, fearing inadvertent disclosure. Senator John Stennis (D-MS) once brushed off a CIA briefer ready to tell him about a covert action by saying, "No, no, my boy, don't tell me. Just go ahead and do it—but I don't want to know."[58]

On the other hand, a fuller historical investigation found much more evidence of congressional knowledge, oversight, and advice to the executive. David M. Barrett concluded that, while oversight was not comprehensive, it was not simply passive or static prior to 1961. There were numerous hearings and briefings, though few records were preserved. Members were often quite hawkish on covert actions when they learned of them. Barrett also notes that Congress in 1951 approved an amendment authorizing $100 million to arm and train residents or escapees from communist countries into military units for North Atlantic Treaty Organization (NATO) defense. Although never put into practice as envisioned, the endorsement of

U.S.-funded forces to overthrow of Soviet and Eastern European governments was a green light for other operational planning.[59]

By the 1970s, however, Congress had grown more skeptical about CIA covert actions and other seeming dirty tricks abroad as more and more information was becoming available. A series of news articles in 1974 revealing U.S. involvement in the overthrow of the Salvador Allende government in Chile prompted Congress to act. One of the first measures was an amendment by Senator Harold Hughes (D-IA) requiring that covert operations could be conducted only if and after the president made a finding that the action was "vital to the defense of the United States" and transmitted a report to Congress. This provision was later merged with a similar one authored by Congressman Leo Ryan (D-CA) and passed by the House. The Hughes–Ryan Amendment was then followed in 1975 by full-scale investigative committees in both chambers and by creation of intelligence committees in each body.

The Senate Select Committee on Intelligence (SSCI, commonly called the *sissy*) and the House Permanent Select Committee on Intelligence (HPSCI, called the *hip-see*) are the oversight panels with regular access to finished intelligence and classified reports circulated widely in the executive branch. To protect sources and methods, they are denied routine access to *raw,* unevaluated reports. Each has a staff of about 40 professionals who arrange briefings and hearings and help prepare authorization bills. Various controversies prevented Congress from enacting an authorization bill between 2004 and 2010, but the 2010 measure broadened congressional access to intelligence information by requiring eventual (after 180 days) notification of all committee members of covert actions, creating an inspector general in the ODNI, and requiring some access by Government Accountability Office (GAO) auditors.

The intelligence panels, like many legislative committees, tend to pay closest attention to scandals and controversies rather than routine reviews of programs—what the political scientists call *fire alarm* hearings rather than *police patrol* oversight.[60] For example, they investigated the Aldrich Ames spy case and intelligence failures connected to the 9/11 attacks and the absence of weapons of mass destruction (WMD) in Iraq.

Congress has also sought out information that the executive branch seemed reluctant to provide, even for itself. Despite administration resistance, Congress created the independent 9/11 Commission in order to get a fuller investigation than was made available to a joint congressional panel. In 2002, lawmakers demanded an NIE on Iraq's WMD before voting on the use of force resolution, something the Bush administration had never prepared. One of the later defenses of that flawed estimate was that it had been done in only four weeks instead of the usual several months. In 2006, Congress required a new NIE on Iranian nuclear programs.

The 9/11 Commission called congressional oversight of intelligence *dysfunctional* and tried to shame lawmakers into creating a single joint committee to do both authorizations and appropriations. The appropriations committees, who routinely review intelligence budgets and approve funds in the Defense Appropriations Bill—along with a detailed classified annex—refused to go along, although the House, for the 110th and 111th Congresses, had a special panel consisting of intelligence and appropriations members. Nevertheless, the authorizing committees have enormous influence over the IC through their hearings and, when enacted, their bills.

Covert actions are probably the intelligence operations of greatest concern to Congress. Regular collection has costs and risks, and analyses can be reviewed and critiqued, but covert actions can lead to diplomatic crises and wars if they go badly. That's why Congress demanded to be informed about such operations. The 1991 law allowed the president to restrict notification in extraordinary cases to only the gang of eight—the Senate and House leadership, plus the two senior intelligence members in each chamber. One reason for the 2010 change in the law to require eventual notification of all intelligence committee members was the Bush administration's routine practice of limiting notifications to the gang of eight. Very sensitive collection activities that do not fall under the definition of covert actions are briefed only to the four senior committee members.

From a congressional perspective, the notifications on covert actions have served their intended purpose. They are consulted, and they usually have an opportunity to give their own advice. That process forces the executive branch to respond to congressional concerns, either with changes or cancellation of the proposed action. On some occasions, the covert action briefings have been so unpersuasive to lawmakers that presidents have decided to cancel the plans. In 1989, for example, the Senate oversight committee specifically voted against a program to assist overthrow Panamanian strongman Manuel Noriega in Panama by aiding opposition military officers. The committee favored nonlethal aid but did not want U.S. complicity in an assassination attempt.[61]

The expanded use since 2001 of SOF and military drones for actions that previously were conducted only by the IC has led some members of Congress to call for an extension of the law to cover Pentagon activities that fall into the covert action category so that Congress will be given timely notification.

Do lawmakers abuse their access to secret information? Journalists say that leaks come from both the executive and legislative branches, usually from people who disagree with the proposed action. But, some members caught divulging classified information have been admonished or punished, so the risks are known. Secrecy is one of the levers each branch has over the other.

\* \* \*

The intelligence instruments are a very important part of a president's foreign policy toolkit. They can reduce uncertainty but not eliminate it. They gather information but still require a process of evaluation that can be influenced by personal and political factors. Some of the instruments can be used to great effectiveness but also at great risk. Their secrecy enhances their value to policy makers even as it leaves outsiders uncertain as to the benefits of the large sums expended.

## Selected Resources

Gateway websites for the DNI and CIA are available at www.dni.gov/ and www.cia.gov/index.html.

Much is available at the CIA's Center for the Study of Intelligence at www.cia.gov/library/center-for-the-study-of-intelligence/index.html.

Each of the components of the IC has its own site with links from ODNI at www.dni.gov/members_IC.htm.

The congressional intelligence committees also have sites with current and historical information at www.intelligence.senate.gov/; http://intelligence.house.gov/.

Several excellent books on the intelligence instruments have been published in recent years: Mark Lowenthal, *Intelligence: From Secrets to Policy, Fifth Edition* (Washington, DC: CQ Press, 2012); Paul R. Pillar, *Intelligence and U.S. Foreign Policy* (New York: Columbia University Press, 2011), and Dana Priest and William M. Arkin, *Top Secret America* (New York: Little, Brown, 2011).

# 10 The Homeland Security Instruments

*Americans will likely die on American soil, possibly in large numbers.*

—Hart-Rudman Commission warning of need for homeland security agency, September 15, 1999[1]

*Terrorism is a tragic fact, an unwelcome but immutable reality of life in the twenty-first century.*

—First Secretary of Homeland Security Tom Ridge[2]

The tools to preserve homeland security have been around since 1789. For the first 212 years, they were called national defense and relied primarily on the armed forces and a federalized militia. The framers empowered the federal government to oppose invasions and insurrections and guaranteed all states a Republican form of government without saying how that should be accomplished. The 9/11 attacks, however, prompted lawmakers to create a cabinet department and other institution specifically focused on homeland security.

Domestic defense is a supreme obligation for any president, but in today's world of globalized transportation and trade, electronic communications, and transnational threats, homeland security requires international cooperation and coordination. Whatever other goals the United States has in dealing with other countries, securing help in fighting terrorists has to rank high. Similarly, American intelligence and security best practices are tools to be shared with others for mutual protection. In short, homeland security instruments are used both at home and abroad for domestic and foreign policy goals. (See Table 10.1.)

## A Brief History of United States Homeland Security

Other than the War of 1812 and some later attacks on places that were U.S. protectorates but not states in the union—such as Pearl Harbor in Hawaii in 1941—all of America's wars with foreign enemies were fought on foreign soil. Many Americans felt protected by large oceans and the absence of

255

| Table 10.1 | Homeland Security Instrument Brief | |
|---|---|---|
| **AREAS OF RESPONSIBILITY** | **ADVANTAGES** | **DISADVANTAGES** |
| Critical infrastructure | Coordinator for government | Requires cooperation from private sector |
| Cybersecurity | Responsible for domestic agencies | Conflicts with Department of Defense (DOD) |
| Biological protection | Narrow responsibilities | Center for Disease Control and Prevention (CDC) has greater role |
| Border security | Coordination for government | Many political and budgetary pressures |
| Transportation security | Broad authority, overseas presence | Costly, often unpopular |
| Emergency preparedness and response | Federal Emergency Management Agency (FEMA) experienced, well resourced | Domestic and budgetary pressures |
| **ROLE OF CONGRESS** | Enabler and overseer, program defender | Multiple overseers |
| **CULTURE** | High priority on homeland security | Components retain prior focus and distinctiveness |

Most of the major activities performed for homeland security are domestically focused, even though many of them involve other nations, either participating in the efforts or reacting to U.S. actions in their diplomatic dealings.

technology that could penetrate naval, coastal, and air defenses to reach the homeland. And, political leaders recognized the imperative of preventing attacks.

The advent of nuclear weapons brought a recognition of U.S. vulnerability to attack. At first, defense planners sought protection through military superiority then through deterrence based on secure retaliatory forces. The United States also developed bits and pieces of a civil defense program but never embraced the concept enthusiastically.

By the 1970s, most U.S. civilian and military leaders concluded that ballistic missiles with nuclear warheads could not be stopped, or at least not at a reasonable cost. That realization led Richard Nixon to conclude a treaty with the Soviet Union banning national missile defenses on both sides. Some Americans still believed in the feasibility and desirability of such defenses. Ronald Reagan proposed a strategic defense initiative that critics labeled *Star Wars*, and George W. Bush abrogated the missile defense treaty in order to continue U.S. programs that still have not produced a deployed nationwide system.

Internal threats have always been dealt with by local law enforcement officials, supplemented by the Federal Bureau of Investigation (FBI) and ultimately backed by the threat of U.S. military force. Congress has always insisted on limiting the intelligence agencies to overseas activities and trusting the FBI to investigate and prosecute domestic lawbreakers, whether they use ordinary criminal or terrorist tactics. The FBI had long (and sometimes highly criticized) experience investigating alleged communists, antiwar activists during Vietnam, violent groups like the Weather Underground, and civil rights organizations considered prone to violence. In the 1980s and 1990s, the FBI set up joint terrorism task forces in New York and other cities, numbering 35 by the time of the 9/11 attacks.[3]

In the late 1990s, several national security analysts began warning of potential terrorist attacks on mainland America and urged actions to protect the homeland. They were divided on whether that threat would be nuclear or conventional, delivered by aircraft or suitcases, but they believed some sort of threat was real, and the United States was woefully unprepared. The Defense Science Board in the mid-1990s forecasted that the United States would face enemies whose command and control system was the Internet with logistics by Federal Express. The Hart–Rudman Commission first warned in 1999 about direct attacks on American soil and then told the incoming Bush administration in March 2001 that it should create a national homeland security agency linking FEMA, the coast guard, customs, and border patrol. The warning was placed on the back burner, not ignored but not considered urgent.

## Creation of the Homeland Security System

The attacks on September 11, 2001, in which a foreign group attacked the United States on its own soil, killing nearly 3,000 people, forced the U.S. government to examine and refashion all of its instruments for homeland security. Previous studies like Hart–Rudman were dusted off and their ideas turned into actions. The most significant idea was the creation of a federal agency with the specific mandate of protecting the homeland from terrorist attacks, such as that proposed by Hart–Rudman. But, there were other ideas as well: changes in the law to allow intelligence agencies to talk to crime-fighting agencies; new measures to protect nationwide networks for power, finance, transportation, and communications from disruption; and better border security to prevent dangerous people or materials from reaching the homeland.

The USA PATRIOT Act (formally the Uniting and Strengthening America by Providing the Appropriate Tools Required to Intercept and Obstruct Terrorism Act, Public Law 107–56) was signed into law six weeks after the 9/11 attacks. One of its most important sections reduced the "wall" separating law enforcement from intelligence officials so that they could share information on potential terrorists. The law also gave expanded authorities for domestic surveillance and investigating money laundering. Several terrorist-related acts were specifically made federal crimes. Several provisions were *sunset* with expiration dates, thus forcing Congress to revisit them and decide on renewal, as was done most recently in 2011.[4]

The goal of initial efforts was simple: to link the disparate agencies and operations, coordinate them with a homeland security focus, and provide them with additional legal and investigative tools. One of President Bush's first actions—on September 20—was to create a Homeland Security Council (HSC) modeled on the National Security Council (NSC)—a White House-based group headed by a presidential aide tasked to coordinate federal actions aimed at protecting against terrorist attacks. As any bureaucrat could tell you, however, coordination is easier said than done. Established agencies had their existing laws, programs, procedures, priorities, clients, and overseers in Congress. They had to be cajoled or coerced into cooperating with others on additional goals while still trying to meet their existing ones.

Members of Congress objected that the presidential assistant for homeland security was not subject to Senate confirmation or congressional testimony or any law setting the rules for the HSC. They pushed for, and after nine months of pressure got the president to support, creation of a Department of Homeland Security (DHS). The law was a compromise, moving 22 government organizations now with more than 180,000 people into the new department. (See Figure 10.1.) The resulting system posed enormous challenges to its initial leaders.

Several long-standing organizations were transferred from their home departments to the new DHS: the U.S. Coast Guard (USCG) from Transportation; the Secret Service from Treasury; and FEMA from the Executive Office of the President (EOP). Several other organizations were split, with only parts going to DHS: the Customs Service, Immigration and Naturalization Service (INS), and Animal and Plant Health Inspection Service (APHIS). Visa issuance stayed in the State Department; the FBI remained in Justice; the Federal Aviation Administration (FAA) remained in Transportation, but the newly created Transportation Security Administration (TSA) was moved to DHS; Health and Human Services (HHS) kept the CDC and the National Institutes of Health (NIH); and the Bureau of Alcohol, Tobacco, Firearms, and Explosives was moved from Treasury to Justice.[5]

The antiterrorist purpose in creating DHS was unmistakably clear in the law:

The primary mission of the Department is to—(A) prevent terrorist attacks within the United States;

(B) reduce the vulnerability of the United States to terrorism;

(C) minimize the damage, and assist in the recovery, from terrorist attacks that do occur within the United States;

(D) carry out all functions of entities transferred to the Department, including by acting as a focal point regarding natural and manmade crises and emergency planning[6]

The mandate from the law was simple: Do everything you've been doing, but worry first about terrorism, both domestic and foreign in origin, that threatens the security of the United States. Congress recognized that this

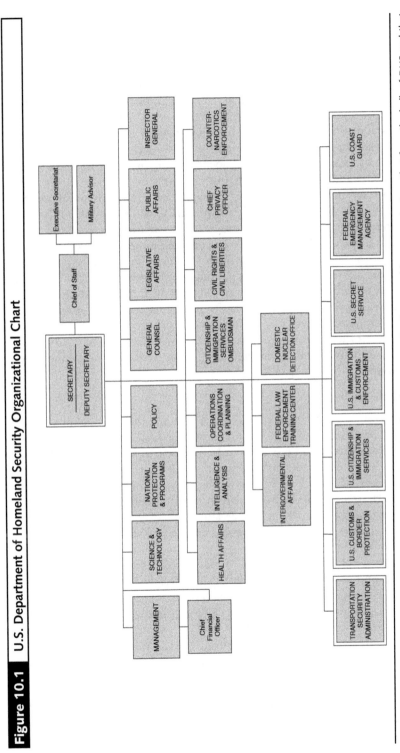

**Figure 10.1** U.S. Department of Homeland Security Organizational Chart

DHS has many special offices reporting directly to the secretary, but they do not supervise the several large organizations that form the bulk of DHS and that have their own distinctive missions and cultures.

*Source:* U.S. DHS, 2010.

259

mission might conflict with existing agency missions but insisted that activities not directly related to homeland security be "not diminished or neglected." That has been hard to achieve in practice, not least because the congressional committees that previously had jurisdiction over DHS components for those other missions retained jurisdiction and oversight even after creation of the new department. Within DHS, there is ongoing competition for resources and influence among the many newly combined organizations and, within them, between legacy and new missions.

The budget process for homeland security is enormously complicated. Only about half the total federal spending for that purpose goes through DHS. DOD and HHS also have major programs, with the rest of the spending scattered among 28 other federal agencies. Only about two thirds of the DHS budget goes specifically for homeland security activities, with the remainder going for traditional programs like maritime safety and mitigation of oil spills. While listing all the spending information across the government, the Office of Management and Budget (OMB) still has not created a separate homeland security budget function.[7] That means that budgeteers trade off homeland security programs against other activities in each agency rather than against homeland security programs across the government. A similar situation prevails in national security, where defense and international affairs activities are in separate functions, making it hard to trade off military and civilian activities that are similar in objectives but separate in execution.

## The Defense Mission

Fears of an attack from abroad arose now and then throughout U.S. history, at first from Canada and later from the sea. Long before the United States had a blue-water navy, it was building coastal forts with artillery and shallow draft gunboats. In World War II, German submarines threatened ships near U.S. ports, and some coastal cities imposed blackout restrictions to thwart attacks. On the Pacific coast, Japanese submarines attacked ships and some shore facilities and later launched fire balloons that did minor damage. These real but minor attacks and numerous false alarms caused major public concern.

Military operations within the United States were strictly limited by the *Posse Comitatus* Act of 1878, which prohibited the use of federal troops for domestic law enforcement. The law halted federal prosecutions of violations of civil rights and other laws in the southern states and marked an end to Reconstruction after the Civil War. Only in recent years were exceptions written into law allowing counterdrug assistance (military personnel can identify drug-trafficking activities but cannot conduct arrests) and emergency assistance in case of the theft of nuclear materials or situations involving chemical or biological weapons of mass destruction (WMD).[8]

One early response to the Soviet nuclear threat was the creation of the North American Air Defense Command (NORAD) in 1958. With Canadian support, the United States built radar systems to detect enemy bombers flying over the North Pole and later upgraded the system to warn of enemy missiles. After the end of the Cold War in the 1990s, some defense officials worked to create military units to deal with threats from smaller nuclear devices—*suitcase bombs*—that might be carried by ships or aircraft.

The 9/11 attacks demonstrated that serious damage could be done using civilian airliners rather than explosive weapons. While DOD remained focused on foreign military threats and defense of American airspace, civilian agencies undertook to defend against threats that traveled on common carriers or were already resident in the United States. The creation of DHS brought most of those agencies under a single umbrella and gave them a new highest priority—preventing terrorist attacks.

DOD spends about 26% of the money counted government-wide as being for homeland security, with the bulk of that going for DOD programs to protect military facilities, personnel, and infrastructure like computer and communications systems. In 2002, DOD created the Northern Command (NORTHCOM) and gave it area responsibilities for the continental United States, Canada, and Mexico and important functional roles including aerial monitoring and defense as well as *military support to civil authorities,* the Pentagon's phrase for everything from disaster relief to riot control. NORTHCOM took over the joint task force that worked on drug interdiction along the Mexican border and expanded its mandate to surveillance and detection for homeland defense. It also controls the joint task force established in 1999 to prepare to deal with any chemical, biological, radiological, or nuclear incident on U.S. soil. NORTHCOM today has about 1,200 personnel regularly assigned and an annual budget of about $70 million. These activities suggest that the Pentagon still treats its domestic security role as secondary to its external security missions and is primarily concerned with dealing with the consequences of threats to the homeland.

The USCG, now part of DHS, has long been an instrument for foreign policy activities as well as for domestic purposes. It has its own military operations at home and overseas. Besides interdiction of drug traffickers and illegal migrants, the USCG has been involved in Haitian earthquake relief and training missions to 51 nations. It has deployed six patrol boats to U.S. Central Command (CENTCOM) for Middle East activities and has sent port security units to Kuwait and Iraq.[9] USCG has 42,000 military personnel and 8,000 civilians, with an annual budget of about $10 billion.

## Intelligence Collection and Integration Mission

Prevention of terrorist attacks relies heavily on what the intelligence community (IC) can learn from its many techniques and sources. But, the intelligence agencies are limited to overseas activities. (For more detailed discussion, see Chapter 9.) One of the government's most important tools to bring together domestic and foreign threat information is the National Counterterrorism Center (NCTC), a 500-person organization drawing on all 16 members of the IC. Its task, basically, is to connect the dots pointing to terrorist threats. Formally, its responsibility is to analyze the threat, share that information, and integrate all instruments of national power to obtain unity of effort.[10] NCTC manages a terrorist identity database and provides regular reports to other parts of the government, including threat reports, incident tracking, and daily teleconferences. It reports directly to the president and the Director of National Intelligence (DNI).

In practice, NCTC has been judged as providing added value to the rest of the government but facing "numerous obstacles," including "systemic impediments" and culture clashes among agencies. A congressionally commissioned study found that planning and operations have been hindered by overlapping authorities, especially among NCTC and State and the CIA. Relations with the NSC staff were also judged "not well institutionalized."[11]

DHS is part of the IC. It has a 1,000-person component for analysis and operations with a budget around $350 million that does both operational planning and intelligence analysis. DHS does not do the foreign intelligence collection that is the responsibility of other parts of the IC, but it does gather unique information as part of its regular activities at airports, seaports, and the border. It also gains information from local law enforcement officials as well as the private sector.

Given these multiple sources of information, the DHS intelligence and analysis unit prepares intelligence warnings and security assessments as well as monthly *security monitors* and an annual threat assessment. The unit's analytic thrusts are narcotics trafficking, alien and human smuggling, money laundering, radicalizations and extremism, groups that could be exploited by terrorists or criminals, critical infrastructure and key resources, WMD; and health threats. The intelligence office is responsible for providing actionable intelligence to departmental officials and for sharing threat information and assessments with state, local, and private-sector partners. As part of this process, DHS has provided people and secure communications equipment to 72 state and local fusion centers across the country.[12] The coast guard has a separate intelligence unit that works with maritime fusion centers and conducts signals intelligence (SIGINT) operations for the National Security Agency (NSA).

In 2010, the Government Accountability Office (GAO) reported to Congress that DHS was making progress on sharing and managing information related to terrorism but still lacked a comprehensive approach. On this activity, as well as on several other DHS functions, GAO for several years has rated DHS problems as "high risk."[13]

## Critical Infrastructure Mission

As terrorist threats became a major concern of the federal government in the 1990s, analysts pointed to several infrastructure systems that seemed potentially vulnerable, such as the electric power grid, oil and gas pipelines, financial networks, key transportation nodes, and various communications networks. Those systems that, if disrupted or destroyed, would have a debilitating effect on the national economy, or homeland security, or public health and safety were deemed critical infrastructures, and DHS was given overall responsibility for prioritizing and executing infrastructure protection programs. It spends about $5 billion per year on such activities.

Presidential directives identified 17 key sectors, each of which is supposed to develop protection plans.[14] These include agriculture and food; banking and finance; chemical; commercial facilities; communications; critical manufacturing; dams; defense industrial base; emergency services; energy; government facilities; healthcare and public health; information technology; national monuments and icons; nuclear reactors, materials, and waste; postal and shipping; transportation systems; and water. While DHS has overall responsibility for developing strategies for protection, other departments have lead agency roles for the sectors they know best—such as the Environmental Protection Agency (EPA) for water and chemical, Justice for emergency services, and Treasury for banking and finance. As sector plans have evolved in recent years, DHS has put added emphasis on resiliency and not just protection. Planners recognize the need to prepare to deal with possible attacks in case preventive measures fail. For example, DHS has now developed web portals for specific incidents for real-time exchange of sensitive information.

The challenge for DHS and the rest of the federal government, of course, is that 85% of the critical infrastructure is privately owned and operated, and businesses resent and resist government interference, especially costly government regulations.[15] There are often major barriers to cooperation, such as from the antitrust laws or competition-sensitive information. Government officials also worry about providing information that is based on classified data. A 2011 study noted the inherent conflict between the electric industry's efforts to build Internet-based, smart grids for more efficient pricing and delivery of power and the heightened vulnerability to disruption such a system would be at risk for without major security features. But, security is a low priority for these efforts, and it is unclear who would have to pay for the enhancements.[16]

## Cybersecurity Mission

The Internet developed from a military program to allow communications even in the event of nuclear war through the use of packet switching. The Pentagon has always had programs for secure command, control, and communications linkages and has recently expanded both its defensive and offensive capabilities against potential threats. Increasing civilian reliance on cyber networks has made their protection against disruption similarly important in recent years. Analysts fear that attackers could hack into computer systems to destroy nuclear reactors, crash trains or planes, or disable banking and financial transactions. A think tank report in 2011 noted that U.S. government networks faced 1.8 billion cyber attacks of varying sophistication each month. It concluded that "cyber attacks are more than a nuisance and more than criminal activity. They constitute a serious challenge to U.S. national security."[17]

Cybersecurity became a special priority of the Obama administration, with nearly $1 billion budgeted for this purpose in the first two years. In 2009 and 2011, the administration announced programs involving DHS in liaison with the private sector and DOD for protecting governmental and allied networks. The White House named a cybersecurity coordinator to manage the interagency process. The Pentagon in 2010 established the U.S. Cyber Command as a component of the strategic command with missions to defend U.S. networks and if necessary conduct "full spectrum military cyberspace operations." The administration also announced plans for working with other nations on a joint cyberspace strategy.[18]

Coordination just within the U.S. government will pose major challenges, however, because several agencies and military commands already have large cyberdivisions. In fact, 21 federal organizations dealing with cybersecurity have been created since 2001.[19]

For its part, DHS is preparing to deploy the EINSTEIN 3 system to prevent and detect intrusions on government computer systems. The department also has been working to identify U.S. companies deemed most important for cyber infrastructure and get them to develop security plans. Additional legislation is needed from Congress to codify and implement the strategic plans and deal with related issues of privacy and intellectual property. There has been some push back from the private sector, however. The U.S. Chamber of Commerce complained that the plans developed so far amount to "regulatory overreach" by imposing heavy burdens on U.S. businesses.[20]

## Biological Protection Mission

There are no easy answers as to how to handle threats to public health. Several civilian agencies have long-standing programs, enormous scientific expertise, and well-established connections to national and local medical communities. On the other hand, DHS has special expertise on biological threats and unique capabilities for integrating whole of government responses to disruptive threats and emergencies. So far, the tendency has been to tilt in favor of the doctors.

Public health and safety programs are divided between DHS and the HHS, which manages the NIH and the CDC. While both departments are supposed to work closely in responding to disasters, HHS was given lead agency status for medical emergencies by Congress in 2006.[21] DHS is mainly responsible for biological defense and surveillance programs. The department also has a $1 billion annual science and technology program that, among other things, funds research and development of biometric detectors and surveillance systems. The federal government is also developing an Early Warning Infectious Disease Program (EWIDS) that seeks early detection, identification, and reporting of infectious diseases associated with bioterrorism agents and other major threats to public health, which may originate at home or abroad.

## Border Security and Immigration Missions

The largest single component of DHS is called U.S. Customs and Border Protection (CBP), with 61,000 people and an annual budget of over $11.5 billion. It combined the customs bureau from Treasury and the border patrol from Justice, along with inspectors from the INS and the Department of Agriculture. CPB's job is to prevent the illegal entry of people and forbidden items at the U.S. borders. CPB officials also work at airports and seaports, both domestic and overseas.

Investigations and law enforcement of immigration and customs matters are handled by a separate part of DHS, the Immigration and Customs Enforcement (ICE), with 20,000 employees and an annual budget over $5.5 billion. ICE goes after transnational criminal organizations and runs deportation programs.

A third agency, Citizenship and Immigration Services (CIS), processes immigration and naturalization requests as well as asylum petitions. It has 11,000 employees and a nearly $3 billion budget.

Managing the CPB, ICE, and CIS has been a major challenge because of the differing cultures and practices developed in their legacy institutions and the need to impose greater commonality for homeland security purposes.[22] The task has been made even more difficult by the political disputes over immigration and naturalization issues. Some political leaders demand tougher entry barriers and more aggressive enforcement of sanctions against undocumented persons and their employers as a precondition; others seek immigration reform and paths to citizenship for some people already resident. This political dispute complicates DHS management as it weighs spending more money on border fencing versus, say, port security or whether to target employers or undocumented workers in their enforcement efforts.

## Transportation Security Mission

The third largest component of DHS is the TSA, with 14% of the budget and 58,000 employees. (CBP is first, with 21% of the budget and 61,000 people. The coast guard is next, with 18% of the budget and 50,000 people.) TSA was created shortly after the 9/11 attacks, combining the existing air marshal program with newly federalized airport screeners. There are more than 500 commercial airports in the United States with airline service, but about 70% of passenger boardings occur at just 31 sites. In 2010, TSA reached its mandated goals of 100% screening of all passengers on designated flights to, from, and within the United States against government watch lists as well as 100% screening of cargo on passenger aircraft. In addition to the airport screeners and their advanced imaging machines, DHS has 3,336 behavior detection officers and 900 canine teams for added security.[23]

TSA is also responsible for developing programs for security of surface transportation in cooperation with state, local, and private operators. There, too, the challenge is huge. There are 45,000 miles of interstate freeways and 600,000 bridges. Freight rail networks extend for 300,000 miles.[24]

TSA faces a no-win problem. Passengers resent the intrusive inspections, even of small children and the disabled, as *security theater,* but inspectors want to avoid blame if they overlook what becomes a threat. Rules have been changed to guard against new techniques, such as liquid chemicals or underwear bombs.

## Emergency Preparedness and Response Missions

Federal help in cases of natural disasters was ad hoc until the 1930s, when federal funds were authorized for repair of public facilities and roads that suffered damage. Broader federal programs were enacted in the 1960s and 1970s, and in 1980, several programs were merged into FEMA.[25] At first, FEMA was under the direct control of the president, but it was moved into DHS when that department was created in 2003. Some observers feared that would lead to a subordination and diminution of an effective government agency. Others argued that it was only logical to link homeland security protection and prevention programs to response planning if those measures fail. FEMA has about 10,000 permanent employees and an annual budget about $10 billion. About half the people are assigned to disaster relief operations, the remainder to other FEMA activities.

While the terrorism focus of DHS adds another set of concerns for FEMA, its actual toolkit would be the same for natural disasters and for terrorist attacks. In either case, it would need to plan for evacuations; search and rescue; medical support; temporary housing; food, water, and fuel supplies; communications; and evacuee registration. There are important differences, however, in how to train and interact with first responders and local communities depending whether the emergencies are terrorism, natural disasters, infectious diseases, or industrial accidents—the broader spectrum of incidents FEMA is now mandated to handle.[26]

When FEMA does well, there are no limits to the praise and budgets it receives. When it does poorly, as after Hurricane Katrina, Congress reacts with predictable anger. Some critics say that FEMA does too much, pushed by Congress and pulled by presidents who want to show their concern and support to local communities. The number of presidential disaster declarations has soared in recent decades, from an average of 43 per year in the 1980s to 130 per year under President Bush the younger and 108 per year in President Obama's first two years. Local officials want such declarations, of course, because then the federal government pays 75% to 100% of the disaster response bills. Congress then helps out by passing supplemental emergency funds.

While FEMA's role remains essentially unchanged, its relation to the rest of DHS is conflicted. Departmental officials don't like to think of failure to prevent and protect against terrorist attacks. They also have a bias in favor of additional protective measures over funding for relief and recovery.

FEMA officials lament their loss of White House status and the need to compete for funds with the rest of DHS.

### The Anomaly of the Secret Service

Also in DHS is the Secret Service with its 7,000 people and nearly $2 billion annual budget. Most people think of the Secret Service primarily as the protectors of the president and other current and former officials. But, the agency was created in 1865 to catch counterfeiters and received the presidential protection mission only after the McKinley assassination in 1901.

Part of its mission remains safeguarding the financial infrastructure and payment systems and the investigation of electronic crimes. While formally under DHS, the Secret Service has substantial autonomy—plus the special benefit of daily access to the president.

## Culture of the Department of Homeland Security

The integration of the 22 agencies moved under the DHS umbrella is still a work in progress. Most of the components had well-honed bureaucratic cultures and practices. Some had a law enforcement mission and viewed the world in black and white. Others performed services for the public and developed strong ties to civilian communities. Still others had technical skills and professionalism, isolating themselves somewhat from outsiders. If there is an emerging DHS culture, it seems to be one emphasizing coordination—coordination of the units and activities within the department and coordination with the many other government agencies who perform related tasks.[27]

A second aspect of DHS organizational culture seems to be a kind of hyper vigilance combined with risk aversion. Officials are right to be worried; that's their primary job. But, that focus on worst-case threats makes it hard for them to perform another important task—reassuring the public. As former counterterrorism official Michael Sheehan has written, "No terrorism expert or government leader wants to appear soft on terrorism. It's always safer to predict the worse; if nothing happens, the exaggerators are rarely held accountable for their nightmare scenarios."[28] The Obama administration discontinued the color-coded threat levels precisely because they were numbingly vague and unhelpful in terms of what ordinary citizens should do.

The risk aversion component of DHS culture can be seen in reviews of its risk assessment methodologies. Critics say there is a preoccupation with "low probability/high consequence" events and that risk assessments exaggerate the probability and likely costs of terrorist incidents. A National Research Council assessment in 2010 placed only "low confidence" in DHS risk analyses and said they were inadequate to support decision making except in the case of natural disasters.[29] Such critiques make it even harder to increase DHS prestige within government or the morale of its employees.

# Homeland Security Council

The law creating DHS also created the HSC and staff to advise the president. The membership was to be the president, vice president, secretary of homeland security, secretary of defense, and "such other individuals as may be designated by the President."[30] President Obama took the advice of national security analysts and decided to merge the HSC and NSC staffs as their subject matters had so much overlap. He retained a separate position for an assistant to the president for homeland security and counterterrorism.[31]

HSC is still an immature organization with no track record of effective planning and execution—in contrast to the NSC. Nor does the special assistant have any directive power over the interagency process. There is little evidence that the HSC has achieved significant bureaucratic status in the White House or that it has created distinctive bureaucratic processes for presidential management of homeland security issues. Presidents can call any meetings they want and then decide whether to call the gathering an HSC or NSC meeting.

# Strengths and Weaknesses of the Homeland Security System

As long as there is no major terrorist attack on U.S. soil, the homeland security system will receive a passing grade from the American public. But, most experts argue that the government needs to do better overall and that DHS in particular needs major improvements. The GAO has repeatedly documented DHS administrative shortfalls and has listed DHS as a "high risk" agency with numerous programs vulnerable to fraud, waste, abuse, and mismanagement and in need of transformational improvements. Some fixes require better management, but others require different laws or more money, both of which are much harder to come by.[32]

The federal system is fragmented, with DHS managing only half of the federal money spent on "homeland security." DHS is the designated principal federal office (PFO) for management of domestic incidents but is not really empowered to integrate and manage an interagency response. As the Project on National Security Reform (PNSR) concluded in its 2008 report, "The DHS lacks the authority necessary to fulfill its national security mission."[33]

While a good case can be made for letting other departments run the programs where they have experience and expertise, the potential problem remains that, in an emergency, there should be an effective coordination mechanism. DHS is really a *department of coordination,* and thus reasonably suited for such a role with other agencies, but coordination works best when someone has directive authority, not merely persuasive opportunities. Still unproven is how well DHS can mobilize cooperation with state, local, and private-sector officials on many of its tasks. There are committees and conferences, but they have not been tested in crises.

DHS itself is still at the toddler stage. There is much staff turnover and low morale. DHS ranks near the bottom of federal agencies in terms of worker satisfaction.[34] The component organizations are still torn between the new structure and missions and the legacy programs they were most comfortable carrying out. While senior leaders know they will be judged primarily on how well they prevent terrorist incidents and protect the nation, their subordinates know they will also be judged on how well they perform those legacy missions.

The president of Rand Corporation has written that DHS goals and strategy are ill defined. "DHS leaders are thus left to 'manage by inbox,' with the dominant mode for DHS behavior being crisis management." James Thomson also said, "DHS implements most of its programs with little or no evaluation of their performance."[35]

Since that was written in 2007, DHS has followed the good government practices of further internal reviews and reorganizations. In 2009, it conducted, on the Pentagon model, a quadrennial homeland security review and, in 2010, did a bottom-up review. Despite those commendable efforts, the GAO and others say much more needs to be done.

Another critic, Stephen Flynn of the Center for National Policy, says, "The United States has made a mess of homeland security." He complains that DHS and other agencies "are subsumed in a world of security clearances and classified documents" and fail to reach out to the people they are supposed to serve. Instead of doing their work behind closed doors in windowless offices, Flynn urges DHS to reach out to the private sector and the public and involve them more actively in planning both protection and responses. "Building societal resilience requires a bottom-up, open and participatory process," he says, "that is, the exact inverse of the way U.S. policymakers have approached homeland security to date."[36]

# Congress and Homeland Security

There is widespread agreement that congressional oversight of DHS is a burden for the department. An estimated 108 congressional committees and subcommittees have some sort of jurisdiction over DHS—compared with 36 for DOD. In addition to the House and Senate homeland security and appropriations committees and their subcommittees, many other panels have legacy jurisdictions over the nonsecurity activities of DHS components, which account for more than one third of the DHS budget. Lawmakers concerned about the coast guard's maritime safety programs or about immigration issues beyond infiltration of terrorists demand continued oversight rights and want to call witnesses from DHS and write new laws.[37]

As a result of the multiple panels with jurisdiction, DHS had to prepare testimony and send witnesses to 376 hearings during the 110th Congress, only half of which involved the two committees with primary homeland security focus. By comparison, the Pentagon, with its much larger budget and range of activities, appeared before only two thirds as many hearings

(261) during the same period.[38] And while the secretary of defense can designate subordinates to testify in most cases, the DHS secretary and the heads of the major agencies find it harder to say "no."

Redrawing jurisdictional lines, as outside observers suggest, is much harder to achieve within Congress. It took four years before the House granted its committee on homeland security legislative authority and then only after protecting the jurisdictional claims of other committees. The Senate counterpart also has primary jurisdiction over laws reorganizing government and was strictly limited in which parts of DHS it could oversee. Members on other committees argued that they have expertise on the legacy operations of the DHS components and that the law required that those programs not be "diminished or neglected." Thus, Congress mirrors the tension within the executive branch between focus on security and prevention, not to mention shared focus on the other activities by the organizations within DHS.

Further evidence of the weakness of the two principal authorizing committees is their failure to pass a homeland security authorization bill since the creation of the department. As with foreign aid, this failure prevents Congress from giving timely guidance and program adjustments except in spending levels through appropriations.

On the other hand, homeland security has had a relatively protected budget in recent years. Both Republicans and Democrats lump DHS spending with defense and veterans affairs and then impose less restraint than for the rest of the civilian portions of the budget. Some lawmakers still criticize some DHS programs; however, preparedness grants have been given to 63 different urban areas, far more than are deemed high risk.

## International Aspects of Homeland Security

Just as America's defense strategy and efforts start far from the shoreline, so does homeland security. The case study in this chapter on Mexico illustrates how cooperation on homeland security requires foreign policy deftness and involves many domestic issues for both the United States and Mexico. DHS has agents at 58 overseas ports that handle 86% of container ship traffic. TSA has negotiated aviation security declarations with African, European, and Latin American nations. The United States has numerous agreements with Canada and Mexico regarding border management. DHS has cooperation agreements on homeland security with 10 other nations.[39] And, the United States has sensitive arrangements with several nations for intelligence sharing and other cooperation regarding terrorist threats.

Reaching these various agreements is as important a diplomatic activity as any other pursued by the State Department. They are part of the network of cooperative relations that bolster U.S. national security overall. While Americans may view functional arrangements for passengers and goods as noncontroversial, other nations treat them as political matters that are part of their overall foreign policy. Immigration laws and visa requirements have long been major foreign policy issues in many countries and have to be dealt with diplomatically. For example, the U.S. government can include visa requirements as part of a larger bargain, granting fewer restrictions as a reward for international cooperation or denying privileges as a punishment.

The homeland security instruments are thus part of America's foreign policy toolkit because their use almost always involves foreign nations or individuals and thus becomes part of the context in which international policies are developed. Since the 9/11 attacks, America has developed techniques and processes for terrorist identification and safety procedures, inspections and monitoring that have been widely shared and adopted by friendly nations. Some parts of DHS can also be sent on overseas missions, as has been done by sending coast guard units to Haiti and the Middle East and by sending TSA to work out aviation security agreements.

If the homeland security instruments are weak or faulty, that could have enormous foreign policy consequences. An insecure America could seek to withdraw from international engagements. America's enemies could be emboldened by even a minor successful attack. U.S. leaders could be shaken and distracted by security challenges. And in case of another significant attack, lawmakers and the public might succumb to demands to deny civil liberties to large segments of the population.

# Areas of Presidential Choice

Within the U.S. government, the president can try to impose integration and coordination. Presidents Bush and Obama have issued executive orders that point in the right direction, but their subordinates have limited powers, and the integrative mechanisms are weak and untested. Going further requires congressional assent and action as well as close executive supervision.

The president can also try to reorient homeland security activities while reassuring the public that best efforts are being made to protect them, their communities, and the economy. He can try to modify the DHS culture's focus on preventing worst-case events so that it can prepare and deal with more likely threats and associated recovery efforts. In 2011, President Obama issued a policy directive ordering the development of a *national preparedness goal* that would weigh specific threats and vulnerabilities, including regional variations, and recommend "concrete, measurable, and prioritized objectives" to mitigate the risks.[40] The administration has also stressed the goal of "build[ing] a ready and resilient Nation,"[41] terminology that suggests a slight shift away from a preoccupation with prevention of attacks. This may be bureaucratic wheel spinning, or it may produce a more nuanced and balanced homeland security strategy.

\* \* \*

The U.S. government has a broad array of institutions involved in some way or another with homeland security. To perform their missions, they often have to work with other nations and thus become part and parcel of

U.S. foreign policy instruments. The largest coordinating entity, DHS, still faces enormous bureaucratic challenges as it tries to fashion integrated plans for the protection of the American people and U.S. infrastructure.

## Case Study: U.S.–Mexican Collaboration on Security

This case study on Mexico illustrates how homeland security is a major tool for both U.S. domestic and foreign policy. The United States and Mexico share a common border nearly 2,000 miles long as well as numerous problems relating to trade, migration, and criminal activities. The Mexican government under President Felipe Calderón launched a major effort to combat drug-trafficking organizations (DTO) that have threatened the governments, judiciary, and law enforcement activities of several Mexican states and communities. He increased Mexico's security budget from about $2 billion in 2006 to $9.3 billion in 2009 and mobilized thousands of soldiers and federal police to arrest drug traffickers, establish checkpoints, and interdict drug shipments. On its side of the border, the United States increased the number of border patrol agents, installed additional detection systems, and deployed 1,200 national guard troops.

Despite Calderón's efforts, between 2007 and 2010, the Mexican government estimated that 34,500 people died in violence related to organized crime. Murders and kidnappings soared within some border cities and spilled over into the United States. Circumstances were so dire that Mexico set aside 150 years of anti-Yanqui feelings and accepted a broad range of U.S. assistance, including U.S. military personnel to train Mexican anti-drug units. The most comprehensive plan was the 2007 Mérida Initiative of counterdrug and anticrime assistance and cooperation.

Presidents George W. Bush and Barack Obama expanded the number and types of collaborative efforts. Today, the two nations work together in a broad range of intergovernmental organizations, from the White House to the border-crossing level. In addition, of course, there are transnational groups in the private sector and between state and local governments. Included among the collaborative efforts of the two countries are meetings among the executive leadership, cabinet-level representatives, and defense and diplomatic contacts. For instance, the U.S. and Mexican presidents meet about once a year, sometimes with the Canadian prime minister, under the umbrella of the North American Free Trade Agreement (NAFTA), and in 2010, Secretary of State Clinton chaired a cabinet-level delegation including the U.S. secretaries of defense and homeland security, the chairman of the Joint Chiefs of Staff (JCS), and the director of national intelligence (DNI) that met with its Mexican counterparts.

The State Department runs numerous contacts and midlevel task forces via the U.S. embassy, while the Pentagon's NORTHCOM regularly meets with its Mexican counterparts. Similar meetings down the ranks address drug trafficking and environmental issues, while more active collaboration includes the creation of 11 border enforcement security task forces containing U.S. and Mexican representatives. Under the 2007 Mérida Initiative to fight drug trafficking and organized crime, the United States provided more than $1.8 billion in assistance through 2011, and between 2008 and 2010, DOD has provided counternarcotics assistance in the form of equipment and training to the total of nearly $100 million. The United States has located offices of 16 agencies in Mexico City to work with partner agencies on these counterdrug programs.

While meetings are not the same thing as progress against the threats, they are a necessary precondition. The breadth of collaboration between the two governments illustrates the importance the two nations place on improving their mutual homeland security. This effort also shows that homeland security instruments have both domestic and foreign policy functions.

*Sources:* David A. Shirk, *The Drug War in Mexico: Confronting a Shared Threat,* Council on Foreign Relations, March 2011; Clare Ribando Seelke, "Mexico–U.S. Relations: Issues for Congress," *CRS Report for Congress,* February 15, 2011.

## Selected Resources

U.S. government sites for homeland security include DHS, which also has links to its component organizations at www.dhs.gov

The two principal congressional committees dealing with homeland security are the Senate Committee on Homeland Security and Governmental Affairs—http://hsgac.senate.gov/public/—and the House Committee on Homeland Security—http://homeland.house.gov/.

Many think tanks have active programs in homeland security. A list is here at www.hlswatch.com/thinktanks/.

Two books with deeper backgrounds are: Donald F. Kettl, *System Under Stress: Homeland Security and American Politics, Second Edition* (Washington, DC: CQ Press, 2007) and Gordon Adams and Cindy Williams, *Buying National Security* (Routledge, 2010).

# 11 The International Institutions Instrument

*The United States should invest time and resources into building international relationships and institutions that can help manage local crises when they emerge.*

—President George W. Bush, 2002[1]

*Indeed, our ability to advance peace, security, and opportunity will turn on our ability to strengthen both our national and our multilateral capabilities. We need to spur and harness a new diversity of instruments, alliances, and institutions in which a division of labor emerges on the basis of effectiveness, competency, and long-term reliability. This requires enhanced coordination among the United Nations, regional organizations, international financial institutions, specialized agencies, and other actors that are better placed or equipped to manage certain threats and challenges.*

—President Barack Obama, 2010[2]

International organizations are part of America's foreign policy toolkit. They can be partners, leveraging U.S. capabilities and power, or substitutes, carrying the burdens the United States would prefer not to bear. Using such organizations, however, creates a separate set of challenges. International organizations can be valuable partners in the pursuit of shared goals, but their participation may impose constraints on U.S. actions. They can be force multipliers for U.S. diplomacy, but they can also be impediments, limiting freedom or speed of action by a need for consensus. Multinational groups may also create expectations, norms, and opportunities that affect American decisions. The United States may be pressured to use or support these organizations when America might prefer to act on its own.

U.S. leaders tend to be pragmatic, embracing international cooperation when it seems to be helpful and avoiding it when it limits U.S. choices. This chapter examines some of the major international institutions and the ways they have been used or could be used as instruments of U.S. foreign policy.

Established institutions are ready forums for consultations and negotiations as well as venues for collective action. They can help in many ways to reduce the risk of conflict by the rules and norms they set, such as the United Nations (UN) Charter's provisions on resort to force and the UN's more

274

recent declaration of a "right to protect" civilians. They can help to prevent crises by actions such as monitoring elections and political transitions (as in several African nations); working to ease ethnic tensions (as in Central and Eastern Europe); helping to resolve boundary disputes (as in Africa, Latin America, and Southeast Asia); and by special investigations (as in Lebanon and Sri Lanka). And, they can work to mitigate conflicts that do break out both through diplomacy and by sending military peacekeepers.[3]

When problems arise, the United States can sometimes choose deliberately to use one or more of the major international organizations. The president can turn the issue over to others to avoid the costs and the hassles or to take advantage of the organization's special capabilities. At other times, however, the president will have to act defensively when an organization asserts itself into a foreign policy matter in ways that complicate or influence U.S. decisions. (See Table 11.1.)

It helps to share burdens and responsibilities. But, sharing also entails consultation and coordination, and sometimes, partners have differing perspectives and goals. On more than one occasion—including Lebanon in 1983 and Somalia in 1993—the United States suffered major military disasters because of confused lines of authority and differing approaches among the international partners. On the other hand, the UN has been an indispensable neutral force in many peacekeeping operations, and the North Atlantic Treaty Organization (NATO) has shared major burdens in Kosovo and Afghanistan. As is so often the case, the value of multilateral actions depends on the particular circumstances.

# The Role of International Institutions

For major security issues, the UN will be involved whether or not the United States wishes. Only the UN can give an international imprimatur to arms embargoes or comprehensive economic sanctions. Only the UN Security Council (UNSC) can authorize major peacekeeping operations or the use of force against violent dictators and aggressive regimes. Acting with UN support gives legitimacy and moral standing to a nation's own policies.

Regional organizations like NATO, the OAS, and ASEAN can also be useful vehicles for security and other policies. They can mobilize political coalitions and even military forces to police problem areas in their regions. Annual meetings can be important venues for exchanging views, resolving problems, and launching initiatives. Where they have established infrastructures, they can be used to plan and implement agreed policies.

Economic crises and problems requiring economic solutions can often best be handled through the existing multilateral economic institutions—the G-8 and G-20 for high-level economic policy coordination, the IMF for advice and assistance on currency problems and debt, the World Bank and regional banks for development advice and assistance, and the WTO for managing trade disputes.

| Table 11.1 | International Institutions as U.S. Instruments Brief | |
|---|---|---|
| **MAJOR INSTITUTIONS** | **ADVANTAGES** | **DISADVANTAGES** |
| United Nations (UN) | Broad membership, much experience in relief and peacekeeping | Security Council veto, resistance to some U.S. views |
| International Atomic Energy Agency (IAEA) | Professional, authoritative | May self-censor reports |
| North Atlantic Treaty Organization (NATO) | Capable military forces | Requires consensus |
| Organization for Security and Co-operation in Europe (OSCE) | Broad forum | Little real power |
| Organization of American States (OAS) | Symbolic power when it acts | Limited by regional rivalries |
| Association of Southeast Asian Nations (ASEAN); ASEAN Regional Forum (ARF); Asia–Pacific Economic Cooperation (APEC) | Valuable forums | Little beyond meetings, small staffs |
| Group of Eight (G-8); Group of Twenty (G-20) | Valuable economic forums | Limited follow-through |
| International Monetary Fund (IMF) and international financial institutions (IFIs) | Experienced, powerful | May provoke local resentment |
| World Trade Organization (WTO) | Authoritative | Slow, technical |
| International courts | Symbolic | No enforcement powers |
| Nonstate actors | United States can help or keep distance | Groups limited; may be competitive with others |
| **ROLE OF CONGRESS** Funding and oversight | Necessary supporter | Reflects domestic political pressures |

This list of some of the major international organizations includes many that the United States has deliberately chosen to use for its own foreign policy purposes as well as ones where others have challenged U.S. policies and forced American engagement. Each has its particular advantages and disadvantages as an instrument for U.S. policy.

The very fact that most of these organizations have regular meetings and expert staff make them useful for diplomacy. Meetings are action-forcing events for government agencies, prompting them to develop agendas and find measures that can be resolved as signs of success at the meeting. This is true also of bilateral meetings, such as presidential visits, but those lack the regularity of organizational summits. Whether a president or cabinet officer takes the time to attend one of these periodic meetings often depends on whether things will be accomplished—usually after having been worked out in advance by subordinates—that can be portrayed as justifying the trip.

International organizations also function as interest groups trying to influence U.S. policy decisions. (For different types of IOs, see Box 11.1.) They make demands, exert pressure, and offer rewards for support. They become part of the policy calculus as a matter of course.

# Ad Hoc Versus Institutional Multilateralism

Too often, policy debates focus on *multilateral* or *unilateral* as if that were an enduring binary strategic choice. Even the most committed multilateralist cannot always rely on IOs. Even the most determined unilateralist will at times find multilateral approaches necessary or at least useful. The multilateral condemnation of Iraq in 1990 and 2002 by the UNSC empowered and strengthened U.S. foreign policy and added to the roster of nations willing to lend support to the subsequent military operations. UN reluctance to authorize combat operations against Serbia over Kosovo in 1999 was partially offset by the willingness of another IO, NATO, to endorse the mission.

Most international problems are either bilateral, between two parties alone, or multilateral and multifaceted. Bilateral disputes can be resolved without the involvement of third parties, but sometimes, those onlookers can be helpful in facilitating exchanges or weighing in on behalf of one of

---

**Box 11.1**

## International Instruments and Entities

Given the widespread use of *international* in the naming of things, it's useful to keep several distinctions in mind. *International organizations* (IOs) as used in this book are organizations with national governments, and sometimes other international organizations, as members. They are usually established by treaties, have permanent staff, and perform regular activities, like the UN and its specialized agencies. They may be used as instruments of U.S. foreign policy as a forum for debate or negotiation or as a means of acting, such as giving aid or conducting military operations.

*Nongovernmental organizations* (NGOs) are groups separate from governments, usually not for profit, that conduct activities in other nations. They may deliver services, like Doctors Without Borders, or advocate for particular policies, like Amnesty International and numerous environmental groups. For U.S. foreign policy purposes, NGOs function either as advocacy groups or as potential instruments abroad when their goals coincide with the U.S. government's.

*Multinational corporations* (MNCs) are business organizations operating in more than one country. For U.S. foreign policy purposes, they are usually stakeholders and policy advocates, seeking support and favorable treatment by government. As such, they more often try to use the U.S. government as an instrument for their purposes than the other way around.

the disputants. Issues involving more than one country often benefit from having several participants involved in the discussions and actions. How to proceed thus depends on numerous factors that need to be considered, not simply a *go it alone* or *let's all work this out together* approach. *Coalitions of the willing* can act with fewer constraints than coalitions that form within a particular IO, but coalitions of the willing already trained and practiced can act even better and faster.

Different organizations have different strengths and weaknesses that make them more or less suitable for particular activities. The UN, for example, was designed to resolve disputes among smaller powers on the assumption of great power unanimity. When the Cold War fractured that agreement, the organization lost much of its effectiveness. The UN has become stronger and more effective since great power unity became more common in the 1990s. The G-8 served as a useful forum for economically advanced countries to coordinate policies among themselves but had to be broadened to the G-20 when economic problems became more global in both cause and remedy. APEC has made formal statements on North Korean nuclear programs and has taken preliminary actions on infectious disease control as well as other issues not directly related to its primary focus on economic relations and trade.

Some IOs have large staffs; others make do with small staffs. Some make decisions by formal votes; others require consensus and thus unanimity in order to act. While a few have the capacity to act to implement their decisions, most are limited to making recommendations to member states.[4] All these factors affect how and whether the United States can work with an organization in pursuit of its own foreign policy goals.

Other nations face similar choices and often choose to utilize IOs for their own purposes. They can shop for the forum most likely to be sympathetic to their positions. They can build coalitions within and among international groups. And, they can resort to *ad hoc multilateralism* for particular issues. The United States has joined several of these entities, often called *contact groups,* to deal with issues like Bosnia and Kosovo, Tajikistan, and Haiti. They can be a useful supplement to the established, larger organizations.[5]

# International Institutions

For U.S. foreign policy, the most important international institutions are those concerned with international politics and security. These are the ones that can give international legal authorization for sanctions and military operations and that serve as venues for negotiations. Because other member nations can also use these organizations to challenge U.S. policy, America needs to engage with them and understand their capabilities.

### United Nations

The UN is an important and at times unavoidable instrument for American foreign policy. Designed in 1945 to protect U.S. interests with a UNSC veto, headquartered in New York City, and funded to a significant extent—currently 22% of its core budget—by U.S. contributions, the UN is *the* global organization, with 192 member nations, and the symbolic guarantor of peace and security in a turbulent world. Its other members often disagree with U.S. policies, but their support, when it comes, can legitimate and leverage American actions.

The UN is a large organization with a $2.6 billion annual budget, not counting the costs of peacekeeping operations (around $8 billion in 2010) and the various specialized agencies (about $3 billion). The professional staff of the Secretariat has about 2,500 people, chosen both for their expertise and for geographical diversity. There are four major action centers at the UN: the General Assembly (UNGA), the UNSC, the Secretary-General (S-G) and the Secretariat, plus the specialized agencies.

**General Assembly.** The UNGA is the forum for discussion of the UN's 192 member nations. While it can be disparaged as a toothless debating society that ritually passes high-sounding resolutions that are then mostly ignored, the assembly's annual session, starting in September, is a major venue for international discussions. Leaders of many nations come to speak—and to use the occasion for private meetings with other officials. The U.S. president usually spends a day or two in high-level meetings in addition to his annual address, and the secretary of state regularly spends one to two weeks in New York in talks with foreign officials.

UNGA votes are important indicators of international sentiment on some topics, and even the United States can respond to opponents by ignoring them or by working harder to persuade or accommodate them. In 2009, the United States voted against UNGA resolutions more than any other member. Over all, the American position was supported by other members 39% of the time on recorded votes. (The State Department is required to report to Congress each year on UN voting patterns.) The level of support has varied over time and by particular issue, from about 50% support in the mid-1990s to around 23% to 25% in the mid-2000s. The most frequent disagreements have come on Middle East issues, where other members have voted with the United States only about 10% to 11% of the time since 2003. Not surprisingly, the nation voting with the U.S. most often is Israel at 97% of the time.[6]

Despite its many divisions and factions, the UNGA has acted in at least two important ways on peace and security issues. In 1950, it adopted the Uniting for Peace resolution that declared the GA's right to act to restore peace and security when the UNSC was unable to agree. (The United States pushed for the resolution as a way of getting around the usual Soviet veto in the UNSC.) And in 2005, at the world summit commemorating the UN's 50th anniversary, national leaders approved an *outcome document* that included a declaration that both individual states and the international community have a "responsibility to protect" their citizens. This doctrine underpinned the UNSC's decision in 2011 authorizing military intervention in Libya. The GA also acted to promote the Ottawa Convention banning antipersonnel mines when the major powers were reluctant to support it.[7]

**Security Council.** The UNSC is the most powerful UN body because it can vote binding measures on all UN members on matters of war, peace, and security. Such votes are subject to a veto by any of the five permanent members: the United States, United Kingdom, Russia, China, and France. Avoiding a veto, therefore, often requires crucial negotiations among the Perm 5 (P-5) as they are called. The UNSC has developed a series of informal practices for consultations and negotiations, sometimes among the whole membership, sometimes just among the P-5.[8] There is even a special room for such meetings separate from the regular UNSC chamber.

Corralling votes in the UN is similar to winning votes in Congress: The president and senior officials make arguments, listen to concerns that often relate to side issues, and then respond with arguments, threats, promises, or changes. U.S. officials made major efforts to win support for the UNSC resolutions against Iraq in 1990, and in subsequent years, they bypassed the UNSC when they knew they lacked the votes for action against Kosovo in 1999 and for tougher language against Iraq in 2003.

The UNSC has authorized numerous major policy actions over the decades since 1945. (See Table 11.2 for a listing of major UN military operations.) In 1950 it authorized, while the Soviet delegate was boycotting the organization, an American-led force to counter the North Korean invasion of South Korea. In 1992 it authorized *all necessary means*—the phrase permitting military force—to create safe havens and a no-fly zone in Bosnia. In 2001, it approved the British-led international force helping the United States in Afghanistan. In 2008, it authorized all necessary means against piracy and armed robbery at sea. In 2011, it authorized use of force to protect Libyan civilians and establish a no-fly zone there.[9]

In addition to authorizing hostile force, in what are called *Chapter VII peace-building operations*, the UNSC has approved many Chapter VI peacekeeping operations, where the opposing sides have agreed to stop fighting but need outside forces to keep them compliant or apart. The United States welcomed each one of these either as the best available means to reduce the level of violence or the threat of war or as a way of avoiding direct U.S. military involvement in the conflict. These have included more than 3,000 troops sent to the Suez Canal and Sinai Peninsula in 1956–1957 and another 7,000 in 1973–1979; 6,400 military observers sent to Cyprus in 1964, with 1,000 still there; 1,400 military observers sent to the Golan Heights in 1974 and still there; 6,150 military observers sent to Lebanon in 1978 and more than 12,000 still there; and more than 4,000 troops sent to the Ethiopian–Eritrean border in 2000, with more than 600 still there. Sizable UN operations with both troops and civilians have also been conducted in Namibia, Somalia, Cambodia, East Timor, Bosnia–Croatia, Kosovo, Sudan–Darfur, and the Democratic Republic of Congo. In fact, of the 74 peacekeeping operations voted by the UN since 1948, 12 are still in

| Table 11.2 | Major United Nations Military Operations, 1948–2011 | |
|---|---|---|
| **PLACE** | **NAME** | **DATES** |
| Palestine, Israel | UNTSO | 1948–present |
| India/Pakistan border | UNMOGIP | 1949–present |
| Korea | UNC | 1950–present |
| Suez, Sinai | UNEF | 1956–1967 |
| Cyprus | UNFICYP | 1964–present |
| Suez, Sinai | UNEF II | 1973–1979 |
| Syria, Golan Heights | UNDOF | 1974–present |
| Lebanon | UNIFIL | 1978–present |
| Namibia | UNTAG | 1989–1990 |
| Cambodia | UNTAC | 1991–1995 |
| Bosnia/Croatia | UNPROFOR | 1992–1995 |
| Somalia | UNOSOM II | 1993–1995 |
| East Timor | UNTAET | 1999–2002 |
| Democratic Republic of Congo | MONUC | 1999–present |
| Kosovo | UNMIK | 1999–present |
| Ethiopia/Eritrea | UNMEE | 2000–2008 |
| Liberia | UNMIL | 2003–present |
| Cote d'Ivoire | UNOCI | 2004–present |
| Haiti | MNUSTAH | 2004–present |
| Sudan | UNMIS | 2005–present |
| Central African Republic/Chad | MNURCAT | 2007–present |
| Darfur | UNAMID | 2007–present |

This list shows how many UN military operations have become semipermanent as well as how many have been started in recent years, especially in Africa. It illustrates as well how the UN gets stuck with a lot of operations that nations prefer to outsource, such as Darfur. Many nations eagerly participate in these operations because it gives their military forces valuable training, free equipment, and UN-paid salaries.

being, 7 of them dating from before 2000. In 2010, more than 100,000 UN personnel were involved.[10] While the United States has paid about 25% of UN peacekeeping costs as part of its regular assessment, it has made major troop contributions only in Korea, the Sinai, Somalia, and the Balkans. The U.S.-led Gulf War coalition against Iraq in 1991 was not a UN operation, though force had been authorized by the UNSC.

Short of the use of force, the UNSC has enacted comprehensive sanctions against pariah regimes, including Southern Rhodesia, Iraq, Yugoslavia, and Haiti. It also has approved at different times arms embargoes against South

Africa, Angola, Libya, Afghanistan, Haiti, Sierre Leone, al Qaeda and the Taliban, Iran, and North Korea.[11] Some of these actions can be considered successful, but others fell short. Achievement of international sanctions has been a major U.S. goal, especially in confronting Libya, North Korea, Iran, and al Qaeda and the Taliban as sanctions tend to be ineffective unless broadly applied.

An important reason for seeking UN sanctions even if the prospects are limited is to build momentum and international support. The UNSC adopted a series of progressively tougher sanctions against Iraq prior to the U.S.-led invasion of 2003. The same process has been followed with regard to Iran's nuclear program, allowing the United States to win support for ever-tighter sanctions as Iran fails to comply with earlier resolutions.

Avoiding a veto often requires delicate diplomacy with the other permanent members, but sometimes, the pressure of the international community can be effective, as appeared to be the case in the Russian and Chinese abstentions from the resolution imposing a no-fly zone in Libya in 2011. While those nations did not really want to endorse UN action on general principles, they were reluctant to ignore the Arab League's call for action to protect civilians. (See the case study for this chapter for more details.)

**Secretary-General.** The S-G is the chief administrative officer of the UN, and he has the crucial power of initiative to raise issues before the UNSC and otherwise engage UN organizations. Forbidden to seek or receive instructions from member states, he can be the impartial facilitator of the peaceful resolution of disputes and the management of crises. He can be actively involved himself, or he can name special envoys or representatives to mediate particular conflicts or monitor certain issues. More than 60 people have been assigned to such tasks in recent years.[12]

The S-G has to work most closely with members of the UNSC and is beholden to them for his job. While the UNGA votes him into office, the UNSC must first approve the nomination on a vote subject to a P-5 veto. The United States has worked hard to see that friendly, or at least non-hostile, people are chosen for that position. In 1996, after clashing repeatedly with the S-G, Clinton administration officials worked openly to deny Boutros Boutros-Ghali a second term, replacing him with Kofi Annan.[13]

The United States conducts its UN operations through a special mission in New York, headed by an ambassador who, in many administrations, is given cabinet rank by the president. The American delegate has often been a controversial figure who has strongly criticized the organization to which he or she has been posted. Jeane Kirkpatrick, UN ambassador under President Reagan, once said, "What takes place in the Security Council more closely resembles a mugging than either a political debate or an effort at problem-solving." One of George W. Bush's nominees for the post, John Bolton, said, "If the U.N. building in New York lost 10 stories, it wouldn't make a bit of difference." Another indicator of controversy is that Bolton was never confirmed by the Senate and had to leave his post after 15 months.

One of his predecessors, Richard Holbrooke, faced a Senate delay of over a year before winning confirmation. Opposition to both men was partly in an assertion of senatorial power and partly in disagreement with the nominee's policy positions, but in both cases, the message received abroad was that filling the UN post was not that important.

## Congress and the United Nations

Congress blows hot and cold toward the UN, usually hot with criticism and cold in terms of support. During the Cold War, members frequently criticized the UN as ineffective because it was often stymied by the U.S.–Soviet rivalry. Individual countries earned praise or blame on Capitol Hill on the basis of their voting percentage in agreement with the United States.

Starting in the 1980s, Congress began voting cuts in U.S. contributions to the UN in response to programs and activities it strongly disfavored, including actions that seemed to benefit the Palestine Liberal Organization (PLO) and the UNGA resolution equating Zionism with racism. A 1985 law required a 20% cut in U.S. contributions unless certain reforms were adopted. This measure seemed to work, and similar efforts were enacted in the 1990s to achieve additional reforms. Further reform-forcing bills and amendments were adopted in the mid-2000s, but they did not become law.

What was achieved was a reduction in the U.S. share of basic UN costs from 25% to 22% and a cut in the share of peacekeeping costs from about 30% to 27%. (By comparison, the top contributors to the regular UN budget in 2010 were: Japan, 16.6%; Germany, 8.6%; UK, 6.6%; France, 6.3%; Italy, 5.1%; Canada, 3.0%; Spain 3.0%; China, 2.7%; and Mexico, 2.3%.) Nevertheless, in dollar terms, the United States now pays more than $6 billion each year for the UN, and pressures are rising in Congress to cut U.S. contributions further. The major current costs include $1.2 billion in regularly assessed contributions, $450 million in voluntary contributions to specialized agencies like the UN Development Program and UNICEF, and $2.1 billion for peacekeeping. As of 2010, the UN calculated that the United States still owed $860 million in arrearages that accrued during the earlier congressionally mandated ceilings.

Less controversial, most of the time, are the activities of the UN's specialized agencies and programs. The World Food Program spends about $3 billion each year feeding the hungry in more than 80 nations. The Food and Agricultural Organization spends more than $900 million in technical assistance to fight hunger. The UN Children's Fund, UNICEF, spends about $2.4 billion in long-term humanitarian and development assistance for children and mothers. The High Commissioner for Refugees spends about $1.2 billion in relief and resettlement of more than 20 million people in 116 countries. The World Health Organization (WHO) has global vaccination campaigns and responses to pandemics and other health emergencies, spending more than $470 million. Many of these activities are partnered with charitable groups and NGOs. The UN also runs many other programs, some of a technical nature like the World Meteorological Organization and the Universal Postal Union, as well as programs on drug control, the environment, and prevention of HIV/AIDS. The World Bank and IMF are also legally part of the UN system.

In 2011, however, the UN's Educational, Scientific and Cultural Organization (UNESCO), which runs programs in literacy and science education and designates World Heritage Sites, admitted the Palestinian Authority to membership, triggering U.S. laws passed in the 1990s that required the United States to stop funding the organization. Prior to that action, UNESCO had an annual budget of $653 million and 1,955 regular personnel.

As these examples indicate, the UN and the S-G are important actors in international affairs that can affect U.S. decisions and actions. UNSC disagreements over Kosovo in 1999 led the United States to get NATO approval instead for the operations against Serbia. Similarly, UNSC divisions over sanctions on Iran have prevented the United States from achieving the breadth and severity of sanctions that America preferred. If the president chooses to work with or through the UN, the United States can gain valuable legitimacy for its policies. Its membership also requires the United States to engage with those who want to use the UN and its components against U.S. policies and interest. International organizations are a two-way street.

## International Atomic Energy Agency

The IAEA is part of the UN system, though autonomous, and reports to the UNGA and the UNSC. Created in 1957 and headquartered in Vienna, it now has 151 member states, a staff of 2,300 people, and an annual budget of more than $450 million. Its original mandate was to promote safe, secure, and peaceful nuclear technologies, but it gained significant additional responsibilities under the 1968 Non-Proliferation Treaty (NPT) because that pact requires signatories to conclude comprehensive safeguard agreements with the IAEA. There are now 171 states with safeguard agreements.

Policing those agreements has put the IAEA at the center of international efforts to limit the spread of nuclear weapons. In 1991, with strong U.S. support, the UNSC tasked the IAEA with inspecting and dismantling suspected Iraqi nuclear programs. The UNSC adopted additional resolutions to force Iraqi compliance with IAEA inspections in 1993 and 1997. When Saddam Hussein refused further cooperation in 1998, inspectors were pulled out of the country.

In November 2002, after a UNSC resolution declaring Iraq in "material breach" of its obligations under various prior resolutions, UN and IAEA teams were again allowed back. When the teams reported lack of evidence of Iraqi weapons of mass destruction (WMD) in early March 2003, the United States insisted on the withdrawal of inspectors so that military operations could begin.

IAEA has also been a key player in international efforts to limit North Korea's nuclear capabilities. Pyongyang withdrew from membership in

1994 after a long dispute over IAEA inspections but reached an *agreed framework* with the United States allowing renewed inspections in return for fuel assistance and two light-water nuclear reactors. In 2002, after evidence emerged that North Korea had a secret uranium enrichment program that would have been in violation of its earlier agreements, the government dismantled the inspection devices and expelled the IAEA inspectors. They were allowed to return in July 2007 but left in April 2009 after North Korea decided to cease all cooperation with the IAEA.

When Iran began building its first nuclear reactor in 2002, the IAEA criticized Tehran and was allowed to send inspection teams. This was the start of a series of IAEA findings and UNSC resolutions that has continued for several years. Each time the IAEA found that Iran had failed to meet important obligations, the UNSC voted additional, tougher sanctions.

This history shows that the IAEA is an important tool for the United States and the international community to try to enforce and then verify compliance with nonproliferation promises. Once the agency gets engaged, it seems to act on professional and institutional bases without the need for diplomatic vote gathering.

# Regional Institutions

There are many organizations with regional focuses and memberships that are important actors in international affairs. The European Union (EU), for example, is a supranational government with its own, albeit fledgling, institutions for diplomacy and foreign affairs. In this chapter, however, we consider only organizations of which the United States is a member and which, therefore, might be utilized as instruments of U.S. foreign policy.

### North Atlantic Treaty Organization

The most robust and operational regional group is NATO. Formed in 1949 as a defensive military alliance against the Soviet bloc, NATO has grown in size to 28 nations and has deployed military forces both in Europe and beyond. It has a civilian secretariat, a military committee and staff, and even a parliamentary assembly that functions as a liaison to national legislatures and the broader public. The large 13,000-person staff is slated to be cut to 9,000 over the next few years. The current budget totals $2.2 billion annually, $1.8 billion for military activities and $390 million for the civil budget, of which the U.S. share is about 22%. These figures do not include the operational costs of deployed units.

The original membership of 12 was expanded in 1952 by the addition of Greece and Turkey, in 1955 by West Germany, and in 1982 by Spain. See the full list in Table 11.3. After the end of the Cold War, the alliance created a process for grooming former Warsaw Pact nations for membership. In 1999, the Czech Republic, Hungary, and Poland joined. Several more countries were added in 2004: Bulgaria, Estonia, Latvia, Lithuania, Romania, Slovakia, and Slovenia. Albania and Croatia joined in 2009, bringing the total to the current 28. Georgia and Ukraine are considered future members, pending resolution of various issues, and active negotiations are under way with Macedonia, Montenegro, and Bosnia–Herzegovina. On many foreign policy issues, the longtime members of NATO have different views from the newer members that were formerly part of the Soviet bloc.

During the Cold War, NATO organized and equipped itself for war with the Soviet Union and its allies. It developed institutions for consultation—the ambassadorial-level North Atlantic Council—and for military planning, with a military committee with representatives of member chiefs of staff, a defense planning committee, and a nuclear planning group. It developed programs for weapons standardization and logistics and created 11 command bases, now slated to be cut to 7.

Although some NATO members contributed troops to the conflicts in Korea and the 1991 Gulf War, the first NATO-authorized military operations were in the Balkans in the 1990s. Allied aircraft conducted operations in August through September 1995, which led to the Dayton peace talks and accords. NATO then contributed peacekeepers to the implementation force (IFOR) that became the stabilization force (SFOR), which lasted until 2005. The most recent major NATO military operation was in Libya in 2011, as described in the case study for this chapter. In each case, the United States joined with its allies and provided key capabilities, but NATO involvement allowed burden sharing of the costs and risks of the operation.

The North Atlantic Council, the senior decision body composed of ambassadors from the member nations, decides matters largely by consensus. No formal votes are taken. Instead of requiring formal unanimity, however, an objecting nation must file a formal notice of opposition. Because the pressure for agreement can be high, as it was when missions were launched in Kosovo in 1999, some countries preferred to abstain rather than become obstructionists.

When the UNSC was unable to agree on measures to halt Serbian repression of ethnic Albanians in Kosovo in 1999, the United States pressed for, and NATO agreed to take action in, what became a 78-day air campaign. U.S. forces delivered more than 80% of the weapons used in the attacks. NATO troops then formed the UNSC-blessed Kosovo Force (KFOR), which remained in place as of 2011. KFOR units also deployed to Albania during 2001–2003, when they were succeeded by the EU force.

On September 12, 2001, the North Atlantic Council, for the first time in NATO's history, formally invoked Article 5 of the 1949 Washington Treaty, which declared the "an armed attack against one" member "shall be considered an attack against them all." Despite that show of solidarity, the U.S. government consciously decided to bypass NATO in forming its coalition to fight in Afghanistan.[14] Nevertheless, several NATO members participated in the U.S.-led Operation Enduring Freedom in Afghanistan and then in the UN-mandated International Security Assistance Force (ISAF) created in December 2001 and likely to remain in Afghanistan at least until 2014.

The International Institutions Instrument

In 2011, NATO members accounted for about 90% of the non-U.S. military personnel in ISAF.

While NATO members were sharply divided over the 2003 U.S.-led Iraq war, NATO agreed in 2004 to operate a training mission in Iraq. The numbers involved were small—only 170 troops in 2011—but there has been broad symbolic support and participation by 23 member nations.

As further evidence of the alliance's willingness to conduct out-of-area operations, NATO forces gave support to the African Union's mission in Sudan during 2005–2007 and in Somalia in 2007. Since 2008, NATO has also conducted antipiracy operations in the Gulf of Aden. These operations, strongly supported by the United States, allowed others to shoulder the burden while U.S. forces remained committed in large numbers in Iraq and Afghanistan.

In 2011, NATO undertook to conduct military operations in support of the UNSC resolution calling for the protection of civilians in rebellious Libya. NATO aircraft imposed a no-fly zone, and ships enforced an arms embargo. Between March 19 and October 31, NATO aircraft conducted more than 26,500 sorties, of which 9,700 were strike sorties. After taking the lead in the initial weeks, the United States deliberately switched to a supporting role. In the end, only 25% of the air sorties were flown by U.S. aircraft.

In 2003, the alliance formally decided to create a NATO Response Force (NRF) so that it would have some readily deployable units to contribute to international coalitions. The plan is to have an immediate response force of about 13,000 that could grow to as much as 25,000 in a short period. The NRF, composed of units assigned on rotation, took shape over the following years and was used for humanitarian relief after a major earthquake in Pakistan in 2005 and even after Hurricane Katrina in the United States in 2005.

Some Europeans see the NRF as a means of having a military force separate from the United States, while many U.S. analysts see it as a welcome addition to NATO's usable capabilities.

NATO faces several political challenges as well as the practical military one of maintaining ready and modernized forces at a time of severe governmental austerity throughout the alliance. While formally open to membership for all European democracies, Russia is still strongly opposed to NATO expansion. While concerned about nuclear proliferation, terrorism, cyber attacks, and instability outside Europe, alliance members often disagree among themselves or with the United States on how to proceed. Nevertheless, NATO remains a strong institution, a ready forum for consultations and decision with a diverse set of military and diplomatic instruments.

## Organization for Security and Co-operation in Europe

Larger in membership than NATO but more limited in institutional capacity is the OSCE. Of its 56 members, the United States is the only non-European nation, but OSCE has partnership arrangements with Japan,

South Korea, and Australia as well as with Israel and some North African nations. It has an annual budget of about $215 million, derived from voluntary contributions by members, and a staff of 2,900, most of whom are assigned to one of 18 field missions in Central Asia and the nations of the former Yugoslavia.

The organization began as the forum for promulgating the Helsinki Final Act in 1975, which codified post–World War II European borders but also endorsed civil rights, leading to the growth of dissident groups in the Soviet Union. The organization continued as the Conference for Security and Cooperation in Europe until renamed and given permanent institutional status in 1995. It served as a useful venue for East–West dialogue during the Cold War, and has since undertaken programs to help many former Soviet bloc nations develop national capacities to manage their borders, regulate the transfer of weapons, and promote media freedom and other aspects of good governance. It is one of the leading organizations in providing international election observers.

These numerous activities make OSCE a good vehicle for outsourcing some nation-building tasks that the host nations request as well as a forum for multinational dialogue of issues that directly involve members. Some nations apparently hoped that OSCE would become the hub of security cooperation in Europe, especially because it was more inclusive in membership, but in recent years, Russia has complained that the organization was too much dominated by the United States and NATO.[15] The United States uses OSCE mechanisms to oversee several arms control agreements involving Europe and to engage in its weekly *security dialogue* on regional issues.

## Organization of American States

The OAS is the world's oldest continuous regional organization that serves as a forum for hemispheric dialogue and an institution to resolve conflicts among members and promote democratic practices. Begun in 1889–1890, then reorganized as the Pan American Union in 1914, the OAS charter of 1948 created the modern institution. It has 35 members, a staff of nearly 700, and an annual core budget of about $90 million that does not include voluntary contributions to particular programs and activities. The U.S. share is around 59%. The OAS operates under a secretary-general, has a permanent council and an annual general assembly, and is the vehicle for annual Summits of the Americas since 1995.

The organization suspended Cuba and imposed sanctions in 1962 but, in 2009, lifted the suspension and opened a dialogue with Havana that is aimed at returning Cuba to the group if it meets certain conditions. The United States has regularly tried to use the OAS as a tool for hemisphere-wide pressure on the Castro regime but has also felt counterpressure to be more flexible.

There is an inter-American defense pact—the Rio Treaty of 1947—that contains language similar to NATO, declaring an attack on one to be an attack on all, but the OAS has never developed military institutions to buttress that treaty. Instead, as part of its work, the OAS has been a forum for hemispheric dialogue and for trying to resolve conflicts among members. It regularly sends missions of election observers throughout the hemisphere as part of efforts to promote democratic practices. Under a 1992 amendment to the OAS charter, members can be suspended if their democratically elected governments are overthrown by force. This provision was broadened in 2001 and has led to a series of high-level missions, conflict resolution actions, multilateral diplomacy, and sanctions in several countries. In 2009, for example, the OAS, with strong U.S. support, condemned the ouster of the Honduran president and arranged mediation leading to free elections of a successor.

While the OAS has been involved in various border disputes and the defense of democracy against coups, it has a mixed record and has often been bypassed in favor of subregional ad hoc groups.[16] While other members were divided over U.S. anticommunist policies in the 1980s, with many unwilling to support actions against the leftist government in Nicaragua, they have found more common ground in recent years in counterdrug activities as well as acting against coups.

For military consultation and coordination on counterdrug and humanitarian missions, the United States uses the Southern Command (SOUTHCOM), headquartered in Florida. It is one of the regional military commands and works closely with the military in countries of the Western hemisphere.

### Association of Southeast Asian Nations, the Association of Southeast Asian Nations Regional Forum, and Asia–Pacific Economic Cooperation

Asia has several regional organizations, two of which have the United States as a member and which range in size from 10 members to 27. See Table 11.3 for a list of the different organizations. What they share are limitations in size, focus, and institutional capacity. As Margaret Karns and Karen Mingst say, "Asian and Asia-Pacific regional institutions tend to be informal, having few specific rules, no binding commitments, small secretariats, consensus decisionmaking, and a strong emphasis on process over substance and outcomes. Informal processes include extensive meetings, consultations, and dialogues; informal outcomes typically refer to agreements on general principles and nonbinding codes of conduct."[17]

The oldest of these regional Asian organizations is ASEAN, established in 1967 and limited to nations of the region. In 1994, ASEAN created ARF to consider security questions with a much broader membership, including the United States, the EU, Japan, China, Russia, India, and others. ARF seeks to promote dialogue on issues like maritime security, confidence-building measures such as notification of military exercises, illegal migrations, and terrorist financing.[18]

APEC has economies rather than states as members and includes most of the nations on the rim of the Pacific Ocean. Created in 1989, it has gained visibility and utility because of annual summits and regular meetings of member foreign and trade ministers. The United States has used the

| Table 11.3 | Membership of Asian Regional Organizations | |
|---|---|---|
| **ASEAN** | **ARF (ASEAN members +)** | **APEC (ASEAN members +)** |
| Brunei | Australia | Australia |
| Cambodia | Bangladesh | Canada |
| Indonesia | Canada | Chile |
| Laos | China | China |
| Malaysia | European Union | Hong Kong |
| Myanmar | India | Japan |
| Philippines | Japan | Korea |
| Singapore | N. Korea | Mexico |
| Thailand | S. Korea | New Zealand |
| Vietnam | Mongolia | Papua New Guinea |
| | New Zealand | Peru |
| | Pakistan | Russia |
| | Papua New Guinea | Taiwan |
| | Russia | United States |
| | Sri Lanka | |
| | Timor Leste | |
| | United States | |

There are many overlapping regional organizations in Asia, each providing a forum for collaboration or conflict and thus allowing members some choices for venue shopping when they wish to raise issues. As is shown here, membership is not restricted just to those nations geographically in Asia. For instance, Canada, the EU, and the United States are members of ARF.

summits for dialogue on foreign economic issues, and APEC itself has been a venue for cooperation on contagious diseases and climate change.[19]

The organizations are used, as the members see fit, as forums for regional engagement. The United States has used APEC in particular to push trade and economic cooperation, and it serves as an annual gathering at which to raise current economic and political issues. Insofar as U.S. policy pivots toward Asia and faces rising powers like China, these Asian organizations become important stages where the United States can build support for its policies.

# Economic Institutions

The United States worked to establish the postwar global economic system after 1945 and remains a key player in its many institutions. While each has its own mandate, membership, rules, and goals, the United States has used its memberships to pursue its national policies and its vision of a world economic order. Instead of trying on its own to manage the global economy, it relies on the IMF to promote economic stability, on the World Bank and similar regional banks to promote long-term development, and on the WTO to enforce trading rules and agreements.

## G-8 and G-20

As the global economy entered a series of crises beginning in 2007–2008 and continuing to the present, the United States and other economic powers have made increasing use of groups originally set up just to provide periodic consultations. Regular meetings of the finance ministers and heads of the central banks of the major economic powers began in the 1970s as the Group of Six—France, Germany, Italy, Japan, the United Kingdom, and the United States. In 1975, France formalized the G-6 and hosted a summit of heads of government, a practice that has continued ever since. In 1976, Canada was added to make the G-7, and in 1997—for political more than economic reasons—Russia was invited to be part of the G-8. Together, the member nations account for about 14% of the world's population and 60% of the gross global product.

Now, in addition to the annual summits, there are regular meetings of foreign ministers, finance ministers, and environment ministers. The agenda each year is set by the host government, whose leader heads the G-8 in rotation. There is no permanent secretariat.

As the 2008 financial crisis hit in the United States and began spreading worldwide, President George W. Bush convened a summit in Washington, D.C., of a larger group, now called the G-20. See Table 11.4 for the membership of each group. In addition to the G-8, the G-20 has ten other members, including Argentina, Australia, Brazil, China, India, Indonesia, Mexico, Saudi Arabia, South Africa, South Korea, Turkey, and the EU. Together, those nations and the EU account for 85% of gross global product. But, the organization still has no permanent staff or structure.

The Washington summit created a venue for international cooperation on major financial matters, and at the London summit in April 2009, the leaders committed to add $1.1 trillion for the IMF, the multilateral development banks, and other organizations. At the third summit, in Pittsburgh in September 2009, the G-20 leaders formally declared their organization the premier international economic forum. Spain and the Netherlands have also been allowed to sit in, though they are not yet formal members.

The G-20 held twice-yearly summit meetings through 2010 and one in 2011. These have been supplemented by meetings of finance ministers. The agendas so far have been largely confined to major financial issues like IMF reform, financial regulation, and trade. Meanwhile, the G-8 meetings continue, and the national leaders have added more noneconomic topics to the agenda, like climate change, aid to Africa, and some security issues like piracy and nonproliferation. If this division of focus continues, the United States has two additional forums in which to raise its own foreign policy issues. The value of regular meetings and institutional organizations is that

| Table 11.4 | G-8 and G-20 Members with 2010 Gross Domestic Product in Billions | |
|---|---|---|
| **G-8 MEMBERS** | **G-20 MEMBERS (G-8 MEMBERS +)** | |
| Canada, $1,577 | Argentina, $369 | |
| France, 2,560 | Australia, 924 | |
| Germany, 3,280 | Brazil, 2,088 | |
| Italy, 2,051 | China, 5,927 | |
| Japan, 5,459 | EU*, 16,220 | |
| Russia, 1,480 | India, 1,727 | |
| United Kingdom, 2,249 | Indonesia, 707 | |
| United States, 14,587 | Mexico, 1,035 | |
| | Saudi Arabia, 435 | |
| | South Africa, 364 | |
| | South Korea, 1,014 | |
| | Turkey, 734 | |

* The EU includes G-8 members France, Germany, Italy, and the United Kingdom. The EU gross domestic product (GDP) figure reflects their inclusion. EU GDP minus those states is $6,080 billion.

The original grouping of major economic powers has been expanded in recent years in recognition of the growing economic strength of the additional nations and in order to craft more broadly based economic policies.

Source: GDP figures from the World Bank, Gross Domestic Product 2010, http://databank .worldbank.org/databank/download/GDP.pdf.

they allow for advance planning and consultation so that agreements might be achieved. Ad hoc meetings are usually less effective. A scheduled meeting is also action forcing on governments and their bureaucracies to decide on policies and priorities.

### The International Monetary Fund and Other International Financial Institutions

The IMF and the World Bank were established at the end of World War II to provide a stable monetary system and to finance reconstruction and development, first in Europe and later across the globe. Both make use of financial contributions by members and turn a profit from their operations. Members have voting power proportionate to their contributions—the U.S. leads at about 17%—and votes on major issues require supermajority support of 70% or in some cases 85%.

The IMF has a staff of about 2,650 people and an annual operating budget around $740 million. Most nations are members—186 in all. The IMF performs three main tasks: surveillance of the economic and financial policies of nations and dialogue with them; financial assistance such as lines of credit, currency purchases, and loans; and technical assistance to improve their local financial systems. The IMF helps countries with problems on the basis of conditionality, linking the assistance to acceptance and performance of specific policy actions.[20]

The World Bank, including the subsidiary institutions of the International Finance Corporation and the International Development Association, lends money to development projects—and expects payback. It has a staff of about 10,000 people. Both the IMF and the bank employ many professional economists and have strong organizational cultures described as "apolitical, technocratic, and economic rationality."[21]

Both institutions have come under criticism in recent years—the IMF, for perpetuating the *Washington consensus* (so-called because the two organizations were headquartered in the U.S. capital and their economists were of one mind) requiring loan recipients to impose severe domestic austerity with few deviations from the template, and the bank, for approving loans on narrow criteria with insufficient consideration of social and environmental effects.[22] Both are adopting various reforms in response to these and other criticisms.

In addition to the World Bank, in order to represent its interests, the United States belongs to several regional development banks: the Inter-American Development Bank, the Asian Development Bank, the African Development Bank, and the European Bank for Reconstruction and Development. The Treasury Department represents the U.S. government and votes the U.S. shares in each institution.

The United States has used these institutions for its own foreign policy goals in addition to the specific economic objectives of the banks and the IMF. Scholars have found significant correlations between a country's support for U.S. policies and approval of IMF help, whether or not the United States acted consciously to those ends. For example, analysts point to IMF's support for friendly Zaire (now the Democratic Republic of Congo) during the Cold War; generous help to Egypt; and very favorable conditions on help to Pakistan soon after the 9/11 attacks. Other studies show that countries that voted less often with the United States in the UN received IMF loans less often and that the punishment period for nations falling into noncompliance with the IMF was shorter for U.S.-favored ones. Moreover, U.S. allies tended to receive IMF support with fewer conditions attached.[23]

These studies demonstrate that the United States can—and probably does—use these international financial institutions as an important tool of foreign policy. The mechanisms may be less overt, but their outcomes are visible.

During the global economic crisis of 2008–2009, IFIs were surprisingly responsive and flexible. Pushed by decisions at the G-20 leaders meetings, they mobilized an additional $1.1 trillion in resources to help troubled economies and to buttress trade finance. The IMF provided timely advice and lending commitments of more than $170 billion in the early months and then, urged by the United States, agreed to expand its borrowing pool by up to $500 billion. The multilateral development banks launched a fast-track facility to expedite loans to the poorest countries and, at a time when few institutions were lending, provided $222 billion in financing.[24]

## World Trade Organization

The WTO was established in 1995 to replace the less-structured system of the General Agreement on Tariffs and Trade (GATT) that had been created after World War II. One of the main features of WTO is its Disputes Settlement Body (DSB) that supervises consultations between disputing members and establishes panels to hear disputes and issue reports. Findings by those panels are automatically accepted unless vetoed by all WTO members. When the DSB makes a ruling in favor of the complainant, the responding nation has a period of time to come into compliance, usually by repealing or modifying the law, rule, or policy that was found to be in violation. Delays can trigger punitive tariffs.

As this process indicates, WTO is less of an executive body than a legislative and judicial one. It makes rules to enforce the principle of non-discrimination under various international agreements, and it adjudicates complaints of violations of those rules. It has a secretariat staff of about 600 people and a budget just over $200 million. The U.S. contribution is about 13%. Voting is by unanimity, including the admission of new members beyond the current 153. With Russia and Iran as the most economically significant countries still awaiting approval for membership, WTO members account for 91% of the world's population, 98% of the global GDP, and 96% of world trade.[25]

As discussed in Chapter 7, the United States has several trade remedies including use of the WTO when U.S. firms or workers are harmed by foreign practices, notably enforcement of antidumping and countervailing duty laws, as well as by providing trade adjustment assistance to affected parties. The United States can also raise disputes in the WTO system, though that is a costly and lengthy procedure. As only member states can bring cases, whether or not to raise a dispute for WTO consideration is a significant political choice for a country like the United States, which has numerous political and economic issues with any major trading partner.

According to a 2009 report by the U.S. trade representative (USTR), the United States has won most of the cases it brought before WTO. On the other hand, it has lost a little over half the cases where others complained about U.S. practices. These figures probably reflect the fact that cases are not brought unless the complainant has a strong case and lots of evidence. Of the 90 or so cases where the United States brought the complaint, the U.S. prevailed on the core issue 35% of the time and did not prevail in 4% of the cases. Another 30% of the cases were resolved to U.S. satisfaction without completing the litigation process, and the remaining 30% were ongoing or inactive. In 128 complaints against the United States, the U.S. prevailed only 12.5% of the time, and lost 29%. Another 15% of the cases were resolved to U.S. satisfaction before formal findings. Almost half (44%) were in progress or inactive at the time of the report.[26]

This record suggests that the United States benefits from this professional legal process even if the results sometimes anger lawmakers whose protectionist measures are ruled illegal. Nevertheless, there remains strong domestic political opposition to a more liberalized trading system and to procedures like fast-track or Trade Promotion Authority (TPA) to negotiate free trade agreements (FTAs). The WTO process is nonpolitical at a time when political forces in many nations want to be able to prevail.

Presidents have the freedom to choose to bring WTO cases, but outside observers have detected a recurring practice going back to the days of GATT. Jeffrey Dunoff says there is a "historic American pattern of initiating new disputes when the country is facing negative trade balances, rising protectionist voices at home, or when an administration is about to seek new trade negotiation authority from the Congress."[27] In other words, raising trade disputes can serve domestic political ends as well as economic goals.

# International Courts

There are now about 18 permanent international courts and tribunals, some highly specialized on matters like trade law and human rights, others dealing with general questions of international law. In recent years, in fact, observers have noticed an increasing *judicialization* of international relations.[28] The United States is a member of only some of these bodies and has actively opposed many of the operations of at least one, the International Criminal Court, because of concerns that U.S. military personnel and policy makers might be unfairly subjected to prosecution. Nevertheless, international tribunals are in the toolkit of the United States and other nations to be used when they choose.

Throughout its history, the United States has often created or made use of judicial instruments for the settlement of disputes and claims. The 1794 Jay Treaty with Great Britain, for example, created two commissions that heard claims on ship seizures and colonial era debts. In recent decades, the American government worked actively to create three significant tribunals in order to achieve specific foreign policy goals. One was the Iran–United States Claims Tribunal that paid compensation in numerous cases and functioned despite the continuing break in diplomatic relations between Washington and Tehran. Second was the series of mechanisms created under U.S. pressure to compensate victims of the Holocaust. Third was the UN Compensation Commission set up after the 1991 Gulf War. When it completed its work in 2007, it had paid out about $22 billion in compensation.[29]

As part of the UN system, the United States supported the creation of the International Court of Justice (ICJ) as successor to the League of Nations Permanent Court of International Justice (PCIJ), which the United States had held at arm's length, never ratifying its charter. In joining the ICJ, the U.S. Senate insisted on the Connally Reservation denying jurisdiction to disputes "which are essentially within the domestic jurisdiction of the United States of America as determined by the United States of America."[30]

The United States used the ICJ actively in its early decades then treated it as inconsequential. The United States withdrew from participation after losing a bitterly contested case over Nicaragua in 1986 and wound up on the defensive against cases brought by others in more recent years. Interestingly, the Connally Reservation proved to be a double-edged weapon because the court allowed its applicability to nations the U.S. tried to bring into the dock. Despite some adverse rulings—in cases involving Nicaragua, Libya, Yugoslavia, and Iran—analysts conclude that the ICJ cases have had little or no practical effect on U.S. foreign policy.[31]

America's mixed record in the ICJ does constrain risk-averse political leaders. They recognize that public opinion surveys show majority and sometimes strong majority support for the use of international tribunals, even for U.S. participation in the International Criminal Court (ICC).[32] But, they also recognize the public resonance with notions of American exceptionalism and protection of sovereignty.

The Clinton administration negotiated the ICC treaty and then formally signed on to the pact but declared that it would not seek ratification without further changes. There was sharp division among Clinton's advisers, with opposition in particular from the Joint Chiefs of Staff (JCS) and the Defense Department (DOD). The Bush administration went further and withdrew from signature, thereby freeing it legally from obligations not to undercut its provisions. In 2002, Congress went on to enact the American Servicemembers' Protection Act, which limits U.S. participation in peacekeeping missions unless U.S. personnel are exempt from ICC prosecution and which cuts off certain economic aid to nations that fail to conclude exemption agreements with the United States.[33]

U.S. policy in recent years has become more pragmatic regarding the various criminal courts, including the ICC. Officials say they decide on participation on a case-by-case basis. As Professor John P. Cerone concludes, "The United States has tended to support international criminal courts when the U.S. government has (or is perceived by U.S. officials to have) a significant degree of control over the court or when the possibility of prosecution of U.S. nationals is either expressly precluded or otherwise remote."[34]

Pragmatism has its benefits and its limitations. Avoiding the international courts means the United States cannot help shape their jurisprudence. On the other hand, limiting U.S. involvement helps deal with the problem cited by Professor Cesare Romano: "[N]ot only are international courts just one tool among many, but they are also second best to most. They are unwieldy instruments, difficult to steer and control. If they rule in favor of the United States, their main problem is that they lack their own enforcement powers. If they do have bite, then they are dangerous because they might be used by another state against the United States."[35]

## Major Nonstate Actors

There are many international organizations that are privately organized yet very active in influencing the policies of governments. Further consideration of some of them can be found in Chapter 12 on nongovernmental actors and interest groups. For our purposes here, it is sufficient just to note that these include: multinational corporations (MNCs); foundations; NGOs like the International Committee of the Red Cross and various human rights and environmental groups; and transnational networks and coalitions like the ones that deal with land mines. These groups research and publicize issues, participate in global conferences, and mobilize support for their views. They can be allies or adversaries of national governments, and that's how they will be treated in return.[36]

✳ ✳ ✳

To some extent, IOs can be influenced more by the effects of American *soft power* than by direct actions of U.S. officials. When the United States is widely admired and its policies broadly supported, it is easier for IO leaders to work with Washington. When America falls into international disfavor, however, even routine cooperation can be contentious. However much the U.S. president may want to outsource an issue to an IO, his ability to do so depends crucially on the international political context at the time.

It also helps to have a permanent U.S. presence at the institution, as has long been the case with regard to UN and European institutions and the OAS, but only in 2009 did America assign a resident ambassador to the African Union and ASEAN. Having such representation can help the president better choose whether and when to try to use the organization as an instrument for U.S. policies.

Congress is also a necessary partner in any outreach to IOs. Yet, Congress historically has resisted measures that seemed to risk a loss of domestic sovereignty—hence the Connally Reservation and frequent criticism of the UN. Lawmakers hate to see America outvoted or otherwise embarrassed in international assemblies and hate even more to pay for the privilege of losing in public. Even if U.S. officials weigh the use of IOs on a case-by-case basis, Congress is asked to appropriate money for U.S. contributions to keep the groups in operation. That leads to permanent tension and occasional retribution, as in the case of UNESCO in 2011.

To use international institutions as a policy tool, presidents need to persuade Congress as well as foreign governments of the value of such actions.

# Case Study: Using North Atlantic Treaty Organization as an Instrument of Foreign Policy in Libya, 2011

In February 2011, President Obama made a conscious decision to try to use NATO as a tool of U.S. foreign policy in order to avoid a more direct American combat role in the uprising in Libya. What some called *leading from behind* was also *burden sharing* of costs and risks.

When protests erupted in Libya in mid-February, the Obama administration faced difficult choices. For the previous decade, U.S. policy had been to engage with the regime of longtime leader Muammar Qaddafi, using more carrots than sticks. In 2003, Qaddafi had agreed to dismantle his nuclear weapons and long-range missile programs in return for the lifting of sanctions and diplomatic recognition, thus allowing Western trade and investment. When Qaddafi ordered his troops to fire on protestors and threatened further bloody retaliation, many U.S. officials doubted that he would be toppled, as had just happened to aging leaders in Tunisia and Egypt.

Just in case, Obama ordered the U.S. military to develop some possible options for action. Meanwhile, the State Department arranged for the evacuation of Americans by sea and air, and the Pentagon began moving some warships closer to Libyan waters. But, the president did not really want to launch a third U.S. war against a Muslim nation, especially not when U.S. forces were still heavily committed in Iraq and Afghanistan and the chances of a quick and easy overthrow of Qaddafi seemed remote.

With French President Nicolas Sarkozy and British Prime Minister David Cameron pressing for military action, Obama agreed only to impose economic sanctions. On February 25, within minutes of the evacuation of the last Americans, the president signed an executive order freezing more than $30 billion in Libyan assets held in U.S. banks and imposing sanctions on top-ranking Libyan officials. American and European leaders, after a flurry of conversations, agreed to a UNSC Resolution 1970, adopted unanimously on February 26. That resolution imposed an arms embargo on Libya but did not authorize the use of force.

The most widely discussed military option being considered by the diplomats was a no-fly zone to prevent Qaddafi from attacking opposition forces and civilians from the air. Defense Secretary Gates warned that it would require a major military effort, including suppression of Libyan air defenses, and would probably not, by itself, lead to Qaddafi's overthrow. Secretary of State Clinton was also initially reluctant to support U.S. military action.

Drawing on the other instruments in his foreign policy toolkit, Obama ordered diplomatic efforts to meet key conditions prior to American use of force: strong support from Arab nations, authorization by the UNSC, NATO management of the military operation, and no involvement of U.S. ground troops. Surprisingly, deft diplomacy by Obama, Clinton, and others led to fulfillment of those conditions by mid-March.

On March 7, the Gulf Cooperation Council called for a no-fly zone and demanded that the UN take *all necessary measures* to protect Libyan civilians. That is the phrase historically used by the UN to authorize member states to use force. On March 12, the Arab League, a regional institution, announced support for UN action imposing a no-fly zone and creating safe havens for civilians. Two days later, Secretary Clinton obtained commitments from Qatar and the United Arab Emirates (UAE) to provide warplanes for operations over Libya.

On March 15, the president held a National Security Council (NSC) meeting to review policy options. Intelligence reports suggested that a loyalist attack on Benghazi would succeed and might be followed by a massacre of civilians. There was a consensus that a no-fly zone would be insufficient to prevent widespread slaughter. Obama ordered more robust military options and directed his UN ambassador to seek a new UNSC resolution allowing all necessary measures.

On March 17, after frantic diplomacy to convince Russia and China not to veto and other members to support tough action, the UNSC approved Resolution 1973 allowing force to protect Libyan civilians, imposing a no-fly zone, and freezing of Libyan assets. The measure specifically prohibited, however, any foreign occupation force in Libyan territory.

On March 19, French aircraft launched the first attacks on Libyan forces moving toward Benghazi, and the United States attacked Libyan air defenses and air force in what was called Operation Odyssey Dawn. U.S. officials said that the attacks would last "a matter of days, not weeks" and that operational control would soon be turned over to NATO.

In fact, NATO was involved in military activities from the very start of the Libyan uprising. NATO ministers had agreed on February 25 to deploy its airborne warning and control system (AWACS) aircraft to monitor Libya. Obama and Clinton, as well as other foreign leaders, consulted back and forth throughout March, gradually developing the concept for a NATO-led operation. The difficulty was that NATO operated by unanimity, and several members, notably Germany, were reluctant to support the use of force against the Qaddafi regime. On March 22, NATO ministers agreed to take over only the maritime arms embargo. After the Turkish parliament approved participation in the no-fly zone and arms embargo on March 24, Germany agreed to approve the mission but not participate. Final NATO agreement to take over the military operation was secured on March 28. On March 29, the much larger Libyan Contact Group was established for diplomatic coordination. It included 21 nations from Europe and the Middle East plus several IOs.

On March 31, Operation Unified Protector began under NATO command. U.S. units retreated to primarily support roles: electronic warfare, aerial refueling, logistical support, search and rescue, and intelligence, surveillance, and reconnaissance. American ground attack aircraft were put on a standby basis in Italy. Gradually, the air attacks degraded Qaddafi's forces and the noose tightened. Tripoli fell to rebel forces on August 20. Qaddafi's final defeat and death came on October 20. At that point, NATO voted to end its operations on October 31.

The U.S. Congress was divided over the Libya operation and failed to take a firm or consistent position. The Senate, on March 1, had approved a resolution supporting the idea of a no-fly zone and call for a transition to a democratic government. A subsequent measure supporting U.S. military action was sidetracked by filibuster threats. In June and July, the House defeated measures cutting off funds for the operation but did approve a resolution demanding answers to questions about U.S. policy and later approved a ban on aiding Libyan rebels. Members preferred complaining about Obama's circumvention of the War Powers Act rather than voting for or against the policy.

Over the seven months of Operation Unified Protector, NATO and affiliated aircraft from Sweden, Jordan, Qatar, and UAE conducted more than 26,500 sorties, including more than 9,700 strike sorties against Qaddafi's forces and in defense of civilians. U.S. aircraft conducted only 25% of the sorties. Costs to the United States totaled $1.1 billion.

President Obama achieved his explicit and implicit goals by letting NATO lead the operation against Qaddafi. He avoided the diplomatic and military costs and risks of a U.S.-dominated operation and built instead an international force that not only protected Libyan civilians but also allowed the opposition forces to oust Qaddafi. He used an IO as an instrument of American foreign policy in an ultimately successful operation.

*Sources: The New York Times;* Anthony Bell and David Witter, "The Libyan Revolution: Part 2, Escalation & Intervention," Institute for the Study of War, September 2011, accessible at www .understandingwar.org/report/libyan-revolution-part-2-escalation-intervention.

## Selected Resources

Each of the major IOs has its own website.

APEC, www.aseansec.org/

ASEAN, www.aseansec.org/

G-8, www.g8.utoronto.ca/

G-20, www.g20.0rg/

IAEA, www.iaea.org/

ICJ, www.icj-cij.org/

ICC, www.icc-cpi.int/Menus/ICC/Home

IMF, www.imf.org

NATO, www.nato.int

OSCE, www.osce.org

OAS, www.oas.org

UN, www.un.org

WTO, www.wto.org

In addition, the American Society of International Law has numerous links and background materials, such as at www.asil.org/erg/?page=io, as do think tanks like the Council on Foreign Relations at https://secure.www .cfr.org/issue/international-organizations/ri37.

# Notes

## Chapter 1

1. U.S. Census Bureau, *Census of Governments*, Vol. 1 (Washington, DC: Department of Commerce, 2007).
2. See Lester Salamon, ed., *Handbook of Policy Instruments* (New York: Oxford University Press, 2001), Introduction.
3. Richard Nelson, *The Moon and the Ghetto* (New York: Norton, 1977).
4. Richard Rose, "The Programme Approach to the Growth of Government," *British Journal of Political Science* 15 (1985): 1–28.
5. Jacob Torfing, B. Guy Peters, Jon Pierre, and Eva Sørensen, *Interactive Governance: Advancing the Paradigm* (Oxford: Oxford University Press, 2012).
6. For example, the Department of Defense now has several programs for cleaning up environmental damage from military bases and for creating more environmentally sustainable programs in the military.
7. Brian W. Hogwood and B. Guy Peters, *The Pathology of Public Policy* (Oxford: Oxford University Press, 1985); and Craig W. Thomas, "Public Management as Interagency Cooperation," *Journal of Public Administration Research and Theory* 7 (1997): 221–246.
8. Peter J. May, "Policy Design and Implementation," in *Handbook of Public Administration*, ed. B. G. Peters and Jon Pierre, 2nd ed. (London: Sage); Helen Ingram and Anne Schneider, "Improving Implementation through Framing Smarter Statutes," *Journal of Public Policy* 10 (1990): 67–88.
9. Private actors do, of course, have recourse to law as a means of influencing policy and forcing government action. This is especially true in the United States, where the courts are so important for determining policy. For example, in addition to the enforcement activities of the Federal Trade Commission and the Antitrust Division of the Department of Justice, private individuals also bring suit to enforce antitrust laws.
10. *Bragdon v. Abbott,* 524 U.S. 624 (1998).
11. B. Guy Peters and Martin O. Heisler, "Thinking about Public Sector Growth," in *Why Governments Grow: Measuring Public Sector Size,* ed. C. L. Taylor (Beverly Hills, CA: Sage, 1983). See also Giandomenico Majone, *Regulating Europe* (London: Routledge, 1996).

12. The costs of these regulatory interventions was made popular by Murray Wiedenbaum. See his original article, "The High Costs of Government Regulation," *Challenge,* November 1979, 32–39. More recently the Small Business Administration (2011) estimated the costs of compliance with regulations as $1.7 trillion. These costs were not without their political motivations—for example, to demonstrate the high costs of government—and they usually failed to include the offsetting value of the benefits of regulation.

13. William T. Gormley, *Privatization and Its Alternatives* (Madison: University of Wisconsin Press, 1991).

14. Penelope Lemov, "Jailhouse, INC," *Governing* 6 (May 1993): 44–48; Mildred Warner and Amir Hefetz, "Applying Market Solutions to Public Services," *Urban Affairs Review* 38 (2002): 70–89.

15. Donald F. Kettl, *Government by Proxy: (Mis)Managing Federal Programs?* (Washington, DC: CQ Press, 1988); and Patricia W. Ingraham, "Quality in the Public Services," in *Governance in a Changing Environment,* ed. B. Guy Peters and Donald J. Savoie (Montreal: McGill/Queens University Press, 1995).

16. Charles H. Levine and Paul L. Posner, "The Centralizing Effects of Fiscal Austerity on the Intergovernmental System," *Political Science Quarterly* 96 (1981): 67–85.

17. James D. Chesney, "Intergovernmental Politics in the Allocation of Block Grant Funds for Substance Abuse in Michigan," *Publius* 24 (1994): 39–46; and Doug Peterson, "Block Grant 'Turn-Backs' Revived in Bush Budget," *Nation's Cities Weekly* 15 (February 3, 1992): 6.

18. Brian K. Collins and Brian J. Gerber, "Redistributive Policy and Devolution: Is State Administration a Road Block (Grant) to Equitable Access to Federal Funds," *Journal of Public Administration Research and Theory* 16 (2006): 613–632.

19. Stanley S. Surrey and Paul R. McDaniel, *Tax Expenditures* (Cambridge, MA: Harvard University Press, 1985).

20. Aaron Wildavsky, "Keeping Kosher: The Epistemology of Tax Expenditures," *Journal of Public Policy* 5 (1985): 413–431; Edward D. Kleinbard, "The Congress Within Congress: How Tax Expenditures Distort Our Budget and Political Processes," *University of Southern California Law Review* (2010), Paper 61.

21. Charles L. Schultze, *The Public Use of Private Interest* (Washington, DC: Brookings Institution Press, 1977).

22. Richard Hula, *Market-Based Public Policy* (New York: St. Martin's, 1988).

23. Ibid.; more generally, see Salamon, *Handbook of Policy Instruments.*

24. Douglas F. Elliott, *Uncle Sam in Pinstripes: Evaluating Federal Credit Programs* (Washington, DC: Brookings Institution Press, 2010).

25. Thomas Anton, *Moving Money* (Cambridge, MA: Oelgeschlager, Hain and Gunn, 1980).

26. Johan Fritzell, "Income Inequality Trends in the 1980s: A Five-Country Comparison," *Acta Sociologica* 36 (1993): 47–62; and Daniel Rigney, *The Matthew Effect: How Advantage Begets Further Advantage* (New York: Columbia University Press, 2010).

27. On taxation, see B. Guy Peters, *The Politics of Taxation: A Comparative Perspective* (Oxford: Blackwell, 1991). On conscription, see Margaret Levi, *Consent, Dissent, Patriotism* (Cambridge: Cambridge University Press, 1997).

28. Anthony King, "Ideas, Institutions and Policies of Government: A Comparative Analysis," *British Journal of Political Science* 5 (1975): 418.

29. See Linda M. Bennett and Stephen Earl Bennett, *Living with Leviathan: Americans Coming to Terms with Big Government* (Lawrence: University Press of Kansas, 1990).

30. Lloyd A. Free and Hadley Cantril, *The Political Beliefs of Americans* (New York: Simon and Schuster, 1968).

31. David O. Sears and Jack Citrin, *Tax Revolt: Something for Nothing in California*, rev. ed. (Berkeley: University of California Press, 1991).

32. See chapter 10; ABC News Polls for a number of years have found that Americans think government wastes about half of the money it collects in taxes.

33. Peter Bachrach and Aryeh Botwinick, *Power and Empowerment: A Radical Theory of Participatory Democracy* (Philadelphia: Temple University Press, 1992).

34. Michael Cooper and Megan Thee-Brenan, "Disapproval Rate for Congress at Record 82% After Debt Talks," *The New York Times*, August 4, 2011.

35. Michael T. Hayes, *Incrementalism* (New York: Longman, 1992).

36. See, for example, Charles O. Jones, *The Reagan Legacy* (Chatham, NJ: Chatham House, 1989).

37. Shaan K. Hathiramani, "The Politics of Pensions: Trouble for Both Parties Looms in Social Security Debate," *Harvard Political Review* 32, no. 2 (2005): 24–25.

38. Robin Toner, "House Democrats Support Abortion in Health Plans," *New York Times*, July 14, 1994.

39. See William Schneider, "What Else Do They Want?" *National Journal*, May 16, 1998, 1150; Susan B. Hansen.

40. Morris P. Fiorina, "Parties and Partisanship: A 40-Year Retrospective," *Political Behavior* 24 (2002): 93–115.

41. Jackie Calmes, "House Passes Stimulus Plan with No GOP Votes," *New York Times*, January 28, 2009.

42. See Robert Reich, *The Work of Nations* (New York: Norton, 1991); and Ann O. Kreuger, *The Political Economy of American Trade Policy* (Chicago: University of Chicago Press, 1995).

43. "Race, Class and Hurricane Katrina," *Political Affairs* 84, no. 10 (2005): 36–39.

44. Andrew Hacker, *Two Nations: Black and White, Separate, Hostile, Unequal* (New York: Scribner, 1992).

## Chapter 2

1. Charles H. Levine, "Human Resource Erosion and the Uncertain Future of the U.S. Civil Service: From Policy Gridlock to Structural Fragmentation," *Governance* 1 (1988): 115–143.

2. See Terry Sanford, *Storm over the States* (New York: McGraw-Hill, 1967), 80.

3. Deil S. Wright, *Understanding Intergovernmental Relations,* 3rd ed. (Belmont, CA: Brooks/Cole, 1988), 83–86; the term *multilevel governance* is increasingly used to describe these relationships. See B. Guy Peters, "Developments in Intergovernmental Relations: Towards Multi-level Governance," *Policy and Politics* 29 (2001): 131–135.

4. Ibid.

5. Joseph A. Zimmerman, *Contemporary American Federalism: The Growth of National Power,* 2nd ed. (Albany: State University of New York Press, 2008).

6. John Kincaid, "From Cooperative to Coercive Federalism," *Annals* 509 (1990): 139–152.

7. Angela Antonelli, "Promises Unfilled: Unfunded Mandates Reform Act of 1995," *Regulation* 19, no. 2 (1996): 44–52.

8. U.S. Bureau of the Census, *Census of Governments, 1997* (Washington, DC: U.S. Government Printing Office, 1998).

9. Jerry Mitchell, *Public Authorities and Public Policy: The Business of Government* (New York: Greenwood, 1992); and Kathryn A. Foster, *The Political Economy of Special Purpose Government* (Washington, DC: Georgetown University Press, 1998).

10. During the mid-1980s, the states averaged over 11 percent surpluses in their total budgets. See the Tax Foundation, *Facts and Figures on Government Finance,* vol. 38, 1991 (Baltimore: Johns Hopkins University Press, 2004), Table E2.

11. Linda Greenhouse, "Supreme Court Agrees to Hear Gun Control Case," *New York Times,* November 20, 2007.

12. On the concept of "veto points," see George Tsebelis, *Veto Players: How Institutions Work* (Princeton, NJ: Princeton University Press, 2002).

13. Mark Peterson, *Legislating Together* (Cambridge, MA: Harvard University Press, 1992).

14. See, for example, James Q. Wilson, *Bureaucracy* (New York: Basic Books, 1989); Charles T. Goodsell, *Mission Mystique: Belief Systems in Public Agencies* (Washington, DC: CQ Press, 2011).

15. See Cornelius Kerwin, *Rulemaking,* 4th ed. (Washington, DC: CQ Press, 2011).

16. Daniel Carpenter, *Forging Bureaucratic Autonomy* (Princeton, NJ: Princeton University Press, 2001).

17. George Krause, *A Two-Way Street: The Institutional Dynamics of the Modern Administrative State* (Pittsburgh: University of Pittsburgh Press, 2000).

18. Morris P. Fiorina, "An Era of Divided Government," *Political Science Quarterly* 107 (1992): 387–410; and James L. Sundquist, *Constitutional Reform and Effective Government,* rev. ed. (Washington, DC: Brookings Institution Press, 1992).

19. David Mayhew, *Divided We Govern* (New Haven, CT: Yale University Press, 1991); Charles O. Jones, *The Presidency in a Separated System* (Washington, DC: Brookings Institution Press, 1994); Nelson Polsby, *Policy Innovation in America* (New Haven, CT: Yale University Press, 1984); and John E. Schwartz, *America's Hidden Success,* rev. ed. (New York: Norton, 1988). For a critique, see Alberto Alesina and Howard Rosenthal, *Partisan Politics, Divided Government and the Economy* (Cambridge: Cambridge University Press, 1996).

20. Michael T. Hayes, *Incrementalism* (New York: Longman, 1992); Carter A. Wilson, "Policy Regimes and Policy Change," *Journal of Public Policy* 20, 247–274.

21. Charles E. Lindblom, *The Intelligence of Democracy: Decision Making through Mutual Adjustment* (New York: Free Press, 1965).

22. For example, a poll in late 2003 found that 79 percent of the American populace supported health care for all Americans even if it meant higher taxes; see "Poll," *Washington Post,* October 13, 2003. When faced with the reality of the Obama health care reforms, however, less than half supported the changes in early 2012 (see chapter 11).

23. Brian W. Hogwood and B. Guy Peters, *Policy Dynamics* (Brighton, UK: Wheatsheaf, 1982); and Robert E. Goodin, *Political Theory and Public Policy* (Chicago: University of Chicago Press, 1986).

24. The classic statement is in J. Leiper Freeman, *The Political Process: Executive Bureau–Legislative Committee Relations* (New York: Random House, 1965).

25. The classic statement of this point is in Theodore J. Lowi, *The End of Liberalism,* 2nd ed. (New York: Norton, 1979).

26. Peter L. Hall and C. Lawrence Evans, "The Power of Subcommittees," *Journal of Politics* 52 (1990): 335–355.

27. See D. Roderick Kiewiet and Mathew D. McCubbins, *The Logic of Delegation* (Chicago: University of Chicago Press, 1991).

28. Gregory J. Wawro, *Legislative Entrepreneurship in the U.S. House of Representatives* (Ann Arbor: University of Michigan Press, 2000).

29. D. McCool, "Subgovernments as Determinants of Political Viability," *Political Science Quarterly* 105 (1990): 269–293.

30. André Blais and Stéphane Dion, *The Budget-Maximizing Bureaucrat* (Pittsburgh: University of Pittsburgh Press, 1992).

31. Peter B. Natchez and Irvin C. Bupp, "Policy and Priority in the Budgetary Process," *American Political Science Review* 67 (1973): 951–963.

32. See Robert H. Salisbury, J. P. Heinz, R. L. Nelson, and Edward O. Laumann, "Triangles, Networks and Hollow Cores: The Complex Geometry of Washington Interest Representation," in *The Politics of Interests,* ed. Mark P. Petracca (Boulder, CO: Westview Press, 1992), 141–166.

33. Rufus E. Miles, "A Cabinet Department of Education: An Unwise Campaign Promise or a Sound Idea?" *Public Administration Review* 39 (1979): 103–110.

34. For example, the Cooperative Extension Service in the Department of Agriculture eliminated hundreds of county offices.

35. See D. F. Kettl, *The Department of Homeland Security's First Year: A Report Card* (New York: Century Foundation Press, 2004).

36. Robert Brodsky, "Administration Hopes to Leave Performance Management Legacy," *Government Executive,* April 21, 2008.

37. See Jack L. Walker, *Mobilizing Interest Groups in America* (Ann Arbor: University of Michigan Press, 1991).

38. Charles O. Jones, *The United States Congress* (Homewood, IL: Dorsey, 1982).

39. Try it!

40. Some scholars make a great deal over the differences between these concepts, with a community being a more unified and tightly knit set of groups than a network. See Martin J. Smith, *Pressure, Power and Policy* (Pittsburgh: University of Pittsburgh Press, 1994).

41. James Kuhnhenn, "Congress Proves Unable to Cut Back on Pork," *Knight-Ridder Washington Bureau,* October 2, 2005.

42. See Martin Jaffe, "Earmark Hypocrisy," http://abcnews.go.com/Politics/hypocrisy-alert-abc-news-grills-gop-leaders-earmarks/story?id=12403958.

43. See Richard Rose and B. Guy Peters, *Can Government Go Bankrupt?* (New York: Basic Books, 1976).

44. Richard A. McGowan, *Privatize This? Assessing the Opportunities and Costs of Privatization* (Santa Barbara, CA: Praeger, 2011).

45. See Linda L. M. Bennett and Stephen Earl Bennett, *Living with Leviathan: Americans Come to Terms with Big Government* (Lawrence: University Press of Kansas, 1990); Jeff Madrick, *The Case for Big Government* (Princeton, NJ: Princeton University Press).

46. Jonas Prager, "Contracting Out Government Services: Lessons from the Private Sector," *Public Administration Review* 54 (1994): 176–184; and Steven Rathgeb Smith and Michael Lipsky, *Nonprofits for Hire: The Welfare State in the Age of Contracting* (Cambridge, MA: Harvard University Press, 1993).

47. B. Guy Peters, "Public and Private Provision of Services," in *The Private Provision of Public Services,* ed. Dennis Thompson (Beverly Hills, CA: Sage, 1986).

48. This form of organization has not been typical in the United States. See Robert H. Salisbury, "Why No Corporatism in America?" in *Trends toward Corporatist Intermediation,* ed. Philippe C. Schmitter and Gerhard Lehmbruch (Beverly Hills, CA: Sage, 1979); and Susan B. Hansen, "Industrial Policy and Corporatism in the American States," *Governance* 2 (1989): 172–197.

49. U.S. Government Accountability Office, *Core Principles and a Strategic Approach Would Enhance Stakeholder Participation in Developing Quota-Based Programs* (Washington, DC: USGAO), GAO-06-289, February 24, 2005.

50. Federal Advisory Committee Act Database (General Services Administration, 2011), www.fido.gov/facadatabse.

51. For a more complete treatment of public employment, see Hans-Ulrich Derlien and B. Guy Peters, *Who Works for Government and What Do They Do?* (Bamberg, Germany: University of Bamberg, Administrative Sciences, 1998).

52. See Jonathan R. T. Hughes, *The Governmental Habit Redux: Economic Controls from Colonial Times to the Present* (Princeton, NJ: Princeton University Press, 1993).

53. The figures for later years would be somewhat lower but with a significant number of jobs still being created by defense purchases.

54. Tax Foundation, *Facts and Figures on Government Finance,* 37th ed. (Baltimore: Johns Hopkins University Press, 2004).

55. Thomas D. Hopkins, *Regulatory Costs in Profile* (St. Louis: Weidenbaum Center, Washington University, 2001).

56. See Thomas D. Hopkins, "OMB's Regulatory Accounting Report Falls Short of the Mark," *Policy Study* 142 (St. Louis: Washington University Center for the Study of American Business, November 1997).

## Chapter 3

1. Robert A. Dahl, "The Concept of Power," *Behavioral Science* 2 (1957): 201–215.

2. E. E. Schattschneider, *The Semi-Sovereign People* (New York: Holt, Rinehart, 1960).

3. Peter Bachrach and Morton S. Baratz, "The Two Faces of Power," *American Political Science Review* 56 (1962): 947–952; Steven Lukes, *Power: A Radical View* (Basingstoke, UK: Palgrave, 2005).

4. Charles O. Jones, *An Introduction to the Study of Public Policy* (Monterey, CA: Brooks/Cole, 1984); and Michael J. Hill, *The Public Policy Process* (London: Longman, 2005).

5. John W. Kingdon, *Agendas, Alternatives and Public Policies,* 2nd ed. (New York: HarperCollins, 1995).

6. George Tsebelis, *Veto Players: How Real Institutions Work* (Princeton, NJ: Princeton University Press, 2000).

7. Brian W. Hogwood and B. Guy Peters, *Policy Dynamics* (Brighton, UK: Wheatsheaf, 1983).

8. R. Kent Weaver and Bert A. Rockman, *Do Institutions Matter?* (Washington, DC: Brookings Institution Press, 1994).

9. James G. March and J. P. Olsen, "The New Institutionalism: Organizational Factors in Political Life," *American Political Science Review* 78 (1984): 734–749; and B. Guy Peters, *Institutional Theory in Political Science,* 3rd ed. (London: Continuum, 2011).

10. See Charles T. Goodsell, *Mission Mystique: Belief Systems in Public Agencies* (Armonk, NY: M. A. Sharpe, 2010).

11. Paul Pierson, "Increasing Returns, Path Dependence and the Study of Politics," *American Political Science Review* 94 (2000): 251–267.

12. Wolfgang Streek and Kathleen Thelen, *Beyond Continuity: Institutional Change in Advanced Political Economies* (Oxford: Oxford University Press, 2005).

13. Elinor Ostrom, "Institutional Rational Choice," in *Theories of the Policy Process,* ed. P. A. Sabatier (Boulder, CO: Westview Press, 2007), 21.

14. Kenneth Shepsle, "Institutional Equilibrium and Equilibrium Institutions," in *Political Science: The Science of Politics,* ed. H. F. Weisberg (New York: Agathon Press, 1986), 51.

15. George Tsebelis, *Veto Points: How Institutions Work* (Princeton, NJ: Princeton University Press, 2000).

16. See Vivien Schmidt, "Taking Ideas and Discourse Seriously: Explaining Change through Discursive Institutionalism," *European Political Science Review* 2, 1–25.

17. Paul A. Sabatier and Hank Jenkins-Smith, *Policy Change and Learning: An Advocacy-Coalition Framework* (Boulder, CO: Westview Press, 1993).

18. On wicked problems, see Robert Hoppe, *Puzzling, Power in and Participation* (Cambridge: Policy Press, 2011).

19. B. Guy Peters, Jon Pierre, and Desmond S. King, "The Politics of Path Dependency: Political Conflict and Historical Institutionalism," *Journal of Politics* 67 (2005): 1275–1300.

20. Theodore J. Lowi, "Four Systems of Policy, Politics, Choice," *Public Administration Review* 32 (1972): 298–310.

21. Robert Salisbury and John Heinz, "A Theory of Policy Analysis and Some Preliminary Applications," in *Policy Analysis in Political Science,* ed. Ira Sharkansky (Chicago: Markham, 1970), 59.

22. K. B. Smith, "Typologies, Taxonomies and the Benefits of Policy Classification," *Policy Studies Journal* 30 (2002): 379–395.

23. Claudio Radaelli, "The Europeanization of Public Policy," in *The Politics of Europeanization,* ed. Kenneth Featherstone (Oxford: Oxford University Press, 2004), 27.

24. Jeremy J. Richardson, *Policy Styles in Western Europe* (Boston: Allen and Unwin, 1982).

25. Frans van Waarden, "Persistence of National Policy Styles: A Study of Their Institutional Foundations," in *Convergence of Diversity?* ed. B. Under and F. van Waarden (Aldershot, UK: Avebury, 1995), 333–372.

26. Gary Freeman, "National Styles and Policy Sectors: Explaining Structured Variation," *Journal of Public Policy* 5 (1985): 467–496.

27. The freedom from interest groups would be easy to overstate. Interest groups have become more active in international policy issues as globalization reduces some of the barriers between domestic and international politics.

28. Christopher Hood, *The Tools of Government* (Chatham, NJ: Chatham House, 1978); B. Guy Peters and F. Van Nispen, *Public Policy Instruments: Evaluating the Tools of Public Administration* (Cheltenham, UK: Edward Elgar, 1998); and Lester M. Salamon, Introduction, in *The Handbook of Policy Instruments,* ed. Salamon (New York: Oxford University Press, 2001).

29. Ulrika Morth, *Soft Law in Governance and Regulation* (Cheltenham, UK: Edward Elgar, 2004).

30. Stephen H. Linder and B. G. Peters, "The Analysis of Design or the Design of Analysis," *Policy Studies Review* 7 (1988): 738–750; and Pearl Eliadis, Margaret Hill, and Michael Howlett, eds., *Designing Government: From Instruments to Governance* (Montreal: McGill/Queens University Press, 2005).

31. B. Guy Peters and John A. Hoornbeek, "The Problem of Policy Problems," in *Designing Government: From Instruments to Governance,* ed. Eliadis, Hill, and Howlett (Montreal: McGill/Queens University Press, 2005), 77.

32. Michael Laver, *Private Desires, Public Action* (London: Sage, 1997).

33. William Niskanen, *Bureaucracy and Representative Government* (Chicago: Aldine/Atherton, 1971).

34. E. Patashnik, "After the Public Interest Prevails: The Political Sustainability of Political Reform," *Governance* 16 (2003): 203–234.

35. Michael D. Cohen, James. G. March, and J. P. Olsen, "A Garbage Can Model of Organizational Decision-Making," *Administrative Science Quarterly* 17 (1972): 1–25.

36. Kingdon, *Agendas, Alternatives and Public Policy.*

37. N. Zahariadis, "Multiple Streams Framework: Structure, Limitations, Prospects," in *Theories of the Policy Process,* ed. P. A. Sabatier (Boulder, CO: Westview Press, 2007), 71–108.

38. Jennifer LaFleur, "Infrastructure Spending in Stimulus Bill and Unemployment Rate," *Pro Publica,* January 26, 2009.

39. Davis, M. A. H. Dempster, and Aaron Wildavsky, "A Theory of the Budgetary Process," *American Political Science Review* 60 (1966): 529–547.

40. Charles E. Lindblom, *The Intelligence of Democracy: Policy-Making through Mutual Adjustment* (New York: Free Press, 1965).

41. Leiper Freeman, *The Political Process* (New York: Random House, 1965).

42. H. Brinton Milward and Kevin Provan, "Managing the Hollow State," *Journal of Public Administration Research and Theory* 10 (2000): 359–380.

43. Eva Sorenson and Jacob Torfing, *Theories of Democratic Network Governance* (Basingstoke, UK: Palgrave, 2007).

44. Charles Wolfe, "Market and Non-Market Failures: Comparison and Assessment," *Journal of Public Policy* 7 (1987): 43–70.

45. The standard definition of *public goods* is a good or service from which individuals cannot be excluded—for example, clean air, that and therefore cannot be priced.

46. Even laws against murder may disadvantage psychopaths while making most citizens better off.

47. Helen Ingram, Anne B. Schneider, and Peter DeLeon, "Social Constructivism and Policy Design," in *Theories of the Policy Process,* ed. Paul A. Sabatier (Boulder, CO: Westview Press, 2007), 93.

48. Peters and Hoornbeek, "The Problem of Policy Problems."

49. T. Payan, *Cops, Soldiers and Diplomats: Explaining Agency Behavior in the War on Drugs* (Lanham, MD: Lexington Books, 2006).

50. John S. Dryzek, *Deliberative Democracy and Beyond* (Oxford: Oxford University Press, 2000).

51. Frank Fischer, *Reframing Public Policy: Discursive Politics and Deliberative Practices* (Oxford: Oxford University Press, 2003); and M. Hajer and H. Wagenaar, *Understanding Governance in a Network Society* (Cambridge: Cambridge University Press, 2003).

52. Herbert Gottweiss, "Argumentative Policy Analysis," in *The Handbook of Public Policy*, ed. B. G. Peters and J. Pierre (London: Sage, 2006), 461.

53. Harold D. Lasswell, *Politics: Who Gets What, When, How* (London: Whittlesey House, 1936).

54. See Graham T. Allison and P. Zelikow, *Essence of Decision: Explaining the Cuban Missile Crisis*, 2nd ed. (New York: Longman, 1999).

## Chapter 4

1. See Michael Harrington, *The Other America: Poverty in America* (New York: Macmillan, 1963). The huge number of more recent books explicitly on the topic of poverty includes Loretta Schwartz-Nobel, *Growing Up Empty: The Hunger Epidemic in America* (New York: HarperCollins, 2002); Robert Asen, *Visions of Poverty: Welfare Policy and Political Imagination* (East Lansing: Michigan State University Press, 2002); Judith A. Chafel, *Child Poverty and Public Policy* (Washington, DC: Urban Institute Press, 1993); Marisa Chappell, *The War on Welfare: Family, Poverty and Policy in the United States* (Philadelphia: University of Pennsylvania Press, 2010).

2. But see Barbara J. Nelson, *Making an Issue of Child Abuse* (Chicago: University of Chicago Press, 1984).

3. James Agee, *Let Us Now Praise Famous Men* (Boston: Houghton Mifflin, 1941). This is a book of photographs and text about the plight of rural America during the Great Depression, funded by the Farm Security Administration. The book clearly had some impact, but that impact was more limited than a comprehensive attack on poverty.

4. Anthony Downs, "Up and Down with Ecology: 'The Issue Attention Cycle,'" *Public Interest* 28 (1972): 28–50; and B. Guy Peters and Brian W. Hogwood, "In Search of the Issue-Attention Cycle," *Journal of Politics* 47 (1985): 238–253.

5. Peter Hennessey, Susan Morrison, and Richard Townsend, "Routines Punctuated by Orgies: The Central Policy Review Staff," *Strathclyde Papers on Government and Politics*, no. 30 (1985).

6. Frank Baumgartner and Bryan D. Jones, *Agendas and Instability in American Politics* (Chicago: University of Chicago Press, 1993). The same description that is being applied to the system as a whole could be applied to individual policy areas.

7. See also Bryan D. Jones, *Reconceiving Decision-Making in Democratic Politics* (Chicago: University of Chicago Press, 1994).

8. Michael D. Cohen, James G. March, and Johan P. Olsen, "The Garbage Can Model of Organizational Choice," *Administrative Science Quarterly* 17 (1972): 1–25; and John Kingdon, *Agendas, Alternatives, and Public Policy*, 2nd ed. (Boston: Little, Brown, 2003).

9. Joel Best, *Images of Issues* (New York: Aldine DeGruyter, 1989).

10. T. Payan, *Cops, Soldiers and Diplomats: Explaining Agency Behavior in the War on Drugs* (Lanham, MD: Lexington Books, 2006).

11. Roger W. Cobb and Charles D. Elder, *Participation in American Politics* (Baltimore: Johns Hopkins University Press, 1983), 85.

12. This is what Peter Bachrach and Morton S. Baratz referred to as the "second face of power." See their "Decisions and Nondecisions: An Analytic Framework," *American Political Science Review* 57 (1964): 632–642; and Steven Lukes, *Power: A Radical View* (London: Macmillan, 1974).

13. Cobb and Elder, *Participation in American Politics*, 86.

14. Ibid., 96.

15. U.S. Department of Defense, *Quadrennial Defense Review Report* (Washington, DC: Department of Defense, September 30, 2001). The quadrennial review published September 30, 2001, had relatively little on terrorism, but the one published in early 2006 was dominated by terrorism.

16. This has often been the case for social policy programs, given that in the United States these programs generally have low status, and so politicians may be able to score political points by reducing expenditures and benefits dispensed by them.

17. Jack L. Walker, "Setting the Agenda in the U.S. Senate: A Theory of Problem Selection," *British Journal of Political Science* 7 (1977): 423–445.

18. Glenn Kessler, "Explaining the Debt Ceiling Debate," *Washington Post*, June 29, 2011.

19. See David Dery, "Rethinking Agenda Setting" (unpublished paper, Department of Political Science, Hebrew University of Jerusalem, June 2002).

20. See A. Grant Jordan, "The Pluralism of Pluralism: An Anti-Theory," *Political Studies* 38 (1990): 286–301.

21. For agenda setting in another, similarly disaggregated setting, see B. Guy Peters, "Agenda-Setting in the European Community," *Journal of European Public Policy* 1 (1994): 9–26.

22. C. Wright Mills, *The Power Elite* (New York: Oxford University Press, 1961); and Charles E. Lindblom, *Democracy and the Market System* (New York: Oxford University Press, 1988).

23. Carter A. Wilson, "Policy Regimes and Policy Change," *Journal of Public Policy* 20 (2000): 247–274.

24. E. E. Schattschneider, *The Semi-Sovereign People* (New York: Holt, Rinehart and Winston, 1969).

25. Dave Gibson and Carolyn Perot, "It's the Inequality, Stupid," *Mother Jones* (March 2011).

26. Lance deHaven Smith, *Philosophical Critiques of Policy Analysis: Lindblom, Habermas and the Great Society* (Gainesville: University of Florida Press, 1988). Habermas proposes the development of a more participatory "dialogical democracy" as a means of effectively including all interests. See also Jon Elster, ed., *Deliberative Democracy* (New York: Cambridge University Press, 1998).

27. Bachrach and Baratz, "Decisions and Nondecisions."

28. Martin J. Smith, *Pressure, Power and Policy* (Pittsburgh: University of Pittsburgh Press, 1993).

29. K. Beckett, "Media Depictions of Drug Abuse: The Impact of Official Sources," *Research in Political Sociology* 7 (1995): 161–182.

30. J. Leiper Freeman, *The Political Process: Executive Bureau–Legislative Committee Relations* (New York: Random House, 1965).

31. Advisory Commission in Intergovernmental Relations, *The Federal Role in the Federal System* (Washington, DC: ACIR, 1980).

32. Many of these programs, as noted in chapter 2, confer particular benefits on one constituency or another, but many are also more general.

33. Nelson Polsby, *Policy Innovation in America* (New Haven, CT: Yale University Press, 1984); and John E. Schwartz, *America's Hidden Successes*, rev. ed. (New York: Norton, 1988). More recent is Paul C. Light, *Government's Greatest Achievements* (Washington, DC: Brookings Institution Press, 2002).

34. Samuel Kernell, *Going Public: New Strategies of Presidential Leadership*, 3rd ed. (Washington, DC: CQ Press, 1997); Charles O. Jones, *Separate but Equal Branches: Congress and the Presidency* (Chatham, NJ: Chatham House, 1994).

35. See Robert S. Gilmour and Alexis A. Halley, eds., *Who Makes Public Policy? The Struggle for Control between Congress and the Executive* (Chatham, NJ: Chatham House, 1994).

36. Sarah Cliff, "The Romneycare-Obamacare Connection," *Washington Post*, October 11, 2011.

37. See, for example, Baumgartner and Jones, *Agendas and Instability.*

38. Best, *Images of Issues*; and Anne Schneider and Helen Ingram, "Social Construction of Target Populations: Implications for Policy and Politics," *American Political Science Review* 87 (1993): 34–47.

39. John W. Kingdon, *Agendas, Alternatives and Public Policy* (Boston: Little, Brown, 1984); and Nancy C. Roberts, "Public Entrepreneurship and Innovation," *Policy Studies Review* 11 (1992): 55–73.

40. See Newt Gingrich and Robert Egge, "To Fight the Flu, Change How Government Works," *New York Times*, November 6, 2005.

41. See James Q. Wilson, *The Politics of Regulation* (New York: Basic Books, 1980).

42. Robert H. Salisbury, "The Paradox of Interest Groups in Washington—More Groups, Less Clout," in *The New American Political System*, ed. Anthony King (Washington, DC: American Enterprise Institute, 1990), 203–230; "Three Decades of Lobbying Scandal and Repercussion," *CQ Weekly*, January 20, 2006, 239.

43. Theodore R. Marmor, *The Politics of Medicare* (Chicago: Aldine, 1973).

44. In part because of those choices, the plan appears unnecessarily complex and has been difficult for senior citizens to manage. See Milt Freudenheim, "The Drug Decision," *New York Times*, November 24, 2005.

45. Brian W. Hogwood and B. Guy Peters, *Policy Dynamics* (Brighton, UK: Wheatsheaf, 1983).

46. See Joel Slemrod and Jon Bakija, *Taxing Ourselves: A Citizen's Guide to the Debate over Taxes*, 3rd ed. (Cambridge, MA: MIT Press, 2004).

47. Aaron Wildavsky, "Policy as Its Own Cause," *Speaking Truth to Power* (Boston: Little, Brown, 1979), 62–85.

48. Advocates for the victims of the disease argue that there were significant delays in responding to the issue, in part because of "homophobia." See Gregory M. Herek and Beverly Greene, *AIDS, Identity and Community* (Beverly Hills, CA: Sage, 1995). On the other hand, the National Institutes of Health at one point was spending $33,513 in research for every AIDS death in the country, compared with $1,162 for

each heart disease death. "Panel Criticizes NIH Spending," *USA Today,* July 9, 1998.

49. Jonathan Weisman, "Linking Tax to Death May Have Brought Its Doom," *USA Today,* May 21, 2001.

50. But see Peter Self, *Government by the Market? The Politics of Public Choice* (Boulder, CO: Westview Press, 1991).

51. James M. Buchanan, *The Demands and Supply of Public Goods* (Chicago: Rand McNally, 1958), 3–7.

52. A classic statement of the issue is R. H. Coase, "The Problem of Social Cost," *Journal of Law and Economics* 3 (1960): 1–44.

53. Market approaches to redressing externalities have become increasingly common. See Joseph J. Cordes, "Corrective Taxes, Charges and Tradeable Permits," in *The Tools of Government,* ed. Lester M. Salamon (New York: Oxford University Press, 2002), 255–281.

54. Charles Wolf Jr., *Markets or Governments?* (Cambridge, MA: MIT Press, 1987).

55. Cohen, March, and Olsen, "The Garbage Can Model."

56. Abraham Kaplan, *The Conduct of Inquiry* (San Francisco: Chandler, 1964).

57. See Frank Fischer and Herbert Gottweiss, *The Argumentative Turn Revisited* (Durham, NC: Duke University Press, 2012).

58. On instruments, see Christopher Hood, *Tools of Government* (Chatham, NJ: Chatham House, 1986); Stephen H. Linder and B. Guy Peters, "Instruments of Government: Perceptions and Contexts," *Journal of Public Policy* 9 (1989): 35–58; and Salamon, *The Tools of Government.*

59. See Pearl Eliadas, Margaret Hill, and Michael Howlett, eds., *Designing Government* (Montreal: McGill/Queens University Press, 2004).

60. For example, organizational resistance within government to privatizing Social Security, as well as political pressure from outside, helped save the program when it was under threat. See chapter 12.

61. They are argued to be so by, among others, William Niskanen, *Bureaucracy and Representative Government* (Chicago: Aldine/Atherton, 1971); but see André Blais and Stéphane Dion, *The Budget-Maximizing Bureaucrat* (Pittsburgh: University of Pittsburgh Press, 1991).

62. Kenneth J. Meier, *Politics and the Bureaucracy,* 3rd ed. (Pacific Grove, CA: Brooks/Cole, 1993).

63. Mark A. Eisner, "Bureaucratic Professionalism and the Limits of Political Control Thesis: The Case of the Federal Trade Commission," *Governance* 6 (1992): 127–153.

64. John DiIulio, ed., *Deregulating the Public Service* (Washington, DC: Brookings Institution Press, 1994); and B. Guy Peters, *The Future of Governing,* 2nd ed. (Lawrence: University Press of Kansas, 2002).

65. See Andrew Rich, *Think Tanks, Public Policy and the Politics of Expertise* (Cambridge: Cambridge University Press, 2000).

66. See Charles L. Heatherly, ed., *Mandate for Change: Policy Management in a Conservative Administration* (Washington, DC: Heritage Foundation, 1981).

67. See, for example, *The Work of Nations: Preparing Ourselves for Twenty-First Century Capitalism* (New York: Knopf, 1991); and *Education and the Next Economy* (Washington, DC: National Education Association, 1988).

68. For example, the website of the *National Journal* listed several dozen responses to the 2006 State of the Union address.

69. M. Eshbaugh-Sona, "The Politics of Presidential Agendas," *Political Research Quarterly* 58: 257–268.

70. Michael Malbin, *Our Unelected Representatives* (New York: Basic Books, 1980). For a conservative critique, see Eric Felten, "Little Princes," *Policy Review* 63 (1993): 51–57.

71. David H. Rosenbloom, *Building a Legislative-Centered Public Administration: Congress and the Administrative State* (Tuscaloosa: University of Alabama Press).

72. See W. Kip Viscusi, "The Value of Risks to Life and Health," *Journal of Economic Literature* 31 (1993): 1912–1946; Richard Zeckhauser and W. Kip Viscusi, "Risk within Reason," *Science* 248 (May 4, 1990): 559–564; and R. Hahn, *Risks, Costs and Lives Saved* (Oxford: Oxford University Press, 1996).

73. Robert Eisner, *The Misunderstood Economy* (Cambridge, MA: Harvard Business School, 1994).

74. There have been a number of books and articles about "crises" in Social Security, but the pattern of decision making tends to be more incremental. See Theodore R. Marmor, *Social Security: Beyond the Rhetoric of Crisis* (Princeton: Princeton University Press, 1988); and Martha Derthick, *Agency under Stress, NJ Social Security Administration in American Government* (Washington, DC: Brookings Institution Press, 1990).

75. See Richard Topf, "Science, Public Policy, and the Authoritativeness of the Governmental Process," in *The Politics of Expert Advice,* ed. Anthony Barker and B. Guy Peters (Pittsburgh: University of Pittsburgh Press, 1993).

76. R. Kent Weaver, "Setting and Firing Policy Triggers," *Journal of Public Policy* 9 (1989): 307–336.

77. Paulette Kurzer, "The Politics of Central Banks: Austerity and Unemployment in Europe," *Journal of Public Policy* 8 (1988): 21–48.

78. Indeed, reducing values such as clean air, natural beauty, and social equality to dollars and cents (as is necessary to make cost-benefit analysis work) represents an extreme form of utilitarianism.

79. See Henry J. Aaron, Thomas E. Mann, and Timothy Taylor, *Values and Public Policy* (Washington, DC: Brookings Institution Press, 1994).

80. Moshe F. Rubenstein, *Patterns of Problem Solving* (Englewood Cliffs, NJ: Prentice-Hall, 1975).

81. The political risks for the mayor may be different than the actual risks to the city and its people. The mayor does not want to be seen as panicking in the face of a crisis, but the unnecessary loss of life may be the most damaging possibility of all for a political leader.

82. Stephen H. Linder and B. Guy Peters, "From Social Theory to Policy Design," *Journal of Public Policy* 4 (1984): 237–259; and Davis Bobrow and John S. Dryzek, *Policy Analysis by Design* (Pittsburgh: University of Pittsburgh Press, 1987).

83. Anne L. Schneider and Helen M. Ingram, for example, argue that policy design runs directly opposite to the pluralistic politics that dominates policymaking in the United States. See their *Policy Design for Democracy* (Lawrence: University Press of Kansas, 1997).

## Chapter 5

1. Peter G. Brown, *Restoring the Public Trust* (Boston: Beacon Press, 1994); and Rodney Barker, *Political Legitimacy and the State* (Oxford: Clarendon Press, 1990).
2. The government of the United Kingdom suspended civil liberties in Northern Ireland in response to the sectarian violence there. For at least a portion of the population, this action reduced its legitimacy. For other citizens, the extreme crisis of sectarian violence and terrorism justified the action.
3. Donald L. Westerfield, *War Powers: The President, the Congress, and the Question of War* (Westport, CT: Praeger, 1996).
4. Kathy Kiely, "Some Lawmakers Balk at Proposed Boost in Salaries," *USA Today*, June 26, 2006.
5. Christopher F. Karpowitz, J. Quin Monson, Kelly D. Patterson, and Jeremy C. Pope, "Tea Time in America?: The Impact of the Tea Party Movement in the 2010 Midterm Elections," *PS: Political Science and Politics* 44, 303–309.
6. See, for example, Alan Brinkley, "What's Wrong with American Political Leadership?" *Wilson Quarterly* 18, no. 2 (1994): 46–54; and Paul Krugman, "A Can't Do Government," *New York Times,* September 2, 2005.
7. The very high figure in 1991 appears to be at least in part a function of the Gulf War (see also the figure for the military in that year)—presidents often get a popularity boost from wars. George W. Bush enjoyed the same high levels after September 11, 2001.
8. His approval rating was 22 percent as he left office in the CBS/*Washington Post* poll.
9. Bruce Gilley, *Right to Rule: How Nations Win and Lose Legitimacy* (Cambridge: Cambridge University Press, 2009).
10. In addition to the rational economic dimension of housing, there is the emotional attachment to the "American Dream" of owning a home.
11. This is to some degree what Aaron Wildavsky meant when he argued that policy analysts must "speak truth to power" in his book *Speaking Truth to Power* (Boston: Little, Brown, 1979).
12. Arnold J. Meltsner, "Political Feasibility and Policy Analysis," *Public Administration Review* 32 (1972): 859–867; and Giandomenico Majone, "The Feasibility of Social Policies," *Policy Sciences* 6 (1975): 49–69.
13. For nonmajoritarian legitimation see G. Majone, "Nonmajoritarian Institutions and the Limits of Democratic Governance," *Journal of Institutional and Theoretical Economics* 157: 57–78.
14. Joel D. Aberbach, *Keeping a Watchful Eye: The Politics of Congressional Oversight* (Washington, DC: Brookings Institution Press, 1991).
15. *Immigration and Naturalization Service v. Chadha,* 462 U.S. 919 (1983); and John D. Huber and Charles R. Shipan, "The Costs of Control: Legislators, Agencies and Transaction Costs," *Legislative Studies Quarterly* 25 (2000): 25–52.
16. Jessica Korn, *The Power of Separation: American Constitutionalism and the Myth of the Legislative Veto* (Princeton, NJ: Princeton University Press, 1997); and J. Mitchell Pickerill, *Constitutional Deliberation in Congress* (Durham, NC: Duke University Press, 2005).

17. Walter J. Oleszek, *Congressional Procedures and the Policy Process* (Washington, DC: CQ Press, 1988); and Sarah A. Binder and Steven S. Smith, *Filibustering: Politics or Principle* (Washington, DC: Brookings Institution Press, 1997).

18. There are, therefore, a number of "veto points," a concept similar to "clearance points" in implementation theory. See Ellen Immergut, *Health Care Politics* (Cambridge: Cambridge University Press, 1992).

19. Jeff Flake, "Earmarked Men," *New York Times,* February 9, 2006.

20. There have been majorities in favor of reforming medical care for some time, but there is as yet no major change. Likewise, there has been a majority for stronger handgun control for some time but little policy change.

21. Lori Montgomery and Paul Kane, "Debt-Limit Debate: 43 Republicans Say They Will Reject Reid's Plan?," *Washington Post,* July 29, 2011.

22. Charles E. Lindblom and Edward J. Woodhouse, *The Policy-Making Process,* 3rd ed. (Englewood Cliffs, NJ: Prentice-Hall, 1993).

23. James Buchanan and Gordon Tullock, *The Calculus of Consent* (Ann Arbor: University of Michigan Press, 1962), 120–144.

24. See John A. Hamman, "Universalism, Program Development, and the Distribution of Federal Assistance," *Legislative Studies Quarterly* 18 (1993): 553–568.

25. Morris P. Fiorina, *Congress: Keystone of the Washington Establishment* (New Haven, CT: Yale University Press, 1981).

26. Douglas R. Arnold, *Congress and the Bureaucracy* (New Haven, CT: Yale University Press, 1979).

27. Diana Evans, *Greasing the Wheels: Using the Pork Barrel to Build Majority Coalitions in Congress* (Cambridge: Cambridge University Press, 2005).

28. Many programs will do that; the question is whether there is also a broader public interest involved.

29. James Kitfield, "The Battle of the Depots," *National Journal,* April 4, 1998.

30. Jane Gordon, "In a Hurry to Diversify beyond Submarines and Luck," *New York Times,* December 18, 2005.

31. William R. Riker and Peter Ordeshook, *Positive Political Theory* (Englewood Cliffs, NJ: Prentice-Hall, 1973), 97–114.

32. Kenneth Arrow, *Social Choice and Individual Values,* 2nd ed. (New York: Wiley, 1963).

33. Aberbach, *Keeping a Watchful Eye.*

34. These terms come from Mathew McCubbins and Thomas Schwartz, "Congressional Oversight Overlooked: Police Patrols versus Fire Alarms," *American Journal of Political Science* 28 (1984): 165–179.

35. Cornelius M. Kerwin and Scott Furlong, *Rulemaking: How Government Agencies Write Law and Make Policy,* 4th ed. (Washington, DC: CQ Press, 2011).

36. Marc Allen Eisner, *Regulatory Politics in Transition* (Baltimore: Johns Hopkins University Press, 2000).

37. OMB Watch, "Turning Back the Clock: The Obama Administration and the Legacy of Bush Era Midnight Regulations," February 5, 2009, www.ombwatch.org/node/10497?page=0%2C10.

38. Margaret T. Kriz, "Kibitzer with Clout," *National Journal,* May 30, 1987, 1404–1408.

39. Thomas O. McGarity, *Reinventing Rationality: The Role of Regulatory Analysis in the Federal Bureaucracy* (Cambridge: Cambridge University Press, 1991).

40. Viveca Novak, "The New Regulators," *National Journal,* July 17, 1993, 1801–1804.
41. Reuters, "Six Areas of Obama Regulatory Reform," August 24, 2011.
42. Martin Shapiro, "APA: Past, Present and Future," *Virginia Law Review* 72 (1986): 447–492.
43. Jerry L. Mashaw, "Prodelegation: Why Administrators Should Make Political Decisions," *Journal of Law, Economics and Organization* 5 (1985): 141–164.
44. Even then, there was a concentration of participation, with only a few interest groups taking advantage of this opportunity. See Barry Boyer, "Funding Public Participation in Agency Proceedings: The Federal Trade Commission Experience," *Georgetown Law Journal* 70 (1981): 51–172.
45. See Glen O. Robinson, *American Bureaucracy: Public Choice and Public Law* (Ann Arbor: University of Michigan Press, 1991), 139–147.
46. Stephen Williams, "Hybrid Rulemaking under the Administrative Procedures Act: A Legal and Empirical Analysis," *University of Chicago Law Review* 42 (1975): 401–456.
47. *International Harvester Co. v. Ruckelshaus,* 478 F. 2nd 615 (1973).
48. William Gormley Jr., *Taming the Bureaucracy* (Princeton, NJ: Princeton University Press, 1989), 94–97.
49. Philip Harter, "Negotiated Rulemaking: A Cure for the Malaise," *Georgetown Law Review* 71 (1982): 1–28; "Assessing the Assessors: The Actual Performance of Negotiated Rulemaking," *New York University Environmental Law Journal* 9 (2001), 32–64; and Thomas McGarrity, "Some Thoughts on Deossifying the Rulemaking Process," *Duke Law Journal* 41 (1992): 1385–1462.
50. David Pritzker and Deborah Dalton, *Negotiated Rulemaking Sourcebook* (Washington, DC: Administrative Conference of the United States, 1990).
51. Philippe C. Schmitter, "Still the Century of Corporatism?" *Review of Politics* 36 (1974): 85–131.
52. See Robert Kvavik, *Interest Groups in Norwegian Politics* (Oslo, Norway: Universitetsforlaget, 1980).
53. Mike Mills, "President to Stage Timber Summit," *Congressional Quarterly Weekly Report* 51 (March 13, 1993): 593.
54. This could hardly be corporatist, however, since it involved only the one side of a complex policy debate. See William Schneider, "It's Cheney vs. Carter in the New Energy War," *National Journal,* May 12, 2001, 649.
55. See Colin S. Diver, "A Theory of Regulatory Enforcement," *Public Policy* 29 (1980): 295–296.
56. Theodore J. Lowi, *The End of Liberalism,* 2nd ed. (New York: Norton, 1979).
57. Richard A. Harris and Sidney M. Milkis, *The Politics of Regulatory Change* (New York: Oxford University Press, 1989).
58. David Schoenbrod, *Power without Responsibility* (New Haven, CT: Yale University Press, 1993).
59. Martha Derthick and Paul J. Quirk, *The Politics of Deregulation* (Washington, DC: Brookings Institution Press, 1985).
60. Robert A. Kagan, "Adversarial Legalism and American Government," *Journal of Policy Analysis and Management* 10 (1991): 369–406; and Robert J. Samuelson, "Whitewater: The Law as Bludgeon," *International Herald Tribune,* March 8, 1994.

61. Federal Judge Frank Johnson, in Alabama, literally took over the prisons and mental hospitals of that state. See *Wyatt v. Stickney*, 344 F. Supp. 373 (M.D. Ala. 1972), and *Pugh v. Locke,* 406 F. Supp. 318 (M.D. Ala. 1976).
62. Thomas J. Cronin, *Direct Democracy* (Cambridge, MA: Harvard University Press, 1989). See also Ian Budge, *The New Challenge of Direct Democracy* (Cambridge, MA: Polity Press, 1996).
63. National Council of State Legislatures, "What the Voters Have Decided So Far: The Thicket," (NCSL blog), November 6, 2008, www.ncsl.org/magazine/the-thicket-a-legislative-blog.aspx.
64. Benjamin R. Barber, *Strong Democracy: Participatory Politics in a New Age* (Berkeley: University of California Press, 1984); and James Bohman and William Rehig, *Deliberative Democracy: Essays on Reason and Politics* (Cambridge, MA: MIT Press). For a less philosophical discussion, see Phil Duncan, "American Democracy in Search of Debate," *Congressional Quarterly Weekly Report* 51 (October 16, 1993): 2850.

## Chapter 6

1. Michael Lipsky, *Street Level Bureaucracy* (New York: Russell Sage, 1980).
2. Cass Sunstein, *After the Rights Revolution: Reconceiving the Regulatory State* (Cambridge, MA: Harvard University Press, 1990); John D. Huber and Charles R. Shipan, *Deliberate Discretion: The Institutional Foundations of Bureaucratic Autonomy* (Cambridge: Cambridge University Press, 2002).
3. See U.S. Senate, Committee on Governmental Affairs, *The Federal Executive Establishment: Evolution and Trends* (Washington, DC: U.S. Government Printing Office, 1980), 23–63.
4. Harold Seidman and Robert S. Gilmour, *Politics, Position and Power,* 4th ed. (New York: Oxford University Press, 1986).
5. The degree of central control in the Defense Department can be exaggerated. See C. Kenneth Allard, *Command, Control, and the Common Defense* (New Haven, CT: Yale University Press, 1990); Joseph Metcalf III, "Decision-Making and the Grenada Rescue Operation," in *Ambiguity and Control,* ed. J. G. March and R. Wessinger-Baylon (Boston: Pirman, 1987).
6. John Hart, *The Presidential Branch,* 2nd ed. (Chatham, NJ: Chatham House, 1994).
7. B. Guy Peters, R. A. W. Rhodes, and Vincent Wright, eds., *Administering the Summit* (London: Macmillan, 1998).
8. Frederick C. Mosher, *The GAO* (Boulder, CO: Westview Press, 1979); and Ray C. Rist, *Program Evaluation and Management of Government* (New Brunswick, NJ: Transaction, 1990).
9. Daily reports from the Government Accountability Office can be found at www.gao.gov.
10. Marc Alan Eisner, *Regulatory Politics in Transition* (Baltimore: Johns Hopkins University Press, 1993).
11. The classic statement is Samuel P. Huntington, "The Marasmus of the ICC," *Yale Law Review* 61 (April 1952): 467–509. For a very different perspective, see Jonathan R. Mezey, "Organizational Design and Political Control of Administrative Agencies," *Journal of Law, Economics and Organization* 8 (1992): 93–110.

12. The growth of the consumer movement has placed additional pressures on regulatory agencies to escape capture. See Michael D. Reagan, *Regulation: The Politics of Policy* (Boston: Little, Brown, 1987).

13. Michael Dorf, "Artifactions: The Battle over the National Endowment for the Arts," *Brookings Review* 26 (Winter 1993): 32–35.

14. On June 25, 1998, the Court argued that there is no right to a grant, so artists could not argue that this denied them any fundamental rights. *National Endowment for the Arts v. Finley,* 524 U.S. 569 (1998).

15. Annemarie Hauck Walsh, *Managing the Public's Business* (Cambridge, MA: MIT Press, 1980), 41–44.

16. See Peter Passell, "The Sticky Side of Privatization: Sale of U.S. Nuclear Fuel Plants Raises Host of Conflicts," *New York Times*, August 30, 1997.

17. The level of autonomy of the Federal Reserve has decreased substantially in the economic crisis, as it became more closely linked to the Obama administration's efforts to revive the economy. See "The Fed," Times Topics, *New York Times,* January 29, 2012.

18. Seidman and Gilmour, *Politics, Position and Power,* 274.

19. Charles Duhigg, "Two Mortgage Giants Are Unlikely to Be Restored," *New York Times,* March 3, 2009.

20. Marc Alan Eisner, *Antitrust and the Triumph of Economics* (Chapel Hill: University of North Carolina Press, 1992).

21. Martin Landau, "The Rationality of Redundancy," *Public Administration Review* 29 (1969): 346–358; Jonathan R. Bendor, *Parallel Politics* (Berkeley: University of California Press, 1985).

22. James L. Sundquist, "Needed: A Political Theory for a New Era of Coalition Government in the United States," *Political Science Quarterly* 108 (1988): 613–635.

23. U.S. Federal Reserve Board, "The Role of the Federal Reserve in Preserving Monetary and Financial Stability," joint press release, March 23, 2009, www.federalreserve .gov/newsevents/press/monetary/20090323b.htm.

24. U.S. Senate, Committee on Governmental Affairs, *The Federal Executive Establishment,* 27–30.

25. "In God We Trust," *Harvard Political Review* 28 (2001): 15–27.

26. Woodrow Wilson, "The Study of Administration," *Political Science Quarterly* 1 (1887): 197–222.

27. This is perhaps especially true of American government given the number of "veto points" that exist within the system. See Ellen Immergut, *Health Care Politics: Ideas and Institutions in Western Europe* (Cambridge: Cambridge University Press, 1992).

28. See Else Oyen, S. M. Miller, and S. A. Samad, *Poverty: A Global Review* (Oslo, Norway: Scandinavian University Press, 1996).

29. Daniel Patrick Moynihan, *The Politics of Guaranteed Income* (New York: Vintage, 1973), 240.

30. The importance of laser technologies is demonstrated in William Broad, *Teller's War: The Top-Secret Story behind the Star Wars Initiative* (New York: Simon and Schuster, 1992).

31. David Runk, "Bush Highlights Alternative Energy Plans in Michigan," *USA Today,* February 8, 2006.

32. Bill Vladic, "Obama Reveals Details of Gas Mileage Rules," *New York Times,* July 20, 2011.

33. That difference is discussed well in Richard R. Nelson, *The Moon and the Ghetto* (New York: Norton, 1977).

34. That decision eventually was rescinded after a public outcry. However, in 1998 another decision by the Department of Agriculture made salsa a vegetable for school lunches, provided it was made from fresh vegetables (there's that word again).

35. Tax legislation is sufficiently complex that it is possible to hide benefits for particular groups even in legislation that ostensibly is general tax relief. See Paul Krugman, *Fuzzy Math: The Essential Guide to the Bush Tax Plan* (New York: Norton, 2001).

36. Theodore J. Lowi, *The End of Liberalism,* 2nd ed. (New York: Norton, 1979), 42–63.

37. Christopher Hood, *The Limits of Administration* (New York: Wiley, 1976).

38. Burt Solomon, "Twixt Cup and Lip," *National Journal,* October 24, 1992, 2410–2415; and Paul C. Light, *Thickening Government: Federal Hierarchy and the Diffusion of Accountability* (Washington, DC: Brookings Institution Press, 1995).

39. A classic description of the dangers of this occurring is found in Herbert Kaufman, *The Forest Ranger* (Baltimore: Johns Hopkins University Press, 1960); M. K. Meyers and S. Vorsanger, "Street-Level Bureaucrats and Policy Implementation," in *Handbook of Public Administration,* ed. G. Peters and J. Pierre (London: Sage, 2004).

40. Janet Schrader, "Lost on the Road to Reform: Some of My Clients Can't Do the Jobs Out There," *Washington Post,* May 11, 1997.

41. Peter M. Blau, *The Dynamics of Bureaucracy* (Chicago: University of Chicago Press, 1955), 184–193.

42. Eugene Bardach and Robert A. Kagan, *Going by the Book: The Problem of Regulatory Unreasonableness* (Philadelphia: Temple University Press, 1982).

43. This is now often phrased in terms of a "principal" controlling its agents. See Dan Wood and Richard Waterman, *Bureaucratic Dynamics: The Role of Bureaucracy in a Democracy* (Boulder, CO: Westview Press, 1994).

44. Martha A. Derthick, *Agency under Stress: The Social Security Administration in American Government* (Washington, DC: Brookings Institution Press, 1990).

45. Arthur Stinchcombe, *Information and Organizations* (Berkeley: University of California Press, 1990).

46. James G. March and Herbert A. Simon, *Organizations* (New York: Wiley, 1958).

47. On the other hand, too much similarity in backgrounds and training enhances the possibilities of "groupthink" and an absence of error correction within the organization. See Paul T. Hart, Eric K. Stern, and Bengt Sundelius, *Beyond Groupthink: Political Group Dynamics and Foreign Policy-Making* (Ann Arbor: University of Michigan Press, 1997).

48. The Gore commission (National Performance Review) reforms have had the effect of reducing drastically the number of levels in organizations, with the presumed effect of empowering employees at lower levels and improving internal communications.

49. James McGregor Burns, *Roosevelt: The Lion and the Fox* (New York: Harcourt, Brace, 1956).

50. Harold Wilensky, *Organizational Intelligence* (New York: Basic Books, 1967), 130–145.

51. Hood, *The Limits of Administration,* 85–87.

52. Ibid., 192–197.

53. For a good compilation, see Peter Hall, *Great Planning Disasters* (London: Weidenfield and Nicolson, 1980). We should remember, however, that these failings are as common in large private organizations as in the public sector, but there they tend to be less publicized. See Charles T. Goodsell, *The Case for Bureaucracy: A Public Administration Polemic,* 4th ed. (Chatham, NJ: Chatham House, 2003).

54. Paul R. Schulman, *Large-Scale Policy Analysis* (New York: Elsevier, 1980).

55. Richard A. Rettig, *Cancer Crusade* (Princeton, NJ: Princeton University Press, 1977).

56. This assumes that this disease is similar to cancer in requiring a more decentralized research format.

57. Benny Hjern and David O. Porter, "Implementation Structures: A New Unit of Organisational Analysis," *Organisational Studies* 2 (1981): 211–228.

58. Eugene Bardach, "Turf Barriers to Interagency Collaboration," in *The State of Public Management,* ed. D. F. Kettl and H. B. Milward (Baltimore: Johns Hopkins University Press, 1996), 168.

59. See Kevin P. Kearns, *Private Sector Strategies for Public Sector Success* (San Francisco: Jossey-Bass, 2000).

60. Jeffrey L. Pressman and Aaron Wildavsky, *Implementation* (Berkeley: University of California Press, 1979).

61. Ibid., 145–168.

62. Judith Bowen, "The Pressman-Wildavsky Paradox," *Journal of Public Policy* 2 (1982): 1–22; and Ernst Alexander, "Improbable Implementation: The Pressman-Wildavsky Paradox Revisited," *Journal of Public Policy* 9 (1989): 451–465.

63. See David Osborne and Ted Gaebler, *Reinventing Government* (Reading, MA: Addison-Wesley, 1992); and B. Guy Peters, "Can't Row, Shouldn't Steer: What's a Government to Do?" *Public Policy and Administration* 12, no. 2 (1997): 51–61.

64. Rochelle L. Stanfield, "Between the Cracks," *National Journal,* October 11, 1997, 314–318.

65. William T. Gormley, "Regulating Mr. Rogers's Neighborhood: The Dilemmas of Day Care Regulation," *Brookings Review* 8 (1990): 21–28.

66. Barry Meier, "Fight in Congress Looms on Fishing," *New York Times,* September 19, 1994.

67. R. Lewis Bowman, Eleanor C. Main, and B. Guy Peters, "Coordination in the Atlanta Model Cities Program" (mimeo, Department of Political Science, Emory University, Atlanta, GA, 1971).

68. Jon Pierre, "The Marketization of the State: Citizens, Consumers and the Emergence of Public Markets," in *Governance in a Changing Environment,* ed. Donald Savoie and B. Guy Peters (Montreal: McGill/Queens University Press, 1995), 55.

69. Richard F. Elmore, "Backward Mapping and Implementation Research and Policy Decisions," in *Studying Implementation,* ed. Walter Williams (Chatham, NJ: Chatham House, 1984).

70. M. Kiviniemi, "Public Policies and Their Targets: A Typology of the Concept of Implementation," *International Social Science Quarterly* 108 (1986): 251–265.

71. Elmore, "Backward Mapping"; Paul A. Sabatier, "Top-down and Bottom-up Models of Policy Implementation: A Critical Analysis and Suggested Synthesis," *Journal of Public Policy* 6 (1986): 21–48; and Stephen H. Linder and B. Guy Peters,

"Implementation as a Guide to Policy Formulation: A Question of 'When' Rather Than 'Whether,'" *International Review of Administrative Sciences* 55 (1989): 631–652.

72. Linder and Peters, "Implementation as a Guide."

73. Giandomenico Majone, "The Feasibility of Social Policies," *Policy Sciences* 6 (1975): 49–69.

74. Malcolm L. Goggin, Ann O'M. Bowman, James P. Lester, and Laurence J. O'Toole, *Implementation Theory and Practice: Toward a Third Generation* (New York: Harper-Collins, 1990); and Soren Winter, "The Implementation Perspective," in *Handbook of Public Administration,* ed. G. Peters and J. Pierre (London: Sage, 2004), 212.

75. Laurence O'Toole, "Interorganizational Relations in Implementation," in *Handbook of Public Administration,* ed. G. Peters and J. Pierre (London: Sage, 2004), 234.

# Chapter 7

1. But see David Jackson and John Fritze, "Obama Vows to Cut Pork, Later," *USA Today,* March 11, 2009.

2. Jan-Erik Lane, *The Public Sector: Concepts, Models, and Approaches* (London: Sage, 1994).

3. Rather than a question of the efficient division of resources between the public and private sectors, this is an intergenerational equity question. The huge deficit that the federal government has incurred will impose costs on American citizens for generations to come. See David Rosnick and Dean Parker, *Taming the Deficit: Saving Our Children from Themselves* (Washington, DC: Center for Economic and Policy Research, 2009).

4. In the budget debates after 2009, entitlements are now more subject to careful scrutiny and cuts than in the past. See Helene Cooper, "Obama Offers Plan to Cut Deficit by Over $3 Trillion," *New York Times,* September 11, 2011.

5. Charles Stewart III, *Budget Reform Politics* (New York: Cambridge University Press, 1989).

6. Louis Fisher, *Presidential Spending Power* (Princeton, NJ: Princeton University Press, 1975).

7. "After Years of Wrangling, Accord Is Reached on Plan to Balance Budget by 2002," *New York Times,* May 3, 1997.

8. Nancy Roberts, "The Synoptic Model of Strategic Planning and GPRA," *Public Productivity and Management Review* 23 (2000): 297–311.

9. General Accounting Office, *Biennial Budgeting for the Federal Government* (Washington, DC: U.S. General Accounting Office, October 7, 1993), GAO/T-AIMED-94-4; and Louis Fisher, "Biennial Budgeting in the Federal Government," *Public Budgeting and Finance* 17, no. 3 (1997): 87–97.

10. "Federal Capital Budgeting," *Intergovernmental Perspective* 20 (1994): 8–16; Beverly S. Bunch, "Current Practices and Issues in Capital Budgeting and Reporting," *Public Budgeting and Finance* 16, no. 2 (1996): 7–25. The *Special Analyses of the Budget* also contains information about the investment features of federal spending.

11. See *Washington Post,* "The Long Path to the Federal Budget," February 4, 2002; "The Federal Budget Process," January 31, 2010.

12. Charles L. Schultze, "Paying the Bills," in *Setting Domestic Priorities*, ed. Henry J. Aaron and Charles L. Schultze (Washington, DC: Brookings Institution Press, 1992), 295–317.

13. Paul E. Peterson and Mark Rom, "Macroeconomic Policymaking: Who Is in Control," in *Can the Government Govern?* eds. John E. Chubb and Paul E. Peterson (Washington, DC: Brookings Institution Press, 1989), 167–198.

14. This official was Murray Weidenbaum. See David Stockman, *The Triumph of Politics* (New York: Harper and Row, 1986), 104.

15. See Roy T. Meyers, *Strategic Budgeting* (Ann Arbor: University of Michigan Press, 1994), 52–60.

16. Aaron Wildavsky and Naomi Caiden, *The New Politics of the Budgetary Process*, 5th ed. (New York: Longman, 2004), 50–54.

17. Ibid., 81–82.

18. Office of Management and Budget, *Preparation and Submission of "Current Services" Budget Estimates*, Bulletin 76–4 (Washington, DC: U.S. Office of Management and Budget, August 13, 1975), 2–4.

19. See Thomas W. Wander, F. Ted Hebert, and Gary W. Copeland, *Congressional Budgeting* (Baltimore: Johns Hopkins University Press, 1984); and Robin Toner, "Putting Prices on Congress's Ideas," *New York Times*, August 21, 1994.

20. John W. Ellwood and James A. Thurber, "The Politics of the Congressional Budget Process Re-considered," in *Congress Reconsidered*, ed. Lawrence C. Dodd and Bruce Oppenheimer, 2nd ed. (Washington, DC: CQ Press, 1981), 124–141. There has been some tendency to disperse this power, with appropriations committees now handling only about two-thirds of the total budget. See John F. Cogan, "Congress Has Dispersed the Power of the Purse," *Public Affairs Report* 35 (September 1994): 7–8.

21. Paul Starobin, "Bringing It Home," *National Journal*, June 26, 1993, 1642–1645.

22. D. Roderick Kiewiet and Mathew D. McCubbins, *The Logic of Delegation* (Chicago: University of Chicago Press, 1991).

23. See Irene Rubin, *The Politics of Public Budgeting*, 4th ed. (Chatham, NJ: Chatham House, 2002), 75–76; and James Thurber, "Congressional Budget Reform: Impact on Congressional Appropriations Committees," *Public Budgeting and Finance* 17, no. 3 (1997): 62–73.

24. Carl Hulse, "Whistle-Stops and War Whoops Bury Budget Woes," *New York Times*, October 1, 2002.

25. David Baumann, "Congress—Does a Budget Really Matter?" *National Journal*, April 15, 2006.

26. The dispute concerning the FAA has been over minute points of agency management rather than over fundamental issues concerning the utility of the agency.

27. Fisher, *Presidential Spending Power*.

28. David Baumann, "Line-Item Lite," *National Journal*, April 8, 2006.

29. Gary Therkildsen, "Obama Requests Enhanced Rescission Authority," *OMB Watch*, May 11, 2010.

30. Frederick C. Mosher, *The GAO: The Quest for Accountability in American Government* (Boulder, CO: Westview Press, 1979), 169–200; and Ray C. Rist, "Management Accountability: The Signals Sent by Auditing and Evaluation," *Journal of Public Policy* 9 (1989): 355–369.

31. James D. Savae, *Balanced Budgets and American Politics* (Ithaca, NY: Cornell University Press, 1988); Barry C. Burden and Joseph Neal Rice Sanderg, "Budget Rhetoric in Presidential Campaigns from 1952 to 2000," *Political Behavior* 25 (2003): 97–118.

32. Technically, the general fund is borrowing the money from the Social Security Trust Fund, although the presentation of deficit figures does not make that distinction clear. See General Accounting Office, *Retirement Income: Implications of Demographic Trends for Social Security and Pension Reform* (Washington, DC: U.S. General Accounting Office, July 1997), GAO/HEHS-97-81.

33. Glenn Kessler, "Use of Retirement Funds to Widen Debt Limit Fight," *Washington Post*, April 3, 2002.

34. These changes have been in part in response to accounting fiascos in the private sector, for example, in Enron and WorldCom.

35. See Bruce Bartlett, "The 81 Percent Tax Increase," *Forbes*, May 15, 2009.

36. Jim Cooper, "A Truer Measure of America's Ballooning Deficit," *Financial Times*, May 1, 2006.

37. Stephen Taub, "Accrual Accounting Raises Federal Deficit," *Today in Finance*, March 2, 2004.

38. Else Foley, "House GOP Votes Down Clean Debt Ceiling Limit Increase, Eyes Medicare in Deal," *Huffington Post*, May 31, 2011.

39. See Robert D. Reischauer, "The Unfulfillable Promise: Cutting Nondefense Discretionary Spending," in *Setting National Priorities: Budget Choices for the Next Century*, ed. Robert D. Reischauer (Washington, DC: Brookings Institution Press, 1997), 123–126.

40. Rob Norton, "Every Budget Tells a Story, and This Is No Exception," *Washington Post*, March 10, 2002.

41. Michael D. Shear, "Obama Pledges Entitlement Reform," *Washington Post*, January 16, 2009.

42. Glenn Kessler, "Obama and the Defense Budget," *Washington Post*, February 14, 2012.

43. Jeff Shear, "The Untouchables," *National Journal*, July 16, 1994; "America's Budget: The Elephant in the Room," *Economist*, May 7, 2011.

44. A variety of federal loan programs account for over $200 billion in outstanding direct loans and over $700 billion in guaranteed loans. The Tax Foundation, *Facts and Figures on Government Finance*, 1993 (Washington, DC: Tax Foundation, 1994).

45. Office of Management and Budget, *Analytical Perspectives on the Budget*, 2006 (Washington, DC: U.S. Office of Management and Budget, 2005).

46. Ben Wildavsky, "After the Deficit," *National Journal*, November 29, 1997, 2408–2410.

47. General Accounting Office, *Budgeting for Federal Insurance Programs* (Washington, DC: U.S. General Accounting Office, September 1997), GAO/AIMD-97-16.

48. The federal government has been fortunate that during a period of high deficits the interest rates it has had to pay have been exceptionally low.

49. Office of Management and Budget, *Budget of the United States, FY 2007, Analytical Perspectives* (Washington, DC: U.S. Government Printing Office, 2007).

50. For Germany, see Russell J. Dalton, *Politics in Germany*, 2nd ed. (New York: Harper Collins, 1993), 372–377; More generally, see Wallace Oates, "Toward a Second

Generation Theory of Fiscal Federalism," *International Tax and Public Finance* 12 (2005): 197–215.

51. These surpluses tended to be, on average, 11 percent of total state revenues, although some 15 percent of total state revenues comes from grants from the federal government.

52. Philip J. Candreva and L. R. Jones, "Congressional Delegation of Spending Power to the Defense Department in the Post 9-11 Period," *Public Budgeting and Finance* 25 (2005): 1–19.

53. ABC News, "Classified Spending Still High, Report Says," August 1, 2007, http://blogs.abcnews.com/theblotter/2007/08/classified-spen.html.

54. James McCaffrey and Paul Godek, "Defense Supplementals and the Budget Process," *Public Budgeting and Finance* 23 (2003): 53–72.

55. Marcia Clemmitt, "Pork Barrel Politics," *CQ Researcher,* June 16, 2006, entire issue.

56. Steve Ellis, "Earmark Reform: Understanding the Obligations of Funds Transparency Act," testimony before House Homeland Security and Governmental Affairs Committee, U.S. Congress, March 16, 2006.

57. Citizens against Government Waste, *2010 Congressional Pig Book* (Washington, DC: Citizens against Government Waste, 2011).

58. See Clemmitt, "Pork Barrel Politics."

59. Diana Evans, *Greasing the Wheels: Using Pork Barrel Projects to Build Majority Coalitions in Congress* (Cambridge: Cambridge University Press, 2004).

60. Brian Riedl, "How Pork Corrupts," *Washington Post,* January 29, 2006.

61. Paul Kane and Scott Wilson, "Obama Signs Spending Bill, Promises Earmark Reform," *Washington Post,* March 12, 2009.

62. William D. Berry, "The Confusing Case of Budgetary Incrementalism: Too Many Meanings for a Single Concept," *Journal of Politics* 52 (1990): 167–196.

63. M. A. H. Dempster and Aaron Wildavsky, "On Change: Or, There Is No Magic Size for an Increment," *Political Studies* 28 (1980): 371–389.

64. See David Braybrooke and Charles E. Lindblom, *A Strategy for Decision* (New York: Free Press, 1963).

65. Otto A. Davis, M. A. H. Dempster, and Aaron Wildavsky, "A Theory of the Budgetary Process," *American Political Science Review* 60 (1969): 529–547. These findings are now quite old, but there is little evidence that the process or the outcomes have changed significantly.

66. Aaron Wildavsky, *Budgeting: A Comparative Theory of the Budgetary Process,* rev. ed. (New Brunswick, NJ: Transaction, 1986): 7–27.

67. Michael T. Hayes, *Incrementalism and Public Policy* (New York: Longman, 1992), 131–144; see also Meyers, *Strategic Budgeting.*

68. Peter B. Natchez and Irvin C. Bupp, "Policy and Priority in the Budgetary Process," *American Political Science Review* 64 (1973): 951–963.

69. Dempster and Wildavsky, "On Change."

70. John R. Gist, "'Increment' and 'Base' in the Congressional Appropriation Process," *American Journal of Political Science* 21 (1977): 341–352.

71. Robert E. Goodin, *Political Theory and Public Policy* (Chicago: University of Chicago Press, 1983), 22–38.

72. Brian W. Hogwood and B. Guy Peters, *The Pathology of Public Policy* (New York: Oxford University Press, 1985), 124–126.

73. David Novick, *Program Budgeting: Program Analysis and the Federal Budget* (Cambridge, MA: Harvard University Press, 1967).

74. Robert H. Haveman and Burton A. Weisbrod, "Defining Benefits from Public Programs: Some Guidance from Policy Analysts," in *Public Expenditure and Policy Analysis,* ed. Robert H. Haveman and Julius Margolis, 3rd ed. (Boston: Houghton-Mifflin, 1983), 135; and Philip G. Joyce, "Using Performance Measures for Federal Budgeting: Proposals and Prospects," *Public Budgeting and Finance* 13 (1993): 3–17.

75. Aaron Wildavsky, "Political Implications of Budgetary Reform," *Public Administration Review* 21 (1961): 183–190.

76. Lenneal J. Henderson, "GPRA: Mission, Metrics, and Marketing," *Public Manager* 24, no. 1 (1995): 7–10; and Beryl A. Radin, "The Government Performance and Results Act (GPRA): Hydra-Headed Monster or Flexible Management Tool?" *Public Administration Review* 58 (1998): 307–316.

77. General Accounting Office, *Managing for Results: Agency Progress in Linking Performance Plans with Budgets and Financial Statements* (Washington, DC: U.S. General Accounting Office, January 2002), GAO-02-236. See also Roy T. Meyers and Philip G. Joyce, "Congressional Budgeting at Age 30: Is It Worth Saving?" *Public Budgeting and Finance* 25 (2005): 68–82.

78. See Jon Blondal, Dirk-Jan Kraan, and Michael Ruffner, "Budgeting in the United States," *OECD Journal of Budgeting* 3 (2003): 1–45.

79. These solutions are examples of "formula budgeting," which substitutes formulas for political judgment and political will. See Eric A. Hanushek, "Formula Budgeting: The Economics and Politics of Fiscal Policy under Rules," *Journal of Public Analysis and Management* 6 (1986): 3–19.

80. *James D. Savage, Balanced Budgets and American Politics* (Ithaca, NY: Cornell University Press, 1988).

81. *Bowsher v. Synar,* 478 U.S. 714 (1986); see also Lance T. LeLoup, Barbara Luck Graham, and Stacey Barwick, "Deficit Politics and Constitutional Government: The Impact of Gramm-Rudman-Hollings," *Public Budgeting and Finance* 7 (1987): 83–103.

82. Congressional Budget Office, *The Economic and Budget Outlook, 1992–96* (Washington, DC: U.S. Government Printing Office, 1991).

83. Philip G. Joyce, "Congressional Budget Reform: The Unanticipated Implications of Federal Policy Making," *Public Administration Review* 56 (1996): 317–324.

84. Allen Schick, *The Federal Budget: Politics, Policy and Process* (Washington, DC: Brookings Institution Press, 1995), 40–41.

85. Karl O'Lessker, "The Clinton Budget for FY 1994: Taking Aim at the Deficit," *Public Budgeting and Finance* 13 (1993): 7–19.

86. "The Supercommittee Collapses" *New York Times,* November 21, 2011.

87. Alvin Rabushka, "Fiscal Responsibility: Will Anything Less than a Constitutional Amendment Do?" in *The Federal Budget,* ed. Michael J. Boskin and Aaron Wildavsky (San Francisco: Institute for Contemporary Studies, 1982), 333–350. See also Henry J. Aaron, "The Balanced Budget Blunder," *Brookings Review,* (1994): 41; and James V. Saturno and Richard G. Forgette, "The Balanced Budget Spring Amendment: How Would It Be Enforced?" *Public Budgeting and Finance* 18, no. 1 (1998): 33–53.

88. Rudolph G. Penner and Alan J. Abramson, *Broken Purse Strings: Congressional Budgeting 1974–1988* (Washington, DC: Urban Institute Press, 1989), 95–100. For more recent figures, see Bill Montague, "New Budget Forecasts 'Solid,'" *USA Today,* December 13, 1995.

89. Updated by the author from Rudolph G. Penner, "Forecasting Budget Totals: Why We Can't Get It Right," in *The Federal Budget,* ed. Boskin and Wildavsky, 89–110. See also Donald F. Kettl, *Deficit Politics* (New York: Macmillan, 1992), 109–117.

90. U.S. House of Representatives, Committee on the Budget, *The Line-Item Veto: An Appraisal* (Washington, DC: U.S. Government Printing Office, 1984).

91. See Norman Ornstein, "Why GOP Will Rue Line-Item Veto," *USA Today,* November 18, 1997.

92. Jeff Flake, "Earmarked Men," *New York Times,* February 9, 2006.

93. Eric Lichtblau, "New Earmark Rules Have Lobbyists Scrambling," *New York Times,* March 11, 2010.

94. Viveca Novak, "Defective Remedy," *National Journal,* March 27, 1993.

95. These included one provision that would have provided $84 million to one sugar beet processor in Texas and another that benefited certain potato growers in Idaho. See Robert Pear, "Justice Department Belatedly Finds New Defense of Line-Item Veto," *New York Times,* March 26, 1998.

96. See *Getting Back in the Black: Pew-Peterson Committee on Budget Reform* (Philadelphia: Pew Charitable Trust, November, 2010).

97. Daniel Tarschys, "Rational Decremental Budgeting: Elements of an Expenditure Policy for the 1980s," *Policy Sciences* 14 (1982): 49–58.

98. For some members of Congress, there is also a strong desire to reduce the level of services and to return the federal government to some sort of Acadian past. See Paul Kane, "House GOP Revs Up for a Repeal, Reduce and Rein-in Agenda for the Fall," *Washington Post,* August 28, 2011.

99. President's Private Sector Survey on Cost Containment (Grace Commission), *Report to the President* (Washington, DC: PPSSCC, 1984).

100. Sar A. Levitan and Alexandra B. Noden, *Working for the Sovereign* (Baltimore: Johns Hopkins University Press, 1983), 85.

101. National Performance Review, *Making Government Work Better and Cost Less* (The Gore Report) (Washington, DC: U.S. Government Printing Office, 1993).

102. Robert Pear, "As Deadline Nears, Deficit Panel Still at Deep Impasse," *New York Times,* November 19, 2011.

103. Aaron Wildavsky, "A Budget for All Seasons: Why the Traditional Budget Lasts," *Public Administration Review* 38 (1978): 501–509. See also Dirk-Jan Kraan, *Budgetary Decisions: A Public Choice Approach* (Cambridge: Cambridge University Press, 1996); and Christopher G. Reddick, "Testing Rival Decision-Making Theories on Budget Outputs," *Public Budgeting and Finance* 22 (2002): 1–25.

## Chapter 8

1. For a good summary of the issues involved in evaluating public sector programs, see Evert Vedung, *Public Policy and Program Evaluation* (New Brunswick, NJ: Transaction, 1997).

2. Martin Painter and Jon Pierre, eds., *Challenges to State Policy Capacity* (London: Routledge, 2005).
3. Elaine Morley, Scott P. Bryant, and Harry P. Hatry, *Comparative Performance Measurement* (Washington, DC: Urban Institute, 2001).
4. J. N. Noy, "If You Don't Care Where You Get To, Then It Doesn't Matter Which Way You Go," in *The Evolution of Social Policy,* ed. C. C. Abt (Beverly Hills, CA: Sage, 1976), 97–120.
5. David L. Sills, *The Volunteers* (Glencoe, IL: Free Press, 1956), 253–268.
6. To get some idea of the current orientation of the organization, take a look at the Bureau of Indian Affairs website, www.doi.gov/bureau-indian-affairs.html.
7. Daniel A. Mazmanian and Jeanne Nienaber, *Can Organizations Change?* (Washington, DC: Brookings Institution Press, 1979).
8. There is a growing literature on the means of minimizing and controlling changes in the missions of regulatory agencies. Jonathan R. Mezey, "Organizational Design and the Political Control of Regulatory Agencies," *Journal of Law, Economics and Organization* 8 (1992): 93–110; Patrick D. Schmidt, *Lawyers and Regulation: The Politics of the Administrative Process* (New York: Cambridge University Press, 2005).
9. Robert K. Merton, "Bureaucratic Structure and Personality," *Social Forces* 18 (1940): 560–568.
10. Anthony Downs, *Inside Bureaucracy* (Boston: Little, Brown, 1967), 92–111.
11. See Paul Light, *Tides of Reform* (New Haven, CT: Yale University Press, 1998).
12. Morley, Bryant, and Hatry, *Comparative Performance Measurement.*
13. See Christopher Hood, B. Guy Peters, and Helmutt Wollmann, "Sixteen Ways to Consumerise the Public Sector," *Public Money and Management* 16, no. 4 (1996): 43–50.
14. William Alonzo and Paul Starr, *The Politics of Numbers* (New York: Russell Sage, 1987).
15. Geert Bouckaert, Derry Ormond, and B. Guy Peters, *A Potential Governance Agenda for Finland* (Helsinki: Ministry of Finance, 2000).
16. Richard N. Haass, *The Reluctant Sheriff: The United States after the Cold War* (Washington, DC: Brookings Institution Press, 1997).
17. I. C. R. Byatt, "Theoretical Issues in Expenditure Decisions," in *Public Expenditure: Allocation among Competing Ends,* ed. Michael V. Posner (Cambridge: Cambridge University Press, 1977), 22–27.
18. Michael Woolcock, "The Importance of Time and Trajectories in Understanding Program Effectiveness," *World Bank Blog,* May 5, 2011.
19. Lester M. Salamon, "The Time Dimension in Policy Evaluation: The Case of New Deal Land Reform," *Public Policy, (Spring 1979)*: 129–183.
20. See Robert E. Goodin, *Political Theory and Public Policy* (Chicago: University of Chicago Press, 1983), 26–29.
21. Debra Viadero, "'Fade-Out' in Head Start Gains Linked to Later Schooling," *Education Week,* (April 20, 1994): 9.
22. For a discussion of this point, see Henry J. Aaron, *Politics and the Professors* (Washington, DC: Brookings Institution Press, 1978), 84–85. More recent research indicates that there may be some more durable effects; see Edward Zigler and Susan Muenchow, *Head Start: The Inside Story of America's Most Successful Educational Experiment* (New York: Basic Books, 1992).

23. Gerald Schneider, *Time, Planning and Policymaking* (Bern, Switzerland: Peter Lang, 1991); Christopher Pollitt, *Time, Policy, Management: Governing with the Past* (Oxford: Oxford University Press).

24. On social experiments, see William Dunn, *The Experimenting Society* (New Brunswick, NJ: Transaction, 1998); and Norma R. A. Romm, *Accountability in Social Research: Issues and Debates* (New York: Kluwer, 2001).

25. Donald T. Campbell and Julian C. Stanley, *Experimental and Quasi-Experimental Design for Research* (Chicago: Rand-McNally, 1966); and Richard E. Neustadt and Ernest R. May, *Thinking in Time: The Uses of History for Decision-Makers* (New York: Free Press, 1986).

26. In the economic downturn of 2008–2009, the large majority of home mortgage foreclosures were in suburban areas, perhaps accelerating the downward turn of these areas.

27. Campbell and Stanley, *Experimental and Quasi-Experimental Design for Research*, 44–53.

28. For a discussion of the role of experimentation in assessing social policy, see R. A. Berk et al., "Social Policy Experimentation: A Position Paper," *Education Research* 94 (1985): 387–429.

29. Peter Passell, "Like a New Drug, Social Programs Are Put to the Test," *New York Times*, March 9, 1993. Also, the reforms of Medicare after the Balanced Budget Act involve an experiment of 300,000 using Medical Savings Plans.

30. Helen Ingram and Anne Schneider, "The Choice of Target Populations," *Administration and Society* 23 (1991): 149–167; and Anne Schneider and Helen Ingram, "Social Construction of Target Populations: Implications for Politics and Policy," *American Political Science Review* 87 (1993): 334–347.

31. Government Accountability Office, *Prekindergarten: Four States Expanded Access* (Washington, DC: U.S. Government Accountability Office, September 9, 2004), GAO-04-852.

32. Peter Townsend, ed., *Inequalities in Health* ("The Black Report") (London: Penguin, 1988).

33. Brian W. Hogwood and B. Guy Peters, *The Pathology of Public Policy* (Oxford: Oxford University Press, 1985).

34. Welfare had already tended to be short-term for many of the recipients, so the fact that many people could move on should have been no surprise.

35. Barbara J. Holt, "Targeting in Federal Grant Programs: The Case of the Older Americans Act," *Public Administration Review* 54 (1994): 444–449. Michael Hill and Peter Hupe, *Implementing Public Policy*, 2nd ed. (London: Sage, 2009).

36. P. H. Rossi, M. W. Lipsey, and H. E. Freeman, *Evaluation: A Systematic Analysis* (London: Sage, 2004).

37. Sam D. Sieber, *Fatal Remedies* (New York: Plenum, 1980).

38. Arnold Meltsner, *Policy Analysts in the Bureaucracy* (Berkeley: University of California Press, 1976).

39. See B. Guy Peters, *The Future of Governing: Two Decades of Administrative Reform*, 2nd ed. (Lawrence: University Press of Kansas, 2001).

40. General Accounting Office, *Managing for Results: Critical Issues for Improving Federal Agencies' Strategic Plans* (Washington, DC: U.S. General Accounting Office,

September 16, 1997), GAO/GGD-97-180. A full range of information on GPRA can be obtained from the GAO's website, www.gao.gov/sp/.

41. Donald F. Kettl and John J. DiIulio, eds., *Inside the Reinvention Machine: Appraising Governmental Reform* (Washington, DC: Brookings Institution Press, 1995).

42. Rochelle L. Stanfield, "Education Wars," *National Journal*, March 7, 1998, 506–509.

43. Michael Nelson, "What's Wrong with Policy Analysis," *Washington Monthly*, September 1979, 53–60. See also Dan Durning, "Participatory Policy Analysis in a Social Service Agency: A Case Study," *Journal of Policy Analysis and Management* 12 (1993): 297–322.

44. Brian W. Hogwood and B. Guy Peters, *Policy Dynamics* (Brighton, UK: Wheatsheaf, 1983).

45. Ibid.

46. Janet E. Franz, "Reviving and Revising a Termination Model," *Policy Sciences* 25 (1992): 175–189; Joseph Stewart., D. M. Hedge, and J. P. Lester, *Public Policy: An Evolutionary Approach,* 3rd ed. (Boston: Thompson Wadsworth, 2008).

47. Laurence E. Lynn Jr. and David deF. Whitman, *The President as Policymaker: Jimmy Carter and Welfare Reform* (Philadelphia: Temple University Press, 1981).

48. Downs, *Inside Bureaucracy.*

49. Rufus E. Miles, "Considerations for a President Bent on Reorganization," *Public Administration Review* 37 (1977): 157.

50. Jean-Claude Thoenig and Eduard Friedberg, "The Power of the Field Staff," in *The Management of Change in Government,* ed. Arne F. Leemans (The Hague, Netherlands: Martinus Nijhoff, 1976), 176–188.

51. On networks, see Edward O. Laumann and David Knoke, *The Organizational State: Social Change in National Policy Domains* (Madison: University of Wisconsin Press, 1987); E. Klijn, J. Koopenjaan, and W. J. M. Kickert, *Policy Networks* (London: Routledge, 2004); Jacob Torfing and Eva Sørensen, *Theories of Democratic Network Governance* (Basingstoke, UK: Macmillan, 2007).

52. See Jan Kooiman, "Societal Governance," in *Debating Governance,* ed. Jon Pierre (Oxford: Oxford University Press, 1998), 138.

53. R. Kent Weaver, "Setting and Firing Policy Triggers," *Journal of Public Policy* 9 (1989): 307–336.

54. William T. Gormley Jr., *Taming the Bureaucracy: Muscles, Prayers and Other Strategies* (Princeton, NJ: Princeton University Press, 1989), 205–207.

55. Karen Kaplan and Nbah H. Levey, "Barack Obama to Reverse Bush Policy on Federal Funding for Stem Cell Research," *Chicago Tribune*, March 7, 2009.

## Chapter 9

1. See Michael Stewart, *Keynes and After* (Harmondsworth, UK: Penguin, 1972); and Peter A. Hall, *The Political Power of Economic Ideas: Keynesianism across Nations* (Princeton, NJ: Princeton University Press, 1989).

2. Robert Skidelsky, *Politicians and the Slump* (London: Macmillan, 1967).

3. Walter Heller, *New Dimensions of Political Economy* (Cambridge, MA: Harvard University Press, 1966).

4. This problem has been especially evident with the Bush tax cuts, given that the majority of the benefits have gone to the more affluent who tend to spend a smaller proportion of their income. See Paul Krugman, "Now That's Rich," *New York Times,* August 22, 2010.

5. This trade-off is referred to as the "Phillips Curve." See "A Cruise around the Phillips Curve," *Economist,* February 19, 1994, 82–83; and M. G. Hayes, *The Economics of Keynes: A New Guide to the General Theory* (Cheltenham, UK: Edward Elgar, 2008).

6. In fairness, they often have been promised more of everything by politicians and often without any associated costs. See Isabel V. Sawhill, "Reagonomics in Retrospect," in *Perspectives on the Reagan Years,* ed. John L. Palmer (Washington, DC: Urban Institute Press, 1986), 91.

7. We will point out, however, that although the average has been getting higher, the degree of inequality of distribution of the benefits of growth has also been increasing.

8. For a discussion of this "treble affluence," see Richard Rose and B. Guy Peters, *Can Government Go Bankrupt?* (New York: Basic Books, 1978).

9. Lester Thurow, *The Zero-Sum Society* (New York: Basic Books, 1979).

10. Martin Crutsinger, "Savings Rate at Lowest Level Since 1933," Associated Press, January 30, 2006.

11. U.S. Census Bureau, *Income, Poverty and Health Insurance Coverage in the United States, 2010* (Washington, DC: Census Bureau, September 2011).

12. Organization for Economic Cooperation and Development, *Divided We Stand: Why Inequality Keeps Rising* (Paris: OECD, May 2011).

13. David Leonhardt, "Income Inequality," *New York Times,* January 16, 2011.

14. "The Occupy Movement," *New York Times,* February 12, 2012.

15. Although employment in manufacturing has been declining, value added has been relatively stable. Industries are finding ways to produce with less labor or are shifting toward high-value-added products such as computers and other information technologies. Also, the resurgence of the automobile industry after the intervention of the federal government has returned a significant amount of employment in manufacturing. Jeremy W. Peters, "Bailout Stand Trails Romney in Car Country," *New York Times,* February 16, 2012.

16. Service industries include a wide range of activities such as insurance, medical care, computer services, and banking, in addition to dry cleaners, restaurants, and so forth. For some, wages and benefits are excellent, but many also are minimum-wage jobs with no benefits.

17. Emily Kaiser, "Economists See Longest Recession Since World War II," Reuters News Service, January 10, 2009.

18. Frank Ahrens, "Actual U.S. Unemployment 15.8%," *Washington Post,* May 8, 2009.

19. Fred Hirsch and John H. Goldthorpe, *The Political Economy of Inflation* (Cambridge, MA: Harvard University Press, 1978).

20. R. Kent Weaver, *The Politics of Indexation* (Washington, DC: Brookings Institution Press, 1987).

21. This is the so-called Baumol's disease, named after the economist William J. Baumol; see his "The Macroeconomics of Unbalanced Growth: The Anatomy of Urban Crisis," in *Is Economics Relevant?* eds. Robert L. Heilbroner and A. M. Ford (Pacific Palisades, CA: Goodyear, 1971), 32–45.

22. John T. Woolley, *Monetary Politics: The Federal Reserve and the Politics of Monetary Policy* (Cambridge: Cambridge University Press, 1987).

23. Gøsta Esping-Anderson, *The Three Worlds of Welfare Capitalism* (Princeton, NJ: Princeton University Press, 1990).

24. Simon Johnson, "A Second Great Depression, or Worse?" *New York Times*, August 11, 2011.

25. Yuka Hayashi, "Japan Braces for Protracted Stretch of Deflation," *Wall Street Journal*, May 1, 2009.

26. Nitsan Chorey, *Remaking U.S. Trade Policy: From Protectionism to Globalization* (Ithaca, NY: Cornell University Press, 2006).

27. William S. Harat and Thomas D. Willett, eds., *Monetary Policy for a Volatile Global Economy* (Washington, DC: AEI Press, 1991).

28. Martin Tolchin and Susan Tolchin, *Buying into America: How Foreign Money Is Changing the Face of Our Nation* (New York: Times Books, 1988).

29. David Barboza, "China Urges New Money Reserve to Replace Dollar," *New York Times*, March 24, 2009.

30. See Susan Strange, *The Retreat of the State: The Diffusion of Power in the World Economy* (Cambridge: Cambridge University Press, 1996).

31. Michael M. Weinstein, "Twisting Controls on Currency and Capital," *New York Times*, September 10, 1998; and Martin Wolf, *Why Globalization Works* (New Haven, CT: Yale University Press, 2004).

32. M. Hallerberg and S. Basinger, "Internationalization and Changes in Tax Policy in OECD Countries: The Importance of Domestic Veto Players," *Comparative Political Studies* 31 (1998): 321–352; and David Vogel, *Trading Up: Consumer and Environmental Regulation in a Global Economy* (Cambridge, MA: Harvard University Press, 1995).

33. At least some of this relative success is the result of the Troubled Asset Relief Program (TARP). See Yalman Oranan and Alexis Leondis, "Bank Bailout Yields 8.2%, Beating Treasury Yields," *Bloomberg Financial Reporter*, October 20, 2010.

34. Henry Kaufman, "European Debt Crisis Can Prompt U.S. Credit Squeeze," *Huffington Post*, December 18, 2011.

35. Terry F. Buss, "The Effects of State Tax Incentives on Economic Growth and Firm Location Decisions," *Economic Development Quarterly* 15 (2001): 90–105.

36. Fred R. Bleakley, "Infrastructure Dollars Pay Big Dividends," *Wall Street Journal*, August 12, 1997.

37. Robert J. Reinshuttle, *Economic Development: A Survey of State Activities* (Lexington, KY: Council of State Governments, 1984).

38. N. Edward Coulson, "Sectoral Sources of the Massachusetts Miracle," *Journal of Regional Science* 41 (2002): 617–637; Scott Shane, *Academic Entrepreneurship: Academic Spinoffs and Wealth Creation* (Cheltenham, UK: Edward Elgar, 2006).

39. Federal Reserve Bank of San Francisco, "What Is the Difference between Monetary and Fiscal Policy," September, 2002).

40. See Strange, *The Retreat of the State*; and K. Ohmae, *The End of the Nation State* (New York: Free Press, 1995). For a contrary view, see Linda Weiss, *The Myth of the Powerless State* (Cambridge: Cambridge University Press, 1998).

41. Andrew P. Cortell, *Mediating Globalization: Domestic Institutions and Industrial Policies in the United States and Britain* (Albany, NY: SUNY Press, 2006).

42. For one view, see Robert B. Reich, "Trade Accords That Spread the Wealth," *New York Times,* September 2, 1997.

43. John Maggs, "Back from the Dead," *National Journal,* February 2, 2002, 304–307.

44. See Robert E. Litan, "Trade Policy: What Next?" *Brookings Review* 18 (Fall 2000): 41–44.

45. Paul Magnusson, "Bush Trade Policy: Crazy Quilt Like a Fox," *Business Week,* April 15, 2002.

46. "Jobs and Protectionism in the Stimulus Package," *Business Week,* February 16, 2009.

47. James D. Savage, *Balanced Budgets and American Democracy* (Ithaca, NY: Cornell University Press, 1988).

48. Rose and Peters, *Can Government Go Bankrupt?* 135–141; and James M. Buchanan and Richard Wagner, *Democracy in Deficit: The Political Legacy of Lord Keynes* (New York: Academic Press, 1978), 38–48.

49. When one listens to the debates about the impact of budgets in most parliaments or central agencies, it is clear that the ideas of Keynesianism are far from dead.

50. "The Undeniable Shift to Keynes," *Financial Times,* January 23, 2009.

51. Henry Aaron et al., *Setting National Priorities: The 1980 Budget* (Washington, DC: Brookings Institution Press, 1979). For a critique, see William H. Buiter, "A Guide to Public Sector Deficits," *Economic Policy* 1 (1985): 3–15.

52. Richard W. Stevenson, "House Republicans to Seek Big Tax Cuts," *New York Times,* September 10, 1998.

53. G. Calvin Mackenzie and Saranna Thornton, *Bucking the Deficit: Economic Policymaking in America* (Boulder, CO: Westview Press, 1996).

54. "Budget Resolution Embraces Clinton Plan," *CQ Almanac 1993* (Washington, DC: CQ Press, 1994), 102–121.

55. "Pact Aims to Erase Deficit by 2002," *CQ Almanac 1997* (Washington, DC: CQ Press, 1998), February 18–February 23.

56. Jackie Calmes, "House Passes Stimulus Package with No Republican Votes," *New York Times,* January 28, 2009.

57. Douglas A. Hibbs, *The American Political Economy: Macroeconomics and Electoral Choice* (Cambridge, MA: Harvard University Press, 1987).

58. Paul Craig Roberts, *The Supply-Side Revolution: An Insider's Account of Policymaking in Washington* (Cambridge, MA: Harvard University Press, 1984), esp. 27–33.

59. Yannis Gabriel and Tim Lang, *The Unmanageable Consumer* (Thousand Oaks, CA: Sage, 2006).

60. B. Douglas Bernheim, *The Vanishing Nest Egg: Reflections on Saving in America* (New York: Twentieth Century Fund, 1991).

61. Bruce Bartlett and Timothy P. Roth, eds., *The Supply-Side Solution* (Chatham, NJ: Chatham House, 1983). George H. W. Bush once referred to this assumption as "voodoo economics."

62. For an extended critique see Alice M. Rivlin and Isabel Sawhill, eds., *Restoring Fiscal Sanity 2005* (Washington, DC: Brookings Institution Press, 2005).

63. *New York Times,* "Job Losses in the Public Sector," February 18, 2012.

64. Donald F. Kettl, *Leadership at the Fed* (New Haven, CT: Yale University Press, 1986). For a more muckraking account, see William Greider, *Secrets of the Temple: How the Federal Reserve Runs the Country* (New York: Simon and Schuster, 1987).

65. Sen. Harry Reid, D-NV, called Greenspan "one of the biggest political hacks in Washington," in a CNN interview with Judy Woodruff on March 6, 2005.

66. See topics.nytimes.com/topics/reference/timestopics/organizations/federalreserve-system.

67. Ben Bernanke, "The Crisis and the Policy Response," *Federal Reserve*, January 13, 2009.

68. Robert Shiller, "A Failure of Control of Animal Spirits," *Financial Times*, May 12, 2009.

69. See B. Guy Peters, "Institutionalization and Deinstitutionalization: Regulatory Institutions in American Government," in *Comparative Regulatory Institutions*, ed. G. Bruce Doern and Stephen Wilks (Toronto: University of Toronto Press, 1998), 212–239.

70. Marc Alan Eisner, *Antitrust and the Triumph of Economics* (Chapel Hill: University of North Carolina Press, 1991).

71. The Department of Justice had been the only enforcement agency. It retained its powers after the passage of the Clayton Act, and both it and the Federal Trade Commission enforce antitrust legislation.

72. Joel Brinkley, "Strategies Set in Microsoft Antitrust Case," *New York Times*, September 14, 1998.

73. Some of this argument appears specious given that all firms will face the same wage increases.

74. See Herbert Stein, *Presidential Economics: Making Economic Policy from Roosevelt to Clinton*, 3rd ed. (Washington, DC: AEI Press, 1994).

75. William Pfaff, "Deregulation Is a False God," *Los Angeles Times*, June 27, 2002.

76. June Fletcher, "Is the Party Really Over for the Housing Bubble?" *Wall Street Journal*, February 10, 2007.

77. Viral V. Achrya et al., *Regulating Wall Street: The Dodd-Frank Act and the New Architecture of Global Finance* (New York: Wiley Finance, 2012).

78. Author's calculation based on the federal budget documents.

79. J. C. Gray and D. A. Spina, "State and Local Government Industrial Location Incentives: A Well-Stocked Candy Store," *Journal of Corporation Law* 5 (1980): 517–687; and Andrew Ward, "U.S. States Become Addicted to Use of Economic Sweeteners," *Financial Times*, March 23, 2006.

80. William S. Dietrich, *In the Shadow of the Rising Sun: The Political Roots of American Economic Decline* (University Park: Pennsylvania State University Press, 1991).

81. The most famous was Ross Perot, who characterized the predicted large loss of jobs to Mexico under NAFTA as a "large sucking sound." See also G. Bruce Doern and Brian W. Tomlin, *Faith and Fear: The Free Trade Story* (Toronto: Stoddard, 1991).

82. Edmund L. Andrews and David E. Sanger, "U.S. Finds its Role in Business Hard to Unwind," *New York Times*, September 15, 2009.

83. Nick Bunkley, "GM Still Hopeful of Fully Paying Back the Government," *New York Times*, June 7, 2011.

84. Jonathan T. R. Hughes, *The Governmental Habit Redux: Economic Controls from Colonial Times to the Present*, 2nd ed. (Princeton, NJ: Princeton University Press, 1991).

85. That support may come through direct subsidies or through protection from foreign competition. See David B. Yoffie, "American Trade Policy: An Obsolete Bargain," in *Can the Government Govern?* eds J. Chubb and P. Peterson (Washington, DC: Brookings Institution Press, 1989), 100–138.

86. Jim Rutenberg and Bill Vlasic, "Chrysler Files to Seek Bankruptcy Protection," *New York Times*, May 1, 2009.

87. Bureau of Labor Statistics, *Productivity Statistics*, monthly, www.bls.gov/lpc/.

88. *Business Week*, "Behind America's Jobless Recovery," July 15, 2011.

89. Steven Greenhouse, "The Wageless, Profitable Recovery," *New York Times*, June 30, 2011.

90. See Marie-Louise Bermelmans-Videc, Ray C. Rist, and Evert Vedung, eds., *Carrots, Sticks and Sermons: Policy Instruments and Their Evaluation* (New Brunswick, NJ: Transaction Books, 1998).

## Chapter 10

1. Henry J. Aaron and William G. Gale, eds., *Economic Effects of Fundamental Tax Reform* (Washington, DC: Brookings Institution Press, 1996).

2. Charles E. McLure, *The Value-Added Tax: Key to Deficit Reduction?* (Washington, DC: American Enterprise Institute, 1987); and R. E. Hall, "The Simple, Progressive Value-Added Consumption Tax," in *Toward Fundamental Tax Reform*, ed. K. A. Haslett and A. J. Auerbach (Washington, DC: American Enterprise Institute, 2005), 203–228.

3. B. Guy Peters, *Taxation: A Comparative Perspective* (Oxford: Blackwell, 1991).

4. For example, John Dougherty, "Property Tax Conflict Enters Nevada Governor's Race," *Nevada Journal*, January 28, 2010, http://nevadajournal.com/2010/01/28/property-tax-conflict-enters-nevada-governors-race/.

5. See Cathie Jo Martin, "Business Influence and State Power: The Case of U.S. Corporate Tax Policy," *Politics and Society* 17 (1989): 189–223. For a somewhat polemical account of recent developments, see Christopher Lasch, *The Revolt of the Elites and the Betrayal of Democracy* (New York: Norton, 1995); William F. Holmes, *American Populism* (New York: D. C. Heath, 1994), provides a more *balanced* treatment of populism.

6. David Brunori, *State Tax Policy: A Political Perspective* (Washington, DC: Urban Institute, 2005).

7. Stanley S. Surrey and Paul R. McDaniel, *Tax Expenditures* (Cambridge: Cambridge University Press, 1985).

8. Richard W. Stevenson, "The Secret Language of Social Engineering," *New York Times*, July 6, 1997.

9. Robert Pear, "Now, Special Tax Breaks Get Hidden in Plain Sight," *New York Times*, August 1, 1997.

10. Janet Novack, "The Dirty Little Secret of Tax Reform," *Forbes*, July 29, 2011.

11. Christopher Howard, *The Hidden Welfare State: Tax Expenditures and Social Policy in the United States* (Princeton, NJ: Princeton University Press, 1997); Marie Gottschalk, *The Shadow Welfare State: Labor, Business and the Politics of Health Care* (Ithaca, NY: Cornell University Press).

12. For a useful review of public opinion on tax reform, see "Public Opinion on Taxes," *American Enterprise Institute (AEI) Studies in Public Opinion,* April 10, 2009, www .aei.org/search/Studies+in+Public+Opinion%2C+April+10%2C+2009.

13. ABC News Polls, "Flat Tax Outpaces 9-9-9, Notably among Conservatives," October 25, 2011, http://abcnews.go.com/blogs/politics/2011/10/in-poll-flat-tax-outpaces-9-9-9-notably-among-conservatives/. Less than half the respondents favored a flat tax.

14. The two standard ideas are ability to pay, justifying a progressive system of taxation, and benefits received, which can justify more of a flat-rate system of taxation.

15. See O. Listhaug and Arthur H. Miller, "Public Support for Tax Evasion: Self-Interest or Symbolic Politics?" *European Journal of Political Research* 13 (1985): 265–282. See also John T. Scholz and Mark Lubell, "Adaptive Political Attitudes: Duty, Trust and Fear as Monitors of Tax Policy," *American Journal of Political Science* 42 (1998): 903–920.

16. Gallup Poll, March 24–26, 1997; March 25–27, 2001, available at www.pollingreport .com, a comprehensive listing of U.S. polling results.

17. Robert Greenstein, *How Would Families at Different Income Levels Benefit from the Bush Tax Cut?* (Washington, DC: Center for Budget and Policy Priorities, April 2001). The effects of those tax cuts have been exacerbated since that time. One estimate by the Center for Budget and Policy Priorities (December 2005) is that the average taxpayer in the top 1 percent of income earners has saved $34,900 as a result, while the average saved by the lower 20 percent was $18.

18. See Citizens for Tax Justice, *Overall Tax Rates Have Flattened Sharply under Bush* (Washington, DC: Citizens for Tax Justice, April 2004).

19. Glenn Kessler, "Revisiting the Cost of the Bush Tax Cuts," *Washington Post,* May 10, 2011.

20. It does, of course. Leaving aside how one counts the protective services delivered by the military, there are the Veterans Administration and its hospitals, the Postal Service, the National Park Service, agricultural extension agents, and a host of others.

21. National Center on Alcohol and Drug Dependency, *Washington Report,* December 2005, entire issue.

22. This is, however, bad news for health advocates who are attempting to use the cigarette tax as a means of deterring smoking. It may be more of a deterrent for the main target group—teen smokers—who have less disposable income.

23. See William F. Shugart, ed., *Taxing Choices: The Predatory Politics of Fiscal Discrimination* (New Brunswick, NJ: Transaction, 1997).

24. CBS News poll, April 2001, www.pollingreport.com.

25. ABC News poll, March 2001, www.pollingreport.com.

26. In addition to conventional polling, deliberative polling shows the preference for services and fiscal responsibility as opposed to tax cuts. See Edmund Andrews, "Public's Deficit Fix May Stun Politicians," *New York Times,* July 30, 2006.

27. David O. Sears and Jack Citrin, *Tax Revolt: Something for Nothing in California,* enl. ed. (Cambridge, MA: Harvard University Press, 1985).

28. J. Owens, "Fundamental Tax Reform: An International Perspective," *National Tax Journal* (March 1, 2006): 131–164.

29. Joel Slemrod, "Which Is the Simplest Tax System of Them All?" in *Economic Effects of Fundamental Tax Reform,* ed. Henry J. Aaron and William G. Gale (Washington, DC: Brookings Institution Press, 1996), 355.

30. Scott A. Hodge, J. Scott Moody, and Wendy P. Warcholik, "The Rising Cost of Complying with Federal Income Tax," *Special Report* (Washington, DC: The National Tax Foundation, January 10, 2006).

31. Even at the minimum wage of $7.25 per hour, this would amount to over $7 billion in free work by citizens.

32. Tami Luhby, "Reeling States Hit by April Tax Shortfalls," *CNN Money,* May 7, 2009, http://money.cnn.com/2009/05/07/news/economy/state_budget_gaps/index.htm.

33. Richard A. Musgrave, *Fiscal Systems* (New Haven, CT: Yale University Press, 1969).

34. Laura Sanders, "The Campeau Coup and the May Maneuver," *Forbes,* October 31, 1988, 98–99.

35. L. E. Burman, W. G. Gale, Jeffrey Rohaly, and M. Hall, *Key Points on the Alternative Minimum Tax* (Washington, DC: Urban Institute–Brookings Tax Policy Center, January 21, 2004).

36. Joseph A. Pechman, *Who Paid the Taxes, 1966–85?* (Washington, DC: Brookings Institution Press, 1986).

37. Cathy Dodge and Kate Anderson Brower, "Obama Calls on Wealthy Americans to Pay More Tax to Restore Fairness," *Bloomberg News,* January 2, 2012.

38. Paul E. Peterson and Mark Rom, "Lower Taxes, More Spending and Budget Deficits," in *The Reagan Legacy,* ed. Charles O. Jones (Chatham, NJ: Chatham House, 1988), 213.

39. Calculated from Internal Revenue Service, *Statistics of Income Bulletin* (quarterly), various issues.

40. Harold Wilensky, *The "New Corporatism," Centralization, and the Welfare State* (Beverly Hills, CA: Sage, 1976).

41. The author, for example, pays four separate income taxes, three property taxes, sales and excise taxes, etc. Some of these taxes are small, but they do add up.

42. W. W. Pommerehne and F. Schneider, "Fiscal Illusion, Political Institutions and Local Public Spending," *Kyklos* 31 (1978): 381–408.

43. William H, Gale, *The Value-Added Tax in the United States: Part of the Solution* (Washington, DC: Brookings Institution Press, July 22, 2010).

44. Guy Peters, *The Politics of Taxation: A Comparative Perspective* (Oxford: Blackwell's, 1991), 165–167.

45. Sven Steinmo, *Taxation and Democracy* (New Haven, CT: Yale University Press, 1992).

46. J. M. Verdier, "The President, Congress and Tax Reform: Patterns over Three Decades," *Annals* 499 (1988): 114–123.

47. Even after reform, the federal income tax was considered the least fair tax by a plurality of respondents in surveys. See Advisory Commission on Intergovernmental Relations, *Changing Public Attitudes on Government and Taxes* (Washington, DC: ACIR, 1992).

48. Timothy J. Conlan, Margaret T. Wrightson, and David R. Beam, *Taxing Choices: The Politics of Tax Reform* (Washington, DC: CQ Press, 1989); and J. H. Birnbaum and A. S. Murray, *Showdown at Gucci Gulch* (New York: Random House, 1987).

49. Gary Mucciaroni, "Public Choice and the Politics of Comprehensive Tax Reform," *Governance* 3 (1990): 1–32.

50. Conlan, Wrightson, and Beam, *Taxing Choices*.

51. John W. Kingdon, *Agendas, Alternatives, and Public Policies*, 2nd ed. (Boston: Little, Brown, 2003).

52. For example, if I had invested in a piece of land in 1970 for $100 and then sold it in 1998 for $500, there would be an apparent profit of $400. If, however, inflation were taken into account, the "real" profit would be less than $200 (in 1998 dollars). On what basis should I be taxed?

53. In 1995, 82 percent of all returns reporting capital gains cited incomes less than $100,000, although 76 percent of all capital gains income does go to people earning over $100,000.

54. Henry J. Aaron and William A. Gale, "Truth in Taxes," *Brookings Review* 18 (Spring 2000): 12–15.

55. William Gale and Joel B. Slemrod, *Rethinking the Estate and Gift Tax* (Ann Arbor: University of Michigan Business School, January 2001).

56. Carl Hulse, "Battle on Estate Tax: How Two Well-Organized Lobbies Sprang into Action," *New York Times*, June 14, 2001.

57. Suzanne Malvaux, "Obama to Introduce Tax Reforms That Target Overseas Loopholes," CNN Politics.com, May 4, 2009, http://edition.cnn.com/2009/POLITICS/05/04/obama.tax.code/index.html.

58. Lori Montgomery, "Once Considered Unthinkable, U.S. Sales Tax Gets Fresh Look," *Washington Post*, May 27, 2009.

59. This resentment came to a head in 1997 and 1998 with a series of congressional hearings about the Internal Revenue Service and its treatment of citizens. See Daniel J. Murphy, "IRS: An Agency Out of Control?" *Investor's Business Daily*, October 1, 1997. More recently, it became evident that the IRS was focusing much of its attention on less affluent taxpayers, who were easier targets, not being protected by a phalanx of accountants and lawyers like the more affluent. See David Cay Johnston, "IRS Will Cut Tax Lawyers Who Audit the Richest," *New York Times*, July 23, 2006.

60. In 2002, the effective tax rate for earners with incomes of $100,000 was less than this 17 percent, but the marginal rate was 28 percent. Thus, the flat tax would be a real boon for the very affluent but would produce higher taxes for the middle classes.

61. But see Aaron Wildavsky, "Keeping Kosher: The Epistemology of Tax Expenditures," *Journal of Public Policy* 5 (1985): 413–431.

62. See Robert S. McIntyre, "The 23 Percent Solution," *New York Times*, January 23, 1998.

63. Psychologically that may create demands for increases in wages, even though people should have a great deal more take-home pay with the elimination of the income tax.

64. See David F. Bradford, *Untangling the Income Tax* (Cambridge, MA: Harvard University Press, 1986); and General Accounting Office, *Tax Administration: Potential Impact of Alternate Taxes on Taxpayers and Administrators* (Washington, DC: U.S. General Accounting Office, January 1998), GAO/GGD-98-37, appendix VIII.

65. See Thomas J. DiLorenzo and James T. Bennett, "National Nannies Seek Taxes on All We Consume," *USA Today*, December 23, 1997.

66. That is, 24 million business returns plus 115 million personal returns.

67. Ben Wildavsky, "A Taxing Question," *National Journal*, February 8, 1998: 440–444.

## Chapter 11

1. U.S. Centers for Medicare and Medicaid Services, Office of the Actuary, *Health Accounts* (Washington, DC: Department of Health and Human Services, 2005).
2. Victor R. Fuchs and Ezekiel J. Emmanuel, "Health Care Reform: Why? What? When?" *Health Affairs* 24 (2005): 1399–1414.
3. CBS News/*New York Times* poll, March 1, 2007.
4. "Federal, State, Local, or Private Action," *American Enterprise,* November/December 1997, 94; and Gina Kolata, "An Economist's View of Health Care Reform," *New York Times,* May 2, 2000.
5. Pam Belluck, "Massachusetts Sets Health Plan for Nearly All," *New York Times,* April 5, 2006.
6. Julie Appleby, "States Take Health Care Problems into Their Own Hands," *USA Today,* November 9, 2005.
7. With the loss of welfare also came a loss of Medicaid coverage, but another federal law funded care for children in states that adopted a suitable program. See Peter T. Kilborn, "States to Provide Health Insurance to More Children," *New York Times,* September 21, 1997; and Thomas M. Selden, Jessica S. Bathin, and Joel W. Cohen, "Trends: Medicaid's Problem Children: Eligible but Not Enrolled," *Health Affairs* 17, no. 3 (1998): 192–200.
8. Jonathan Gruber, "Incremental Universalism in the United States: The States Move Fast," *Journal of Economic Perspectives* 22 (2008): 51–68.
9. World Health Organization, *World Health Statistics Annual* (Geneva: World Health Organization, 2011).
10. J. Banks, M. Marmot, Z. Oldfield, and J. P. Smith, "Disease and Disadvantage in the United States and in England," *Journal of the American Medical Association* 295 (May 3, 2006): 2037–2047.
11. "The Public Decides on Health Care Reform," *Public Perspective* 5 (September/ October 1994): 23–28. See also note 4.
12. U.S. Census Bureau, *Current Population Reports,* census data series P60-226 (Washington, DC: U.S. Census Bureau, 2010).
13. Ibid.
14. Ibid.; see also Robert Pear, "Tough Decision on Health Care if Employers Won't Pay the Bill," *New York Times,* July 9, 1994.
15. Despite its good intentions, the indications are that Kennedy-Kassebaum is not as effective as it might be because the rates at which the portable insurance can be charged are not adequately controlled. See Robert Pear, "High Rates Hobble Law to Guarantee Health Insurance," *New York Times,* March 17, 1998.
16. Peter Townsend, ed., *Inequalities in Health: The Black Report* (London: Penguin, 1988).
17. Lisette Alvarez, "A Conservative Battles Corporate Health Care," *New York Times,* February 12, 1998; Alina Tugend, "Hands to Hold When Health Care Becomes a Maze," *New York Times,* October 13, 2007.
18. Peter T. Kilborn, "Black Americans Trailing Whites in Health, Studies Say," *New York Times,* January 26, 1998; see also U.S. Center for Health Statistics, *Health 2006* (Washington, DC: Department of Health and Human Services, 2007).
19. Sheryl Gay Stolberg, "Race Gap Seen in Health Care of Equally Insured Patients," *New York Times,* March 21, 2002.

20. U.S. Centers for Disease Control and Prevention, *Vital Statistics of the United States* (Atlanta, GA: Centers for Disease Control and Prevention, 2006).

21. Rural areas tend to have a number of hospital beds but very low occupancy rates, and that drives up costs.

22. Dan Verango, "The Operation You Get Often Depends on Where You Live," *USA Today*, September 19, 2000; see www.dartmouth.edu/~atlas.

23. Peter T. Kilborn, "Roving Doctors Paying House Calls to Towns," *New York Times*, April 16, 2000.

24. *Rural Health Clinics: Rising Program Expenditures Not Focused on Improving Care in Isolated Areas*, testimony of Bernice Steinhardt (Washington, DC: U.S. General Accounting Office, February 13, 1997), GAO/T-HEHS-97-65.

25. Nicholas Eberstadt, "Why Are So Many American Babies Dying?" *American Enterprise* 2 (September 1991): 37–45. This finding, of course, supports conservative arguments for individual responsibility and minimizes the need for government intervention in the medical marketplace.

26. See Henry J. Aaron, *The Problem That Won't Go Away: Reforming U.S. Health Care Financing* (Washington, DC: Brookings Institution Press, 1995).

27. These constraints on access to referrals were challenged successfully in the courts. Mark Carriden, "High Court Hears Suit on HMO Referrals," *Dallas Morning News*, January 15, 2002.

28. Cathy Cowan, Aaron Catlin, Cynthia Smith, and Arthur Sensening, "National Health Expenditures, 2002," *Health Care Financing Review* 25 (2004): 143–166.

29. Catherine Rampell, "Medicare Care Prices Fell for First Time in 35 Years," *New York Times*, August 13, 2010.

30. Milt Freudenheim, "Many HMOs Easing the Rules on Specialists' Care," *New York Times*, February 2, 1997; Cowan et al., "National Health Expenditures, 2002."

31. See Robert Pear, "Bush Seeks Surplus via Medicare Cuts," *New York Times*, January 31, 2008.

32. Henry J. Aaron and Bruce K. McLaury, *Serious and Unstable Condition: Financing America's Health Care* (Washington, DC: Brookings Institution Press, 1991), 8–37.

33. Service employees, including health services, in both the public and private sectors are the only segment of the labor force with increasing levels of unionization.

34. *Health USA, 2007* (Washington, DC: Department of Health and Human Services, 2008).

35. Spencer Rich, "Hospital Administration Costs Put at 25%," *Washington Post*, August 6, 1993.

36. U.S. Government Accountability Office, *VA Health Care: Status of Inspector General Recommendations for Health Care Services Contracting* (Washington, DC: Government Accountability Office, October 31, 2007).

37. Joshua M. Wiener and Laura Hixon Illston, "Health Care Reform: Six Questions for President Clinton," *Brookings Review* 11 (Spring 1993): 22–25.

38. Aaron and McLaury, *Serious and Unstable Condition*, 45–47.

39. M. M. Mello, D. M. Studdert, and T. A. Brennen, "The New Medical Malpractice Crisis," *New England Journal of Medicine* 348 (2002): 2281–2286.

40. Julie Kosterlitz, "Wanted: GPs," *National Journal*, September 5, 1992.

41. Susan Hosek et al., *The Study of Preferred Provider Organizations* (Santa Monica, CA: RAND, 1990). Doctors are beginning to fight back against managed care. See Reed Abelson, "A Medical Resistance Movement," *New York Times,* March 25, 1998.

42. Health Care Financing Administration, *Health Care Financing Review* (annual) (Washington, DC: Health Care Financing Administration, 2004); figures are for 1995.

43. Garrett Hardin and John Baden, *Managing the Commons* (San Francisco: W. H. Freeman, 1977).

44. Bob Herbert, "Curing Health Costs: Let the Sick Suffer," *New York Times,* September 1, 2005.

45. T. Bodenheimer, "The Oregon Health Plan: Lessons for the Nation," *New England Journal of Medicine* 337 (1997): 651–659.

46. Susan Feigenbaum, "Denying Access to Life-Saving Technologies: Budgetary Implications of a Moral Dilemma," *Regulation* 16, no. 4 (1994): 74–79.

47. On the latter point, see Ivan Illich, *Medical Nemesis* (New York: Pantheon, 1976).

48. Abelson, "A Medical Resistance Movement"; and R. Pear, "The Tricky Business of Keeping Doctors Quiet," *New York Times,* September 22, 1996.

49. As of spring 1997, eight states had comprehensive laws providing managed care rights to citizens, two others had regulations and were writing legislation, and nineteen others had legislation under active consideration.

50. These efforts to regain control often have been less than successful. See Nancy Wolff and Mark Schlesinger, "Clinicians as Advocates: An Exploratory Study of Responses to Managed Care by Mental Health Professionals," *Journal of Behavioral Health Services and Research* 29 (2004): 274–288.

51. The same questions arise concerning developments in medical technology, such as artificial hearts. See "One Miracle, Many Doubts," *Time,* December 10, 1984, 10.

52. Henry R. Glick, *The Right to Die* (New York: Columbia University Press, 1994); Gunther Lewy, *Assisted Death in Europe and America: Four Regimes and Their Lessons* (Oxford: Oxford University Press, 2011).

53. See G. Magill, "Resolving the Case of Terry Schiavo," *Health Care Ethics USA* 11, no. 2 (2005), www.slu.edu/centers/chce/hceusa/.

54. Robert Pear, "Obama Returns to End-of-Life Plan That Caused Stir," *The New York Times,* December 25, 2010.

55. Gregg Bloche. *The Hippocratic Myth: Why Doctors Are Under Pressure to Ration Care, Practice Politics and Compromise Their Oath as They Heal* (New York: Palgrave, 2011).

56. Adam Liptak, "On Day 3, Justices Weigh What-ifs of Health Ruling," *New York Times,* March 28, 2012.

57. Bruce Japsen, "Small Picture Approach Flips Medical Economics," *New York Times,* March 12, 2012.

58. Robert Pear, "House Votes to Kill a Medicare Cost Panel," *New York Times,* March 22, 2012.

59. Elizabeth A. McGlynn et al., "The Quality of Health Care Delivered to Adults in the United States," *New England Journal of Medicine,* 348 (2003): 2635–2645.

60. Amy Goldstein and N. C. Aizenman, "House Votes to Repeal Health Care Law," *Washington Post,* January 20, 2011.

61. Higher-income Medicare enrollees now must pay higher deductibles.

62. Karen Davis, "Equal Treatment and Unequal Benefits," *Milbank Memorial Fund Quarterly* (Fall 1975): 449–488; and Robert Ball, "What Medicare's Architects Had in Mind," *Health Affairs* 14, no. 4 (1995): 62–72.

63. Advisory Council on Social Security, *Report on Medicare Projections by the Health Technical Panel* (Washington, DC: U.S. Government Printing Office, 1991).

64. Marilyn Werber Serafini, "Brave New World," *National Journal,* August 16, 1997.

65. In a medical savings account, Medicare buys the patient a catastrophic care policy and covers part of the deductible payments for care under the policy. If there are any savings over the year—if, for example, the recipient is healthy and actually spends less than under the standard program—then he or she gets to keep the difference.

66. Louise B. Russell and Carrie Lynn Manning, "The Effect of Prospective Payment on Medicare Expenditures," *New England Journal of Medicine* 330 (1989): 439–444.

67. Jeffrey A. Buck and Mark S. Kamlet, "Problems with Expanding Medicaid for the Uninsured," *Journal of Health Politics, Policy and Law* 18 (1993): 1–25. In 1999, Medicaid spending accounted for approximately one dollar in five of state expenditures.

68. Health Care Financing Administration, *Health Care Financing Review,* annual (Washington, DC: Health Care Financing Administration, 2009).

69. Paul Jesilow, Gilbert Geis, and Henry Pontell, "Fraud by Physicians against Medicaid," *Journal of the American Medical Association* 266 (1991): 3318–3322; see also M. K. Wynia, D. S. Cummins, J. B. VanGeest, and I. B. Wilson, "Physician Manipulation of Reimbursement Rules for Patients," *Journal of the American Medical Association* 283 (2000): 1858–1865; Katie Thomas, "Seven Charged in Health Care Fraud," *New York Times,* February 25, 2012.

70. U.S. Government Accountability Office (GAO), *Medicare and Medicaid Fraud Waste and Abuse,* March 9, 2011 (USGAO-11-409T), Washington, DC: Government Printing Office.

71. Karen Davis et al., *Health Care Cost Containment* (Baltimore: Johns Hopkins University Press, 1990), 222ff.

72. Patricia Baumann, "The Formulation and Evolution of Health Maintenance Organization Policy, 1970–73," *Social Science and Medicine* 10 (1976): 129–142.

73. See Lester C. Thurow, "As HMOs Lose Control, Patient Costs Head Skyward," *USA Today,* December 16, 1997.

74. Milt Freudenheim, "Big HMO to Give Decisions on Care Back to Doctors," *New York Times,* November 9, 1999.

75. Julie Appleby, "HMOs: What Happens When the Band Aids Run Out?" *USA Today,* December 8, 2000.

76. Stephen Linder and Pauline Vaillancourt Rousseau, "Health Care Policy," in *Developments in American Politics* 4, ed. Gillian Peele et al. (Basingstoke, England: Palgrave, 2002), 222–233.

77. One of the older forms of health care regulation, the control of facilities through certificates of need, has ceased to be of great relevance, given the emphasis on cost containment in managed care.

78. MedPac, *Report to Congress: Medicare Payment Process* (Washington, DC: Center for Medicare Statistics, March 2006).

79. Peter H. Stone, "Ready for Round Two," *National Journal,* January 3, 1998; and "Health Care Reform," *Public Perspective,* February/March 1998, 39.
80. In particular, Rep. Charles Norwood, R-GA, led a campaign for more extensive regulation of HMOs. This had him making common cause with Sen. Edward Kennedy, D-MA, one of the more liberal members of the Senate.
81. Mark A. Hall, "Managed Care: Patient Protection or Provider Protection?" *American Journal of Medicine* 117 (2004): 932–937.
82. Sam Howe Verhovek, "Texas Is Lowering HMO Legal Shield," *New York Times,* June 5, 1997.
83. There is some evidence that managed care systems do invest more in preventive care. Steven Findlay, "Survey Shows HMO Care Varies Widely," *USA Today,* October 2, 1997.
84. Tort actions may not be as effective as ex ante controls, but they do at least force the industry to consider the long-run costs of any decisions it may make.
85. Peter S. Arno and Karyn L. Feiden, *Against the Odds: The Story of AIDS Drug Development, Politics and Profits* (New York: HarperCollins, 1992).
86. Carol Rados, "The FDA Speeds Medical Treatments for Serious Conditions," *FDA Consumer* 40, no. 2 (2006): 9–12.
87. Susan Okie, "Medical Journals Try to Curb Drug Companies' Influence on Research," *Washington Post,* August 5, 2001; and Dennis Cauchon, "FDA Advisers Tied to Industry," *USA Today,* September 25, 2000.
88. Anna Wilde Mathews, "FDA to Review Drug Marketing to Consumers," *Wall Street Journal,* August 2, 2005.
89. General Accounting Office, *Drug Safety: Most Drugs Withdrawn in Recent Years Have Greater Health Risks for Women* (Washington, DC: U.S. General Accounting Office, January 10, 2001), GAO-01-286R.
90. See Sheryl Gay Stolberg and Jeff Gerth, "How Companies Stall Generics and Keep Themselves Healthy," *New York Times,* July 23, 2000.
91. Andrew Pollack, "Antibiotics Research Subsidies Weighed by U.S.," *New York Times,* November 5, 2010.
92. Howard Leichter, *Health Policy Reform in America: Innovations from the States,* 2nd ed. (Armonk, NY: M. E. Sharpe, 1997).
93. See www.barackobama/issues/healthcare.
94. See Paul Krugman, "Keeping Them Honest," *New York Times,* June 5, 2009.
95. Rebecca Vesely, "AHIP: Surely 30% Possible," *Modern Healthcare,* December 8, 2008.
96. Robert Pear, "Sweeping Health Care Plan Is Drafted by Kennedy," *New York Times,* June 6, 2009.
97. Helene Cooper, "Obama Urges Effort for Health Care," *New York Times,* June 6, 2009.
98. Some aspects of the plan have been implemented in various states under the same name. See, for example, A. C. Enthoven and S. J. Singer, "Managed Competition and California's Health Care Economy," *Health Affairs* 15, no. 1 (1996): 39–57.
99. Robert Pear, "Bill Passed by Panel Would Open Medicare to Millions of Uninsured People," *New York Times,* July 1, 1994.

100. The degree of choice actually existing in the current medical care system appeared to have been exaggerated by the opponents of reform. See Robin Toner, "Ills of Health System Outlive Debate on Care," *New York Times*, October 2, 1994.
101. Victor R. Fuchs, "What's Ahead for Health Insurance in the United States," *New England Journal of Medicine* 346 (2002): 1822–1824.

## Chapter 12

1. See Theodore R. Marmor, Jerry L. Mashaw, and Philip L. Harvey, *America's Misunderstood Welfare State* (New York: Basic Books, 1990).
2. Indeed, in 2011, almost half of American households received some form of government benefit. See Sara Murray, "Nearly Half of U.S. Lives in Households Receiving Government Benefits," *Wall Street Journal*, January 17, 2012.
3. See Allan Sloan, "Bush's Social Security Sleight of Hand," *Washington Post*, February 8, 2006.
4. Donald O. Parsons and Douglas R. Munro, "Intergenerational Transfers in Social Security," in *The Crisis in Social Security*, ed. Michael J. Boskin (San Francisco: Institute for Contemporary Studies, 1977), 65–86.
5. Kaiser Family Foundation, *Survey on Social Security*, February 2005, www.kff.org/newsmedia/washpost/7280.cfm.
6. Ibid.; 81 percent of respondents in 2005 wanted to eliminate the top limit. In a poll in 2011, only 53 percent supported this change.
7. The separation of pensions and other social insurance benefits from general taxation is unusual in the rest of the world. See Margaret S. Gordon, *Social Security Policies in Industrial Countries: A Comparative Analysis* (Cambridge: Cambridge University Press, 1990). The separation also contributes to the somewhat artificial sense that Social Security can go bankrupt, since if general taxation were provided for the system there is no reason for bankruptcy.
8. Social Security Administration, *The Future of Social Security* (Baltimore: Social Security Administration, 2009).
9. Michael D. Hurd and John B. Shoven, "The Distributional Impact of Social Security," in *Pensions, Labor and Individual Choice*, ed. David Wise (Chicago: University of Chicago Press, 1985); Jeffrey Liebman, "Does Social Security Distribute to Low Income Groups?" (NBER Working Paper 8625) (Cambridge, MA: National Bureau of Economic Research, 2002).
10. The actual determination of taxability is somewhat more complicated. See David Pattison and David E. Harrington, "Proposals to Modify the Taxation of Social Security Benefits: Options and Distributional Effects," *Social Security Bulletin* 56 (Summer 1993): 3–13.
11. This program has been, like so many, "path dependent," and its initial formulation has largely determined its development. See B. Guy Peters, *Institutional Theory in Political Science*, 3rd ed. (London: Continuum, 2011), chap. 4.
12. Joseph Bondar, "Beneficiaries Affected by the Annual Earnings Test, 1989," *Social Security Bulletin* 56 (Spring 1993): 20–34.

13. Social Security Administration, Office of the Actuary, *Life Tables for the United States Social Security Area, 1900–2080* (Baltimore: Social Security Administration, 1992).

14. "Commission: Raise Retirement Age to 70," *USA Today,* May 19, 1998.

15. C. Eugene Steuerle and Jon M. Bakija, *Retooling Social Security for the Twenty-first Century* (Washington, DC: Urban Institute Press, 1994), 97.

16. Deborah Stone, *The Disabled State* (Philadelphia: Temple University Press, 1985).

17. General Accounting Office, *SSA Disability Programs: Fully Updating Disability Criteria Has Implications for Program Design* (Washington, DC: U.S. General Accounting Office, July 11, 2002), GAO-02-919T.

18. General Accounting Office, *SSA and VA Disability Programs: Reexamination of Disability Criteria Needed to Help Ensure Program Integrity* (Washington, DC: U.S. General Accounting Office, August 9, 2002), GAO-02-597.

19. Bernadine Weatherford, "The Disability Insurance Program: An Administrative Attack on the Welfare State," in *The Attack on the Welfare State,* ed. Anthony Champagne and Edward J. Harpham (Prospect Heights, IL: Waveland Press, 1984), 37.

20. General Accounting Office, *Social Security Disability: SSA Needs to Improve Continuing Disability Review Program* (Washington, DC: U.S. General Accounting Office, July 1993), GAO/HRD-93-109.

21. "Workers' Compensation," *Social Security Bulletin* 56 (Winter 1993): 28–31.

22. The maximum payment in Iowa is $1,134 per week, while that in Mississippi is $351 per week.

23. Government Accountability Office, *Federal Disability Assistance: Wide Array of Programs Needs to Be Reexamined in Light of 21st Century Challenges* (Washington, DC: U.S. Government Accountability Office, June 2005), GAO-05-626.

24. As noted, Social Security does accumulate funds in its trust fund but not at a rate sufficient to finance future benefits—which continue to be paid largely from current revenues from Social Security taxation.

25. For a detailed analysis, see Henry J. Aaron, Barry P. Bosworth, and Gary Burtless, *Can America Afford to Grow Old? Paying for Social Security* (Washington, DC: Brookings Institution Press, 1989), 55–75.

26. Practical politics, however, prevented President Reagan from doing anything to reduce Social Security benefits. See Paul E. Peterson and Mark Rom, "Lower Taxes, More Spending, and Budget Deficits," in *The Reagan Legacy,* ed. Charles O. Jones (Chatham, NJ: Chatham House, 1988), 224–225.

27. ABC News/*Washington Post* poll, February 19–22, 2009, www.washingtonpost.com/wp-srv/politics/postpoll_022309.html.

28. Jonathan Rauch, "False Security," *National Journal,* February 14, 1987, 362–365, www.nationaljournal.com.

29. Aaron, Bosworth, and Burtless, *Can America Afford to Grow Old?*

30. Paula Span, "Social Security and Younger Americans," *New York Times,* August 25, 2010.

31. Board of Trustees of the Federal Old-Age, Survivors, and Disability Insurance Trust Funds, *Annual Report, 2010* (Washington, DC: U.S. Government Printing Office, 2010). These figures are based on intermediate assumptions about the future of the system. Under less optimistic assumptions, there would be only 1.7 workers per recipient in 2050.

32. Linda E. Demkovich, "Budget Cutters Think the Unthinkable—Social Security Cuts Would Stem Red Ink," *National Journal*, June 23, 1984.

33. George F. Break, "The Economic Effects of Social Security Financing," in *Social Security Financing*, ed. Felicity Skidmore (Cambridge, MA: MIT Press, 1981), 45–80.

34. See B. Guy Peters, *The Politics of Taxation* (Oxford: Basil Blackwell, 1992).

35. Charles E. McLure, "VAT versus the Payroll Tax," in *Social Security Financing*, ed. Felicity Skidmore (Cambridge, MA: MIT Press, 1981), 129.

36. For a review of the proposals, see Henry J. Aaron and Robert D. Reischauer, "Should We Reform Social Security?" *Brookings Review* 17 (Winter 1999): 6–11.

37. These retirement plans take their name from the section of the U.S. Internal Revenue Code that governs their creation and use.

38. Ben Wildavsky, "The Two Percent Solution," *National Journal*, April 11, 1998, 794–797.

39. R. Shep Melnick, *Between the Lines* (Washington, DC: Brookings Institution Press, 1994).

40. Most of these critics are on the political right, for example, Charles Murray, *Losing Ground* (New York: Basic Books, 1984) and his "Stop Favoring Welfare Mothers," *New York Times*, January 16, 1992; and Lawrence M. Mead, *The New Politics of Poverty* (New York: Basic Books, 1992). There are also critics on the left, for example, David T. Ellwood, *Poor Support: Poverty and the American Family* (New York: Basic Books, 1988); and Frances Fox Piven and Richard Cloward, *Regulating the Poor*, 2nd ed. (New York: Vintage, 1993).

41. M. Gilens, *Why Americans Hate Welfare: Race, Media and the Politics of Anti-Poverty Policy* (Chicago: University of Chicago Press, 2000).

42. See James L. Morrison, *The Healing of America: Welfare Reform in a Cyber Economy* (Brookfield, VT: Ashgate, 1997).

43. Penelope Lemov, "Putting Welfare on the Clock," *Governing*, November 1993, 29–30.

44. Edwin W. Witte, *The Development of the Social Security Act* (Madison: University of Wisconsin Press, 1962), 5–39.

45. Julie Kosterlitz, "Behavior Modification," *National Journal*, February 1, 1992, 271–275. The earlier attempts to control behavior pale in comparison to those of the 1996 reforms.

46. Kevin Sack, "Fingerprinting Allowed in Welfare Fraud Fight," *New York Times*, July 9, 1994.

47. Some evidence appearing just as workfare was being implemented placed some doubt on the efficacy of permitting greater earnings. See Jason DeParle, "More Questions about Incentives to Get Those on Welfare to Work," *New York Times*, August 28, 1997.

48. As noted, despite those disincentives to leave, the majority of people on AFDC did not stay long. The other problems with the program, and the relatively meager benefits, attracted few long-term beneficiaries.

49. Julie Kosterlitz, "Reworking Welfare," *National Journal*, September 26, 1992.

50. Michael Wiseman, "Research and Policy: A Symposium on the Family Support Act of 1988," *Journal of Policy Analysis and Management* 10 (1991): 588–589.

51. Kay E. Sherwood and David A. Long, "JOBS Implementation in an Uncertain Environment," *Public Welfare* 49 (1991): 17–27.

52. This problem would, of course, have been rectified if the Clinton plan, or any other plan, for universal health insurance had been adopted.

53. Sherwood and Long, "JOBS Implementation in an Uncertain Environment."

54. Amy L. Sherman, "The Lessons of W-2," *Public Interest* 140 (Summer 2000): 36–46. Tommy Thompson, the governor of Wisconsin responsible for implementing the program, became secretary of health and human services in the Bush administration.

55. The title of the bill is a masterpiece of symbol manipulation in the process of agenda setting and legitimation.

56. For a discussion of this and other myths, see Steven M. Teles, *Whose Welfare? AFDC and Elite Politics* (Lawrence: University Press of Kansas, 1996).

57. Robert Pear, "Governors Limit Revisions Sought in Welfare Law," *New York Times,* February 3, 1997.

58. The political motivation was to please Hispanic voters, given the number of immigrants from Mexico and other Latin countries who had been denied benefits.

59. See Jonathan Rabinowitz, "Connecticut Welfare Law Cuts Hundreds Off the Rolls," *New York Times,* November 3, 1997; and Richard Wolf, "Some States Still at Welfare Impasse," *USA Today,* July 2, 1997.

60. Nina Bernstein, "Giant Companies Enter Race to Run State Welfare Programs," *New York Times,* September 15, 1996.

61. Judith Havemann, "Welfare Reform Still on a Roll as States Bounce It Down to Counties," *Washington Post,* August 29, 1997.

62. Dilys Hills, "Social Policy," in *Developments in American Politics III,* ed. Gillian Peele et al. (New York: Chatham House, 1998), 214–235.

63. Rochelle L. Stanfield, "Valuing the Family," *National Journal,* July 4, 1992, 1562–1566.

64. Marilyn Werber Serafini, "Get Hitched, Stay Hitched," *National Journal,* March 9, 2002, 694–697.

65. Laura Meckler, "Bush Outlining Welfare Plans," Associated Press, February 26, 2002.

66. See General Accounting Office, *Welfare Reform: States Are Restructuring Programs to Reduce Welfare Dependency* (Washington, DC: U.S. General Accounting Office, June 18, 1998), GAO/HEHS-98-109. Oregon, for example, found that half the welfare caseload would require treatment for chemical dependency before they would be likely to be employable.

67. D. Card and R. M. Blank, *Findings Jobs: Work and Welfare Reform* (New York: Russell Sage, 2000).

68. Rochelle L. Stanfield, "Cautious Optimism," *National Journal,* May 2, 1998.

69. Administration for Children and Families, Department of Health and Human Services, *U.S. Welfare Caseloads Information* (Washington, DC: Administration for Children and Families, monthly).

70. Marilyn Werber Serafini, "As More Jobs Vanish, the Worries Mount," *National Journal,* September 29, 2001.

71. Ibid.

72. Sheila Kammerman and Alfred Kahn, "Universalism and Testing in Family Policy: New Perspectives on an Old Debate," *Social Work* 32 (1987): 277–280.

73. Hermione Parker, *Instead of the Dole: An Enquiry into the Integration of Tax and Benefit Systems* (London: Routledge, 1989).

74. M. Kenneth Bowler, *The Nixon Guaranteed Income Proposal: Substance and Process in Policy Change* (Cambridge, MA: Ballinger, 1974).

75. Office of Child Support Enforcement, *Annual Report to Congress, 2006* (Washington, DC: Office of Child Support Enforcement, Department of Health and Human Services, 2006).

76. Irwin Garfinkel, Sara S. McLanahan, and Philip K. Robins, *Child Support and Child Well-Being* (Washington, DC: Urban Institute Press, 1994).

77. General Accounting Office, *Child Support Assurance: Effects of Applying State Guidelines to Determine Fathers' Payments* (Washington, DC: U.S. General Accounting Office, January 1993), GAO/HRD-93-26.

78. Administration for Children and Families, *Annual Report, 2009* (Washington, DC: ACF, 2010).

79. Mimi Hall, "Child Support: States Pay if Parents Don't," *USA Today,* March 28, 1994.

80. At least one state has already done so; see "In Maine, No Child Support, No Driving," *New York Times,* June 28, 1994.

81. For a general discussion of employment policy, see Margaret Weir, *Politics and Jobs* (Princeton, NJ: Princeton University Press, 1992).

82. General Accounting Office, *Multiple Employment Training Programs: Conflicting Requirements Hamper Delivery of Services* (Washington, DC: U.S. General Accounting Office, January 1994), GAO/HEHS-94-78.

83. Sar A. Levitan, *The Great Society's Poor Law: A New Approach to Poverty* (Baltimore: Johns Hopkins University Press, 1969).

84. Some later research, however, found some latent effects of Head Start, much like the "sleeper effects" described in chapter 7. See William Celis III, "Study Suggests Head Start Helps beyond School," *New York Times,* April 20, 1993; see also Carlotta C. Joyner, "Head Start: Research Insufficient to Assess Program Impact," testimony to the Subcommittee on Early Childhood, Youth and Families, Committee on Labor and Human Resources, U.S. Senate, March 26, 1998.

85. Richard Rose and B. Guy Peters, *Can Government Go Bankrupt?* (New York: Basic Books, 1978).

86. For a more recent view, see Michael Harrington, *The New American Poverty* (New York: Holt, Rinehart, and Winston, 1984).

87. Sabrina Tavernise, "Soaring Poverty Casts Spotlight on 'Lost Decade,'" *New York Times,* September 13, 2011.

88. Sar Levitan, Frank Gallo, and Isaac Shapiro, *Working but Poor: America's Contradiction,* rev. ed. (Baltimore: Johns Hopkins University Press, 1993).

89. Ibid., 99–125.

90. Patricia Ruggles, *Drawing the Line: Alternative Poverty Measures and Their Implications for Public Policy* (Washington, DC: Urban Institute Press, 1990).

91. John L. Palmer, Timothy Smeeding, and Barbara Boyle Torrey, eds., *The Vulnerable* (Washington, DC: Urban Institute Press, 1988); Jacob S Hacker and Paul Pierson, *Winner-Take-All Politics: How Washington Makes the Rich Richer and Turned Its Back on the Middle Class* (New York: Simon and Schuster, 2010).

92. National Academy of Sciences, Panel on Poverty and Family Assistance, *Alternative Poverty Measures* (Washington, DC: National Academy of Sciences, 1995).

93. The current fashionable term for these problems, made popular by the Labour government in Britain, is "social exclusion."

94. Maybeth Shinn and Colleen Gillespie, "The Roles of Housing and Poverty in the Origins of Homelessness," *American Behavioral Scientist* 37 (1994): 505–521.

95. Ann Braden Johnson, *Out of Bedlam: The Truth about Deinstitutionalization* (New York: Basic Books, 1990); and Julian Leff, *Care in the Community: Myth or Reality* (New York: John Wiley, 1997).

96. Manny Fernandez, "Helping to Keep Homelessness at Bay as Foreclosures Increase," *New York Times,* February 4, 2009.

97. General Accounting Office, *Homelessness: McKinney Act Programs Provide Assistance but Are Not Designed to Be the Solution* (Washington, DC: U.S. General Accounting Office, May 1994), GAO/RCED-94-37.

98. Jacob S. Hacker, The Divided Welfare State: The Battle over Public and Private Social Benefits in the United States (Cambridge: Cambridge University Press, 2002).

99. General Accounting Office, *Private Pensions: Key Issues to Consider Following the Enron Collapse,* testimony by David M. Walker (Washington, DC: U.S. General Accounting Office, February 27, 2002), GAO-02-480T.

100. J. Dao, "Miners' Benefits Vanish with Bankruptcy Ruling," *New York Times,* October 24, 2004.

101. F. Norris, "As Baby Boom Ages, Era of Guaranteed Retirement Income Fades," *New York Times,* November 12, 2004.

## Chapter 13

1. Richard Hofferbert, "Race, Space and the American Policy Paradox" (paper presented at the conference of the Southern Political Science Association, Atlanta, GA, November 1980).

2. In areas in which parochial schools were important, they also tended to draw from a wide range of social classes, if not religions.

3. Karen DeWitt, "Nation's Schools Learn a Fourth R: Resegregation," *New York Times,* January 19, 1992.

4. For diverse views on this topic, see Gerald Graff, *Beyond the Culture Wars: How Teaching the Conflicts Can Revitalize American Education* (New York: Norton, 1992); and Russell Jacoby, *Dogmatic Wisdom: How the Culture Wars Divert Education and Distract America* (New York: Doubleday, 1994).

5. Andrew Rosenthal, "Oppression Is not a State's Right," *New York Times,* November 8, 2011.

6. Bureau of the Census, *Statistical Abstract of the United States, 2009* (Washington, DC: U.S. Government Printing Office, 2009).

7. Gallup Poll, January 5–8, 2012. Ten percent of respondents said they were completely satisfied, and 30 percent were somewhat satisfied.

8. Students in Iowa and North Dakota, on average, scored as well as those in Korea and better than those in any European country on math and science tests.

9. Diana Jean Schemo, "Public School Students Score Well in Math in Large-Scale Government Study," *New York Times,* January 21, 2006.

10. See William Bennett, *Our Country and Our Children: Improving America's Schools and Affirming Our Common Culture* (New York: Touchstone, 1988). There have been a number of books advocating such a traditional curriculum for American schools,

including Allan Bloom, *The Closing of the American Mind* (New York: Touchstone, 1987).

11. Catherine S. Mangold, "Students Make Strides but Fall Short of Goals," *New York Times,* August 18, 1994. U.S. rankings in elementary and secondary education have, however, been slipping. See "U.S. Slipping in Education Ranking," UPI.com, November 19, 2008.

12. "Poll Readings," *National Journal,* February 14, 1998, 368.

13. See Times Topics, "No Child Left Behind," *New York Times,* n.d., accessed June 23, 2009, http://topics.nytimes.com/top/reference/timestopics/subjects/n/no_child_left_behind_act/index.html.

14. "No Child Left Behind: Obama Administration Grants 10 Waivers," *Los Angeles Times,* February 9, 2012.

15. This is rather paradoxical given that the Republicans have been tending to advocate states rights against the presumed centralizing powers of Washington.

16. Jonathan Kozol, *Savage Inequalities: Children in America's Schools* (New York: Crown, 1991).

17. Michelle Singletary, "Obama's Student Plan Isn't So New," *Washington Post,* October 16, 2011.

18. The states also have taken new steps to assist parents, permitting them to invest in tax-free accounts for their children's education or to pay in the current year, at present rates, for future tuition.

19. Rochelle L. Stanfield, "We Have a Tradition of Not Learning," *National Journal,* September 7, 1991, 2156–2157.

20. David Cay Johnston, "Despite Pledge, Taxes Increase for Teenagers," *New York Times,* May 21, 2006.

21. See *Texas et al. v. Lesage,* 528 U.S. 18 (1999); the Michigan cases are *Gratz v. Bollinger,* 539 U.S. 244 (2003) and *Grutter v. Bollinger,* 539 U.S. 306 (2003).

22. Norman C. Thomas, *Educational Policy in National Politics* (New York: David McKay, 1975).

23. Michael D. Reagan, *The New Federalism* (New York: Oxford University Press, 1972).

24. Jerome T. Murphy, "Title I of ESEA: The Politics of Implementing Federal Educational Reform," *Harvard Education Review* 41 (1971): 35–63.

25. *Title I of ESEA: Is It Helping Poor Children?* (Washington, DC: NAACP Legal Defense Fund, 1969).

26. Stephen Phillips, "Union Joins Attack on Bush Flagship Program," *Times Education Supplement,* April 29, 2004, 20; Diana Jean Schemo, "Group Pushes Education Act as 2004 Issue," *New York Times,* August 12, 2004.

27. Lance D. Fusarelli, "Gubernatorial Reactions to No Child Left Behind: Politics, Pressure and Educational Reform," *Peabody Journal of Education* 80 (2005): 120–136.

28. James E. Ryan, "The Perverse Incentives of the No Child Left Behind Act," *New York University Law Review* 79 (2004): 932–989.

29. Kathryn A. McDermott and Laura S. Jensen, "Dubious Sovereignty: Federal Conditions of Aid and No Child Left Behind," *Peabody Journal of Education* 80 (2005): 39–56.

30. Kenneth Jost, "Revising No Child Left Behind," *CQ Researcher,* April 16, 2010, 337–360.

31. Shelley Dietz, "How Many Schools Have Not Met Adequate Yearly Progress Standards," *Center on Education Policy*, March 10, 2011.

32. Some polls show that minority parents, like majority parents, want good basic education instead of a distinctive curriculum. See "Minority Parents Seek Quality over Diversity," *USA Today*, July 29, 1998. The support from minority parents for vouchers and charter schools is further support for this contention.

33. Rochelle L. Stanfield, "Making the Grade?" *National Journal*, April 17, 1993.

34. Neil King, Jr. and Barbara Martinez, "Squaring Off on U.S Schools," *Wall Street Journal*, March 15, 2010.

35. U.S. Department of Education, "The Race to the Top Fund," n.d., www2.ed.gov/programs/racetothetop/index.html.

36. It seems that in Milwaukee there has been a good deal of effective and committed leadership in the schools. Emily Van Dunk and Anneliese Dickman, "School Choice Accountability," *Urban Affairs Review* 37 (2002): 844–856.

37. Myron Lieberman, *Privatization and Educational Choice* (New York: St. Martin's, 1989).

38. John Witte, "The Milwaukee Parental Choice Program Third Year Report," *LaFollette Policy Report* 6 (1994): 6–7.

39. John E. Chubb and Terry M. Moe, *Politics, Markets, and America's Schools* (Washington, DC: Brookings Institution Press, 1990); see also Paul E. Peterson, *Choice and Competition in American Education* (Lanham, MD: Rowman and Littlefield, 2005).

40. Rochelle L. Stanfield, "Education Wars," *National Journal*, March 7, 1998.

41. See Sean Lengell, "House Votes to Restart D.C. Vouchers," *Washington Times*, March 30, 2011.

42. Jeffrey R. Henig, *Rethinking School Choice: Limits of the Market Metaphor* (Princeton, NJ: Princeton University Press, 1994); Clive Belfield and Henry M. Levin, "Vouchers and Public Policy: When Ideology Trumps Evidence," *American Journal of Education* III (2005): 548–567.

43. James S. Coleman, *Equality of Educational Opportunity* (Washington, DC: U.S. Government Printing Office, 1966). Since that time, Coleman has modified his view to be substantially less supportive of busing.

44. Gallup Poll, "Public Attitudes to Education" (Princeton, NJ: Gallup Organization, 2005).

45. For a positive view, see James N. Goenner, "Charter Schools: The Revitalization of Public Education," *Phi Delta Kappan* 78 (September 1996): 32, 34–36.

46. "States Ignore Traps Tripping Up Charter Schools," *USA Today*, April 2, 2002.

47. See U.S. Department of Education, *The Evaluation of the Public Charter School Program* (Washington, DC: U.S. Department of Education, 2004); Institute of Educational Sciences, *The Evaluation of Charter School Impacts: Final Report* (Washington, DC: U.S. Department of Education, June, 2010).

48. D. M. Lewis, "Certifying Functional Literacy: Competency and the Implications for Due Process and Equal Educational Opportunity," *Journal of Law and Education* 8 (1979): 145–183; and Chubb and Moe, *Politics, Markets, and America's Schools*, 197–198.

49. Educational Testing Service, *One-Third of a Nation: Rising Dropout Rates and Declining Opportunities* (Princeton, NJ: Educational Testing Service, 2005).

50. Tamar Lewin, "Obama Wades into Issue of Raising Dropout Rate," *New York Times*, January 29, 2012.

51. Jessica Portner, "Educators Keeping Eye on Measures Designed to Combat Youth Violence," *Education Week*, February 9, 1994, 21.

52. For some discussion of the lengths to which school systems may go to recruit teachers, see Jacques Steinberg, "As Demand for Teachers Exceeds Supply, Schools Sweeten Their Offers," *New York Times*, September 7, 1998.

53. General Accounting Office, *School Facilities: America's Schools Report Differing Conditions* (Washington, DC: U.S. General Accounting Office, June 1996), GAO/HEHS-96-103.

54. Richard W. Stevenson, "Clinton Proposes Spending $25 Billion on Education," *New York Times*, January 27, 1998.

55. David Branham, "The Wise Man Builds His House upon the Rock: The Effects of Inadequate School Building Infrastructure on School Attendance," *Social Science Quarterly* 85 (2004): 1112–1128.

56. Michael D. Simpson, "Voucher Victory," *NEA Today*, March 2006, 19.

57. See, for example, Lonnie Harp, "Michigan Bill Penalizes Teachers for Job Actions," *Education Week*, April 27, 1994, 9.

58. Monica Davey, "Wisconsin Court Reinstates Law on Union Rights," *New York Times*, June 14, 2011.

59. Morgan Smith, "Texas Schools Face Bigger Classes and Smaller Staffs," *New York Times*, March 16, 2012.

60. Stephen M. Barro, "Countering Inequity in School Finance," in *Federal Policy Options for Improving the Education of Low-Income Students*, vol. 3 (Santa Monica, CA: Rand, 1994).

61. Another equity funding case was contested in Alabama—*Alabama Coalition for Equity, Inc. v. Guy Hunt*, 1992.

62. Sam Howe Verhovek, "Texas to Hold Referendum on School-Aid Shift to Poor," *New York Times*, February 16, 1993.

63. Lonnie Harp, "Texas Voters Reject Finance Plan: Consolidation Called Last Resort," *Education Week*, May 12, 1993, 1, 16.

64. Lonnie Harp, "Texas Finance Ruling Angers Both Rich, Poor Districts," *Education Week*, January 12, 1994, 18.

65. Tamar Lewin, "Patchwork of School Financing Schemes Offers Few Answers and Much Conflict," *New York Times*, April 8, 1998.

66. William Schneider, "Voters Get an Offer They Can't Refuse," *National Journal*, March 26, 1994, 754.

67. Rochelle L. Stanfield, "Equity and Excellence," *National Journal*, November 23, 1991, 3860–3864.

68. Reagan Walker, "Blueprint for State's New School System Advances in Kentucky," *Education Week*, March 7, 1990, 1, 21.

69. Dirk Johnson, "Study Says Small Schools Are Key to Learning," *New York Times*, September 21, 1994.

70. The Spearman rank-order correlation is −0.26. This finding is to some degree confounded by the different percentages of students taking the SAT in different states. Many of the high-scoring states had a small percentage of students taking the SAT.

71. De Witt, "Nation's Schools Learn a Fourth R."

72. Tom Loveless, *Test-Based Accountability: The Promise and the Perils* (Washington, DC: Brown Center on Educational Policy, Brookings Institution, 2005).

73. Rochelle L. Stanfield, "Reform by the Book," *National Journal,* December 4, 1994, 2885–2887.

74. Peter Schmidt, Jeffrey Selingo, Sara Hebel, and Jeffrey R. Young, "The Michigan Cases: The Repercussions," *Chronicle of Higher Education* 49 (July 2003): 3.

75. For example, in 1998, blacks constituted 17 percent of the school population but had 31 percent of all expulsions (U.S. Department of Education, Office of Civil Rights, unpublished data). In 2010, black students were three and a half times more likely to be severely disciplined than whites (U.S. Department of Education, Office of Civil Rights).

76. College Board, *Trends in Student Aid, 2005* (Washington, DC: College Board, 2006).

## Chapter 14

1. Timothy Wirth, "Hot Air over Kyoto: The United States and the Politics of Global Warming," *Harvard International Review* 23 (2002): 72–77.

2. John M. Broder, "Obama Affirms Climate Change Goals," *New York Times,* November 18, 2008.

3. Clifford Krauss and Eric Lipton," U.S. Inches Toward Goal of Energy Independence," *New York Times,* March 23, 2012.

4. See, for example, Glennda Chui, "Scientific American Gives California High Marks for Technology," *San Jose Mercury News,* November 12, 2002.

5. *America's Energy Needs and Our National Security Policy,* hearing before the Subcommittee on Energy and Resources, Committee on Government Reform, U.S. House of Representatives, April 6, 2006.

6. U.S. Energy Information Administration, *International Energy Statistics,* 2006 (Washington DC: Department of Energy, 2007).

7. Energy Information Agency, *Annual Energy Review 2010* (Washington, DC: U.S. Dept. of Energy, 2011).

8. Eric Pianin, "A Stinging Repudiation Engineered by Three Democrats," *Washington Post,* April 19, 2002.

9. Dan Morgan and Ellen Nakashima, "Search for Oil Targets Rockies," *Washington Post,* April 19, 2002.

10. See Michael Janofsky, "House Votes to Allow Drilling in Alaska Refuge," *New York Times,* May 26, 2006.

11. John M. Broder, "Obama Shifts to Speed Oil and Gas Drilling," *New York Times,* May 14, 2011.

12. Peter H. Stone, "Mixing Oil and Instability," *National Journal,* November 10, 2001.

13. Bureau of Economic Analysis, *International Economic Accounts,* Table 2a, U.S. Trade in Goods (Washington, DC: Department of Commerce, June 17, 2009).

14. Christime Burmma, "U.S. Cuts Estimate of Marcellus Shale Gas by 66 percent," *Bloomberg News,* January 12, 2012.

15. Traci Watson, "EPA: Power Plant Plan Could Save 12,000 Lives per Year," *USA Today,* July 3, 2002.

16. Brad Plumer, "Get Ready for a Wave of Coal Plant Shutdowns," *Washington Post*, August 19, 2011.

17. James M. McElfish and Ann E. Beier, *Environmental Regulation of Coal Mining* (Washington, DC: Environmental Law Institute, 1990); Robert F. Duffy, "King Coal vs Reclamation: Federal Regulation of Mountaintop Removal in Appalachia," *Administration & Society* 41 (October 2009): 573–592.

18. Processes of this type have existed for some time; Germany used a process like this in World War II. It is not, however, economically feasible at anything like current energy prices.

19. Felicity Barringer, "Four Years Later, Soviets Reveal Wider Scope to Chernobyl Horror," *New York Times*, April 28, 1990; and David Marples, *The Social Impact of the Chernobyl Disaster* (New York: St. Martin's, 1988); "One Year Post Fukushima Americans Are Divided about the Risks of Nuclear Power," *New York Times*, March 14, 2012.

20. See Shankar Vendantum, "Storage of Spent Nuclear Fuel Criticized," *Washington Post*, March 28, 2005.

21. John L. Campbell, *Collapse of an Industry: Nuclear Power and the Contradictions of U.S. Policy* (Ithaca, NY: Cornell University Press, 1988).

22. Richard Balzhiser, "Future Consequences of Nuclear Non-Policy," in *Energy: Production, Consumption, Consequences*, ed. John L. Helm (Washington, DC: National Academy Press, 1990), 184.

23. General Accounting Office, *Nuclear Waste: Uncertainties about the Yucca Mountain Repository Project* (Washington, DC: U.S. General Accounting Office, March 21, 2000), GAO-02-539T; and Alison M. McFarlane and Rodney C. Ewings, *Uncertainty Underground: Yucca Mountain and the Nation's High-Level Energy Waste* (Cambridge, MA: MIT Press, 2006).

24. Henry F. Bedford, *Seabrook Station: Citizen Politics and Nuclear Power* (Amherst: University of Massachusetts Press, 1990).

25. Matthew L. Wald, "License Is Granted to Nuclear Plant in New Hampshire," *New York Times*, March 2, 1990.

26. Testimony of Deputy Energy Secretary Clay Sell before Senate Committee on Energy and Natural Resources, hearing on Department of Energy Nuclear Power Program for 2010, April 26, 2005.

27. The "fracking" technology associated with recovering natural gas from shale involves the use of fluids that, along with the gas itself, may pollute water supplies.

28. Rodman D. Griffin, "Nuclear Fusion," *CQ Researcher* 3 (January 22, 1993): 51–64.

29. Michael Kenward, "Fusion Becomes a Hot Bet for the Future," *New Scientist* 132 (November 1991): 10–11.

30. Scott Wilson, "Obama Touts Solar in Nev. as Part of Four State Energy Tour," *Washington Post*, March 22, 2012.

31. The hydrogen would essentially be converted back into water. See Matthew Wald, "Questions about a Hydrogen Economy," *Scientific American*, May 2004, 64, 73.

32. Greg Schneider, "Automakers Put Hydrogen Power on the Fast Track," *Washington Post*, January 9, 2005.

33. Jeremy Rifkin, *The Hydrogen Economy* (New York: Tarcher Putnam, 2005).

34. Todd Wilkinson, "Gone with the Wind," *Backpacker*, September 1992, 11.

35. "Briefing on Energy Policy," *Weekly Compilation of Presidential Documents* 27 (February 25, 1991): 188–190.

36. *Reliable, Affordable and Environmentally Sound Energy for America's Future: Report of the National Energy Development Group* (Washington, DC: Executive Office of the President, May 2001).

37. Natural Resources Defense Council, "Energy Department Documents Verify Industry Influence over Bush Policies," press release, May 21, 2002.

38. See "Wasteful Handouts Skew Energy Benefit's Plan," *USA Today,* May 30, 2001.

39. An NBC/*Wall Street Journal* poll in April 2001 showed that 25 percent of the respondents thought there was a crisis, but 60 percent did see a distinct problem.

40. Michael Janofsky, "Democrats Offer Alternative to Republican Energy Plan," *New York Times,* May 18, 2006.

41. Ibid.

42. Jim Rutenberg, "Solution to Greenhouse Gases Is New Nuclear Plants, Bush Says," *New York Times,* May 25, 2006.

43. David E. Sanger, "Bush Takes Steps to Stem Increase in Energy Prices," *New York Times,* April 26, 2006.

44. *New York Times*/CBS News poll, February 22–26, 2006, www.nytimes.com/packages/pdf/national/20060228_poll_results.pdf.

45. Judith Mantel, "Energy Efficiency," *CQ Researcher* 16 (May 19, 2006): 19.

46. Deborah Henry, "Republicans Highly Critical of Obama Energy Bill," *New York Times,* June 29, 2009.

47. Many of these provisions were added by members of Congress attempting to protect industries in their home districts.

48. This policy became more attractive in spring 2012, when gasoline reached $4.00 per gallon. This is a huge price for Americans, if only a third or less than what most Europeans pay.

49. Claudia Golden and Gary D. Libecap, *The Regulated Economy* (Chicago: University of Chicago Press, 1994).

50. Center for the Advancement of Energy Markets, www.caem.org, February 1, 2001.

51. T. Munroe and L. Baroody, "California's Flawed Deregulation: Implications for the State and Nation," *Journal of Energy and Development* 26 (2001): 159–179.

52. S. George Philander, *Is the Temperature Rising? The Uncertain Science of Global Warming* (Princeton, NJ: Princeton University Press, 1998); and Marcel Leroux, *Global Warming: Myth or Reality* (Berlin: Springer, 2005).

53. The journal *Diversity* is a good source of information about the resources existing in these settings.

54. Keith Bradsher and David Barboza, "Pollution from Chinese Coal Casts a Global Shadow," *New York Times,* June 11, 2006.

55. One can, however, identify over thirty federal organizations with environmental responsibilities; see Walter A. Rosenbaum, *Environmental Politics and Policy,* 8th ed. (Washington, DC: CQ Press, 2010).

56. Riley E. Dunlap, "Trends in Public Opinion toward Environmental Issues, 1965–1990," *Society and Natural Resources* 4 (1991): 285–312; and Jerry Spangler, "Survey Shows Environmental Values Deeply Rooted," *Deseret News* [Utah], October 9, 1997.

57. Gallup Poll, January 5–8, 2012.

58. Margaret E. Kriz, "Jobs vs. Owls," *National Journal,* November 30, 1993, 2913–2916.

59. Another manifestation of the issue was the congressional use of a rider on an EPA appropriations act in 1996 to permit more lumbering of old-growth forests. For the consequences of these conflicts, see E. Niemi and E. Whitelaw, "Bird of Doom, or Was It?" *Amicus Journal* 22 (1997): 19–25.

60. On the caribou issue, see Paul Feine, "Beware Porcupine Caribou," *Energy Economist* 2 (1995): 2–19; more generally, see Kolson L. Schlosser, "U.S. National Security Discourse and the Political Construction of the Arctic National Wildlife Refuge," *Society and Natural Resources* 19 (2006): 3–18.

61. Murray Weidenbaum, "Return of the 'R' Word: The Regulatory Assault on the Economy," *Policy Review* 59 (1992): 40–43.

62. See John Hoornbeek, "Runaway Bureaucracies or Congressional Control: Water Pollution Policies in the American States" (PhD diss., University of Pittsburgh, PA., 2004).

63. For example, the Safe Drinking Water Act requires monitoring for eighty-three substances, although a number have never been found in any public water supply. See Margaret E. Kriz, "Cleaner than Clean?" *National Journal,* April 23, 1994, 946–949.

64. Christopher J. Bosso, "After the Movement: Environmental Activism in the 1990s," in *Environmental Policy in the 1990s,* 3rd ed., ed. Norman J. Vig and Michael E. Kraft (Washington, DC: CQ Press, 1997), 60. Updated from websites, personal conversations. See also Jacqueline Vaughan, *Environmental Politics: Domestic and Global Dimensions* (New York: Wadsworth, 2011).

65. Vice President Gore's book on environmental politics became a part of the presidential campaign in 1992. See Al Gore, *Earth in the Balance: Ecology and the Human Spirit* (Boston: Houghton Mifflin, 1992).

66. Margaret Kriz, "That Was the Week That Was," *National Journal,* February 2, 1994, 393.

67. Christine Todd Whitman, "This Land Is Our Land," *Environmental Forum* 22 (2005): 24–35.

68. "A Light in the Forest," *New York Times,* September 9, 2005; and Margaret Kriz, "Working the Land: Bush Aggressively Opens Doors to New Drilling and Logging in Federal Lands," *National Journal,* February 23, 2002.

69. Government Accountability Office, *Greater EPA Enforcement and Reporting Are Needed to Enhance Cleanup of DOD Sites* (Washington, DC: U.S. General Accounting Office, March 13, 2009), GAO-09-728.

70. This has been described as "bureaucratic pluralism," with some even within the EPA itself. See Walter A. Rosenbaum, "Into the 1990s at EPA," in *Environmental Policy in the 1990s,* 3rd ed., Norman J. Vig and Michael E. Kraft. (Washington, DC: CQ Press, 1997), 146.

71. Evan Ringquist, Environmental Protection at the State Level (Armonk, NY: M. E. Sharpe, 1994); John A. Hoornbeek, *Water Pollution Policies and the American States: Runaway Bureaucracies or Congressional Control* (Albany: State University of New York Press, 2010).

72. See W. Michael Hanneman, "How California Came to Pass AB 32, the Global Warming Solutions Act of 2006" (unpublished manuscript, University of California, Berkeley, School of Law, January 2007).

73. On the possibilities of a "race to the bottom," see Mary Graham, "Environmental Protection and the States," *Brookings Review* 16 (Winter 1998): 22–25.

74. Margaret Kriz, "Feuding with the Feds," *National Journal*, August 9, 1997, 1598–1601.

75. Michael Janofsky, "Judges Overturn Bush Bid to Ease Pollution Rules," *New York Times*, March 18, 2006.

76. Richard N. L. Andrews, "Risk-Based Decisionmaking," in *Environmental Policy in the 1990s*, ed. Norman J. Vig and Michael E. Kraft, 3rd ed. (Washington, DC: CQ Press, 1997), 208.

77. Donald T. Hornstein, "Reclaiming Environmental Law: A Normative Critique of Comparative Risk Analysis," *Columbia Law Review* 29 (1992): 562–633.

78. Margaret Kriz, "The Greening of Environmental Regulation," *National Journal*, June 18, 1994, 1464–1467.

79. Janet Pelley, "Is EPA's Performance Track Running Off the Rails?" *Environmental Science and Technology* 40 (2006): 2499–2550.

80. *Lujan v. Defenders of Wildlife*, 504 U.S. 555 (1992). The courts tend to limit suits to those who have experienced a direct loss because of an action.

81. See Michael E. Kraft, "Environmental Policy in Congress," in *Environmental Policy*, Norman J. Vig and Michael E. Kraft (Washington, DC: CQ Press, 2010), 124.

82. James R. Kahn, *An Economic Approach to the Environment and Natural Resources* (New York: Dryden Press, 1995).

83. For a review of developments, see Debra S. Knopman and Richard A. Smith, "Twenty Years of the Clean Water Act," *Environment* 35 (1993): 17–20, 34–41.

84. "Oil Officials Fear Stricter Water Act Provisions from New Congress," *Oilgram News* 74, no. 218 (1986): 2.

85. James P. Lester, "New Federalism and Environmental Policy," *Publius* 16 (1986): 149–165.

86. Margaret E. Kriz, "Clashing over Chlorine," *National Journal*, March 19, 1994, 659–661.

87. Tom Arrandale, "The Pollution Puzzle," *Governing*, August 2002, 22–26.

88. Paul Raeburn, "Hybrid Care: Less Fuel but More Costs," *Business Week*, April 15, 2002, 107.

89. Margaret Kriz, "Clean Machines," *National Journal*, November 16, 1991, 2789–2794.

90. Mary H. Cooper, "Air Pollution Conflict," *CQ Researcher* 13 (November 2003): 20–26.

91. James C. McKinley Jr., "Ten States Agree on a Program for Air Quality," *New York Times*, October 2, 1994.

92. Denny A. Ellerman and Paul L. Joskow, "Clearing the Polluted Sky," *New York Times*, May 1, 2002.

93. National Academy of Sciences, *Interim Report on Changes in New Source Programs for Stationary Sources of Air Pollution* (Washington, DC: National Academy of Sciences, 2005).

94. Mireya Navarro, "E.P.A. Is Sued over Delays in Soot Standards," *New York Times*, February 10, 2012.

95. Mark Crawford, "Hazardous Waste: Where to Put It?" *Science* 235 (January 9, 1987): 156.
96. Peter A. A. Berle, "Toxic Tornado," *Audubon* 87 (1985): 4.
97. See Charles E. Davis, *The Politics of Hazardous Waste* (Englewood Cliffs, NJ: Prentice Hall, 1993).
98. Steven Cohen, "Federal Hazardous Waste Programs," in *Environmental Policy in the 1990s,* ed. Norman J. Vig and Michael E. Kraft, 3rd ed. (Washington, DC: CQ Press, 1997), 45.
99. Thomas Church and Robert Nakamura, *Cleaning Up the Mess: Implementation Strategies in Superfund* (Washington, DC: Brookings Institution Press, 1993).
100. Environmental Protection Agency, Office of Emergency and Remedial Response, *Superfund Facts* (Washington, DC: EPA, annual).
101. Environmental Protection Agency, *A Preliminary Analysis of the Public Costs of Environmental Protection, 1981–2000* (Washington, DC: U.S. Environmental Protection Agency, May 1990); and Milton E. Russell, William Colglazier, and Bruce E. Tonn, "U.S. Hazardous Waste Legacy," *Environment* 34 (1992): 12–15, 34–39.
102. Katharine Q. Seelye, "Bush Slashing Aid of EPA Cleanup at 33 Toxic Sites," *New York Times,* July 1, 2002.
103. Government Accountability Office, *Environmental Liabilities: EPA Should Do More to Ensure That Liable Parties Meet Their Cleanup Obligations* (Washington, DC: U.S. Government Accountability Office, August 17, 2005), GAO-05-658.
104. Zachary A. Smith, *The Environmental Policy Paradox* (Englewood Cliffs, NJ: Prentice Hall, 1991), 179–186.
105. Church and Nakamura, *Cleaning Up the Mess* (Washington, DC: Brookings Institution Press, 1993).
106. General Accounting Office, *Environmental Contamination: Corps Needs to Reassess Its Determination That Many Former Defense Sites Do Not Need Cleanup* (Washington, DC: U.S. General Accounting Office, August 23, 2002), GAO-02-658.
107. Environmental Protection Agency, "Superfund Program Implements the Recovery Act" (May 15, 2009), www.epa.gov/superfund/eparecovery/index.html.
108. Douglas Bevington, *The Rebirth of Environmentalism: From the Spotted Owl to the Polar Bear* (Washington, DC: Island Press, 2009).
109. Shannon Petersen, *Acting for Endangered Species: The Statutory Ark* (Lawrence: University Press of Kansas, 2002).
110. Richard A. Epstein, *Takings: Private Property and the Power of Eminent Domain* (Cambridge, MA: Harvard University Press, 1985).
111. Nancie G. Marzulla and Roger J. Marzulla, *Property Rights: Understanding Takings and Environmental Regulation* (Rockville, MD: Government Institutes, 1997).
112. Lara Parker, "Species on the Endangered List Challenged," *USA Today,* June 1, 2006.
113. Cornelia Dean, "Bid to Undo Bush Memo on Threat to Species," *New York Times,* March 3, 2009.
114. Charles O. Jones, "Speculative Augmentation in Federal Air Pollution Policymaking," *Journal of Politics* 42 (1975): 438–464.
115. Graeme Browning, "Taking Some Risks," *National Journal,* June 1, 1991, 1279–1282.

116. L. J. Lindquist, *The Hare and the Tortoise* (Ann Arbor: University of Michigan Press, 1986).

117. Some analysts have argued that there may be *insufficient* negotiation in the enforcement of environmental legislation and that better compliance could be achieved through bargaining rather than conventional regulatory enforcement. See Eugene Bardach and Robert Kagan, *Going by the Book* (Philadelphia: Temple University Press, 1983); and David Vogel, *Trading Up: Consumer and Environmental Regulation in a Global Economy* (Cambridge, MA: Harvard University Press, 1995).

118. Robert N. Stavins, "Lessons from the American Experience with Market-Based Environmental Policies," in *Market-Based Governance,* ed. John D. Donahue and Joseph S. Nye (Washington, DC: Brookings Institution Press, 2002), 173.

119. Barnaby J. Feder, "Sold: $21 Million of Air Pollution," *New York Times,* March 30, 1993. For a somewhat skeptical view, see General Accounting Office, *Environmental Protection: Implications for Using Pollution Taxes to Supplement Regulation* (Washington, DC: U.S. General Accounting Office, February 1993), GAO/RCED-93-13; and Peter Berck and Gloria E. Helfland, "The Case for Markets versus Standards for Pollution Policy," *Natural Resources Journal* 45 (2005): 345–368.

120. See Walter A. Rosenbaum, *Environmental Politics and Policy,* 5th ed. (Washington, DC: CQ Press, 2001), 109–110; and Stavins, "Lessons from the American Experiment with Market-Based Environmental Policies."

121. Margaret Kriz, "Emission Control," *National Journal,* July 3, 1993, 1696–1701.

122. See Renee Rico, "The U.S. Allowance Trading System for Sulphur Dioxide: An Update on Market Experience," *Environmental and Resource Economics* 5 (1995): 115–129.

## Chapter 15

1. For some sense of the ups and downs of defense employment (civilian and uniformed), see B. Guy Peters, "Public Employment in the United States," in *Public Employment in Western Democracies,* ed. Richard Rose et al. (Cambridge: Cambridge University Press, 1985), 125–145; and H.-U. Derlien and B. Guy Peters, eds., "The United States," in *Who Works for Government and What Do They Do?* (Cheltenham, UK: Edward Elgar, 2009).

2. See "Building Arms for the Wrong War," *New York Times,* May 10, 2002.

3. Elizabeth Bumiller and Thom Shanker, "Obama Puts His Stamp on Strategy for a Leaner Military," *The New York Times,* January 5, 2012.

4. John D. Steinbruner and William W. Kaufmann, "International Security Reconsidered," in *Setting National Priorities: Budget Choices for the Next Century,* ed. Robert D. Reischauer (Washington, DC: Brookings Institution Press, 1997).

5. Graham Allison, "How to Stop Nuclear Terror," *Foreign Affairs* 83, no. 1 (2004): 64–74.

6. See, for example, Robert K. Jervis, *Perception and Misperception in International Politics* (Princeton, NJ: Princeton University Press, 1976).

7. For example, there have been a number of assertions about marked differences in policy preferences among members of the Bush administration following September 11.

8. Joseph S. Nye, *Bound to Lead: The Changing Nature of American Power* (New York: Basic Books, 1992).

9. Gregory L. Schulte, "Bringing Peace to Bosnia and Change to the Alliance," *NATO Review* 45 (March 1997): 22–25.

10. Ivo Daalder and James M. Lindsay, *America Unbound: The Bush Revolution in Foreign Policy* (Washington, DC: Brookings Institution Press, 2003).

11. *Does UN Peacekeeping Serve U.S. Interests?* Hearing before the Committee on International Relations, U.S. House of Representatives, April 9, 1997.

12. See, for example, James A. Nathan and James K. Oliver, *United States Foreign Policy and World Order*, 2nd ed. (Boston: Little, Brown, 1981).

13. Paul Boyer, *Fallout: A Historian Reflects on America's Half-Century Encounter with Nuclear Weapons* (Columbus: Ohio State University Press, 1998).

14. Dunbar Lockwood, "Purchasing Power," *Bulletin of the Atomic Scientists* 50 (March 1994): 10–12; and "Former Soviet Republics Clear Way for Nunn-Lugar Monies," *Arms Control Today* 24 (1994): 28–29.

15. At the same time, this amounted to the end of the Anti-Ballistic Missile Treaty, one of the early attempts to negotiate arms control in the Cold War. See D. E. Sanger and M. Wines, "With a Shrug, a Monument to Cold War Fades Away," *New York Times*, June 14, 2002.

16. Recent evidence points to continuing nuclear weapons development in North Korea, despite agreements with both South Korea and the United States. See Steven Lee Meyers and Choe San-Hun, "North Koreans Agree to Freeze Nuclear Work," *New York Times*, February 26, 2012.

17. Bradley Graham, "Missile Threat to U.S. Greater Than Thought," *International Herald Tribune*, July 17, 1998.

18. Patrick E. Tyler, "As Fear of a Big War Fades, Military Plans for Little Ones," *New York Times*, February 3, 1992.

19. David C. Morrison, "Bottoming Out?" *National Journal*, September 17, 1994, 2126–2130; see also Donald J. Savoie and B. Guy Peters, "Comparing Programme Review," in *Programme Review in Canada*, ed. E. Lundquist and D. J. Savoie (Ottawa: Canadian Centre for Management Development, 1999), 56–75.

20. Mark Sappenfield, "How Iraq, Afghanistan Have Changed War 101," *Christian Science Monitor*, June 28, 2006.

21. As always, generals run the risk of learning the lessons of the last conflict but not anticipating adequately what the next conflict will be. See Brad Knickerbocker, "How Iraq Will Change U.S. Military Doctrine," *Christian Science Monitor*, July 2, 2004.

22. Julian Critchley, *The North Atlantic Alliance and the Soviet Union in the 1980s* (London: Macmillan, 1982).

23. Joshua B. Spero, "Beyond Old and New Europe," *Current History* 103 (2004): 103–105.

24. Robert L. Bernstein and Richard Dicker, "Human Rights First," *Foreign Policy* 94 (1994): 43–47; and William Korey, *The Promises We Keep: Human Rights, the Helsinki Process and American Foreign Policy* (New York: St. Martin's, 1993).

25. See Christoph Bluth, Emil Kirchner, and James Sperling, *The Future of European Security* (Aldershot, England: Dartmouth, 1995).

26. Bumiller and Shanker, "Obama Puts His Stamp on Strategy."

27. For example, the much-heralded accuracy of "smart bombs" during the Gulf War apparently would be crude in comparison to that of contemporary weapons.

28. For an analysis of the famous Reagan Strategic Defense Initiative program, see Congressional Budget Office, *Analysis of the Costs of the Administration's Strategic Defense Initiative, 1985–89* (Washington, DC: Congressional Budget Office, May 1984). This idea was revived in the 1990s.

29. James Dao and Andrew C. Revkin, "Machines Are Filling In for Troops," *New York Times,* April 16, 2000; and Government Accountability Office, *Several Factors Limited the Production and Installation of Army Truck Armor during Current Wartime Operations* (Washington, DC: U.S. Government Accountability Office, March 2006), Report No. GAO-06-160.

30. Michael E. O'Hanlon, "Too Big a Buck for the Bang," *Washington Post,* January 6, 2003.

31. Gordon Adams, *The Politics of Defense Contracting: The Iron Triangle* (New Brunswick, NJ: Transaction, 1981); and "Mission Implausible," *U.S. News & World Report,* October 14, 1991, 24–31.

32. Of course, the United States is the only country that has ever used these weapons in war.

33. See, for example, the Pew Center poll "Defense and International Relations" of July 8–18, 2004 (Washington, DC: Pew Center on the Press and the Public).

34. William Newman, "Causes of Change in National Security Processes: Carter, Reagan, Bush Decision Making on Arms Control," *Presidential Studies Quarterly* 31 (2001): 69–103.

35. Owen Cote, "The Trident and the Triad," *International Security Quarterly* 16 (1991): 117–136.

36. Ria Novosti, "Iran Tests Indigenous Anti-Ship Missile in Gulf Drills," *Defense Talk,* July 7, 2011.

37. Pat Towell, "Pentagon Banking on Plans to Reinvent Procurement," *Congressional Quarterly Weekly Report,* April 16, 1994, 899; and Lauren Holland, "Explaining Weapons Procurement: Matching Operational Performance and National Security Needs," *Armed Forces and Society* 19 (1993): 353–376.

38. Clifford J. Levy and Peter Baker, "Russian Reaction on Missile Plan Leaves Iran Issue Hanging," *New York Times,* September 11, 2009.

39. The Government Accountability Office has done a number of evaluations of these and other poorly performing weapons systems—for example, *Defense Acquisition: Major Weapons Systems Continue to Experience Cost and Schedule Problems* (Washington, DC: U.S. Government Accountability Office, April 2006), Report No. USGAO-06-368. See also Scott Shuger, "The Stealth Bomber Story You Haven't Heard," *Washington Monthly* 23 (January 1991): 1–2, 14–22.

40. Moshe Schwartz, *Defense Acquisition: How DOD Acquires Weapons Systems and Recent Efforts to Reform the Process* (Washington, DC: Congressional Research Service, April 23, 2010).

41. Frank Rich, "The Road from K Street to Yusufiya," *New York Times,* June 5, 2006.

42. Eric Schmitt, "Military Proposes to End Production of Most New Arms," *New York Times,* January 24, 1992.

43. Leslie Wayne, "Runaway Arms Costs: Threat to U.S. Security?" *New York Times,* July 11, 2006.
44. Andrew Taylor, "Obama Defense Contractor Battle Only Just Begun," Associated Press, April 22, 2009.
45. Eric Schmitt, "Run Silent, Run Deep, Beat Foes (Where?)," *New York Times,* January 30, 1992.
46. Beth L. Bailey, *America's Army: Making the All Volunteer Force* (Cambridge, MA: Harvard University Press, 2009).
47. David McCormick, *The Downsized Warrior: America's Army in Transition* (New York: New York University Press, 1998).
48. See Cindy Williams, "Paying Tomorrow's Military," *Regulation* 29 (Summer 2006): 26–31.
49. For example, Molly Pitcher played a partly real, partly mythical part in the Battle of Monmouth during the Revolutionary War.
50. See Andrea Stone, "They're 'Not an Experiment Anymore,'" *USA Today,* January 11, 2002.
51. Linda Bird Francke, *Ground Zero: The Gender Wars in the Military* (New York: Simon and Schuster, 1997).
52. See James Kitfield, "Front and Center," *National Journal,* October 25, 1997, 1097–1111.
53. The Department of Defense argued that the fundamental reason for dismissal of the female pilot was her lying about the existence of a relationship and then continuing once ordered to terminate it.
54. Michael R. Gordon, "Pentagon Spells Out Rules for Ousting Homosexuals; Rights Group Vows a Fight," *New York Times,* December 23, 1993.
55. Tamar Lewin, "At Bases, Debate Rages over Impact of New Gay Policy," *New York Times,* December 24, 1993.
56. Eric Schmitt, "How Is This Strategy Working? Don't Ask," *New York Times,* December 19, 1999.
57. Lara Jakes, "Court Rejects Challenge to Don't Ask Don't Tell," Associated Press, June 8, 2009.
58. Tim Weiner, "Proposal Cuts Back on Some Weapons to Spend More on Personnel," *New York Times,* February 8, 1994. Another version of this is to fight one war while maintaining a holding action in another.
59. William W. Kaufmann, "'Hollow' Forces," *Brookings Review* 12 (1994): 24–29.
60. Other estimates show substantially greater employment generated by defense purchases. These are rather conservative estimates from the Department of Labor.
61. James Kitfield, "The New Partnership," *National Journal,* August 6, 1994, 8749.
62. David C. Morrison, "Painful Separation," *National Journal,* March 3, 1990, 768–773.
63. John DiIulio Jr., "Federal Crime Policy," *Brookings Review* 19 (Winter 1999): 17–21; and Michael E. Dupre and David A. Mackey, "Crime in the Public Mind," *Journal of Criminal Justice and Popular Culture* 8 (2001): 1–24.
64. V. Beiser, "Why the Big Apple Feels Safer," *Maclean's,* September 11, 1995, 39ff.
65. Generally, young adults are the most prone to commit crimes; this group has been declining rapidly as a percentage of the American population.

66. James Risen and Eric Lichtblau, "Bush Secretly Lifted Limits on Spying in U.S. after 9/11, Officials Say," *New York Times,* December 15, 2005.

67. Hoover himself had a somewhat more complex career. See Anthony Summers, *Official and Confidential* (New York: Putnam, 1993).

68. This organization became very visible during the siege of the Branch Davidian compound in Waco, Texas, in 1993.

69. Actually, it does not exhaust the list of federal enforcement activities, which also include, for example, law enforcement by park rangers (Department of the Interior) in national parks.

70. John DiIulio, "Crime," in *Setting Domestic Priorities: What Can Government Do?* ed. Henry J. Aaron and Charles L Schultze (Washington, DC: Brookings Institution Press, 1992), 101.

71. Included here was the (in)famous "midnight basketball"—keeping recreation centers in poorer areas open long hours to give young people something more constructive to do than commit crimes.

72. For a discussion of this controversy in the context of the Clinton crime bill, see W. John Moore, "Shooting in the Dark," *National Journal,* February 2, 1994, 358–363.

73. See "Crime in California: Three Strikes, You're Out," *Economist,* January 15, 1994, 29–32; and Michael G. Turner, "Three Strikes and You're Out Legislation: A National Assessment," *Federal Probation* 59 (1995): 16–35.

74. Committee on Ways and Means, U.S. House of Representatives, *Children and Families at Risk* (Washington, DC: U.S. Government Printing Office, January 1994).

75. This appears to be especially true for child and spousal abuse. See David J. Kolko, "Characteristics of Child Victims of Physical Abuse," *Journal of Interpersonal Violence* 7 (1992): 244–276; and Cathy Spatz Widom, "Avoidance of Criminality in Abused and Neglected Children," *Psychiatry* 54 (1991): 162–174.

76. Government Accountability Office, *Community Policing Grants: COPS Grants Were a Modest Contributor to Declines in Crime in the 1990s* (Washington, DC: U.S. Government Accountability Office, October 2005), Report No. GAO-05-104.

77. U.S. Bureau of Justice Statistics, *State Prison Expenditures* (Washington, DC: BJS, annual).

78. Most correctional officials oppose these changes, arguing that all this will do is make the prison population more restive and difficult to control.

79. The amendment is worded as follows: "A well regulated Militia, being necessary to the security of a free State, the right of the people to keep and bear Arms, shall not be infringed."

80. Federal Bureau of Investigation, *Crime in the United States* (Washington, DC: U.S. Government Printing Office, annual).

81. The act was named after James Brady, President Reagan's press secretary, who was wounded severely in the attempted assassination of Reagan in 1981. After that experience, his wife, Sarah Brady, became a vigorous advocate of gun control.

82. Peter H. Stone, "Under the Gun," *National Journal,* June 5, 1993, 1334–1338; and Holly Idelson and Paul Nyhan, "Gun Rights and Restrictions: The Territory Reconfigured," *Congressional Quarterly Weekly Report,* April 24, 1993, 1021–1027.

83. Bob Adams, "The Gun Control Debate," *CQ Researcher* 40, no. 14 (November 2004).

84. *2004 National Annenberg Election Survey* (Philadelphia: Annenberg Center), www.srbi.com/election_2004.html.

85. CBS News/*New York Times* poll, April 22–26, 2009, www.nytimes.com.

86. CNN/Opinion Research Corporation poll, June 4–5, 2008, www.pollingreport.com/guns.htm.

87. George Pettinico, "Crime and Punishment: America Changes Its Mind," *Public Perspective* 5 (September/October 1994): 29; Gallup Poll, October 3–5, 2008, www.gallup.com/.

88. Welsh S. White, *The Death Penalty in the Nineties: An Examination of the Modern System of Capital Punishment* (Ann Arbor: University of Michigan Press, 1991).

89. Stanley Cohen, *The Wrong Men: America's Epidemic of Wrongful Death Row Convictions* (New York: Carroll and Graf, 2003); Franklin E. Zimring, *The Contradictions of American Capital Punishment* (New York: Oxford University Press, 2003).

90. James Dao, "Governor Finds New Middle Ground in Capital Punishment Debate," *New York Times,* January 14, 2006.

91. *Furman v. Georgia,* 408 U.S. 238 (1972).

92. Linda Greenhouse, "Justices Bar Death Penalty for Retarded Defendants," *New York Times,* June 21, 2002; and Adam Liptak, "Inmate's Rising IQ Score Could Mean His Death," *New York Times,* February 6, 2005.

93. Gregory D. Russell, *The Death Penalty and Racial Bias: Overturning Supreme Court Assumptions* (Westport, CT: Greenwood, 1994).

94. This may not be strictly a constitutional argument, since the Constitution and its amendments do not mention economics as a forbidden category for differentiating among individuals.

95. Hugo Adam Bedau and Paul G. Casswell, *Debating the Death Penalty: Should America Have Capital Punishment?* (New York: Oxford University Press, 2004).

96. Stephen Reinhardt, "The Supreme Court, the Death Penalty and the Harris Case," *Yale Law Journal* 102 (1992): 205–222.

97. Marcia Coyle, "Blackmun's Turnabout on the Death Penalty," *National Law Journal* 16 (March 7, 1994): 39.

98. Robbie Brown, "Tennessee Exoneration after 22 Years on Death Row," *New York Times,* May 13, 2009.

99. This is called "Mirandizing" an arrestee, after Ernesto Miranda, whose conviction was overturned because he was not told of his right to remain silent (*Miranda v. Arizona,* 384 U.S. 436 [1966]).

100. Kenneth B. Noble, "Ruling Helps Prosecution of Simpson," *New York Times,* September 20, 1994.

101. Prisons are already dangerous enough. See Mark S. Fleisher, *Warehousing Violence* (Newbury Park, CA: Sage, 1989); and George M. Anderson, "Prison Violence: Victims behind Bars," *America,* November 26, 1988, 430–433.

102. W. A. Corbitt, "Violent Crimes among Juveniles," *FBI Law Enforcement Bulletin* 69 (June 2000): 18–21.

103. Center for Disease Control and Prevention, *Youth Violence Facts, 2009* (Atlanta, GA: CDCP, June 29, 2009).

104. See Richard Rose, "On the Priorities of Government," *European Journal of Political Research* 4 (1973): 247–289.

## Chapter 16

1. See John Kenneth White, *The Values Divide: American Politics and Culture in Transition* (New York: Chatham House, 2002); and Raymond Tatlovich and Byron W. Daynes, *Moral Controversies in American Politics* (Armonk, NY: M. E. Sharpe, 2004).

2. Jonathan Zimmerman, *Whose America: Culture Wars in the Public Schools* (Cambridge, MA: Harvard University Press, 2002).

3. See Gilbert Meilaender, "The Point of a Ban, or How to Think about Stem Cell Research," *Hastings Center Report* 31 (2001): 9–16; Thomas F. Banchoff, *Embryo Politics: Ethics and Policy in Atlantic Democracies* (Ithaca, NY: Cornell University Press).

4. By *line*, scientists mean a collection of cells derived from a common background. The common genetic background of the cells makes research less subject to possible spurious findings.

5. In 2006, Harvard University decided to go ahead with a large-scale program in stem cell research using private resources rather than wait for more federal funds that may or may not materialize.

6. "The Politics of Genes: America's Next Ethical War," *Economist*, April 14, 2001, 21–24.

7. School prayer may approach being bargainable in this way: If enough vouchers are made available, parents who want their children in schools where prayer is permitted may be able to find those opportunities, while the public schools remain secular. Some advocates, however, believe that the absence of school prayer undermines the fundamental values of the country. Opponents argue that public support for religious schools is fundamentally wrong.

8. On policy framing, see D. A. Schon and M. Rein, *Frame Selection: On Solving Intractable Policy Disputes* (New York: Basic Books, 1994).

9. John E. Thompson, "What's the Big Deal: The Unconstitutionality of God in the Pledge of Allegiance," *Harvard Civil Rights–Civil Liberties Law Review* 38 (2003): 563–574.

10. Julie Preston, "Partial Birth Abortion Act Ruled Unconstitutional by U.S. Courts," *New York Times*, February 1, 2006.

11. The right of privacy is itself implied rather than stated in the Constitution. See Madeleine Mercedes Plascenia, *Privacy and the Constitution* (New York: Garland, 1999).

12. Lawrence Tribe, *Abortion: The Clash of Absolutes* (New York: Norton, 1992), 29.

13. In *Doe v. Bolton* (1973), the Court ruled that not only could abortions not be criminalized but also the states could not make them unreasonably difficult to obtain.

14. Karen O'Connor, *No Neutral Ground: Abortion Politics in an Age of Absolutes* (Boulder, CO: Westview Press, 1996).

15. NBC News/*Wall Street Journal* poll conducted by the polling organizations of Peter Hart (D) and Neil Newhouse (R), September 6–8, 2008, http://topics.wsj.com/subject/W/wall-street-journal/nbc-news-polls/6052. Note: The more recent polls do not ask the questions in precisely the same ways.

16. The logic is that this is a major decision that is irreversible. Moreover, many other medical procedures for males or females may require parental approval. The intended effect, of course, is to prevent the female minor from having the procedure, either

because the parent will not approve it or because there is fear of even discussing the possibility.

17. The Interstate Commerce Clause (Article 1, section 8, clause 3) has been used to provide Congress with the power to regulate in a variety of areas that might not appear to be directly economic—for example, civil rights.

18. Justice David Souter was assumed to oppose abortion when President George H. W. Bush appointed him in 1990, but he tended to side with the pro–abortion rights majority on the Court.

19. "Judge Alito on Abortion," *Washington Post*, November 6, 2005.

20. Robert Pear, "U.S. Clarifies Policy on Birth Control for Religious Groups," *New York Times*, March 16, 2012.

21. See *Health, United States, 2005* (Atlanta, GA: Centers for Disease Control and Prevention, 2005), Table 16.

22. Barry D. Adam, *The Rise of the Gay and Lesbian Movement* (New York: Twayne, 1995).

23. The position, along with that of most mainstream Protestant churches, has been to "hate the sin but love the sinner."

24. One of the more extreme examples occurred after the 2001 terrorist attacks in New York and Washington, D.C. Religious right leaders Jerry Falwell and Pat Robertson argued that the terrorists were facilitated by the undermining of the moral fiber of the country by gay rights advocates, as well as other "secularists." See Gustav Niebuhr, "Falwell Apologizes for Saying an Angry God Allowed Attacks," *New York Times*, September 18, 2001.

25. Mike Allen, "Bush Allows Death Benefits to Gays," *Washington Post*, June 26, 2002.

26. See, for example, John Schwartz, "After New York, New Look at Defense of Marriage Act," *New York Times*, June 27, 2010.

27. The U.S. Constitution (Article IV) mandates that states give "full faith and credit" to the legal actions of the other states, so failure to accept the marital status of a gay couple may violate that provision.

28. Jim Ruttenberg and Carl Hulse, "Conservatives Watching Senate Debate on Gay Marriage," *New York Times*, June 6, 2006.

29. Engel v. Vitale, 370 U.S. 421 (1962).

30. See *Wallace v. Jaffree*, 472 U.S. 38 (1985).

31. *Cochran v. Board of Education*, 281 U.S. 370 (1930).

32. *Everson v. Board of Education*, 330 U.S. 1 (1947).

33. *Lemon v. Kurzman*, 403 U.S. 602 (1971).

34. *Roemer v. Maryland*, 426 U.S. 736 (1976).

35. See *Mitchell v. Helms*, 530 U.S. 793 (2000).

36. *Board of Education of the Kiryas Joel School District v. Grument*, 512 U.S. 708 (1994).

37. Charles Lane, "Court Upholds Ohio School Vouchers," *Washington Post*, June 28, 2002.

38. In fairness, a number of scientists are concerned about those gaps. For a defense, see Stephen Jay Gould, *The Structure of Evolutionary Theory* (Cambridge, MA: Harvard University Press, 2002).

39. Bill Toland, "Intelligent Design Goes on Trial in Pennsylvania," *Pittsburgh Post Gazette*, September 27, 2005.

## Chapter 17

1. Edward C. Gramlich, *Benefit-Cost Analysis for Government Programs* (Englewood Cliffs, NJ: Prentice Hall, 1981); R. O. Zerbe, *Benefit Cost Analysis in Theory and Practice* (New York: HarperCollins, 1994).

2. Steven Kelman, "Cost-Benefit Analysis: An Ethical Critique," *Regulation* 4 (1981): 33–40.

3. Kenneth Arrow, *Social Choice and Individual Values* (New York: Wiley, 1963); and Allan Feldman, *Welfare Economics and Social Choice Theory* (Boston: Martinus Nijhoff, 1986).

4. P. Hennipman, "Pareto Optimality: Value Judgment or Analytical Tool?" in *Relevance and Precision,* ed. J. S. Cramer, A. Heertje, and P. Venekamp (New York: North-Holland, 1976), 39; E. J. Mishan and Euston Quah, *Cost Benefit Analysis,* 5th ed. (London: Routledge, 2007), 45–56.

5. Nicholas Kaldor, "Welfare Propositions of Economics and Interpersonal Comparisons of Utility," *Economic Journal* 49 (1939): 549–552; and John R. Hicks, "The Valuation of the Social Income," *Economica* 7 (1940): 105–124.

6. Richard Posner, "Cost-Benefit Analysis: Definition, Justifications and Comments," in *Cost Benefit Analysis,* ed. R. Posner (Cambridge, MA: Harvard University Press, 2001).

7. Richard Posner, *The Economics of Justice* (Cambridge, MA: Harvard University Press, 1983).

8. E. J. Mishan, *Cost-Benefit Analysis,* expanded ed. (New York: Praeger, 1967), 24–54.

9. David Whittington and Duncan MacRae Jr., "The Issue of Standing in Cost-Benefit Analysis," *Journal of Policy Analysis and Management* 5 (1986): 665–682; R. O. Zerbe, "A Place to Stand for Environmental Law and Economic Analysis," (n.d.), www .cserge.ucl.ac.uk/Zerbe.pdf.

10. E. J. Mishan, "The Post-War Literature on Externalities: An Interpretative Essay," *Journal of Economic Literature* 16 (1978): 1–28; and Neva R. Goodwin, *As if the Future Mattered: Translating Social and Economic Theory into Human Behavior* (Ann Arbor: University of Michigan Press, 1996).

11. John Martin Gilroy, "The Ethical Poverty of Cost-Benefit Methods: Autonomy, Efficiency and Public Policy Choice," *Policy Sciences* 25 (1992): 83–102.

12. "The TVA—Hardy Survivor," *Economist,* July 1, 1989, 22–23.

13. Edith Stokey and Richard Zeckhauser, *A Primer for Policy Analysis* (New York: Norton, 1978), 149–152; and J. Frykblom, "Hypothetical Question Modes and Real Willingness to Pay," *Journal of Environmental Economics and Management* 34 (1998), 275–287.

14. This is referred to as a "hedonic price model," in which the contributions of intangibles to price are assessed. See Paul Portney, "Housing Prices, Health Effects and Valuing Reductions in the Risk of Death," *Journal of Environmental Economics and Management* 8 (1981): 72–78.

15. Robin Gregory, Donald McGregor, and Sarah Lichtenstein, "Assessing the Quality of Expressed Preference Measures of Value," *Journal of Economic Behavior and Organization* 17 (1992): 277–292.

16. *The Road Back: Endangered Species Recovery* (Washington, DC: U.S. Department of the Interior, 1998), see chap. 13.

17. Peter Passell, "Polls May Help Government Decide the Worth of Nature," *New York Times,* September 6, 1993. See also J. A. Hausman, *Contingent Valuation: A Critical Assessment* (Amsterdam, Netherlands: North-Holland, 1993).

18. Robert E. Niewijk, "Misleading Quantification: The Contingent Valuation of Environmental Quality," *Regulation* 17, no. 1 (1994): 60–71.

19. Steven E. Rhoads, ed., *Valuing Life: Public Policy Dilemmas* (Boulder, CO: Westview Press, 1980); and W. Kip Viscusi, "Alternative Approaches to Valuing the Health Impact of Accidents: Liability Law and Prospective Evaluations," *Law and Contemporary Problems* 46 (1983): 49–68.

20. "What's a Life Worth? 9/11 Fund Stirs Anger," *USA Today,* January 8, 2002; and David W. Chen, "Hundreds of 9/11 Families File for Right to Sue Port Authority," *New York Times,* July 10, 2002.

21. Jack Hirschleifer and David L. Shapiro, "The Treatment of Risk and Uncertainty," in *Public Expenditure and Policy Analysis,* 3rd ed., ed. Robert H. Haveman and Julius Margolis (Boston: Houghton Mifflin, 1983), 145–166.

22. For a general discussion of the problems of discounting, see Robert E. Goodin, "Discounting Discounting," *Journal of Public Policy* 2 (1982): 53–71; Hal R. Varian, "Recalculating the Costs of Global Climate Change," *New York Times* December 14, 2006.

23. William J. Baumol, "On the Social Rate of Discount," *American Economic Review* 10 (1968): 788–802.

24. Marthe R. Gold et al., *Cost-Effectiveness in Health and Medicine* (New York: Oxford University Press, 1996).

25. Ray Robinson, "Cost-Effectiveness Analysis," *British Medical Journal* 307 (September 25, 1993): 793–795.

26. David M. Eddy, "Cost-Effectiveness Analysis: Will It Be Accepted?" *Journal of the American Medical Association* 268 (1992): 132–136.

27. See Sidney A. Shapiro and Robert L. Glicksman, *Risk Regulation at Risk: Restoring a Pragmatic Approach* (Stanford, CA: Stanford University Press, 2005).

28. Alphonse G. Holtman, "Beyond Efficiency: Economists and Distributional Analysis," in *Policy Analysis and Economics: Developments, Tensions, Prospects,* ed. David L. Weimer (Boston: Kluwer, 1991); and Elio Londero, *Benefits and Beneficiaries: An Introduction to Estimating Distributional Effects in Cost-Benefit Analysis,* 2nd ed. (Washington, DC: Inter-American Development Bank, 1996).

29. Peter Self, *Econocrats and the Policy Process: The Politics and Philosophy of Cost-Benefit Analysis* (London: Macmillan, 1975).

30. Peter Self, "Nonsense on Stilts: Cost-Benefit Analysis and the Roskill Commission," *Political Quarterly* 10 (1970): 30–63; and Kelman, "Cost-Benefit Analysis."

31. See Bruce Ackerman, "The Emergency Constitution," *Yale Law Journal* 113 (2004): 1029–1088.

32. Charlie Savage, "Secret U.S. Memo Made Legal Case to Kill a Citizen," *New York Times,* October 8, 2011.

33. Russell Hardin, *Morality within the Limit of Reason* (Chicago: University of Chicago Press, 1988).

34. See Martin E. Marty, *The One and the Many: America's Struggle for the Common Good* (Cambridge, MA: Harvard University Press, 1997).

35. Victor Grassian, *Moral Reasoning* (Englewood Cliffs, NJ: Prentice Hall, 1981).

36. Arnold Meltsner, *Policy Analysts in the Bureaucracy* (Berkeley: University of California Press, 1976), 3–25.

37. Abraham Kaplan, "Social Ethics and the Sanctity of Life," in *Life or Death: Ethics and Options*, ed. D. H. Labby (London: Macmillan, 1968), 58–71.

38. Guido Calabresi and Phillip Bobbitt, *Tragic Choices* (New York: Norton, 1978), 21. See also B. Guy Peters, "Tragic Choices: Administrative Rulemaking and Policy Choice," in *Ethics in Public Service*, ed. Richard A. Chapman (Edinburgh, UK: University of Edinburgh Press, 1993), 43.

39. Sheryl Gay Stolberg, "Live and Let Die over Transplants," *New York Times*, April 5, 1998; Philip Newton, "Do Alcoholics Deserve Liver Transplants," *Psychology Today*, February 15, 2009.

40. As a part of its rationing program, the state of Oregon made this determination. The justification was primarily utilitarian, based on the assumption that the treatment would be less beneficial for people with substance abuse problems.

41. Dave Davis, Ted Wendling, and Joan Mazzolini, "U.S. Orders Revisions in Rules on Transplants: Current System's Range of Waits Is Called Unfair," *Cleveland Plain Dealer*, March 27, 1998.

42. Bonnie Steinbock, *Life before Birth: The Moral and Legal Status of Embryos and Fetuses* (New York: Oxford University Press, 1992).

43. Ronald Dworkin, *Life's Dominion: An Argument about Abortion, Euthanasia and Individual Freedom* (New York: Knopf, 1993).

44. For a detailed account see Rebecca Dresser, "A Hard Case Makes Questionable Law," *Hastings Center Report* 34 (2004): all; Michael Patrick Allen, "Congress and Terri Schiavo: A Primer on the American Constitutional Order," *West Virginia Law Review* 108 (2006): 309–360.

45. Individuals have the option of making "living wills" specifying their choices about such end-of-life issues; there was not a formal document present in this case.

46. Steven H. Miles, "Doctors and Their Patients' Suicides," *Journal of the American Medical Association* 271 (June 8, 1994): 1786–1788; and Daniel Avila, "Medical Treatment Rights of Older Persons and Persons with Disabilities," *Issues in Law and Medicine* 9 (1994): 345–360.

47. Jonathan Glover, *Causing Deaths and Saving Lives* (Harmondsworth, UK: Penguin, 1977).

48. Robert Nozick, *Anarchy, State, and Utopia* (New York: Basic Books, 1974).

49. This individualistic and conservative interpretation of the law was common during the late nineteenth and early twentieth centuries. See, for example, *Lochner v. New York*, 198 U.S. 45 (1905).

50. Robert E. Goodin, *Reasons for Welfare* (Princeton, NJ: Princeton University Press, 1988), 312–331; and Christian Bay, *The Structure of Freedom* (New York: Athenaeum, 1965).

51. John Kultgen, *Autonomy and Intervention: Paternalism in the Caring Life* (New York: Oxford University Press, 1994).

52. Desmond King, *Illiberal Policies in Liberal States* (Oxford: Oxford University Press, 1999).

53. See Dennis A. Robbins, *Ethical and Legal Issues in Home Health and Long-Term Care: Challenges and Solutions* (Gaithersburg, MD: Aspen, 1996); and Bonnie Steinbock

and Alastair Norcross, *Killing and Letting Die,* 2nd ed. (New York: Fordham University Press, 1994).

54. Some conservatives have argued, for example, that even professional licensure of doctors and lawyers should be abandoned in the name of free choice. In the long run, it is argued, the market would take care of the problem.

55. Jerome S. Legge, *Traffic Safety Reform in the United States and Great Britain* (Pittsburgh: University of Pittsburgh Press, 1991); and Kenneth E. Warner, "Bags, Buckles and Belts: The Debate over Mandatory Passive Restraints in Automobiles," *Journal of Health Politics, Policy and Law* 8 (1983): 44–75.

56. Howard M. Leichter, *Free to be Foolish* (Princeton, NJ: Princeton University Press, 1991).

57. For one perspective, see Mario Loyola, "Challenging Obamacare's Coercive Medicaid Provisions," *National Review,* June 7, 2011.

58. The FDA has to some extent relaxed its usual guidelines for drugs that may help victims of AIDS and a few other extremely deadly diseases—for example, Lou Gehrig's Disease. See Harold Edgar and David J. Rothman, "New Rules for New Drugs: The Challenge of AIDS to the Regulatory Process," in *A Disease of Society,* ed. Dorothy Nelkin, David P. Willis, and Scott V. Parris (Cambridge: Cambridge University Press, 1991), 84; see also Peter Davis, *Contested Ground: Public Purpose and Private Interest in the Regulation of Prescription Drugs* (New York: Oxford University Press, 1996).

59. Sissela Bok, *Lying: Moral Choice in Public and Private Life* (New York: Vintage, 1979).

60. Loch K. Johnson, *Secret Agencies: U.S. Intelligence in a Hostile World* (New Haven, CT: Yale University Press, 1996); James P. Pfiffner, "Did President Bush Mislead the Country in His Arguments for War in Iraq?" *Presidential Studies Quarterly* 34 (2004): 25–46.

61. See Raymond L. Goldstein and John K. Schoor, *Demanding Democracy after Three Mile Island* (Gainesville: University of Florida Press, 1991).

62. James C. Petersen, *Whistleblowing: Ethical and Legal Issues in Expressing Dissent* (Dubuque, IA: Kendall/Hunt, 1986); Daniel P. Westman, *Whistleblowing: The Law of Retaliatory Discharge* (Washington, DC: Bureau of National Affairs, 1991); and U.S. Merit Systems Protection Board, *Whistleblowing in the Federal Government* (Washington, DC: U.S. Merit Systems Protection Board, 1993).

63. See, respectively, Edward Weisband and Thomas M. Franck, *Resignation in Protest* (New York: Penguin, 1975); and David Burnham, "Paper Chase of a Whistleblower," *New York Times,* October 16, 1982.

64. See Joseph S. Nye, Philip D. Zelikow, and David C. King, eds., *Why People Don't Trust Government* (Cambridge, MA: Harvard University Press, 1997).

65. Michael Walzer, "Political Action: The Problem of Dirty Hands," *Philosophy and Public Affairs* 1 (1973): 160–180; and Thomas Nagel, "Ruthlessness in Public Life," in *Public and Private Life,* ed. Stuart Hampshire (Cambridge: Cambridge University Press, 1978), 145–168.

66. Jan-Erik Lane, *The Public Sector: Concepts, Models and Approaches* (Newbury Park, CA: Sage, 1993).

67. See Robert E. Goodin, *Protecting the Vulnerable: A Re-Analysis of Our Social Responsibilities* (Chicago: University of Chicago Press, 1985). Even such a committed conservative as Charles Murray could argue that "There is no such thing as an

undeserving five-year-old"; see his *Losing Ground* (New York: Basic Books, 1984).

68. Richard Allen Epstein, *Takings: Private Property and the Power of Eminent Domain* (Cambridge, MA: Harvard University Press, 1985); and William A. Fischel, *Regulatory Takings: Law, Economics and Politics* (Cambridge, MA: Harvard University Press, 1995).

69. Karl Marx, *Criticism of the Gotha Program* (New York: International Universities Press, 1938), vol. 929, 14.

70. For an important attempt to provide such a justification, see Goodin, *Reasons for Welfare*, 287–305. See also Bo Rothstein, *Just Institutions Matter: The Moral and Political Logic of the Universal Welfare State* (Cambridge: Cambridge University Press, 1998).

71. Edith Brown Weiss, *In Fairness to Future Generations: International Law, Common Patrimony, and Intergenerational Equity* (Tokyo: United Nations University, 1988).

72. Peter S. Burton, "Intertemporal Preferences and Intergenerational Equity Considerations in Optimal Resource Harvesting," *Journal of Environmental Economics and Management* 24 (1993): 119–132; and Laurence J. Kotlikoff, *Generational Accounting* (New York: Free Press, 1992).

73. John Rawls, "Justice as Fairness," *Philosophical Review* 77 (1958): 164–194, esp. 166.

74. John Rawls, *A Theory of Justice* (Cambridge, MA: Harvard University Press, 1971), esp. 57, 65, 72, 93.

75. Ibid., 19.

76. For an earlier literary treatment of this view of fairness, see L. P. Hartley, *Facial Justice* (London: Hamish Hamilton, 1960). On desert, see George Bernard Shaw's *Doctor's Dilemma: A Tragedy* (London: Penguin, 1957).

77. Epstein, *Takings*.

78. Roberto Alejandro, *The Limits of Rawlsian Justice* (Baltimore: Johns Hopkins University Press, 1998).

79. Richard A. Epstein, *Forbidden Grounds: The Case against Employment Discrimination Laws* (Cambridge, MA: Harvard University Press, 1992); and Russell Nieli, ed., *Racial Preference and Racial Justice: The New Affirmative Action Controversy* (Washington, DC: Ethics and Public Policy Center, 1991).

80. Douglas E. Ashford, *The Emergence of the Welfare State* (Oxford: Basil Blackwell, 1986). But see T. H. Marshall, *Class, Citizenship, and Social Development* (New York: Doubleday, 1965).

81. See Gareth Davies, *From Opportunity to Entitlement* (Lawrence: University Press of Kansas, 1996).

82. In a few places—for example, the City University of New York—there was once free higher education as well, but budget constraints have forced the imposition of fees in those institutions.

83. See also Kimberly J. Cook, *Divided Passions: Public Opinions on Abortion and the Death Penalty* (Boston: Northeastern University Press, 1997).

84. Frances Fox Piven and Richard A. Cloward, *Regulating the Poor*, 2nd ed. (New York: Viking, 1993).

85. Amitai Etzioni, ed., *New Communitarian Thinking: Virtues, Institutions, and Communities* (Charlottesville: University Press of Virginia, 1995).

# Notes

## Introduction

1. Jack Anderson, *Peace, War & Politics: An Eyewitness Account* (New York: Forge Books, 1999), 134.
2. Bob Woodward, *Bush at War* (New York: Simon & Schuster, 2002), 38; *The 9/11 Commission Report* (New York: W. W. Norton, 2004), 330.
3. Donald Rumsfeld, *Known and Unknown: A Memoir* (New York: Sentinel, 2011), 346; Hugh Shelton, *Without Hesitation* (New York: St. Martin's Press, 2010), 440.
4. *The 9/11 Commission Report,* 333, www.911commission.gov/report/911Report.pdf
5. Public Law 107–40.
6. Public Law 107–56.
7. Charles A. Stevenson, *Congress at War: The Politics of Conflict since 1789* (Washington, DC: Potomac Books, 2007), 18.
8. Public Law 107–296.
9. Graham Allison and Philip Zelikow, *Essence of Decision: Explaining the Cuban Missile Crisis, Second Edition,* (New York: Longman, 1999), 6, 300–301.

## Chapter 1

1. George C. Herring, *From Colony to Superpower: U.S. Foreign Relations Since 1776* (New York: Oxford University Press, 2008), 53.
2. Christopher Collier and James Lincoln Collier, *Decision in Philadelphia* (New York: Ballantine Books, 1986), 348.
3. Quoted in Richard B. Morris, *The Forging of the Union, 1781–1789* (New York: Harper & Row, 1987), 266.
4. Morris, 130–132, 154–159; Frederick W. Marks, III, *Independence on Trial: Foreign Affairs and the Making of the Constitution* (Baton Rouge, LA: State University Press, 1973), 59.
5. Marks 111, 113; Morris, 209.
6. Marks, 16; *Journal of Continental Congress,* June 21, 1786; October 30, 1786; and July 18, 1787.
7. Marks, 37–44, 49.
8. *Journal of the Continental Congress,* February 8, 1786.
9. *Journal of the Continental Congress,* October 18, 1786.

10. Quoted in Morris, 266.

11. Address of the Annapolis Convention, September 1786.

12. Marks, xvii–xix, citing Forrest McDonald, Page Smith, James MacGregor Burns, and Merrill Jensen.

13. Herring, 49.

14. Marks, 170, 142–145; Richard H. Kohn, ed., *The United States Military Under the Constitution, 1789–1989* (New York University Press, 1991), 63–71.

15. Collier & Collier, 103–4; Richard Beeman, *Plain, Honest Men: The Making of the American Constitution* (New York: Random House, 2009), 67.

16. Collier & Collier, 114–115.

17. Collier & Collier, 198–200.

18. David O. Stewart, *The Summer of 1787: The Men Who Invented the Constitution* (New York: Simon & Schuster, 2007), 103–104.

19. The original allocation of seats in the House of Representatives gave Southern states 45% of the seats and Northern states 55%. After the first census in 1790, along with the addition of Vermont and Kentucky, Southern states had 46.5% using the three-fifths ratio. The actual house apportionment was 44.8%. If only free inhabitants had been counted, the Southern percentage would have dropped to 41.0%. If slaves had been counted wholly, the figure would have been 49.9%. George William Van Cleve, *A Slaveholders' Union* (University of Chicago Press, 2010), 121.

20. Farrand's *Records of the Federal Convention*, vol. 1, 24–26, http://memory.loc.gov/ammem/amlaw/lwfr.html

21. Collier & Collier, 121, 123.

22. Collier & Collier, 316, 322–323.

23. *Federalist 51*, http://thomas.loc.gov/home/histdox/fed_51.html

24. Quoted in Cecil V. Crabb, Jr., and Pat M. Holt, *Invitation to Struggle* (Washington, DC: CQ Press, 1992), ix.

25. Quoted in Collier & Collier, 340–341.

26. Beeman, 373–376.

27. Pauline Maier, *Ratification: The People Debate the Constitution, 1787–1788* (New York: Simon & Schuster, 2010), 124; Marks, 197.

28. Beeman, 386–90.

29. Beeman, 391–392; Maier, 459.

30. Beeman, 394.

31. Beeman, 395–400.

32. Beeman, 400–403.

33. Maier, 429, 433.

34. Quoted in David P. Currie, *The Constitution in Congress: The Federalist Period, 1789–1801* (University of Chicago Press, 1997), 4n.

35. Maier, 446.

36. Maier, 446.

37. Statutes at Large, I Stat. 119, http://memory.loc.gov/ammem/amlaw/lwsl.html; Richard H. Kohn, *Eagle and Sword* (New York: Free Press, 1975), 108, 126.

38. Currie, 42.

## Chapter 2

1. Charles A. Stevenson, *Congress at War: The Politics of Conflict Since 1789* (Washington, DC: Potomac Books, 2007), 1.

2. Fred I. Greenstein, "The Policy-Driven Leadership of James K. Polk: Making the Most of a Weak Presidency," *Presidential Studies Quarterly*, vol. 40, no. 4, December 2010, 725.

3. Charles A. Stevenson, *Warriors and Politicians: U.S. Civil–Military Relations Under Stress* (London: Rutledge, 2006), 31.

4. Leonard D. White, *The Federalists: A Study in Administrative History, 1789–1801* (New York: Free Press, 1948), 103, 106.

5. White, *Federalists*, 210–236.

6. White, *Federalists*, 61–63; George C. Herring, *From Colony to Superpower: U.S. Foreign Relations Since 1776* (New York: Oxford University Press, 2008), 77–79; Gordon S. Wood, *Empire of Liberty* (New York: Oxford University Press, 2009), 196–199.

7. Kenneth J. Hagan, *This People's Navy* (New York: Free Press, 1991), 32–34, 36–37.

8. Stevenson, *Warriors*, 79–92.

9. Stevenson, *Warriors*, 88–92.

10. Leonard D. White, *The Jeffersonians: A Study in Administrative History, 1801–1829* (New York: Free Press, 1951), 4, 213; Wood, 292.

11. White, *Jeffersonians*, 35, 48, 52.

12. Stevenson, *Congress*, 16.

13. White, *Jeffersonians*, 30–31, 36–37; Stevenson, *Congress*, 38.

14. White, *Jeffersonians*, 248.

15. Herring, 134, 144–151.

16. Herring, 138; 74. William Barnes and John Heath Morgan, *The Foreign Service of the United States* (Washington, DC: Department of State Historical Office, 1961), 74.

17. Herring, 139–143, 155–157.

18. White, *Jeffersonians*, 94, 99.

19. Herring, 178–183.

20. Kinley J. Brauer, "1821–1860: Economics and the Diplomacy of American Expansionism," in William H. Becker and Samuel F. Wells, Jr., eds., *Economics and World Power: An Assessment of American Diplomacy since 1789* (New York: Columbia University Press, 1984), 56–60, 82–83.

21. Herring, 182–183.

22. Herring, 164, 169; Russell F. Weigley, *History of the United States Army, Enlarged Edition* (Bloomington: Indiana University Press, 1984), 161–162.

23. Greenstein, 725.
24. Herring, 191–192.
25. Herring, 198–201.
26. Leonard D. White, *The Jacksonians: A Study in Administrative History, 1829–1861* (New York: Free Press, 1954), 53–54, 63–65.
27. Henry Bartholomew Cox, *War, Foreign Affairs, and Constitutional Power, 1829–1901* (Cambridge, MA: Ballinger, 1984), 147–148; Herring, 201–205.
28. White, *Jacksonians,* 69, 92; Greenstein, 731.
29. Herring, 214–221; Brauer, 104–112.
30. Herring, 210–213, 221; Stevenson, *Congress,* 20.
31. Herring, 228–230, 236–237.
32. Herring, 240–245.
33. See Stevenson, *Warriors,* 230–251.
34. W. Stull Holt, *Treaties Defeated by the Senate* (Baltimore, MD: Johns Hopkins University Press, 1933), 122–124, 139.
35. Leonard D. White, *The Republican Era: A Study in Administrative History, 1869–1901* (New York: Free Press, 1958), 49.
36. Holt, 142–145, 148.
37. David M. Pletcher, "1861–1898: Economic Growth and Diplomatic Adjustment," in Becker & Wells, 120–124, 136, 146.
38. White, *Republican Era,* 158–160.
39. Herring, 308.
40. Herring, 310.
41. Herring, 328; Stevenson, *Congress,* 13–14, 36–37.
42. Herring, 317; White, *Republican Era,* 147–148.
43. Herring, 316–320.
44. Holt, 165–177.
45. Herring, 321–325, 332, 364.
46. Stevenson, *Warriors,* 141; Herring, 367–372.
47. Herring, 345–346; Warren Frederick Ilchman, *Professional Diplomacy in the United States, 1779–1939* (University of Chicago Press, 1961), 3; Barnes, 154.
48. Stevenson, *Warriors,* 143–146, 148.
49. Stevenson, *Warriors,* 149–150.
50. Herring, 372–374.
51. Herring, 358.
52. Herring, 351–352, 356.
53. Herring, 382.
54. Herring, 381, 386, 388–389, 395–396.
55. Herring, 399–401; William H. Becker, "1899–1920: America Adjusts to World Power," in Becker & Wells, 209.
56. Herring, 404–405; Weigley, 348; Hagan, 253.
57. Stevenson, *Congress,* 40, 48.

58. Ernest R. May, *The Ultimate Decision: The President as Commander in Chief* (New York: George Braziller, 1960), 117; Herring, 417–431.

59. Herring, 429–434.

60. Herring, 436.

61. Stevenson, *Congress,* 69; Herring, 439, 452.

62. Herring, 453–455, 489.

63. Richard B. Morris, ed., *Encyclopedia of American History* (New York: Harper & Brothers, 1953), 322–324; Herring, 504–505.

64. Herring, 470–474, 487; Melvyn P. Leffler, "1921–1932: Expansionist Impulses and Domestic Constraints," in Becker & Wells, 254.

65. Becker, in Becker & Wells, 213; Herring, 443.

66. Stevenson, *Warriors,* 96.

67. Ernest R. May, "The Development of Political-Military Consultation in the United States," *Political Science Quarterly,* vol. 70, no. 2 (June 1955), 166–173.

68. May, *Political Science Quarterly,* 172–175; Henry L. Stimson and McGeorge Bundy, *On Active Service in Peace and War* (New York: Harper & Brothers, 1947–48), 495.

69. See Stevenson, *Warriors,* 99–108.

70. Stevenson, *Warriors,* 93, 108–112; Herring, 526, 533–534.

71. Herring, 556–559.

## Chapter 3

1. Morton Halperin, *Bureaucratic Politics and Foreign Policy, Second Edition* (Washington, DC: Brookings, 2006), 226–227.

2. Foreign Assistance Act of 1961, Public Law 87–195, sect. 620G and sect. 602.

3. Public Law 105–277, sect. 103.

4. 1 Statutes at Large 96, 561.

5. Public Law 104–201, sect. 1411.

6. Richard E. Neustadt, *Presidential Power and the Modern Presidents, Revised Edition* (New York: Free Press, 1991).

7. See John Yoo memo at www.justice.gov/olc/warpowers925.htm

8. Theodore Sorensen, *Decision-Making in the White House* (New York: Columbia University Press, 1964), 44.

9. Alexander L. George, *Presidential Decision-Making in Foreign Policy: The Effective Use of Information and Advice* (New York: Westview, 1980).

10. Thomas Preston, *The President and His Inner Circle* (New York: Columbia University Press, 2001).

11. Gordon M. Goldstein, *Lessons in Disaster: McGeorge Bundy and the Path to War in Vietnam* (New York: Henry Holt, 2008), 207.

12. Henry L. Stimson and McGeorge Bundy, *On Active Service in Peace and War* (New York: Harper & Brothers, 1947–48), 495.

13. Mark A. Stoler, *Allies and Adversaries* (Chapel Hill: University of North Carolina Press, 2000), 103.

14. See Charles A. Stevenson, "Underlying Assumptions of the National Security Act of 1947," *Joint Forces Quarterly*, 48 (1st quarter 2008), 129–133.

15. Public Law 80–253, sect. 101(a).

16. Ivo M. Saalder and I. M. Destler, *In the Shadow of the Oval Office* (New York: Simon & Schuster, 2009), 70; David Auerswald, "The Evolution of the NSC Process," in Roger Z. George and Harvey Rishikof, *The National Security Enterprise: Navigating the Labyrinth* (Washington, DC: Georgetown University Press, 2011), 40; David Rothkopf, *Running the World* (Public Affairs, 2005), 267; John P. Burke, *Honest Broker?* (College Station: Texas A&M University Press, 2009), 347.

17. Saalder & Destler, 68.

18. Auerswald, 35.

19. See Burke, *Honest Broker?*

20. Saalder & Destler, 70.

21. Rothkopf, 407.

22. Memorandum from James L. Jones, "The 21st Century Interagency Process," March 18, 2009, www.fas.org/irp/offdocs/ppd/nsc031909.pdf

23. Auerswald, 33.

24. Rothkopf, 405.

25. This section is based on www.ndu.edu/icaf/outreach/publications/nspp/docs/icaf-nsc-policy-process-report-10–2010.pdf, 35–45.

26. Morton H. Halperin et al., *Bureaucratic Politics and Foreign Policy, Second Edition* (Washington, DC: Brookings, 2006), 131.

27. George Tenet, *At the Center of the Storm* (New York: HarperCollins, 2007), 449–475.

28. Saalder & Destler, 218.

29. See Peter Feaver and William Inboden, "A Strategic Planning Cell on National Security at the White House," in Daniel W. Drezner, ed., *Avoiding Trivia: The Role of Strategic Planning in American Foreign Policy* (Washington, DC: Brookings, 2009), 98–112.

## Chapter 4

1. Cecil V. Crabb, Jr., and Pat M. Holt, *Invitation to Struggle* (Washington, DC: CQ Press, 1992), 242, 187.

2. Rebecca K. C. Hersman, *Friends and Foes* (Washington, DC: Brookings, 2000), 67–70.

3. Crabb & Holt, 237–238; Patrick J. Haney, "Why Do We Still Have an Embargo of Cuba?" in Ralph G. Carter, *Contemporary Cases in U.S. Foreign Policy: From Terrorism to Trade, Fourth Edition,* (Washington, DC: CQ Press, 2011), 340.

4. Michael John Garcia and R. Chuck Mason, "Congressional Oversight and Related Issues Concerning International Security

Agreements Concluded by the United States," *CRS Report for Congress,* October 1, 2009, 3.

5. Glen S. Krutz and Jeffrey S. Peake, *Treaty Politics and the Rise of Executive Agreements* (Ann Arbor: University of Michigan Press, 2009), 71–73.

6. U.S. Congress, Senate Committee on Foreign Relations, *Treaty With Russia on Measures for Further Reduction and Limitation of Strategic Offensive Arms (The New START Treaty),* Executive Report, 111th Cong., 2d sess., October 1, 2010, Exec. Rept. 111–6.

7. Lee H. Hamilton with Jordan Tama, *A Creative Tension: The Foreign Policy Roles of the President and Congress* (Washington, DC: Woodrow Wilson Center Press, 2002), 56.

8. See Thomas E. Mann and Norman J. Ornstein, *The Broken Branch: How Congress Is Failing America and How to Get It Back on Track* (New York: Oxford University Press, 2006); David Epstein and Sharyn O'Halloran, *Delegating Powers: A Transaction Cost Politics Approach to Policy Making Under Separate Powers* (New York: Cambridge University Press, 1999).

9. Gerald Felix Warburg, "Congress; Checking Presidential Power," in Roger Z. George and Harvey Rishikof, eds., *The National Security Enterprise: Navigating the Labyrinth* (Washington, DC: Georgetown University Press, 2011), 230–234.

10. Hamilton, 7.

11. Hamilton, 60.

12. Alexis de Tocqueville, *Democracy in America,* vol. 1 (New York: Vintage Books, 1945), 243.

13. David R. Mayhew, "Actions in the Public Sphere," in Paul J. Quirk and Sarah A. Binder, *The Legislative Branch* (New York: Oxford University Press, 2005), 71.

14. James M. Lindsay, *Congress and the Politics of U.S. Foreign Policy* (Baltimore, MD: Johns Hopkins University Press, 1994), 4.

15. Quoted in Stephen R. Weissman, *A Culture of Deference* (New York: Basic Books, 1995), 14.

16. Quoted in Weissman, 12.

17. Weissman, 14.

18. Bruce W. Jentleson and Rebecca L. Britton, "Still Pretty Prudent," *Journal of Conflict Resolution,* vol. 42, no. 4 (August 1998), 395–417.

19. Ralph G. Carter and James M. Scott, *Choosing to Lead: Understanding Congressional Foreign Policy Entrepreneurs* (Durham, NC: Duke University Press, 2009), 27, 224–225.

20. See Charles A. Stevenson, *Congress at War: The Politics of Conflict Since 1789* (Washington, DC: Potomac Books, 2007), 11–33.

21. Hamilton, 64.

22. David P. Auerswald and Peter F. Cowhey, "Ballotbox Diplomacy: The War Powers Resolution and the Use of Force," *International Studies Quarterly,* vol. 41 (1997), 507.

23. Stevenson, *Congress at War,* 54–55.
24. Stevenson, *Congress at War,* 4.
25. Crabb & Holt, ix.

## Chapter 5

1. *John Quincy Adams Memoirs,* vol. vii (Philadelphia, PA: Lippincott, 1875), 359.
2. Shelley Lynne Tomkin, *Inside OMB* (Armonk, NY: M.E. Sharpe, 1998), 55, 62.
3. Gordon Adams, "The Office of Management and Budget: The President's Policy Tool," in Roger Z. George and Harvey Rishikof, *The National Security Enterprise: Navigating the Labyrinth* (Washington, DC: Georgetown University Press, 2011), 58. For a comprehensive look at budgeting for defense, international affairs, and homeland security, see Gordon Adams and Cindy Williams, *Buying National Security* (New York: Routledge, 2009).
4. Adams, 56, 63–64; Tomkin, 118–137.
5. Tomkin, 121–125.
6. See "How Government Plays the Budget Game," *National Journal,* September 30, 2002.
7. Adams, 76.
8. Louis Fisher, *Presidential Spending Power* (Princeton University Press, 1975), 238; William C. Banks and Peter Raven-Hansen, *National Security Law and the Power of the Purse* (New York: Oxford University Press, 1994), 71–72.
9. Public Law 112–81, sect. 1207.
10. The HELP Commission Report on Foreign Assistance Reform, Beyond Assistance, December 2007, 30.
11. Fisher, 204–207.
12. See www.wired.com/dangerroom/2009/05/pentagons-black-budget-grows-to-more-than-50-billion/. For more on secret spending, see Banks & Raven-Hansen, 51–52, 100–105.

## Chapter 6

1. Arthur M. Schlesinger, Jr., *A Thousand Days: John F. Kennedy in the White House* (Boston: Houghton Mifflin, 1965), 406.
2. *Foreign Relations of the United States, 1969–76,* vol. II (Washington, DC: U.S. Government Printing Office), 768.
3. U.S. Statutes, I, 28–29; 22 U.S. Code 2656.
4. Leonard D. White, *The Federalists* (New York: Free Press, 1948), 136.
5. Center for Strategic and International Studies (CSIS), *The Embassy of the Future* (Washington, DC: Center for Strategic and International Studies, 2007), 47.
6. Edward Peck, "Chief of Mission Authority: A Powerful but Underused Tool," *Foreign Service Journal,* December 2007, 30; Robert B. Oakley

and Michael Casey, Jr., "The Country Team: Restructuring America's First Line of Engagement," *JFQ*, 47 (4th quarter 2007), 150.

7. Oakley & Casey, 150.

8. Oakley & Casey, 146.

9. See U.S. Senate Foreign Relations Committee, "Iraq: The Transition From a Military Mission to a Civilian-Led Effort," Committee Print, S. Prt. 112–3, January 31, 2011, 7; Karen DeYoung, "U.S. Evaluating Size of Baghdad Embassy, Officials Say," *Washington Post*, February 17, 2012.

10. Marc Grossman, "The State Department: Culture as Interagency Destiny?" in Roger Z. George and Harvey Rishikof, eds., *The National Security Enterprise: Navigating the Labyrinth* (Washington, DC: Georgetown University Press, 2011), 80.

11. Advisory Committee on Transformational Diplomacy, *Final Report of the State Department in 2025 Working Group*, U.S. Department of State, 2008, 28.

12. Frederick C. Smith and Franklin C. Miller, "The Office of Secretary of Defense: Civilian Masters?" in George & Rishikof, 109.

13. Data from American Foreign Service Association.

14. William Barnes and John Heath Morgan, *The Foreign Service of the United States* (Washington, DC: Department of State, 1961), 207.

15. Harry W. Kopp and Charles A. Gillespie, *Career Diplomacy: Life and Work in the U.S. Foreign Service* (Washington, DC: Georgetown University Press, 2008), 20.

16. "A More Representative Foreign Service," Association for Diplomatic Studies and Training, www.usdiplomacy.org

17. Grossman, 83.

18. Henry A. Kissinger, *Years of Upheaval* (New York: Little, Brown, 1982), 442–443.

19. Alexander M. Haig, Jr., *Caveat: Realism, Reagan, and Foreign Policy* (New York: Scribner, 1984), 27; James A. Baker, III, *The Politics of Diplomacy: Revolution, War, and Peace, 1989–1992* (New York: G.P. Putnam's Sons, 1995), 31.

20. Col. Rickey L. Rife, "Defense Is From Mars, State Is From Venus," Army War College, 1998.

21. Rife, "Defense Is From Mars, State Is From Venus."

22. Jim Hoagland, "Fighting Iran—With Patience," *Washington Post*, February 25, 2007.

23. Project on National Security Reform, "Ensuring Security in an Unpredictable World, Preliminary Findings," July 2008, 36–37.

24. Center for Strategic and International Studies (CSIS) Report, *A Steep Hill: Congress and U.S. Efforts to Strengthen Fragile States*, March 2008, 23.

25. Figures based on congressional action in annual budget resolutions as reported in *CQ Almanacs*.

26. Charles Flickner, "Removing Impediments to an Effective Partnership With Congress," in Lael Brainard, ed., *Security by Other Means* (Washington, DC: Brookings, 2007), 242; CSIS Report, *A Steep Hill,* app. G, 85.

## Chapter 7

1. Stephen D. Cohen, *The Making of United States International Economic Policy, Fifth Edition* (Westport, CT: Praeger, 2000), 263.
2. David A. Baldwin, *Economic Statecraft* (Princeton, NJ: Princeton University Press, 1985), 41–42.
3. Lael Brainard, *Security by Other Means* (Washington, DC: CSIS & Brookings, 2007), 18.
4. The Fed is legally independent of the Treasury Department, though they try to harmonize their operations. Decentralization is built into the system, with 5 of the 12 members of the Fed's key open market committee chosen by regional banks dominated by local banking interests.
5. Cohen, 5.
6. Commerce Department figures; Benn Steil and Robert E. Litan, *Financial Statecraft* (New Haven, CT: Yale University Press, 2006), 3.
7. Joan E. Spero and Jeffrey A. Hart, *The Politics of International Economic Relations, Sixth Edition* (New York: Thomson/Wadsworth, 2003), 387–388.
8. Index of Global Philanthropy and Remittances 2010, www.hudson.org/files/pdf_upload/Index_of_Global_Philanthropy_and_Remittances_2010
9. See KeithHennessey.com, "Roles of the President's White House Economic Advisors," August 8, 2010.
10. Brian Katz, "International Trade and Economic Policy, Planning and Strategy in the USG: The National Economic Council (NEC)," paper for the Project on National Security Reform, 2008.
11. George Thomas Kurian, ed., *A Historical Guide to the U.S. Government* (New York: Oxford University Press, 1998), 235–241.
12. Cohen, 47.
13. Gordon Adams and Cindy Williams, *Buying National Security* (New York: Routledge, 2010), 55.
14. Department of Commerce homepage, www.commerce.gov/about-department-commerce
15. Cohen, 55–57.
16. Cohen, 12.
17. Steven Radelet, "Strengthening U.S. Development Assistance," in Brainard, 94.
18. Adams & Williams, 86–90.
19. Adams & Williams, 64.
20. Adams & Williams, 90–92.

21. Adams & Williams, 62–64.
22. Gary Clyde Hufbauer et al., *Economic Sanctions Reconsidered, Third Edition* (Washington, DC: Peterson Institute for International Economics, 2009), 148–154.
23. Steil & Litan, 27.
24. Vivian C. Jones et al., "Trade Preferences: Economic Issues and Policy Options," *CRS Report for Congress,* September 24, 2010.
25. William H. Cooper, "Free Trade Agreements: Impact on U.S. Trade and Implications for U.S. Trade Policy," *CRS Report for Congress,* February 23, 2010.
26. Vivian C. Jones, "Trade Remedies: A Primer," *CRS Report for Congress,* July 30, 2008.
27. Radelet in Brainard, 94.
28. Gerald F. Hyman, "A Cabinet-Level Development Agency: Right Problem, Wrong Solution," Center for Strategic and International Studies (CSIS), January 2009, 2.
29. Brainard, 33.
30. For QDDR, see www.state.gov/s/dmr/qddr/index.htm
31. Brainard, 5.
32. Curt Tarnoff et al., "Foreign Aid: An Introduction to U.S. Programs and Policy," *CRS Report for Congress,* February 10, 2009.
33. Public Law 112–81, sect. 1207.
34. Adams & Williams, 67–77.
35. Adams & Williams, 46–49.
36. Adams & Williams, 86–90.
37. Spero & Hart, 14–24.
38. Steil & Litan, 3.
39. Steil & Litan, 32–41.
40. Steil & Litan, 64–66.
41. Spero & Hart, 148.
42. James K. Jackson, "U.S. Direct Investment Abroad: Trends and Current Issues," *CRS Report for Congress,* February 1, 2011.
43. James K. Jackson, "Foreign Direct Investment in the United States: An Economic Analysis," *CRS Report for Congress,* February 1, 2011; Michael V. Seitzinger, "Foreign Investment in the United States: Major Federal Statutory Restrictions," *CRS Report for Congress,* January 26, 2009.
44. James K. Jackson, "The Committee on Foreign Investment in the United States (CFIUS)," *CRS Report for Congress,* February 4, 2010; CFIUS Report to Congress, November, 2010.
45. Edward M. Graham and David M. Marchick, *U.S. National Security and Foreign Direct Investment* (Washington, DC: Institute for International Economics, May 2006), 128–141.
46. See Graham & Marchick, 95–121.

## Chapter 8

1. Dana Priest, *The Mission* (New York: W. W. Norton, 2003), 14.
2. Oral history interview, Historical Office of the Secretary of Defense, May 18, 2001, 9.
3. Joint publication 3–0, Joint Operations, 22 March 2010, I-2.
4. Joint Publication 1, Doctrine for the Armed Forces of the United States, 20 March 2009, xi.
5. Joint Publication 1, x.
6. Carl von Clausewitz, Michael Howard, and Peter Paret, eds., *On War* (Princeton, NJ: Princeton University Press, 1982), 87.
7. Michael Meese and Isaiah Wilson III, "The Military: Forging a Joint Warrior Culture," in Roger Z. George and Harvey Rishikof, eds., *The National Security Enterprise: Navigating the Labyrinth* (Washington, DC: Georgetown University Press, 2011), 125.
8. Charles A. Stevenson, *Congress at War: The Politics of Conflict Since 1789* (Washington, DC: Potomac Books, 2007), 38.
9. Kenneth J. Hagan, *This People's Navy* (New York: Free Press, 1991), 194–195, 208–209; John Whiteclay Chambers II, ed., *The Oxford Companion to American Military History* (Oxford University Press, 1999), 488–489.
10. Charles A. Stevenson, *SecDef: The Nearly Impossible Job of Secretary of Defense* (Washington, DC: Potomac Books, 2006), 7.
11. See Charles A. Stevenson, *Warriors and Politicians: U.S. Civil–Military Relations Under Stress* (New York: Routledge, 2006), 205–209.
12. Bradley Graham, *By His Own Rules* (New York: Public Affairs, 2009), 216.
13. 2010 U.S. Census; Population Representation in the Military Services, Defense Equal Opportunity Management Institute (DEOMI), Fiscal Year 2008 Report.
14. Population Representation in the Military Services, Fiscal Year 2008 Report.
15. Harvey M. Sapolsky et al., *U.S. Defense Politics* (New York: Routledge, 2009), 31.
16. Lawrence Kapp, "Reserve Component Personnel Issues: Questions and Answers," *CRS Report for Congress,* February 10, 2009; Michael Waterhouse and JoAnne O'Bryant, "National Guard Personnel and Deployments: Fact Sheet," *CRS Report for Congress,* January 17, 2008.
17. Col. Rickey L. Rife, "Defense Is From Mars, State Is From Venus," Army War College, 1998.
18. Meese & Wilson, 127–130.
19. Frederick C. Smith and Franklin C. Miller, "The Office of the Secretary of Defense: Civilian Masters?" in George & Rishikof, 109–111.
20. DOD FY 2011 Budget Presentation, 7–11.
21. Stevenson, *SecDef,* 190.

22. R. Chuck Mason, "Securing America's Borders: The Role of the Military," *CRS Report for Congress,* June 16, 2010.
23. See Charles A. Stevenson, *Congress at War* (Washington, DC: Potomac Books, 2007), 4.
24. Walter Pincus, "The Pentagon's New View of Warfare," *Washington Post,* February 6, 2012.
25. Richard A. Best, Jr., and Andrew Feickert, "Special Operations Forces (SOF) and CIA Paramilitary Operations: Issues for Congress," *CRS Report for Congress,* August 3, 2009.
26. U.S. Statistical Abstract, 2011, 338.
27. Gordon Adams and Cindy Williams, *Buying National Security* (New York: Routledge, 2010), 86–90.
28. Smith & Miller, 111–113.
29. David Rothkopf, *Running the World* (New York: Public Affairs, 2005), 419.

**Chapter 9**

1. James B. Steinberg, "The Policymaker's Perspective: Transparency and Partnership," in Roger Z. George and James B. Bruce, eds., *Analyzing Intelligence* (Washington, DC: Georgetown University Press, 2008), 83.
2. William J. Daugherty, "The Role of Covert Action," in Loch K. Johnson, ed., *Handbook of Intelligence Studies* (New York: Routledge, 2007), 279.
3. Dana Priest and William M. Arkin, *Top Secret America* (New York: Little, Brown, 2011), 18.
4. Robert M. Gates, *From the Shadows* (New York: Simon & Schuster, 1996), 33.
5. I Statutes at Large, 128–129, July 1, 1790. A similar provision allowing secret expenditures is still on the books (31 USC 3526 [e]).
6. Godfrey Hodgson, *The Colonel: The Life and Wars of Henry Stimson, 1867–1950* (New York: Knopf, 1990), 203.
7. Priest & Arkin, 100, 103. Their figure for the Office of the Director of National Intelligence (ODNI) staff also includes personnel attached to the National Counterterrorism Center (NCTC).
8. Public Law 108–458, sect. 1018, of the Intelligence Reform and Terrorism Prevention Act of 2004.
9. Thomas Fingar, "Office of the Director of National Intelligence: Promising Start Despite Ambiguity, Ambivalence, and Animosity," in Roger Z. George and Harvey Rishikof, *The National Security Enterprise: Navigating the Labyrinth* (Washington, DC: Georgetown University Press, 2011), 139, 149; Richard A. Best, Jr., "Intelligence Reform After Five Years: The Role of the Director of National Intelligence (DNI)," *CRS Report for Congress,* June 22, 2010.
10. Priest & Arkin, 97.

11. Fingar, 142.
12. Fingar, 148.
13. Roger Z. George, "Central Intelligence Agency: The President's Own," in George & Rishikof, 158.
14. Gates, 563–564.
15. Richard A. Clarke, *Against All Enemies* (New York: Free Press, 2004), 277; George, 161.
16. Gordon Adams and Cindy Williams, *Buying National Security* (New York: Routledge, 2010), 123.
17. George, 160.
18. Quoted in George, 159.
19. George, 164; Walter Pincus and Dana Priest, "Some Iraq Analysts Felt Pressure From Cheney Visits," *Washington Post,* June 5, 2003.
20. Adams & Williams, 124.
21. Adams & Williams, 123. Another recent source says NSA has "35,000+" personnel. Matthew Aid, *Intel Wars: The Secret History of the Fight Against Terror* (New York: Bloomsbury Press, 2012), 44, also has higher figures for other parts of the IC: CIA, 25,000; NRO, 4,500; NGIA, 16,000.
22. Adams & Williams, 124–125.
23. Adams & Williams, 125–126.
24. Adams & Williams, 127–128.
25. Adams & Williams, 126–129.
26. Greg Miller, "27% of U.S. Spy Work Is Outsourced," *Los Angeles Times,* August 28, 2008. Priest & Arkin, 181, say the figure is 29% of the workforce in the IC are contractors.
27. Mark M. Lowenthal, *Intelligence: From Secrets to Policy, Fourth Edition,* (Washington, DC: CQ Press, 2009), 66.
28. Lowenthal, 82–107.
29. Priest & Arkin, 77.
30. Presidential Policy Directive (PPD) 35 Intelligence Requirements, March 2, 1995, www.fas.org/irp/offdocs/pdd35.htm
31. Paul R. Pillar, "Adapting Intelligence to Changing Issues," in Johnson, *Handbook,* 151–152; Lowenthal, 59, 73–74.
32. See Paul R. Pillar, *Intelligence and U.S. Foreign Policy* (New York: Columbia University Press, 2011) and Joshua Rovner, *Fixing the Facts* (New York: Cornell University Press, 2011).
33. Quoted in Lowenthal, 111.
34. Lowenthal, 186.
35. Lowenthal, 120–121, 125–126.
36. Gates, 56.
37. Pillar, *Intelligence and U.S. Foreign Policy,* 139.
38. Lowenthal, 63.
39. George, 163, 159; Walter Pincus, "Measuring a President's Approach on Foreign Policy," *Washington Post,* January 17, 2012.
40. Priest & Arkin, 80, 81.

41. Pillar, 200.
42. George, 160.
43. Quoted in William J. Daugherty, *Executive Secrets* (Lexington: University Press of Kentucky, 2006) 13.
44. Daugherty, *Executive Secrets,* 14.
45. Daugherty, *Executive Secrets,* 71–89; Daugherty, *Handbook,* 280–283, 291.
46. Jeffrey T. Richelson, *The U.S. Intelligence Community, Fifth Edition,* (New York: Westview, 2008), 420–424; Yochi Dreazen and Marc Ambinder, "CIA Deploys to Libya as White House Authorizes Direct Assistance to Rebels," *National Journal,* March 30, 2011.
47. Jennifer D. Kibbe, "Covert Action, Pentagon Style," in Loch K. Johnson, ed., *The Oxford Handbook of National Security Intelligence* (New York: Oxford University Press, 2010), 571, 576.
48. Public Law 102–88.
49. Daugherty, *Executive Secrets,* 101–107.
50. Daugherty, *Executive Secrets,* 34.
51. Gates, 567–568.
52. Steinberg, 83–84.
53. John McLaughlin, "Serving the National Policymaker," in George & Bruce, 72.
54. Mark M. Lowenthal, "The Policymaker–Intelligence Relationship, in Johnson, *Oxford Handbook,* 439–440.
55. McLaughlin, 74–78.
56. David Ignatius, "Obama's Intelligence Retooling," *Washington Post,* June 9, 2010; Josh Gerstein, "Panel Found 'Distracted' DNI," *Politico,* June 2, 2010.
57. Pillar, 5.
58. Quotations are in David M. Barrett, *The CIA and Congress* (Lawrence: University Press of Kansas, 2005), 3, and Daugherty, *Executive Secrets,* 92.
59. Barrett, 458–460, 102–112.
60. Loch K, Johnson, "A Shock Theory of Congressional Accountability for Intelligence," in Johnson, *Handbook,* 343.
61. Daugherty, *Executive Secrets,* 95; L. Britt Snider, *The Agency and the Hill,* CIA Center for the Study of Intelligence, www.cia.gov/library/center-for-the-study-of-intelligence/csi-publications/books-and-monographs/agency-and-the-hill/index.html

## Chapter 10

1. Hart–Rudman Commission, *New World Coming: American Security in the 21st Century,* September 15, 1999, i–vii.
2. Tom Ridge, *The Test of Our Times* (New York: St. Martin's Press, 2009), 277.
3. Richard H. Ward, Kathleen L. Kiernan, and Daniel Mabrey, *Homeland Security: An Introduction* (LexisNexis, 2006), 11.

4. Donald F. Kettl, *System Under Stress: Homeland Security and American Politics, Second Edition* (Washington, DC: CQ Press, 2007), 106–107; Ward et al., 246.

5. Kettl, 54–55.

6. Public Law 107–296, sect. 101.

7. Gordon Adams and Cindy Williams, *Buying National Security* (Routledge, 2010), 141–143; Office of Management and Budget, 2012 Budget, Analytical Perspectives, 403–410.

8. Ward et al., 110–111.

9. Department of Homeland Security, 2012 Budget in Brief, 95–97, www.dhs.gov/xlibrary/assets/budget-bib-fy2012.pdf

10. See www.nctc.gov/about_us/about_nctc.html

11. Project on National Security Reform (PNSR), Toward Integrating Complex National Missions Lessons From the National Counterterrorism Center's Directorate of Strategic Operational Planning, February 2010, www.pnsr.org/data/files/pnsr_nctc_dsop_report.pdf

12. Mark A. Randol, "The Department of Homeland Security Intelligence Enterprise: Operational Overview and Oversight Challenges for Congress," *CRS Report for Congress,* March 19, 2010.

13. Government Accountability Office, "High-Risk Series: An Update," Report to Congressional Committees, February 2011, 91–110, www.gao.gov/new.items/d11278.pdf

14. A list of the various sector plans can be found at www.dhs.gov/files/programs/gc_1179866197607.shtm

15. Ward et al., 118.

16. McAfee/CSIS Report, *In the Dark: Crucial Industries Confront Cyberattacks,* April 2011, http://www.mcafee.com/us/resources/reports/rp-critical-infrastructure-protection.pdf

17. Center for a New American Security, "America's Cyber Future: Security and Prosperity in the Information Age," vol. 1, June 2011, www.cnas.org/files/documents/publications/CNAS_Cyber_VolumeOI_0.pdf

18. See White House Fact Sheet: "The Administration's Cybersecurity Accomplishments," May 12, 2011.

19. Dana Priest and William M. Arkin, *Top Secret America* (Little, Brown, 2011), 88.

20. Siobahn Gorman, "Chamber Critical of White House Cybersecurity Plan," *Wall Street Journal,* May 26, 2011.

21. Gary M. Shiffman and Jonathan Hoffman, "The Department of Homeland Security: Chief of Coordination," in Roger Z. George and Harvey Rishikof, eds., *The National Security Enterprise: Navigating the Labyrinth* (Washington, DC: Georgetown University Press, 2011), 216.

22. Shiffman & Hoffman, 209.

23. Statement for the Record, The Honorable Janet Napolitano, Secretary, U.S. Department of Homeland Security, Before the U.S. Sen-

ate Committee on Homeland Security and Governmental Affairs, February 17, 2011.

24. Ward et al., 142.

25. Ward et al., 234.

26. Kettl, 79; Shiffman & Hoffman, 217.

27. Shiffman & Hoffman, 204, 219.

28. Michael A. Sheehan, *Crush the Cell: How to Defeat Terrorism Without Terrorizing Ourselves* (New York: Crown, 2008), 7.

29. John Mueller and Mark G. Stewart, "Terror, Security, and Money: Balancing the Risks, Benefits, and Costs of Homeland Security," paper prepared for Annual Convention of the Midwest Political Science Association, Chicago, IL, April 1, 2011.

30. Public Law 107–296, sect. 903.

31. Statement by the president on the White House Organization for Homeland Security and Counterterrorism, May 26, 2009.

32. See GAO report at www.gao.gov/new.items/d11278.pdf

33. Project on National Security Reform (PNSR), *Forging a New Shield Executive Summary*, December 2008, 486.

34. See agency rankings at http://bestplacestowork.org/BPTW/rankings/overall/large

35. James A. Thomson, "DHS AWOL?" RAND Review, Spring 2007.

36. Stephen Flynn, "Recalibrating Homeland Security," *Foreign Affairs*, May–June 2011, 130–140.

37. Paul Rosenzweig, Jena Baker McNeill, and James Jay Califano, "Stopping the Chaos: A Proposal for Reorganization of Congressional Oversight of the Department of Homeland Security," Web-Memo by the Heritage Foundation, November 4, 2010.

38. Timothy Balunis, Jr., and William Hemphill, "Escaping the Entanglement: Reversing Jurisdictional Fragmentation Over the Department of Homeland Security," *Journal of Homeland Security and Emergency Management*, vol. 6, is. 1 (2009), art. 58.

39. See DHS list at http://www.dhs.gov/files/international/counter terrorism.shtm

40. Presidential Policy Directive (PPD) 8, "National Preparedness," March 30, 2011.

41. Napolitano testimony, February 17, 2011.

## Chapter 11

1. George W. Bush, *The National Security Strategy of the United States*, September 2002.

2. Barack Obama, *The National Security Strategy of the United States*, May 2010.

3. For more on these activities, see Paul B. Stares and Micah Zenko, "Partners in Preventive Action: The United States and International Institutions," Council on Foreign Relations, September 2011.

4.  Margaret P. Karns and Karen A. Mingst, *International Organizations, Second Edition* (Boulder, CO: Kynne Rienner, 2010), 17, 26.

5.  Karns & Mingst, 274–279.

6.  Linda Fasulop, *An Insider's Guide to the UN, Second Edition,* (New Haven CT: Yale University Press, 2009), 96; the State Department voting report can be found at www.state.gov/documents/organization/139481.pdf

7.  J. Samuel Barkin, *International Organizations* (New York: Palgrave Macmillan, 2006), 59.

8.  Karns & Mingst, 111.

9.  Karns & Mingst, 312–315.

10. Karns & Mingst, 329, 331; Fasulo, 114–118; Marjorie Ann Browne, "United Nations Peacekeeping: Issues for Congress," *CRS Report for Congress,* August 13, 2010.

11. Karns & Mingst, 319.

12. Barkin, 72.

13. Fasulo, 203–207.

14. Ellen Hallams, *The United States and NATO Since 9/11* (New York: Routledge, 2010), 58.

15. International Institute for Strategic Studies, *Strategic Survey 2010: The Annual Review of World Affairs* (London: Routledge, 2010), 77–80.

16. Karns & Mingst, 182–183.

17. Karns & Mingst, 189–190.

18. Karns & Mingst, 198.

19. Karns & Mingst, 200–201.

20. Barkin, 95.

21. Karns & Mingst, 403.

22. Karns & Mingst, 403–405; Barkin, 106.

23. James Raymond Vreeland, *The International Monetary Fund* (London: Routledge, 2007), 41–44.

24. 2009 Report to Congress by the National Advisory Council on International Monetary and Financial Policies, U.S. Treasury Department, August 5, 2010.

25. Barkin, 91–93; Karns & Mingst, 415; Kent Jones, *The Doha Blues* (New York: Oxford University Press, 2010), 51.

26. Raymond J. Ahearn and Ian F. Fergusson, "World Trade Organization (WTO): Issues in the Debate on Continued U.S. Participation," *CRS Report for Congress,* June 16, 2010.

27. Jeffrey L. Dunoff, "Does the United States Support International Tribunals? The Case of the Multilateral Trade System," in Cesare P. R. Romano, ed., *The Sword and the Scales: The United States and International Courts and Tribunals* (New York: Cambridge University Press, 2009), 354.

28. Romano, xiii.

29. John R. Crook, "The U.S. and International Claims and Compensation Bodies," in Romano, 297–321.

30. Sean D. Murphy, "The United States and the International Court of Justice: Coping With Antinomies," in Romano, 65–66.
31. Murphy, 78, 66–67; Romano, 429–430.
32. Steven Kull and Clay Ramsay, "American Public Opinion on International Courts and Tribunals," in Romano, 12–29.
33. John P. Cerone, "U.S. Attitudes Toward International Criminal Courts and Tribunals," in Romano, 150–156.
34. Cerone, 182.
35. Romano, 423.
36. Karns & Mingst, 222, 235.

## Chapter 12

1. Thomas Knecht, *Paying Attention to Foreign Affairs: How Public Opinion Affects Presidential Decision Making* (Pennsylvania State University Press, 2010), 3.
2. Quoted in Timothy E. Cook, *Governing With the News: The News Media as a Political Institution* (University of Chicago Press, 1998), 131, and dated May 12, 1992.
3. Quoted in Gary J. Andres, *Lobbying Reconsidered* (New York: Pearson Longman, 2009), 192.
4. Knecht, 9.
5. Knecht, 205.
6. Douglas C. Foyle, *Counting the Public In: Presidents, Public Opinion, and Foreign Policy* (Columbia University Press, 1999), 267–268.
7. Foyle, 268.
8. Steven W. Hook, *U.S. Foreign Policy: The Paradox of World Power, Third Edition* (CQ Press, 2010), 214.
9. See www.worldpublicopinion.org/pipa/articles/brunitedstatescanadara/238.php?nid=&id=&pnt=238 and www.cbsnews.com/stories/2007/09/12/opinion/pollpositions/main3253552.shtml
10. First examples at www.publicagenda.org; Liberia examples in George F. Bishop, *The Illusion of Public Opinion* (Rowman & Littlefield, 2005), xiii–xiv.
11. Yankelovich's views are discussed in Jim Willis, *The Media Effect* (Praeger, 2007), 63.
12. See report at www.cfr.org/thinktank/iigg/pop/about.html
13. Bruce W. Jentleson and Rebecca L. Britton, "Still Pretty Prudent," *Journal of Conflict Resolution*, vol. 42, no. 4 (August 1998), 395–417.
14. Wolfowitz quote cited in *USA Today*, May 30, 2003; Shoon Kathleen Murray and Christopher Spinosa, "The Post-9/11 Shift in Public Opinion: How Long Will It Last?" in Eugene R. Wittkopf and James M. McCormick, eds., *The Domestic Sources of American Foreign Policy, Fourth Edition* (Lanham, MD: Rowman & Littlefield 2004), 103, 105; Hook, 230.

15. Foyle, 46–47.
16. Peter D. Feaver and Christopher Gelpi, *Choosing Your Battles* (Princeton University Press, 2004), 103–105, 134–140, 185–186; Feaver document quoted in Hook, 229.
17. Bob Woodward, *State of Denial* (New York: Simon & Schuster, 2006), 326.
18. Foyle, 208.
19. Knecht, 215.
20. Quoted in Brandon Rottinghaus, "Presidential Leadership on Foreign Policy, Opinion Polling, and the Possible Limits of 'Crafted Talk,'" *Political Communication*, 25 (2008), 139.
21. A point made in the 1960s by Douglass Cater, who called the press "the fourth branch of government." Cater is quoted and discussed in Cook, 1–2.
22. Doris A. Graber, *Mass Media and American Politics, Eighth Edition* (CQ Press, 2010), 228–230.
23. Graber, 305.
24. Morton Halperin, *Bureaucratic Politics and Foreign Policy, Second Edition,* (Brookings, 2006), 182–183.
25. Richard T. Cooper and Faye Fiore, "In Politics, Leaking Stories Is a Fine Art," *Los Angeles Times,* April 9, 2006.
26. Halperin, 185–188.
27. Graber, 307.
28. Alex Mintz and Karl DeRouen, Jr., *Understanding Foreign Policy Decision Making* (Cambridge University Press, 2010), 161.
29. Data are from Pew Center reports available at www.journalism.org
30. Pew report for 2011 at http://stateofthemedia.org/2011/overview-2/
31. Allan J. Cigler and Burdett A. Loomis, eds., *Interest Group Politics, Eighth Edition* (CQ Press, 2012), 3–4.
32. David M. Paul and Rachel Anderson Paul, *Ethnic Lobbies and U.S. Foreign Policy* (Lynne Rienner, 2009), 14.
33. Frank R. Baumgartner et al., *Lobbying and Policy Change* (University of Chicago Press, 2009), 239, 193.
34. Within government, stakeholders are those agencies and offices that have some authorities or responsibilities related to the issue under review, such as all the entities related to policy toward, say, China or export of warplanes to Saudi Arabia. Outside of government, stakeholders are those who believe their interests are already affected, or likely to be affected, by a policy being considered.
35. Paul & Paul, 24.
36. Thomas Ambrosio, ed., *Ethnic Identity Groups and U.S. Foreign Policy* (Westport, CT: Praeger, 2002), 10.
37. Quoted in Thomas, 151.
38. Thomas, 152–153.
39. Thomas, 177.
40. Data at www.opensecrets.org

41. Gerald Warburg, "Lobbyists: U.S. National Security and Special Interests," in Roger Z. George & Harvey Rishikof, *The National Security Enterprise: Navigating the Labyrinth* (Washington, DC: Georgetown University Press, 2011), 270; Kim Eisler, "Hired Guns: The City's 50 Top Lobbyists," *Washingtonian Magazine,* June 2007.

42. Lobbying and campaign contribution data are available at www .opensecrets.org

43. William D. Hartung, *Prophets of War: Lockheed Martin and the Making of the Military Industrial Complex* (New York: Nation Books, 2011), 29.

44. Lobbying and campaign contribution data are available at www .opensecrets.org

45. Thomas, 142–143; Anthony J. Nownes, *Total Lobbying* (Cambridge University Press, 2006), 28; Andres, 200.

46. Quoted in Nicholas W. Allard, "Lobbying Is an Honorable Profession: The Right to Petition and the Competition to Be Right," *Stanford Law and Policy Review,* vol. 19, 1 (2008), 48.

47. Baumgartner et al., 193.

48. Data at www.opensecrets.org

49. Matthew R. Kambrod, *Lobbying for Defense: An Insider's View* (Annapolis, MD: Naval Institute Press, 2008), 115; data at www .opensecrets.org

50. Thomas, 148–149.

51. James G. McGann, "The Global Go-To Think Tanks, 2010" The Think Tanks and Civil Societies Program, University of Pennsylvania; Ellen Laipson, "Think Tanks: Supporting Cast Players in the National Security Enterprise," in Roger Z. George & Harvey Rishikof, 290–291.

52. Eliot A. Cohen, "How Government Looks at Pundits" *Wall Street Journal,* January 23, 2009.

53. Laipson, 289.

54. Laipson, 293.

## Chapter 13

1. Committee on Government Operations, U.S. Senate, "Organizing for National Security," vol. 3, Staff Reports and Recommendations, 1961, 4.

2. Hart–Rudman Commission, *Road Map for National Security: Imperative for Change,* March 15, 2001, xiii.

3. Reorganization authority lapsed in 1984. President Obama requested a renewal in 2012 in order to restructure the trade-related organizations in the executive branch.

4. Dean Acheson, *Present at the Creation* (New York: W. W. Norton, 1969), 243; Thomas D. Boettcher, *First Call: The Making of the Modern U.S. Military, 1945–1953* (Boston: Little, Brown, 1992), 176.

5. Acheson, 244–246.

6. See "Organizing for National Security," vol. 3; Cody M. Brown, *The National Security Council,* Project on National Security Reform (PNSR), 2008, 27.

7. Murphy Commission, "Commission on the Organization of the Government for the Conduct of Foreign Policy," Washington, 1975.

8. *The Tower Commission Report* (Bantam Book and Times Books, 1987).

9. Report of the National Defense Panel, *Transforming Defense: National Security in the 21st Century,* December 1997, i–vii.

10. Hart–Rudman Commission, 2001; *New World Coming: American Security in the 21st Century,* September 15, 1999.

11. Center for Strategic and International Studies (CSIS), *Beyond Goldwater–Nichols, Phase 2 Report,* July 2005, 1–8.

12. CSIS, *CSIS Commission on Smart Power,* 2007, 61–69.

13. PNSR, *Forging a New Shield,* November 2008, http://pnsr.org/data/files/pnsr%20forging%20a%20new%20shield.pdf

14. See Peter Feaver and William Inboden, "A Strategic Planning Cell on National Security at the White House," in Daniel W. Drezner, ed., *Avoiding Trivia: The Role of Strategic Planning in American Foreign Policy* (Brookings, 2009), 98–112.

15. See PNSR report on this at www.pnsr.org/data/images/pnsr_the_power_of_people_report.pdf

16. For a critique of DNI, see Amy Zegart, *Spying Blind* (Princeton University Press, 2007), and Richard A. Best, Jr., and Alfred Cumming, "Director of National Intelligence Statutory Authorities: Status and Proposals," *CRS Report for Congress,* January 12, 2011, http://assets.opencrs.com/rpts/RL34231_20110112.pdf; for Department of Homeland Security (DHS), see Government Accountability Office (GAO) high risk report, www.gao.gov/highrisk/agency/dhs/; for National Counterterrorism Center (NCTC), see PNSR, *Toward Integrating Complex National Missions: Lessons From the National Counterterrorism Center's Directorate of Strategic Operational Planning,* February 2010, www.pnsr.org/data/files/pnsr_nctc_dsop_report.pdf

17. A fuller description of these teams is at PNSR, *Forging a New Shield,* 442–459.

18. Public Law 112–81, sect. 1207.

19. See Andrew F. Krepinevich and Barry D. Watts, *Regaining Strategic Competence,* Center for Strategic and Budgetary Assessments, 2009, intro., chap. 4, and conc., www.csbaonline.org/4Publications/PubLibrary/R.20090901.Regaining_Strategi/R.20090901.Regaining_Strategi.pdf; Jones memo to NSC members is at www.fas.org/irp/offdocs/ppd/nsc031909.pdf

20. See www.fas.org/irp/offdocs/ppd/nsc031909.pdf